Foundations of Financial Management

Foundations of Financial Management

Stanley B. Block
Texas American Bank/Fort Worth Chair of Finance
Texas Christian University

Geoffrey A. Hirt
Chairman of the Department of Finance
DePaul University

1989   Fifth Edition

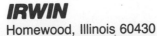
Homewood, Illinois 60430

For our fathers

Cover photo: © 1988 Philip Mrozinski

©RICHARD D. IRWIN, INC., 1978, 1981, 1984, 1987, and 1989

All rights reserved. No part of this publication may be
reproduced, stored in a retrieval system, or transmitted,
in any form or by any means, electronic, mechanical,
photocopying, recording, or otherwise, without the prior
written permission of the publisher.

Sponsoring editor: Gary L. Nelson
Project editor: Jane Lightell
Production manager: Irene H. Sotiroff
Cover designer: Paula Lang
Compositor: Carlisle Communications, Ltd.
Typeface: 10.5/13 Plantin
Printer: R. R. Donnelley & Sons Company

LIBRARY OF CONGRESS
Library of Congress Cataloging-in-Publication Date

Block, Stanley B.
    Foundations of financial management / Stanley B. Block, Geoffrey
  A. Hirt — 5th ed.
      p. cm.
    Includes bibliographies and index.
    ISBN 0-256-06844-5
    1. Corporations Finance. I. Hirt, Geoffrey A. II. Title.
HG4026.B589 1989
658.1'5—dc19   88–8857
                                           CIP

Printed in the United States of America

4 5 6 7 8 9 0 DO 5 4 3 2 1

Editor's Note

Over 250,000 students strong—and growing. The past four editions of Block and Hirt's *Foundations of Financial Management* have been used by over 250,000 students. Impressed by its clear and thorough treatment of financial theory and its applications, an increasing number of instructors are turning to *Foundations of Financial Management*. The exponential growth of the book can be attributed to one basic factor: It works! After adopting Block and Hirt, few instructors find other approaches to be as successful in teaching basic financial concepts.

The fifth edition builds on the strengths of previous editions, but it has been comprehensively revised and updated to incorporate the most significant new developments in the financial environment. We are grateful for the large numbers of instructors who have decided to let *Foundations of Financial Management* enhance their students' financial education. We challenge you to use this edition of *Foundations of Financial Management* and let it work for you!

Preface

For the fifth edition of *Foundations of Financial Management,* we wrote a two-year revision primarily because we wanted to include the Tax Reform Act of 1986. This reform act is having a substantial impact on corporations and the U.S. economy, and its integration into financial management concepts is crucial. We also thoroughly revised and updated the entire text—to maintain the high quality that the market has come to expect from Block and Hirt's *Foundations of Financial Management.* We remain strongly committed to presenting the concepts of finance in an enlightening and interesting manner, without sacrificing important aspects of theory.

Reinforcing Prerequisite Knowledge

Employers in finance report that the most successful financial analysts and planners have both facility and confidence in their financial skills. The authors of this text concur. One of the best ways to increase the students' facility in financial planning is to have them integrate their knowledge from prerequisite courses. So the text is designed to build on the students' knowledge from such courses as accounting, basic math, and economics. By applying tools from these courses, the student can develop a conceptual and analytical understanding of financial management.

We realize, however, that for some students two years have passed since they completed their accounting courses. For such students, we included Chapter 2, a thorough review of accounting principles, finance terminology, and financial statements.

With a working knowledge of Chapter 2, students will have a more complete understanding of financial decisions and the impact of those decisions on financial statements. Furthermore, students soon to begin their careers in finance will be much better prepared after reviewing and applying financial concepts learned throughout their college years.

Module Format Adds Flexibility

The text is organized into six major parts:

- Introduction (goals and functions of financial management).
- Financial Analysis and Planning.
- Working Capital Management.
- The Capital Budgeting Process.
- Long-term Financing.
- Expanding the Perspective of Corporate Finance (mergers and international financial management).

Each of these parts begins with a short introductory essay. For example, the essay that precedes "The Capital Budgeting Process" explains the relationship between the time value of money, valuation, the cost of capital, the decision process, and the goals of the firm.

Foundations of Financial Management covers virtually every possible topic taught in a financial management course. In fact, it is almost impossible for the instructor to cover every topic in this text. So, as is true when using almost any introductory text, the instructor must make some choices about course content and organization. We have been careful in crafting a book that is flexible and can be used in a variety of ways. The text works well as it is, but it can be adapted to a variety of teaching approaches. For instance, instructors who prefer a different order of topical coverage find that the book can easily be taught in a modular format. That is, they can reorganize the parts without losing continuity or clarity. The following sequences of major parts present two popular alternatives for professors wishing to cover the quantitative and valuation material early in the course.

Alternate Sequencing of the Major Sections

Alternative I

Goals of the firm, financial analysis followed by valuation and long-term finance, working capital, mergers, and international finance.

Under this alternative, time value of money is the sixth chapter covered.

Part 1   Introduction (1 chapter).

Part 2   Financial Analysis and Planning (4 chapters).

Part 4   The Capital Budgeting Process (5 chapters). (includes valuation)

Part 5   Long-term Financing (6 chapters).

Part 3   Working Capital Management (3 chapters).

Part 6   Expanding the Perspective of Corporate Finance (2 chapters).

Alternative II

Goals of the firm, valuation, and long-term finance followed by financial analysis, working capital, mergers and international finance.

Under this alternative, time value of money is the second chapter covered.

Part 1   Introduction (1 chapter).

Part 4   The Capital Budgeting Process (5 chapters). (includes valuation)

Part 5   Long-term Financing (6 chapters).

Part 2   Financial Analysis and Planning (5 chapters).

Part 3   Working Capital Management (3 chapters).

Part 6   Expanding the Perspective of Corporate Finance (2 chapters).

Obviously, this text works very well in the sequence provided, and most instructors will be satisfied with the text as it is. However, if you find that the text does not directly parallel your course syllabus, realize that the organization to parts and chapters is very flexible.

Changes in the Fifth Edition of *Foundations of Financial Management*

One of the major changes in the fifth edition is the comprehensive coverage of the **Tax Reform Act of 1986** and its effects on the financial decision-making process. The tax law changes are incorporated into material on corporate tax rates, depreciation, dividends and capital gains taxes, leasing, corporate dividend exclusions on stock held by a corporation, and other areas. According to the tax law schedule, 1987 was the year for blended taxes. By 1989, when this book is first used, the transition period should be over and the new tax law should be fully implemented.

We have also included the new **Statement of Cash Flows** to replace the Statement of Changes in Financial Position in the firm's financial statements. As spelled out by FASB Standard 95, released in November of 1987, the statement of cash flows is broken down into operations, investments, and financing sections. This new standard, explained thoroughly in this fifth edition text, is a straightforward method for analyzing cash flow.

In Part 4, we have revised Appendix 11A, **The Cost of Capital** and the **Capital Asset Pricing Model,** to include current financial data. In the discussion of the equity-risk premium ($K_m - R_f$), we have more accurately indicated an equity–risk premium instead of treating K_m and R_f separately. We have also added Appendix 11B, **Capital Structure Theory and Modigliani and Miller.** This appendix presents the net income approach, the net operating income approach, and the traditional approach, as well as the issues of bankruptcy and tax effects on the capital structure. This appendix has been carefully written, so the presentation level is consistent with the other chapters in the text. Faculty who wish to cover this classic discussion will now be able to expose the undergraduate student to these thought-provoking issues in the cost of capital literature.

We have expanded our use of **real-world examples** throughout the book and have provided a list of real-world illustrations on pages *xvii* through *xix* for your convenience. These actual examples are integrated throughout the text. Pedagogically, this approach makes more sense than simply putting an illustration at the beginning of each chapter as a teaser.

Some adopters have requested information on the use of **financial or business calculators.** So we have included a calculator appendix (Appendix E) at the end of the book. For greater flexibility, instructions are included for both the Texas Instruments Business Analysts' 35 (an algebraic calculator) and the Hewlett-Packard 12C Financial Calculator. Even though the appendix covers financial calculations for four chapters (Chapters 9–12), we felt that four separate appendices were not feasible. Instead, we leave it up to the instructor to decide if he or she wishes to assign the appropriate parts of Appendix E to coincide with material covered in Chapters 9–12.

The rapid **internationalization** of the capital markets and its impact on the U.S. economy and corporations has been included in this edition. Although we still have a separate chapter on international finance, not all professors will be able to include a whole chapter on international finance in their course. Integrating international material into a number of earlier chapters allows the student to realize, at least, that financial decisions are becoming more global in scope.

Other contemporary issues include updates and revisions on corporate restructuring and divestitures, leveraged buy-outs, the changing nature of the investment banking and financial services industries, corporate stock repurchases, and uses of electronic funds transfer in cash management. The material on shelf registrations, floating rate, and zero-coupon debt, as well as Euro-convertible debt, has been revised. Although we set out to do a two-year revision to cover the Tax Reform Act of 1986, we thoroughly revised and updated the entire text to meet the market's high expectations for Block and Hirt's *Foundations of Financial Management*.

End-of-Chapter Material

At the end of every chapter that includes equations, we have provided a list of all equations used in that chapter. This summary list should help the student review the mathematics of financial analysis. Similarly, the student can use the list of terms as a self-test, because every term listed at the end of the chapter is fully defined in the Glossary, at the end of the book.

The material in the text is supported by an unusually large number of questions and problems, particularly in the areas of financial analysis and capital budgeting. There are approximately 200 questions and 350 problems in the fifth edition. Well over half of the old problems are rewritten. Many of the problems better reflect the changing corporate environment. Risk–return considerations also are given increased attention. Of course, all problems that have tax implications have been rewritten to reflect the Tax Reform Act of 1986.

Several chapters have optional comprehensive problems that integrate a number of financial concepts into one problem. Sometimes, these comprehensive problems cover the material in one chapter. Occasionally, a comprehensive problem at the end of the last chapter in a section (such as Chapter 5, problem 17) includes material from as many as four chapters.

Teaching Support Package

We have developed a very comprehensive and integrated learning system. There are 11 teaching support items in the overall package, several new to this edition:

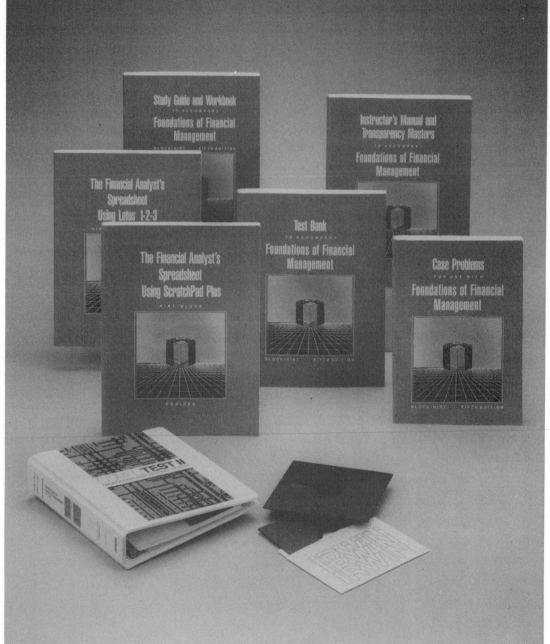

1. The *Instructor's Manual* contains detailed solutions to all problems and questions at the end of the chapters. It also includes teaching notes or strategies for each of the 21 chapters. At the end of the *Instructor's Manual* are about 50 transparency masters, which can be used to make overhead transparencies.

NEW 2. A set of supplemental *teaching transparencies* will be available to all adopters of Block and Hirt's *Foundations of Financial Management.* The transparencies will reproduce **all odd-numbered exercises, selected text illustrations,** as well as **charts, tables,** and **figures not included in the text.** A **chapter outline** for each chapter will also appear on transparencies, to serve as a classroom overview and lecture guide to each chapter.

3. A *Test Bank* of over 1,300 new and revised multiple-choice and true-false questions is available. Additionally, there are quiz problems and 10 question-matching quizzes, geared to test the student's knowledge of the terms at the end of the chapter.

4. A computerized test bank, "CompuTest II," includes all questions found in the test bank. Using CompuTest II, the instructor can construct exams by randomly selecting questions from a set of chapters. Instructors can also choose their own questions or even edit or add new questions to the computer test bank.

5. An excellent student *Study Guide* has been developed by Dwight C. Anderson. This guide outlines the chapters and presents and solves sample questions and problems.

NEW 6. In this edition, we have added a casebook, *Case Problems For Use with Foundations of Financial Management,* with 12 short cases. The cases vary in length from three to six pages and can be used for in-depth analysis and discussion. The cases correspond to issues from each major section of the text. These cases vary in degrees of difficulty; advanced cases are most easily solved on Lotus® 1-2-3®. Unlike many casebooks, these cases are perfectly tailored to the text and contain the same terminology used in the text. These cases add value and flexibility to the teaching package.

7. "The Financial Analyst's Spreadsheet Using ScratchPad Plus™" is a computer workbook that is totally integrated with the textbook. This package was designed, developed, and programmed by the authors, so the terminology is totally compatible with *Foundations of Financial Management.* "The Financial Analyst's Spreadsheet" has 28 different templates on disk. Students can use these templates to solve the workbook problems and test the sensitivity of financial decision variables. Templates include ratios, financial forecasting,

cash budgeting, capital budgeting and capital budgeting under uncertainty, time value of money, net present value and internal rate of return calculations, bond refunding, and more. This package includes the ScratchPad Plus™ Spreadsheet software: a very powerful spreadsheet that includes all functions, as well as 125,000 cells for configuration. For students unable to afford their own software package, this spreadsheet is a bargain.

8. "The Financial Analyst's Spreadsheet Using Lotus® 1-2-3®" was developed by Fredric Shipley using ScratchPad based templates as a model. Its templates and sensitivity problems are identical to ScratchPad, except that they're in the Lotus® 1-2-3® format. The templates and graphical presentation of template results are on disk, while the workbook gives the sensitivity problems. The spreadsheet package, like the ScratchPad Plus™ version, can be used to solve over 200 end-of-chapter problems in the textbook. We indicate which textbook problems may be solved in the computerized workbook. Users will need their own copy of Lotus® 1-2-3®.

9. Both versions of "The Financial Analyst's Spreadsheet" have a complete instructor's manual. Solutions are presented in the same format as the student worksheets. The essays are answered and the results of the sensitivity analysis are discussed.

NEW 10. To all adopters of the fifth edition, we'll provide free Lotus® 1-2-3® templates for selected problems and basic financial decisions. This software, new to this edition, is designed for professors who want only to introduce the student to the basics of spreadsheet analysis and who find "The Financial Analyst's Spreadsheet" workbook too comprehensive for their needs.

NEW 11. Also available free to adopters of the fifth edition is a new student self-help program, *SelfTest*. *SelfTest* randomly generates 40 true-false and multiple-choice questions for each chapter. *SelfTest* provides text page references for incorrect answers. After completing the test, the program repeats these page references and gives a final score. *SelfTest* contains questions similar but not identical to those in the *Test Bank*. *SelfTest* works with IBM PC and most compatibles.

All of the items in the supplement package have been thoroughly reviewed, checked, and classroom tested.

Acknowledgments

We wish to thank those finance professors who have contributed directly to the preparation of the manuscript, particularly Tim Gallagher for his help in problem development and G. N. Naidu for his work in the area of international financial management.

For their valuable reviews and helpful comments, we are grateful to:

Dwight C. Anderson
Eric Anderson
Brian T. Belt
Joseph Bentley
William J. Bertin
Debela Birru
Ezra Byler
Rolf Christensen
Allan Conway
LaVerne Cox (deceased)
Fred Ebeid
Jim Gahlon
Tim Gallagher
Bernie J. Grablowsky

John R. Hall
Charles Higgins
Stanley Jacobs
Peter R. Kensicki
Tom Kewley
Bill Kitrell (deceased)
Joseph Levitsky
John H. Lewis
Joe Lipscomb
John P. Listro
Paul Marciano
Michael Matukonis
Wayne E. McWee
Heber Moulton

Jerry D. Miller
John D. Markese
Joe Massa
John Meador (deceased)
Dimitrios Pachis
Coleen C. Pantalone
Harlan Platt
Roger Potter
Franklin Potts
Chris Prestopino
Frederick Rommel

Abu Selimuddin
Joanne Sheridan
Fred Shipley
William Smith
Mark Sunderman
Robert Swanson
Mike Tuberose
Donald E. Vaughn
Gary Wells
Don Wort
Ergun Yener

We wish to express our thanks to Joyce Dompke, Jeff Ryan, and Dave Ritzwoller for their help in proofreading the manuscripts; and to Joe Andrew for his special work in case development. We also express our thanks to our respective institutions for their administrative support and encouragement, and last, to our editor, Gary Nelson, for his feedback, support, and enduring commitment to excellence.

Stanley B. Block
Geoffrey A. Hirt

Table of Real World Examples

CHAPTER **Title, Table Number or Company Name**

1 Ivan Boesky and Dennis Levine—Insider Trading   9
Corporate Restructuring—Exxon, Ford, Phillips Petroleum,
   CBS, Chevron, EDS, Boone Pickins   14
Government Economic Policy—Deficits, Crash of 1929 and 1987   15
Tax Reform Example—Table 1–1   16

2 Price-Earnings Ratios—Table 2–3   28
Market Price to Book Value—Table 2–5   33
New Tax Law Changes   42

3 Compaq and Tandem Computers—DuPont Analysis   62
Ratios and Computer Industry—IBM, UNISYS, Apple Computer   67

6 Cyclical Sales—Houghton Mifflin and Macmillan   149
Cyclical Earnings—J. C. Penney and K mart   150
Term Structure examples—Interest Rates and Government Policy   159
Current Assets—U.S. Nonfinancial Corporations   168

7 Short-Term Investments—Table 7–3   185
Inventory Management—General Motors, Ford, and Chrysler   193

8 General Electric—Credit Operations   208
Prime Rate Data   209
Commercial Paper—GMAC, GE Credit, CIT Financial   215
Commercial Paper Outstanding—Figure 8–2   216
Commercial Paper Rates versus Prime Rate—Table 8–1   218
Foreign Borrowing—IBM   218

Asset-Backed Public Offerings—GMAC, Bank America,
  Mack Trucks   221

10 Price-Earnings Ratios and Valuation—Capital Cities
      Communications Corp.   284

11 Standard & Poor's Bond Guide—Table 11–2   304
    Debt as a Percentage of Total Assets—Table 11–3 List of 16
    Companies   315

12 New Tax Law on Depreciation   369

13 Beta-List of 10 Companies—Table 13–2   395

14 Composition of Capital Market Long-Term Funds—Figure 14–1   424
    Long-Term Corporate Financing—Figure 14–2   428
    Corporate Sources of Funds Internal versus External—
      Figure 14–3   429
    Foreign Capital Markets   435
    Examples of Over-the-Counter Companies   436

15 Investment Banking Data—Table 15–1   446
    Leading Underwriters—Table 15–4   453
    Public Offerings—Classic Example Electronic Data Systems   456
    Rockefeller Properties   457
    Publicly and Privately Placed Bonds—Figure 15–3   460
    Large Firms Going Private—Table 15–6   461
    Miraculous Changes in Market Value   462

16 Example of Pfizer Bond—Moody's Bond Record   478
    High Grade Corporate Bond Yields   481
    Actual Bond Ratings   483
    Zero Coupon Examples—Bank America, Pepsi-Cola   488
    Leasing—Clark Equipment, Citicorp, U.S. Leasing International 494

17 Institutional Ownership of U.S. Companies   515
    Common Stock Class and Rights—Wang, Ford, General Motors   516
    Poison Pills—International Paper   525
    Bond Yield versus Preferred Stock Yield—Table 17–2   528

18 Dividend Policies—Growth versus Slow Growth Companies   547
    Dividend Payout Example—Monsanto   551
    Stock Repurchase—List of 34 Companies—Table 18–7   558

19   Pricing Patterns of Convertible Bonds—List of 6 Companies—
         Table 19–1   571
     Forcing Conversion—Table 19–3   575
     Convertible Eurobonds   576
     Warrants—8 Companies—Table 19–6   580

20   Unfriendly Takeover—Example   596
     Ten Biggest Acquisitions—Table 20–1   596
     Merger Record—Table 20–2   597
     Tender Offer—Examples   614

21   Foreign Sales—U.S. International companies—Table 21–1   632
     Exchange Rates   636
     Tax Reform Act and Foreign Investment   659
     International Equity Markets   659

CONTENTS

PART ONE **Introduction**

1 The Goals and Functions of Financial Management   3

The Field of Finance   3
Evolution of Finance as a Field of Study   4
   Current Emphasis   6
Goals of Financial Management   7
   A Valuation Approach   7
   Maximizing Stockholder Wealth   8
   Social Responsibility   9
Functions of Financial Management   10
   Forms of Organization   10
Recent Economic Developments   13
   Inflation and Disinflation   13
   Reliance on Debt   13
   Corporate Restructuring   14
   High Deficits   15
   Tax Reform   16
Format of the Text   17
   Parts   18

PART TWO **Financial Analysis and Planning**

2 Review of Accounting   25

Income Statement   25
   Return to Capital   27
   Price-Earnings Ratio Applied to Earnings Per Share   28
   Limitations of the Income Statement   29

Balance Sheet   29
  Interpretation of Balance Sheet Items   30
  Concept of Net worth   32
  Limitations of the Balance Sheet   32
Statement of Cash Flows   33
  Developing an Actual Statement   34
  Determining Cash Flows from Operating Activities   35
  Determining Cash Flows from Investing Activities   39
  Determining Cash Flows from Financing Activities   39
  Combine the Three Sections of the Statement   39
Depreciation and Funds Flow   41
Income Tax Considerations   42
  Corporate Tax Rates   42
  Corporate versus Individual Taxes   44
  Cost of a Tax-Deductible Expense   44
  Depreciation as a Tax Shield   45

3   Financial Analysis   55

Ratio Analysis   56
  Classification System   57
  The Analysis   58
  Trend Analysis   65
Impact of Inflation on Financial Analysis   67
  Disinflation Effect   69
Other Elements of Distortion in Reported Income   70
  Explanation of Discrepancies   71
  Net Income   72

4   Financial Forecasting   85

Constructing Pro Forma Statements   86
Pro Forma Income Statement   86
  Establish a Sales Projection   87
  Determine a Production Schedule and the Gross Profit   88
  Other Expense Items   90
  Actual Pro Forma Income Statement   91
Cash Budget   91
  Cash Receipts   92
  Cash Payments   92
  Actual Budget   93
Pro Forma Balance Sheet   95
  Analysis of Pro Forma Statement   98
Percent-of-Sales Method   98

5 Operating and Financial Leverage 112

Leverage in a Business 112
Operating Leverage 113
  Break-Even Analysis 113
  A More Conservative Approach 115
  The Risk Factor 116
  Cash Break-Even Analysis 118
  Degree of Operating Leverage 118
  Leveraged Firm 119
  Conservative Firm 119
  Limitations of Analysis 121
Financial Leverage 121
  Impact on Earnings 122
  Degree of Financial Leverage 125
  Limitations to Use of Financial Leverage 126
Combining Operating and Financial Leverage 126
  Degree of Combined Leverage 128
  A Word of Caution 129

PART THREE **Working Capital Management**

6 Working Capital and the Financing Decision 145

The Nature of Asset Growth 146
Controlling Assets - Matching Sales and Production 147
  Temporary Assets under Level Production - An Example 151
Patterns of Financing 156
  Alternative Plans 157
  Long-Term Financing 157
  Short-Term Financing (opposite approach) 158
The Financing Decision 159
  Term Structure of Interest Rates 159
A Decision process 165
  Introducing Varying Conditions 166
  Expected Value 166
Shifts in Asset Structure 167
Toward an Optimal Policy 168

7 Current Asset Management 178

Cash Management 178
Float 179
  Improving Collections 180
  Extending Disbursements 181

Cost-Benefit Analysis   181
Electronic Funds Transfer   182
International Cash Management   183
Marketable Securities   184
Management of Accounts Receivable   188
Accounts Receivable as an Investment   188
Credit Policy Administration   189
An Actual Credit Decision   192
Inventory Management   193
Level versus Seasonal Production   193
Inventory Policy in Inflation (and Deflation)   194
The Inventory Decison Model   194

8 Sources of Short-Term Financing   205

Trade Credit   205
Payment Period   206
Cash Discount Policy   206
Net Credit Position   207
Bank Credit   207
Prime Rate   208
Compensating Balances   209
Maturity Provisions   211
Cost of Commercial Bank Financing   211
Interest Costs with Compensating Balances   212
Rate on Installment Loans   213
Annual Percentage Rate   214
The Credit Crunch Phenomenon   214
Financing through Commercial Paper   215
Advantages of Commercial Paper   217
Limitations on the Issuance of Commercial Paper   217
Foreign Borrowing   218
Use of Collateral in Short-Term Financing   219
Accounts Receivable Financing   219
Pledging Accounts Receivable   220
Factoring Receivables   220
Asset-Backed Public Offerings   221
Inventory Financing   222
Stages of Production   223
Nature of Lender Control   223
Appraisal of Inventory Control Devices   224
Hedging to Reduce Borrowing Risk   224

PART FOUR **The Capital Budgeting Process**

9 The Time Value of Money   239

Relationship to Capital Outlay Decision   240
Compound Sum—Single Amount   240
Present Value—Single Amount   241
Compound Sum—Annuity   242
Present Value—Annuity   244
Determining the Annuity Value   245
 Annuity Equaling a Compound Sum   246
 Annuity Equaling a Present Value   246
Determining the Yield on an Investment   248
 Yield—Present Value of a Single Amount   248
 Yield—Present Value of an Annuity   250
Special Considerations in Time Value Analysis   250
 Patterns of Payment   251
Special Review of the Chapter   253

10 Valuation and Rates of Return   262

Valuation Concepts   262
Valuation of Bonds   263
 Concept of Yield to Maturity   265
 *Changing the Yield to Maturity and the Impact on Bond
  Valuation*   267
 Time to Maturity   270
 Determining Yield to Maturity from the Bond Price   271
 Semiannual Interest and Bond Price   275
Valuation and Preferred Stock   276
 *Determining the Required Rate of Return (Yield) from the Market
  Price*   277
Valuation of Common Stock   278
 No Growth in Dividends   279
 Constant Growth in Dividends   279
 *Determining the Required Rate of Return from the Market
  Price*   282
 The Price-Earning Ratio Concept and Valuation   283
 Variable Growth in Dividends   285
Summary and Review of Formulas   286
 Bonds   286
 Preferred Stock   287
 Common Stock   288
Appendix 10A: The Bond Yield to Maturity Using Interpolation
 Problem   295
Appendix 10B: Valuation of a Supernormal Growth Firm
 Problem   297

11 Cost of Capital   301

The Overall Concept   302
Cost of Debt   303
Cost of Preferred Stock   306
Cost of Common Equity   307
  Valuation Approach   307
  *Alternate Calculation of the Required Return on Common
    Stock*   308
  Cost of Retained Earnings   309
  Cost of New Common Stock   311
  Overview of Common Stock Costs   312
Optimal Capital Structure—Weighting Costs   312
Capital Acquisition and Investment Decision Making   315
  Cost of Capital in the Capital Budgeting Decision   316
The Marginal Cost of Capital   317

Appendix 11A: Cost of Capital and the Capital Asset   335

Appendix 11B: Capital Structure Theory and Modigliani and Miller   343

12 The Capital Budgeting Decision   352

Administrative Considerations   353
Accounting Flows versus Cash Flows   354
Methods of Ranking Investment Proposals   356
  Payback Method   356
  Internal Rate of Return   357
  Net Present Value   360
Selection Strategy   361
  Reinvestment Assumption   363
Capital Rationing   364
Net Present Value Profile   364
  Characteristics of Investment C   367
Combining Cash Flow Analysis and Selection Strategy   368
  The New Rules on Depreciation   369
Actual Investment Decision   372
The Replacement Decision   374
  Sales of Old Asset   374
  Incremental Depreciation   376
  Cost Savings   377

13 Risk and Capital Budgeting   389

Definition of Risk in Capital Budgeting   389
The Concept of Risk Averse   390
Actual Measurement of Risk   392
Risk and the Capital Budgeting Process   395
  Risk-Adjusted Discount Rate   395

Increasing Risk over Time   396
  Qualitative Measures   397
Simulation Models   399
  Decision Trees   401
The Portfolio Effect   402
  Portfolio Risk   402
  Evaluation of Combinations   405
The Share Price Effect   406

PART FIVE   Long-Term Financing

14   Capital Markets   423
Competition for Funds in the Capital Markets   424
  Government Securities   425
  Corporate Securities   426
  Internal versus External Sources of Funds   429
The Supply of Capital Funds   430
  The Role of the Security Markets   431
The Organization of the Security Markets   432
  The Organized Exchanges   432
  The New York Stock Exchange   434
  Foreign Exchanges   435
  The Over-the-Counter Markets   436
Market Efficiency   437
  Criteria of Efficiency   437
  The Efficient Market Hypothesis   437
Regulation of the Security Markets   438
  Securities Act of 1933   438
  Securities Exchange Act of 1934   439
  The Securities Acts Amendments of 1975   440
  Current Legislative Issues   441

15   Investment Banking: Public and Private Placement   445
The Role of Investment Banking   445
Enumeration of Functions   446
The Distribution Process   447
Pricing the Security   450
  Dilution   450
  Market Stabilization   451
  Aftermarket   451
Changes in the Investment Banking Industry   452
  Shelf Registration   454
Public versus Private Financing   454

Advantages of Being Public   454
Disadvantages of Being Public   455
Public Offerings   456
  A Classic Example of Instant Wealth—EDS Goes Public   456
  Rockefeller Center Properties, Inc.   457
Private Placement   459
  Going Private and Leveraged Buy-Outs   459

16   Long-Term Debt and Lease Financing   472

The Expanding Role of Debt   472
The Debt Contract   473
  Security Provisions   474
  Unsecured Debt   475
  Methods of Repayment   475
Bond Prices, Yields and Ratings   477
  Bond Yields   480
  Bond Ratings   482
  Examining Actual Bond Ratings   483
The Refunding Decision   483
  A Capital Budgeting Problem   484
Innovative Forms of Bond Financing   488
Advantages and Disadvantages of Debt   490
  Benefits of Debt   490
  Drawbacks of Debt   491
  Eurobond Market   491
Leasing as a Form of Debt   491
  Capital Lease versus Operating Lease   493
  Income Statement Effect   494
  Advantages of Leasing   494

Appendix 16A: Financial Alternatives for Distressed Firm   502

Appendix 16B: Lease versus Purchase Decision   511

17   Common and Preferred Stock Financing   514

Common Stockholders' Claim to Income   516
The Voting Right   517
  Cumulative Voting   518
The Right to Purchase New Shares   520
  The Use of Rights in Financing   520
  Effect of Rights on Stockholders' Position   523
  Desirable Features of Rights Offerings   524
  Poison Pill   525
Preferred Stock Financing   526
  Justification for Preferred Stock   526
Provisions Associated with Preferred Stock   528
Comparing Features of Common and Preferred Stock and Debt   530

18 Dividend Policy and Retained Earnings 542

The Marginal Principle of Retained Earnings 542
Life Cycle Growth and Dividends 543
Dividends as a Passive Variable 544
An Incomplete Theory 544
Arguments for the Relevance of Dividends 545
Dividend Stability 546
Other Factors Influencing Dividend Policy 548
Legal Rules 548
Cash Position of the Firm 549
Access to Capital Markets 549
Desire for Control 550
Tax Position of Shareholders 550
Dividend Payment Procedures 551
Stock Dividend 552
Accounting Considerations for a Stock Dividend 552
Value to the Investor 553
Possible Value of Stock Dividends 554
Use of Stock Dividends 555
Stock Splits 555
Repurchase of Stock as an Alternative to Dividends 556
Other Reasons for Repurchase 557
Dividend Reinvestment Plans 559

19 Convertibles and Warrants 568

Convertible Securities 568
Value of the Convertible Bond 569
Is This Fool's Gold? 572
Advantages and Disadvantages to the Corporation 573
Forcing Conversion 574
Euro-Convertible Bonds 576
Accounting Considerations with Convertibles 576
Financing through Warrants 579
Valuation of Warrants 580
Use of Warrants in Corporate Finance 582
Accounting Considerations with Warrants 583

PART SIX Expanding the Perspective of Corporate Finance

20 External Growth through Mergers 595

Motives for Business Combinations 597
Financial Motives 598
Nonfinancial Motives 600
Motives of Selling Stockholders 600

Terms of Exchange   601
   Cash Purchases   601
   Stock-for-Stock Exchange   603
   Long-Term Considerations   605
   Buying a Company at a Higher P/E Ratio   607
   Market Value Maximization   610
   Portfolio Effect   611
Accounting Considerations in Mergers and Acquisitions   612
Negotiated versus Tendered Offers   614
Premium Offers and Stock Price Movements   616
Two-Step Buy-Out   618
Holding Companies   619
   Drawbacks   620

21   International Financial Management   631

Introduction   631
The Multinational Corporation: Nature and Environment   633
Foreign Exchange Rates   635
   Factors Influencing Exchange Rates   636
   Spot Rates and Forward Rates   639
Managing Foreign Exchange Risk   641
Foreign Investment Decisions   645
   Analysis of Political Risk   647
Cash Flow Analysis and the Foreign Investment Decision   649
The Tax Reform Act of 1986 and Foreign Investment Decisions   653
Financing International Business Operations   654
   Funding of Transactions   655
Some Unsettled Issues in International Finance   662

Appendix A   Compound Sum of \$1, IF_s 672

Appendix B   Present Value of \$1, IF_{pv} 674

Appendix C   Compound Sum of an Annuity of \$1, IF_{sa} 676

Appendix D   Present Value of an Annuity of \$1, IF_{pva} 678

Appendix E   Using Calculators for Financial Analysis   680

Glossary   689

Index   719

Introduction

1 The Goals and Functions of Financial Management

1

The Goals and Functions of Financial Management

The financial manager's contribution to directing the operations of the firm has become increasingly critical in the last decade. Some have referred to the era we live in as the morning after the biggest credit binge in U.S. history. In a time of unpredictable economic turns, fluctuating interest rates, inflation and disinflation, painful shortages and excesses, and extreme optimism and pessimism, the chief financial officer must maintain the financial viability of the firm. As financial markets become more international, the chief financial officer must also manage the global financial affairs of the firm. The board of directors and the president look to the financial division to provide a precious resource—capital—and to manage it in an efficient and profitable fashion.

The Field of Finance

The field of finance is closely related to economics and accounting, and financial managers need to have an understanding of the relationships between these fields. Economics provides a structure for decision making in such areas as risk analysis, pricing theory through supply and demand relationships, comparative return analysis, and many other important areas. Economics also provides the broad picture of the economic

3

environment in which corporations are continually making decisions. A financial manager must understand the institutional structure of the Federal Reserve System, the commercial banking system, and the interrelationships between the various sectors of the economy. Economic variables, such as gross national product, industrial production, disposable income, unemployment, inflation, interest rates, and taxes (to name a few), must fit into the financial manager's decision model and be applied correctly. These terms will be presented throughout the text and integrated into the financial process.

Accounting is sometimes said to be the language of finance in that it provides financial data through income statements, balance sheets, and the statement of cash flows. The financial manager must know how to interpret and use these statements in the allocation of the firm's financial resources to generate the best return possible in the long run. Finance is the link that integrates economic theory with the numbers of accounting, and all corporate managers—whether in the area of production, sales, research, marketing, management, or long-run strategic planning—must know what it means to assess the financial performance of the firm.

Many students approaching the field of finance for the first time might wonder what career opportunities exist. For those who develop the necessary skills and training, job positions in the field include corporate financial officer, banker, stockbroker, financial analyst, portfolio manager, investment banker, financial consultant, or personal financial planner. As the student progresses through the text, he or she will become increasingly familiar with the important role of the various participants in the financial decision-making process. A financial manager addresses such varied issues as decisions on plant location, the raising of capital, or simply, how to get the highest return on x million dollars between five o'clock this afternoon and eight o'clock tomorrow morning. Training in finance has served as a stepping-stone to a number of the top corporate positions in the country.

Evolution of Finance as a Field of Study

To appreciate and understand the shifting emphasis in finance as a field of study, some historical perspective is essential. We see a field that has matured with the passage of time.

At the turn of the century, finance emerged as a field separate from economics but still closely linked. The major focus of study reflected the developments of the time, namely the building of giant industrial corporations by Rockefeller, Carnegie, Du Pont, and others. A student of finance would have spent much time learning about the financial instruments that were essential to mergers and acquisitions.

With the development and implementation of antitrust legislation, corporate consolidations became less important, and more normal patterns of growth were emphasized. Attention shifted to stocks and bonds and other securities utilized for raising capital. The role of the investment banker or middleman in a security offering also received much attention. No doubt, the great bull market of the 1920s contributed to the emphasis in raising capital.

In the 1930s the shock of the Depression ushered in an era of conservatism, and attention shifted to such topics as preservation of capital, maintenance of liquidity, reorganization of financially troubled corporations, and the bankruptcy process. The federal government assumed a much larger role in regulating business through the Securities Act of 1933 and the Securities Exchange Act of 1934. A by-product of this regulation was the development of published data related to corporate performance. The groundwork was laid for the sophisticated analysis of corporate information that would take place in later decades.

The 1940s and early 1950s offered little new in the study or practice of corporate finance. However, in the mid-50s a major shift in emphasis took place. Up to that time, the study procedures of finance had been descriptive or definitional in nature. Furthermore, the orientation had been from the viewpoint of a third party or outsider looking in. This all changed in the mid-50s as a more analytical, decision-oriented approach began to evolve.

The first area of study to generate the newfound enthusiasm for decision-related analysis was capital budgeting.[1] The financial manager was presented with analytical techniques for allocating resources among the various assets of the firm. The enthusiasm spread to other decision-making areas of the firm—such as cash and inventory management, capital structure formulation, and dividend policy. The emphasis shifted from that of the outsider looking in to that of the financial manager forced to make tough day-to-day decisions affecting the performance of the firm.

---

[1] A starting point was Joel Dean's *Capital Budgeting* (New York: Columbia University Press, 1951).

Current Emphasis

From the late 1960s through today, the emphasis of financial management has also sharply focused on risk–return relationships and the maximization of return for a given level of risk. This risk–return emphasis was accompanied by corporate implementation of portfolio management strategies. In an attempt to reduce risk, companies in the 1960s began to diversify their portfolio of assets into unrelated industries, thus creating conglomerates. High inflation from the 1970s to 1982 created low profitability and caused large increases in debt for many companies. Firms were forced to replace plant and equipment (at inflated prices) with borrowed money since they did not have the benefit of large earnings from operations. By 1981–82, this borrowing binge caught up with many companies, and the increased financial risk showed up in record numbers of corporate bankruptcies. By the late 1980s, firms were emphasizing the return aspect of the risk–return trade-off; they did so by focusing on high-profit products while selling off their marginal and losing divisions. Such restructuring of assets resulted in many firms moving away from a strategy of conglomerate diversification to a more narrow focus on "doing what you do well, profitably." This shift toward the return side of the equation has been partially caused by increased international competition and the use of advanced technology in the production process. Accompanying these developments has been a sharpened focus on the financial objectives of the firm.

A new area of financial research that is also receiving more attention in the late 1980s is agency theory. This theory examines the relationship between the owners of the firm and the managers of the firm. In privately owned firms, management and the owners are usually the same people. Management operates the firm to satisfy its own goals, needs, financial requirements, and the like. As a company moves from private to public ownership, management now represents all the owners. This places management in an agency agreement to make decisions in the best interests of all stockholders. Because of the diversified ownership interests, conflicts between managers and stockholders can arise that impact on the financial decisions of the firm. Also, because of the increased level of corporate stock repurchases, corporate restructuring, and mergers and acquisitions taking place in the 1980s, agency theory has become more important in assessing whether stockholder goals are being achieved by management in the long run.

Goals of Financial Management _____

One may suggest that the most important goal for financial management is to "earn the highest possible profit for the firm." Under this criterion, each decision would be evaluated on the basis of its overall contribution to the firm's earnings. While this seems to be a desirable approach, there are some serious drawbacks to profit maximization as the primary goal of the firm.

First, a change in profit may also represent a change in risk. A conservative firm that earned $1.25 per share may be a less desirable investment if its earnings per share increases to $1.50, but the risk inherent in the operation increases even more.

A second possible drawback to the goal of maximizing profit is that it fails to take into account the timing of the benefits. For example, if we could choose between the following two alternatives, we might be indifferent if our emphasis were solely on maximizing earnings.

	Earnings per Share		
	Period One	Period Two	Total
Alternative A	$1.50	$2.00	$3.50
Alternative B	2.00	1.50	3.50

Both investments would provide $3.50 in total earnings, but Alternative B is clearly superior because the larger benefits occur earlier. We could reinvest the difference in earnings for Alternative B one period sooner.

Finally, the goal of maximizing profit suffers from the almost impossible task of accurately measuring the key variable in this case, namely, "profit." As you will observe throughout the text, there are many different economic and accounting definitions of profit, each open to its own set of interpretations. Furthermore, new problems related to inflation and international currency transactions complicate the issue. Constantly improving methods of financial reporting offer some hope in this regard, but many problems remain.

A Valuation Approach

While there is no question that profits are important, the key issue is how to use them in setting a goal for the firm. The ultimate measure of performance is not what we earned but how the earnings are *valued* by the investor. In making an analysis of the firm, the investor will also consider the risk inherent in the firm's operation, the time pattern over which the firm's earnings increase or decrease, the quality and reliability of reported earnings, and many other factors. The financial manager, in turn, must be sensitive to all of these considerations. He or she must question the impact of each decision on the firm's overall valuation. If a decision maintains or increases the firm's overall value, it is acceptable from a financial viewpoint; otherwise, it should be rejected. This principle is demonstrated throughout the text.

Maximizing Stockholder Wealth

The broad goal of the firm can be brought into focus if we say that the financial manager should attempt to *maximize the wealth of the firm's shareholders* through achieving the highest possible value for the firm. This is not a simple task, since the financial manager cannot directly control the firm's stock price, but can only act in a way that is consistent with the desires of the shareholders in general. Since stock prices are affected by expectations of the future as well as by the economic environment, much of what affects stock prices is beyond management's direct control. Even firms with good earnings and favorable financial trends do not always perform well in a declining stock market over the short term.

The concern is not so much with daily fluctuations in stock value as with long-term wealth maximization. This can be a difficult task in light of changing investor expectations. In the 1950s and 1960s the investor emphasis was on maintaining rapid rates of earnings growth. In the 1970s and 1980s, investors have become more conservative, putting a premium on lower risk and, at times, high current dividend payments.

Does modern corporate management actually follow the goal of maximizing shareholder wealth as we have defined it? In many large corporations stock ownership is diffused and fragmented and management, with a relatively small ownership position, often controls policy. Under these circumstances, management may be more interested in maintaining its own tenure and protecting "private spheres of influence" than in maximizing stockholder wealth. For example, suppose the management of a corporation receives a tender offer to merge the corporation into a second firm; while this offer might be attractive to stockholders, it might be quite unpleasant to present management. Management is often more willing to satisfy, while maintaining the status quo, than to maximize.

The answer to this issue is twofold. First, in most cases "enlightened management" is aware that the only way to maintain its position over the long run is to be sensitive to shareholder concerns. Poor stock price performance relative to other companies often leads to undesirable take-overs and proxy fights for control. Second, management often has sufficient stock option incentives that motivate them to achieve market value maximization for their own benefit.

Social Responsibility

Is our goal of stockholder wealth maximization consistent with a concern for social responsibility for the firm? In most instances the answer is yes. By adopting policies that maximize values in the market, the firm is able to attract capital, provide employment, and offer benefits to its community. This is the basic strength of the private enterprise system.

Nevertheless, certain socially desirable actions such as pollution control, equitable hiring practices, and fair pricing standards may at times be inconsistent with earning the highest possible profit or achieving maximum valuation in the market. For example, pollution control projects frequently offer a very low return. Does this mean that firms should not exercise social responsibility in regard to pollution control? The answer is no—but certain cost-increasing activities may have to be mandatory rather than voluntary, at least initially, to ensure that the burden falls equally over all business firms.

Insider trading is one area of finance that is considered to be not socially responsible. Insider trading occurs when someone has information that is not available to the public and then uses this information to profit from trading in a company's common stock. This practice is illegal and protected against by the Securities and Exchange Commission (SEC). Unfortunately, the definition of an inside trade is not as well defined as many would like, and this has become a hot issue. Sometimes, the insider is a company manager; other times, it is the company's lawyer, investment banker, or even the printer of the company's financial statement. Anyone who has knowledge before public dissemination of that information stands to benefit from either good news or bad news. Several dominant Wall Street news stories involved insider trading by Ivan Boesky and Dennis Levine. Both were sentenced to jail, and Ivan Boesky was barred from trading stock and forced to return over $100 million in illegal insider trading profits. A large ring of insiders was found and prosecuted. Such activities as these serve no beneficial economic or financial purpose, and it could be argued that they have a negative impact on shareholder interests. Some of you may have seen the issue of insider trading highlighted in the 1987 movie, *Wall Street*.

Functions of Financial Management

Having examined the goals and objectives of financial management, let us turn our attention to the functions that it must perform. It is the responsibility of financial management to allocate funds to current and fixed assets, to obtain the best mix of financing alternatives, and to develop an appropriate dividend policy within the context of the firm's objectives. These functions are performed on a day-to-day basis as well as through infrequent approaches to the capital markets to acquire new funds. The daily activities of financial management include credit management, inventory control, and the receipt and disbursement of funds. Less routine functions encompass the sale of stocks and bonds and the establishment of a capital budgeting and dividend plan.

As indicated in Figure 1–1, all these functions are carried out while balancing the profitability and risk components of the firm.

The appropriate risk–return trade-off must be determined in order to maximize the market value of the firm for its shareholders. The risk–return decision will influence not only the operational side of the business (capital versus labor or product A versus product B) but also the financing mix (stocks versus bonds versus retained earnings).

Forms of Organization

The finance function may be carried out within a number of different forms of organizations. Of primary interest are the sole proprietorship, the partnership, and the corporation.

Figure 1–1
Functions of the
financial manager

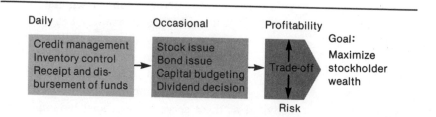

Sole proprietorship   This form of organization represents single-person ownership and offers the advantages of simplicity of decision making and low organizational and operating costs. Most small businesses with 1 to 10 employees are sole proprietorships. The major drawback of the sole proprietorship is that there is unlimited liability to the owner. In settlement of the firm's debts, he or she can lose not only the capital that has been invested in the business, but also personal assets. This drawback can be serious, and the student should realize that few lenders are willing to advance funds to a small business without a personal liability commitment.

The profits or losses of a sole proprietorship are taxed as though they belong to the individual owner. Thus, if a sole proprietorship makes $25,000, the owner will claim the profits in his or her tax return. (In the corporate form of organization, the corporation first pays a tax on profits, and then the owners of the corporation pay a tax on any distributed profits.) Approximately 75 percent of the 12 million business firms in this country are organized as sole proprietorships, and these produce approximately 10 percent of the total revenue and 25 percent of the total profits of the U.S. economy.

Partnership   This second form of organization is similar to a sole proprietorship except that there are two or more owners. Multiple ownership makes it possible to raise more capital and to share ownership responsibilities. Most partnerships are formed through an agreement between the participants, known as the *articles of partnership*, which specifies the ownership interest, the methods for distributing profits, and the means for withdrawing from the partnership. For taxing purposes, partnership profits or losses are allocated directly to the partners, and there is no double taxation, as there is in the corporate form.

Like the sole proprietorship, the partnership arrangement carries unlimited liability for the owners. While the partnership offers the advantage of *sharing* possible losses, it presents the problem of owners with unequal wealth having to absorb losses. If three people form a partnership with a $10,000 contribution each and the business loses $100,000, one wealthy partner may have to bear a disproportionate share of the losses if the other two partners do not have sufficient personal assets.

To circumvent this shared unlimited liability feature, a special form of partnership, called a *limited partnership*, can be utilized. Under this arrangement, one or more partners are designated general partners and have unlimited liability for the debts of the firm; other partners are designated limited partners and are only liable for their initial contribution. The limited partners are normally prohibited from being active in the management of the firm. You may have heard of limited partnerships in real estate syndications in which a number of limited partners are doctors, lawyers, and CPAs and there is one general partner who is a real estate professional. Not all financial institutions will extend funds to a limited partnership.

Corporation   In terms of revenue and profits produced, the corporation is by far the most important type of economic unit. While only 17 percent of U.S. business firms are corporations, over 80 percent of sales and over 65 percent of profits can be attributed to the corporate form of organization. The corporation is unique—it is a legal entity unto itself. Thus the corporation may sue or be sued, engage in contracts, and acquire property. A corporation is formed through *articles of incorporation*, which specify the rights and limitations of the entity.

A corporation is owned by stockholders who enjoy the privilege of limited liability, meaning that their liability exposure is generally no greater than their initial investment.[2] A corporation also has a continual life and is not dependent on any one stockholder for maintaining its legal existence.

A key feature of the corporation is the easy divisibility of the ownership interest through the issuance of shares of stock. While it would be nearly impossible to have more than 50 or 100 partners in most businesses, a corporation may have more than a million shareholders. A current example of a firm with over 1 million stockholders is General Motors.

The shareholders' interests are ultimately managed by the corporation's board of directors. The directors, who may include key management personnel of the firm as well as outside directors not permanently employed by it, serve in a stewardship capacity and may be liable for the mismanagement of the firm or for the misappropriation of funds. Outside directors of large public corporations may be paid more than $15,000 a year to attend meetings and share in important decisions.

Because the corporation is a separate legal entity, it reports and pays taxes on its *own* income. As previously mentioned, any remaining income that is paid to the stockholders in the form of dividends will require the payment of a second tax by the stockholders. One of the key disadvantages to the corporate form of organization is this potential double taxation of earnings.

There is, however, one way to circumvent the double taxation of a normal corporation and that is through formation of a Subchapter S

---

[2]An exception to this rule is made if they buy their stock at less than par value. Then they would be liable for up to the par value.

corporation. With a Subchapter S corporation, the income is taxed as direct income to the stockholders and thus is taxed only once, as in a partnership. Nevertheless, the stockholders receive all the organizational benefits of a corporation, including limited liability. The Subchapter S designation, as amended by 1982 tax legislation, can apply to corporations with up to 35 stockholders.[3] Thus only relatively small entities can elect Subchapter S status.

While the proprietorship, traditional partnership, and various forms of limited partnerships are all important, the corporation will be given the primary emphasis in this text. Because of the all-pervasive impact of the corporation on our economy, and because most growing businesses eventually become corporations, the effects of most decisions in this text are considered from the corporate viewpoint.

Recent Economic Developments

Inflation and Disinflation

A number of key issues of the late 1970s and 1980s are given special attention in the text. Even though inflation has been significantly reduced from double digits to the 3–4 percent range during the 1980s, leading economists and financial analysts now accept some degree of inflation as a way of life in the United States and throughout the world. A 3–4 percent inflation rate is still several times the average rate from 1925 to 1965. Inflation-induced profits of the late 1960s and 1970s are somewhat in the past, but the student should not ignore the lessons of inflated phantom profits and undervalued assets of the past two decades. The student should be equally aware of the benefits, drawbacks, and implications of disinflation (a slowing down of price increases). The problems and opportunities related to inflation and disinflation receive particular attention in the later discussion of financial analysis.

Reliance on Debt

A second aspect of contemporary finance is the extreme reliance that financial managers have placed on the use of debt. Debt-to-asset ratios have moved from 25 percent to approximately 45 percent of assets in the

---

[3]The 1982 legislation also eliminated restrictions on the type of income that could be earned by a Subchapter S corporation.

last 20 years, and the typical firm's ability to cover its interest expenses has eroded. This is not a short-term, cyclical phenomenon but rather a slow, steady process that has taken place in good times as well as bad. While many firms that were formerly in financial trouble have recovered miraculously (Chrysler, for instance), other firms in industries such as farm equipment, steel, trucks, and oil well drilling equipment are suffering from low profitability, international competition, faltering domestic markets, and high debt.

Corporate Restructuring

Third, restructuring of the balance sheet is possibly one of the most important phenomena currently taking place in corporate America, and one of the results is an increase in the use of debt relative to ownership capital. Firms are repurchasing shares of common stock in the open market either because they do not have better investment opportunities (Exxon); because management thinks that the stock is underpriced (Ford, Amoco); or because management is trying to avoid an unfriendly takeover (Phillips Petroleum, Revlon, CBS).[4] The shares may be repurchased with excess cash or through the issuance of new debt. In the 1980s, Exxon bought back 46.6 million common shares worth $2.3 billion, Ford repurchased 20 million shares for $980 million, and Phillips Petroleum thwarted a takeover by T. Boone Pickens by repurchasing 81.5 million shares of stock valued at $4.1 billion.

Restructuring was not just confined to stock repurchases in the 1980s but also included mergers and acquisitions of gigantic proportions unheard of in other decades. Firms were buying or merging with companies in similar and related industries. Rather than just seeking risk reduction through diversification, firms were acquiring greater market share, brand name products, hidden asset values, or technology—or they were simply looking for size to help them "play the game" in an international arena. In the biggest of all combinations, Standard Oil of California acquired Gulf Oil in 1984 for $13.3 billion and, in the process, increased the firm's debt by billions of dollars and changed the company name to Chevron. Philip Morris, the consumer products company that holds such brand names as Miller Beer and Philip Morris cigarettes, acquired General Foods for $5.8 billion in a merger that expanded its existing market emphasis.

---

[4]The corporate repurchase of shares may also be viewed as an alternative to paying a cash dividend. This topic is covered more thoroughly in Chapter 18, Dividend Policy and Retained Earnings.

On the other hand, General Motors went after technology by buying Electronic Data Systems (a computer services company, for $2.5 billion) and Hughes Aircraft (a huge defense and electronics company, for $5.8 billion). Many of these stories are covered in more detail in later chapters. You should also be aware that some corporations have restructured their balance sheets by selling off (divesting) unprofitable or unwanted divisions over a period of time.

High Deficits

Another economic problem facing corporations has been the foreign trade deficit and the federal deficit. Americans have been buying more foreign goods than American companies have been selling to foreigners. This trade imbalance impacts on the U.S. economy by keeping U.S. workers less than fully employed, by not being able to fully utilize plant and equipment in the production process, and by making the United States a net borrower of foreign capital. This imbalance of trade has caused the U.S. dollar to decline relative to foreign currencies (most notably the Japanese yen and German deutsche mark) and has forced the United States to keep domestic interest rates at levels high enough to attract foreign capital into the United States to help finance both the trade deficit and federal deficit.

The federal deficit represents the difference between U.S. government revenues and expenses. The annual deficit of $100–200 billion a year in the 1980s indicates the government needs more revenue (perhaps higher taxes), less spending, or a combination of the two strategies. No one seems to be willing to adequately address this issue.

In the midst of these two deficit problems, the U.S. stock markets, as well as international stock markets, crashed on October 19, 1987. To put the crash of 1987 into perspective, the "Great Crash of 1929" accounted for a one-day decline on the Dow Jones Industrial Average of 30 high-quality stocks of 12.9 percent while the "Crash of 1987" saw common stock prices decline 22.6 percent (the Dow Jones Industrial Average fell 508 points, from the previous close of 2,246.74, to 1,738.74). This total erosion in confidence caused many companies to cancel or postpone planned sales of common stock whose proceeds would have been used for capital expansion, debt reduction, or other corporate purposes. As we write this chapter, the fallout from the "Crash of 87" has not been fully measured. One obvious thing, however, is that we live in a world where capital flows from country to country faster than ever thought possible; where computers interact in a vast international financial network, and where markets are more vulnerable to the emotions of the players than they have been in the past. The corporate financial manager has an increasing number of external impacts that are outside of management control. Future financial managers will need to have the sophistication to understand international capital flows, computerized electronic funds transfer systems, foreign currency hedging strategies, and many other such factors.

Tax Reform

In 1986, Congress passed major new tax legislation. Initially, the 1986 tax legislation was intended to represent not only tax reform but tax simplification as well. In the early stages of the legislative process, some proponents of tax revision even went so far as to suggest that individuals might be able to inform the government of their tax obligation on a three by five index card. But the final document drawn up by the Congress and signed by the president was approximately one thousand pages long with all the standard "ands, ifs, and buts" that have appeared in prior tax legislation.

The main thrust of the Tax Reform Act of 1986 was to eliminate or reduce many of the abuses of the tax code. Because of some of the tough provisions in the law, progress is being made along these lines. Observe in Table 1–1, the low percentage tax rate that a number of corporations paid prior to tax reform. Please keep in mind that corporations were

Table 1–1
Tax rates paid by selected corporations in 1985

Company	1985 Actual Profits (millions of $)	1985 Taxes Paid (millions of $)	Tax Rate (%)
AT&T	$2,362.8	$ 103.0	4.4%
Bankers Trust	198.4	3.7	1.9
Boeing	863.0	38.0	4.4
Digital Equipment Corp.	202.6	3.8	1.9
General Electric	3,350.0	258.0	7.7
Georgia-Pacific Corp.	304.0	13.0	4.3
Houston Industries	730.4	52.3	7.2
IBM	5,945.0	594.0	10.0
Johnson & Johnson	439.4	27.4	6.2
Litton Industries	400.4	42.7	10.7
McDonnell-Douglas Corp.	531.1	9.5	1.8
Ohio Edison Co.	543.5	19.5	3.6
Tenneco	527.0	9.0	1.7
Westinghouse	723.7	24.7	3.4

Source: *The Wall Street Journal* (August 18, 1986), p. 9.

exposed to a tax rate of 46 percent during this time period (the rate is currently 34 percent).

Historically corporations and individuals have been able to reduce taxes through the use of tax credits, rapid depreciation write-offs, preferential tax treatment accorded to long-term capital gains from investments, passive losses from tax shelters, and a number of other devices. It is not really essential that you understand all these terms for now, only that you recognize that many of the most popular vehicles for sheltering income have been eliminated or reduced in importance. This normally would mean more revenue for the government, but instead Congress has decided to pass on the benefits through lower overall tax rates for all. Presumably those who took advantage of tax loopholes in the past will pay more taxes in the future. However, many other taxpayers will pay less taxes as the result of lower rates.

Industries that will be particularly hard hit by tax reform include those dependent on heavy investment in plant and equipment and real estate. The first category includes firms in such industries as steel, machine tools, and auto manufacturing; they will be hurt by the elimination of the investment tax credit (a percentage of the purchase price of equipment that can be deducted from tax obligations), and the requirement that they depreciate assets over a longer time period for tax purposes. Real estate will also be adversely affected by longer depreciation schedules and by severe restrictions on deducting tax losses from limited partnership investments, which traditionally have been quite popular in real estate.

Industries that will benefit are those that previously had limited tax deductions associated with investment in plant and equipment or other tax sheltered write-offs and therefore were paying the maximum tax rate. Now that overall rates are lower, they will have approximately the same taxable income, but lower rates will apply. Examples of industries that fall into this category are retailing, publishing, and life insurance. As an example, Tandy Corporation (retail electronics, personal computers) announced that it anticipates saving 45 to 50 million dollars a year under the tax reform legislation. The funds are being passed on to stockholders in the form of a cash dividend.

Format of the Text

The material in this text is covered under six major headings. The student progresses from the development of basic analytical skills in accounting and finance to the utilization of decision-making techniques in working capital management, capital budgeting, long-term financing, and other related areas. A total length of 21 chapters should make the text appropriate for one-semester coverage.

The student is given a thorough grounding in financial theory in a highly palatable and comprehensive fashion—with careful attention to definitions, symbols, and formulas. The intent is, above all, that the student develop a thorough understanding of the basic concepts in finance.

Although we prefer to cover the chapters in the order presented, other faculty have moved working capital management so that it follows Part Five. This permits covering the topics of time value of money, valuation, cost of capital, and capital budgeting earlier in the course.

Parts

1. Introduction   This section examines the goals and objectives of financial management. The present-day emphasis on decision making and risk management is stressed, with an update of significant events influencing the study of finance.

2. Financial analysis and planning   The student is first given the opportunity to review the basic principles of accounting as they relate to finance (emphasis is placed on financial statements and funds flow). This review material, in Chapter 2, is optional—and the student may judge whether he or she needs this review before progressing through the section.

Additional material in this part includes a thorough study of ratio analysis, budget construction techniques, and the development of comprehensive pro forma statements. The effect of heavy fixed commitments, in the form of either debt or plant and equipment, is examined in a discussion of leverage.

3. Working capital management   The techniques for managing the short-term assets of the firm and the associated liabilities are examined. The material is introduced in the context of risk–return analysis. The financial manager must constantly choose between liquid, low-return assets (perhaps marketable securities) and more profitable, less liquid assets (such as inventory). Sources of short-term financing are also considered.

4. The capital budgeting process   The decision on capital outlays is among the most significant that a firm will have to make. In terms of study procedure, we attempt to carefully lock down "time value of money" calculations, then proceed to the valuation of bonds and stocks, emphasizing present-value techniques. The valuation chapter develops the traditional dividend valuation model and examines bond price sensitivity in response to discount rates and inflation. An appendix presents the supernormal dividend growth model, or what is sometimes called the "two-stage" dividend model. After careful grounding in valuation practice and theory, we move into an examination of the cost of capital and capital structure. The text then moves to the actual capital budgeting decision, making generous use of previously learned material and employing the concept of marginal analysis. The concluding chapter in this part covers risk–return analysis in capital budgeting, with a brief exposure to portfolio theory and a consideration of market value maximization.

5. Long-term financing   The student is introduced to U.S. financial markets as they relate to corporate financial management. The student considers the sources and uses of funds in the capital markets—with coverage given to warrants and convertibles, as well as the more conventional methods of financing. The guiding role of the investment banker in the distribution of securities is also analyzed. Furthermore, the student is encouraged to think of leasing as a form of debt.

6. Expanding the perspective of corporate finance   A chapter on corporate mergers considers external growth strategy and serves as an integrative tool to bring together such topics as profit management, capital budgeting, portfolio considerations, and valuation concepts. A second chapter on international financial management describes the growth of the international financial markets, the rise of multinational business, and the effects on corporate financial management. The issues discussed in these two chapters highlight corporate diversification and risk-reduction attempts prevalent in the 1970s and continuing well into the 1980s.

List of Terms

agency theory	Subchapter S corporation
stockholder wealth maximization	conglomerate
insider trading	inflation
sole proprietorship	disinflation
partnership	restructuring
limited partnership	Tax Reform Act of 1986
corporation	"Crash of 1987"

Discussion Questions

1. How has the finance discipline changed since the 1940s and early 1950s?

2. What is meant by the goal of maximization of stockholder wealth? Why is profit maximization, by itself, an inappropriate goal?

3. What issue does agency theory examine? Why has it become more important in recent times?

4. When does insider trading occur? What government agency is charged with the responsibility of protecting against insider trading?

5. Suggest two forms of daily functions and two forms of occasional functions that the financial manager performs.

6. Contrast the liability provisions for a sole proprietorship, a partnership, a limited partnership, and a corporation.

7. Why is the corporate form of organization best suited to a large organization?

8. Why does the financial manager need to be concerned with inflation? With disinflation?

9. What are some ways in which corporations are restructuring their balance sheets and other related activities?

10. What is meant by the U.S. foreign trade deficit? How does the trade deficit affect the U.S. economy?

11. What was the main thrust of the Tax Reform Act of 1986? Will the act by itself tend to increase tax revenue?

Selected References

Branch, Ben. "Corporate Objectives and Market Performance." *Financial Management* 2 (Summer 1973), pp. 22–29.

Brennen, Michael J., and Eduardo S. Schwartz. "Regulation and Corporate Investment Policy." *Journal of Finance* 37 (May 1982), pp. 289–300.

Business Conditions Digest. U.S. Department of Commerce, December 1987.

"Compensation for Outside Directors." *Harvard Business Review* 57 (November–December 1979), pp. 18–28.

Collins, J. Markham, and Roger P. Bey. "The Master Limited Partnership: An Alternative to the Corporation." *Financial Management* 15 (Winter 1986), pp. 5–14.

Davis, Keith. "Social Responsibility Is Inevitable." *California Management Review* 19 (Fall 1976), pp. 14–20.

Donaldson, Gordon. "Financial Goals: Management vs. Stockholders." *Harvard Business Review* 41 (May–June 1963), pp. 16–29.

Gitman, Lawrence J., and Charles E. Maxwell. "Financial Activities of Major U.S. Firms: Survey and Analysis of Fortune's 1000." *Financial Management* 14 (Winter 1985), pp. 57–65.

Hill, Lawrence W. "The Growth of the Corporate Finance Function." *Financial Executive* 44 (July 1976), pp. 38–43.

Hirt, Geoffrey A. "Integrating Financial Theory and Practice with Institutional–Descriptive Finance." *Journal of Financial Education* 13 (Fall 1984), pp. 19–27.

Lewellen, Wilbur G. "Management and Ownership of Large Firms." *Journal of Finance* 24 (May 1969), pp. 299–322.

Seitz, Neil. "Shareholder Goals, Firm Goals and Firm Financing Decisions." *Financial Management* 11 (Autumn 1982), pp. 20–26.

Solomon, Ezra. *The Theory of Financial Management.* New York: Columbia University Press, 1963, pp. 15–26.

Weston, J. Fred. "The Development of Finance Theory." *Financial Management* 10 (Tenth Anniversary Issue, 1981), pp. 5–22.

PART

2

Financial Analysis and Planning

2   Review of Accounting

3   Financial Analysis

4   Financial Forecasting

5   Operating and Financial Leverage

Introduction

In this day of ever-increasing pressures to "tell the truth" from the Securities and Exchange Commission, the Federal Trade Commission, and various investor and consumer groups, the presentation and understanding of financial data are critical. Furthermore, increasing complexities in the business environment mean that new methods of reporting the financial condition of the firm are certain to take place. The student must be well positioned to understand the old rules of the game and to appreciate new developments on the horizon.

In Chapter 2, we review some of the basic principles of accounting. The student should have a reasonable understanding of financial statements and related concepts before studying the more analytical material. Students with a strong background in accounting may choose to merely gloss over this material.

We then proceed to a study of company performance through ratio analysis in Chapter 3. The purpose of ratio analysis is to examine financial data on a relative basis. Net profit means very little unless it is compared to some other measure such as sales, total assets, or net worth in an appropriate ratio format. Net income of $100,000 offers little insight, but a ratio of net income to sales of 5 percent may suggest a great deal in comparison to past performance and other companies.

An important dimension in financial analysis is a consideration of the impact of inflation and disinflation on the financial fortunes of the firm. The authors present examples showing how changing prices may distort the normally reported income of the firm.

In Chapter 4, we shift the emphasis from "what was" to "what will be" as we go through the process of financial forecasting. To anticipate future financing requirements, the firm must determine what the income statement, balance sheet, and cash budget will look like for the planning period. In the process of financial forecasting, we are forced to make predictions about future sales, inventory levels, receivables, and other accounts, and then to combine our forecasts into a structured set of financial statements. Upon completion of Chapter 4, the student should have a better understanding not only of forecasting but also of all the elements that make up the financial structure of the firm.

As a last topic of consideration in Part 2, we look at management's use of leverage to magnify the results of the firm. By leverage, we mean the utilization of a high percentage of fixed assets or "fixed cost" debt in the management and operation of the firm. As indicated in Chapter 5, if we are able to achieve a high volume of operation, our fixed costs should allow for strong profitability as our revenues go up while much of our costs remain constant. At a low level of operation, perhaps in a recession, the opposite results will take place, and our heavy fixed costs could force us into bankruptcy. We must learn how to handle this two-edged sword in an effective fashion.

2

Review of Accounting

The language of finance flows logically from accounting. In order to ensure that the student is adequately prepared to study important financial concepts, we must lock in the preparatory material from the accounting area. Much of the early frustration suffered by students who have difficulty with finance can be overcome if such concepts as retained earnings, stockholders' equity, depreciation, and historical/replacement cost accounting are brought into focus.

In this chapter, we examine the three basic types of financial statements—the income statement, the balance sheet, and the statement of cash flows—with particular attention paid to the interrelationships among these three measurement devices. As special preparation for the financial manager, we briefly examine income tax considerations affecting financial decisions.

Income Statement

The income statement is the major device for measuring the profitability of a firm over a period of time. An example of the income statement is presented in Table 2–1 for the Kramer Corporation.

Table 2–1

KRAMER CORPORATION
Income Statement
For the Year Ended December 31, 1989

1. Sales	$2,000,000
2. Cost of goods sold	1,500,000
3. Gross profits	500,000
4. Selling and administrative expense	220,000
5. Depreciation expense	50,000
6. Operating profit (EBIT)*	230,000
7. Interest expense	20,000
8. Earnings before taxes (EBT)	210,000
9. Taxes	99,500
10. Earnings after taxes (EAT)	110,500
11. Preferred stock dividends	10,500
12. Earnings available to common stockholders	$ 100,000
13. Shares outstanding	100,000
14. Earnings per share	$1.00

*Earnings before interest and taxes.

First, note that the income statement covers a defined period of time, whether it be one month, three months, or a year. The statement is presented in a stair-step or progressive fashion so that we can examine the profit or loss after each type of expense item is deducted.

We start with sales and deduct cost of goods sold to arrive at gross profit. The $500,000 thus represents the difference between what we bought or manufactured our goods for and the sales price. We then subtract selling and administrative expense and depreciation from gross profit to determine our profit (or loss) purely from operations of $230,000.[1] It is possible for a company to enjoy a high gross profit margin (25–50 percent) but a relatively low operating profit because of heavy expenses incurred in marketing the product and managing the company.

Having obtained operating profit (essentially a measure of how efficient management is in generating revenues and controlling expenses), we now adjust for revenues and expenses not related to operational matters. In this case we pay $20,000 in interest and arrive at earnings before taxes of $210,000. Our tax payments are $99,500, leaving aftertax income of $110,500.

---

[1]Depreciation was not treated as part of cost of goods sold in this instance, but rather as a separate expense. All or part of depreciation may be treated as part of cost of goods sold, depending on the circumstances.

Return to Capital

Before proceeding further, we should note that there are three primary sources of capital—the bondholders, who received $20,000 in interest (item 7); the preferred stockholders, who will receive $10,500 in dividends (item 11); and the common stockholders. After the $10,500 dividend has been paid to the preferred stockholders, there will be $100,000 in earnings available to the common stockholders (item 12). In computing earnings per share, we must interpret this in terms of the number of shares outstanding. As indicated in item 13, there are 100,000 shares outstanding, so the $100,000 of earnings available to the common stockholders may be translated into earnings per share of $1. Needless to say, common stockholders are sensitive to the number of shares outstanding—the more shares, the lower the earnings per share. A corollary to this is that, before any new shares are issued, the financial manager must be sure they will eventually generate sufficient earnings to avoid reducing earnings per share.

The $100,000 of profit ($1 earnings per share) may be paid out to the common stockholders in the form of dividends or retained in the company for subsequent reinvestment. The reinvested funds theoretically belong to the common stockholders, who hope they will provide future earnings and dividends. In the case of the Kramer Corporation, we assume that $50,000 in dividends will be paid out to the common stockholders, with the balance retained in the corporation for their benefit. A short supplement to the income statement, a statement of retained earnings (see Table 2–2), usually indicates the disposition of earnings.[2]

We see that $50,000 has been added to previously accumulated earnings of $250,000.

Table 2–2

Statement of Retained Earnings
For the Year Ended December 31, 1989

Retained earnings, balance, January 1, 1989	$250,000
Add: Earnings available to common stockholders, 1989	100,000
Deduct: Cash dividends declared in 1989	50,000
Retained earnings, balance, December 31, 1989	300,000

[2]The statement may also indicate any adjustments to previously reported income as well as any restrictions on cash dividends.

Price–Earnings Ratio Applied to Earnings per Share

A concept utilized throughout the text is the price–earnings ratio. This refers to the multiplier applied to earnings per share to determine current value. In the case of the Kramer Corporation, earnings per share were $1. If the firm enjoyed a price–earnings ratio of 12, the market value of each share would be $12. The price–earnings ratio (or P/E ratio, as it is commonly called) is influenced by the earnings and the sales growth of the firm, the risk (or volatility in performance), the debt–equity structure of the firm, the dividend payment policy, the quality of management, and a number of other factors. Since companies have various levels of earnings per share, price–earnings ratios allow us to compare the relative market value of many companies based on $1 of earnings per share.

The P/E ratio indicates expectations about the future of a company. Firms expected to provide returns greater than those for the market in general with equal or less risk often have P/E ratios higher than the market P/E ratio. Expectations of returns and P/E ratios do change over time, as Table 2–3 illustrates.

Price–earnings ratios can be confusing at times. When a firm's earnings are dropping rapidly or perhaps even approaching zero, its stock price, though declining too, may not match the magnitude of falloff in earnings. This process can give the appearance of an increasing P/E ratio under adversity. This happens from time to time in the auto industry and other cyclical industries. For example, in late 1987 B. F. Goodrich Tire Company was trading at a P/E over 50, because of cyclically low earnings. At

Table 2–3   P/E ratios for selected U.S. companies

Corporation	Industry	Jan. 2, 1980	Jan. 2, 1983	Jan. 2, 1986	Jan. 2, 1988
CBS	Broadcasting	7	12	18	16
Digital Equipment	Computers	12	15	16	14
Exxon	International oil	6	10	9	11
General Cinema	Movies	8	11	19	25
Holiday Corp.	Hotels, motels	8	15	16	5
IBM	Computers	12	15	16	14
Macmillan	Publishing	20	13	18	24
McDonald's	Restaurants	9	10	16	15
Texas Utilities	Public utilities	7	6	7	6
Upjohn	Drugs	10	19	20	17
Winn-Dixie	Retail	8	11	14	14
Standard & Poor's (500 Stock Index)		7	11	14	15

the time, the average P/E, as measured by Standard & Poor's 500 Stock Index, was 15.

Limitations of the Income Statement

The economist defines income as the change in real worth that takes place between the beginning and the end of a specified time period. To the economist, an increase in the value of a firm's land as a result of a new airport being built on adjacent property is an increase in the real worth of the firm and therefore represents income. Similarly, the elimination of a competitor might also increase the firm's real worth and therefore result in income in an economic sense. The accountant does not ordinarily employ such broad definitions. Accounting values are established primarily by actual transactions, and income that is gained or lost during a given period is a function of verifiable transactions. While the potential sales price of your property may go from $100,000 to $200,000 as a result of new developments in your area, your stockholders may only perceive a much smaller gain or loss from operations.

Also, as will be pointed out in Chapter 3, Financial Analysis, there is some flexibility in the reporting of transactions, so that similar events may result in differing measurements of income at the end of a time period. The intent of this section is not to criticize the accounting profession, for it is certainly among the best-organized, trained, and paid professions, but to alert students to imperfections already well recognized within the profession.

Balance Sheet

The balance sheet indicates what the firm owns and how these assets are financed in the form of liabilities or ownership interest. While the income statement purports to show the profitability of the firm, the balance sheet delineates the firm's holdings and obligations. Together these statements are intended to answer two questions: How much did the firm make or lose, and what is a measure of its worth? A balance sheet for the Kramer Corporation is presented in Table 2–4.

Note that the balance sheet is a picture of the firm at a point in time— in this case December 31, 1989. It does not purport to represent the result of transactions for a specific month, quarter, or year, but rather is a cumulative chronicle of all transactions that have affected the corporation since its inception. In contrast, the income statement measures results

Table 2–4

KRAMER CORPORATION
Statement of Financial Position (Balance Sheet)
December 31, 1989

Assets

Current assets:

Cash		$ 40,000
Marketable securities		10,000
Accounts receivable	$ 220,000	
Less: Allowance for bad debts	20,000	200,000
Inventory		180,000
Prepaid expenses		20,000
Total current assets		450,000

Other assets:

Investments		50,000

Fixed assets:

Plant and equipment, original cost	1,100,000	
Less: Accumulated depreciation	600,000	
Net plant and equipment		500,000
Total assets		$1,000,000

Liabilities and Stockholders' Equity

Current liabilities:

Accounts payable	$ 80,000
Notes payable	100,000
Accrued expenses	30,000
Total current liabilities	210,000

Long-term liabilities:

Bonds payable, 1998	90,000
Total liabilities	300,000

Stockholders' equity:

Preferred stock, $100 par value, 500 shares	50,000
Common stock, $1 par value, 100,000 shares	100,000
Capital paid in excess of par (common stock)	250,000
Retained earnings	300,000
Total stockholders' equity	700,000
Total liabilities and stockholders' equity	$1,000,000

only over a short, quantifiable period of time. Generally, balance sheet items are stated on an original cost basis rather than at present worth.

Interpretation of Balance Sheet Items

Asset accounts are listed in order of liquidity. The first category of current assets covers items that may be converted to cash within one year (or within the normal operating cycle of the firm). A few items are worthy of mention. *Marketable securities* are temporary investments of excess cash. The value shown in the account is the lower of cost or current market value. *Accounts receivable* include an allowance for bad debts (based on historical evidence) to determine their anticipated collection value. *Inventory* may be in the form of raw material, goods in process, or finished goods, while *prepaid expenses* represent future expense items that have already been paid, such as insurance premiums or rent.

Investments, unlike marketable securities, represent a longer-term commitment of funds (at least one year). They may include stocks, bonds, or investments in other corporations. Frequently, the account will contain stock in companies that the firm is acquiring.

Plant and equipment is carried at original cost minus accumulated depreciation. Accumulated depreciation is not to be confused with the depreciation expense item indicated in the income statement in Table 2–1. Accumulated depreciation is the sum of all past and present depreciation charges on currently owned assets, while depreciation expense is the current year's charge. If we subtract accumulated depreciation from the original value, the balance ($500,000) tells us how much of the original cost has not been expensed in the form of depreciation.

Total assets are financed through either liabilities or stockholders' equity. Liabilities represent financial obligations of the firm and move from current liabilities (due within one year) to longer-term obligations, such as bonds payable in 1998.

Among the short-term obligations, *accounts payable* represent amounts owed on open account to suppliers, while *notes payable* are generally short-term signed obligations to the banker or other creditors. An *accrued expense* is generated when a service has been provided or an obligation incurred and payment has not yet taken place. The firm may owe workers additional wages for services provided or the government taxes on earned income.

In the balance sheet presented in Table 2–4, we see the $1,000,000 in total assets of the Kramer Corporation was financed by $300,000 in debt and $700,000 in the form of stockholders' equity. Stockholders' equity represents the total contribution and ownership interest of preferred and common stockholders.

The *preferred stock* investment position is $50,000, based on 500 shares at $100 par. In the case of *common stock*, 100,000 shares have been issued at a total par value of $100,000, plus an extra $250,000 in *capital paid in excess of par* for a sum of $350,000. We can assume that the 100,000 shares were originally sold at $3.50 each.

100,000 shares	$1.00	Par value	$100,000
	2.50	Capital paid in excess of par	250,000
	$3.50	Price per share	$350,000

Finally, there is $300,000 in *retained earnings*. This value, previously determined in the statement of retained earnings (Table 2–2), represents the firm's cumulative earnings since inception minus dividends and any other adjustments.

Concept of Net Worth

Stockholders' equity minus the preferred stock component represents the *net worth*, or *book value*, of the firm. There is some logic to the approach. If you take everything that the firm owns and subtract the debt and preferred stock obligation,[3] the remainder belongs to the common stockholder and represents net worth. In the case of the Kramer Corporation, we show:

Total assets	$1,000,000
Total liabilities	300,000
Stockholders' equity	700,000
Preferred stock obligation	50,000
Net worth assigned to common	$ 650,000
Common shares outstanding	100,000
Net worth, or book value, per share	$6.50

The original cost per share was $3.50; the net worth, or book value, per share is $6.50; and the market value (based on a P/E ratio of 12 and earnings per share of $1) is $12. It is this last value that is of primary concern to the financial manager and the security analyst.

Limitations of the Balance Sheet

Lest we attribute too much significance to the balance sheet, we need to examine some of the underlying concepts supporting its construction. Most of the values on the balance sheet are stated on a historical or original cost basis. This may be particularly troublesome in the case of plant and equipment and inventory, which may now be worth two or three times

---

[3]An additional discussion of preferred stock is presented in Chapter 17, Common and Preferred Stock Financing. Preferred stock represents neither a debt claim nor an ownership interest in the firm. It is a hybrid, or intermediate, type of security.

Table 2–5 Comparison of market value to book value per share, December 1987	Corporation	Market Value per Share	Book Value per Share	Ratio of Market Value to Book Value
	Lotus	$25.00	$ 4.30	5.81
	Playboy	10.50	2.40	4.38
	American Home Products . . .	70.75	17.50	4.04
	Automatic Data	41.25	11.50	3.59
	Lilly (Eli)	66.25	22.00	3.01
	Outboard Marine	17.75	22.50	0.79
	Inland Steel	23.50	35.00	0.67
	Best Products	7.00	15.50	0.45
	Long Island Lighting	7.25	30.80	0.24
	CityFed Financial	4.25	18.80	0.23

the original cost or—from a negative viewpoint—may require many times the original cost for replacement.

The accounting profession has been grappling with this problem for decades, and the discussion becomes particularly intense each time inflation rears its ugly head. In October 1979 the Financial Accounting Standards Board (FASB) issued a ruling that required large companies to disclose inflation-adjusted accounting data in their annual reports. This information was to be disclosed in addition to the traditional historical cost data and could show up in footnotes or in a separate full-fledged financial section with detailed explanations. However, the standard is no longer in force, and the inclusion of inflation-adjusted data is no longer required in any form. If a company wishes to adjust its balance sheet or income statement data for inflation, it is purely a voluntary act.

In Table 2–5 we look at large disparities between market value per share and historical book value per share for a number of publicly traded companies at the end of 1987. Besides asset valuation, a number of other factors may explain the wide differences between per share values, such as industry outlook, growth prospects, quality of management, and risk–return expectations.

Statement of Cash Flows

In November 1987, the accounting profession designated the "Statement of Cash Flows" as the third required financial statement, along with the balance sheet and income statement. Referred to as Financial Accounting Standards Board (FASB) Standard 95, it replaces the old statement of changes in financial position (and the sources and uses of funds statement).

The purpose of the new statement of cash flows is to emphasize the critical nature of cash flow to the operations of the firm. Cash flow generally represents cash or cash equivalent items that can easily be converted into cash within 90 days (such as a money market fund).

The income statement and balance sheet that we have studied thus far are normally based on the accrual method of accounting, in which revenues and expenses are recognized as they occur, rather than when cash actually changes hands. For example, a $100,000 credit sale may be made in December of 1988 and shown as revenue for that year—in spite of the fact that the cash payment would not be received until March of 1989. When the actual payment is finally received under accrual accounting, no revenue is recognized (it has already been accounted for previously). The primary advantage of accrual accounting is that it allows us to match revenues and expenses in the period in which they occur in order to appropriately measure profit; but a disadvantage is that there is not adequate attention directed to the actual cash flow position of the firm.

One can think of situations in which a firm made a $1 million profit on a transaction, but will not receive the actual cash payment for two years. Or, perhaps, the $1 million profit is in cash, but the firm increased its asset purchases by $3 million (a new building). If you merely read the income statement, you might assume the firm is in a strong $1 million cash position; but if you go beyond the income statement to cash flow considerations, you would observe the firm is $2 million short of funds for the period.

As a last example, a firm might show a $100,000 loss on the income statement; but if there were a depreciation expense write-off of $150,000, the firm would actually have $50,000 in cash. Since depreciation is a noncash deduction, the $150,000 deduction in the income statement for depreciation can be added back to net income to determine cash flow.

The statement of cash flows addresses these issues by translating income statement and balance sheet data into cash flow information. A corporation that has $1 million in accrual-based accounting profits can determine whether it can actually afford to pay a cash dividend to stockholders, buy new equipment, or undertake new projects. In the low-profit and cash-tight era of the 1980s, cash flow analysis has taken on a very special meaning.

Developing an Actual Statement

We shall use the information previously provided for the Kramer Corporation in this chapter to illustrate how the statement of cash flows is developed.

But first, let's identify the three primary sections of the statement of cash flows:

1. Cash flows from operating activities.
2. Cash flows from investing activities.
3. Cash flows from financing activities.

After each of these sections is completed, the results are added together to compute the net increase or decrease in cash flow for the corporation. An example of the process is shown in Figure 2–1. Let's begin with cash flows from operating activities.

Determining Cash Flows from Operating Activities

Basically, we are going to translate *income from operations* from an accrual to a cash basis. According to FASB 95, there are two ways to accomplish this objective. First, the firm may use a *direct method*, in which each and every item on the income statement is adjusted from accrual accounting

Figure 2–1
Illustration of concepts behind statement of cash flows

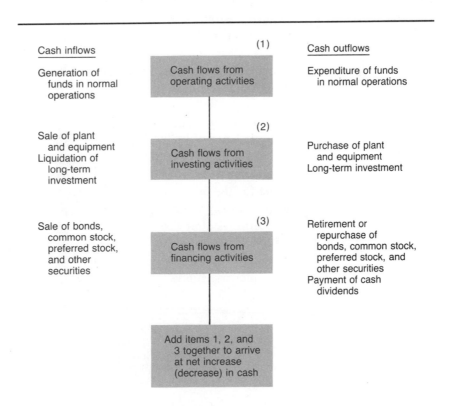

to cash accounting. This is a tedious process, in which all sales must be adjusted to cash sales, all purchases must be adjusted to cash purchases, and so on. A more popular method is the *indirect method,* in which net income represents the starting point and then adjustments are made to convert net income to cash flows from operations.[4] This is the method we will use. Regardless of whether the direct or indirect method is used, the same final answer will be derived.

We follow these procedures in computing cash flows from operating activities using the indirect method.[5]

- Start with net income.
- Recognize that depreciation is a noncash deduction in computing net income and should be added back to net income to *increase* the cash balance.
- Recognize that increases in current assets are a use of funds and *reduce* the cash balance (indirectly)—as an example, the firm spends more funds on inventory.
- Recognize that decreases in current assets are a source of funds and *increase* the cash balance (indirectly)—that is, the firm reduces funds tied up in inventory.
- Recognize that increases in current liabilities are a source of funds and increase the cash balance (indirectly)—the firm gets more funds from creditors.
- Recognize that decreases in current liabilities are a use of funds and *decrease* the cash balance (indirectly)—that is, the firm pays off creditors.

These steps are illustrated in Figure 2–2.

We will follow these procedures for the Kramer Corporation, drawing primarily on material from Table 2–1 on page 26 (the previously presented income statement) and from Table 2–6 on page 38 (which shows balance sheet data for the most recent two years).

The analysis is presented in Table 2–7 on page 38. We begin with net income (earnings after taxes) of $110,500 and add back depreciation of $50,000. We then show that increases in current assets (accounts receivable and inventory) reduce funds and decreases in current assets (prepaid expenses) increase funds. Also, we show increases in current liabilities

---

[4]The indirect method is very similar to procedures used to construct the old sources and uses of funds statement.

[5]In addition to the items mentioned, we may need to recognize the *gains* or *losses* on the sale of operating and nonoperating assets. We exclude these for ease of analysis.

Figure 2–2
Steps in computing
net cash flows from
operating activities
using the indirect
method

(accounts payable) as an addition to funds and decreases in current liabilities (accrued expenses) as a reduction of funds.

We see in Table 2–7 that the firm generated $150,500 in cash flows from
operating activities. Of some significance is that this figure is $40,000 larger
than the net income figure reported to stockholders ($150,500 – $110,500).
You can also envision that a firm with little depreciation and a massive
buildup of inventory might show lower cash flow than reported net income.
Once cash flows from operating activities are determined, management has
a better feel for what can be allocated to investing or financing needs (such
as paying cash dividends).

Table 2–6

KRAMER CORPORATION
Comparative Balance Sheets

	Year-End 1988	Year-End 1989
Assets		
Current assets:		
Cash	$ 30,000	$ 40,000
Marketable securities	10,000	10,000
Accounts receivable (net)	170,000	200,000
Inventory	160,000	180,000
Prepaid expenses	30,000	20,000
Total current assets	400,000	450,000
Investments (long-term)	20,000	50,000
Plant and equipment	1,000,000	1,100,000
Less: Accumulated depreciation	550,000	600,000
Net plant and equipment	450,000	500,000
Total assets	$ 870,000	$1,000,000
Liabilities and Stockholders' Equity		
Current liabilities:		
Accounts payable	$ 45,000	$ 80,000
Notes payable	100,000	100,000
Accrued expenses	35,000	30,000
Total current liabilities	180,000	210,000
Long-term liabilities:		
Bonds payable, 1998	40,000	90,000
Total liabilities	220,000	300,000
Stockholders' equity:		
Preferred stock, $100 par value	50,000	50,000
Common stock, $1 par value	100,000	100,000
Capital paid in excess of par	250,000	250,000
Retained earnings	250,000	300,000
Total stockholders' equity	650,000	700,000
Total liabilities and stockholders' equity	$ 870,000	$1,000,000

Table 2–7
Cash flows from operating activities

Net income (earnings after taxes) (Table 2–1)		$110,500
Adjustments to determine cash flow from operating activities:		
Add back depreciation (Table 2–1)	50,000	
Increase in accounts receivable (Table 2–6)	(30,000)	
Increase in inventory (Table 2–6)	(20,000)	
Decrease in prepaid expenses (Table 2–6)	10,000	
Increase in accounts payable (Table 2–6)	35,000	
Decrease in accrued expenses (Table 2–6)	(5,000)	
Total adjustments		40,000
Net cash flows from operating activities		$150,500

Determining Cash Flows from Investing Activities

This represents the second section in the statement of cash flows. The section relates to long-term investment activities in other issuers' securities or, more importantly, in plant and equipment. Increasing investments represent a *use* of funds and decreasing investments represent a *source* of funds.

Examining Table 2–6 for the Kramer Corporation, we show the following information in Table 2–8.

Table 2–8
Cash flows from
investing activities

Increase in investments (long-term securities) (Table 2–6)	($30,000)
Increase in plant and equipment (Table 2–6)	(100,000)
Net cash flows from investing activities	($130,000)

Determining Cash Flows from Financing Activities

In the third section of the statement of cash flows, we show the effects of financing activities on the corporation. Financing activities apply to the sale or retirement of bonds, common stock, preferred stock, and other corporate securities. Also, the payment of cash dividends is considered as a financing activity. The sale of the firm's securities represents a *source* of funds and the retirement or repurchase of such securities represents a *use* of funds. The payment of dividends also represents a *use* of funds.

Using data from Table 2–1, Table 2–2, and Table 2–6, the financing activities of the Kramer Corporation are shown in Table 2–9.

Table 2–9
Cash flows from
financing activities

Increase in bonds payable (Table 2–6)	$50,000
Preferred stock dividends paid (Table 2–1)	(10,500)
Common stock dividends paid (Table 2–2)	(50,000)
Net cash flows from financing activities	($10,500)

Combining the Three Sections of the Statement

We now combine the three sections of the statement on cash flows to arrive at the one overall statement that the corporation provides to security analysts and stockholders. The information is shown in Table 2–10.

We see in Table 2–10 that the firm created excess funds from operating activities that were utilized heavily in investing activities and somewhat in financing activities. As a result, there is a $10,000 increase in the cash balance, and this can also be reconciled with the increase in the cash balance of $10,000 from $30,000 to $40,000, as indicated in Table 2–6.

One might also do further analysis on how the buildups in various accounts were financed. For example, if there is a substantial increase in inventory or accounts receivable, is there an associated buildup in accounts payable and short-term bank loans? If not, the firm may have to utilize long-term financing to carry part of the short-term needs. An even more important question might be: How are increases in long-term assets being financed? Most desirably, there should be adequate long-term financing and profits to carry these needs. If not, then short-term funds (trade credit and bank loans) may be utilized to carry long-term needs. This is a potentially high risk situation, in that short-term sources of funds may dry up while long-term needs continue to demand funding. In problems at the back of the chapter, you will have an opportunity to further consider these points.

Table 2–10

KRAMER CORPORATION
Statement of Cash Flows
For the Year Ended December 31, 1989

Cash flows from operating activities:		
Net income (earnings after taxes)		$110,500
Adjustments to determine cash flow from operating activities:		
Add back depreciation	$ 50,000	
Increase in accounts receivable	(30,000)	
Increase in inventory	(20,000)	
Decrease in prepaid expenses	10,000	
Increase in accounts payable	35,000	
Decrease in accrued expenses	(5,000)	
Total adjustments		40,000
Net cash flows from operating activities		$150,500
Cash flows from investing activities:		
Increase in investments (long-term securities)	(30,000)	
Increase in plant and equipment	(100,000)	
Net cash flows from investing activities		($130,000)
Cash flows from financing activities:		
Increase in bonds payable	50,000	
Preferred stock dividends paid	(10,500)	
Common stock dividends paid	(50,000)	
Net cash flows from financing activities		($10,500)
Net increase (decrease) in cash flows		$10,000

Depreciation and Funds Flow

One of the most confusing items to finance students is whether depreciation is a source of funds to the corporation. In Table 2–7, we listed depreciation as a source of funds (cash flow). This item deserves further clarification. The reason we added back depreciation was not that depreciation was a new source of funds, but rather that we subtracted this noncash expense in arriving at net income and now have to add it back to determine the amount of actual funds on hand.

Depreciation represents an attempt to allocate the initial cost of an asset over its useful life. In essence, we attempt to match the annual expense of plant and equipment ownership against the revenues that are being produced. Nevertheless, the charging of depreciation is purely an accounting entry and does not directly involve the movement of funds. To go from accounting flows to cash flows in Table 2–7, we restored the noncash deduction of $50,000 for depreciation that was subtracted in Table 2–1, the income statement.

Let us examine a very simple case involving depreciation in Table 2–11. Assume that we purchase a machine for $500 with a five-year life and that we pay for it in cash. Our depreciation schedule calls for equal annual depreciation charges of $100 per year for five years. Assume further that our firm has $1,000 in earnings before depreciation and taxes and that

Table 2–11
Comparison of accounting and cash flows

	Year 1	
	(1) Accounting Flows	*(2)* Cash Flows
Earnings before depreciation and taxes (EBDT) . . .	$1,000	$1,000
Depreciation	100	100
Earnings before taxes (EBT)	900	900
Taxes	300	300
Earnings after taxes (EAT)	$ 600	600
Purchase of equipment		−500
Depreciation charged without cash outlay		+100
Cash flow		$ 200

	Year 2	
Earnings before depreciation and taxes (EBDT) . . .	$1,000	$1,000
Depreciation	100	100
Earnings before taxes	900	900
Taxes	300	300
Earnings after taxes (EAT)	$ 600	600
Depreciation charged without cash outlay		+100
Cash flow		$ 700

the tax obligation is $300. Note the difference between accounting flows and cash flows for the first two years in Table 2–11.

Since we took $500 out of cash flow originally to purchase equipment (in column 2), we do not wish to take it out again. Thus, we add back $100 in depreciation each year for five years to "wash out" the subtraction in the income statement.

Income Tax Considerations

Virtually every financial decision is influenced by federal income tax considerations. Primary examples are the lease versus purchase decision, the issuance of common stock versus debt decision, and the decision to replace an asset. While the intent of this section is not to review the rules, regulations, and nuances of the Federal Income Tax Code, we will examine how tax matters influence corporate financial decisions. The primary orientation will be toward the principles governing "corporate" tax decisions, though many of the same principles apply to a sole proprietorship or a partnership.

Corporate Tax Rates

The new corporate tax rates under the Tax Reform Act of 1986 are as follows. (The marginal tax rate is the rate that applies to each new dollar of income within the bracket.)

Income Level	Marginal Tax Rate
0–$50,000	15%
$50,000–75,000	25
over $75,000	34

Also, on income between $100,000 and $335,000 there is an additional 5 percent surtax, resulting in a 39 percent tax over that range.[6] (Is this really called simplification?)

Assume a corporation has income of $200,000; what would its tax obligation be? The answer is provided in Table 2–12.

---

[6]The purpose of this surtax is to eliminate the benefits of the lower rates (15 percent and 25 percent) for corporations that have income over $100,000. By adding the 5 percent surtax up to $335,000, the beneficial effects of the lower rates are completely wiped out. That is, the surtax adds $11,750 to taxes between $100,000 and $335,000, which is exactly equal to the benefit of paying only 15 percent on the first $50,000 and 25 percent on the next $25,000 instead of 34 percent over this sum.

**Table 2–12
Corporate tax
obligation on
$200,000**

	Amount	Marginal Tax Rate	Incremental Taxes
Ist	$ 50,000	15%	$ 7,500
next	$ 25,000	25	6,250
next	$ 25,000	34	8,500
next	$100,000	39	39,000
		Total taxes	$61,250

The total tax bill would be $61,250. Observe that, although the marginal tax rate extends between 15 and 39 percent in this case, the average tax rate for $200,000 of earnings is 30.625 percent.

$$\text{Average tax rate} = \frac{\text{Total taxes}}{\text{Total income}} = \frac{\$61,250}{\$200,000} = 30.625 \text{ percent}$$

At income levels of $335,000 or over, the marginal tax rate and average tax rate are always the same: 34 percent. Let's once again compute the tax obligation to demonstrate this point. An income level of $400,000 is utilized in Table 2–13.

**Table 2–13
Corporate tax
obligation on
$400,000**

	(1) Amount	(2) Total Amount	(3) Marginal Tax Rate	(4) Incremental Taxes
Ist	$ 50,000	$ 50,000	15%	$ 7,500
next	$ 25,000	75,000	25	6,250
next	$ 25,000	100,000	34	8,500
next	$235,000	335,000	39	91,650
next	$ 65,000	400,000	34	22,100
			Total taxes	$136,000

In this example, the amount of income subject to the marginal tax rate is shown in column 1, the cumulative total income is presented in column 2, the marginal tax rate is shown in column 3, and the incremental tax is presented in column 4. The incremental tax is, of course, equal to the value in column 1 times the marginal tax rate in column 3.

The total tax of $136,000 represents an average tax of 34 percent on $400,000 of income.

$$\frac{\text{Total taxes}}{\text{Total income}} = \frac{\$136,000}{\$400,000} = 34 \text{ percent}$$

The 34 percent average tax rate is equal to the marginal tax rate of 34 percent at this $400,000 level.

Corporate versus Individual Taxes

For the first time in U.S. history, the maximum corporate tax rate is higher than the maximum individual tax rate. The maximum corporate rate is 34 percent (with a possible 5 percent surtax) and the maximum individual tax rate is 33 percent.[7] As recently as 1980, the maximum individual tax rate was 24 percent *higher* than the maximum corporate tax rate (70 percent versus 46 percent).

	1980	1988
Maximum individual tax rate	70%	33%
Maximum corporate tax rate	46	34

With the maximum individual tax rate now lower than the maximum corporate tax rate, it is possible that some small corporations may consider converting to limited partnerships or elect to be taxed under Subchapter S corporate rules. They not only will avoid double taxation but will also enjoy a lower rate on the first tax (33 percent versus 34 percent).

Cost of a Tax-Deductible Expense

The businessman often states that a tax-deductible item such as interest on business loans, travel expenditures, or salaries costs substantially less than the amount expended, on an aftertax basis. We shall investigate how this process works. Let us examine the tax statements of two corporations—the first pays $100,000 in interest, and the second has no interest expense. An average tax rate of 40 percent is used for each computation. (The 40 percent rate is a bit easier to follow than the new 34 percent corporate rate for this example, so we use it for ease of presentation.)

	Corporation A	Corporation B
Earnings before interest and taxes	$400,000	$400,000
Interest	100,000	0
Earnings before taxes (taxable income)	300,000	400,000
Taxes (40%)	120,000	160,000
Earnings after taxes	$180,000	$240,000
Difference in earnings after taxes—$60,000		

---

[7]To be technically correct, the maximum individual rate is only 28 percent with a 5 percent surtax; but this surtax effectively creates a third bracket for the individual taxpayer, which carries a 33 percent marginal tax rate. The surtax is much more meaningful for upper-income individual taxpayers than it is for corporations.

Although Corporation A paid out $100,000 more in interest than Corporation B, its earnings after taxes are only $60,000 less than those of Corporation B. Thus, we say that the $100,000 in interest cost the firm only $60,000 in aftertax earnings. The aftertax cost of a tax-deductible expense can be computed as the actual expense times one minus the tax rate. In this case, we show $100,000 (1 − Tax rate), or $100,000 × 0.60 = $60,000. The reasoning in this instance is that the $100,000 is deducted from earnings before determining taxable income, thus saving us $40,000 in taxes and only costing $60,000 on a net basis.

Because a dividend on common stock is not tax deductible, we say that it cost us 100 percent of the amount paid. From a purely corporate cash flow viewpoint, the firm would be indifferent between paying $100,000 in interest and $60,000 in dividends.

Depreciation as a Tax Shield

Although depreciation is not a new source of funds, it does provide the important function of shielding part of our income from taxes. Let us examine Corporation A and B again, this time with an eye toward depreciation rather than interest. Corporation A charges off $100,000 in depreciation, while Corporation B charges off none.

	Corporation A	Corporation B
Earnings before depreciation and taxes	$400,000	$400,000
Depreciation	100,000	0
Earnings before taxes	300,000	400,000
Taxes (40%)	120,000	160,000
Earnings after taxes	180,000	240,000
+Depreciation charged without cash outlay	100,000	0
Cash flow	$280,000	$240,000
Difference—$40,000		

We compute earnings after taxes and then add back depreciation to get cash flow. The difference between $280,000 and $240,000 indicates that Corporation A enjoys $40,000 more in cash flow. The reason is that depreciation shielded $100,000 from taxation in Corporation A and saved $40,000 in taxes, which eventually showed up in cash flow. Though depreciation is not a new source of funds, it does provide tax shield benefits that can be measured as depreciation times the tax rate, or in this case $100,000 × 0.40 = $40,000. A more comprehensive discussion of depreciation's effect on cash flow is presented in Chapter 12, as part of the long-term capital budgeting decision.

Summary

The financial manager must be thoroughly familiar with the language of accounting in order to administer the financial affairs of the firm. The income statement provides a measure of the firm's profitability over a specified period of time. Earnings per share represents residual income to the common stockholder that may be paid out in the form of dividends or reinvested to generate future profits and dividends. A limitation of the income statement is that it reports income and expense primarily on a transaction basis and thus may not recognize certain major economic events as they occur.

The balance sheet is a snapshot of the financial position of the firm at a point in time, with the stockholders' equity section purporting to represent ownership interest. Because the balance sheet is presented on a historical-cost basis, it may not necessarily reflect the true value of the firm.

The statement of cash flows, the third major statement that the corporation presents to stockholders and security analysts, emphasizes the importance of cash flows data to the operations of the firm. It translates the information on the income statement and balance sheet that was prepared on an accrual accounting basis to a cash basis. From this data, the firm can better assess its ability to pay cash dividends, invest in new equipment, and so on.

Finally, we examine the corporate tax structure and the tax implications of interest, dividends, and depreciation. The aftertax cost and cash flow implications of these items are important throughout the text.

List of Terms

income statement	net worth, or book value
earnings per share	cash flow
price–earnings ratio (P/E ratio)	statement of cash flows
	cash flows from operating activities
balance sheet	cash flows from investing activities
stockholders' equity	cash flows from financing activities
liquidity	marginal corporate tax rate

Discussion Questions ————————————————————

1. Discuss some of the financial variables that have an effect on the price–earnings ratio.

2. What is the difference between book value per share of common stock and market value per share? Why does this disparity occur?

3. Explain how depreciation generates actual cash flows for the company.

4. What is the difference between accumulated depreciation and depreciation expense? How are they related?

5. How is the income statement related to the balance sheet?

6. Comment on why inflation may restrict the usefulness of the balance sheet as normally presented.

7. Explain why the statement of cash flows provides useful information that goes beyond income statement and balance sheet data.

8. What are the three primary sections of the statement of cash flows? In what section would the payment of a cash dividend be shown?

9. Explain why the limited partnership enjoys additional popularity as a result of the change in the tax rates under the Tax Reform Act of 1986.

10. Why is interest expense said to cost the firm substantially less than the actual expense, while dividends cost it 100 percent of the outlay?

Problems ————————————————————————

1. Quack Medical Supplies has income of $260,000.
   a. Compute the total tax obligation.
   b. What is the average tax rate on the income? (Round to two places to the right of the decimal point.)

2. Reynolds Enterprises has income of $500,000.
   a. Compute the total tax obligation.
   b. What is the average tax on the income?

3. Given the following information, prepare, in good form, an income statement for Overton, Inc. Use the corporate tax rates in Chapter 2 to calculate taxes.

Selling and administrative expense	$ 50,000
Depreciation expense	80,000
Sales	390,000
Interest expense	30,000
Cost of goods sold	140,000

4. The Lane Book Company sold 1,200 finance textbooks to State University for $45 each. These books cost Lane $30 each to produce. In addition, Lane spent $2,000 to convince the university to buy its books. Lane borrowed $10,000 on January 1, 1988, on which it paid 12 percent interest. Both principal and interest were paid on December 31, 1988. Lane's tax rate is 30 percent. Depreciation expense for the year was $4,000.

   Did Lane make a profit in 1988? Verify with an income statement presented in good form.

5. Classify the following balance sheet items as current or noncurrent:

   Inventory
   Accounts payable
   Preferred stock
   Prepaid expenses
   Bonds payable

   Retained earnings
   Marketable securities
   Accounts receivable
   Plant and equipment
   Accrued wages payable

6. Arrange the following income statement items so that they are in the proper order of an income statement:

   Depreciation expense
   Gross profit
   Interest expense
   Taxes
   Preferred stock dividends
   Shares outstanding
   Earnings per share
   Earnings after taxes

   Operating profit
   Selling and administrative expense
   Sales
   Earnings before taxes
   Cost of goods sold
   Earnings available to common stockholders

7. Identify whether each of the following items increases or decreases cash flow:

   Increase in inventory
   Decrease in prepaid expenses
   Decrease in accounts receivable
   Increase in cash
   Decrease in inventory

   Dividend payment
   Increase in notes payable
   Depreciation expense
   Decrease in accounts payable
   Increase in investments

8. The Gourmet Restaurant has an operating profit of $180,000. Interest expense for the year was $10,000; preferred dividends paid were

$12,050; and common dividends paid were $30,000. The tax was $57,950. The Gourmet Restaurant has 20,000 shares of common stock outstanding.

    a. Calculate the earnings per share and the common dividends per share for the Gourmet Restaurant.

    b. What was the increase in retained earnings for the year?

9. Meredith Office Supplies had $600,000 of retained earnings on December 31, 1989. The company paid dividends of $50,000 in 1989 and had retained earnings of $520,000 on December 31, 1988. How much did Meredith earn during 1989, and what would earnings per share be if 50,000 shares of common stock are outstanding?

10. Fill in the blank spaces with categories 1 through 7 below:

    1. Balance sheet (BS).   5. Current liabilities (CL).
    2. Income statement (IS).   6. Long-term liabilities (LL).
    3. Current assets (CA).   7. Stockholders' equity (SE).
    4. Fixed assets (FA).

Indicate Whether Item Is on Balance Sheet (BS) or Income Statement (IS)	If on Balance Sheet, Designate Which Category	Item
_____	_____	Retained earnings
_____	_____	Income tax expense
_____	_____	Accounts receivable
_____	_____	Common stock
_____	_____	Capital in excess of par value
_____	_____	Bonds payable, maturity 1999
_____	_____	Notes payable (six months)
_____	_____	Net income
_____	_____	Selling and administrative expenses
_____	_____	Inventories
_____	_____	Accrued expenses
_____	_____	Cash
_____	_____	Plant and equipment
_____	_____	Sales
_____	_____	Operating expenses
_____	_____	Marketable securities
_____	_____	Accounts payable
_____	_____	Interest expense
_____	_____	Income tax payable

11. The Eastern Corporation has a gross profit of $960,000 and $340,000 in depreciation expense. The Western Corporation also has $960,000 in gross profit, with $40,000 in depreciation expense. Selling and administrative expense is $220,000 for each company.

   Given that the tax rate is 40 percent, compute the cash flow for both companies. Explain the difference in cash flow between the two firms.

12. The Simmons Corporation has assets of $400,000, current liabilities of $50,000, and long-term liabilities of $100,000. There is $40,000 in preferred stock outstanding. Twenty thousand shares of common stock have been issued.
   a. Compute book value (net worth) per share.
   b. If there is $44,000 in earnings available to common stockholders and Simmon's stock has a P/E ratio of seven times earnings per share, what is the current price of the stock?
   c. What is the ratio of market value per share to book value per share?

13. Arrange the following items in proper balance sheet presentation:

Accumulated depreciation	$300,000
Retained earnings	96,000
Cash	10,000
Bonds payable	136,000
Accounts receivable	48,000
Plant and equipment—original cost	680,000
Accounts payable	35,000
Allowance for bad debts	6,000
Common stock, $1 par, 100,000 shares outstanding	100,000
Inventory	66,000
Preferred stock, $50 par, 1,000 shares outstanding	50,000
Marketable securities	20,000
Investments	20,000
Notes payable	33,000
Capital paid in excess of par (common stock)	88,000

14. Tandem Paper Products has assets of $1,200,000, current liabilities of $315,000, and long-term liabilities of $460,000. There is $135,000 in preferred stock outstanding. Twenty-five thousand shares of common stock have been issued.
   a. Compute book value (net worth) per share.
   b. If there is $30,000 in earnings available to common stockholders and Tandem's stock has a P/E of 15 times earnings per share, what is the current price of the stock?

c. What is the ratio of market value per share to book value per share?

15. In problem 14, if the firm sells at two times book value per share, what will the P/E ratio be?

16. For December 31, 1988, the balance sheet of the Gardner Corporation is as follows:

Current Assets			Liabilities		
Cash		$ 15,000	Accounts payable		$ 20,000
Accounts receivable		22,500	Notes payable		30,000
Inventory		37,500	Bonds payable		75,000
Prepaid expenses		18,000			

Fixed Assets			Stockholders' Equity		
Plant and equipment			Common stock		112,500
(gross)		375,000	Paid-in capital		37,500
Less: Accumulated			Retained earnings		118,000
depreciation		75,000	Total liabilities and		
Net plant and equipment		300,000	stockholders' equity		$393,000
Total assets		$393,000			

Sales for 1989 were $330,000, with cost of goods sold being 60 percent of sales. Depreciation expense was 10 percent of plant and equipment (gross) at the beginning of the year. Interest expense for the bonds payable was 12 percent, while interest on the notes payable was 10 percent. These are based on December 31, 1988, balances. Selling and administrative expenses were $33,000, and the tax rate averaged 20 percent.

During the year 1989, the cash balance and prepaid expense balance were unchanged. Accounts receivable and inventory each increased by 20 percent, and accounts payable increased by 30 percent. A new machine was purchased on December 31, 1989, at a cost of $60,000. A cash dividend of $6,100 was paid to common stockholders at the end of 1989. Also notes payable increased by $10,000 and bonds payable decreased by $15,000. The common stock and paid-in capital accounts did not change.

a. Prepare an income statement for 1989.
b. Prepare a balance sheet as of December 31, 1989.

17. Prepare a statement of cash flows for the Crosby Corporation. Follow the general procedures indicated in Table 2–10 of the chapter.

CROSBY CORPORATION
Income Statement
For the Year Ended December 31, 1989

Sales	$2,200,000
Cost of goods sold	1,300,000
Gross profits	900,000
Selling and administrative expense	420,000
Depreciation expense	150,000
Operating income	330,000
Interest expense	90,000
Earnings before taxes	240,000
Taxes	80,000
Earnings after taxes	160,000
Preferred stock dividends	10,000
Earnings available to common stockholders	150,000
Shares outstanding	120,000
Earnings per share	$1.25

Statement of Retained Earnings
For the Year Ended December 31, 1989

Retained earnings, balance, January 1, 1989	$500,000
Add: Earnings available to common stockholders, 1989	150,000
Deduct: Cash dividends declared and paid in 1989	50,000
Retained earnings, balance, December 31, 1989	$600,000

Comparative Balance Sheets
for 1988 and 1989

	Year-End 1988	Year-End 1989
Assets		
Current assets:		
Cash	$70,000	$100,000
Accounts receivable (net)	300,000	350,000
Inventory	410,000	430,000
Prepaid expenses	50,000	30,000
Total current assets	830,000	910,000
Investments (long-term securities)	80,000	70,000
Plant and equipment	2,000,000	2,400,000
Less: Accumulated depreciation	1,000,000	1,150,000
Net plant and equipment	1,000,000	1,250,000
Total assets	$1,910,000	$2,230,000

Liabilities and Stockholders' Equity

Current liabilities:		
Accounts payable	$250,000	$440,000
Notes payable	400,000	400,000
Accrued expenses	70,000	50,000
Total current liabilities	720,000	890,000
Long-term liabilities:		
Bonds payable, 2004	70,000	120,000
Total liabilities	790,000	1,010,000
Stockholders' equity:		
Preferred stock, $100 par value	90,000	90,000
Common stock, $1 par value	120,000	120,000
Capital paid in excess of par	410,000	410,000
Retained earnings	500,000	600,000
Total stockholders' equity	1,120,000	1,220,000
Total liabilities and stockholders' equity	$1,910,000	$2,230,000

(The following questions apply to the Crosby Corporation, as presented in problem 17.)

18. Describe the general relationship between net income and net cash flows from operating activities for the firm.

19. Has the buildup in plant and equipment been financed in a satisfactory manner? Briefly discuss.

20. Compute the book value per common share for 1988 and 1989 for the Crosby Corporation.

21. If the market value of a share of common stock is 1.8 times book value for 1989, what is the firm's P/E ratio for 1989?

Selected References

Arthur Andersen & Co. Study. "Objectives of Financial Statements for Business Enterprises." Chicago, 1972.

Bierman, Harold, Jr. "Toward a Constant Price–Earnings Ratio." *Financial Analysis Journal* 38 (September–October 1982), pp. 62–65.

Craig, Darryl; Glen Johnson; and Maurice Joy. "Accounting Methods and P/E Ratios." *Financial Analysts Journal* 43 (March–April 1987), pp. 41–45.

Haugen, Robert A., and Lemma W. Senbet. "Corporate Finance and Taxes: A Review." *Financial Management* 15 (Winter 1986), pp. 5–21.

Helfert, Erich A. *Techniques of Financial Analysis.* 6th ed. Homewood, Ill.: Richard D. Irwin, 1987.

Lambert, S. J. III., and Christine V. Zavgren. "The Objectives of the Statement of Financial Accounting Concepts No. 1." *Financial Executive*, May 1982, pp. 26–30.

Kroll, Yoman. "On the Differences between Accrual Accounting Figures and Cash Flows: The Case of Working Capital." *Financial Management* 13 (Spring 1985), pp. 33–35.

Norby, William C. "Accounting for Financial Analysis." *Financial Analysis Journal* 38 (July–August 1982), pp. 33–35.

Opinions and Statement of the American Institute of Certified Public Accountant (AICPA) and the Financial Accounting Standards Boards (FASB).

Welsch, Glenn, A.; Charles T. Zlatkovich; and John A. White. *Intermediate Accounting.* 7th ed. Homewood, Ill.: Richard D. Irwin, 1986.

3

Financial Analysis

In Chapter 2, Review of Accounting, we examined the basic assumptions of accounting and the various components that make up the financial statements of the firm. We now use this fundamental material as a springboard into financial analysis—to evaluate the financial performance of the firm.

The format for the chapter is twofold. In the first part we will use financial ratios to evaluate the relative success of the firm. Various measures such as net income to sales and current assets to current liabilities will be computed for a hypothetical company and examined in light of industry norms and past trends.

In the second part of the chapter we explore further the impact of inflation and disinflation on financial operations over the last decade. The student begins to appreciate the impact of rising prices (or at times, declining prices) on the various financial ratios. The chapter concludes with a discussion of how other factors—in addition to price changes—may distort the financial statements of the firm. Terms such as net income to sales, return on investment, and inventory turnover take on much greater meaning when they are evaluated through the eyes of a financial manager who does more than merely pick out the top or bottom line of an income statement. The examples in the chapter are designed from the viewpoint of a financial manager (with only minor attention to accounting theory).

Ratio Analysis

Ratios are used in much of our daily life. We buy cars based on miles per gallon; we evaluate baseball players by earned run averages and batting averages, basketball players by field goal and foul-shooting percentages, and so on. These are all ratios constructed to judge comparative performance. Financial ratios serve a similar purpose, but you must know what is being measured in order to construct a ratio and to understand the significance of the resultant number.

Financial ratios are used to weigh and evaluate the operating performance of the firm. While an absolute value such as earnings of $50,000 or accounts receivable of $100,000 may appear satisfactory, its acceptability can only be measured in relation to other values. For this reason, financial managers place heavy emphasis on ratio analysis.

For example, are earnings of $50,000 actually good? If we earned $50,000 on $500,000 of sales (10 percent "profit margin" ratio), that might be quite satisfactory—whereas earnings of $50,000 on $5,000,000 could be disappointing (a meager 1 percent return). After we have computed the appropriate ratio, we must compare our results to those achieved by similar firms in our industry as well as to our own past record of performance. Even then, this "number crunching" process is not fully adequate, and we are forced to supplement our financial findings with an evaluation of company management, physical facilities, and numerous other factors.

For comparative purposes, a number of organizations provide industry data. For example, Dun & Bradstreet compiles data on 800 different lines of business, while Robert Morris Associates provides ratios on over 150 industry classifications. Quite often the most valuable industry figures come from the various trade organizations to which firms belong (for example, the National Retail Furniture Association or the National Hardware Association).

Many libraries and universities subscribe to financial services such as Standard & Poor's Industry Surveys and Corporate Reports, the Value Line Investment Survey, and Moody's Investment Service. Standard & Poor's also leases a computer data base called Compustat to banks, corporations, investment organizations, and universities. Compustat contains financial statement data on over 3,000 companies for a 20-year period. These data can be used to make countless ratios to measure corporate performance. The ratios classified in this text are a sample of the major ratio categories, but others can also be constructed.

Classification System

We will separate 13 significant ratios into four primary categories.

A. Profitability ratios.
    1.   Profit margin.
    2.   Return on assets (investment).
    3.   Return on equity.
B. Asset utilization ratios.
    4.   Receivable turnover.
    5.   Average collection period.
    6.   Inventory turnover.
    7.   Fixed asset turnover.
    8.   Total asset turnover.
C. Liquidity ratios.
    9.   Current ratio.
   10.   Quick ratio.
D. Debt-utilization ratios.
   11.   Debt to total assets.
   12.   Times interest earned.
   13.   Fixed charge coverage.

The first grouping, the profitability ratios, allows us to measure the ability of the firm to earn an adequate return on sales, total assets, and invested capital. Many of the problems related to profitability can be explained, in whole or in part, by the firm's ability to effectively employ its resources. Thus the next category of ratios is asset utilization. Under this heading, we measure the speed at which the firm is turning over accounts receivable, inventory, and longer-term assets. In other words, asset utilization ratios measure how many times per year a company sells its inventory or collects its entire accounts receivable. For long-term assets, the utilization ratio tells us how productive the fixed assets are in terms of sales generation.

In Category C, the liquidity ratios, the primary emphasis moves to the firm's ability to pay off short-term obligations as they come due. In Category D, debt-utilization ratios, the overall debt position of the firm is evaluated in light of its asset base and earning power.

The users of financial statements will attach different degrees of importance to the four categories of ratios. To the potential investor or security analyst, the critical consideration is profitability, with secondary consideration given to such matters as liquidity and debt utilization. For the banker or trade creditor, the emphasis shifts to the firm's current ability to meet debt obligations. The bondholder, in turn, may be primarily influenced by debt to total assets—while also eyeing the profitability of the firm in terms of its ability to cover debt obligations. Of course, the shrewd analyst looks at all the ratios, but with different degrees of attention.

The Analysis

Definitions alone carry little meaning in analyzing or dissecting the financial performance of a company. For this reason, we shall apply our four categories of ratios to a hypothetical firm, the Saxton Company, as presented in Table 3–1. The use of ratio analysis is rather like solving a mystery in which each clue leads to a new area of inquiry.

A. Profitability ratios   We first look at the profitability ratios. The appropriate ratio is computed for the Saxton Company and is then compared to representative industry data.

A. *Profitability ratios*—

		Saxton Company	*Industry Average*
1. Profit margin $= \dfrac{\text{Net income}}{\text{Sales}}$		$\dfrac{\$200{,}000}{\$4{,}000{,}000} = 5\%$	6.7%
2. Return on assets (investment) $=$			
a.	$\dfrac{\text{Net income}}{\text{Total assets}}$	$\dfrac{\$200{,}000}{\$1{,}600{,}000} = 12.5\%$	10%
b.	$\dfrac{\text{Net income}}{\text{Sales}} \times \dfrac{\text{Sales}}{\text{Total assets}}$	$5\% \times 2.5 = 12.5\%$	$6.7\% \times 1.5 = 10\%$
3. Return on equity $=$			
a.	$\dfrac{\text{Net income}}{\text{Stockholders' equity}}$	$\dfrac{\$200{,}000}{\$1{,}000{,}000} = 20\%$	15%
b.	$\dfrac{\text{Return on assets (investment)}}{(1 - \text{Debt/Assets})}$	$\dfrac{0.125}{1 - 0.375} = 20\%$	$\dfrac{0.10}{1 - 0.33} = 15\%$

The Saxton Company shows a lower return on the sales dollar (5 percent) than the industry average of 6.7 percent. However, its return on assets (investment) of 12.5 percent exceeds the industry norm of 10 percent. There is only one possible explanation for this occurrence—a more rapid turnover of assets than that generally found within the industry. This is verified in ratio 2*b*, in which sales to total assets is 2.5 for the Saxton Company and only 1.5 for the industry. Thus, Saxton earns less on each sales dollar, but it compensates by turning over its assets more rapidly.

Table 3–1
Financial statement
for ratio analysis

SAXTON COMPANY
Income Statement
For the Year Ended December 31, 1989

Sales (all on credit)	$4,000,000
Cost of goods sold	3,000,000
Gross profit	1,000,000
Selling and administrative expense*	450,000
Operating profit	550,000
Interest expense	50,000
Extraordinary loss	200,000
Net income before taxes	300,000
Taxes (33%)	100,000
Net income	$ 200,000

*Includes $50,000 in lease payments.

Balance Sheet
As of December 31, 1989
Assets

Cash	$ 30,000
Marketable securities	50,000
Accounts receivable	350,000
Inventory	370,000
Total current assets	800,000
Net plant and equipment	800,000
Total assets	$1,600,000

Liabilities and Stockholders' Equity

Accounts payable	$ 50,000
Notes payable	250,000
Total current liabilities	300,000
Long-term liabilities	300,000
Total liabilities	600,000
Common stock	400,000
Retained earnings	600,000
Total liabilities and stockholders' equity	$1,600,000

Return on total assets as described through the two components of profit margin and asset turnover is part of the Du Pont system of financial analysis.

Return on assets (investment) = Profit margin × Asset turnover

The Du Pont company was a forerunner in stressing that satisfactory return on assets may be achieved through high profit margins or rapid turnover of assets, or a combination of both. We shall also soon observe that under the Du Pont system of analysis, the use of debt may be important. The Du Pont system causes the analyst to examine the sources of a company's profitability. Since the profit margin is an income statement ratio, a high profit margin indicates good cost control, whereas a high asset turnover ratio demonstrates efficient use of the assets on the balance sheet. Different industries have different operating and financial structures. For example, in the heavy capital goods industry the emphasis is on a high profit margin with a low asset turnover—whereas in food processing, the profit margin is low and the key to satisfactory returns on total assets is a rapid turnover of assets.

Equally important to a firm is its return on equity or ownership capital. For the Saxton Company, return on equity is 20 percent, versus an industry norm of 15 percent. Thus the owners of Saxton Company are more amply rewarded than are other shareholders in the industry. This may be the result of one or two factors: a high return on total assets or a generous utilization of debt or a combination thereof. This can be seen through Equation 3b, which represents a modified or second version of the Du Pont formula.

$$\text{Return on equity} = \frac{\text{Return on assets (investment)}}{(1 - \text{Debt/Assets})}$$

Note the numerator, return on assets, is taken from Formula 2, which represents the initial version of the Du Pont formula (Return on assets = Net income/Sales × Sales/Total assets). Return on assets is then divided by [1 − (Debt/Assets)] to account for the amount of debt in the capital structure. In the case of the Saxton Company, the modified version of the Du Pont formula shows:

$$\text{Return on equity} = \frac{\text{Return on assets (investment)}}{(1 - \text{Debt/Assets})}$$

$$= \frac{12.5\%}{1 - 0.375} = 20\%$$

Actually the return on assets of 12.5 percent in the numerator is higher than the industry average of 10 percent, and the ratio of debt to assets in the denominator of 37.5 percent is higher than the industry norm of 33 percent. Both the numerator and denominator contribute to a higher return on equity than the industry average (20 percent versus 15 percent). Note that if the firm had a 50 percent debt-to-assets ratio, return on equity would go up to 25 percent.[1]

---

[1]The return could be slightly different from 25 percent because of changing financing costs with higher debt.

$$\text{Return on equity} = \frac{\text{Return on assets (investment)}}{(1 - \text{Debt/Assets})}$$

$$= \frac{12.5\%}{1 - 0.50} = 25\%$$

This does not necessarily mean that debt is a positive influence, only that it can be used to boost return on equity. The ultimate goal for the firm is to achieve maximum valuation for its securities in the marketplace, and this goal may or may not be advanced by using debt to increase return on equity. Because debt represents increased risk, a lower valuation of higher earnings is possible.[2] Every situation must be evaluated individually.

The reader may wish to review Figure 3–1, which illustrates the key points in the Du Pont system of analysis.

As an example of the Du Pont analysis, in Table 3–2, we compare Compaq Computer and Tandem Computers, two well-positioned firms in the personal computer and data systems industry. It is clear for the year 1986 that Tandem outperformed Compaq in regard to the profit margin (8.3 percent versus 6.9 percent). But observe that, in terms of return on assets, Compaq is clearly ahead (12.3 percent versus 9.9 percent). This is a result of the higher asset turnover for Compaq, as indicated in the table. Finally, Compaq dominates Tandem in the return on equity ratio (26.6 percent versus 13.0 percent). We see the higher return on assets ratio that Compaq enjoys is translated into a substantially higher return on equity, because Compaq has a debt–assets ratio of 53.8 percent, compared to 23.8 percent for Tandem. The larger debt ratio may, of course, be a cause of concern to some analysts.

Figure 3–1
Du Pont analysis

[2]Further discussion of this point is presented in Chapter 5, Operating and Financial Leverage, and Chapter 10, Valuation and Rates of Return.

Table 3–2
Position of Compaq
versus Tandem using
the Du Pont method
of analysis

	Profit margin	×	Asset turnover	=	Return on assets	÷	(1 − Debt/Assets)	=	Return on equity
Compaq	6.9%	×	1.78	=	12.3%	÷	(1 − .538)	=	26.6%
Tandem	8.3%	×	1.19	=	9.9%	÷	(1 − .238)	=	13.0%

Finally as a general statement in computing all the profitability ratios, the analyst must be sensitive to the age of the assets. Plant and equipment purchased 15 years ago may be carried on the books far below its replacement value in an inflationary economy. A 20 percent return on assets purchased in the 1970s may be inferior to a 15 percent return on newly purchased assets.

B. Asset utilization ratios   The second category of ratios relates to asset utilization, and the ratios in this category may well explain why one firm is able to turn over its assets more rapidly than another. Notice that all of these ratios below relate the balance sheet (assets) to the income statement (sales). The Saxton Company's rapid turnover of assets is explained in ratios 4, 5, and 6.

B. *Asset utilization ratios*—

	Saxton Company	Industry Average
4. Receivables turnover = $\dfrac{\text{Sales (credit)}}{\text{Receivables}}$	$\dfrac{\$4,000,000}{\$350,000} = 11.4$	10 times
5. Average collection period = $\dfrac{\text{Accounts receivable}}{\text{Average daily credit sales}}$	$\dfrac{\$350,000}{\$11,111} = 32$	36 days
6. Inventory turnover = $\dfrac{\text{Sales}}{\text{Inventory}}$	$\dfrac{\$4,000,000}{\$370,000} = 10.8$	7 times
7. Fixed asset turnover = $\dfrac{\text{Sales}}{\text{Fixed assets}}$	$\dfrac{\$4,000,000}{\$800,000} = 5$	5.4 times
8. Total asset turnover = $\dfrac{\text{Sales}}{\text{Total assets}}$	$\dfrac{\$4,000,000}{\$1,600,000} = 2.5$	1.5 times

Saxton collects its receivables faster than does the industry. This is shown by receivables turnover of 11.4 times versus 10 times for the industry, and in daily terms by the average collection period of 32 days, which is 4 days faster than that of the industry norm. The average collection period suggests how long, on the average, our customers' accounts stay on our books. The Saxton Company has $350,000 in accounts receivable and $4,000,000 in credit sales, which when divided by 360 days yields average daily credit sales of $11,111. We divide accounts receivable of $350,000 by average daily credit sales of $11,111 to determine how many days that credit sales are on the books (32 days).

In addition, the firm turns over its inventory 10.8 times per year as contrasted with an industry average of 7 times.[3] This tells us that Saxton is able to generate more sales per dollar of inventory than the average company in the industry does, and we can assume that the firm uses very efficient inventory-ordering and cost-control methods.

The firm maintains a slightly lower ratio of sales to fixed assets (plant and equipment) than does the industry (5 versus 5.4). This is a relatively minor consideration in view of the rapid movement of inventory and accounts receivable. Finally, the rapid turnover of total assets is again indicated (2.5 versus 1.5).

C. Liquidity ratios After considering profitability and asset utilizaiton, the analyst needs to examine the liquidity of the firm. The Saxton Company's liquidity ratios fare quite well in comparison with the industry. Further analysis might call for a cash budget to determine if we can meet each maturing obligation as it comes due.

C. Liquidity ratios—

	Saxton Company	Industry Average
9. Current ratio = $\dfrac{\text{Current assets}}{\text{Current liabilities}}$	$\dfrac{\$800,000}{\$300,000} = 2.67$	2.1
10. Quick ratio = $\dfrac{\text{Current assets} - \text{Inventory}}{\text{Current liabilities}}$	$\dfrac{\$430,000}{\$300,000} = 1.43$	1.0

D. Debt utilization ratios The last grouping of ratios, debt utilization, allows the analyst to measure the prudence of the debt management policies of the firm.

Debt to total assets of 37.5 percent as shown on page 64 is slightly above the industry average of 33 percent, but well within the prudent

[3]This ratio may also be computed by using "cost of goods sold" in the numerator. While this offers some theoretical advantages in terms of using cost figures in both the numerator and denominator, Dun & Bradstreet and other credit reporting agencies generally show turnover as in ratio 6.

range of 50 percent or less. One of the ways to benefit from an inflationary economy is through the utilization of heavy long-term debt, enabling long-standing obligations to be repaid in inflated dollars with the passage of time.

D. Debt utilization ratios—

	Saxton Company	Industry Average
11. Debt to total assets = $\dfrac{\text{Total debt}}{\text{Total assets}}$	$\dfrac{\$600{,}000}{\$1{,}600{,}000} = 37.5\%$	33%
12. Times interest earned = $\dfrac{\text{Income before interest and taxes}}{\text{Interest}}$	$\dfrac{\$550{,}000}{\$50{,}000} = 11$	7 times
13. Fixed charge coverage = $\dfrac{\text{Income before fixed charges and taxes}}{\text{Fixed charges}}$	$\dfrac{\$600{,}000}{\$100{,}000} = 6$	5.5 times

Ratios for times interest earned and fixed charge coverage show that the Saxton Company debt is being well managed compared to the debt management of other firms in the industry. Times interest earned indicates the number of times that our income before interest and taxes covers the interest obligation (11 times). The higher the ratio, the stronger is the interest-paying ability of the firm. The figure for income before interest and taxes in the ratio is the equivalent of the operating profit figure presented in Table 3–1.

Fixed charge coverage measures the firm's ability to meet all fixed obligations rather than interest payments alone, on the assumption that failure to meet any financial obligation will endanger the position of the firm. In the present case the Saxton Company has lease obligations of $50,000 as well as the $50,000 in interest expenses. Thus the total fixed charge financial obligation is $100,000. We also need to know the income before all fixed charge obligations. In this case, we take income before interest and taxes (operating profit) and add back the $50,000 in lease payments.

Income before interest and taxes	$550,000
Lease payments	50,000
Income before fixed charges and taxes	$600,000

The fixed charges are safely covered 6 times, exceeding the industry norm of 5.5 times. The various ratios are summarized in Table 3–3. The conclusions reached in comparing the Saxton Company to industry averages are generally valid, though exceptions may exist. For example, a

Table 3–3
Ratio analysis

		Saxton Company	Industry Average	Conclusion
A. Profitability				
1.	Net income to sales	5%	6.7%	Below average
2.	Net income to total assets . .	12.5%	10%	Above average due to high turnover
3.	Net income to stockholders' equity	20%	15%	Good due to ratios 2 and 10
B. Asset Utilization				
4.	Receivable turnover	11.4	10	Good
5.	Average collection period . . .	32	36	Good
6.	Inventory turnover	10.8	7	Good
7.	Fixed asset turnover	5	5.4	Below average
8.	Total asset turnover	2.5	1.5	Good
C. Liquidity				
9.	Current ratio	2.67	2.1	Good
10.	Quick ratio	1.43	1.0	Good
D. Debt Utilization				
11.	Debt to total assets	37.5%	33%	Slightly more debt
12.	Times interest earned	11	7	Good
13.	Fixed charge coverage	6	5.5	Good

high inventory turnover is considered "good" unless it is achieved by maintaining unusually low inventory levels, which may hurt future profitability.

In summary, the Saxton Company more than compensates for a lower return on the sales dollar by a rapid turnover of assets, principally inventory and receivables, and a wise use of debt. The student should be able to use these 13 measures to evaluate the financial performance of any firm.

Trend Analysis

Over the course of the business cycle, sales and profitability may expand and contract, and ratio analysis for any one year may not present an accurate picture of the firm. Therefore, we look at trend analysis of performance over a number of years. However, without industry comparisons even trend analysis may not present a complete picture. For example, in Figure 3–2 we see that the profit margin for the Saxton Company has improved, while asset turnover has declined. This by itself may look good for the profit margin and bad for asset turnover. However,

Figure 3–2
Trend analysis

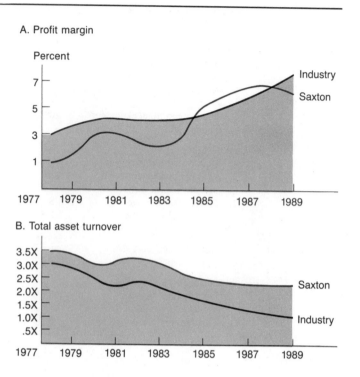

A. Profit margin

Percent

[Chart showing "Industry" and "Saxton" profit margin trends from 1977 to 1989, with percent axis marked 1, 3, 5, 7]

B. Total asset turnover

[Chart showing "Saxton" and "Industry" total asset turnover from 1977 to 1989, with axis marked .5X, 1.0X, 1.5X, 2.0X, 2.5X, 3.0X, 3.5X]

when compared to industry trends, we see that the firm's profit margin is still below the industry average. On asset turnover, Saxton has improved in relation to the industry even though it is in a downward trend. Similar data could be generated for the other ratios.

By analyzing companies in the same industry, one company can compare its performance to the industry leader. In the case of the computer industry, IBM is the largest and one of the most consistent performers. In Table 3–4, we compare selected profitability measures for IBM, Unisys (the firm created by the merger of Burroughs and Sperry Corporation), and Apple Computer.

The first pattern to note is that all three companies have generally shown decreasing profitability over the last decade (though they are still quite profitable). Increasing competition between the three firms—and also with Hewlett-Packard, Tandy, NCR, Digital Equipment, Data General, Compaq Computer, Tandem Computers, Data General, Cray Research, Wang, Prime Computers, and others—have tended to hold down profit margins in the industry. Note that IBM has fairly consistently outperformed Unisys in terms of profit margin and return on equity. However, the same point cannot be made about Apple Computer. While

Table 3–4   Trend analysis using an industry leader

	IBM		Unisys		Apple Computer	
	Profit Margin	Return on Equity	Profit Margin	Return on Equity	Profit Margin	Return on Equity
1978	14.8%	23.1%	10.5%	13.3%	10.1%	35.1%
1979	13.2	20.1	11.0	14.3	10.6	52.4
1980	13.6	21.7	2.9	3.9	10.0	45.1
1981	11.4	18.2	4.5	6.8	11.8	22.2
1982	12.8	22.1	2.2	4.5	10.5	23.9
1983	13.7	23.6	4.6	8.8	7.8	20.3
1984	14.3	24.9	5.1	10.7	3.9	12.7
1985	13.1	20.5	4.9	10.0	3.2	11.1
1986	9.3	13.9	3.1	6.0	8.1	22.2
1987	9.6	14.5	6.3	13.5	8.2	24.5
1988 (est.) . . .	10.7	16.0	6.5	14.5	9.1	26.0

IBM has normally enjoyed a higher profit margin, Apple Computer had a higher return on equity in 8 of the 11 years shown. This superior performance is due to both better asset turnover and higher debt utilization.

Impact of Inflation on Financial Analysis

Prior to, coincident with, or following the computation of financial ratios, we should explore the impact of inflation and other sources of distortion on the financial reporting of the firm. As illustrated in this section, inflation causes phantom sources of profit that may mislead even the most alert analyst. Disinflation also causes certain problems and we shall eventually consider these as well.

The major problem during inflationary times is that revenue is almost always stated in current dollars, whereas plant and equipment or inventory may have been purchased at lower price levels. Thus, profit may be more a function of increasing prices than of satisfactory performance.

An Illustration

The Stein Corporation shows the accompanying income statement for 1988 (Table 3–5). At year-end the firm also has 100 units still in inventory at $1 per unit and $200 worth of plant and equipment with a 20-year life.

Assume that in 1989 the number of units sold remains constant at 100. However, inflation causes a 10 percent increase in price, from $2 to $2.20.

Table 3–5

STEIN CORPORATION
Net Income for 1988

Sales	$200 (100 units at $2)
Cost of goods sold	100 (100 units at $1)
Gross profit	100
Selling and administrative expense	20
Depreciation	10
Operating profit	70
Taxes (40%)	28
Aftertax income	$ 42

Total sales will go up to $220 as shown in Table 3–6, but with no actual increase in physical volume. Further assume the firm uses FIFO inventory pricing, so that inventory first purchased will be written off against current sales. In this case 1988 inventory will be written off against 1989 sales revenue.

The 1989 income statement of the Stein Corporation is fully shown below.

Table 3–6

STEIN CORPORATION
Net Income for 1989

Sales	$220 (100 units at 1989 price of $2.20)
Cost of goods sold	100 (100 units at $1.00)
Gross profit	120
Selling and administrative expense	22 (10% of sales)
Depreciation	10
Operating profit	88
Taxes (40%)	35
Aftertax income	$ 53

The company appears to have increased profit by $11 simply as a result of inflation. But not reflected is the increased cost of replacing inventory and plant and equipment. Presumably, their replacement costs have increased in an inflationary environment.

As mentioned in Chapter 2, inflation-related information was formerly required by the FASB for large companies, but this is no longer the case. It is now purely voluntary. What are the implications of this type of inflation adjusted data? From a study[4] of 10 chemical firms and 8 drug

---

[4]Jeff Garnett and Geoffrey A. Hirt, "Replacement Cost Data: A Study of the Chemical and Drug Industry for Years 1976 through 1978." Replacement cost is but one form of current cost. Nevertheless, it is widely used as a measure of current cost.

companies, using current cost (replacement cost) data found in the financial 10K statements that these companies filed with the Securities and Exchange Commission, it was found that the changes shown in Table 3–7 occurred in their assets, income, and selected ratios.

Table 3–7
Comparison of replacement cost accounting and historical cost accounting

	Ten Chemical Companies		Eight Drug Companies	
	Replacement Cost	Historical Cost	Replacement Cost	Historical Cost
Increase in assets	28.4%	—	15.4%	—
Decrease in net income before taxes	45.8%	—	(19.3%)	—
Return on assets	2.8%	6.2%	8.3%	11.4%
Return on equity	4.9%	13.5%	12.8%	19.6%
Debt-to-assets ratio	34.3%	43.8%	30.3%	35.2%
Interest coverage ratio (times interest earned)	7.1×	8.4×	15.4×	16.7×

The comparison of replacement cost and historical cost accounting methods in the table shows that replacement cost reduces income but at the same time increases assets. This increase in assets lowers the debt-to-assets ratio since debt is a monetary asset that is not revalued because it is paid back in nominal dollars. The decreased debt-to-assets ratio would indicate that the financial leverage of the firm is decreased, but a look at the interest coverage ratio tells a different story. Because the interest coverage ratio measures the operating income available to cover interest expense, the declining income penalizes this ratio and the firm has decreased its ability to cover its interest cost.

Disinflation Effect

As long as prices continue to rise in an inflationary environment, profits appear to feed on themselves. The main objection is that when price increases moderate (disinflation), there will be a rude awakening for management and unsuspecting stockholders as expensive inventory is charged against softening retail prices. A 15 or 20 percent growth rate in earnings may be little more than an "inflationary illusion." Industries most sensitive to inflation-induced profits are those with cyclical products, such as lumber, copper, rubber, and food products, and also those in which inventory is a significant percentage of sales and profits.

A leveling off of prices is, of course, not necessarily bad. Even though inflation-induced corporate profits may be going down, investors may be more willing to place their funds in financial assets such as stocks and bonds. The reason for the shift may be a belief that declining inflationary pressures will no longer seriously impair the purchasing power of the dollar. Lessening inflation means that the required return that investors demand on financial assets will be going down, and with this lower demanded return, future earnings or interest should receive a higher current valuation.

None of the above happens with a high degree of certainty. To the extent that investors question the permanence of disinflation (leveling off of price increases), they may not act according to the script. That is, lower rates of inflation will not necessarily produce high stock and bond prices unless the price pattern appears sustainable over a reasonable period of time.

Whereas financial assets such as stocks and bonds have the potential (whether realized or not) to do well during disinflation, such is not the case for tangible (real) assets. Precious metals, such as gold and silver, gems, and collectibles, that boomed in the highly inflationary environment of the late 1970s fell off sharply in the mid-1980s, as softening prices caused less perceived need to hold real assets as a hedge against inflation. The shifting back and forth by investors between financial and real assets may take place many times over a business cycle.

Other Elements of Distortion in Reported Income

The effect of changing prices is but one of a number of problems the analyst must cope with in evaluating a company. Other issues, such as the reporting of revenue, the treatment of nonrecurring items, and the tax write-off policy, cause dilemmas for the financial manager or analyst. The point may be illustrated by considering the income statements for two hypothetical companies in the same industry (Table 3–8). Both firms had identical operating performances for 1989—but Company A is very conservative in reporting its results, while Company B has attempted to maximize its reported income.

If both companies had reported income of $280,000 in the prior year of 1988, Company B would be thought to be showing substantial growth in 1989 with net income of $700,000, while Company A is reporting a "flat" or no-growth year of $280,000 in 1989. However, we have already established the fact that the companies have equal operating performance.

Table 3–8

**Income Statement
For the Year 1989**

	Conservative A	High Reported Income B
Sales	$4,000,000	$4,200,000
Cost of goods sold	3,000,000	2,700,000
Gross profit	1,000,000	1,500,000
Selling and administrative expense	450,000	450,000
Operating profit	550,000	1,050,000
Interest expense	50,000	50,000
Extraordinary loss	100,000	—
Net income before taxes	400,000	1,000,000
Taxes (30%)	120,000	300,000
Net income	280,000	700,000
Extraordinary loss (net of tax)	—	70,000
Net income transferred to retained earnings	$ 280,000	$ 630,000

Explanation of Discrepancies

Let us examine how the inconsistencies in Table 3–8 could take place. Emphasis is given to a number of key elements on the income statement.

Sales Company B reported $200,000 more in sales, although actual volume was precisely the same. This may be the result of different concepts of revenue recognition.

For example, certain assets may be sold on an installment basis over a long period of time. A conservative firm may defer recognition of the sales or revenue until each payment is received, while other firms may attempt to recognize a fully effected sale at the earliest possible date. Similarly, firms that lease assets may attempt to consider a long-term lease as the equivalent of a sale, while more conservative firms, such as IBM or Digital Equipment, only recognize as revenue each lease payment as it comes due. Although the accounting profession attempts to establish appropriate methods of financial reporting through generally accepted accounting principles, there is variation of reporting among firms.

Cost of goods sold The conservative firm (Company A) may well be using LIFO accounting in an inflationary environment, thus charging the last-purchased, more expensive items against sales, while Company B uses FIFO accounting—charging off less expensive inventory against sales. The $300,000 difference in cost of goods sold may also be explained by varying treatment of research and development costs and other items.

Extraordinary gains/losses   Nonrecurring gains or losses may occur from the sale of corporate fixed assets, lawsuits, or similar nonrecurring events. Some analysts argue that such extraordinary events should be included in computing the current income of the firm, while others would leave them off in assessing operating performance. Unfortunately, there is some inconsistency in the manner in which nonrecurring losses are treated in spite of determined attempts by the accounting profession to ensure uniformity of action. The conservative firm A has written off its $100,000 extraordinary loss against normally reported income, while firm B carries a subtraction against net income only after the $700,000 amount has been reported. Both had similar losses of $100,000, but firm B's is shown net of tax implications at $70,000.

Extraordinary gains and losses occur among large companies more often than you might think. In the 1980s (1983–85) Chrysler Corporation has been a good example of a firm whose earnings have been affected by tax loss carry-forwards from the accumulated losses of more than $3.5 billion suffered during 1978–82. Chevron had nonrecurring per-share losses of 24¢ in 1982, 50¢ in 1983, 46¢ in 1984, and 56¢ in 1986. These losses arose from its consolidation and disposition of assets when it acquired the Gulf Oil Corporation. In this age of mergers, tender offers, and buyouts, understanding the finer points of financial statements becomes even more important.

Net Income

Firm A has reported net income of $280,000, while Firm B claims $700,000 before subtraction of extraordinary losses. The $420,000 difference is attributed to different methods of financial reporting, and it should be recognized as such by the analyst. No superior performance has actually taken place. The analyst must remain ever alert in examining each item in the financial statements, rather than accepting bottom-line figures.

Summary

The subject of financial analysis was divided into two categories: an examination of ratio analysis and a study of the shortcomings in reported financial data from the viewpoint of a financial manager. Under ratio analysis, we developed four categories of ratios: profitability, asset utilization, liquidity, and debt utilization. Each ratio for the firm should be compared to industry measures and analyzed in light of past trends. The use of ratio analysis is rather like the solving of a mystery in which each clue leads to a new area of inquiry.

Financial analysis also calls for an awareness of the impact of inflation and disinflation on the reported income of the firm. Inflation leads to phantom profits which are created as a result of buying goods and reselling them at inflation-induced higher prices. The process is further magnified by the use of FIFO accounting, in which older inventory items are costed against current prices. Alternate methods of financial reporting may allow firms with equal performance to report different results.

List of Terms

FIFO

LIFO

replacement cost

inventory profits

Du Pont system of ratio analysis

disinflation

trend and analysis

Dun & Bradstreet

profitability ratios

asset utilization ratios

liquidity ratios

debt utilization ratios

Discussion Questions

1. If we divide users of ratios into short-term lenders, long-term lenders, and stockholders, which ratios would each group be *most* interested in, and for what reasons?

2. Inflation can have significant effects on income statements and balance sheets, and therefore on the calculation of ratios. Discuss the possible impact of inflation on the following ratios, and explain the direction of the impact based on your assumptions.

   a. Return on investment.
   b. Inventory turnover.
   c. Fixed asset turnover.
   d. Debt-to-assets ratio.

3. Explain how the Du Pont system of analysis breaks down return on assets. Also explain how it breaks down return on stockholders' equity.

4. What advantage does the fixed-charge coverage ratio offer over simply using times interest earned?

5. Is there any validity in rule-of-thumb ratios for all corporations, for example, a current ratio of 2 to 1 or debt to assets of 50 percent?

6. Why is trend analysis helpful in analyzing ratios?

7. What effect will disinflation following a highly inflationary period have on the reported income of the firm?

8. Why might disinflation prove to be favorable to financial assets?

9. Comparisons of income can be very difficult for two companies even though they sell the same products in equal volume. Why?

Problems

1. Hurtz, Inc., is considering expansion into a new product line. New assets to support this expansion will cost $450,000. It is estimated that Hurtz can generate $1 million in annual sales, with a 5 percent profit margin. What would net income and return on assets (investment) for the year be?

2. Staley Cosmetics has a return on assets (investment) ratio of 10 percent.
   a. If the debt to total assets ratio is 40 percent, what is the return on equity?
   b. If the firm had no debt, what would the return on equity ratio be?

3. Using the Du Pont method, please evaluate the effects of the following relationships for the Butters Corporation.
   a. Butters Corporation has a profit margin of 7 percent and its return on assets (investment) is 25.2 percent. What is its assets turnover?
   b. If Butters Corporation has a debt to total assets ratio of 50 percent, what would the firm's return on equity be?
   c. What would happen to the return on equity if the debt to total assets ratio decreased to 35 percent?

4. Fleming Enterprises had an asset turnover of 1.8 times per year.
   a. If the return on total assets (investment) was 14.4 percent, what was Fleming's profit margin?
   b. The following year, on the same level of assets, Fleming's asset turnover declined to 1.6 times and its profit margin was 9 percent.
      How did the return on total assets change from that of the previous year?

5. A firm has sales of $2 million, and 10 percent of the sales are for cash. The year-end accounts receivable balance is $210,000. What is the average collection period? (Use a 360-day year.)

6. The Russell Corporation has accounts receivable turnover equal to 12 times. If accounts receivable are equal to $75,000, what is the value for average daily credit sales?

7. The balance sheet for the Hatton Corporation is given here. Sales for the year were $1,750,000, with 90 percent of sales sold on credit.

HATTON CORPORATION
Balance Sheet 198x

Assets		Liabilities and Equity	
Cash	$ 45,000	Accounts payable	$180,000
Accounts receivable	155,000	Accrued taxes	20,000
Inventory	260,000	Bonds payable	
Plant and equipment	300,000	(long-term)	100,000
		Common stock	50,000
		Paid-in capital	150,000
		Retained earnings	260,000
		Total liabilities and	
Total assets	$760,000	equity	$760,000

Compute the following ratios:
a. Current ratio.
b. Quick ratio.
c. Debt to total assets.
d. Asset turnover.
e. Average collection period.

8. Titan Electronics income statement is given below.
a. What is the times-interest-earned ratio?
b. What would be the fixed-charge-coverage ratio?

TITAN ELECTRONICS

Sales	$200,000
Cost of goods sold	134,000
Gross profit	66,000
Fixed charges (other than interest)	18,000
Income before interest and taxes	48,000
Interest	12,000
Income before taxes	36,000
Taxes (34%)	12,240
Income after taxes	$ 23,760

9. Using the income statement for the Sports Car Tire Company on page 76, compute the following ratios.
a. The interest coverage.
b. The fixed charge coverage.

The total assets for the Sports Car Tire Company equal $40,000. Set up the equation for the Du Pont system of ratio analysis, and compute *c, d,* and *e.*

c. Return on investment (assets).
d. Profit margin.
e. Total asset turnover.

THE SPORTS CAR TIRE COMPANY

Sales	$20,000
Less: Cost of goods sold	9,000
Gross profit	$11,000
Less: Selling and administrative expense	4,000
Less: Lease expense	1,000
Operating profit*	$ 6,000
Less: Interest expense	500
Earnings before taxes	$ 5,500
Less: Taxes (40%)	2,200
Earnings after taxes	$ 3,300

*Equals income before interest and taxes.

10. A firm has net income before taxes of $120,000 and interest expense of $24,000.
    a. What is the times-interest-earned ratio?
    b. If the firm's lease payments are $40,000, what is the fixed charge coverage?

11. In January 1979, the Status Quo Company was formed. Total assets were $500,000, of which $300,000 consisted of depreciable fixed assets. Status Quo uses straight-line depreciation, and in 1979 it estimated its fixed assets to have useful lives of 10 years. Aftertax income has been $26,000 per year each of the last 10 years. Other assets have not changed since 1979.
    a. Compute return on assets at year-end for 1979, 1981, 1984, 1986, and 1988. (Use $26,000 in the numerator for each year.)
    b. To what do you attribute the phenomenon shown in part *a?*
    c. Now assume that income increased by 10 percent each year. What effect would this have on your above answers? Comment.

12. Viceroy Healthcare, Inc., has the following data. Industry information is also shown.

Year	Net Income	Total Assets	Industry Data on Net Income / Total Assets
1987	$250,000	$2,000,000	11%
1988	260,000	2,400,000	8
1989	260,000	2,600,000	5

Year	Debt	Total Assets	Industry Data on Debt / Total Assets
1987	$1,125,000	$2,000,000	52%
1988	1,250,000	2,400,000	40
1989	1,300,000	2,600,000	31

As an industry analyst comparing the firm to the industry, are you likely to praise or criticize the firm in terms of:
a. Net income/total assets
b. Debt/total assets

13. The United World Corporation has three subsidiaries.

	Computers	Magazines	Cable TV
Sales	$16,000,000	$4,000,000	$8,000,000
Net income (after taxes)	1,000,000	160,000	600,000
Assets	5,000,000	2,000,000	5,000,000

a. Which division has the lowest return on sales?
b. Which division has the highest return on assets?
c. Compute the return on assets for the entire corporation.
d. If the $5,000,000 investment in the Cable TV division is sold off and redeployed in the computer subsidiary at the same rate of return on assets currently achieved in the computer division, what will be the new return on assets for the entire corporation?

14. Bard Corporation shows the following income statement. The firm uses FIFO inventory accounting.

BARD CORPORATION
Income Statement for 1988

Sales	$200,000 (10,000 units at $20)
Cost of goods sold	100,000 (10,000 units at $10)
Gross profit	100,000
Selling and administrative expense	10,000
Depreciation	20,000
Operating profit	70,000
Taxes (34%)	23,800
Aftertax income	$ 46,200

a. Assume in 1989 the same 10,000 unit volume is maintained, but that the sales price increases by 10 percent. Because of FIFO inventory policy, old inventory will still be charged off at $10 per unit. Also assume that selling and administrative expense will be 5 percent of sales and depreciation will be unchanged. The tax rate is 34 percent. Compute aftertax income for 1989.

b. In part *a,* by what percent did aftertax income increase as a result of a 10 percent increase in the sales price? Explain why this impact took place.

c. Now assume in 1990 the volume remains constant at 10,000 units, but that the sales price decreases by 15 percent from its 1989 level. Also, because of FIFO inventory policy, cost of goods sold reflects the inflationary conditions of the prior year and is $11 per unit. Further assume that selling and administrative expense will be 5 percent of sales and depreciation will be unchanged. The tax rate is 34 percent. Compute aftertax income.

15. Construct the current assets section of the balance sheet from the following data:

Yearly sales (credit)	$540,000
Inventory turnover	6 times
Current liabilities	$ 90,000
Current ratio	2
Quick ratio	1
Average collection period	34 days

Current assets:

Cash	$ _____
Accounts receivable	_____
Inventory	_____
Total current assets	_____

16. The Griggs Corporation has credit sales of $1,200,000. Given the following ratios, fill in the balance sheet below:

Total assets turnover	2.4 times
Cash to total assets	2.0 %
Accounts receivable turnover	8.0 times
Inventory turnover	10.0 times
Current ratio	2.0 times
Debt to total assets	61.0 %

GRIGGS CORPORATION
Balance Sheet, 198x

Assets		Liabilities and Stockholders' Equity	
Cash	_____	Current debt	_____
Accounts receivable	_____	Long-term debt	_____
Inventory	_____	Total debt	_____
Total current assets . . .	_____	Net worth	_____
Fixed assets	_____	Total liabilities and	
Total assets	_____	stockholders' equity . . .	_____

17. We are given the following information for the Eaton Equipment Corporation.

Sales (credit)	$6,000,000
Cash	275,000
Inventory	1,550,000
Current liabilities	1,200,000
Asset turnover	1.25 times
Current ratio	2.50 times
Debt-to-assets ratios	45%
Receivables turnover	7.5 times

Current assets are composed of cash, marketable securities, accounts receivable and inventory. Calculate the following balance sheet items:

  a. Accounts receivable.
  b. Marketable securities.
  c. Fixed assets.
  d. Long-term debt.

18. The following data are from U Guessed It Company's financial statements. U Guessed It is a manufacturer of board games for young adults, and it competes with Marker Brothers and Bilton Radley. Sales (all credit) were $20 million for 1988.

Sales to total assets	2 times
Total debt to assets	40%
Current ratio	3.0 times
Inventory turnover	5.0 times
Average collection period	18 days
Fixed asset turnover	5.0 times

Fill in the brief balance sheet:

Cash	_____	Current debt	_____
Accounts receivable	_____	Long-term debt	_____
Inventory	_____	Total debt	_____
Total current assets	_____	Net worth	_____
Fixed assets	_____	Total liabilities	
Total assets	_____	and equity	_____

19. Using the financial statements of the Hot Air Company, calculate the 13 basic ratios found in this chapter.

THE HOT AIR COMPANY
Balance Sheet
December 31, 1988
Assets

Current assets:

Cash	$ 40,000
Marketable securities	30,000
Accounts receivable (net)	120,000
Inventory	180,000
Total current assets	370,000
Investments	40,000
Plant and equipment	450,000
Less: Accumulated depreciation	(100,000)
Net plant and equipment	350,000
Total assets	$760,000

Liabilities and Stockholders' Equity

Current liabilities:

Accounts payable	$ 90,000
Notes payable	10,000
Accrued expenses	10,000
Total current liabilities	110,000

Long-term liabilities:

Bonds payable	170,000
Total liabilities	280,000

Stockholders' equity:

Preferred stock, $100 par value	90,000
Common stock, $1 par value	60,000
Capital paid in excess of par	230,000
Retained earnings	100,000
Total stockholders' equity	480,000
Total liabilities and stockholders' equity	$760,000

THE HOT AIR COMPANY
Income Statement
For the Year Ending December 31, 1988

Sales (on credit)	$2,000,000
Less: Cost of goods sold	1,300,000
Gross profit	700,000
Less: Selling and administrative expenses	400,000*
Operating profit (EBIT)	300,000
Less: Interest expense	20,000
Earnings before taxes (EBT)	280,000
Less: Taxes	112,000
Earnings after taxes (EAT)	$ 168,000

*Includes $10,000 in lease payments.

20. (*Comprehensive problem.*)

Given the financial statements for Jones Corporation and Smith Corporation shown here:

a. To which one would you, as credit manager for a supplier, approve the extension of (short-term) trade credit? Why? Compute all ratios before answering.

b. In which one would you buy stock? Why?

JONES CORPORATION

Current Assets		Liabilities	
Cash	$ 20,000	Accounts payable	$100,000
Accounts receivable . . .	80,000	Bonds payable—10% . . .	80,000
Inventory	50,000		

Long-term Assets		Stockholders' Equity	
Fixed assets	$500,000	Common stock	$150,000
Less: Accum. dep. . .	(150,000)	Paid-in capital	70,000
Net fixed assets	350,000	Retained earnings	100,000
	$500,000		$500,000

Sales (on credit)	$1,250,000
Cost of goods sold	750,000
Gross profit	500,000
Selling and administrative expense	257,000*
Less: Depreciation expense	50,000
Operating profit	193,000
Interest expense	8,000
Earnings before taxes	185,000
Tax expense (50%)	92,500
Net income	92,500

*Includes $7,000 in lease payments.

Jones Corporation has 75,000 shares outstanding.

SMITH CORPORATION

Current Assets		Liabilities	
Cash	$ 35,000	Accounts payable	$ 75,000
Marketable securities	7,500	Bonds payable—10%	210,000
Accounts receivable	70,000		
Inventory	75,000		

Long-term Assets		Stockholders' Equity	
Fixed assets	$500,000	Common stock	$75,000
Less: Accum. dep.	(250,000)	Paid-in capital	30,000
Net fixed assets	250,000	Retained earnings	47,500
	$437,500		$437,500

Sales (on credit)	$1,000,000
Cost of goods sold	600,000
Gross profit	400,000
Selling and administrative expense	224,000*
Depreciation expense	50,000
Operating profit	126,000
Interest expense	21,000
Earnings before taxes	105,000
Tax expense	52,500
Net income	52,500

*Includes $7,000 in lease payments.

Smith Corporation has 75,000 shares outstanding.

21. (*Comprehensive problem on trend analysis and industry comparisons.*)

Al Thomas has recently been approached by his brother-in-law, Robert Watson, with a proposal to buy 20 percent interest in Watson Leisure Time Sporting Goods. The sporting goods company manufactures golf clubs, baseball bats, basketball goals, and other similar items.

Mr. Watson is quick to point out the increase in sales that have taken place over the last three years as indicated in the income statement, Exhibit 1. The annual growth rate is 20 percent. A balance sheet for a similar time period is shown in Exhibit 2, and selected industry ratios are presented in Exhibit 3. Note the industry growth rate in sales is only approximately 10 percent per year.

There was a steady real growth of 3–4 percent in gross national product during the period under study. The rate of inflation was in the 5–6 percent range.

Exhibit 1

WATSON LEISURE TIME SPORTING GOODS
Income Statement

	198x	*198y*	*198z*
Sales (all on credit)	$1,500,000	$1,800,000	$2,160,000
Cost of goods sold	950,000	1,120,000	1,300,000
Gross profit	550,000	680,000	860,000
Selling and administrative expense*	380,000	490,000	590,000
Operating profit	170,000	190,000	270,000
Interest expense	30,000	40,000	85,000
Net income before taxes	140,000	150,000	185,000
Taxes	46,120	48,720	64,850
Net income	$ 93,880	$ 101,280	$ 120,150
Shares	40,000	40,000	46,000
Earnings per share	$2.35	$2.53	$2.61

*Includes $20,000 in lease payments for each year.

Exhibit 2

WATSON LEISURE TIME SPORTING GOODS
Balance Sheet

	198x	198y	198z
Assets			
Cash	$ 20,000	$ 30,000	$ 20,000
Marketable securities	30,000	35,000	50,000
Accounts receivable	150,000	230,000	330,000
Inventory	250,000	285,000	325,000
Total current assets	450,000	580,000	725,000
Net plant and equipment	550,000	720,000	1,169,000
Total assets	$1,000,000	$1,300,000	$1,894,000
Liabilities and Stockholders' Equity			
Accounts payable	$ 100,000	$ 225,000	$ 200,000
Notes payable (bank)	100,000	100,000	300,000
Total current liabilities	200,000	325,000	500,000
Long-term liabilities	250,000	331,120	550,740
Total liabilities	450,000	656,120	1,050,740
Common stock ($10 par)	400,000	400,000	460,000
Capital paid in excess of par	50,000	50,000	80,000
Retained earnings	100,000	193,880	303,260
Total stockholders' equity	550,000	643,880	843,260
Total liabilities and stockholders' equity	$1,000,000	$1,300,000	$1,894,000

Exhibit 3

Selected Industry Ratios

	198x	198y	198z
Growth in sales	—	9.98%	10.02%
Profit margin	5.75%	5.80%	5.81%
Return on assets (investment)	8.22%	8.24%	8.48%
Return on equity	13.26%	13.62%	14.16%
Receivable turnover	10×	9.5×	10.1×
Average collection period	36 days	37.9 days	35.6 days
Inventory turnover	5.71×	5.62×	5.84×
Fixed asset turnover	2.75×	2.66×	2.20×
Total asset turnover	1.43×	1.42×	1.46×
Current ratio	2.10×	2.08×	2.15×
Quick ratio	1.05×	1.02×	1.10×
Debt to total assets	38%	39.5%	40.1%
Times interest earned	5.00×	5.20×	5.26×
Fixed charge coverage	3.85×	3.95×	3.97×
Growth in EPS	—	9.7%	9.8%

The stock in the corporation has become available due to the ill health of a current stockholder, who is in need of cash. The issue here is not to determine the exact price for the stock, but rather whether Watson Leisure Time Sporting Goods represents an attractive investment situation. Although Mr. Thomas has a primary in-

interest in the profitability ratios, he will take a close look at all the ratios. He has no fast and firm rules about required return on investment, but rather wishes to analyze the overall condition of the firm. The firm does not currently pay a cash dividend, and return to the investor must come from selling the stock in the future. After doing a thorough analysis (including ratios for each year and comparisons to the industry), what comments and recommendations can you offer to Mr. Thomas?

Selected References

Altman, Edward I. "Financial Ratios, Discriminant Analysis, and the Prediction of Corporate Bankruptcy." *Journal of Finance* 23 (September 1968), pp. 586–609.

Benishay, Haskell. "Economic Information in Financial Ratio Analysis." *Accounting and Business Research* 2 (Spring 1971), pp. 174–79.

Callard, Charles G., and David C. Kleinman. "Inflation-Adjustment Accounting: Does It Matter?" *Financial Analysts Journal* 41 (May–June 1985), pp. 51–59.

Chen, Kung H., and Thomas A. Shimerda. "An Empirical Analysis of Financial Ratios." *Financial Management* 10 (Spring 1981), pp. 51–60.

Copeland, Ronald M.; Joseph F. Wojdak; and John K. Shank. "The Use of LIFO to Offset Inflation." *Harvard Business Review* 49 (May–June 1971), pp. 91–100.

D'Ambrosio, Charles A. "Truth Reality and Financial Analysis." *Financial Analysts Journal* 38 (July–August 1982), pp. 24–25.

Davidson, S., and R. L. Weil. "Inflation Accounting." *Financial Analysts Journal* 31 (January–February 1975), pp. 27–31, 70–84.

Estep, Tony. "Security Analysis and Stock Selection: Turning Financial Information Into Return Forecasts." *Financial Analysts Journal* 43 (July–August 1987), pp. 34–43.

Gandolfi, Arthur E. "Inflation, Taxation, and Interest Rates." *Journal of Finance* 37 (June 1982), 797–807.

Garnett, Jeff, and Geoffrey A. Hirt. "Replacement Costs Data: A Study of the Chemical and Drug Industry for Years 1976 Through 1978." An unpublished study at Illinois State University, January 1980.

Malburg, Chris, and Steve Wagner. "Using Financial Projections." *Cash Flow* 8 (July 1987), pp. 25–37.

Modigliani, Franco, and Richard A. Cohn. "Inflation, Rational Valuation and the Market." *Financial Analysts Journal* 35 (March–April 1979), pp. 24–44.

Siegel, Joel G. "The 'Quality of Earnings' Concept—A Survey." *Financial Analysts Journal* 38 (March–April 1982), 60–68.

Von Furstenberg, George M., and Burton G. Malkiel. "Financial Analysis in an Inflationary Environment." *Journal of Finance* 32 (May 1977), pp. 575–88.

Wallich, Henry C. "Investment Income during Inflation." *Financial Analysts Journal* 34 (March–April 1978), pp. 34–37.

4

Financial Forecasting

The old notion of the corporate treasurer burning the midnight oil in order to find new avenues of financing before dawn is no longer in vogue. If there is one talent that is essential to the financial manager, it is the ability to plan ahead and to make necessary adjustments before actual events occur. Quite likely, we could construct the same set of external events for two corporations (inflation, recession, severe new competition, and so on), and one would survive, while the other would not. The outcome might be a function not only of their risk-taking desires, but also of their ability to hedge against risk with careful planning.

While we may assume that no growth or a decline in volume is the primary cause for a shortage of funds, this is not necessarily the case. A rapidly growing firm may witness a significant increase in accounts receivable, inventory, and plant and equipment that cannot be financed in the normal course of business. Assume that sales go from $100,000 to $200,000 in one year for a firm that has a 5 percent profit margin on sales. At the same time, assume that assets represent 50 percent of sales and go from $50,000 to $100,000 as sales double. The $10,000 of profit (5 percent × $200,000) will hardly be adequate to finance the $50,000 asset growth. The remaining $40,000 must come from suppliers, the bank, and perhaps stockholders. The student should recognize that profit alone is generally inadequate to finance significant growth and that a comprehensive financing plan must be developed. All too often, the small businessman (and sometimes the big one as well) is mystified by an increase in sales and profits but less cash in the till.

Constructing Pro Forma Statements

The most comprehensive means of financial forecasting is to go through the process of developing a series of pro forma, or projected, financial statements. We will give particular attention to the *pro forma income statement,* the *cash budget,* and the *pro forma balance sheet.* Based on the projected statements, the firm is able to judge its future level of receivables, inventory, payables, and other corporate accounts as well as its anticipated profits and borrowing requirements. The financial officer can then carefully track actual events against the plan and make necessary adjustments. Furthermore, the statements are often required by bankers and other lenders as a guide for the future.

A systems approach is necessary for the development of pro forma statements. We first construct a pro forma income statement based on sales projections and the production plan, then translate this material into a cash budget, and finally assimilate all previously developed material into a pro forma balance sheet. The process of developing pro forma financial statements is depicted in Figure 4–1. We will use a six-month time frame to facilitate the analysis, though the same procedures could be extended to one year or longer.

Pro Forma Income Statement

Assume that the Goldman Corporation has been requested by its bank to provide pro forma financial statements for midyear 1989. The pro forma income statement will provide a projection of how much profit the firm anticipates making over the ensuing time period. In developing the pro forma income statement, we will follow four important steps.

1. Establish a sales projection.
2. Determine a production schedule and the associated use of new material, direct labor, and overhead, to arrive at gross profit.
3. Compute other expenses.
4. Determine profit by completing the actual pro forma statement.

**Figure 4–1
Development of pro
forma statements**

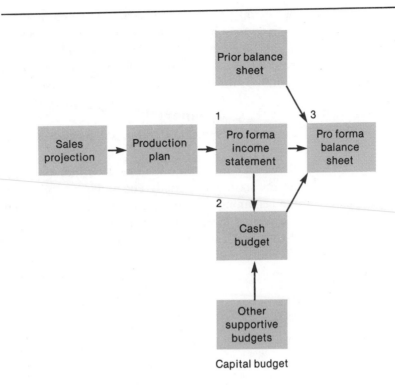

Capital budget

Establish a Sales Projection

For purposes of analysis, we shall assume that the Goldman Corporation
has two primary products: wheels and casters. Our sales projection calls
for the sale of 1,000 wheels and 2,000 casters at prices of $30 and $35,
respectively. As indicated in Table 4–1, we anticipate total sales of
$100,000.

It is assumed that the sales projections were derived from both an
external and internal viewpoint. Using the former, we analyze our prospective sales in light of economic conditions affecting our industry and

**Table 4–1
Projected wheel and
caster sales (first six
months, 1989)**

	Wheels	*Casters*	
Quantity	1,000	2,000	
Sales price	$30	$35	
Sales revenue	$30,000	$70,000	
Total			$100,000

our company. Statistical techniques such as regression and time series analysis may be employed in the process. Internal analysis calls for surveying our own salespeople within their territories. Ideally, we would proceed along each of those paths in isolation of the other and then assimilate the results into one meaningful projection.

Determine a Production Schedule and the Gross Profit

Based on anticipated sales, we determine the necessary production plan for the six-month period. The number of units produced will depend on the beginning inventory of wheels and casters, our sales projection, and the desired level of ending inventory. Assume that on January 1, 1989, the Goldman Corporation has in stock the items shown in Table 4–2.

Table 4–2
Stock of beginning inventory

	Wheels	*Casters*
Quantity	85	180
Cost	$16	$20
Total value	$1,360	$3,600
Total		$4,960

We will add the projected quantity of unit sales for the next six months to our desired ending inventory and subtract our stock of beginning inventory (in units) to determine our production requirements.

Units

  + Projected sales
  + Desired ending inventory
  – *Beginning* inventory
  = Production requirements

In Table 4–3, we see a required production level of 1,015 wheels and 2,020 casters.

Table 4–3
Production requirements for six months

	Wheels	*Casters*
Projected unit sales (Table 4–1)	+1,000	+2,000
Desired ending inventory (assumed to represent 10% of unit sales for the time period)	+100	+200
Beginning inventory (Table 4–2)	–85	–180
Units to be produced	1,015	2,020

We must now determine the cost to produce these units. In Table 4–2 we saw that the cost of units in stock was $16 for wheels and $20 for casters. However, we shall assume that the price of materials, labor, and overhead going into the products is now $18 for wheels and $22 for casters, as indicated in Table 4–4.

Table 4–4
Unit costs

	Wheels	Casters
Materials	$10	$12
Labor	5	6
Overhead	3	4
Total	$18	$22

The *total* cost to produce the required items for the next six months is shown in Table 4–5.

Table 4–5
Total production costs

	Wheels	Casters	
Units to be produced (Table 4–3)	1,015	2,020	
Cost per unit (Table 4–4)	$18	$22	
Total cost	$18,270	$44,440	$62,710

Cost of goods sold The main consideration in constructing a pro forma income statement is the costs specifically associated with units sold during the time period. Note that in the case of wheels we anticipate sales of 1,000 units, as indicated in Table 4–1, but are producing 1,015, as indicated in Table 4–5, to increase our inventory level by 15 units. For profit measurement purposes, we will *not* charge these extra 15 units against current sales.[1] Furthermore, in determining the cost of the 1,000 units sold during the current time period, we will *not* assume that all of the items sold represent inventory manufactured in this period. In the case of the Goldman Corporation, we shall assume that it uses FIFO (first-in, first-out) accounting and that it will first allocate the cost of current sales to beginning inventory and then to goods manufactured during the period.

In Table 4–6, we look at the revenue, associated cost of goods sold, and gross profit for both products. For example, 1,000 units of wheels

---

[1] Later on in the analysis we will show the effect that these extra units have on the cash budget and the balance sheet.

Table 4–6
Allocation of
manufacturing cost
and determination of
gross profits

	Wheels	Casters	Combined
Quantity sold (Table 4–1)	1,000	2,000	3,000
Sales price	$30	$35	
Sales revenue	$30,000	$70,000	$100,000
Cost of goods sold:			
Old inventory (Table 4–2)			
Quantity (units)	85	180	
Cost per unit	$16	$20	
Total	$ 1,360	$ 3,600	
New inventory (the remainder)			
Quantity (units)	915	1,820	
Cost per unit (Table 4–4)	$18	$22	
Total	16,470	40,040	
Total cost of goods sold	17,830	43,640	$ 61,470
Gross profit	$12,170	$26,360	$ 38,530

are to be sold at a total revenue of $30,000. Of the 1,000 units, 85 units are from beginning inventory at a $16 cost (Table 4–2) and the balance of 915 units are from current production at an $18 cost. The total cost of goods sold for wheels is $17,830, yielding a gross profit of $12,170. The pattern is the same for casters, with sales of $70,000, cost of goods sold of $43,640, and gross profit of $26,360. The combined sales for the two products are $100,000, with cost of goods sold of $61,470 and gross profit of $38,530.

At this point, we also compute the value of ending inventory for later use in constructing financial statements. As indicated in Table 4–7, the value of ending inventory will be $6,200.

Other Expense Items

Having computed total revenue, cost of goods sold, and gross profits, we must now subtract other expense items to arrive at a net profit figure. We deduct general and administrative expenses as well as interest expenses

Table 4–7
Value of ending
inventory

+ Beginning inventory (Table 4–2)	$ 4,960
+ Total production costs (Table 4–5)	62,710
Total inventory available for sales	67,670
− Cost of goods sold (Table 4–6)	61,470
Ending inventory	$ 6,200

from gross profit to arrive at earnings before taxes, then subtract taxes to determine aftertax income, and finally deduct dividends to ascertain the contribution to retained earnings. For the Goldman Corporation, we shall assume that general and administrative expenses are $12,000, interest expense is $1,500, and dividends are $1,500.

Actual Pro Forma Income Statement

Combining the gross profit in Table 4–6 with our assumptions on other expense items, we arrive at the pro forma income statement presented in Table 4–8. We anticipate earnings after taxes of $20,024, dividends of $1,500, and an increase in retained earnings of $18,524.

Cash Budget

As previously indicated, the generation of sales and profits does not necessarily ensure that there will be adequate cash on hand to meet financial obligations as they come due. A profitable sale may generate accounts receivables in the short run, but no immediate cash to meet maturing obligations. For this reason, we must translate the pro forma income statement into cash flows. In this process we divide the longer-term pro forma income statement into smaller and more precise time frames in order to appreciate the seasonal and monthly patterns of cash inflows and outflows. Some months may represent particularly high or low sales volume or may require dividends, taxes, or capital expenditures.

Table 4–8

Pro Forma Income Statement
June 30, 1989

Sales revenue	$100,000
Cost of goods sold	61,470
Gross profit	38,530
General and administrative expense	12,000
Operating profit (EBIT)	26,530
Interest expense	1,500
Earnings before taxes (EBT)	25,030
Taxes (20%)*	5,006
Earnings after taxes (EAT)	20,024
Common stock dividends	1,500
Increase in retained earnings	$ 18,524

*Though profit before taxes is slightly over $25,000, a convenient rate of 20 percent is applied to the full amount.

Cash Receipts

In the case of the Goldman Corporation, we break down the pro forma income statement for the first half of 1989 into a series of monthly cash budgets. In Table 4–1 we showed anticipated sales of $100,000 over this time period; we shall now assume that these sales can be divided into monthly projections, as indicated in Table 4–9.

A careful analysis of past sales and collection records indicates that 20 percent of sales are collected in the month of sales and 80 percent in the following month. The cash receipt pattern related to monthly sales is shown in Table 4–10. It is assumed that sales for December 1988 were $12,000.

The cash inflows will vary between $11,000 and $23,000, with the high point in receipts coming in May.

We now examine the monthly outflows.

Cash Payments

The primary considerations for cash payments are monthly costs associated with inventory manufactured during the period (material, labor, and overhead) and disbursements for general and administrative expenses, interest payments, taxes, and dividends. We must also consider cash payments for any new plant and equipment, an item that does not show up on our pro forma income statement.

Table 4–9
Monthly sales pattern

January	February	March	April	May	June
$15,000	$10,000	$15,000	$25,000	$15,000	$20,000

Table 4–10   Monthly cash receipts

	Dec.	Jan.	Feb.	March	April	May	June
Sales	$12,000	$15,000	$10,000	$15,000	$25,000	$15,000	$20,000
Collections: (20% of current sales)		$ 3,000	$ 2,000	$ 3,000	$ 5,000	$ 3,000	$ 4,000
Collections: (80% of previous month's sales)		9,600	12,000	8,000	12,000	20,000	12,000
Total cash receipts		$12,600	$14,000	$11,000	$17,000	$23,000	$16,000

Costs associated with units manufactured during the period may be taken from the data provided in Table 4–5, Total Production Costs. In Table 4–11, we simply recast these data in terms of material, labor, and overhead.

Table 4–11   Component costs of manufactured goods

	Wheels			Casters			
	Units Produced	Cost per Unit	Total Cost	Units Produced	Cost per Unit	Total Cost	Combined Cost
Materials	1,015	$10	$10,150	2,020	$12	$24,240	$34,390
Labor	1,015	5	5,075	2,020	6	12,120	17,195
Overhead	1,015	3	3,045	2,020	4	8,080	11,125
							$62,710

We see that the total costs for components in the two products are materials $34,390, labor $17,195, and overhead $11,125. We shall assume that all of these costs are incurred on an equal monthly basis over the six-month period. Even though the sales volume varies from month to month, we assume that we are employing level monthly production to ensure maximum efficiency in the use of various productive resources. Average monthly costs for materials, labor, and overhead are as shown in Table 4–12.

Table 4–12
Average monthly
manufacturing costs

	Total Costs	Time Frame	Average Monthly Cost
Materials	.$34,390	6 months	$5,732
Labor	17,195	6 months	2,866
Overhead	11,125	6 months	1,854

We shall pay for materials one month after the purchase has been made. Labor and overhead represent direct monthly cash outlays, as is true of interest, taxes, dividends, and assumed purchases of $8,000 in new equipment in February and $10,000 in June. We summarize all of our cash payments in Table 4–13. Past records indicate that $4,500 in materials was purchased in December.

Actual Budget

We are now in a position to bring together our monthly cash receipts and payments into a cash flow statement, illustrated in Table 4–14. The

Table 4–13   Summary of all monthly cash payments

	Dec.	Jan.	Feb.	March	April	May	June
From Table 4–12:							
Monthly material purchase	$4,500	$ 5,732	$ 5,732	$ 5,732	$ 5,732	$ 5,732	$ 5,732
Payment for material							
(prior month's purchase)		$ 4,500	$ 5,732	$ 5,732	$ 5,732	$ 5,732	$ 5,732
Monthly labor cost		2,866	2,866	2,866	2,866	2,866	2,866
Monthly overhead		1,854	1,854	1,854	1,854	1,854	1,854
From Table 4–8:							
General and administrative							
expense ($12,000 over							
6 months)		2,000	2,000	2,000	2,000	2,000	2,000
Interest expense							1,500
Taxes (two equal payments)				2,503			2,503
Cash dividend							1,500
Also:							
New equipment purchases			8,000				10,000
Total payments		$11,220	$20,452	$14,955	$12,452	$12,452	$27,953

Table 4–14   Monthly cash flow

	Jan.	Feb.	March	April	May	June
Total receipts (Table 4–10)	$12,600	$14,000	$11,000	$17,000	$23,000	$16,000
Total payments (Table 4–13)	11,220	20,452	14,955	12,452	12,452	27,953
Net cash flow	$ 1,380	($ 6,452)	($ 3,955)	$ 4,548	$10,548	($11,953)

difference between monthly receipts and payments is net cash flow for the month.

The primary purpose of the cash budget is to allow the firm to anticipate the need for outside funding at the end of each month. In the present case, we shall assume that the Goldman Corporation wishes to have a minimum cash balance of $5,000 at all times. If it goes below this amount, the firm will borrow funds from the bank. If it goes above $5,000 and the firm has a loan outstanding, it will use the excess funds to reduce the loan. This pattern of financing is demonstrated in Table 4–15—a fully developed cash budget with borrowing and repayment provisions.

The first line in Table 4–15 shows our net cash flow, which is added to the beginning cash balance to arrive at the cumulative cash balance. The fourth entry is the additional monthly loan or loan repayment, if any, required to maintain a minimum cash balance of $5,000. In order to keep track of our loan balance, the fifth entry represents cumulative

Table 4–15   Cash budget with borrowing and repayment

	Jan.	Feb.	March	April	May	June
1. Net cash flow	$1,380	($6,452)	($3,955)	$4,548	$10,548	($11,953)
2. Beginning cash balance	5,000*	6,380	5,000	5,000	5,000	11,069
3. Cumulative cash balance	6,380	(72)	1,045	9,548	15,548	(884)
4. Monthly loan or (repayment)	—	5,072	3,955	(4,548)	(4,479)	5,884
5. Cumulative loan balance	—	5,072	9,027	4,479	—	5,884
6. Ending cash balance	6,380	5,000	5,000	5,000	11,069	5,000

*We assume that the Goldman Corporation has a beginning cash balance of $5,000 on January 1, 1989, and that it desires a minimum monthly ending cash balance of $5,000.

loans outstanding for all months. Finally, we show the cash balance at the end of the month, which becomes the beginning cash balance for the next month.

At the end of January the firm has $6,380 in cash, but by the end of February the cumulative cash position of the firm is negative, necessitating a loan of $5,072 to maintain a $5,000 cash balance. The firm has a loan on the books until May, at which time there is an ending cash balance of $11,069. During the months of April and May the cumulative cash balance is greater than the required minimum cash balance of $5,000, so loan repayments of $4,548 and $4,479 are made to retire the loans completely in May. In June, the firm is once again required to borrow $5,884 in order to maintain a $5,000 cash balance.

Pro Forma Balance Sheet

Now that we have developed a pro forma income statement and a cash budget, it is relatively simple to integrate all of these items into a pro forma balance sheet. Because the balance sheet represents cumulative changes in the corporation over time, we first examine the *prior* period's balance sheet and then translate these items through time to represent June 30, 1989. The last balance sheet, dated December 31, 1988, is shown in Table 4–16.

In constructing our pro forma balance sheet for June 30, 1989, some of the accounts from the old balance sheet will remain unchanged, while others will take on new values, as indicated by the pro forma income statement and cash budget. The process is depicted in Figure 4–2.

We present the new pro forma balance sheet as of June 30, 1989, in Table 4–17 on page 97.

Table 4–16

Balance Sheet
December 31, 1988

Assets

Current assets:

Cash	$ 5,000
Marketable securities	3,200
Accounts receivable	9,600
Inventory	4,960
Total current assets	22,760
Plant and equipment	27,740
Total assets	$50,500

Liabilities and Stockholders' Equity

Accounts payable	$ 4,500
Notes payable	0
Long-term debt	15,000
Common stock	10,500
Retained earnings	20,500
Total liabilities and stockholders' equity	$50,500

Figure 4–2
Development of a pro
forma balance sheet

Table 4–17

Pro Forma Balance Sheet
June 30, 1989

Assets

Current assets:

1. Cash	$ 5,000
2. Marketable securities	3,200
3. Accounts receivable	16,000
4. Inventory	6,200
Total current assets	30,400
5. Plant and equipment	45,740
Total assets	$76,140

Liabilities and Stockholders' Equity

6. Accounts payable	$ 5,732
7. Notes payable	5,884
8. Long-term debt	15,000
9. Common stock	10,500
10. Retained earnings	39,024
Total liabilities and stockholders' equity	$76,140

Explanation of pro forma balance sheets Each item in Table 4–17 can be explained on the basis of a prior calculation or assumption.

1. Cash ($5,000)—minimum cash balance as shown in Table 4–15.
2. Marketable securities ($3,200)—remains unchanged from prior period's value in Table 4–16.
3. Accounts receivable ($16,000)—based on June sales of $20,000 in Table 4–10. Twenty percent will be collected that month, while 80 percent will become accounts receivable at the end of the month.

$$\begin{array}{rl} \$20,000 & \text{sales} \\ \times\ 80\% & \text{receivables} \\ \hline \$16,000 & \end{array}$$

4. Inventory ($6,200)—ending inventory as shown in Table 4–7.
5. Plant and equipment ($45,740).

Initial value (Table 4–16) . . .	$27,740
Purchases* (Table 4–13) . . .	18,000
Plant and equipment	$45,740

*For simplicity, depreciation is not explicitly considered.

6. Accounts payable ($5,732)—based on June purchases in Table 4–13. They will not be paid until July, and thus are accounts payable.

7. Notes payable ($5,884)—the amount we must borrow to maintain our cash balance of $5,000, as shown in Table 4–15.
8. Long-term debt ($15,000)—remains unchanged from prior period's value in Table 4–16.
9. Common stock ($10,500)—remains unchanged from prior period's value in Table 4–16.
10. Retained earnings ($39,024)

Initial value (Table 4–16)	$20,500
Transfer of pro forma income to retained	
earnings (Table 4–8)	18,524
Retained earnings	$39,024

Analysis of Pro Forma Statement

In comparing the pro forma balance sheet (Table 4–17) to the prior balance sheet (Table 4–16), we note that assets are up by $25,640.

Total assets (June 30, 1987) . . .	$76,140
Total assets (Dec. 31, 1986) . . .	50,500
Increase	$25,640

The growth must be financed by accounts payable, notes payable, and profit (as reflected by the increase in retained earnings). Though the company will enjoy a high degree of profitability, it must still look to bank financing of $5,884 to support the increase in assets. This represents the difference between the $25,640 buildup in assets, and the $1,232 increase in accounts payable as well as the $18,524 buildup in retained earnings.

Percent-of-Sales Method

An alternative to going through the process of tracing cash and accounting flows to determine financial needs is to assume that accounts on the balance sheet will maintain a given percentage relationship to sales. We then indicate a change in the sales level and ascertain our related financing needs. This is known as the *percent-of-sales method*. For example, for the Howard Corporation, introduced in Table 4–18, we show the following balance sheet accounts in dollars and their percent of sales, based on a sales volume of $200,000.

We observe that cash of $5,000 represents 2.5 percent of sales of $200,000; receivables of $40,000 is 20 percent of sales; and so on. No percentages are computed for notes payable, common stock, and retained earnings because they are not assumed to maintain a direct relationship with sales volume. Note that any dollar increase in sales will necessitate

Table 4–18

HOWARD CORPORATION
Balance Sheet and Percent-of-Sales Table

Assets		Liabilities and Stockholders' Equity	
Cash	$ 5,000	Accounts payable	$ 40,000
Accounts receivable	40,000	Accrued expenses	10,000
Inventory	25,000	Notes payable	15,000
Total current assets	$ 70,000	Common stock	10,000
Equipment	50,000	Retained earnings	45,000
		Total liabilities and	
Total assets	$120,000	stockholders' equity	$120,000

$200,000 sales
Percent of Sales

Cash	2.5%	Accounts payable	20.0%
Accounts receivable	20.0	Accrued expenses	5.0
Inventory	12.5		25.0%
Total current assets	35.0		
Equipment	25.0		
	60.0%		

a 60 percent increase in assets,[2] of which 25 percent will be spontaneously or automatically financed through accounts payable and accrued expenses, leaving 35 percent to be financed by profit or additional outside sources of financing. We will assume that the Howard Corporation has an aftertax return of 6 percent on the sales dollar and that 50 percent of profits are paid out as dividends.[3]

If sales increase from $200,000 to $300,000, the $100,000 increase in sales will necessitate $35,000 (35 percent) in additional financing. Since we will earn 6 percent on total sales of $300,000, we will show a profit of $18,000. With a 50 percent dividend payout, $9,000 will remain for internal financing. This means that $26,000 out of the $35,000 must be financed from outside sources. Our formula to determine the need for new funds is:

Required new funds—

$$(\text{RNF}) = \frac{A}{S}(\Delta S) - \frac{L}{S}(\Delta S) - PS_2(1 - D) \qquad (4\text{–}1)$$

[2]We are assuming equipment increases in proportion to sales. In certain cases, there may be excess capacity, and equipment (or plant and equipment) will not increase.

[3]Some may wish to add back depreciation under the percent-of-sales method. Most, however, choose the assumption that funds generated through depreciation (in the sources and uses of funds sense) must be used to replace the fixed assets to which depreciation is applied.

where

$\dfrac{A}{S}$ = Percentage relationship of variable assets to sales [60%]

ΔS = Change in sales [$100,000]

$\dfrac{L}{S}$ = Percentage relationship of variable liabilities to sales [25%]

P = Profit margin [6%]

S_2 = New sales level [$300,000]

D = Dividend payout ratio [.50]

Plugging in the values, we show:

$$
\begin{aligned}
RNF &= 60\% \ (\$100,000) - 25\%(\$100,000) - 6\% \ (\$300,000) \ (1-0.5) \\
&= \$60,000 - \$25,000 - \$18,000 \ (0.5) \\
&= \$35,000 - \$9,000 \\
&= \$26,000 \ \text{required sources of new funds}
\end{aligned}
$$

Presumably the $26,000 can be financed at the bank or through some other appropriate source.

The student will observe that using the percent-of-sales method is a much easier task than tracing through the various cash flows to arrive at the pro forma statements. Nevertheless, the output is much less meaningful and we do not get a month-to-month breakdown of the data. The percent-of-sales method is a "broad brush" approach, while the development of pro forma statements is more exacting. Of course, whatever method we use, the results are only as meaningful or reliable as the assumptions about sales and production that went into the numbers.

Summary

The process of financial forecasting allows the financial manager to anticipate events before they occur, particularly the need for raising funds externally. An important consideration is that growth itself may call for additional sources of financing because profit is often inadequate to cover the net buildup in receivables, inventory, and other asset accounts.

We develop pro forma financial statements from an overall corporate systems viewpoint. The time perspective is usually six months to a year in the future. In developing a pro forma income statement, we begin by making sales projections, then we construct a production plan, and finally we consider all other expenses. From the pro forma income statement we proceed to a cash budget, in which the monthly or quarterly cash inflows and outflows related to sales, expenditures, and capital outlays are portrayed. All of this information can be assimilated into a pro forma balance sheet in which asset, liability, and stockholders' equity accounts are shown. Any shortage of funds is assumed to be financed through notes payable (bank loans).

We may take a shortcut to financial forecasting through the use of the percent-of-sales method. Under this approach, selected balance sheet accounts are assumed to maintain a constant percentage relationship to sales, and thus for any given sales amount we can ascertain balance sheet values. Once again a shortage of funds is assumed to be financed through notes payable.

List of Terms

pro forma balance sheet	cost of goods sold
pro forma income statement	percent-of-sales method
cash budget	

Discussion Questions

1. What are the basic benefits and purposes of developing pro forma statements and a cash budget?

2. Explain how the collections and purchases schedules are related to the borrowing needs of the corporation.

3. With inflation, what are the implications of using LIFO and FIFO inventory methods? How do they affect the cost of goods sold?

4. Explain the relationship between inventory turnover and purchase needs.

5. Rapid corporate growth in sales and profits can cause financing problems. Elaborate on this statement.

6. Discuss the advantage and disadvantage of level production schedules in firms whose sales are cyclical.

7. What conditions would help make a percent-of-sales forecast as accurate as pro forma financial statements and cash budgets?

Problems

1. Sales for Gallagher Lazer Printers, Inc., are expected to be 8,000 units for the coming month. The company likes to maintain 10 percent of unit sales for each month in ending inventory. Beginning inventory is 2,000 units. How many units should Gallagher produce for the coming month?

2. Fluke Manufacturing anticipates sales of 40,000 units for the first six months of the year. Beginning inventory is maintained at 12 percent of anticipated sales. Ending inventory will be equal to 15 percent of the projected sales of 56,000 units for the last six months of the year. How many units should Fluke produce during the first six months of the year?

3. On December 31 of last year, Wolfson Corporation had in inventory 400 units of its product, which cost $21 per unit to produce. During January, the company produced 800 units at a cost of $24 per unit. Assuming that Wolfson Corporation sold 700 units in January, what was cost of goods sold (assume FIFO inventory method)?

4. At the end of January, Evans Corporation had an inventory of 500 units, which cost $15 per unit to produce. During February, the company produced 750 units at a cost of $17 per unit. If Evans Corporation sold 900 units in February, what was its cost of goods sold (assume LIFO inventory accounting)?

5. The Beck Corporation produces a product with the following costs as of July 1, 1988:

Material	$3 per unit
Labor	4 per unit
Overhead	2 per unit

Beginning inventory on July 1 was 4,000 units. From July 1 to December 31, 1988, Beck produced 15,000 units. These units had a material cost of $4 per unit. Other costs were the same. Cox uses FIFO inventory accounting.

Assuming that Cox sold 16,000 units during the last six months of the year at $18 each, what will gross profit be? What is the value of ending inventory?

6. Pete's Rose and Flower Shop has forecasted credit sales for the third quarter of the year.

June (actual)	$30,000

July (forecast) 25,000
August (forecast) 20,000
September (forecast) 40,000

Experience has shown that 20 percent of sales are collected in the month of sale, 70 percent in the following month, and 10 percent are never collected. Prepare a schedule of cash receipts covering the third quarter (July through September).

7. The Denver Corporation has forecast the following sales for the first seven months of the year:

January	$10,000	May	$10,000
February	12,000	June	16,000
March	14,000	July	18,000
April	20,000		

Monthly material purchases are set equal to 30 percent of forecasted sales for the next month. Of the total material costs, 40 percent are paid in the month of purchase and 60 percent in the following month. Labor costs will run $4,000 per month, and fixed overhead is $2,000 per month. Interest payments on the debt will be $3,000 for both March and June. Finally, the Denver salesmen will receive a 1.5 percent commission on total sales for the first six months of the year, to be paid on June 30.

Prepare a monthly summary of cash payments for the six-month period from January through June. (Note: Compute prior December purchases to help get total material payments for January.)

8. Acme Anvil Company forecasts its sales in units for the next four months to be as follows:

April	3,000
May	5,000
June	2,500
July	2,000

Acme maintains an ending inventory for each month in the amount of one and one half times the expected sales in the following month. The ending inventory for March (April's beginning inventory) reflects this policy. Materials cost $200 per unit and are paid for in the month after purchase. Labor cost is $80 per unit and is paid for in the month the cost is incurred. Fixed overhead is $30,000 per month. Dividends of $45,000 are scheduled to be paid in June. Three thousand units were produced in March.

Complete a production schedule and a summary of cash payments for April, May, and June. Remember that production in any month is equal to sales plus desired ending inventory minus beginning inventory.

9. The Pushman Car Company has forecast its sales in units as follows:

January	500	May	920
February	450	June	1,100
March	450	July	1,000
April	800		

Pushman always keeps an ending inventory equal to 120 percent of the next month's expected sales. The ending inventory for December (January beginning inventory) is 600 units, which is consistent with this policy.

Materials cost $8 per unit and are paid for in the month after purchase. Labor cost is $4 per unit and is paid in the month the cost is incurred. Overhead costs are $3,500 per month. Interest of $5,000 on Pushman's bonds is scheduled to be paid in June.

Prepare a monthly production schedule and a monthly summary of cash payments for the period January through June. Pushman produced 400 units in December.

10. The Prill Pencil Company has made the following sales projections for the next six months. All sales are credit sales.

April	$6,000	July	$5,500
May	5,400	August	8,000
June	5,000	September	8,500

Sales in February and March were $6,800 and $6,200, respectively.

Experience has shown that of total sales, 10 percent are uncollectible, 20 percent are collected in the month of sale, 50 percent are collected in the following month, and 20 percent are collected two months after the sale.

Prepare a monthly cash receipts schedule for Prill Pencil Company for April through September.

Of the sales expected to be made during the six months from April through September, how much will still be due at the end of September? How much of this amount is expected to be collected?

11. Gerber Ammunitions and Baby Food, a highly diversified company, has expected sales of $8,000 in September, $10,000 in October, $15,000 in November, and $12,000 in December. Of the company's sales, 20

percent are for cash and 80 percent are on credit. Experience shows that 30 percent of accounts receivable are paid in the month after the sale, while the remaining 70 percent are paid two months after. Determine collections for November and December.

Also assume Gerber's cash payments for November and December are $13,000 and $8,000, respectively. The beginning cash balance in November is $5,000, which is the desired minimum balance.

Prepare a cash budget with borrowing needed or repayments made for November and December.

12. Paco's Pizza Company has restaurants in five college towns. Paco wants to expand into Normal and French Lick and needs a bank loan to do this. Mr. Sousse, the banker, will finance construction if Paco can present an acceptable three-month financial plan for January through March. Following are actual and forecasted sales figures:

Actual		Forecast		Additional information
November	$120,000	January	$190,000	April forecast $230,000
December	140,000	February	210,000	
		March	230,000	

Of Paco's sales, 30 percent are for cash and the remaining 70 percent are on credit. Of credit sales, 40 percent are paid in the month after sale and 60 percent are paid in the second month after the sale. Materials cost 20 percent of sales and are purchased and received each month in an amount sufficient to cover the following month's expected sales. Materials are paid for in the month after they are received. Labor expense is 50 percent of sales and is paid in the month of sales. Selling and administrative expense is 5 percent of sales and is also paid in the month of sales. Overhead is $12,000 in cash per month; depreciation expense is $25,000 per month. Taxes of $20,000 and dividends of $16,000 will be paid in March. Cash at the beginning of January is $70,000 and the minimum desired cash balance is $65,000.

For January, February, and March, prepare a schedule of monthly cash receipts, monthly cash payments, and a complete monthly cash budget with borrowings and repayments.

13. Ellis Electronics Company's actual sales and purchases for April and May are shown here along with forecasted sales and purchases for June through September.

	Sales	Purchases
April (actual)	$320,000	$130,000
May (actual)	300,000	120,000
June (forecast)	275,000	120,000
July (forecast)	275,000	180,000
August (forecast)	290,000	200,000
September (forecast)	330,000	170,000

The company makes 10 percent of its sales for cash and 90 percent on credit. Of the credit sales, 20 percent are collected in the month after the sale and 80 percent are collected two months after. Ellis pays for 40 percent of its purchases in the month after purchase and 60 percent two months after.

Labor expense equals 10 percent of the current month's sales. Overhead expense equals $12,000 per month. Interest payments of $30,000 are due in June and September. A cash dividend of $50,000 is scheduled to be paid in June. Taxes of $25,000 are due in June and September. There is a scheduled capital outlay of $300,000 in September.

Ellis Electronics' ending cash balance in May is $20,000. The minimum desired cash balance is $15,000. Prepare a schedule of monthly cash receipts, monthly cash payments, and a complete monthly cash budget with borrowing and repayments for June through September. The maximum desired cash balance is $50,000. Excess cash (above $50,000) is used to buy marketable securities. Marketable securities are sold before borrowing funds in case of a cash shortfall (less than $15,000).

14. Carter Paint Company has plants in nine midwestern states. Sales for last year were $100 million, and the balance sheet at year-end is similar in percentage of sales to that of previous years (and this will continue in the future). All assets and current liabilities will vary directly with sales.

Balance Sheet
(in $ millions)

Assets		Liabilities and Stockholders' Equity	
Cash	$ 5	Accounts payable	$15
Accounts receivable	15	Accrued wages	6
Inventory	30	Accrued taxes	4
Current assets	50	Current liabilities	25
Fixed assets	40	Notes payable	30
		Common stock	15
		Retained earnings	20
		Total liabilities and	
Total assets	$90	stockholders' equity	$90

Carter Paint has an aftertax profit margin of 5 percent and a dividend payout ratio of 30 percent.

If sales grow by 10 percent next year, determine how many dollars of new funds are needed to finance the expansion. (Assume Carter Paint is already using assets at full capacity and that plant must be added.)

15. The Longbranch Western Wear Company has the following financial statements, which are representative of the company's historical average.

Income Statement

Sales	$200,000
Expenses	158,000
Earnings before interest and taxes	$ 42,000
Interest	2,000
Earnings before taxes	$ 40,000
Taxes	20,000
Earnings after taxes	$ 20,000
Dividends	10,000

Balance Sheet

Assets		Liabilities and Stockholders' Equity	
Cash	$ 5,000	Accounts payable	$ 5,000
Accounts receivable	10,000	Accrued wages	1,000
Inventory	15,000	Accrued taxes	2,000
Current assets	$ 30,000	Current liabilities	$ 8,000
Fixed assets	70,000	Notes payable	7,000
		Long-term debt	15,000
		Common stock	20,000
		Retained earnings	50,000
		Total liabilities and	
Total assets	$100,000	stockholders' equity	$100,000

Longbranch is expecting a 20 percent increase in sales next year, and management is concerned about the company's need for external funds. The increase in sales is expected to be carried out without any expansion of fixed assets, but rather through more efficient asset utilization in the existing store. Only current liabilities vary directly with sales.

Using a percent-of-sales method, determine whether Longbranch Western Wear has external financing needs. (Hint: A profit margin and payout ratio must be found from the income statement.)

16. Cambridge Prep Shops, a national clothing chain, had sales of $200 million last year. The business has a steady net profit margin of 12

percent and a dividend payout ratio of 40 percent. The balance sheet for the end of last year is shown below.

Balance Sheet
End of Year
($ millions)

Assets		Liabilities and Stockholders' Equity	
Cash	$10	Accounts payable	$ 15
Accounts receivable	15	Accrued expenses	5
Inventory	50	Other payables	40
Plant and equipment	75	Common stock	30
		Retained earnings	60
		Total liabilities and	
Total assets	$150	stockholders' equity	$150

Cambridge's marketing staff tell the president that in this coming year there will be a large increase in the demand for tweed sportcoats and various shoes. A sales increase of 15 percent is forecast for the Prep Shop.

All balance sheet items are expected to maintain the same percent-of-sales relationships as last year, except for common stock and retained earnings. No change in the number of common stock shares outstanding is scheduled, and retained earnings will change as dictated by the profits and dividend policy of the firm. (Remember that the net profit margin is 12 percent.)

a. Will external financing be required for the Prep Shop during the coming year?

b. What would the need for external financing be if the net profit margin went up to 14 percent and the dividend payout ratio was increased to 70 percent? Explain.

17. *(Comprehensive problem—external funds.)*

The Landis Corporation had 1988 sales of $100 million. The balance sheet items that vary directly with sales and the profit margin are as follows:

	Percent
Cash	5%
Accounts receivable	15
Inventory	25
Net fixed assets	40
Accounts payable	15
Other payables	10
Profit margin after taxes	6

The dividend payout rate is 50 percent of earnings, and the balance in retained earnings at the beginning of 1989 was $33 million. Common stock and the company's long-term bonds are constant at $10 million and $5 million, respectively. Notes payable are currently $12 million.

a. How much additional external capital will be required for next year if sales increase 15 percent? (Assume that the company is already operating at full capacity.)

b. What will happen to external fund requirements if Landis Corporation reduces the payout ratio, grows at a slower rate, or suffers a decline in its profit margin? Discuss each of these separately.

c. Prepare a pro forma balance sheet for 1989, assuming that any external funds being acquired will be in the form of notes payable. Disregard the information in part *b* in answering this question (that is, use the original information and part *a* in constructing your pro forma balance sheet.)

18. (*Comprehensive financial forecasting problem—seasonal production.*)

The difficult part of solving a problem of this nature is to know what to do with the information contained within a story problem. Therefore, this problem will be easier to complete if you rely on Chapter 4 for the format of all required schedules.

The Adams Corporation makes standard-size two-inch fasteners which it sells for $155 per thousand. Mr. Adams is the majority owner and manages the inventory and finances of the company. He estimates sales for the following months to be:

January	$263,500 (1,700,000 fasteners)
February	$186,000 (1,200,000 fasteners)
March	$217,000 (1,400,000 fasteners)
April	$310,000 (2,000,000 fasteners)
May	$387,500 (2,500,000 fasteners)

Last year Adams Corporation's sales were $175,000 in November and $232,500 in December (1,500,000 fasteners).

Mr. Adams is preparing for a meeting with his banker to arrange the financing for the first quarter. Based on his sales forecast and the following information provided by him, your job as his new financial analyst is to prepare a monthly cash budget, a monthly and quarterly pro forma income statement, a pro forma quarterly balance sheet, and all necessary supporting schedules for the first quarter.

Past history shows that the Adams Corporation collects 50 percent of its accounts receivable in the normal 30-day credit period (the month after the sale) and the other 50 percent in 60 days (two months after the sale). It pays for its materials 30 days after receipt. In general,

Mr. Adams likes to keep a two-month supply of inventory on hand in anticipation of sales. Inventory at the beginning of December was 2,600,000 units. (This was not equal to his desired two-month supply.)

The major cost of production is the purchase of raw materials in the form of steel rods which are cut, threaded, and finished. Last year raw material costs were $52 per 1,000 fasteners, but Mr. Adams has just been notified that material costs have risen, effective January 1, to $60 per 1,000 fasteners. The Adams Corporation uses FIFO inventory accounting. Labor costs are relatively constant at $20 per thousand fasteners since workers are paid on a piecework basis. Overhead is allocated at $10 per thousand units, and selling and administrative expense is 20 percent of sales. Labor expense and overhead are direct cash outflows paid in the month incurred, while interest and taxes are paid quarterly.

The corporation usually maintains a minimum cash balance of $25,000, and it puts its excess cash into marketable securities. The average tax rate is 40 percent, and Mr. Adams usually pays out 50 percent of net income in dividends to stockholders. Marketable securities are sold before funds are borrowed when a cash shortage is faced. Ignore the interest on any short-term borrowings. Interest on the long-term debt is paid in March, as are taxes and dividends.

As of year-end, the Adams Corporation balance sheet was as follows:

ADAMS CORPORATION
Balance Sheet
December 31, 198X

Assets

Current assets:		
Cash	$ 30,000	
Accounts receivable	320,000	
Inventory	237,800	
Total current assets		$ 587,800
Fixed assets:		
Plant and equipment	1,000,000	
Less: Accumulated depreciation	200,000	
		800,000
Total assets		$1,387,800

Liabilities and Stockholder's Equity

Accounts payable	$ 93,600
Notes payable	0
Long-term debt, 8 percent	400,000
Common stock	504,200
Retained earnings	390,000
Total liabilities and stockholders' equity	$1,387,800

Selected References

Brown, Lawrence D.; Gordon D. Richardson; and Stephen J. Schwager. "An Information Interpretation of Financial Analysts Superiority in Forecasting Earnings." *Journal of Accounting Research* 51 (Spring 1987), pp. 49–67.

Chambers, John C.; Satinder K. Mullick; and Donald D. Smith. "How to Choose the Right Forecasting Technique." *Harvard Business Review* 49 (July–August 1971), pp. 45–71.

Donaldson, Gordon. "Strategy for Financial Emergencies." *Harvard Business Review* 47 (November–December 1969), pp. 67–69.

Francis, Jack Clark, and Dexter T. Rowell. "A Simultaneous Equation Model of the Firm for Financial Analysis and Planning." *Financial Management* 7 (Spring 1978), pp. 29–44.

Higgins, Robert C. "How Much Growth Can a Firm Afford?" *Financial Management* 6 (Fall 1977), pp. 7–16.

Jennings, Robert. "Unsystematic Security Price Movements, Management Earnings Forecasts and Revisions in Consensus Analysts Earnings Forecasts." *Journal of Accounting Research* 51 (Spring 1987), pp. 90–110.

Lerner, Eugene M. "Simulating a Cash Budget." *California Management Review* 11 (Winter 1968), pp. 79–86.

Lyneis, James M. "Designing Financial Policies to Deal with Limited Financial Resources." *Financial Management* 4 (Spring 1975), pp. 13–24.

Maier, Steven F.; David W. Robinson; and James H. Vander Weide. "A Short-Term Disbursement Forecasting Method." *Financial Management* 10 (Spring 1981), pp. 9–19.

Parker, George C., and Edilberto L. Segura. "How to Get a Better Forecast." *Harvard Business Review* 49 (March–April 1971), pp. 99–109.

Stilwell, Martin C. "Prospective Reporting and Small Business Clients." *Journal of Accountancy* 161 (May 1986), pp. 68–87.

Wild, John J. "The Prediction Performance of a Structural Model of Accounting Numbers." *Journal of Accounting Research* 51 (Spring 1987), pp. 139–60.

5

Operating and Financial Leverage

In the physical sciences as well as in politics, the term *leverage* has been popularized to mean the use of special force and effects to produce more than normal results from a given course of action. In business, the same concept is applied, with the emphasis on the employment of "fixed cost" items in anticipation of magnifying returns at high levels of operation. The student should recognize that leverage is a two-edged sword—producing highly favorable results when things go well, and quite the opposite under negative conditions.

Leverage in a Business

Assume that you are approached with an opportunity to start your own business. You are to manufacture and market industrial parts, such as ball bearings, wheels, and casters. You are faced with two primary decisions.

First, you must determine the amount of fixed-cost plant and equipment that you wish to use in the production process. By installing modern, sophisticated equipment, you can virtually eliminate labor in the production of inventory. At high volume, you will do quite well, as most of your costs are fixed. At low volume, however, you could face difficulty in making your fixed payments for plant and equipment. If you decide to use expensive labor rather than machinery, you will lessen your opportunity for profit, but at the same time you will lower your exposure to risk (you can lay off part of the work force).

Second, you must determine how you will finance the business. If you rely on debt financing and the business is successful, you will generate substantial profits as an owner, paying only the fixed costs of debt. Of course, if the business starts off poorly, the contractual obligations related to debt could mean bankruptcy. As an alternative, you might decide to sell equity rather than borrow, a step that will lower your own profit potential (you must share with others) but minimize your risk exposure.

In both decisions, you are making very explicit decisions about the use of leverage. To the extent that you go with a heavy commitment to fixed costs in the operation of the firm, you are employing operating leverage. To the extent that you utilize debt in the financing of the firm, you are engaging in financial leverage. We shall carefully examine each type of leverage and then show the combined effect of both.

Operating Leverage

Operating leverage reflects the extent to which fixed assets and associated fixed costs are utilized in the business firm. As indicated in Table 5–1, a firm's operational costs may be classified as fixed, variable, or semivariable.

For purposes of analysis, variable and semivariable costs will be combined. In order to evaluate the implications of heavy fixed asset use, we employ the technique of break-even analysis.

Break-Even Analysis

How much will changes in volume affect cost and profit? At what point does the firm break even? What is the most efficient level of fixed assets to employ in the firm? A break-even chart is presented in Figure 5–1 to answer some of these questions. The number of units produced and sold are shown along the horizontal axis, and revenue and costs are shown along the vertical axis.

**Table 5–1
Classification
of costs**

Fixed	Variable	Semivariable
Rental	Raw material	Utilities
Depreciation	Factory labor	Repairs and maintenance
Executive salaries	Sales commissions	
Property taxes		

**Figure 5–1
Break-even chart:
Leveraged firm**

Fixed costs ($60,000)
Price ($2)
Variable costs per unit ($0.80)

Note, first of all, that our fixed costs are $60,000, regardless of volume, and that our variable costs (at $0.80 per unit) are added to fixed costs to determine total costs at any point. The total revenue line is determined by multiplying price ($2) times volume.

Of particular interest is the break-even *(BE)* point at 50,000 units, where the total costs and total revenue lines intersect. The numbers are as follows:

		Units = 50,000		
Total Variable Costs (TVC)	Fixed Costs (FC)	Total Costs (TC)	Total Revenue (TR)	Operating Income (loss)
(50,000 × $0.80) $40,000	$60,000	$100,000	(50,000 × $2) $100,000	0

The break-even point for the company may also be determined by use of a simple formula—in which we divide fixed costs by the contribution margin on each unit sold, with the contribution margin defined as price minus variable cost per unit.

$$BE = \frac{\text{Fixed costs}}{\text{Contribution margin}} = \frac{\text{Fixed costs}}{\text{Price} - \text{variable cost per unit}} = \frac{FC}{P - VC} \qquad (5\text{--}1)$$

$$\frac{\$60,000}{\$2.00 - \$0.80} = \frac{\$60,000}{\$1.20} = 50,000 \text{ units}$$

Since we are getting a \$1.20 contribution toward covering fixed costs from each unit sold, minimum sales of 50,000 units will allow us to cover our fixed costs (50,000 units × \$1.20 = \$60,000 fixed costs). Beyond this point, we move into a highly profitable range in which each unit of sales brings a profit of \$1.20 to the company. As sales increase from 50,000 to 60,000 units, operating profits increase by \$12,000 as indicated in Table 5–2; as sales increase from 60,000 to 80,000 units, profits increase by another \$24,000; and so on. As further indicated in Table 5–2, at low volumes such as 40,000 or 20,000 units our losses are substantial (\$12,000 and \$36,000 in the red).

It is assumed that the firm depicted in Figure 5–1 is operating with a high degree of leverage. The situation is analogous to that of an airline which must carry a certain number of people on board to break even, but beyond that point is in a very profitable range.

A More Conservative Approach

Not all firms would choose to operate at the high degree of operating leverage exhibited in Figure 5–1. Fear of not reaching the 50,000-unit

Table 5–2
Volume-cost-profit analysis: Leveraged firm

Units Sold	Total Variable Costs	Fixed Costs	Total Costs	Total Revenue	Operating Income (loss)
0	0	\$60,000	\$ 60,000	0	\$(60,000)
20,000	\$16,000	60,000	76,000	\$ 40,000	(36,000)
40,000	32,000	60,000	92,000	80,000	(12,000)
50,000	40,000	60,000	100,000	100,000	0
60,000	48,000	60,000	108,000	120,000	12,000
80,000	64,000	60,000	124,000	160,000	36,000
100,000	80,000	60,000	140,000	200,000	60,000

break-even level may discourage some companies from heavy utilization of fixed assets. More expensive variable costs may be substituted for automated plant and equipment. Assume that fixed costs for a more conservative firm can be reduced to $12,000—but that variable costs will go from $0.80 to $1.60. If the same price assumption of $2 per unit is employed, the break-even level is 30,000 units.

$$BE = \frac{\text{Fixed costs}}{\text{Price} - \text{Variable cost per unit}} = \frac{FC}{P - VC} = \frac{\$12,000}{\$2 - \$1.60}$$

$$= \frac{\$12,000}{\$0.40}$$

$$= 30,000 \text{ units}$$

With fixed costs reduced from $60,000 to $12,000, the loss potential is small. Furthermore, the break-even level of operations is a comparatively low 30,000 units. Nevertheless, the use of a virtually unleveraged approach has cut into the potential profitability of the more conservative firm, as indicated in Figure 5–2.

Even at high levels of operation, the potential profit is rather small. As indicated in Table 5–3, at a 100,000-unit volume, operating income is only $28,000—some $32,000 less than that for the "leveraged" firm previously analyzed in Table 5–2.

The Risk Factor

Whether management follows the path of the leveraged firm or of the more conservative firm depends on its perceptions about the future. If the vice president of finance is apprehensive about economic conditions, the conservative plan may be undertaken. For a growing business, in times of relative prosperity, management might maintain a more aggressive, leveraged position. The firm's competitive position within its industry will also be a factor. Does the firm desire to merely maintain stability or to become a market leader? To a certain extent, management should tailor the use of leverage to meet its own risk-taking desires. Those who are risk averse (prefer less risk to more risk) should anticipate a particularly high return before contracting for heavy fixed costs. Others, less averse to risk, may be willing to leverage under more normal conditions. Simply taking risks is not a virtue—our prisons are full of risk takers. The important idea, which is stressed throughout the text, is to match an acceptable return with the desired level of risk.

**Figure 5–2
Break-even chart:
Conservative firm**

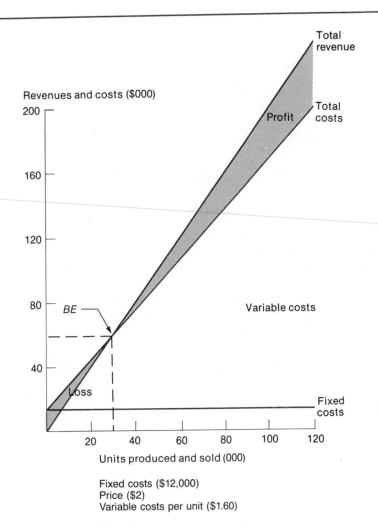

Fixed costs ($12,000)
Price ($2)
Variable costs per unit ($1.60)

**Table 5–3
Volume-cost-profit
analysis:
Conservative firm**

Units Sold	Total Variable Costs	Fixed Costs	Total Costs	Total Revenue	Operating Income (loss)
0	0	$12,000	$ 12,000	0	$(12,000)
20,000	$ 32,000	12,000	44,000	$ 40,000	(4,000)
30,000	48,000	12,000	60,000	60,000	0
40,000	64,000	12,000	76,000	80,000	4,000
60,000	96,000	12,000	108,000	120,000	12,000
80,000	128,000	12,000	140,000	160,000	20,000
100,000	160,000	12,000	172,000	200,000	28,000

Cash Break-Even Analysis

Our discussion to this point has dealt with break-even analysis in terms of accounting flows rather than cash flows. For example, depreciation has been implicitly included in fixed expenses, but it represents an accounting entry rather than an explicit expenditure of funds. To the extent that we were doing break-even analysis on a strictly cash basis, depreciation would be excluded from fixed expenses. In the example of the leveraged firm in Formula 5–1, if we eliminate $20,000 of "assumed" depreciation from fixed costs, the break-even level is reduced to 33,333 units.

$$\frac{FC}{P - VC} = \frac{(\$60,000 - \$20,000)}{\$2.00 - \$0.80} = \frac{\$40,000}{\$1.20} = 33,333 \text{ units}$$

Other adjustments could also be made for noncash items. For example, sales may initially take the form of accounts receivable rather than cash, and the same can be said for the purchase of materials and accounts payable. An actual weekly or monthly cash budget would be necessary to isolate these items.

While cash break-even analysis is helpful in analyzing the short-term outlook of the firm, particularly when it may be in trouble, most break-even analysis is conducted on the basis of accounting flows rather than strictly cash flows. Most of the assumptions throughout the chapter are based on concepts broader than pure cash flows.

Degree of Operating Leverage

Degree of operating leverage (*DOL*) may be defined as the percentage change in operating income that takes place as a result of a percentage change in units sold.

$$DOL = \frac{\text{Percent change in operating income}}{\text{Percent change in unit volume}} \qquad (5\text{--}2)$$

Highly leveraged firms, such as those in the auto or construction industry, are likely to enjoy a rather substantial increase in income as volume expands, while more conservative firms will participate to a lesser extent. Degree of operating leverage should only be computed over a profitable range of operations. However, the closer *DOL* is computed to the company break-even point, the higher the number will be due to a large percentage increase in operating income.[1]

Let us apply the formula to the leveraged and conservative firms previously discussed. Their income or losses at various levels of operation are summarized in Table 5-4.

Table 5-4
Operating income or loss

Units	Leveraged Firm (Table 5-2)	Conservative Firm (Table 5-3)
0	$(60,000)	$(12,000)
20,000	(36,000)	(4,000)
40,000	(12,000)	4,000
60,000	12,000	12,000
80,000	36,000	20,000
100,000	60,000	28,000

We will now consider what happens to operating income as volume moves from 80,000 to 100,000 units.

Leveraged Firm

$$DOL = \frac{\text{Percent change in operating income}}{\text{Percent change in unit volume}} = \frac{\dfrac{\$24,000}{\$36,000} \times 100}{\dfrac{20,000}{80,000} \times 100}$$

$$= \frac{67\%}{25\%} = 2.7$$

Conservative Firm

$$DOL = \frac{\text{Percent change in operating income}}{\text{Percent change in unit volume}} = \frac{\dfrac{\$8,000}{\$20,000} \times 100}{\dfrac{20,000}{80,000} \times 100}$$

$$= \frac{40\%}{25\%} = 1.6$$

[1]While the value of *DOL* varies at each level of output, the beginning level of volume determines the *DOL* regardless of the location of the end point.

We see the *DOL* is much greater for the leveraged firm, indicating at 80,000 units, a 1 percent increase in volume will produce a 2.7 percent change in operating income versus a 1.6 percent increase for the conservative firm.

The formula for degree of operating leverage may be algebraically manipulated to read:

$$DOL = \frac{Q(P - VC)}{Q(P - VC) - FC} \qquad (5\text{--}3)$$

where

Q = Quantity at which *DOL* is computed.
P = Price per unit.
VC = Variable costs per unit.
FC = Fixed costs.

Using the newly stated formula for the first firm at $Q = 80,000$, with $P = \$2$, $VC = \$0.80$, and $FC = \$60,000$:

$$DOL = \frac{80,000\,(\$2.00 - \$0.80)}{80,000\,(\$2.00 - \$0.80) - \$60,000}$$

$$= \frac{80,000\,(\$1.20)}{80,000\,(\$1.20) - 60,000} = \frac{96,000}{96,000 - 60,000}$$

$$= 2.7$$

We once again derive an answer of 2.7.[2] The same type of calculation could also be performed for the conservative firm.

---

[2]The formula for *DOL* may also be rewritten as:

$$DOL = \frac{Q(P - VC)}{Q(P - VC) - FC} = \frac{QP - QVC}{QP - QVC - FC}$$

We can rewrite the second terms as:

$QP = S$, or Sales (Quantity × Price)
$QVC = TVC$, or Total variable costs (Quantity × Variable costs per unit)
FC = Total fixed costs (remains the same term)

We then have:

$$DOL = \frac{S - TVC}{S - TVC - FC}, \text{ or } \frac{\$160,000 - \$64,000}{\$160,000 - \$64,000 - \$60,000} = \frac{\$96,000}{\$36,000} = 2.7$$

Limitations of Analysis

Throughout our analysis of operating leverage, we have assumed that a constant or linear function exists for revenues and costs as volume changes. For example, we have used $2 as the hypothetical sales price at all levels of operation. In the "real world," however, we may face price weakness as we attempt to capture an increasing market, or we may face cost overruns as we move beyond an optimum-size operation. Relationships are not so fixed as we have assumed.

Nevertheless, the basic patterns we have studied are reasonably valid for most firms over an extended operating range (in our example that might be between 20,000 and 100,000 units). It is only at the extreme levels that linear assumptions break down, as indicated in Figure 5–3.

Financial Leverage ─────────────────────────────

Having discussed the effect of fixed costs on the operations of the firm (operating leverage), we now turn to the second form of leverage. Financial

Figure 5–3
Nonlinear break-even analysis

leverage reflects the amount of debt used in the capital structure of the firm. Because debt carries a fixed obligation of interest payments, we have the opportunity to greatly magnify our results at various levels of operation. You may have heard of the real estate developer who borrows 100 percent of the costs of his project and will enjoy an infinite return on his zero investment if all goes well.

It is helpful to think of *operating leverage* as primarily affecting the left-hand side of the balance sheet and *financial* leverage as affecting the right-hand side.

Balance Sheet

Assets	Liabilities and Net Worth
Operating leverage	Financial leverage

Whereas operating leverage influences the mix of plant and equipment, financial leverage determines how the operation is to be financed. It is entirely possible for two firms to have equal operating capabilities and yet show widely different results because of the use of financial leverage.

Impact on Earnings

In studying the impact of financial leverage, we shall examine two financial plans for a firm, each employing a significantly different amount of debt in the capital structure. Financing totaling $200,000 is required to carry the assets of the firm.

Total assets—$200,000

	Plan A (leveraged)	Plan B (conservative)
Debt (8% interest)	$150,000 ($12,000 interest)	$ 50,000 ($4,000 interest)
Common stock	50,000 (8,000 shares at $6.25)	150,000 (24,000 shares at $6.25)
Total financing	$200,000	$200,000

Under *leveraged* Plan A we will borrow $150,000 and sell 8,000 shares of stock at $6.25 to raise an additional $50,000, whereas *conservative* Plan B calls for borrowing only $50,000 and acquiring an additional $150,000 in stock with 24,000 shares.

In Table 5–5, we compute earnings per share for the two plans at various levels of "earnings before interest and taxes" (*EBIT*). These

Table 5–5
Impact of financing plan on earnings per share

	Plan A (leveraged)	Plan B (conservative)
1. EBIT (0)		
Earnings before interest and taxes (EBIT)	0	0
− Interest (I)	$(12,000)	$ (4,000)
Earnings before taxes (EBT)	(12,000)	(4,000)
− Taxes (T)*	(6,000)	(2,000)
Earnings after taxes (EAT)	$ (6,000)	$ (2,000)
Shares	8,000	24,000
Earnings per share (EPS)	$(0.75)	$(0.08)
2. EBIT ($12,000)		
Earnings before interest and taxes (EBIT)	$ 12,000	$ 12,000
− Interest (I)	12,000	4,000
Earnings before taxes (EBT)	0	8,000
− Taxes (T)	0	4,000
Earnings after taxes (EAT)	$ 0	$ 4,000
Shares	8,000	24,000
Earnings per share (EPS)	0	$0.17
3. EBIT ($16,000)		
Earnings before interest and taxes (EBIT)	$ 16,000	$ 16,000
− Interest (I)	12,000	4,000
Earnings before taxes (EBT)	4,000	12,000
− Taxes (T)	2,000	6,000
Earnings after taxes (EAT)	$ 2,000	$ 6,000
Shares	8,000	24,000
Earnings per share (EPS)	$0.25	$0.25
4. EBIT ($36,000)		
Earnings before interest and taxes (EBIT)	$ 36,000	$ 36,000
− Interest (I)	12,000	4,000
Earnings before taxes (EBT)	24,000	32,000
− Taxes (T)	12,000	16,000
Earnings after taxes (EAT)	$ 12,000	$ 16,000
Shares	8,000	24,000
Earnings per share (EPS)	$1.50	$0.67
5. EBIT ($60,000)		
Earnings before interest and taxes (EBIT)	$ 60,000	$ 60,000
− Interest (I)	12,000	4,000
Earnings before taxes (EBT)	48,000	56,000
− Taxes (T)	24,000	28,000
Earnings after taxes (EAT)	$ 24,000	$ 28,000
Shares	8,000	24,000
Earnings per share (EPS)	$3.00	$1.17

*The assumption is that large losses can be written off against other income, perhaps in other years, thus providing the firm with a tax savings benefit. The tax rate is 50 percent for ease of computation.

earnings represent the operating income of the firm—before deductions have been made for financial charges or taxes. We assume *EBIT* levels of 0, $12,000, $36,000, and $60,000.

The impact of the two financing plans is dramatic. Although both plans assume the same operating income, or *EBIT,* for comparative purposes at each level (say $36,000 in calculation 4) the reported income per share is vastly different ($1.50 versus $0.67). It is also evident that the conservative plan will produce better results at low income levels—but that the leveraged plan will generate much better earnings per share as operating income, or *EBIT,* goes up. The firm would be indifferent between the two plans at an *EBIT* level of $16,000 as indicated in Table 5–5.

In Figure 5–4, we graphically demonstrate the effect of the two financing plans on earnings per share.

With an *EBIT* of $16,000, we are earning *8 percent* on total assets of $200,000—precisely the percentage cost of borrowed funds to the firm. The use or nonuse of debt does not influence the answer. Beyond $16,000,

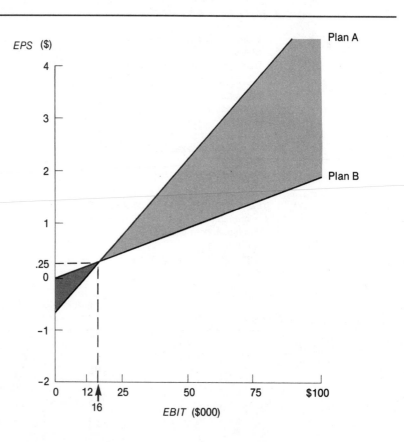

**Figure 5–4
Financing plans and
earnings per share**

Plan A, employing heavy financial leverage, really goes to work, allowing the firm to greatly expand earnings per share as a result of a change in *EBIT*. For example, at the *EBIT* level of $36,000, an 18 percent return on assets of $200,000 takes place—and financial leverage is clearly working to our benefit as earnings greatly expand.

Degree of Financial Leverage

As was true of operating leverage, degree of financial leverage measures the effect of a change in one variable on another variable. Degree of financial leverage (*DFL*) may be defined as the percentage change in earnings (*EPS*) that takes place as a result of a percentage change in earnings before interest and taxes (*EBIT*).

$$DFL = \frac{\text{Percent change in } EPS}{\text{Percent change in } EBIT} \qquad (5\text{--}4)$$

For purposes of computation, the formula for *DFL* may be conveniently restated as:

$$DFL = \frac{EBIT}{EBIT - I} \qquad (5\text{--}5)$$

Let's compute the degree of financial leverage for Plan A and Plan B, presented in Table 5–5, at an *EBIT* level of $36,000. Plan A calls for $12,000 of interest at all levels of financing, and Plan B requires $4,000.

Plan A (leveraged)

$$DFL = \frac{EBIT}{EBIT - I} = \frac{\$36,000}{\$36,000 - \$12,000} = \frac{\$36,000}{\$24,000} = 1.5$$

Plan B (conservative)

$$DFL = \frac{EBIT}{EBIT - I} = \frac{\$36,000}{\$36,000 - \$4,000} = \frac{\$36,000}{\$32,000} = 1.1$$

As expected, Plan A has a much higher degree of financial leverage. At an *EBIT* level of $36,000, a 1 percent increase in earnings will produce a 1.5 percent increase in earnings per share under Plan A, but only a 1.1 percent increase under Plan B. *DFL* may be computed for any level of operation, and it will change from point to point, but Plan A will always exceed Plan B.

Limitations to Use of Financial Leverage

The alert student may quickly observe that if debt is such a good thing, why sell any stock at all? (Perhaps one share to yourself.) With exclusive debt financing at an *EBIT* level of $36,000, we would have a degree of financial leverage factor (*DFL*) of 1.8.

$$DFL = \frac{EBIT}{EBIT - I} = \frac{\$36,000}{\$36,000 - \$16,000} = \frac{\$36,000}{\$20,000} = 1.8$$

(With no stock, we would borrow the full $200,000.)

$$(8\% \times \$200,000 = \$16,000 \text{ interest})$$

As stressed throughout the text, debt financing and financial leverage offer unique advantages, but only up to a point—beyond that point, debt financing may be detrimental to the firm. For example, as we expand the use of debt in our capital structure, lenders will perceive a greater financial risk for the firm. For that reason, they may raise the average interest rate to be paid and they may demand that certain restrictions be placed on the corporation. Furthermore, concerned common stockholders may drive down the price of the stock—forcing us away from the *objective of maximizing the firm's overall value* in the market. The impact of financial leverage must be carefully weighed.

This is not to say that financial leverage does not work to the benefit of the firm—it very definitely does if properly used. Further discussion of appropriate debt-equity mixes is covered in Chapter 11, Cost of Capital. For now, we accept the virtues of financial leverage, knowing that all good things must be used in moderation. For firms in industries that offer some degree of stability, are in a positive stage of growth, and are operating in favorable economic conditions, the use of debt is recommended.

Combining Operating and Financial Leverage _____

If both operating and financial leverage allow us to magnify our returns, then we will get maximum leverage through their combined use. We have said that operating leverage affects primarily the asset structure of the firm, while financial leverage affects the debt–equity mix. From an income statement viewpoint, operating leverage determines return from operations, while financial leverage determines how the "fruits of our labor" will be allocated to debt holders and, more importantly, to stockholders in the form of earnings per share. In Table 5–6, we show the combined influence of operating and financial leverage on the income statement. The values in Table 5–6 are drawn from earlier material in the chapter

Table 5–6
Income statement

Sales (total revenue) (80,000 units @ $2)	$160,000
– Fixed costs	60,000
– Variable costs ($0.80 per unit)	64,000
Operating income	$ 36,000

Operating leverage

Earnings before interest and taxes	$ 36,000
– Interest	12,000
Earnings before taxes	24,000
– Taxes	12,000
Earnings after taxes	$ 12,000
Shares	8,000
Earnings per share	$1.50

Financial leverage

(Tables 5–2 and 5–5). We assumed in both cases a high degree of operating and financial leverage. The sales volume is 80,000 units.

The student will observe, first, that operating leverage influences the top half of the income statement—determining operating income. The last item under operating leverage, operating income, then becomes the initial item for determination of financial leverage. "Operating income" and "earnings before interest and taxes" are one and the same, representing the return to the corporation after production, marketing, and so forth—but before interest and taxes are paid. In the second half of the income statement, we then show the extent to which earnings before interest and taxes are translated into earnings per share. A graphical representation of these points is provided in Figure 5–5.

Figure 5–5
Combining operating and financial leverage

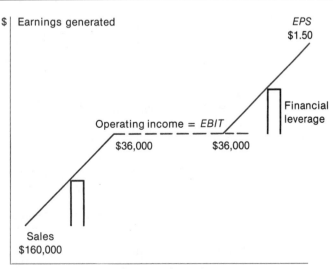

Degree of Combined Leverage

Degree of combined leverage utilizes the entire income statement and shows the impact of a change in sales or volume on bottom-line earnings per share. Degree of operating leverage and degree of financial leverage are, in effect, being combined. Table 5–7 shows what happens to profitability as the firm's sales go from $160,000 (80,000 units) to $200,000 (100,000 units).

Table 5–7
Operating and
financial leverage

		(Taken from Table 5–6)	
Sales—$2 per unit (80,000 units)	$160,000	(100,000 → units)	$200,000
– Fixed costs	60,000		60,000
– Variable costs ($0.80 per unit)	64,000		80,000
Operating income = *EBIT*	36,000		60,000
– Interest	12,000		12,000
Earnings before taxes	24,000		48,000
– Taxes	12,000		24,000
Earnings after taxes	$ 12,000		$ 24,000
Shares	8,000		8,000
Earnings per share	$1.50		$3.00

The formula for degree of combined leverage is stated as:

$$\text{Degree of combined leverage } (DCL) = \frac{\text{Percent change in } EPS}{\text{Percent change in sales (or volume)}} \qquad (5\text{–}6)$$

$$\frac{\text{Percent change in } EPS}{\text{Percent change in sales}} = \frac{\dfrac{\$1.50}{\$1.50} \times 100}{\dfrac{\$40,000}{\$160,000} \times 100} = \frac{100\%}{25\%} = 4$$

Every percentage point change in sales will be reflected in a 4 percent change in earnings per share at this level of operation (quite an impact). An algebraic statement of the formula is:

$$DCL = \frac{Q(P - VC)}{Q(P - VC) - FC - I} \qquad (5\text{–}7)$$

From Table 5–7: Q (quantity) = 80,000; P (price per unit) = $2.00; VC (variable costs per unit) = $0.80; FC (fixed costs) = $60,000; and I (interest) = $12,000.

$$DCL = \frac{80{,}000\ (\$2.00 - \$0.80)}{80{,}000\ (\$2.00 - \$0.80) - \$60{,}000 - \$12{,}000}$$

$$= \frac{80{,}000\ (\$1.20)}{80{,}000\ (\$1.20) - \$72{,}000}$$

$$= \frac{\$96{,}000}{\$96{,}000 - \$72{,}000} = \frac{\$96{,}000}{\$24{,}000} = 4$$

The answer is once again shown to be 4.[3]

A Word of Caution

In a sense, we are piling risk upon risk as the two different forms of leverage are combined. Perhaps a firm carrying heavy operating leverage may wish to moderate its position financially, and vice versa. One thing is certain—the decision will have a major impact on the operations of the firm.

Summary

Leverage may be defined as the use of fixed cost items to magnify returns at high levels of operation. Operating leverage primarily affects fixed versus variable cost utilization in the operation of the firm. An important concept—degree of operating leverage (*DOL*)—measures the percentage change in operating income as a result of a percentage change in volume. The heavier the utilization of fixed cost assets, the higher *DOL* is likely to be.

---

[3] The formula for *DCL* may be rewritten as:

$$DCL = \frac{Q(P - VC)}{Q(P - VC) - FC - I} = \frac{QP - QVC}{QP - QVC - FC - I}$$

We can rewrite the second terms as:

$\quad QP = S$, or Sales (Quantity $\times$ Price)
$\quad QVC = TVC$, or Total variable costs (Quantity $\times$ Variable cost per unit)
$\quad FC = $ Total fixed costs (remains the same term)
$\quad I = $ Interest (remains the same term)

We then have:

$$DCL = \frac{S - TVC}{S - TVC - FC - I}$$

$$= \frac{\$160{,}000 - \$64{,}000}{\$160{,}000 - \$64{,}000 - \$60{,}000 - \$12{,}000} = \frac{\$96{,}000}{\$24{,}000} = 4$$

Financial leverage reflects the extent to which debt is used in the capital structure of the firm. Substantial use of debt will place a great burden on the firm at low levels of profitability, but it will help to magnify earnings per share as volume or operating income increases. We combine operating and financial leverage to assess the impact of all types of fixed costs on the firm. There is a multiplier effect when we use the two different types of leverage.

Because leverage is a two-edged sword, management must be sure that the level of risk assumed is in accord with its desires for risk and its perceptions of the future. High operating leverage may be balanced off against lower financial leverage if this is deemed desirable, and vice versa.

Review of Formulas

1. $BE = \dfrac{FC}{P - VC}$ (5–1)

   BE is break-even point
   FC is fixed costs
   P is price per unit
   VC is variable cost per unit

2. $DOL = \dfrac{Q(P - VC)}{Q(P - VC) - FC}$ (5–3)

   DOL is degree of operating leverage
   Q is quantity at which DOL is computed
   P is price per unit
   VC is variable cost per unit
   FC is fixed costs

3. $DOL = \dfrac{S - TVC}{S - TVC - FC}$ (footnote 2)

   DOL is degree of operating leverage
   S is sales (QP) at which DOL is computed
   TVC is total variable costs
   FC is fixed costs

4. $DFL = \dfrac{EBIT}{EBIT - I}$ \hfill (5–5)

       DFL is degree of financial leverage
       EBIT is earnings before interest and taxes
           I is interest

5. $DCL = \dfrac{Q(P - VC)}{Q(P - VC) - FC - I}$ \hfill (5–7)

       DCL is degree of combined leverage
         Q is quantity at which DCL is computed
         P is price per unit
       VC is variable cost per unit
       FC is fixed costs
         I is interest

6. $DCL = \dfrac{S - TVC}{S - TVC - FC - I}$ \hfill (footnote 3)

       DCL is degree of combined leverage
         S is sales (QP) at which DCL is computed
      TVC is total variable costs
       FC is fixed costs
         I is interest

List of Terms

break-even analysis	operating leverage
fixed costs	degree of operating leverage (*DOL*)
variable costs	financial leverage
contribution margin	degree of financial leverage (*DFL*)
nonlinear break-even analysis	combined leverage
leverage (concept in general)	degree of combined leverage (*DCL*)

Discussion Questions

1. Discuss the various uses for break-even analysis.

2. What factors would cause a difference in the use of financial leverage for a utility company and an automobile company?

3. Explain how the break-even point and operating leverage are affected by the choice of manufacturing facilities (labor intensive versus capital intensive).

4. What role does depreciation play in break-even analysis based on accounting flows? Based on cash flows? Which perspective is longer term in nature?

5. What does risk taking have to do with the use of operating and financial leverage?

6. Discuss the limitations of financial leverage.

7. How does the interest rate on new debt influence the use of financial leverage?

8. Explain how combined leverage brings together operating income and earnings per share.

9. Explain why operating leverage decreases as a company increases sales and shifts away from the break-even point.

10. Why does the starting level of sales determine the degree of operating leverage rather than the ending level of sales?

11. One could say that financial leverage has its most important impact on earnings per share rather than net income after taxes. How would you support this statement?

12. Does being at the *EPS* indifference point mean that you are always indifferent between two financing plans? Explain.

Problems

1. The Ripley Company produces boomerangs which sell for $6 each and have a variable cost of $5.50. Fixed costs are $10,000.
   a.   Compute the break-even point in units.
   b.   Find the sales (in units) needed to earn a profit of $20,000.

2. Draw two break-even graphs—one for a conservative firm using labor-intensive production and another for a capital-intensive firm. Assuming that these companies compete within the same industry and have identical sales, explain the impact of changes in sales volume on both firms' profits.

3. The Prima Donna Company provides studios for musicians to give music lessons. The company's income statement for the year 1989 is as follows:

PRIMA DONNA COMPANY
Income Statement
For the Year Ended December 31, 1989

Sales (10,000 lessons @ $20 each)	$200,000
Less: Variable costs (10,000 lessons at $5)	50,000
Fixed costs	50,000
Earnings before interest and taxes (*EBIT*)	100,000
Interest expense	20,000
Earnings before taxes (*EBT*)	80,000
Income tax expense (40%)	32,000
Earnings after taxes (*EAT*)	$ 48,000

Given this income statement, compute the following:
a. Degree of operating leverage.
b. Degree of financial leverage.
c. Degree of combined leverage.
d. Break-even point in units (number of music lessons).

4. Freudian Slips and Gowns, Inc., income statement for 1989 is as follows:

FREUDIAN SLIPS AND GOWNS
Income Statement
For the Year Ended December 31, 1989

Sales (30,000 units at $25)	$750,000
Less: Variable costs (30,000 units at $7)	210,000
Fixed costs	270,000
Earnings before interest and taxes	270,000
Interest expense	170,000
Earnings before taxes (*EBT*)	100,000
Income tax expense (34%)	34,000
Earnings after taxes (*EAT*)	$ 66,000

Given this income statement, compute the following:
a. Degree of operating leverage.
b. Degree of financial leverage.
c. Degree of combined leverage.
d. Break-even point in units.

5. Tony O's Pizza and Bernie's Sub Shop compete for the college crowd in a small university town. Their capital structures are presented here.

	Tony O's Pizza			Bernie's Sub Shop	
Debt @ 12%	$ 500		Debt @ 12%		$1,000
Common stock, $10 par	$1,500		Common stock, $10 par		$1,000
Total assets	$2,000		Total assets		$2,000
Common shares	150		Common shares		100

   a. Compute earnings per share if earnings before interest and taxes are $150, $240, and $500 (assume a 30 percent tax rate).

   b. Explain the relationship between earnings per share and the level of *EBIT*.

6. In problem 5, compute the stock price for Tony O's Pizza if it sells at 16 times earnings per share, and earnings before interest and taxes are $360.

7. University Catering sells 50-pound bags of popcorn to university dormitories for $10 a bag. The fixed costs of this operation are $80,000, while the variable costs of the popcorn are $0.10 per pound.

   a. What is the break-even point in bags?

   b. Calculate the profit or loss on 12,000 bags and 25,000 bags.

   c. What is the degree of operating leverage at 20,000 bags and 25,000 bags? Why does the degree of operating leverage change as quantity sold increases?

   d. If University Catering has an annual interest payment of $10,000, calculate the degree of financial leverage at both 20,000 and 25,000 bags.

   e. What is the degree of combined leverage at both sales levels?

8. Firms in Japan often employ both high operating and financial leverage because of the use of modern technology and close borrower–lender relationships. Assume the Susaki Company has a sales volume of 100,000 units at a price of $25 per unit; variable costs are $5 per unit and fixed costs are $1,500,000. Interest expense is $250,000. What is the degree of combined leverage for this Japanese firm?

9. Hunt Resources and Newell Products are both involved in the production of chemical products. Their financial information is as follows:

Capital Structure

	Hunt	Newell
Debt @ 10%	$1,200,000	0
Common stock, $20 per share	800,000	2,000,000
Total	$2,000,000	$2,000,000
Common shares	40,000	100,000

Operating Plan

	Hunt	Newell
Sales (100,000 units at $10 each)	$1,000,000	$1,000,000
Less: Variable costs	700,000	400,000
	($7 per unit)	($4 per unit)
Fixed costs	0	300,000
Earnings before interest and		
taxes (*EBIT*)	$ 300,000	$ 300,000

a.   If you combine Hunt's capital structure with Newell's operating plan, what is the degree of combined leverage? (Round to two places to the right of the decimal point.)

b.   If you combine Newell's capital structure with Hunt's operating plan, what is the degree of combined leverage?

c.   Explain why you got the result you did in parts *a* and *b*.

d.   In part *b*, if sales double, by what percent will *EPS* increase?

10. DeSoto Tools, Inc., is planning to expand production. The expansion will cost $300,000, which can either be financed by bonds at an interest rate of 14 percent or by selling 10,000 shares of common stock at $30 per share. Their current income statement before expansion is as follows:

DESOTO TOOLS, INC.
Income Statement
198x

Sales		$1,500,000
Less: Variable costs	$450,000	
Fixed costs	550,000	1,000,000
Earnings before interest		
and taxes		500,000
Less: Interest expense . . .		100,000
Earnings before taxes		400,000
Less: Taxes @ 34%		136,000
Earnings after taxes		$ 264,000
Shares		100,000
Earnings per share		$2.64

After the expansion, sales are expected to increase by $1,000,000. Variable costs will be 30 percent of sales, and fixed costs will increase to $800,000. The tax rate is 34 percent.

a.   Calculate the degree of operating leverage, the degree of financial leverage, and the degree of combined leverage before expansion. (For the degree of operating leverage, use the formula developed in footnote 2; for the degree of combined leverage, use the formula developed in footnote 3. These instructions apply throughout this problem.)

b. Calculate the income statement for the two alternative financing plans.

c. Calculate the degree of operating leverage, the degree of financial leverage, and the degree of combined leverage after expansion.

d. Explain which financing plan you favor and the risks involved with each plan.

11. Dickinson Company has $12 million in assets. Currently half of these assets are financed with long-term debt at 10 percent and half with common stock having a par value of $8. Ms. Smith, vice president of finance, wishes to analyze two refinancing plans, one with more debt (D) and one with more equity (E). The company earns a return on assets before interest and taxes of 10 percent. The tax rate is 45 percent.

Under plan D, a $3 million long-term bond would be sold at an interest rate of 12 percent and 375,000 shares of stock would be purchased in the market at $8 per share and retired.

Under plan E, 375,000 shares of stock would be sold at $8 per share and the $3,000,000 in proceeds would be used to reduce long-term debt.

a. How would each of these plans affect earnings per share? Consider the current plan and the two new plans.

b. Which plan would be most favorable if return on assets fell to 5 percent? Increased to 15 percent? Consider the current plan and the two new plans.

c. If the market price for common stock rose to $12 before the restructuring, which plan would then be most attractive? Continue to assume that $3 million in debt will be used to retire stock in plan D and $3 million of new equity will be sold to retire debt in plan E. Also assume for calculations in part *C* that return on assets is 10 percent.

12. The Lopez-Portillo Company has $10 million in assets, 80 percent financed by debt and 20 percent financed by common stock. The interest rate on the debt is 15 percent and the par value of the stock is $10 per share. President Lopez Portillo is considering two financing plans for an expansion to $15 million in assets.

Under plan A, the debt to total assets ratio will be maintained, but new debt will cost a whopping 18 percent! Under plan B, only new common stock at $10 per share will be issued. The tax rate is 40 percent.

a. If *EBIT* is 15 percent on total assets, compute earnings per share (*EPS*) before the expansion and under the two alternatives.

b. What is the degree of financial leverage under each of the three plans?

c. If stock could be sold at $20 per share due to increased expectations for the firms sales and earnings, what impact would this have on earnings per share for the two expansion alternatives? Compute earnings per share for each.

d. Explain why corporate financial officers are concerned about their stock values!

13. Use Standard & Poor's data or annual reports and compare the financial and operating leverage of Ford Motor Company, Merck and Company, and Delta Airlines for the most current year. Explain the relationship between operating and financial leverage for each company and the resultant combined leverage. What accounts for the differences in leverage of these companies?

14. Mr. Katz is in the widget business. He currently sells 2 million widgets a year at $4 each. His variable cost to produce the widgets is $3 per unit, and he has $1,500,000 in fixed costs. His sales-to-assets ratio is four times, and 40 percent of his assets are financed with 9 percent debt, with the balance financed by common stock at $10 per share. The tax rate is 34 percent.

His brother-in-law, Mr. Doberman, says he is doing it all wrong. By reducing his price to $3.75 a widget, he could increase his volume of units sold by 40 percent. Fixed costs would remain constant, and variable costs would remain $3 per unit. His sales-to-assets ratio would be 5 times. Furthermore, he could increase his debt-to-assets ratio to 50 percent, with the balance in common stock. It is assumed that the interest rate would go up by 1 percent and that the price of stock would remain constant.

a. Compute earnings per share under the Katz plan.

b. Compute earnings per share under the Doberman plan.

c. Mr. Katz's wife does not think that fixed costs would remain constant under the Doberman plan, but that they would go up by 20 percent. If this is the case, should Mr. Katz shift to the Doberman plan based on earnings per share?

15. Physics Fulcrum Laboratories (PFL) is in the process of evaluating the company's break-even position and its operating and financial leverage. PFL has been selling 100,000 fulcrums per year for the last five years at $5 each. The fixed costs associated with this production

level are $200,000, and the variable costs are $1 per fulcrum. PFL is currently producing at full capacity, and it has no debt. Management is expecting sales to increase by 20,000 units per year for the next five years. To plan for this increase over the next five years, PFL is considering an expansion program which would increase capacity to 200,000 units per year. The company would borrow $1 million at 8 percent to finance a portion of the expansion. They currently have no debt. Fixed costs would increase to $500,000, and variable costs would remain $1 per unit. The price would remain at $5 per unit.

a. What is the break-even point before expansion and after expansion?

b. What is the operating leverage before expansion, and what will it be two years after expansion? Five years after expansion? (Use the formula in footnote 2.)

c. Calculate the financial leverage and the combined leverage before expansion and what it will be two years and five years after expansion. (For combined leverage, use the formula in footnote 3.)

d. Explain what causes the changes in break-even and leverage measures in the calculations for parts *a, b,* and *c.*

16. Phelps Canning Company is considering an expansion of its facilities. Its current income statement is as follows:

Sales	$5,000,000
Less: Variable expense (50% of sales)	2,500,000
Fixed expense	1,800,000
Earnings before interest and taxes (*EBIT*)	700,000
Interest (10% cost)	200,000
Earnings before taxes (*EBT*)	500,000
Tax (34%)	170,000
Earnings after taxes (*EAT*)	$ 330,000
Shares of common stock—200,000	
Earnings per share	$1.65

Phelps Canning Company is currently financed with 50 percent debt and 50 percent equity (common stock, par value of $10). In order to expand its facilities, Mr. Phelps estimates a need for $2 million in additional financing. His investment banker has laid out three plans for him to consider:

1. Sell $2 million of debt at 13 percent.
2. Sell $2 million of common stock at $20 per share.
3. Sell $1 million of debt at 12 percent and $1 million of common stock at $25 per share.

Variable costs are expected to stay at 50 percent of sales, while fixed expenses will increase to $2,300,000 per year. Mr. Phelps is not sure how much this expansion will add to sales, but he estimates that sales will rise by $1 million per year for the next five years.

Mr. Phelps is interested in a thorough analysis of his expansion plans and methods of financing. He would like you to analyze the following:

a. The break-even point for operating expenses before and after expansion (in sales dollars).

b. The degree of operating leverage before and after expansion. Assume sales of $5 million before expansion and $6 million after expansion.

c. The degree of financial leverage before expansion and for all three methods of financing after expansion. Assume sales of $6 million for this question.

d. In addition, he would like an indifference graph of the three financing methods as sales go from $5 million to $10 million, and your selection of the financing method which best suits his objective of maximizing shareholders' wealth.

17. (*Comprehensive problem for Chapters 2–5.*)

ASPEN SKI COMPANY
Balance Sheet
December 31, 1988

Assets		Liabilities and Stockholders' Equity	
Cash	$ 40,000	Accounts payable	$1,800,000
Marketable securities	60,000	Accrued expenses	100,000
Accounts receivable	1,000,000	Notes payable (current)	600,000
Inventory	3,000,000	Bonds (10%)	2,000,000
Gross plant and		Common stock (1.5 million	
equipment	5,000,000	shares, par value $1)	1,500,000
Less: Accumulated		Retained earnings	1,100,000
depreciation	2,000,000		
		Total liabilities and	
Total assets	$7,100,000	stockholders' equity	$7,100,000

Income Statement 1988

Sales (credit)	$6,000,000
Fixed costs*	1,800,000
Variable costs (0.60)	3,600,000
Earnings before interest and taxes	600,000
Less: Interest	200,000
Earnings before taxes	400,000
Less: Taxes (@ 40%)	160,000
Earnings after taxes	240,000

| Dividends . . . . | 43,200 |
| Increased retained earnings . . . . | $ 196,800 |

*Fixed costs include (a) lease expense of $190,000 and (b) depreciation of $400,000.

Note: Aspen Ski also has $100,000 per year in sinking fund obligations associated with its bond issue. The sinking fund represents an annual repayment of the principal amount of the bond. It is not tax deductible.

Ratios

	Aspen Ski (To be filled in)	Industry
Profit margin		6.1%
Return on assets		6.5%
Return on equity		8.9%
Receivables turnover		4.9 ×
Inventory turnover		4.4 ×
Fixed-asset turnover		2.1 ×
Total-asset turnover		1.06 ×
Current ratio		1.4 ×
Quick ratio		1.1 ×
Debt to total assets		27%
Interest coverage		4.2 ×
Fixed-charge coverage		3.0 ×

a. Analyze Aspen Ski Company, using ratio analysis. Compute the ratios above for Aspen and compare them to the industry data that is given. Discuss the weak points, strong points, and what you think should be done to improve the company's performance.

b. In your analysis, calculate the overall break-even point in sales dollars and the cash break-even point. Also compute the degree of operating leverage, degree of financial leverage, and degree of combined leverage.

c. Use the information in parts a and b to discuss the risk associated with this company. Given the risk, decide whether a bank should loan funds to Aspen Ski.

Aspen Ski Company is trying to plan their funds needed for 1989. The management anticipates an increase in sales of 20 percent, which can be absorbed without increasing fixed assets.

d. What would be Aspen's needs for external funds, based on the current balance sheet? Compute RNF (required new funds).

e. What would be the required new funds if the company brings its ratios into line with the industry average during 1989? Specifically examine receivables turnover, inventory turnover, and the profit margin. Use the new values to recompute the factors in RNF (assume liabilities stay the same).

f. Do not calculate, only comment on these questions. How would required new funds change if the company:
(1) Were at full capacity?
(2) Raised the dividend payout ratio?
(3) Suffered a decreased growth in sales?
(4) Faced an accelerated inflation rate?

Selected References

Hunt, Pearson. "A Proposal for Precise Definitions of 'Trading on Equity'; and 'Leverage.' " *Journal of Finance* 16 (September 1961), pp. 377–86.

Lev, Baruch. "On the Association between Operating Leverage and Risk." *Journal of Financial and Quantitative Analysis* 9 (September 1974), pp. 627–42.

Levy, Haim, and Robert Brooks. "Financial Break-Even Analysis and the Value of the Firm." *Financial Management* 15 (Autumn 1986), pp. 22–26.

Maur, David C., and Wilbur G. Lewellen. "Debt Management Under Corporate and Personal Taxation." *Journal of Finance* 42 (December 1987), pp. 1,275–92.

O'Brien, Thomas J., and Paul A. Vanderheiden. "Empirical Measurement of Operating Leverage for Growing Firms." *Financial Management* 16 (Summer 1987), pp. 43–53.

Percival, John R. "Operating Leverage and Risk." *Journal of Business Research* 2 (April 1974), pp. 223–27.

Prezas, Alexandros P. "Effects of Debt on the Degree of Operating and Financial Leverage." *Financial Management* 16 (Summer 1987), pp. 329–44.

Rendleman, Richard J., Jr. "The Effect of Default Risk on the Firm's Investment and Financing Decisions." *Financial Management* 7 (Spring 1978), pp. 45–53.

Sarig, Oded, and James Scott. "The Puzzle of Financial Leverage Clienteles." *Journal of Finance* 40 (December 1985), pp. 1,459–67.

Scott, David F., and J. D. Martin. "Industry Influence on Financial Structure." *Financial Management* 4 (Spring 1975), pp. 67–73.

————, **and Dana J. Johnson.** "Financing Policies and Practices in Large Corporations." *Financial Management* 11 (Summer 1982), pp. 51–57.

P A R T

3

Working Capital Management

6 Working Capital and the Financing Decision

7 Current Asset Management

8 Sources of Short-Term Financing

Introduction

Working capital policy involves the management of the current assets of the firm and the acquisition of the appropriate financing for those assets. While a firm may be able to sustain a decrease in sales or profitability for some period of time, the need for current assets and the associated financing is now.

Typical working capital decisions involve a determination of the appropriate level of cash, accounts receivable, and inventory that the firm should maintain. On the financing side, we must determine whether to carry these assets through credit extension from our supplier, short-term bank loans, or longer-term credit arrangements. The smaller firm usually has a limited number of options.

As we shall see, one of the unfortunate choices of terms in the vernacular of finance and accounting is the phrase "current asset." The normal definition of a current asset is a short-term asset that can be converted to cash within one year or within the normal operating cycle of the firm. As a business begins to grow, some current assets become more "permanent" in nature—some inventory is always on hand, and, as sales on credit increase, so do accounts receivable. These so-called current assets become more and more permanent and remain on the books of the firm. All too often, firms think of current assets as being temporary, when, in fact, those that become more permanent in nature may require longer-term financing.

The U.S. economy has not experienced a credit crunch (drying up of credit sources) in recent years as the economy has been expanding slowly and adequate supplies of money are available for corporate expansion. One of the most dramatic changes in corporate financing patterns in the last several years is the maturing of the international capital markets and the ability and willingness of international bankers and lenders to extend credit to U.S. firms. Much of the financing of credit needs has come from Japan. This does not necessarily mean that we have entered a new era where corporate managers should no longer expect a credit crunch. Financing can dry up fast if international and domestic lenders find more promising areas for lending than U.S. corporations.

In the initial chapter on working capital, Chapter 6, we examine some of the basic conceptual items related to working capital and the financing decision, with an eye toward the various risk–return alternatives that are available to the financial manager. Some real world examples of the publishing and retail industries demonstrate the concept of cyclical sales and earnings on a quarterly basis.

In Chapter 7 we look at specific techniques for the management of cash, marketable securities, accounts receivable, and inventory. Our focus is on the use of efficient management techniques in the allocation of funds.

Finally, in Chapter 8, we examine the various sources of short-term financing that are available to the firm. The emphasis is on trade credit, bank financing, and the use of secured loans through the pledging of receivables or inventory as collateral. The relative costs, advantages, and disadvantages of these financing outlets are considered. Also, at the end of the chapter, we examine how the financial futures market can be used to hedge the firm's exposure to changing interest rates.

6
Working Capital and the Financing Decision

The rapid growth of business firms in the last two decades has challenged the ingenuity of financial managers to provide adequate financing. Rapidly expanding sales may cause intense pressure for inventory and receivables buildup—draining the cash resources of the firm. As indicated in Chapter 4, Financial Forecasting, a large sales increase creates an expansion of current assets, especially accounts receivable and inventory. Some of the increased current assets can be financed by the firm's retained earnings, but in most cases internal funds will not provide enough financing and some external sources of funds must be found. In fact, the faster the growth in sales, the more likely it is that an increasing percentage of financing will be external to the firm. These funds could come from the sale of common stock, preferred stock, long-term bonds, short-term securities, and bank loans, or from a combination of short- and long-term sources of funds.

Working capital management involves the financing and management of the current assets of the firm. The financial executive probably devotes more time to working capital management than to any other activity. Current assets, by their very nature, are changing daily, if not hourly, and managerial decisions must be made. "How much inventory is to be carried, and how do we get the funds to pay for it?" Unlike long-term

145

decisions, there can be no deferral of action. While long-term decisions, involving plant and equipment or market strategy, may well determine the eventual success of the firm, short-term decisions on working capital determine whether the firm gets to the long term.

In this chapter, we examine the nature of asset growth, the process of matching sales and production, financial aspects of working capital management, and finally, the factors that go into the development of an optimum policy.

The Nature of Asset Growth

Any company that produces and sells a product, whether the product is consumer or manufacturer oriented, will have current assets and fixed assets. If a firm grows, those assets are likely to increase over time. The key to current asset planning is the ability of management to forecast sales accurately and then to match the production schedules with the sales forecast. Whenever actual sales are different from forecasted sales, unexpected buildups or reductions in inventory will occur that will eventually affect receivables and cash flow.

In the simplest case, all of the firm's current assets will be self-liquidating (sold off at the end of a specified time period). Assume that at the start of the summer you buy 100 tires to be disposed of by September. It is your intention that all tires will be sold, receivables collected, and bills paid over this time period. In this case, your working capital (current asset) needs are truly short term.

Now let us begin to expand the business. In stage two, you add radios, seat covers, and batteries to your operation. Some of your inventory will again be completely liquidated, while other items will form the basic stock for your operation. In order to stay in business, you must maintain floor displays and multiple items for selection. Furthermore, not all items will sell. As you eventually grow to more than one store, this "permanent" aggregate stock of current assets will continue to increase. Problems of inadequate financing arrangements are often the result of the businessperson's failure to realize that the firm is carrying not only self-liquidating inventory—but also the anomaly of "permanent" current assets.

The movement from stage one to stage two growth for a typical business is depicted in Figure 6–1. In Panel A, the buildup in current assets is temporary—while in Panel B, part of the growth in current assets is temporary and part is permanent. (Fixed assets are included in the illustrations, but they are not directly related to the present discussion.)

**Figure 6–1
The nature of asset
growth**

A. Stage I: Limited or no growth

B. Stage II: Growth

Controlling Assets—Matching Sales and Production

In most firms, fixed assets grow slowly as productive capacity is increased and old equipment is replaced, but current assets fluctuate in the short run, depending on the level of production versus the level of sales. When the firm produces more than it sells, inventory rises. When sales rise faster than production, inventory declines and receivables rise.

As discussed in the treatment of the cash budgeting process in Chapter 4, some firms employ level production methods to smooth production schedules and use manpower and equipment efficiently at a lower cost. One consequence of level production is that current assets go up and down when sales and production are not equal. Other firms may try to match sales and production as closely as possible in the short run. This allows current assets to increase or decrease with the level of sales and eliminates the large seasonal bulges or sharp reductions in current assets that occur under level production.

Publishing companies are good examples of companies with seasonal sales and an inventory problem. By the nature of the textbook market, heavy sales are made in the third quarter of the year for Fall semester sales. The bulk of the sales occurs in July and August, and again in December for the second semester. The actual printing and binding of a book has fixed costs that make printing a large number of copies more efficient. Since publishing companies cannot reproduce books on demand, they contract with the printing company to print a fixed number of copies, depending upon expected sales over at least a one-year time period and sometimes based on sales over several years. If the books sell better than expected, the publishing company will order a second or third printing. Orders may have to be placed as much as nine months before the books will actually be needed, and reorders will be placed as much as three or four months ahead of actual sales. If the book declines in popularity, the publisher could get stuck with a large inventory of obsolete books.

Figure 6–2 depicts quarterly sales and earnings per share of two book publishers, Houghton Mifflin and Macmillan. These are good examples of companies with seasonal sales. Houghton Mifflin has all of its earnings and most of its sales in the second and third quarters. The heavy fixed costs of publishing, force first and fourth quarter earnings into a deficit position. Macmillan's pattern is similar, but its third and fourth quarters are the strongest and it only exhibits deficit earnings in the first quarter. Macmillan's more stable earnings and less cyclical sales can be accounted for by its more diversified and less seasonal products than Houghton Mifflin. Because of the seasonal nature of the textbook publishing business, lenders as well as financial managers need to understand the need for inventory financing and inventory management. If management has not planned their inventory correctly, the lost sales or excess inventory could be a serious problem.

Retail firms, such as J. C. Penney and K mart Corporation, also have seasonal sales patterns. Figure 6–3 shows the quarterly sales and earnings per share of these two companies, with the quarters ending in January, April, July, and October. These retail companies do not stock a year or more of inventory at one time as do the publishers. They are either selling products manufactured for them by others or manufactured by their subsidiaries. Most retail stores are not involved in deciding on level versus seasonal production but rather in matching sales and inventory. Their suppliers must make the decision to produce on either a level or a seasonal production basis. Since the selling seasons are very much impacted by the weather and holiday periods, the suppliers and retailers cannot avoid the inventory risk. The fourth quarter beginning in October and ending

Figure 6–2
Sales and earnings
per share, Houghton
Mifflin and Macmillan

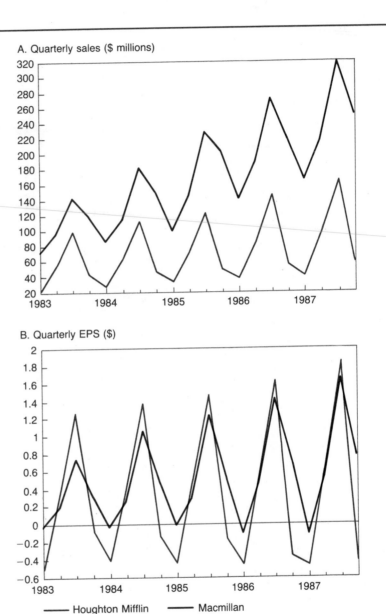

A. Quarterly sales ($ millions)

B. Quarterly EPS ($)

——— Houghton Mifflin   ——— Macmillan

in December is the biggest quarter for retailers and accounts for as much as one half of their earnings. You can be sure that inventory not sold during the Christmas season will be put on sale during January.

Figure 6–3 demonstrates that over several years, each peak and trough in quarterly sales is higher for both companies. These seasonal peaks and

Figure 6–3
Sales and earnings
per share for K mart
and J. C. Penney

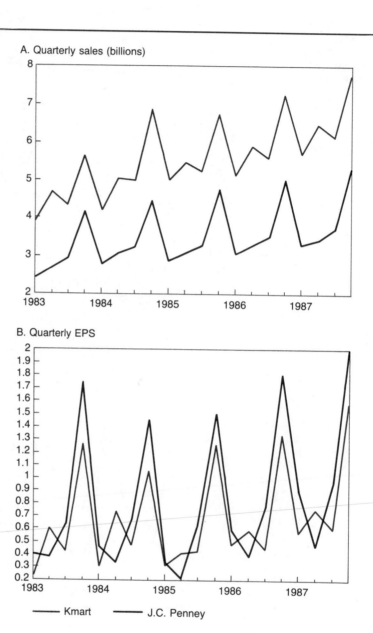

A. Quarterly sales (billions)

B. Quarterly EPS

——— Kmart   ——— J.C. Penney

troughs will also be reflected in cash, receivables, and inventory. Both companies demonstrate the impact of leverage on earnings as discussed in Chapter 5. Notice that when J. C. Penney's sales surge, earnings per share rise by a far greater percentage. We shall see as we go through the chapter that seasonal sales can cause asset management problems. A financial manager must be aware of these to avoid getting caught short of cash or unprepared to borrow when necessary.

Many retail-oriented firms have been more successful in matching sales and orders in recent years because of new, computerized inventory control systems linked to on-line point-of-sales terminals. These point-of-sales terminals either allow digital input or use of optical scanners to record the inventory code numbers and the amount of each item sold. At the end of the day, managers are able to examine sales and inventory levels item by item and, if need be, to adjust orders or production schedules. The predictability of the market will influence the speed with which the the manager reacts to this information, while the length and complexity of the production process will dictate just how fast production levels can be changed.

Temporary Assets under Level Production—An Example

In order to get a better understanding of how current assets fluctuate, let us use the example of the Yawakuzi Motorcycle Company, which manufactures and sells in the snowy U.S. Midwest. Not too many people will be buying motorcycles during October through March, but sales will pick up in early spring and summer and will trail off during the fall. Because of the fixed assets and the skilled labor involved in the production process, Yawakuzi decides that level production is the least expensive and the most efficient production method. The marketing department provides a sales forecast for October through September (Table 6–1).

Table 6–1   Yawakuzi sales forecast (in units)

1st Quarter		2nd Quarter		3rd Quarter		4th Quarter	
October	300	January	0	April . . .	1,000	July	2,000
November	150	February	0	May	2,000	August	1,000
December	50	March	600	June	2,000	September	500

Total sales of 9,600 units at $3,000 each = $28,800,000 in sales.

After reviewing the sales forecast, Yawakuzi decides to produce 800 motorcycles per month, or one year's production of 9,600 divided by 12. A look at Table 6–2 shows how level production and seasonal sales combine to create fluctuating inventory. Assume that October's beginning inventory is one month's production of 800 units. The ending inventory level is computed for each month and then multiplied by the production cost per unit of $2,000.

**Table 6–2
Yawakuzi's
production schedule
and inventory**

	Beginning inventory	+	Production (level production)	–	Sales	=	Ending inventory		Inventory (at cost of $2,000 per unit)
October	800		800		300		1,300		$2,600,000
November	1,300		800		150		1,950		3,900,000
December	1,950		800		50		2,700		5,400,000
January	2,700		800		0		3,500		7,000,000
February	3,500		800		0		4,300		8,600,000
March	4,300		800		600		4,500		9,000,000
April	4,500		800		1,000		4,300		8,600,000
May	4,300		800		2,000		3,100		6,200,000
June	3,100		800		2,000		1,900		3,800,000
July	1,900		800		2,000		700		1,400,000
August	700		800		1,000		500		1,000,000
September . . .	500		800		500		800		1,600,000

The inventory level at cost fluctuates from a high of $9 million in March, the last consecutive month in which production is greater than sales, to a low of $1 million in August, the last month in which sales are greater than production. Table 6–3 combines a sales forecast, a cash receipts schedule, a cash payments schedule, and a brief cash budget in order to examine the buildup in accounts receivable and cash.

In Table 6–3 the *sales forecast* is based on assumptions in Table 6–1. The unit volume of sales is multiplied by a sales price of $3,000 to get sales dollars in millions. Next, *cash receipts* represent 50 percent collected in cash during the month of sale and 50 percent from the prior month's sales. For example, in October this would represent $0.45 million from the current month plus $0.75 million from the prior month's sales.

Cash payments in Table 6–3 are based on an assumption of level production of 800 units per month at a cost of $2,000 per unit, or $1.6 million, plus payments for overhead, dividends, interest and taxes.

Finally, the *cash budget* in Table 6–3 represents a comparison of the cash receipts and cash payments schedules to determine cash flow. We further assume that the firm desires a minimum cash balance of $0.25 million. Thus in October, a negative cash flow of $1.1 million brings the cumulative cash balance to a negative $0.85 million and $1.1 million must be borrowed to provide an ending cash balance of $0.25 million. Similar negative cash flows in subsequent months necessitate expanding the bank loan. For example, in November there is a negative cash flow of $1.325 million. This brings the cumulative cash balance to $−1.075 million, requiring additional borrowings of $1.325 million to ensure a minimum

Table 6–3   Sales forecast, cash receipts and payments, and cash budget

	Oct.	Nov.	Dec.	Jan.	Feb.	March	April	May	June	July	Aug.	Sept.
Sales Forecast ($ millions)												
Sales (units)	300	150	50	0	0	600	1,000	2,000	2,000	2,000	1,000	500
Sales (unit price, $3,000)	$0.9	$0.45	$0.15	$0	$0	$1.8	$3.0	$6.0	$6.0	$6.0	$3.0	$1.5
Cash Receipts Schedule ($ millions)												
50% cash	$0.45	$0.225	$0.075	$0	$0	$0.9	$1.5	$3.0	$3.0	$3.0	$1.5	$0.75
50% from prior month's sales	0.75*	0.450	0.225	0.075	0	0	0.9	1.5	3.0	3.0	3.0	1.50
Total cash receipts	$1.20	$0.675	$0.300	$0.075	0	$0.9	$2.4	$4.5	$6.0	$6.0	$4.5	$2.25

*Assumes September sales of $1.5 million.

	Oct.	Nov.	Dec.	Jan.	Feb.	March	April	May	June	July	Aug.	Sept.
Cash Payments Schedule ($ millions)												
Constant production of 800 units/month (cost, $2,000 per unit)	$1.6	$1.6	$1.6	$1.6	$1.6	$1.6	$1.6	$1.6	$1.6	$1.6	$1.6	$1.6
Overhead	0.4	0.4	0.4	0.4	0.4	0.4	0.4	0.4	0.4	0.4	0.4	0.4
Dividends and interest	—	—	—	—	—	—	—	—	—	—	1.0	—
Taxes	0.3	—	—	0.3	—	—	0.3	—	—	0.3	—	—
Total cash payments	$2.3	$2.0	$2.0	$2.3	$2.0	$2.0	$2.3	$2.0	$2.0	$2.3	$3.0	$2.0

	Oct.	Nov.	Dec.	Jan.	Feb.	March	April	May	June	July	Aug.	Sept.
Cash Budget ($ millions; required minimum balance is $0.25 million)												
Cash flow	$(1.1)	$(1.325)	$(1.7)	$(2.225)	$(2.0)	$(1.1)	$0.1	$2.5	$4.0	$3.7	$1.5	$0.25
Beginning cash	0.25†	0.25	0.25	0.250	0.25	0.25	0.25	0.25	0.25	0.25	1.1	2.60
Cumulative cash balance	$(0.85)	$(1.075)	$(1.45)	$(1.975)	$(1.75)	$(0.85)	$0.35	$2.75	$4.25	$3.95	$2.6	$2.85
Monthly loan or (repayment)	1.1	1.325	1.7	2.225	2.0	1.1	(0.1)	(2.5)	(4.0)	(2.85)	0	0
Cumulative loan	1.1	2.425	4.125	6.350	8.35	9.45	9.35	6.85	2.85	0	0	0
Ending cash balance	0.25	0.25	0.25	0.25	0.25	0.25	0.25	0.25	0.25	1.1	2.6	2.85

†Assumes cash balance of $0.25 million at the beginning of October and that this is the desired minimum cash balance.

cash balance of $0.25 million. The cumulative loan through November (October and November borrowings) now adds up to $2.425 million. Our cumulative bank loan is highest in the month of March.

We now wish to ascertain our total current asset buildup as a result of level production and fluctuating sales for October through September. The analysis is presented in Table 6–4. The cash figures come directly from the last line of Table 6–3. The accounts receivable balance is based on the assumption that accounts receivable represent 50 percent of sales in a given month, as the other 50 percent is paid for in cash. Thus, the accounts receivable figure in Table 6–4 represents 50 percent of the sales figure from the second numerical line in Table 6–3. Finally, the inventory figure is taken directly from the last column of Table 6–2, which presented the production schedule and inventory data.

Total current assets start at $3.3 million in October and rise to $10.35 million in the peak month of April. From April through August, sales are larger than production and inventory falls to its low of $1 million in August, but accounts receivables peak at $3 million in the highest sales months of May, June, and July. The cash budget in Table 6–3 explains the cash flows and external funds borrowed to finance asset accumulation. From October to March, Yawakuzi borrows more and more money to finance the inventory buildup, but from April to July it eliminates all borrowing as inventory is liquidated and cash balances rise to complete the cycle. In October the cycle starts all over again; but now the firm has accumulated cash which it can use to finance next year's asset accumulation, pay a larger dividend, replace old equipment, or—if growth in sales is anticipated—invest in new equipment to increase productive capacity. Table 6–5 presents the cash budget and total current assets for

Table 6–4
Total current assets, first year ($ millions)

	Cash	Accounts Receivable	Inventory	Total Current Assets
October	$0.25	$0.450	$2.6	$ 3.30
November	0.25	0.225	3.9	4.375
December	0.25	0.075	5.4	5.725
January	0.25	0.00	7.0	7.25
February	0.25	0.00	8.6	8.85
March	0.25	0.90	9.0	10.15
April	0.25	1.50	8.6	10.35
May	0.25	3.00	6.2	9.45
June	0.25	3.00	3.8	7.05
July	1.10	3.00	1.4	5.50
August	2.60	1.50	1.0	5.10
September	2.85	0.75	1.6	5.20

Table 6-5 Cash budget and assets for second year with no growth in sales ($ millions)

	End of First Year Sept.	Second Year Oct.	Nov.	Dec.	Jan.	Feb.	March	April	May	June	July	Aug.	Sept.
Cash flow	$0.25	$(1.1)	$(1.325)	$(1.7)	$(2.225)	$(2.0)	$(1.1)	$0.1	$2.5	$4.0	$3.7	$1.5	$0.25
Beginning cash	2.60	2.85	1.750	0.425	0.25	0.25	0.25	0.25	0.25	0.25	0.25	3.7	5.2
Cumulative cash balance . . .		1.75	0.425	(1.275)	(1.975)	(1.75)	(0.85)	0.35	2.75	4.25	3.95	5.2	5.45
Monthly loan or (repayment)		—	—	1.525	2.225	2.0	1.1	(0.1)	(2.5)	(4.0)	(0.25)	—	—
Cumulative loan		—	—	1.525	3.750	5.75	6.85	6.75	4.25	0.25	0	—	—
Ending cash balance	$2.85	$1.75	$0.425	$0.25	$0.25	$0.25	$0.25	$0.25	$0.25	$0.25	$3.70	$5.2	$5.45
Total Current Assets													
Ending cash balance . . .	$2.85	$1.75	$0.425	$0.25	$0.25	$0.25	$0.25	$0.25	$0.25	$0.25	$3.70	$5.2	$5.45
Accounts receivable	0.75	0.45	0.225	0.075	0	0	0.90	1.50	3.0	3.0	3.0	1.5	0.75
Inventory	1.6	2.6	3.9	5.4	7.0	8.6	9.0	8.6	6.2	3.8	1.4	1.0	1.60
Total current assets . . .	$5.2	$4.8	$4.55	$5.725	$7.25	$8.85	$10.15	$10.35	$9.45	$7.05	$8.1	$7.7	$7.80

Figure 6–4
The nature of asset growth (Yawakuzi)

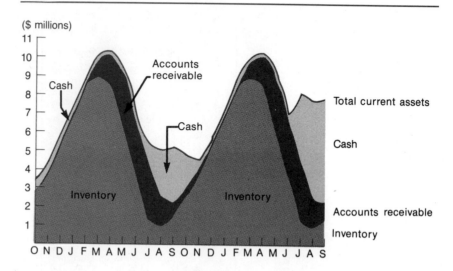

the second year. Under a simplified no-growth assumption, the monthly cash flow is the same as that of the first year, but beginning cash in October is much higher from the first year's ending cash balance and this lowers the borrowing requirement and increases the ending cash balance and total current assets at year-end. Higher current assets are present in spite of the fact accounts receivable and inventory do not change.

Figure 6–4 is a graphic presentation of the current asset cycle. It includes the two years covered in Tables 6–4 and 6–5 assuming level production and no sales growth.

Patterns of Financing

The financial manager's selection of external sources of funds to finance assets may be one of the firm's most important decisions. The axiom that all current assets should be financed by current liabilities (accounts payable, bank loans, commercial paper, etc.) is subject to challenge when one sees the permanent buildup that can take place in current assets. In the Yawakuzi example, the buildup in inventory was substantial, at $9 million. The example had a logical conclusion in that the motorcycles were sold, cash was generated, and current assets became very liquid. What if a much smaller level of sales had occurred? Yawakuzi would be sitting on a large inventory which needed to be financed and would be generating no cash. Theoretically, the firm could be declared technically insolvent (bankrupt) if short-term sources of funds were used but were unable to be renewed when they came due. How would the interest and principal be paid without cash flow from inventory liquidation? The most appropriate financing pattern would be one in which asset buildup and length of financing terms are perfectly matched, as indicated in Figure 6–5.

In the upper part of Figure 6–5 we see that the temporary buildup in current assets is financed by short-term funds. More importantly, however, permanent current assets, as well as fixed assets, are financed with long-term funds from the sale of stock, the issuance of bonds, or retention of earnings.

Alternative Plans

Only a financial manager with unusual insight and timing could construct a financial plan for working capital that adhered perfectly to the design in Figure 6–5. The difficulty rests in precisely determining what part of current assets is temporary and what part is permanent. Even if dollar amounts could be ascertained, the exact timing of asset liquidation is a difficult matter. To compound the problem, we are never quite sure how much short-term or long-term financing is available at a given point in time. While the precise synchronization of temporary current assets and short-term financing depicted in Figure 6–5 may be the most desirable and logical plan, other alternatives must be considered.

Long-Term Financing

To protect against the danger of not being able to provide adequate short-term financing in tight money periods, the financial manager may rely

Figure 6–5
Matching long-term and short-term needs

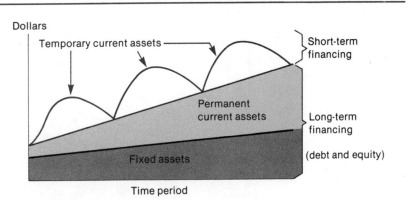

on long-term funds to cover some short-term needs. As indicated in Figure 6–6, long-term capital is now being used to finance fixed assets, permanent current assets, and part of *temporary current assets*.

By using long-term capital to cover short-term needs, the firm virtually assures itself of having adequate capital at all times. The firm may prefer to borrow a million dollars for 10 years—rather than attempt to borrow a million dollars at the beginning of each year for 10 years and paying it back at the end of each year.

Short-Term Financing (opposite approach)

This is not to say that all financial managers utilize long-term financing on a large scale. In order to acquire long-term funds, the firm must generally go to the capital markets with a bond or stock offering or must privately place longer-term obligations with insurance companies, wealthy individuals, and so forth. Many small businesses do not have access to such long-term capital and are forced to rely heavily on short-term bank and trade credit. In the capital shortage era of the last decade, even some large businesses were forced to operate with short-term funds.

Furthermore, short-term financing does offer some advantages over more extended financial arrangements. As a general rule, the interest rate on short-term funds is lower than that on long-term funds. We might surmise then that a firm could develop a working capital financing plan in which short-term funds are used to finance not only temporary current assets but also part of the permanent working capital needs of the firm. As depicted in Figure 6–7, bank and trade credit as well as other sources of short-term financing are now supporting part of the permanent capital asset needs of the firm.

Figure 6–6
Using long-term financing for part of short-term needs

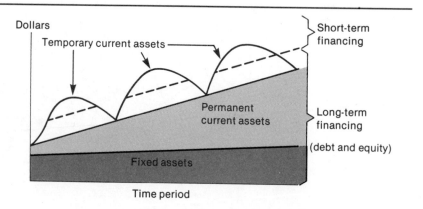

Figure 6–7
Using short-term
financing for part of
long-term needs

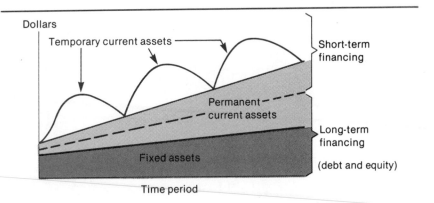

The Financing Decision _____

Some corporations are more flexible than others because they are not locked into a few available sources of funds. Corporations would like many financing alternatives in order to minimize their cost of funds at any point in time. Unfortunately, not many firms are in this enviable position through the duration of a business cycle. During an economic boom period, a shortage of low-cost alternatives exists and firms often minimize their financing costs by raising funds in advance of forecasted asset needs.

Not only does the financial manager encounter a timing problem, but he also needs to select the right type of financing. Even for companies having many alternative sources of funds, there may be only one or two decisions that will look good in retrospect. At the time the financing decision is made, the financial manager is never sure it is the right one. Should the financing be long-term or short-term, debt or equity, and so on? Figure 6–8 is a decision-tree diagram which shows many of the financing decisions that can be made. At each point a decision is made until a final financing method is reached. In most cases a corporation will use a combination of these financing methods. At all times the financial manager will balance short-term versus long-term considerations against the composition of the firm's assets and the firm's willingness to accept risk. The ratio of long-term financing to short-term financing at any point in time will be greatly influenced by the *term structure of interest rates*.

Term Structure of Interest Rates

The term structure of interest rates is often referred to as a yield curve. It shows the relative level of short-term and long-term interest rates at a

**Figure 6–8
Decision tree of the
financing decision**

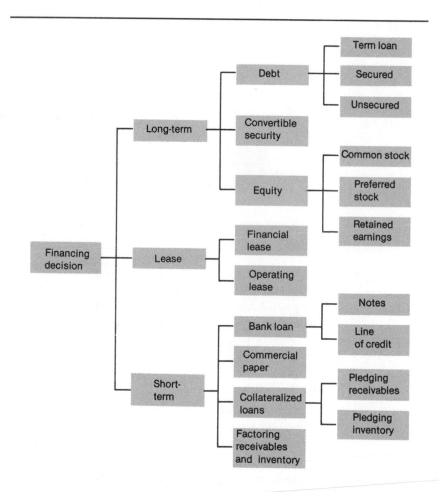

point in time. Generally U.S. government securities are used to construct yield curves because they have many maturities and each of the securities has an equally low risk of default. Corporate securities will move in the same direction as government securities, but will have higher interest rates because of their greater financial risk. Yield curves for both corporations and government securities change daily to reflect current competitive conditions in the money and capital markets, expected inflation, and changes in economic conditions.

There are three basic theories describing the shape of the yield curve. The first theory is called the *liquidity premium theory* and states that long-term rates should be higher than short-term rates. This premium of long-term rates over short-term rates exists because short-term securities have greater liquidity and, therefore, higher rates have to be offered to potential long-term bond buyers to entice them to hold these less liquid and more price sensitive securities. The *segmentation theory* (the second theory) states that Treasury securities are divided into market segments by the various financial institutions investing in the market. Commercial banks prefer short-term securities of one year or less to match their short-term lending strategies. Savings and loans and other mortgage-oriented financial institutions prefer the intermediate length securities of between 5–7 years, while life insurance companies prefer long-term 20–30 year securities to offset the long-term nature of their commitments to policyholders. The changing needs, desires, and strategies of these investors tend to strongly influence the nature and relationship of short-term and long-term interest rates.

The third theory describing the term structure of interest rates is called the *expectations hypothesis*. This theory explains the yields on long-term securities as a function of the short-term rates. The expectations theory says that long-term rates reflect the average of short-term expected rates over the time period that the long-term security is outstanding. Using a four-year example and a simple arithmetic mean, we will demonstrate this theory in Table 6–6. In the left-hand panel of the table, we show the anticipated one-year rate on T-bill (Treasury bill) securities at the beginning of each of four years in the future. Treasury bills are short-term securities issued by the government. In the right-hand panel, we show averages of the one-year anticipated rates.

Table 6–6   The expectations theory

1 yr. T-bill at beginning of yr. 1 = 7%	
1 yr. T-bill at beginning of yr. 2 = 8%	2 yr. security (7% + 8%) / 2 = 7.5%
1 yr. T-bill at beginning of yr. 3 = 9%	3 yr. security (7% + 8% + 9%) / 3 = 8%
1 yr. T-bill at beginning of yr. 4 = 10%	4 yr. security (7% + 8% + 9% + 10%) / 4 = 8.5%

For example, the two-year security rate is the average of the expected yields of two one-year T-bills, while the rate on the four-year security is the average of all four one-year rates. In this example, the progressively higher rates for two-, three- and four-year securities represent a reflection of higher anticipated one-year rates in the future. The expectations hypothesis is especially useful in explaining the shape and movement of the yield curve. The result of the expectations hypothesis is that, when long-term rates are much higher than short-term rates, the market is saying that it expects short-term rates to rise. When long-term rates are lower than short-term rates, the market is expecting short-term rates to fall. This theory is useful to financial managers in helping them set expectations for the cost of financing over time and, especially, in making choices about when to use short-term debt or long-term debt.

In fact, all three theories presented have some impact on interest rates. At times, the liquidity premium or segmentation theory dominate the shape of the curve and, at other times, the expectations theory is most important. The financial manager cannot escape making judgments about future developments and, sometimes, knowledge of yield curve theories provides a managerial edge for more accurate judgment.

Figure 6–9 depicts four panels of term structures (yield curves) covering various time periods. These four panels present very different pictures of interest rate cycles.

Panel A shows five yield curves in a period of falling interest rates—from August 1974 to November 1976. Each yield curve in Panel A has a different shape. The August 1974 curve is called *downward sloping*, or *inverted*, because short-term interest rates are higher than long-term rates. This shape is usually presented at peak periods in economic expansions and sometimes well into economic recessions. The September 1975 curve is called a *humped* curve, because the intermediate rates are higher than both the short- and long-term rates. The other three yield curves are all *upward sloping*, which is considered to be the normal case.

Panel B represents interest rate changes in a period of rising rates. If you start with the December 1976 yield curve and move to each successive curve, you will trace the most dramatic rise in interest rates in U.S. history, caused by record high inflation rates. In Panel C, you can see that short-term rates on U.S. Treasury bills reached historic levels in September of 1981. The Federal Reserve Board maintained high interest rates during this period in an attempt to break the back of inflation even though the economy was quite weak. By 1982 Federal Reserve Board policy had reduced inflation to its lowest level since 1971 but had also created a 16-month recession that ended in November of 1982. However, the recession finally caused interest rates to decline, as evidenced by the May, November, and December 1982 yield curves. One interesting observation is that interest rates can change dramatically in a short time. Between November and December of 1982, interest rates on intermediate- and long-term securities dropped as much as 2 percent. This rapid drop in interest rates during 1982 caused long-term bond prices to rise substantially and rewarded long-term bond investors with over a 35 percent annual return.

A business recovery began in December of 1982 and the yield curve in Panel C bottomed out in that month. Gross national product (GNP) grew at a rate of over 6 percent in 1983, and the economic expansion increased the demand for funds. Panel D shows the resulting rise in rates

Figure 6–9   Yield curves: Yields on U.S. government securities

A. Falling term structure

C. Falling term structure

B. Rising term structure

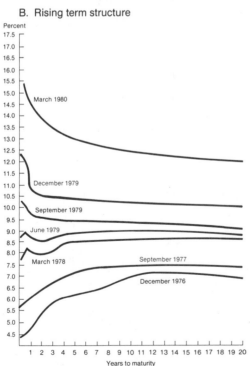

D. Reversals in the term structure

by August of 1983 and March of 1984. By 1985, the economy was growing at a slow rate of about 2.5 percent per year, and inflation came down to a 1.1 percent annual rate for 1986. The slow economy and low inflation rates combined to decrease the yield curve (September 1986) but by August of 1987, rates were moving back up in response to increased economic growth and renewed inflationary pressures.

In designing working capital policy, the astute financial manager is interested not only in the term structure of interest rates but also in the relative volatility and the historical level of short-term and long-term rates. The four panels in Figure 6–9 indicate that interest rates have been on a roller coaster ride since 1974. Figure 6–10 covers a longer time period but still demonstrates the large historical differences in relative volatility, with short-term rates being much more volatile than long-term rates. This volatility is what makes a short-term financing strategy so risky. On top of this volatility, most economists will admit to the great uncertainty of forecasting more than one year ahead. The record of the professionals for accurate interest rate predictions is spotty at best for periods longer than six months.

How should the financial manager respond to fluctuating interest rates and changing term structures? When interest rates are high, the financial manager generally tries to borrow short term (if funds are available). As

**Figure 6–10
Long- and short-term
interest rates
(annually)**

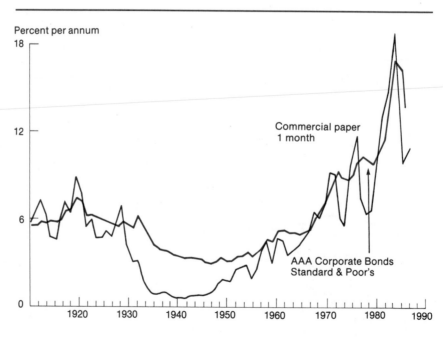

rates decline, the chief financial officer will try to lock in the lower rates with heavy long-term borrowing. Some of these long-term funds will be used to reduce short-term debt and the rest will be available for future expansion of plant and equipment and working capital if necessary.

A Decision Process

Assume that we are comparing alternative financing plans for working capital. As indicated in Table 6–7, $500,000 of working capital (current assets) must be financed for the Edwards Corporation. Under Plan A, we will finance all our current asset needs with short-term funds, while under Plan B we will finance only a relatively small portion of current assets with short-term money—relying heavily on long-term funds. In either case, we will carry $100,000 of fixed assets with long-term financing commitments. As indicated in part 3 of Table 6–7, under Plan A we will finance total needs of $600,000 with $500,000 of short-term financing and $100,000 of long-term financing, whereas with Plan B we will finance $150,000 short term and $450,000 long term.

Plan A carries the lower cost of financing, with interest of 6 percent on $500,000 of the $600,000 required. We show the impact of both plans on bottom-line earnings in Table 6–8.[1] Assuming that the firm generates

Table 6–7 Alternative financing plans	EDWARDS CORPORATION		
		Plan A	*Plan B*
Part 1. Current assets			
Temporary		$250,000	$250,000
Permanent		250,000	250,000
Total current assets		500,000	500,000
Short-term financing (6%)		500,000	150,000
Long-term financing (10%)		0	350,000
		$500,000	$500,000
Part 2. Fixed assets		$100,000	$100,000
Long-term financing (10%)		$100,000	$100,000
Part 3. Total financing (summary of parts 1 and 2)			
Short-term (6%)		$500,000	$150,000
Long-term (10%)		100,000	450,000
		$600,000	$600,000

---

[1]Common stock is eliminated from the example to simplify the analysis. If it were included, all of the basic patterns would still hold.

Table 6–8
Impact of financing
plans on earnings

EDWARDS CORPORATION

Plan A

Earnings before interest and taxes	$200,000
Interest (short-term), 6% × $500,000	− 30,000
Interest (long-term), 10% × $100,000	− 10,000
Earnings before taxes	160,000
Taxes (50%)	80,000
Earnings after taxes	$ 80,000

Plan B

Earnings before interest and taxes	$200,000
Interest (short-term), 6% × $150,000	− 9,000
Interest (long-term), 10% × $450,000	− 45,000
Earnings before taxes	146,000
Taxes (50%)	73,000
Earnings after taxes	$ 73,000

$200,000 in earnings before interest and taxes, Plan A will provide aftertax earnings of $80,000, while Plan B will generate only $73,000.

Introducing Varying Conditions

Although Plan A, employing cheaper short-term sources of financing, appears to provide $7,000 more in return, this is not always the case. During tight money periods, short-term financing may be difficult to find or may carry exorbitant rates. Furthermore, inadequate financing may mean lost sales or financial embarrassment. For these reasons, the firm may wish to evaluate Plans A and B based on differing assumptions about the economy and the money markets.

Expected Value

Past history combined with economic forecasting may indicate an 80 percent probability of normal events and a 20 percent chance of extremely tight money. Using Plan A, under normal conditions the Edwards Corporation will enjoy a $7,000 superior return over Plan B (as indicated in Table 6–8). Let us now assume that under disruptive tight money conditions, Plan A would provide a $15,000 lower return than Plan B because of high short-term interest rates. These conditions are summarized in Table 6–9, and an expected value of return is computed. The expected

Table 6–9
Expected returns
under different
economic conditions

EDWARDS CORPORATION					
1. Normal conditions	Expected higher return under Plan A $7,000	×	Probability of normal conditions .80	=	Expected outcome +$5,600
2. Tight money	Expected lower return under Plan A ($15,000)	×	Probability of tight money .20	=	(3,000)
Expected value of return for Plan A versus Plan B				=	+$2,600

value represents the sum of the expected outcomes under the two conditions.

We see that even when downside risk is considered, Plan A carries a higher expected return of $2,600. For another firm in the same industry that might suffer $50,000 lower returns during tight money conditions, Plan A becomes too dangerous to undertake, as indicated in Table 6–10. Plan A's expected return is now $4,400 less than that of Plan B.

Table 6–10
Expected returns for
high-risk firm

1. Normal conditions	Expected higher return under Plan A $7,000	×	Probability of normal conditions .80	=	Expected outcome +$5,600
2. Tight money	Expected lower return under Plan A ($50,000)	×	Probability of tight money .20	=	(10,000)
Negative expected value of return for Plan A versus Plan B				=	($4,400)

Shifts in Asset Structure

Thus far, our attention has been directed to the risk associated with various financing plans. Risk–return analysis must also be carried to the asset side. A firm with heavy risk exposure due to short-term borrowing may compensate in part by carrying highly liquid assets. Conversely, a firm with established long-term debt commitments may choose to carry a heavier component of less liquid, highly profitable assets.

Either through desire or compelling circumstances, business firms have decreased the liquidity of their current asset holdings since the early 1960s. The rise in interest rates and the cost of financing current assets may be a major reason for this decline. For example, in Table 6–11 we see that,

Table 6–11   Current asset positions ($ billions): U.S. nonfinancial corporations

Year	Cash and Equivalents			Inventory		
	Amount	Percent of Current Assets	Percent of Current Liabilities	Amount	Percent of Current Assets	Percent of Current Liabilities
1963	$ 66.7	18.98%	35.44%	$107.0	30.44%	56.85%
1974	84.3	11.48	18.66	318.9	43.41	70.58
1979	134.7	11.09	16.69	505.1	41.58	62.57
1981	153.1	10.79	15.78	583.7	41.15	60.18
1983	196.4	12.61	18.83	599.3	38.48	57.46
1985	189.1	11.16	16.31	664.6	39.23	57.73
1987	195.3	10.88	15.98	679.6	37.85	55.60

for U.S. nonfinancial corporations, cash and equivalents have decreased from 18.98 percent of current assets in 1963 to 10.88 percent in 1987, while inventory increased from 30.44 percent of current assets in 1963 to 37.85 percent in 1987. The ratio of cash and cash equivalents to current liabilities has fallen from 35.44 percent at the end of 1963 to approximately 16 percent by 1987, or over a 50 percent decline. Clearly, U.S. nonfinancial corporations are less liquid today than two decades ago.

The reasons for diminishing liquidity can be traced in part to more sophisticated, profit-oriented financial management as well as better utilization of cash balances via the computer. Less liquidity can also be traced to the long-term effect inflation has had on corporate balance sheets—forcing greater borrowing to carry more expensive assets and to decreasing profitability during recessions. The average current ratio for nonfinancial corporations is presented in Figure 6–11. After the recession in 1974–75, corporate liquidity increased to the highest level of the 1970s in 1976. Since reaching that peak, corporate liquidity has been squeezed. Generally speaking, corporations are relying more and more on short-term borrowings to carry less liquid assets—a potentially dangerous situation.

Toward an Optimal Policy

As previously indicated, the firm should attempt to relate asset liquidity to financing patterns, and vice versa. In Table 6–12, a number of different working capital alternatives are presented. Along the top of the table, we show asset liquidity; along the side, the type of financing arrangement.

**Figure 6–11
Nonfinancial
corporations' current
ratio**

Quarterly data

The combined impact of the two variables is shown in each of the four panels of the table.

Each firm must decide how it wishes to combine asset liquidity and financing needs. The aggressive, risk-oriented firm in Panel 1 of Table 6–12 will borrow short term and maintain relatively low levels of liquidity, hoping to increase profit. It will benefit from low-cost financing and high-return assets, but it will be vulnerable to a credit crunch. The more conservative firm, following the plan in Panel 4, will utilize established long-term financing and maintain a high degree of liquidity. In Panels 2 and 3, we see more moderate positions in which the firm compensates for short-term financing with highly liquid assets (2) or balances off low liquidity with precommitted, long-term financing (3).

**Table 6–12
Asset liquidity and
financing assets**

Financing Plan	Low Liquidity	High Liquidity
Short-term	1 High profit High risk	2 Moderate profit Moderate risk
Long-term	3 Moderate profit Moderate risk	4 Low profit Low risk

Each financial manager must structure his or her working capital position and the associated risk–return trade-off to meet the company's needs. For firms whose cash flow patterns are predictable, typified by the public utilities sector, a low degree of liquidity can be maintained. Immediate access to capital markets, such as that enjoyed by large, prestigious firms, also allows a greater risk-taking capability. In each case, the ultimate concern must be for maximizing the overall valuation of the firm through a judicious consideration of risk–return options.

In the next two chapters, we will examine the various methods for managing the individual components of working capital. In Chapter 7 we consider the techniques for managing cash, marketable securities, receivables, and inventory. In Chapter 8 we look at trade and bank credit and also at other sources of short-term funds.

Summary

Working capital management involves the financing and management of the current assets of the firm. A firm's ability to properly manage current assets and the associated liability obligations may determine how well it is able to survive in the short run. To the extent that part of the buildup in current assets is permanent, financial arrangements should carry longer maturities.

The financial manager must also give careful attention to the relationship of the production process to sales. Level production in a seasonal sales environment increases operating efficiency, but it also calls for more careful financial planning. The astute financial manager must also keep an eye on the general cost of borrowing, the term structure of interest rates, and the relative volatility of short- and long-term rates.

The firm has a number of risk–return decisions to consider. Though long-term financing provides a safety margin in availability of funds, its higher cost may reduce the profit potential of the firm. On the asset side, carrying highly liquid current assets assures the bill-paying capability of the firm—but detracts from profit potential. Each firm must tailor the various risk–return trade-offs to meet its own needs. The peculiarities of a firm's industry will have a major impact on the options open to management.

List of Terms

working capital management   term structure of interest rates
self-liquidating assets   expected value
"permanent" current assets   tight money
temporary current assets   normal yield curve
trade credit   inverted yield curve
level production   liquidity premium theory
point-of-sales terminals   segmentation theory
liquidity   expectations hypothesis

Discussion Questions

1. Explain how rapidly expanding sales can drain the cash resources of the firm.

2. Discuss the relative volatility of short- and long-term interest rates.

3. What is the significance to working capital management of matching sales and production?

4. How is a cash budget used to help manage current assets?

5. "The most appropriate financing pattern would be one in which asset buildup and length of financing terms are perfectly matched." Discuss the difficulty involved in achieving this financing pattern.

6. By using long-term financing to finance part of temporary current assets, a firm may have less risk but lower returns than a firm with a normal financing plan. Explain the significance of this statement.

7. A firm that uses short-term financing methods for a portion of permanent current assets is assuming more risk but expects higher returns than a firm with a normal financing plan. Explain.

8. What does the term *structure of interest rates* indicate?

9. What are three theories for describing the shape of the term structure of interest rates (the yield curve)? Briefly describe each theory.

10. Since the early 1960s, corporate liquidity has been declining. What reasons can you give for this trend?

Problems

1. Gary's Pipe and Steel Company expects next year's sales to be $800,000 if the economy is strong, $500,000 if the economy is steady, and $350,000 if the economy is weak. Gary believes there is a 20 percent probability that the economy will be strong, a 50 percent probability of a steady economy, and a 30 percent probability of a weak economy. What is the expected level of sales for next year?

2. Tobin Supplies Company expects sales next year to be $500,000. Inventory and accounts receivable will have to be increased by $90,000 to accommodate this sales level. The company has a steady profit margin of 12 percent with a 40 percent dividend payout. How much external funding will Tobin Supplies Company have to seek? Assume there is no increase in liabilities other than that which will occur with the external financing.

3. Doris Daycare Centers, Inc., has decided to buy a new computer system with an expected useful life of three years. The cost is $200,000. The company can borrow $200,000 for three years at 12 percent annual interest or for one year at 10 percent annual interest.

   How much would Doris Daycare Centers save in interest over the three-year life of the computer system if the one-year loan is utilized, and the loan is rolled over (reborrowed) each year at the same 10 percent rate? Compare this to the 12 percent three-year loan. What if one-year interest rates go up to 15 percent in year two and 18 percent in year three? What is the total interest cost now compared to the 12 percent, three-year loan?

4. Assume that Elco Instruments has $3 million in assets. If it goes with a low liquidity plan for the assets, it can earn 16 percent; but with a high liquidity plan, the return will be 13 percent. If the firm uses a short-term financing plan, the financing costs on the $3 million will be 9 percent; and with a long-term financing plan, the financing costs on the $3 million will be 11 percent. (Review Table 6–12 for parts *a, b* and *c.*)
   a. Compute the anticipated return after financing costs on the most aggressive asset-financing mix.
   b. Compute the anticipated return after financing costs on the most conservative asset-financing mix.
   c. Compute the anticipated return after financing costs on the two moderate approaches to the asset-financing mix.
   d. Would you necessarily accept the plan with the highest return after financing costs? Briefly explain.

5. Cummings Enterprises, a manufacturer of low-cost housing, has $5 million in assets.

Temporary current assets	$1,500,000
Permanent current assets	1,500,000
Fixed assets	2,000,000
Total assets	$5,000,000

   Short-term rates are 8 percent. Long-term rates are 13 percent. Earnings before interest and taxes are $920,000. The tax rate is 30 percent.
   If long-term financing is perfectly matched (synchronized) with long-term asset needs, and the same is true of short-term financing, what will earnings after taxes be? For an example of perfectly matched plans, see Figure 6–5.

6. In problem 5, assume the term structure of interest rates becomes inverted, with short-term rates going to 14 percent and long-term rates staying constant at 13 percent.
   If all other factors in the problem do not change, what will earnings after taxes be?

7. Guardian, Inc., is trying to develop an asset-financing plan. The firm has $400,000 in temporary current assets and $300,000 in permanent current assets. Guardian also has $500,000 in fixed assets. Assume a tax rate of 40 percent.
   a. Construct two alternative financing plans for Guardian. One of the plans should be conservative, with 75 percent of assets financed by long-term sources, and the other should be aggressive, with only 56.25 percent of assets financed by long-term sources. The current interest rate is 15 percent on long-term funds and 10 percent on short-term financing.
   b. Given that Guardian's earnings before interest and taxes are $200,000, calculate earnings after taxes for each of your alternatives.
   c. What would happen if the short- and long-term rates were reversed?

8. Lear, Inc., has $800,000 in current assets, $350,000 of which are considered permanent current assets. In addition, the firm has $600,000 invested in fixed assets.
   a. Lear wishes to finance all fixed assets and one half of its permanent current assets with long-term financing costing 10 percent. Short-term financing currently costs 5 percent. Lear's earnings before interest and taxes are $200,000. Determine Lear's

earnings after taxes under this financing plan. The tax rate is 30 percent.

b. As an alternative, Lear might wish to finance all fixed assets and permanent current assets plus one half of its temporary current assets with long-term financing. The same interest rates apply as in part *a*. Earnings before interest and taxes will be $200,000. What will be Lear's earnings after taxes. The tax rate is 30 percent.

c. What are some of the risks associated with each of these alternative financing strategies?

9. Liz's Health Food Store has estimated monthly financing requirements for the next six months as follows:

January	. . . . $8,000	April	. . . . . $8,000
February	 2,000	May	 9,000
March	 3,000	June	 4,000

Short-term financing will be utilized for the next six months. Projected annual interest rates are:

January	. . . . 8.0%	April	. . . . 15.0%
February	. . . . 9.0%	May .	. . . . 12.0%
March	. . . . . 12.0%	June	. . . . 12.0%

a. Compute total dollar interest payments for the six months. To convert an annual rate to a monthly rate, divided by 12.

b. If long-term financing at 12 percent had been utilized throughout the six months, would the total-dollar interest payments be larger or smaller?

10. In problem 9, what long-term interest rate would represent a break-even point between using short-term financing as described in part *a* and long-term financing? Hint: Divide the interest payments in 9*a* by the amount of total funds provided for the six months and multiply by 12.

11. Spike's Machine Tools Company expects to sell 400 units in January, 350 units in February, and 600 units in March. December's ending inventory is 500 units. Expected sales for the whole year are 6,000 units. Spike has decided on a level monthly production schedule of 500 units (6,000 units/12 months = 500 units per month). What is the expected end-of-month inventory for January, February, and March? Show the beginning inventory, production, and sales for each month.

12. Bombs Away Video Games Corporation has forecasted the following monthly sales:

January	$95,000	July	$ 40,000
February	88,000	August	40,000
March	20,000	September	50,000
April	20,000	October	80,000
May	15,000	November	100,000
June	30,000	December	118,000

Total sales = $696,000

Bombs Away Video Games sells the popular Strafe and Capture video game cartridge. It sells for $5 per unit and costs $2 per unit to produce. A level production policy is followed. Each month's production is equal to annual sales (in units) divided by 12.

Of each month's sales, 30 percent are for cash and 70 percent are on account. All accounts receivable are collected in the month after the sale is made.

  a. Construct a monthly production and inventory schedule in units. Beginning inventory in January is 20,000 units. (Note: To do part *a*, you should work in terms of units of production and units of sales.)

  b. Prepare a monthly schedule of cash receipts. Sales in the December before the planning year were $100,000. Work part *b* using dollars.

  c. Determine a cash payments schedule for January through December. The production costs of $2 per unit are paid for in the month in which they occur. Other cash payments, besides those for production costs, are $40,000 per month.

  d. Prepare a monthly cash budget for January through December. The beginning cash balance is $5,000 and that is also the minimum desired.

13. Seasonal Products Corporation expects the following monthly sales:

January	$20,000	May	$ 1,000	September	$20,000
February	15,000	June	3,000	October	25,000
March	5,000	July	10,000	November	30,000
April	3,000	August	14,000	December	22,000

Total sales = $168,000

Sales are 20 percent for cash in a given month, with the remainder going into accounts receivable. All 80 percent of the credit sales are collected in the month following the sale. Seasonal Products sells all of its goods for $2 each and produces them for $1 each. Seasonal

Products uses level production, and average monthly production is equal to annual production divided by 12.

a.   Generate a monthly production and inventory schedule in units. Beginning inventory in January is 5,000 units. (Note: To do part *a*, you should work in terms of units of production and units of sales.)

b.   Determine a cash receipts schedule for January through December. Assume that dollar sales in the prior December were $15,000. Work part *b* using dollars.

c.   Determine a cash payments schedule for January through December. The production costs ($1 per unit produced) are paid for in the month in which they occur. Other cash payments, besides those for production costs, are $6,000 per month.

d.   Construct a cash budget for January through December. The beginning cash balance is $1,000, and that is also the required minimum.

e.   Determine total current assets for each month. (Note: Accounts receivable equal sales minus 20 percent of sales for a given month.)

14. Pick a day within the past week and construct a yield curve for that day. Pick a day approximately a year ago and construct a yield curve for that day. How are interest rates different? *The Wall Street Journal* and *Federal Reserve Bulletin* should be of help in solving this problem.

15. Using the expectations hypothesis theory for the term structure of interest rates, determine the expected return for securities with maturities of two, three, and four years based on the following data. Do an analysis similar to that in Table 6–6.

1-year T-bill at beginning of year 1	9%
1-year T-bill at beginning of year 2	10%
1-year T-bill at beginning of year 3	12%
1-year T-bill at beginning of year 4	14%

Selected References

Brick, John R., and Howard E. Thompson.   "Time Series Analysis of Interest Rates: Some Additional Evidence." *Journal of Finance* 33 (March 1978), pp. 93–103.

Cossaboom, Roger A.   "Let's Reassess the Profitability-Liquidity Tradeoff." *Financial Executive* 39 (May 1971), pp. 46–51.

Gentry, James A., and Darrel Greitzu.   "Short-Run Financial Management Model on Lotus 1–2–3." *Journal of Financial Education* 14 (Fall 1985), pp. 75–85.

Glautier, M. W. E. "Towards a Reformation of the Theory of Working Capital." *Journal of Business Finance1* 3 (Spring 1971), pp. 37–42.

Jennings, Joseph A. "A Closer Look at Corporate Liquidity." *Financial Executive* 39 (February 1971), pp. 26–32.

Jones, Edward B. "Building the Bank Corporate Relationship." *Cash Flow* 8 (November 1987), pp. 64–74.

Knight, W. D. "Working Capital Management—Satisfying versus Optimization." *Financial Management* 1 (Spring 1972), pp. 33–40.

Rush, Ned C., and Daniel M. Ferguson. "EDI: Time for a Win-Win Change in Credit Terms." *Cash Flow* 8 (October 1987), pp. 30–47.

Stewart, G. Bennet III, and David M. Glassman. "Why Restructuring Adds Value: Shedding All too-Tempting Cash Flow." *Cash Flow* 8 (December 1987), pp. 44–47.

Van Horne, James C. "A Risk-Return Analysis of a Firm's Working Capital Position." *Engineering Economist* 14 (Winter 1969), pp. 71–89.

Welter, Paul. "How to Calculate Savings Possible through Reduction of Working Capital." *Financial Executive*, October 1970, pp. 50–58.

7

Current Asset Management

The financial manager must carefully allocate resources among the current assets of the firm—cash, marketable securities, accounts receivable, and inventory. In managing cash and marketable securities, the primary concern should be for safety and liquidity—with secondary attention placed on maximizing profitability. As we move to accounts receivable and inventory, a stiffer profitability test must be met. The investment level should not be a matter of happenstance or historical determination, but must meet the same return-on-investment criteria applied to any decision. We may need to choose between a 20 percent increase in inventory and a new plant location or a major research program. We shall examine the decision techniques that are applied to the various forms of current assets.

Cash Management

In the parlance of corporate financial management, the less cash you have, the better off you are. In spite of whatever lifelong teachings you might have learned about the virtues of cash, the corporate manager actively seeks to keep this nonearning asset to a minimum.

The first consideration is to ensure that inflows and outflows of cash are properly synchronized for transaction purposes. Interest-paying marketable securities, held for precautionary purposes, should only be transferred into cash when there is a scheduled need for disbursement. In determining the appropriate cash balance, the firm must carefully assess the payment pattern of customers, the speed at which suppliers and creditors process checks, and the efficiency of the banking system.

Float

Some people are shocked to realize that even the most trusted asset on a corporation's books, "cash," may not portray actual dollars at a given point in time. There are, in fact, two cash balances of importance: the corporation's recorded amount and the amount credited to the corporation by the bank. The difference between the two is labeled *float*, and it exists as a result of the lag between the time when a check is written and the eventual clearing of the check against a corporate bank account.

Let us examine the use of float. A firm has deposited $1,000,000 in checks received from customers during the week and has written $900,000 in checks to suppliers. If the initial balance were $100,000, the corporate books would show $200,000. But what will the bank records show in the way of usable funds? Perhaps $800,000 of the checks from customers will have cleared their accounts at other banks and been credited to us, while only $400,000 of our checks may have completed a similar cycle. As indicated in Table 7–1, we have used "float" to provide us with $300,000 extra in available short-term funds.

Some companies actually operate with a negative cash balance on the corporate books, knowing that float will carry them through at the bank. In the above example, the firm may write $1.2 million in checks on the assumption that only $800,000 will clear by the end of the week, thus leaving it with surplus funds in its bank account. The results, shown in Table 7–2, represent the phenomenon known as "playing the float." A float of $200,000 turns a negative balance on the corporation's books into a positive temporary balance on the bank's books. Obviously, float can

Table 7–1
The use of float to provide funds

	Corporate Books	Bank Books (usable funds) (amounts actually cleared)
Initial amount	$ 100,000	$100,000
Deposits	+ 1,000,000	+ 800,000
Checks	− 900,000	− 400,000
Balance	+$ 200,000	+$500,000
	+$300,000 float	

Table 7–2
Playing the float

	Corporate Books	Bank Books (usable funds) (amounts actually cleared)
Initial amount	$ 100,000	$100,000
Deposits	+ 1,000,000*	+ 800,000*
Checks	− 1,200,000	− 800,000
Balance	−$ 100,000	+$100,000
		+$200,000 float

*Assumed to remain the same as in Table 7–1.

also work against you if checks going out are being processed more quickly than checks coming in.

Improving Collections

We may expedite the collection and check-clearing process through a number of strategies.[1] A popular method is to utilize a variety of collection centers throughout our marketing area. A dress manufacturer with headquarters in Chicago may have 75 collection offices disbursed throughout the country, each performing a billing and collection-deposit function. One of the collection offices in San Francisco, using a local bank, may be able to clear a check on a San Jose bank in one day—whereas a Chicago bank would require a substantially longer time to remit and clear the check at the California bank.[2] Excess cash balances at the local banks throughout the collection system are remitted to the home office bank through a daily wire transfer.

For those who wish to enjoy the benefits of expeditious check clearance at lower costs, a *lockbox system* may replace the network of regional collection offices. Under this plan, customers are requested to forward their checks to a post-office box in their geographic region and a local bank picks up the checks and processes them to other banks in the locality for rapid collection. Funds are then wired to the corporate home office for immediate use. The company retains many of the benefits of regional collection centers, but with reduced corporate overhead.

[1] Larger banks have cash management advisory groups that can offer valuable consultation on these matters.

[2] Checks deposited with a bank are cleared through the Federal Reserve System, through a correspondent bank, or through a locally established clearinghouse system. A check is collected when it is remitted to the payer's bank and actually paid by that bank to the payee's bank.

Extending Disbursements

Perhaps you have heard of the multimillion-dollar corporation with its headquarters located in the most exclusive office space in downtown Manhattan, but with its primary check disbursement center in Fargo, North Dakota. Though the firm may engage in aggressive speedup techniques in the processing of incoming checks, a slowdown pattern more aptly describes the payment procedures.

While the preceding example represents an extreme case, the slowing of disbursements is not an uncommon practice in cash management. It has even been given the title "extended disbursement float."[3] Many full-service banks offer customers consulting services pointing out structural defects in the Federal Reserve and other collection systems that allow the firm to extend the payment period. While it is not the intent of this text to encourage or discourage such practices, their fairly widespread use is worthy of note.

Cost-Benefit Analysis

An efficiently maintained cash management program can be an expensive operation. The utilization of remote collection and disbursement centers involves additional costs, and banks involved in the process will require that the firm maintain adequate deposit balances or pay sufficient fees to justify their services. Though the use of a lockbox system may reduce total corporate overhead, the costs may still be substantial.

These expenses must be compared to the benefits that may accrue. If a firm has an average daily remittance of $2 million and 1.5 days can be saved in the collection process by establishing a sophisticated collection network, the firm has freed up $3 million for investment elsewhere. Also, through stretching the disbursement schedule by one day, perhaps another $2 million will become available for alternate uses. An example of this process is shown in Figure 7–1. If the firm is able to earn 10 percent on the $5 million that is freed up, as much as $500,000 may be expended on the administrative costs of cash management before the new costs are equal to the generated revenue.

---

[3]"Making Millions by Stretching the Float," *Business Week*, November 23, 1974, p. 88.

**Figure 7–1
Cash management
network**

Electronic Funds Transfer

As we move into the next decade, some of the techniques of delaying payment will be reduced through the techniques of *electronic funds transfer,* a system in which funds are moved between computer terminals without the use of a "check." Through the use of terminal communication between the store and the bank, your payment to the supermarket will be automatically charged against your account at the bank before you walk out the door.

Many large corporations have computerized cash management systems. For example, a firm may have 55 branch offices and 56 banks, one bank for each branch office and a lead bank in which the major corporate account is kept. At the end of each day the financial manager can check all the company's bank accounts through an on-line computer terminal. He or she can then transfer through the computer all excess cash balances from each branch or regional bank to the corporate lead bank for overnight investment in money market securities.

It has been estimated that close to 77 percent of large companies use computers to initiate money transfers and that about 70 percent now use computers to receive reports from their banks on lockbox receipts and bank balances to judge the amount of float available.

Automated clearinghouses (ACHs) are becoming an important element in electronic funds transfer. An ACH transfers information between one financial institution and another and from account to account via computer tape. There are approximately 30 regional automated clearinghouses throughout the United States, claiming total membership of over 10,000 financial institutions. The biggest use of ACHs so far has been in payroll processing, as more banks are offering direct deposit options. In the future more companies will use these automated clearinghouses for transfer of payments between the company and customers, suppliers, and utilities.

International Cash Management

Multinational corporations can shift funds around from country to country much as a firm may transfer funds from regional banks to the lead bank. Just as financial institutions in the United States have become more involved in electronic funds transfer there has also developed an international payments system. This international funds transfer system is called SWIFT.

A company may prefer to hold cash balances in one currency rather than another or to take advantage of the high interest rates that are available in a particular country for short-term investments in marketable securities. In periods in which one country's currency is rising in value relative to other currencies, an astute financial manager will try to keep as much cash as possible in the country with the strong currency. In periods in which the dollar is rising relative to other currencies, many balances are held in U.S. bank accounts or in dollar-denominated bank accounts in foreign banks, more commonly known as Eurodollar deposits. The international money markets have been growing in scope and size, so that these markets have become a much more important aspect of efficient cash management. Cash management at the international level employs the same techniques as domestic cash management, using such forecasting devices as the cash budget and daily cash reports, so that excess funds may be collected and invested until needed in Eurodollar money market securities or other appropriate investments in securities denominated by strong currencies. An in-depth coverage of international cash and asset management is presented in Chapter 21.

Marketable Securities _____

The firm may hold excess funds in anticipation of some major cash outlay, such as a dividend payment or partial retirement of debt or as a precaution against an unexpected event. When funds are being held for other than immediate transaction purposes, they should be converted from cash into interest-earning marketable securities.[4]

The financial manager has a virtual supermarket of securities from which to choose. Among the factors influencing that choice are yield, maturity, minimum investment required, safety, and marketability. Under normal conditions, the longer the maturity period of the security, the higher the yield, as indicated in Figure 7–2.

**Figure 7–2
An examination of
yield and maturity
characteristics**

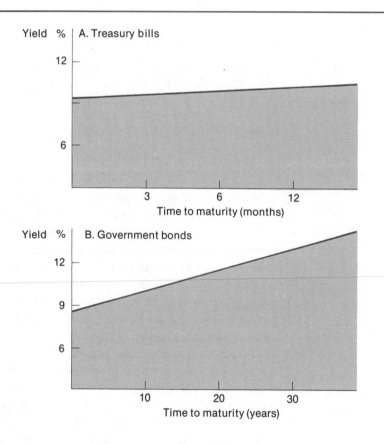

---

[4]The one possible exception to this principle is found in the practice of holding compensating balances at commercial banks—a topic for discussion in Chapter 8.

The problem in "stretching out" the maturity of your investment is not that you are legally locked in (you can generally sell your security when you need funds), but that you may have to take a loss. A $5,000 Treasury note issued initially at 8.5 percent, with three years to run, may only bring $4,500 if the going interest rate climbs to 10 percent. This risk is considerably greater as the maturity date is extended. A complete discussion of the "interest rate risk" is presented in Chapter 16, Long-Term Debt and Lease Financing.

The various forms of marketable securities and investments, emphasizing the short term, are presented in Table 7–3. The key characteristics of each investment are delineated along with examples of yields at two different time periods. Yields on March 22, 1980, were extremely high but dropped over the next seven years as the U.S. economy entered a period of disinflation. By August 6, 1987, many rates were one half to two thirds the rates of seven years earlier.

Let us examine the characteristics of each security. *Treasury bills* are short-term obligations of the federal government and are a popular place

Table 7–3   Types of short-term investments

Investment	Maturity*	Minimum Amount	Safety	Market-ability	Yield March 22, 1980	Yield August 6, 1987
Federal government securities:						
Treasury bills	3 months	$ 10,000	Excellent	Excellent	14.76	5.80
Treasury bills	1 year	10,000	Excellent	Excellent	13.89	6.81
Treasury notes	3–5 years	5,000	Excellent	Excellent	13.86	8.15
Federal agency securities:						
Federal Home Loan Bank	1–5 years	5,000	Excellent	Excellent	14.40	8.45
Federal Land Bank	1–5 years	5,000	Excellent	Excellent	14.32	8.47
Nongovernment securities:						
Certificates of deposit (large)	1 month	100,000	Good	Good	16.97	6.65
Certificates of deposit (small)	90 days	500	Good	Poor	15.90	6.56
Commercial paper	3 months	25,000	Good	Fair	17.04	6.65
Banker's acceptances	90 days	None	Good	Good	17.22	6.66
Eurodollar deposits	3 months	25,000	Good	Excellent	18.98	7.00
LIBOR (London Interbank Offered Rates)	3 months	100,000	Good	Excellent	—	7.06
Savings accounts	Open	None	Excellent	None†	5–5½	5.13
Money market funds	Open	500	Good	None†	14.50	5.80
Money market deposit accounts (financial institutions)	Open	1,000	Excellent	None†	—	5.47

*Several of the above securities can be purchased with maturities longer than those indicated. The above maturities are the most commonly quoted.
†Though not marketable, these investments are still highly liquid in that funds may be withdrawn without penalty.

to "park funds" because of a large and active market. Although these securities are originally issued with maturities of 91 days, 182 days, and one year, the investor may buy an outstanding T-bill with as little as one day remaining (perhaps two prior investors have held it for 45 days each). With the government issuing new Treasury bills weekly, a wide range of choices is always available. Treasury bills are unique in that they trade on a discount basis—meaning that the yield you receive takes place as a result of the difference between the price you pay and the maturity value.

Treasury notes are government obligations with a maturity of three to five years, and they may be purchased with short- to intermediate-term funds. *Federal agency* securities represent the offerings of such governmental organizations as the Federal Home Bank Board and the Federal Land Bank. Though lacking the direct backing of the U.S. Treasury, they are guaranteed by the issuing agency and provide all the safety that one would normally require. There is an excellent secondary market for agency securities which allows investors to sell an outstanding issue in an active and liquid market prior to the maturity date. Government agency issues pay slightly higher yields than direct Treasury issues.

Another outlet for investment is the *certificates of deposit* (CDs), offered by commercial banks, savings and loans, and other financial institutions. The investor places his or her funds on deposit at a specified rate over a given time period as evidenced by the certificate received. This is a two-tier market, with small CDs ($500 to $10,000) carrying lower interest rates, while larger CDs ($100,000 and more) have higher interest provisions and a degree of marketability for those who wish to turn over their CDs prior to maturity. The CD market became fully deregulated by the federal government in 1986. CDs are normally insured (guaranteed) by the federal government for up to $100,000.

Comparable in yield and quality to large certificates of deposit, *commercial paper* represents unsecured promissory notes issued to the public by large business corporations. When Ford Motor Credit Corporation is in need of short-term funds, it may choose to borrow at the bank or expand its credit resources by issuing its commercial paper to the general public in minimum units of $25,000. Commercial paper is usually held to maturity by the investor, with no active secondary market in existence.

Banker's acceptances are short-term securities that generally arise from foreign trade. The acceptance is a draft which is drawn on a bank for payment when presented to the bank. The difference between a draft and a check is that a company does not have to deposit funds at the bank to cover the draft until the bank has accepted the draft for payment and presented it to the company. In the case of banker's acceptances arising from foreign trade, the draft may be accepted by the bank for *future* payment of the required amount. This means that the exporter who now holds the banker's acceptance may have to wait 30, 60, or 90 days to collect the money. Because there is an active market for banker's acceptances, the exporter can sell the acceptance on a discount basis to any buyer and in this way receive the money before the importer receives the goods. This provides a good investment opportunity in banker's acceptances. Banker's acceptances rank close behind Treasury bills and certificates of deposits as a vehicle for viable short-term investments.

Another popular international short-term investment arising from foreign trade is the *Eurodollar certificate of deposit.* The rate on this investment is usually higher than the rates on U.S. Treasury bills and bank certificates of deposit at large U.S. money market banks. Eurodollars are U.S. dollars held on deposit by foreign banks and in turn loaned out by those banks to anyone seeking dollars. Since the U.S. dollar is the only international currency that is also used as a domestic currency abroad, any country can use it to help pay for goods. Therefore, there is a large market for Eurodollar deposits and loans, mostly centered in the London international banking market.

In this edition we have included *LIBOR* (London Interbank Offered Rate) as part of the investment table. The LIBOR rate is the rate offered for dollar deposits in the London market. While this is essentially a Eurodollar deposit, the difference is that the deposit is centered in London rather than Paris or Frankfurt or some other part of Europe. LIBOR is often used as a base lending rate for U.S. companies who may borrow abroad at a floating interest rate of LIBOR plus a small premium. LIBOR is even being used as a base rate for some U.S. domestic loans to corporations. The use of LIBOR is discussed further in Chapter 21, International Financial Management.

The lowest yielding investment may well be a passbook *savings account* at a bank or a savings and loan. Although rates on savings accounts are no longer prescribed by federal regulation, they are still a relatively unattractive form of investment in terms of yield.

Of particular interest to the smaller investor is the *money market fund—* a product of the tight money periods of the 1970s and early 1980s. For as little as $500 or $1,000, an investor may purchase shares in a money market fund, which in turn reinvests the proceeds in high-yielding $100,000 bank CDs, $25,000–$100,000 commercial paper, and other large-denomination, high-yielding securities. The investor then receives his pro rata portion of the interest proceeds daily as a credit to his shares.

The money market funds allow the small businessperson or investor to participate directly in higher yielding securities. All too often in the past, the small investor was forced to place funds in savings accounts yielding 5–5.5 percent, while "smart" money was parked at higher yields in large-unit investments. Examples of money market funds are Dreyfus Liquid Assets, Inc., and Fidelity Daily Income Trust.

Beginning in December 1982, money market funds got new competition when commercial banks, savings and loans, and credit unions were permitted by the regulatory agencies and Congress to offer new *money market accounts* modeled after the money market funds. Due to deregulation, financial institutions are now able to pay competitive market rates on money market deposit accounts. While there is no longer a federally prescribed minimum balance, the normal minimum is $1,000. Terms do vary from institution to institution. Generally these accounts may have only three deposits and three withdrawals per month, and are not meant to be transaction accounts, but a place to keep minimum and excess cash balances. They may be used by individuals or corporations, but are more attractive to smaller firms than to larger firms (which have many more alternatives available). These accounts are insured up to $100,000 by federal agencies, which make them slightly less risky than money market funds.

Although not a short-term investment as such, most financial institutions also offer NOW accounts. NOW accounts are checking accounts that pay interest. (These accounts are not included in Table 7–3 because their primary purpose is for check writing.)

Management of Accounts Receivable

An increasing portion of the investment in corporate assets has been in accounts receivable as expanding sales, fostered at times by inflationary pressures, have placed additional burdens on firms to carry larger balances for their customers. Frequently, recessions have also stretched out the terms of payment as small customers have had to rely on suppliers for credit. Accounts receivable as a percentage of total assets has almost doubled between 1950 and the late 1980s, representing over 20 percent of total assets for the average U.S. corporation.[5]

Accounts Receivable as an Investment

As is true of other current assets, accounts receivable should be thought of as an investment. The level of accounts receivable should not be ad-

---

[5]Federal Trade Commission and Securities and Exchange Commission, *Quarterly Report for Manufacturing Corporations*, 4th quarter, 1951, and 2nd quarter, 1988.

judged too high or too low based on historical standards of industry norms, but rather the test should be whether the level of return we are able to earn from this asset equals or exceeds the potential gain from other commitments. For example, if we allow our customers five extra days to clear their accounts, our accounts receivable balance will increase—draining funds from marketable securities and perhaps drawing down the inventory level. We must ask whether we are optimizing our return, in light of appropriate risk and liquidity considerations.

An example of a buildup in accounts receivable is presented in Figure 7–3, with supportive financing provided through reducing lower yielding assets and increasing lower cost liabilities.

Credit Policy Administration

In considering the extension of credit, there are three primary policy variables to consider in conjunction with our profit objective.

1. Credit standards.
2. Terms of trade.
3. Collection policy.

Figure 7–3
Financing growth in
accounts receivable

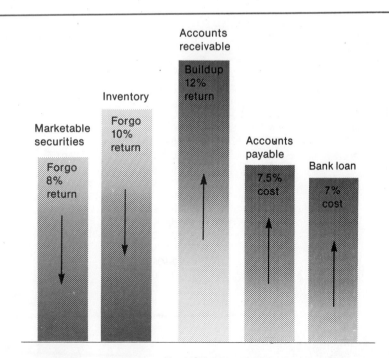

Credit standards   The firm must determine the nature of the credit risk on the basis of prior record of payment, financial stability, current net worth, and other factors. An extensive network of credit information has been developed by credit agencies throughout the country (Big Brother is watching). The most prominent source is Dun & Bradstreet, which publishes a *Reference Book* listing over 3 million business establishments. Information is given on the firm's line of business, net worth, and credit-worthiness. An example of the rating system used by Dun & Bradstreet is presented in Table 7–4.

A firm with a BB2 rating has estimated financial strength, based on net worth, of $200,000–$300,000, with an overall composite credit rating of "Good." Besides the *Reference Book*, Dun & Bradstreet can also provide extensive individualized credit reports on potential customers.

Certain industries have also developed their own special credit reporting agencies, such as the Lyon Furniture Mercantile Agency and the National Credit Office (textiles). Even more important are the local credit bureaus that keep close tabs on day-to-day transactions in a given community.

Terms of trade   The stated terms of credit extension will have a strong impact on the eventual size of the accounts receivable balance. If a firm averages $5,000 in daily credit sales and allows 30-day terms, the average accounts receivable balance will be $150,000. If customers are carried for

Table 7–4
Dun & Bradstreet
credit rating system

	Key to Ratings					
	Estimated Financial Strength		Composite Credit Appraisal			
			High	Good	Fair	Limited
5A	Over	$50,000,000	1	2	3	4
4A	$10,000,000 to	50,000,000	1	2	3	4
3A	1,000,000 to	10,000,000	1	2	3	4
2A	750,000 to	1,000,000	1	2	3	4
1A	500,000 to	750,000	1	2	3	4
BA	300,000 to	500,000	1	2	3	4
BB	200,000 to	300,000	1	(2)	3	4
CB	125,000 to	200,000	1	2	3	4
CC	75,000 to	125,000	1	2	3	4
DC	50,000 to	75,000	1	2	3	4
DD	35,000 to	50,000	1	2	3	4
EE	20,000 to	35,000	1	2	3	4
FF	10,000 to	20,000	1	2	3	4
GG	5,000 to	10,000	1	2	3	4
HH	Up to	5,000	1	2	3	4

60 days, we must maintain $300,000 in receivables and much additional financing will be required.

In establishing credit terms the firm should also consider the use of a cash discount. Offering the terms 2/10, net 30, enables the customer to deduct 2 percent from the face amount of the bill when paying within the first 10 days, but if the discount is not taken, the customer must remit the full amount within 30 days. As later demonstrated in Chapter 8, Sources of Short-Term Financing, the annualized cost of not taking a cash discount may be substantial.

Collection policy A third area for consideration under credit policy administration is the collection function. A number of quantitative measures may be applied to the credit department of the firm.

$$a. \text{ Average collection period} = \frac{\text{Accounts receivable}}{\text{Average daily credit sales}}$$

(See ratio 5 in Chapter 3.) An increase in the average collection period may be the result of a predetermined plan to extend credit terms or the consequence of poor credit administration.

b. Ratio of bad debts to credit sales.

An increasing ratio may indicate too many weak accounts or an aggressive market expansion policy.

c. Aging of accounts receivables.

We may wish to determine the amount of time that the various accounts have been on our books. If there is a buildup in receivables beyond our normal credit terms, we may wish to take remedial action. Such a buildup is shown in the table presented here.

Age of receivables, May 31, 1989

Month of Sales	Age of Account (days)	Amounts
May	0–30	$ 60,000
April	31–60	25,000
March	61–90	5,000
February	91–120	10,000
Total receivables		$100,000

If our normal credit terms are 30 days, we may be doing a poor job of collecting our accounts, with particular attention required on accounts over 90 days outstanding.

An Actual Credit Decision

We now examine a credit decision that brings together the various elements of accounts receivable management. Assume that a firm is considering selling to a group of customers that will bring $10,000 in new annual sales, of which 10 percent will be uncollectible. While this is a very high rate of nonpayment, the critical question is, What is the potential contribution to profitability?

Assume the collection cost on these accounts is 5 percent and the cost of producing and selling the product is 77 percent of the sales dollar. We are in a 40 percent tax bracket. The profit on new sales is as follows:

Additional sales	$10,000
Accounts uncollectible (10% of new sales)	1,000
Annual incremental revenue	9,000
Collection costs (5% of new sales)	500
Production and selling costs (77% of new sales)	7,700
Annual income before taxes	800
Taxes (40%)	320
Annual incremental income after taxes	$ 480

Though the return on sales is only 4.8 percent ($480/$10,000), the return on invested dollars may be considerably higher. Let us assume that the only new investment in this case is a buildup in accounts receivable. (Present working capital and fixed assets are sufficient to support the higher sales level.) Assume analysis of our accounts indicates a turnover ratio of 6 to 1 between sales and accounts receivable. Our new accounts receivable balance will average $1,667.

$$\frac{\text{Sales}}{\text{Turnover}} = \frac{\$10,000^6}{6} = \$1,667$$

Thus, we are committing an average investment of only $1,667 to provide an aftertax return of $480, so that the yield is a very attractive 28.8 percent. If the firm had a minimum required aftertax return of 10 percent, this would clearly be an acceptable investment. We might ask next if we should consider taking on 12 percent or even 15 percent in uncollectible accounts—remaining loyal to our concept of maximizing profit and forsaking any notion about risky accounts being inherently good or bad.

---

[6]We could actually argue that our out-of-pocket commitment to sales is 82 percent (77 percent production and sales costs plus 5 percent collection costs) times $10,000, or $8,200. This would indicate an even smaller commitment to receivables.

Inventory Management

Inventory can create financing and profit problems for a company. The automobile industry is a case in point. In the Fall of 1985, with bulging inventories of 1985 models, the automobile industry instituted a discount financing plan of 7.9 percent interest when market rates were closer to 12 percent for auto financing. While this stimulated sales and cleared 1985 cars out of the dealer showrooms, profits suffered—at General Motors, especially. Financing incentives, as they became known, occurred again in early 1986 at 7.9 percent, in late 1986 at 3.9 percent, and in August of 1987 at a 1.9 percent financing cost. In all cases, GM led the industry in an attempt to clear out overstocked models. Ford and Chrysler followed the lead, even though they were not as overstocked as GM. General Motor's inventory buildup was a function of lagging sales and of overbuilding. Ford used a different strategy and simply chose to produce at a level that might mean the dealers did not always have the car in stock that the customer wanted. While they were willing to suffer the lost sale, they were not forced to discount cars and sell them at low profit margins. Ford's strategy showed up on the bottom line as they achieved record profits for 1986 and 1987.

Because inventory is the least liquid of current assets, it should provide the highest yield to justify investment. While the financial manager may have direct control over the cash management, marketable securities, and accounts receivable, control over inventory policy is generally shared with production management and marketing. Let us examine some key factors influencing inventory management.

Level versus Seasonal Production

A manufacturing firm must determine whether a plan of level or seasonal production should be followed. Level production was discussed in Chapter 6. While level (even) production throughout the year allows for maximum efficiency in the use of manpower and machinery, it may result in unnecessarily high inventory buildups prior to shipment, particularly in a seasonal business. We may have 10,000 bathing suits in stock in November.

If we produce on a seasonal basis, the inventory problem is eliminated, but we will then have unused capacity during slack periods. Furthermore, as we shift to maximum operations to meet seasonal needs, we may be forced to pay overtime wages to labor and to sustain other inefficiencies as equipment is overused.

We have a classic problem in financial analysis. Are the cost savings from level production sufficient to justify the extra expenditure in carrying inventory? Let us look at a typical case.

	Production	
	Level	Seasonal
Average inventory	$100,000	$70,000
Operating costs—after tax . . .	50,000	60,000

Though we will have to invest $30,000 more in average inventory under level production, we will save $10,000 in operating costs. This represents a 33 percent return on investment. If our required rate of return is 10 percent, this would clearly be an acceptable alternative.[7]

Inventory Policy in Inflation (and Deflation)

The price of copper went from $0.50 to $1.40 a pound and back again in the 1980s. Similar price instability has taken place in wheat, sugar, lumber, and a number of other commodities. Only the most astute inventory manager can hope to prosper in this type of environment. The problem can be partially controlled by taking moderate inventory positions (do not fully commit at one price).

Another way of protecting your inventory position would be by hedging with a futures contract to sell at a stipulated price some months from now.

Rapid price movements in inventory may also have a major impact on the reported income of the firm, a process described in Chapter 3, Financial Analysis. A firm using FIFO (first-in, first-out) accounting may experience large inventory profits when old, less expensive inventory is written off against new high prices in the marketplace. The benefits may be transitory, as the process reverses itself when prices decline.

The Inventory Decision Model

Substantial research has been devoted to the problem of determining optimum inventory size, order quantity, usage rate, and similar consid-

---

[7]The problem may be further evaluated by using the capital budgeting techniques presented in Chapter 12.

erations. An entire branch in the field of operations research is dedicated to the subject.

In developing an inventory model, we must evaluate the two basic costs associated with inventory: the carrying costs and the ordering costs. Through a careful analysis of both of these variables, we can determine the optimum order size to place to minimize costs. Carrying costs include interest on funds tied up in inventory, the cost of warehouse space, insurance premiums, and material handling expenses. There is also an implicit cost associated with the dangers of obsolescence and rapid price change. The larger the order we place, the greater the average inventory we will have on hand, and the higher the carrying cost.

As a second factor, we must consider the cost of ordering and processing inventory into stock. If we maintain a relatively low average inventory in stock, we must order many times and total ordering cost will be high. The opposite patterns associated with the two costs are portrayed in Figure 7–4.

As the order size increases, carrying costs go up because we have more inventory on hand. With larger orders, of course, we will order less frequently and overall ordering costs will go down. The approximate trade-off between the two can best be judged by examining the total cost

**Figure 7–4
Determining the
optimum inventory
level**

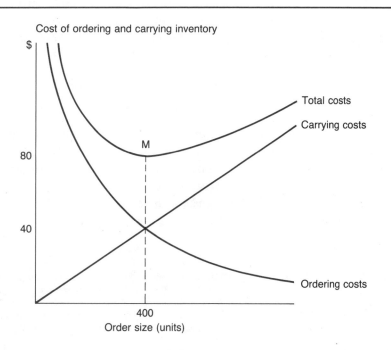

curve. At point *M,* we have appropriately played the advantages and disadvantages of the respective costs against each other. With larger orders, carrying costs will be excessive, while at a reduced order size, constant ordering will put us at an undesirably higher point on the ordering cost curve.

The question becomes, How do we mathematically determine the minimum point (*M*) on the total cost curve? Under certain fairly reasonable assumptions,[8] we may use the following formula as the first step.

$$EOQ = \sqrt{\frac{2SO}{C}} \qquad\qquad (7\text{--}1)$$

EOQ is the "economic ordering quantity," the amount which it is most advantageous for the firm to order each time. We will determine this value, translate it into average inventory size, and determine the minimum total cost amount (M). The terms in the *EOQ* formula are defined as follows:

S = Total sales in units
O = Ordering cost for each order
C = Carrying cost per unit in dollars

Let us assume that we anticipate selling 2,000 units, that it will cost us $8 to place each order, and that the price per unit is $1, with a 20 percent carrying cost to maintain the average inventory (the carrying charge per unit is $0.20). Plugging these values into our formula, we show:

$$EOQ = \sqrt{\frac{2SO}{C}} = \sqrt{\frac{2 \times 2,000 \times \$8}{\$0.20}} = \sqrt{\frac{\$32,000}{\$0.20}} = \sqrt{160,000}$$

$$= 400 \text{ units}$$

The optimum order size is 400 units. On the assumption that we will use up inventory at a constant rate throughout the year, our average inventory on hand will be 200 units, as indicated in Figure 7–5. Average inventory equals *EOQ*/2.

Our total costs with an order size of 400 and an average inventory size of 200 units are computed in Table 7–5.

---

[8]The assumptions are that inventory usage is at a constant rate, that the amount of time to deliver each order is consistent, and that the delivery date coincides with the point at which we reach a zero level of inventory. It does not consider the problem of stock-outs. A stock-out occurs when a firm is out of a specific inventory item and is unable to sell or deliver the product. Relaxation of these assumptions does not greatly change the calculations.

**Figure 7–5
Inventory usage
pattern**

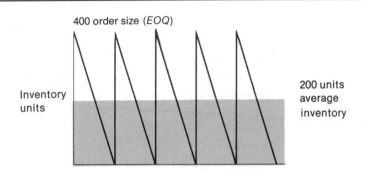

400 order size (*EOQ*)

Inventory
units

200 units
average
inventory

**Table 7–5
Total costs for
inventory**

1. Ordering costs = $\dfrac{2,000 \text{ units}}{400 \text{ order size}}$ = 5 orders

   5 orders at $8 per order = $40

2. Carrying costs = Average inventory in units × Carrying
   cost per unit

   200 × $0.20 = $40

3. Order cost $40
   Carrying cost . . . . +40
   Total cost $80

Point *M* on Figure 7–4 (page 195) can be equated to a total cost of $80 at an order size of 400 units. At no other order point can we hope to achieve lower costs. The same basic principles of total cost minimization that we have applied to inventory can be applied to other assets as well. For example, we may assume that cash has a carrying cost (opportunity cost of lost interest on marketable securities as a result of being in cash) and an ordering cost (transaction costs of shifting in and out of marketable securities) and then work toward determining the optimum level of cash. In each case we are trying to minimize the overall costs and increase the profit and valuation of the firm.

Summary

In cash management our primary goal should be to keep our balances as low as possible consistent with the notion of maintaining adequate funds for transaction purposes. We try to speed the inflow of funds and defer their outflow. Excess short-term funds may be placed in marketable securities—with a wide selection of issues, maturities, and yields from which to choose.

The management of accounts receivable calls for the determination of credit standards and the forms of credit to be offered as well as the development of an effective collection policy. There is no such thing as bad credit—only unprofitable credit extension. Inventory is the least liquid of the current assets, so it should provide the highest yield. We determine the economic ordering quantity and the optimum average inventory size to minimize the total costs of ordering and carrying inventory.

Other assets may also be subjected to decision models similar to that provided for inventory. In each instance we look at the cost of holding the asset versus the cost of transacting in the asset and we strive for a minimum value.

List of Terms

float
lockbox system
electronic funds transfer
cost–benefit analysis
Treasury bills
Treasury notes
certificates of deposit
commercial paper
Dun & Bradstreet
hedging
futures contract
LIBOR (London Interbank
    Offered Rate)

automated clearinghouse (ACH)
economic ordering quantity (*EOQ*)
carrying costs
trade credit
credit terms
average collection period
aging of accounts receivable
Eurodollars
banker's acceptances
money market accounts
money market funds

Discussion Questions

1. In the management of cash and marketable securities, why should the primary concern be for safety and liquidity rather than maximization of profit?

2. Briefly explain how a corporation may use float to its advantage.

3. Why does float exist at all, and what effect would electronic funds transfer systems have on float?

4. How can a firm operate with a negative cash balance on its corporate books?

5. Explain the similarities and differences of lockbox systems and regional collection offices.

6. Why would a financial manager want to slow down disbursements?

7. Use *The Wall Street Journal* or some other financial publication to find the going interest rates for the list of marketable securities in Table 7–3. Which security would you choose for a short-term investment? Why?

8. Why are Treasury bills a favorite place for financial managers to invest excess cash?

9. Explain why the bad debt percentage or any other similar credit-control percentage is not the ultimate measure of success in the management of accounts receivable. What is the key consideration?

10. Precisely what does the *EOQ* formula tell us? What assumption is made about the usage rate for inventory?

Problems

1. City Farm Insurance has collection centers around the country to speed up cash collections. The company also makes its disbursements from remote disbursement centers so that checks written by City Farm take longer to clear the bank. Collection time has been reduced by two days and disbursement time increased by one day because of these policies. Excess funds are being invested in short-term instruments yielding 12 percent per annum.
   a. If City Farm has $5 million per day in collections and $3 million per day in disbursements, how many dollars has the cash management system freed up?
   b. How much can City Farm earn per year on short-term investments made possible by the freed-up cash?

2. Darla's Cosmetics has annual credit sales of $1,440,000 and an average collection period 45 days in 1988. Assume a 360-day year.
   What is the company's average accounts receivable balance? Accounts receivable are equal to the average daily sales times the average collection period.

3. In problem 2, if accounts receivable change to $200,000 in 1989, while credit sales are $1,800,000, should we assume the firm has a more lenient credit policy?

4. Salomon Brothers Shirts has an average collection period of 30 days. Their accounts receivable balance is $60,000. What is the value of their credit sales?

5. Porland Tire Company has expected sales of 36,000 tires this year, an ordering cost of $12 per order, and carrying cost of $2.40 per tire.
   a. What is the economic order quantity?
   b. How many orders will be placed during the year?
   c. What will the average inventory be?

6. Howe Corporation is trying to improve its inventory control system and has installed an online computer at its retail stores. Howe anticipates sales of 126,000 units per year, an ordering cost of $4 per order, and carrying costs of $1.008 per unit.
   a. What is the economic ordering quantity?
   b. How many orders will be placed during the year?
   c. What will the average inventory be?
   d. What is the total cost of inventory expected to be?

7. (See problem 6 for basic data.) In the second year, Howe Corporation finds that it can reduce ordering costs to $1 per order but that carrying costs stay the same at $1.008 per unit.
   a. Recompute a, b, c, and d in problem 6 for the second year.
   b. Now compare years one and two and explain what happened.

8. Johnson Electronics is considering extending trade credit to some customers previously considered poor risks. Sales would increase by $100,000 if credit is extended to these new customers. Of the new accounts receivable generated, 10 percent will prove to be uncollectible. Additional collection costs will be 3 percent of sales, and production and selling costs will be 79 percent of sales. Assume a tax rate of 40 percent.
   a. Compute the incremental income after taxes.
   b. What will Johnson's incremental return on sales be if these new credit customers are accepted?
   c. If the receivable turnover ratio is 6 to 1, and no other asset buildup is needed to serve the new customers, what will Johnson's incremental return on new average investment be?

9. Ron's checkbook shows a balance of $400. A recent statement from the bank (received last week) shows all checks written as of the date of the statement have been paid, except numbers 325 and 326, which were for $35 and $58, respectively. Since the statement

date, checks 327, 328, and 329 have been written for $22, $45, and $17, respectively.

There is an 80 percent probability that checks 325 and 326 have been paid by this time. There is a 50 percent probability that checks 327, 328, and 329 have been paid.

a. What is the total value of the five checks outstanding?
b. What is the expected value of payments for the five checks outstanding?
c. What is the difference between parts *a* and *b*? This represents a type of float.

10. Dimaggio Sports Equipment, Inc., is considering a switch to level production. Cost efficiencies would occur under level production and aftertax costs would decline by $35,000, but inventory would increase by $400,000. Dimaggio would have to finance the extra inventory at a cost of 10.5 percent. (*a*) Should the company go ahead and switch to level production? (*b*) How low would interest rates need to fall before level production would be feasible?

11. Collins Office Supplies is considering a more liberal credit policy to increase sales, but expects 9 percent of the new accounts will be uncollectible. Collection costs are 5 percent of new sales, production and selling costs are 78 percent, and accounts receivable turnover is five times. Assume an income tax rate of 30 percent and an increase in sales of $80,000. No other asset buildup will be required to service the new accounts.

a. What is the level of accounts receivable to support this sales expansion?
b. What would be Collins's incremental aftertax return on investment?
c. Should Collins liberalize credit if a 15 percent aftertax return on investment is required?

Assume that Collins also needs to increase its level of inventory to support new sales and that inventory turnover is four times.

d. What would be the total incremental investment in accounts receivable and inventory to support a $80,000 increase in sales?
e. Given the income determined in part *b* and the investment determined in part *d*, should Collins extend more liberal credit terms?

12. Curtis Toy Manufacturing Company is evaluating the extension of credit to a new group of customers. Although these customers will

provide $240,000 in additional credit sales, 12 percent are likely to be uncollectible. The company will incur $21,000 in additional collection expenses. Production and marketing expenses represent 72 percent of sales. The company is in a 30 percent tax bracket and has a receivables turnover of six times. No other asset buildup will be required to service the new customers. The firm has a 10 percent desired return on investment.

a. Should Curtis extend credit to these customers?

b. Should credit be extended if 14 percent of the new sales prove uncollectible?

c. Should credit be extended if the receivable turnover drops to 1.5 and 12 percent of the accounts are uncollectible (as was the case in part *a*)?

13. Reconsider problem 12. Assume the average collection period is 120 days. All other factors are the same (including 12 percent uncollectibles). Should credit be extended?

(Problems 14–17 are a series and should be taken in order.)

14. Dome Metals has credit sales of $144,000 yearly with credit terms of net 30 days, which is also the average collection period. Dome does not offer a discount for early payment, so its customers take the full 30 days to pay.

What is the average receivables balance? Receivables turnover?

15. If Dome offered a 2 percent discount for payment in 10 days and every customer took advantage of the new terms, what would the new average receivables balance be? Use the full sales of $144,000 for your calculation of receivables.

16. If Dome reduces its bank loans, which cost 10 percent, by the cash generated from reduced receivables, what will be the net gain or loss to the firm (don't forget the 2 percent discount)? Should it offer the discount?

17. Assume that the new trade terms of 2/10, net 30 will increase sales by 15 percent because the discount makes Dome price competitive. If Dome earns 20 percent on sales before discounts, should it offer the discount? (Consider the same variables as you did for Problems 14 through 16.)

18. (*Comprehensive problem on receivables and inventory policy.*)

Bailey Distributing Company sells small appliances to hardware stores in the southern California area. Michael Bailey, the president of the company, is thinking about changing the credit policies offered by the firm in order to attract customers away from competitors. The current policy calls for a 1/10, net 30, and the new policy would call for a 3/10, net 50. Currently 40 percent of Bailey customers are taking the discount, and it is anticipated that this number would go up to 50 percent with the new discount policy. It is further anticipated that annual sales would increase from a level of $200,000 to $250,000 as a result of the change in the cash discount policy.

The increased sales would also affect the inventory level carried by Bailey. The average inventory carried by Bailey is based on a determination of an *EOQ*. Assume unit sales of small appliances will increase from 20,000 to 25,000 units. The ordering cost for each order is $100 and the carrying cost per unit is $1 (these values will not change with the discount). The average inventory level is based on *EOQ*/2. Each unit in inventory has an average cost of $6.50.

Cost of goods sold is equal to 65 percent of net sales, general and administrative expenses are equal to 10 percent of net sales, and interest payments of 12 percent will only be necessary for the increase in the accounts receivable and inventory balances. Taxes will equal 25 percent of before-tax income.

a. Compute the accounts receivable balance before and after the change in the cash discount policy. Use the net sales (Total sales − Cash discounts) to determine the average daily sales and the accounts receivable balances.

b. Determine *EOQ* before and after the change in the cash discount policy. Translate this into average inventory (in units and dollars) before and after the change in the cash discount policy.

c. Complete the income statement.

	Before Policy Change	After Policy Change
Net sales (sales − cash discounts)		
Cost of goods sold		
Gross profit		
General and administrative expense		
Operating profit		
Interest on increase in accounts receivable and inventory (12%)		
Income before taxes		
Taxes		
Income after taxes		

d. Should the new cash discount policy be utilized? Briefly comment.

Selected References _____

Batlin, C. A., and Susan Hinko. "Lockbox Management and Value Maximization." *Financial Management* 10 (Winter 1981), pp. 39–44.

Baumol, William J. "The Transactions Demand for Cash: An Inventory Theoretic Approach." *Quarterly Journal of Economics* 65 (November 1952), pp. 545–56.

Beman, Lewis. "A Big Payoff from Inventory Controls." *Fortune* 104 (July 27, 1981), pp. 76–80.

Block, Stanley B. "Accounts Receivable as an Investment." *Credit and Financial Management* 76 (May 1974), pp. 32–35, 40.

Brown, Keith C., and Scott L. Lummer. "A Re-examination of the Covered Call Option Strategy for Corporate Cash Management." *Financial Management* 15 (Summer 1986), pp. 13–17.

Cornell, Bradford. "Inflation Measurements, Inflation Risk, and the Pricing of Treasury Bills." *Journal of Financial Research* 39 (Fall 1986), 193–202.

Devine, Matthew E. "Managing a Corporate Short-Term Portfolio." *Cash Management* 7 (May–June 1987), pp. 46–48.

Emery, Gary W. "Some Empirical Evidence on the Properties of Daily Cash Flows." *Financial Management* 10 (Spring 1981), pp. 21–28.

Hofer, C. F. "Analysis of Fixed Costs in Inventory." *Management Accounting* (September 1970), pp. 15–17.

Gallinger, George W., and A. James Ifflander. "Monitoring Accounts Receivables Using Variance Analysis. *Financial Management* 16 (Winter 1987), pp. 69–76.

Gentry, James A., and Jesus M. DeLa Garza. "A Generalized Model for Monitoring Accounts Receivable." *Financial Management* 14 (Winter 1985), pp. 28–38.

Kamath, Ravindra R.; Shahriar Khaksari; Heidi Hylton Meier; and John Winklepleck. "Management of Excess Cash: Practices and Developments." *Financial Management* 14 (Autumn 1985), pp. 70–77.

Kim, Young H.; Joseph C. Atkins; and Walter Dolde. "Evaluating Investments in Accounts Receivable: A Maximizing Framework." *Journal of Finance* 33 (May 1978), pp. 403–12.

Miller, Merton H., and Daniel Orr. "The Demand for Money by Firms: Extension of Analytic Results." *Journal of Finance* 23 (December 1968), pp. 735–59.

———. "A Model of the Demand of Money by Firms." *Quarterly Journal of Economics* 80 (August 1966), pp. 413–35.

Miller, Tom W., and Bernell K. Stone. "Daily Cash Modeling and Seasonal Resolution: Alternative Models and Techniques for Using the Distribution Approach." *Journal of Financial and Quantitative Analysis* 20 (September 1985), pp. 335–51.

Patterson, Harlan R. "New Life in Management of Corporate Receivables." *Credit and Financial Management* 72 (February 1970), pp. 15–18.

Schiff, Michael. "Credit and Inventory Management." *Financial Executive* 40 (November 1972), pp. 28–33.

Zivney, Terry L., and Michael J. Alderson. "Hedged Dividend Capture with Stock Index Options." *Financial Management* 15 (Summer 1986), pp. 5–12.

8

Sources of Short-Term Financing

In Chapter 8 we examine the cost and availability of the various outlets for short-term funds, with primary attention to trade credit from suppliers, bank loans, corporate promissory notes, foreign borrowing, and loans against receivables and inventory. It is sometimes said the only way to be sure a bank loan will be approved is to convince the banker that you don't really need the money. The learning objective of this chapter will be quite the opposite—namely, to demonstrate how badly needed funds can be made available on a short-term basis from the various suppliers of credit.

Trade Credit

The largest provider of short-term credit is usually at the firm's doorstep—the manufacturer or seller of goods and services. Approximately 40 percent of short-term financing is in the form of accounts payable or trade credit. Accounts payable is a spontaneous source of funds, growing as the business expands on a seasonal or long-term basis and contracting in a like fashion.

Payment Period

Trade credit is usually extended for 30 to 60 days. Many firms attempt to "stretch the payment period" in order to provide additional short-term financing. This is an acceptable form of financing as long as it is not carried to an abusive extent. Going from a 30 to a 35-day average payment period may be tolerated within the trade, while stretching payments to 65 days might alienate suppliers and cause a diminishing credit rating with Dun & Bradstreet and local credit bureaus. A major variable in determining the payment period is the possible existence of a cash discount.

Cash Discount Policy

A cash discount allows for a reduction in price if payment is made within a specified time period. A 2/10, net 30 cash discount means that we can deduct 2 percent if we remit our funds 10 days after billing, but failing this, we must pay the full amount by the 30th day.

On a $100 billing, we could pay $98 up to the 10th day or $100 at the end of 30 days. If we fail to take the cash discount, we will get to use $98 for 20 more days at a $2 fee. The cost is a whopping 36.72 percent. Note that we first consider the interest cost and then convert this to an annual basis. The standard formula is:

$$\begin{matrix} \text{Cost of failing} \\ \text{to take a} \\ \text{cash discount} \end{matrix} = \frac{\text{Discount percent}}{100 \text{ percent} - \text{Discount percent}} \times$$

$$\frac{360}{\text{Final due date} - \text{Discount period}} \qquad (8\text{--}1)$$

$$= \frac{2\%}{100\% - 2\%} \times \frac{360}{(30 - 10)}$$

$$= 2.04\% \times 18 = 36.72\%$$

Cash discount terms may vary. For example, on a 2/10, net 90 basis, it would cost us only 9.18 percent not to take the discount and to pay the full amount after 90 days.

$$\frac{2\%}{100\% - 2\%} \times \frac{360}{(90 - 10)} = 2.04\% \times 4.5 = 9.18\%$$

In each case, we must ask ourselves whether bypassing the discount and using the money for a longer period of time is the cheapest means of financing. In the first example, with a cost of 36.72 percent, it probably is not. We would be better off borrowing $98 for 20 days at some lesser rate. For example, at 10 percent interest we would pay 54 cents[1] in interest as opposed to $2 under the cash discount policy. With the 2/10, net 90 arrangement, the cost of missing the discount is only 9.18 percent and we may choose to let our suppliers carry us for an extra 80 days.

Net Credit Position

In Chapter 2, Review of Accounting, we defined accounts receivable as a use of funds and accounts payable as a source of funds. The firm should closely watch the relationship between the two to determine its net credit position. If a firm has average daily sales of $5,000 and collects in 30 days, the accounts receivable balance will be $150,000. If this is associated with average daily purchases of $4,000 and a 25-day average payment period, the average accounts payable balance is $100,000—indicating $50,000 more in credit extended than received. Changing this situation to an average payment period of 40 days increases the accounts payable to $160,000 ($4,000 × 40). Accounts payable now exceeds accounts receivable by $10,000, thus leaving funds for other needs. Larger firms tend to be net providers of trade credit (relatively high receivables), with smaller firms in the user position (relatively high payables).

Bank Credit

Banks may provide funds to finance seasonal needs, product line expansion, and long-term growth. The typical banker prefers a self-liquidating loan in which the use of funds will ensure a built-in or automatic repayment scheme. Actually, two thirds of bank loans are short term in nature. Nevertheless, through the process of renewing old loans, many of these 90- or 180-day agreements take on the characteristics of longer-term financing.

Major changes are taking place in banking today that are centered on the concept of "full-service banking." The modern banker's function is much broader than merely accepting deposits, making loans, and processing checks. At present, a banking institution may be providing trust and investment services, a credit card operation, real estate lending, data

---

[1] $\dfrac{20}{360} \times 10\% \times \$98 = 54¢.$

processing services, and helpful advice in cash management or international trade. This wide array of services has been made possible through the development of the bank holding company—a legal entity in which one key bank owns a number of affiliate banks as well as other non-banking subsidiaries engaged in closely related activities. Additionally, the banking scene today has become more international to accommodate increased world trade and the rise of the international corporation.

In the late 1980s, more banks were engaging in interstate banking activities as legislative barriers came down. Even Illinois, which has been a bastion of unit banks (no statewide branching), has entered into a regional agreement with several neighboring Midwest states to allow interregional banking. Bank deregulation has also created greater competition among financial institutions, such as commercial banks, savings and loans, credit unions, brokerage houses, and new companies offering financial services.

General Electric Corporation is an example of the new type of competition facing the traditional banker. General Electric's financial services group now generates almost 20 percent of General Electric's earnings. The company purchased Kidder Peabody, Inc., an old-line stockbroker and investment banker (investment banking is covered in Chapter 15), and Employers Reinsurance Corporation. In addition, GE Credit has large-scale activities in leasing and asset management. It is diversifying into commercial real estate and corporate financial services and is considered one of the top 10 financial services companies in the United States. GE's large size, combined with its top credit rating, gives it an edge over less creditworthy competitors in raising low-cost funds. The "cost of funds" issue has many traditional bankers worried.

We will look at a number of terms generally associated with banking (and other types of lending activity) and consider the significance of each. Attention is directed to the prime interest rate, compensating balances, the term loan arrangement, and methods of computing interest.

Prime Rate

This is the rate that the bank charges its most creditworthy customers, and it is scaled up proportionally to reflect the various credit classes. At certain slack loan periods in the economy, banks may actually charge top customers less than the published prime rate; however, such activities are difficult to track. The average customer can expect to pay 1 or 2 percent above prime, while in tight money periods a builder in a speculative construction project may pay 5 or more percentage points over prime.

Figure 8–1 presents the annual average prime rate from 1961 through 1987. While the period before 1961 does not show up, it should be pointed out that interest rates in the 1950s and early 1960s were relatively stable, hovering between 3 percent and 5 percent. Beginning in 1965 and continuing into the present, the prime rate has become highly volatile, moving as much as 8 percentage points in a 12-month period. In the early 1980s, the prime rate went above 20 percent for several months (the annual average in 1981 reached 18.87 percent) before sharply declining. With lower inflation from 1982 to 1987, interest rates followed the same pattern, and the prime began 1986 at 9.5 percent and reached 7.5 percent by September 1986 before rebounding to 8.75 percent in December 1987.

Compensating Balances

In providing loans and other services, a bank may require that *business* customers either pay a fee for the service or maintain a minimum average account balance, referred to as a compensating balance. In some cases, both fees and compensating balances will be required. According to a recent survey of over 100 major commercial banks in large cities, the

**Figure 8–1
Pattern of prime
interest rate
movements**

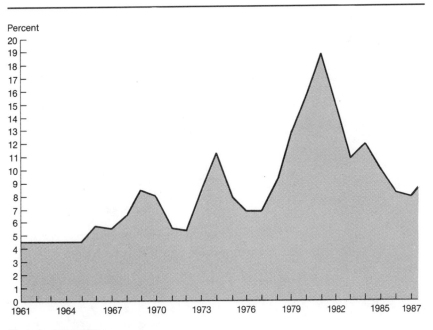

*Annual average rates.
Source: selected Federal Reserve bulletins.

average compensating balance these banks required to offset $100 in service fees was $23,379.[2] For a large company that generates service fees of $100,000, the compensating balance would be $23,379,000.

When compensating balances are required to receive a loan, the required amount is usually computed as a percentage of customer loans outstanding, or as a percentage of bank commitments toward future loans to a given account. A common ratio is 20 percent against outstanding loans or 10 percent against total future commitments, though market conditions tend to influence the percentages.

Some view the compensating balance requirement as an unusual arrangement. Where else would you walk into a business establishment, buy a shipment of goods, and then be told that you could not take 20 percent of the purchase home with you? If you borrow $100,000, paying 8 percent interest on the full amount with a 20 percent compensating balance requirement, you will be paying $8,000 for the use of $80,000 in funds, or an effective rate of 10 percent.

The amount that must be borrowed to end up with the desired sum of money is simply figured by taking the needed funds and dividing by $(1 - c)$, where c is the compensating balance expressed as a decimal. For example, if you need $100,000 in funds, you must borrow $125,000 to ensure that the intended amount will be available. This would be calculated as follows:

$$\text{Amount to be borrowed} = \frac{\text{Amount needed}}{(1 - c)}$$

$$= \frac{\$100,000}{(1 - 0.2)}$$

$$= \$125,000$$

A check on this calculation could be done to see if we actually end up with the use of $100,000

$125,000	Loan
−25,000	20% compensating balance requirement
$100,000	Available funds

The intent here is not to suggest that the compensating balance requirement represents an unfair or hidden cost. If it were not for com-

---

[2]Barry B. Burr, "Services Anything but Uniform," *Pensions & Investment Age*, August 10, 1987, p. CM1.

pensating balances, quoted interest rates would be higher or gratuitous services now offered by banks would carry a price tag.

Of banks responding to a *Pensions & Investment Age* survey, 27 percent of corporate clients paid a fee for cash management services while the other 73 percent eliminated the direct fee with compensating balances.[3] There was a wide variance in fees and compensating balances between banks. As the competition heats up among the providers of financial services, corporations can be expected to selectively shop for high-quality, low-cost institutions.

Maturity Provisions

As previously indicated, bank loans have been traditionally short term in nature (though perhaps renewable). In the last decade there has been a movement to the use of the term loan, in which credit is extended for a period of one to seven years. The loan is usually repaid in monthly or quarterly installments over its life rather than in one single payment. Only superior credit applicants, as measured by working capital strength, potential profitability, and competitive position, can qualify for term loan financing. Here the banker and the business firm are said to be "climbing into bed together" because of the length of the loan.

Bankers are hesitant to fix a single interest rate to a term loan. The more common practice is to allow the interest rate to change with market conditions. Thus the interest rate on a term loan may be tied to the prime rate and will change (float) with it. Perhaps it is set at prime plus 1 percent.

Cost of Commercial Bank Financing

The effective interest rate on a loan is based on the loan amount, the dollar interest paid, the length of the loan, and the method of repayment. It is easy enough to observe that $60 interest on a $1,000 loan for one year would carry a 6 percent interest rate, but what if the same loan were for 120 days? We use the formula:

---

[3] See prior footnote.

$$\text{Effective rate} = \frac{\text{Interest}}{\text{Principal}} \times \frac{\text{Days in the year (360)}}{\text{Days loan is outstanding}} \quad (8\text{--}2)$$

$$= \frac{\$60}{\$1000} \times \frac{360}{120} = 6\% \times 3 = 18\%$$

Since we have use of the funds for only 120 days, the effective rate is 18 percent. To highlight the effect of time, if you borrowed $20 for only ten days and paid back $21, the effective interest rate would be 180 percent—a violation of almost every usury law.

$$\frac{\$1}{\$20} \times \frac{360}{10} = 5\% \times 36 = 180\%$$

Not only is the time dimension of a loan important, but also the way in which interest is charged. We have assumed that interest would be paid when the loan comes due. If the bank deducts the interest in advance (discounts the loan), the effective rate of interest increases. For example, a $1,000 one-year loan with $60 of interest deducted in advance represents the payment of interest on only $940, or an effective rate of 6.38 percent.

$$\begin{aligned} \text{Effective rate on} \atop \text{discounted loan} &= \frac{\text{Interest}}{\text{Principal} - \text{Interest}} \times \\[2mm] &\quad \frac{\text{Days in the year (360)}}{\text{Days loan is outstanding}} \quad (8\text{--}3) \end{aligned}$$

$$= \frac{\$60}{\$1,000 - \$60} \times \frac{360}{360} = \frac{\$60}{\$940} = 6.38\%$$

Interest Costs with Compensating Balances

When a loan is made with compensating balances, the effective interest rate is the stated interest rate divided by $(1 - c)$, where c is the compensating balance expressed as a decimal. Assume that 6 percent is the stated annual rate and that a 20 percent compensating balance is required.

$$\text{Effective rate with} \atop \text{compensating balances} = \frac{\text{Interest rate}}{(1 - c)} \quad (8\text{--}4)$$

$$= \frac{6\%}{(1 - 0.2)}$$

$$= 7.5\%$$

If dollar amounts are used and the stated rate is unknown, Formula 8–5 can be used. The assumption is that we are paying $60 interest on a $1,000 loan, but are only able to use $800 of the funds. The loan is for a year.

$$\begin{array}{l} \text{Effective rate} \\ \text{with} \\ \text{compensating} \\ \text{balances} \end{array} = \frac{\text{Interest}}{\begin{array}{c} \text{Principal} - \text{Compensating} \\ \text{balance in dollars} \end{array}} \times \frac{\begin{array}{c} \text{Days in the} \\ \text{year (360)} \end{array}}{\begin{array}{c} \text{Days loan is} \\ \text{outstanding} \end{array}} \quad (8\text{--}5)$$

$$= \frac{\$60}{\$1,000 - \$200} \times \frac{360}{360} = \frac{\$60}{\$800} = 7.5\%$$

Only when a firm has idle cash balances that can be used to cover compensating balance requirements would the firm not use the higher effective-cost formulas (formulas 8–4 and 8–5).

Rate on Installment Loans

The most confusing borrowing arrangement to the average bank customer or a consumer is the installment loan. An installment loan calls for a series of equal payments over the life of the loan. Though federal legislation prohibits a misrepresentation of interest rates on loans to customers, a loan officer or an overanxious salesperson may quote a rate on an installment loan that is approximately half the true rate.

Assume that you borrow $1,000 on a 12-month installment basis, with regular monthly payments to apply to interest and principal, and that the interest requirement is $60. Though it might be suggested that the rate on the loan is 6 percent, this is clearly not the case. Though you are paying a total of $60 in interest, you do not have the use of $1,000 for one year—rather, you are paying back the $1,000 on a monthly basis, with an average outstanding loan balance for the year of approximately $500. The effective rate of interest is 11.08 percent.

$$\begin{array}{l} \text{Effective} \\ \text{rate on} \\ \text{installment} \\ \text{loan} \end{array} = \frac{2 \times \text{Annual no. of payments} \times \text{Interest}}{(\text{Total no. of payments} + 1) \times \text{Principal}} \quad (8\text{--}6)$$

$$= \frac{2 \times 12 \times \$60}{13 \times \$1,000} = \frac{\$1,440}{\$13,000} = 11.08\%$$

Annual Percentage Rate

Because the many ways that interest is calculated makes the effective rate different from the stated rate, Congress passed the Truth in Lending Act in 1968. This act required that the actual annual percentage rate (APR) be given to the borrower. The APR is really a measure of the effective rate we have presented. Congress was primarily trying to protect the unwary consumer from paying more than the stated rate without his or her knowledge. For example, the stated rate on an installment loan might be 8 percent but the APR might be 14.8 percent. It has always been assumed that businesses should be well versed in business practices and financial matters and, therefore, the Truth in Lending Act was not intended to protect business borrowers but, rather, individuals.

The annual percentage rate requires the use of the actuarial method of compounded interest when calculating the APR. This requires knowledge of the time value of money techniques presented in Chapter 9. For our purposes in this chapter, it is enough to know that the lender must calculate interest for the period on the outstanding loan balance at the beginning of the period. Any payments are first credited against interest due, and any amount left is used to reduce the principal or loan balance. Because there are so many ways to structure loan repayment schedules, no one formula is applicable for computing the APR. For example, loans do not all have 365 days—some have only 10 or 15 days or other portions of a year.

Since most consumer loans are installment types, the APR is usually based upon the assumption of amortization. Amortization assumes that an equal dollar amount is paid each period to retire principal and interest. According to the law, a loan amortization schedule is the final authority in the calculation of the APR. The amortization schedule always has an annual percentage rate that diminishes the principal to zero over the loan period. You will learn how to develop an amortization schedule in Chapter 9.

The Credit Crunch Phenomenon

In 1969–70, 1973–74, and 1979–81, the economy went through a period of extreme credit shortage in the banking sector and other financial markets. We seem to find ourselves in the midst of a tight money situation every three to five years. The anatomy of a credit crunch is as follows. The Federal Reserve tightens the growth in the money supply in its battle against inflation, causing a decrease in lendable funds and an increase in interest rates. To compound the difficulty, business requirements for funds may be increasing to carry inflation-laden inventory and receivables. A third problem is the massive withdrawal of savings deposits at our banking and thrift institutions, all in search of higher returns. There simply are not enough lendable funds to "go around."

Recent history has taught us that the way *not* to deal with credit short-ages is to impose artificial limits on interest rates in the form of restrictive usury laws or extreme governmental pressure. In 1969–70, the prime rate went to 8.5 percent in a tight money period—a level not high enough to bring the forces of demand and supply together, and little credit was available. In 1974, the prime rose to 12 percent, a rate truly reflecting market conditions, and funds were available. The same was true in 1980 and 1981 as the prime went to 20 percent and higher, but lendable funds were available.

In 1979, the Federal Reserve began putting increasing emphasis on "attempting" to control the rate of growth in the money supply at a steady pace and allowing interest rates to move freely. This helps to explain part of the volatility in interest rates during the late 70s and early 80s. However, during the 1982–87 period, the Fed has kept money supply growth quite volatile while emphasizing stable to lower interest rates over time. With Alan Greenspan, the new chairman of the Board of Governors of the Federal System, at the head, no one can be sure what future Fed policy will be, based upon past behavior.

Financing through Commercial Paper

For large and prestigious firms, commercial paper may provide an outlet for raising funds. Commercial paper represents a short-term, unsecured promissory note issued to the public in minimum units of $25,000. As Figure 8–2 indicates, the total amount of commercial paper outstanding has increased dramatically, rising from $83 billion in 1978 to over $360 billion in 1987. This large increase in the commercial paper market reflects the willingness of qualified companies to borrow at the lowest rate available. The larger market that has emerged in the last five years has improved the ability of corporations to raise short-term funds.

Commercial paper falls into two categories. First, there are finance companies, such as General Motors Acceptance Corporation (GMAC), General Electric Credit, and CIT Financial Corporation, that issue paper primarily to institutional investors such as pension funds, insurance companies, and money market mutual funds. It is probably the growth of

Figure 8–2
Total commercial
paper outstanding

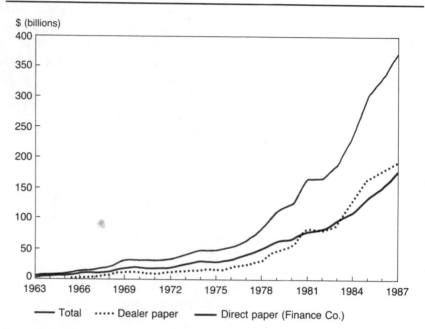

$ (billions)

Total ·····Dealer paper Direct paper (Finance Co.)

Source: Federal Reserve bulletins, *Business Statistics*.

money market mutual funds that has had such a great impact on the ability of companies to sell such an increased amount of commercial paper in the market. Paper sold by financial firms such as GMAC is referred to as *finance paper*, and since it is usually sold directly to the lender by the finance company, it is also referred to as *direct paper*. The second type of commercial paper is sold by industrial companies, utility firms, or finan- cial companies too small to have their own selling network. These firms use an intermediate dealer network to distribute their paper and so this type of paper is referred to as *dealer paper*.

Traditionally commercial paper is just that. A paper certificate is issued to the lender to signify the lender's claim to be repaid. This certificate could be lost, stolen, misplaced, or damaged and, in rare cases, someone could fail to cash it in at maturity. There is a growing trend among companies that sell commercial paper directly to computerize the handling of commercial paper with what is called *book-entry transactions*, in which no actual certificate is created. All transactions simply take place on the books. The use of computer-based electronic issuing methods lowers cost and simplifies administration, as well as linking the lender or lender's bank and the issuing company. General Motors Acceptance Corporation, the largest single issuer of commercial paper, has been a heavy user of the book entry method and currently has over 40 percent of its $31 billion commercial paper in this form. As the market becomes more accustomed to this electronic method, large users ($500 million or more) will likely find it profitable to switch from physical paper to the book entry system, where all transfers of money are done by wiring cash between lenders and commercial paper issuers.

Advantages of Commercial Paper

The growing popularity of commercial paper can be attributed to other factors besides the rapid growth of money market mutual funds and their need to find short-term securities for investment. For example, commercial paper may be issued at below the prime interest. As indicated in the last column of Table 8–1, this rate differential reached over 5 percent in the tight money markets of 1981.

A second advantage of commercial paper is that no compensating balance requirements are associated with its issuance, though the firm is generally required to maintain commercial bank lines of approved credit equal to the amount of the paper outstanding (a procedure somewhat less costly than compensating balances). Finally, a number of firms enjoy the prestige associated with being able to float their commercial paper in what is considered a "snobbish market" for funds.

Limitations on the Issuance of Commercial Paper

The commercial paper market is not without its problems. When the Penn Central Railroad went bankrupt in 1970 with its $85 million in "bad" commercial paper floating around, many lenders in the market panicked and refused to roll over (renew) existing paper as it came due. The market shrank by 15 percent from May to December, and the unnerving situation almost caused Chrysler Financial Corporation to be towed away.

The lesson to be learned is that although the funds provided through the issuance of commercial paper are cheaper than bank loans, they are also less predictable. Although a firm may pay a higher rate for a bank loan, it is also buying a degree of loyalty and commitment that is unavailable in the commercial paper market.

Table 8–1
Comparison of
commercial paper
rate to bank prime
rate (annual rate)*

Year	Finance Co. Paper (directly placed) 4–6 months	Other Paper (dealer-placed) 4–6 months	Average Bank Prime Rate	Prime Rate Minus Dealer Paper
1961	2.97	2.68	4.50	1.82
1962	3.26	3.07	4.50	1.43
1963	3.55	3.40	4.50	1.10
1964	3.97	3.83	4.50	0.67
1965	4.38	4.27	4.50	0.23
1966	5.55	5.42	5.75	0.33
1967	5.10	4.89	5.50	0.61
1968	5.90	5.69	6.50	0.81
1969	7.83	7.16	8.50	1.34
1970	7.72	7.20	8.00	0.80
1971	5.11	4.89	5.50	0.61
1972	4.59	4.55	5.25	0.70
1973	8.15	7.38	8.30	0.92
1974	9.84	8.61	11.12	2.51
1975	6.32	6.16	7.86	1.70
1976	5.35	5.22	6.84	1.62
1977	5.60	5.50	6.82	1.32
1978	7.99	7.78	9.06	1.28
1979	10.91	10.25	12.67	2.42
1980	12.29	11.28	15.27	3.99
1981	14.76	13.73	18.87	5.14
1982	11.89	11.20	14.86	3.66
1983	8.89	8.69	10.79	2.10
1984	10.16	9.65	12.04	2.39
1985	8.11	7.81	9.93	2.12
1986	6.31	6.39	8.33	1.94
1987	6.37	6.85	8.50	1.65

*Averages for the year.
Source: Federal Reserve bulletins. *Business Statistics.*

Foreign Borrowing

An increasing source of funds for U.S. firms has been the large Eurodollar market. Loans from foreign banks denominated in dollars are called Eurodollar loans. Such loans are usually short term to intermediate term in maturity. Many multinational corporations are finding cheaper ways of borrowing in foreign markets. A new approach has been for financial managers to borrow *foreign currencies* either directly or through foreign subsidiaries at very favorable interest rates. The companies *convert* the borrowed francs or marks to dollars, which are then sent to the United States to be used by the parent company. There is, however, foreign exchange exposure risk associated with these loans. This topic is given greater coverage in Chapter 21.

As an example of an international loan, IBM arranged a seven-year loan in Swiss francs at an interest rate of 6 percent at a time when the prime rate in the United States was 19 percent. Because of the different financial practices in foreign countries, the differential is not as great as it seems, but this did save IBM several percent in borrowing costs. A foreign subsidiary of a large U.S. drug and medical supply company borrowed from its foreign banks at rates below prevailing U.S. interest rates and then loaned the money back to its parent firm. These examples simply show that the world financial markets have become more sophisticated, and so must financial managers.

Use of Collateral in Short-Term Financing

Almost any firm would prefer to borrow on an unsecured (no-collateral) basis; but if the borrower's credit rating is too low or its need for funds too great, the lending institution will require that certain assets be pledged. A secured credit arrangement might help the borrower to obtain funds that would otherwise be unavailable.

In any loan the lender's primary concern, however, is whether the borrower's capacity to generate cash flow is sufficient to liquidate the loan as it comes due. Few lenders would make a loan strictly on the basis of collateral. Collateral is merely a stopgap device to protect the lender when all else fails. The bank or finance company is in business to collect interest, not to repossess and resell assets.

Though a number of different types of assets may be pledged, our attention will be directed to accounts receivable and inventory. All states have now adopted the Uniform Commercial Code, which standardizes and simplifies the procedures for establishing the security on a loan.

Accounts Receivable Financing

Accounts receivable financing may include *pledging* accounts receivable as collateral for a loan or an outright *sale* (factoring) of receivables. Receivables financing is popular because it permits borrowing to be tied directly to the level of asset expansion at any point in time. As the level of accounts receivable goes up, we are able to borrow more.

A drawback is that this is a relatively expensive method of acquiring funds, so that it must be carefully compared to other forms of credit. Accounts receivable represent one of the firm's most valuable short-term assets, and they should be committed only where the appropriate circumstances exist. An ill-advised accounts receivable financing plan may exclude the firm from a less expensive bank term loan. Let us investigate more closely the characteristics and the costs associated with the pledging and selling of receivables.

Pledging Accounts Receivable

The lending institution will generally stipulate which of the accounts receivable are of sufficient quality to serve as collateral for a loan. On this basis, we may borrow 60–80 percent of the value of the acceptable collateral. The loan percentage will depend on the financial strength of the borrowing firm and on the creditworthiness of its accounts. The lender will have full recourse against the borrower in the event that any of the accounts go bad. The interest rate in a receivables borrowing arrangement is generally well in excess of the prime rate.

The interest is computed against the loan balance outstanding, a figure that may change quite frequently, as indicated in Table 8–2. In the illustration, interest is assumed to be 12 percent annually, or 1 percent per month. In month 1, we are able to borrow $8,000 against $10,000 in acceptable receivables and we must pay $80 in interest. Similar values are developed for succeeding months.

Table 8–2
Receivable loan balance

	Month 1	Month 2	Month 3	Month 4
Total accounts receivable	$11,000	$15,100	$19,400	$16,300
Acceptable accounts receivable (to finance company)	10,000	14,000	18,000	15,000
Loan balance (80%)	8,000	11,200	14,400	12,000
Interest 12% annual—1% per month	80	112	144	120

Factoring Receivables

When we factor our receivables, they are sold outright to the finance company. Our customers may be instructed to remit the proceeds directly to the purchaser of the account. The factoring firm generally does not have recourse against the seller of the receivables. As a matter of practice, the finance company may do part or all of the credit analysis directly to ensure the quality of the accounts. As a potential sale is being made, the factoring firm may give immediate feedback to the seller on whether the account will be purchased.

When the factoring firm accepts an account, it may forward funds immediately to the seller, in anticipation of receiving payment 30 days later as part of the normal billing process. The factoring firm is not only absorbing risk, but is actually advancing funds to the seller a month earlier than the seller would normally receive them.

For taking the risk, the factoring firm is generally paid on a fee or commission basis equal to 1 to 3 percent of the invoices accepted. In addition, it is paid a lending rate for advancing the funds early. If $100,000 a *month* is processed at a 1 percent commission and a 12 percent annual borrowing rate, the total effective cost will be 24 percent on an *annual* basis.

1%	Commission
1%	Interest for one month (12% annual/12)
2%	Total fee monthly
2%	Monthly × 12 = 24% annual rate

If one considers that the firm selling the accounts is transferring risk as well as receiving funds early, which may allow it to take cash discounts, the rate may not be considered exorbitant. Also, the firm is able to pass on much of the credit-checking cost to the factor.

Asset-Backed Public Offerings

A new wrinkle in accounts receivable financing is the sale of receivables by large firms in public offerings. While factoring has long been one way of selling receivables, public offerings of securities backed by receivables as collateral gained respectability when General Motors Acceptance Corporation made a public offering of $500 million of asset-backed securities in December of 1985.

These asset-backed securities are nothing more than the sale of receivables. In former years, companies that sold receivables were viewed as short of cash, financially shaky, or in some sort of financial trouble. This negative perception has been diminished by new issues of receivables-backed securities by such companies as Unisys (computer receivables), Bank of America (credit-card receivables), GMAC (car-loan receivables), and Mack Truck (truck-loan receivables). In the two years 1986 and 1987, the outstanding balance on these asset-backed financings soared from a little more than $1 billion to over $12 billion. This phenomenal growth shows no immediate sign of stopping, and investment bankers who package and sell these securities are optimistic that any loan with predictable cash flows can be sold to investors in some sort of asset-backed security.

One of the benefits to the issuer is that they trade future cash flows for immediate cash. The asset-backed security is likely to carry a high credit rating of AA or better, even when the issuing firm may have a low credit rating. This allows the issuing firm to acquire lower cost funds than it could with a bank loan or a bond offering. While this short-term market is still relatively small by money market standards, it could provide an important avenue for corporate liquidity and short-term financing.

There are also several problems facing the public sale of receivables. Computer systems need to be upgraded to service securities and handle the paperwork. For GMAC to offer such a large public issue, it had to change its whole data processing system to keep track of the loans for the investors in the securities. A second consideration for the buyer of these securities is the probability that the receivable will actually be paid. Even though the loss rates on loans were about one half of 1 percent in the 1980s, bad debts can be as much as 5 to 10 percent in tight money markets.[4] For example, a serious recession might cause many car owners to default on their car payments to GMAC and thus leave the owners of the asset-backed security without the promised cash flows. To counteract these fears, many issuers set up a loan-loss reserve fund to partially insure the probability of loss. In markets this new, only time will tell what the future growth will be.

Figure 8–3 shows the 1987 issue by Mack Trucks for $215,140,000 of TRUCS (truck receivables underlying certificates). Notice that these securities are short-term, having one year and five years to maturity.

Inventory Financing

We may also borrow against inventory to acquire funds. The extent to which inventory financing may be employed is based on the marketability of the pledged goods, their associated price stability, and the perishability of the product. Another significant factor is the degree of physical control that can be exercised over the product by the lender. We can relate some of these factors to the stages of inventory production and the nature of lender control.

---

[4]Ann Monroe, "Sales of Receivables by Big Firms Gain Respect in Public Offerings," *The Wall Street Journal*, December 2, 1985, p. 41.

Figure 8–3

$215,140,000

Mack Trucks Receivables Corporation

Truck Receivables Underlying Certificates
TRUCS℠ Series 1

Collateralized by Truck and Other Commercial Vehicle Receivables

$103,685,000   7.15% Class 1-A Notes Due June 15, 1988

Price 99.9925%

$111,455,000   8.05% Class 1-B Notes Due June 15, 1992

Price 100%

(Plus accrued interest at the applicable rate from June 15, 1987)

Copies of the Prospectus and the related Prospectus Supplement may be obtained only from
the undersigned in any State where the undersigned may lawfully offer the securities.

Shearson Lehman Brothers Inc.   Lazard Frères & Co.

July 7, 1987

Stages of Production

Raw materials and finished goods are likely to provide the best collateral, while goods in process may only qualify for a small percentage loan. To the extent that a firm is holding such widely traded raw materials as lumber, metals, grain, cotton, and wool, a loan of 70–80 percent or higher is possible. The lender may only have to place a few quick phone calls to dispose of the goods at market value if the borrower fails to repay the loan. For standardized finished goods, such as tires, canned goods, and building products, the same principle would apply. Goods in process, representing altered but unfinished raw materials, may qualify for a loan of only one fourth their value or less.

Nature of Lender Control

The methods for controlling pledged inventory go from the simple to the complex, providing ever greater assurances to the lender but progressively higher administrative costs.

Blanket inventory liens   The simplest method is for the lender to have a general claim against the inventory of the borrower. Specific items are not identified or tagged, and there is no physical control.

Trust receipts   A trust receipt is an instrument acknowledging that the borrower holds the inventory and proceeds from sales in trust for the lender. Each item is carefully marked and specified by serial number. When sold, the proceeds are transferred to the lender and the trust receipt is cancelled. Also known as *floor planning*, this financing device is very popular among auto and industrial equipment dealers and in the television and home appliance industries. Although it provides tighter control than does the blanket inventory lien, it still does not give the lender direct control over inventory—only a better and more legally enforceable system of tracing the goods.

Warehousing   Under this arrangement, goods are physically identified, segregated, and stored under the direction of an independent warehousing company. The firm issues a warehouse receipt to the lender, and goods can be moved only with the lender's approval.

   The goods may be stored on the premises of the warehousing firm, an arrangement known as *public warehousing*, or on the *borrower's premises—* under a *field warehousing* agreement. When field warehousing is utilized, it is still an independent warehousing company that exercises control over inventory.

Appraisal of Inventory Control Devices

While the more structured methods of inventory financing appear somewhat restrictive, they are well accepted in certain industries. For example, field warehousing is popular in grain storage and food canning. Well-maintained control measures do involve substantial administrative expenses, and they raise the overall costs of borrowing. The costs of inventory financing may run 15 percent or higher. As is true of accounts receivable financing, the extension of funds is well synchronized with the need.

Hedging to Reduce Borrowing Risk _____

Those who are in continual need of borrowed funds for the operations of their firm are exposed to the risk of interest rate changes. One way to partially reduce that risk is through interest rate hedging activities in the financial futures market. Hedging means to engage in a transaction that partially or fully reduces a prior risk exposure.

The financial futures market is set up to allow for the trading of a financial instrument at a future point in time. For example, in January of 1989, one might sell a Treasury bond contract that is to be closed out in June of 1989. The sales price of the June 1989 contract is established by the initial January transaction. However, a subsequent purchase of a June 1989 contract at a currently unknown price will be necessary to close out the transaction. In the futures market, you do not physically deliver the goods; you merely execute a later transaction that reverses your initial position. Thus, if you initially sell a futures contract, you later buy a contract that covers your initial sale. If you initially buy a futures contract, the opposite is true and you later sell a contract that covers your initial purchase position.

In the case of selling a Treasury bond futures contract, the subsequent pattern of interest rates will determine whether it is profitable or not. If interest rates go up, Treasury bond prices will go down and you will be able to buy a subsequent contract at a lower price than the sales value you initially established. This will result in a profitable transaction. Note the following example.

Sales price, June 1989 Treasury bond contract[5]
(sale takes place in January 1989) $95,000
Purchase price, June 1989 Treasury bond contract
(the purchase takes place in June 1989) 90,000
Profit on futures contract . . . . $ 5,000

The reason Treasury bond prices went down is that, as previously mentioned, interest rates and bond prices move in opposite directions, and interest rates went up. The lesson to be learned from this example is that rising interest rates can mean profits in the financial futures market if you initially sell a contract and later buy it back.

The financial manager who continually needs to borrow money and fears changes in interest rates can partially hedge his or her position by engaging in the type of futures contract described above. If interest rates do rise, the extra cost of borrowing money to actually finance the business can be offset by the profit on a futures contract. If interest rates go down, there will be a loss on the futures contract as bond prices go up, but this

---

[5]Only a small percentage of the actual dollars involved must be invested to initiate the contract. This is known as margin.

will be offset by the more desirable lower borrowing costs of financing the firm.

The financial futures market can be used to partially or fully hedge against almost any financial event. In addition to Treasury bonds, trades may be initiated in Treasury bills, certificates of deposits, GNMA certificates[6] and many other instruments.[7] The trades may be executed on such exchanges as the Chicago Board of Trade, the Chicago Mercantile Exchange, or the New York Futures Exchange.

Summary

A firm in search of short-term financing must be aware of all the institutional arrangements that are available. The easiest access is to trade credit provided by suppliers as a natural outgrowth of the buying and reselling of goods. Larger firms tend to be net providers of trade credit, while smaller firms are net users.

Bank financing is usually in the form of short-term, self-liquidating loans. A financially strong customer will be offered the prime, or lowest rate, with the rates to other accounts scaled up appropriately. The use of compensating balances tends to increase the effective yield to the bank and serves as a device to compensate the bank for the many services it provides to a commercial account.

An alternative to bank credit for the large, prestigious firm is the use of commercial paper. Though generally issued at a rate below prime, it is an impersonal means of financing that may "dry up" during difficult financing periods.

Firms are also turning to foreign sources of funds, either through the Eurodollar market (foreign dollar loans) or through borrowing foreign currency directly.

By using a secured form of financing, the firm ties its borrowing requirements directly to its asset buildup. We may pledge our accounts receivable as collateral or sell them outright, as well as borrow against inventory. Though secured-asset financing devices may be expensive, they may well fit the credit needs of the firm, particularly those of a small firm that cannot qualify for premium bank financing or the commercial paper market.

---

[6]GNMA stands for Government National Mortgage Association, also known as Ginnie Mae.

[7]For a more complete discussion of corporate hedging in the futures market, see "Commodities and Financial Futures" in Chapter 15 of Geoffrey Hirt and Stanley Block, *Fundamentals of Investment Management*, 2nd ed. (Homewood, Ill.: Richard D. Irwin, 1986).

Finally, the financial manager may wish to consider the use of hedging through the financial futures market. The consequences of rapid interest rate changes can be reduced through participation in the financial futures market.

Review of Formulas

1. Cost of failing to take a cash discount

$$= \frac{\text{Discount percent}}{100 \text{ percent} - \text{Discount percent}} \times$$

$$\frac{360}{\text{Final due date} - \text{Discount period}} \qquad (8\text{--}1)$$

2. Amount of funds to be borrowed to meet needs under compensating balances

$$= \frac{\text{Amount needed}}{(1 - c)}$$

c is compensating balance requirement expressed as a decimal.

3. Effective rate on a loan

$$= \frac{\text{Interest}}{\text{Principal}} \times \frac{\text{Days in the year}}{\text{Days loan is outstanding}} \qquad (8\text{--}2)$$

4. Effective rate on a *discounted* loan

$$= \frac{\text{Interest}}{\text{Principal} - \text{Interest}} \times$$

$$\frac{\text{Days in the year } (360)}{\text{Days loan is outstanding}} \qquad (8\text{--}3)$$

5. Effective loan rate with compensating balances

$$= \frac{\text{Interest rate}}{(1 - c)} \qquad (8\text{--}4)$$

c is compensating balance requirement expressed as a decimal.

6. Effective loan rate with compensating balances (based on dollar values)

$$= \frac{\text{Interest}}{\text{Principal} - \text{Compensating balance in dollars}} \times$$

$$\frac{\text{Days in the year } (360)}{\text{Days loan is outstanding}} \qquad (8\text{--}5)$$

7. Effective loan rate on an installment loan $= \dfrac{2 \times \text{Annual no. of payments} \times \text{Interest}}{(\text{Total no. of payments} + 1) \times \text{Principal}}$ (8–6)

List of Terms

spontaneous sources of funds
net trade credit
self-liquidating loan
prime rate
compensating balances
term loan
commercial paper
installment loan
Eurodollar loan
discounted loan

annual percentage rate (APR)
factoring receivables
asset-backed public offerings
pledging receivables
blanket inventory liens
trust receipt
public warehousing
field warehousing
financial futures market
hedging

Discussion Questions

1. Under what circumstances would it be advisable to borrow money to take a cash discount?

2. Discuss the relative use of credit between large and small firms. Which group is generally in the net creditor position, and why?

3. What is the prime interest rate? How does the average bank customer fare in regard to the prime interest rate? Are companies ever allowed by banks to borrow at less than prime?

4. What advantages do compensating balances have for banks? Are the advantages to banks necessarily disadvantages to corporations?

5. A borrower is often confronted with a stated interest rate and an effective interest rate. What is the difference, and which one should the financial manager recognize as the true cost of borrowing?

6. Commercial paper may show up on corporate balance sheets as either a current asset or a current liability. Explain this statement.

7. What are the advantages of commercial paper in comparison with bank borrowing at the prime rate? What are the disadvantages?

8. Discuss the major types of collateralized short-term loans.

9. What is an asset-backed public offering?

10. What is meant by hedging in the financial futures market to offset interest-rate risks?

Problems

1. Your bank will lend you $2,000 for 45 days at a cost of $25 interest. What is your effective rate of interest?

2. Compute the cost of not taking the following trade discounts.
   a. 2/10, net 40.
   b. 2/15, net 30.
   c. 2/10, net 45.
   d. 3/10, net 180.

3. Dr. Sixkiller is going to borrow $3,000 for one year at 12 percent interest. What is the effective rate of interest if the loan is discounted?

4. Carey Company is borrowing $200,000 for one year at 12 percent from Second Intrastate Bank. The bank requires a 20 percent compensating balance. What is the effective rate of interest? What would the effective rate be if Carey were required to make twelve equal monthly payments to retire the loan? The principal, as used in Formula 8–6, refers to funds the firm can effectively utilize (amount borrowed – compensating balance).

5. Douglas Corporation is borrowing $150,000 for one year at 10 percent from the Corpus Christi State Bank. There is a 20 percent compensating balance requirement. Douglas Corporation keeps minimum transactions balances of $7,500 in the normal course of business. These idle cash balances count toward meeting the compensating balance requirement. What is the effective rate of interest?

6. Spicer Corporation plans to borrow $100,000. Northwest Bank will lend the money at 0.5 percent over the prime rate of 11.5 percent (12 percent total) and requires a compensating balance of 20 percent. What is the effective rate of interest? What would the effective rate be if Spicer were required to make four quarterly payments to retire the loan? Principal in this case refers to funds that the firm can effectively use in the business.

7. Your company needs to borrow $5 million for 12 months, and your banker gives you a stated rate of 14 percent interest. You would like

to know the effective rate of interest for the following types of loans. (Each of the following parts stands alone.)
a. Simple 14 percent interest with a 10 percent compensating balance.
b. Discounted interest.
c. An installment loan (12 payments).
d. Discounted interest with a 5 percent compensating balance.

8. Vroom Motorcycle Company is borrowing $30,000 from First State Bank. The total interest charge is $9,000. The loan will be paid by making equal monthly payments for the next three years. What is the effective rate of interest on this installment loan?

9. If you borrow $3,000 at $250 interest for one year, what is your effective interest cost for the following payment plans:
a. Annual payment.
b. Semiannual payments.
c. Quarterly payments.
d. Monthly payments.

10. Mr. Roland is a very cautious businessman. His suppliers offer trade credit terms of 3/10, net 90. Mr. Roland never takes the discount offered, but he pays his suppliers in 80 days rather than the 90 days allowed so he is sure the payments are never late. What is Mr. Roland's cost of not taking the discount?

11. The Beeler Corporation buys from its suppliers on terms of 2/10, net 45. Beeler has not been taking the discount offered and has been taking 60 days to pay its bills. The suppliers seem to accept this payment pattern, and Beeler's credit rating has not been adversely affected.

   Mr. Carson, a Beeler Corporation vice president, has suggested that the company begin to take the discount offered. In order to do this, Carson is proposing that the company borrow from its bank at a stated rate of 12 percent. The bank requires a 25 percent compensating balance on these loans. Current account balances would not be available to meet any of this compensating balance requirement.

   Do you agree with Mr. Carson's proposal?

12. In problem 11, if the compensating balance requirement were 10 percent instead of 25 percent, would you change your answer? Do the appropriate calculation.

13. Bosworth Petroleum needs $500,000 to take a cash discount of 2/10, net 70. A banker will loan the money for 60 days at an interest cost of $8,100.

a. What is the effective rate on the bank loan?
b. How much would it cost (in percentage terms) if Bosworth did not take the cash discount, but paid the bill in 70 days instead of 10 days?
c. Should Bosworth borrow the money to take the discount?
d. If the banker requires a 20 percent compensating balance, how much must Bosworth borrow to end up with the $500,000?
e. What would be the effective interest rate in part *d* if the interest charge for 60 days were $13,000? Should Bosworth borrow with the 20 percent compensating balance? (He has no funds to count against the compensating balance requirement.)

14. Ajax Box Company is negotiating with two banks for a $100,000 loan.
   Midland Bank requires a 20 percent compensating balance, discounts the loan, and wants to be paid back in four quarterly payments. Central Bank requires a 10 percent compensating balance, does not discount the loan, but wants to be paid back in 12 monthly installments. The stated rate for both banks is 8 percent. Compensating balances will be subtracted from the $100,000 in determining the available funds in part *a*.
   a. Which loan should Ajax accept?
   b. Recompute the effective cost of interest, assuming that Ajax ordinarily maintains at each bank $20,000 in deposits which will serve as compensating balances.
   c. How much did the compensating balances inflate your interest costs? Does your choice of banks change if the assumption in part *b* is correct?

15. Ewing Oil Supplies sells to the 12 accounts listed below.

Account	Receivable Balance Outstanding	Average Age of the Account over the Last Year
A	$ 50,000	35
B	80,000	25
C	120,000	47
D	10,000	15
E	250,000	35
F	60,000	51
G	40,000	18
H	180,000	60
I	15,000	43
J	25,000	33
K	200,000	41
L	60,000	28

J&R Financial Corporation will lend 90 percent against account balances that have averaged 30 days or less; 80 percent for account balances between 30 and 40 days; and 70 percent for account balances between 40 and 45 days. Customers that take over 45 days to pay their bills are not considered as adequate accounts for a loan.

The current prime rate is 12 percent, and J&R Financial Corporation charges 3 percent over prime to Ewing Oil Supplies as its annual loan rate.

  a. Determine the maximum loan for which Ewing Oil Supplies could qualify.

  b. Determine how much one month's interest expense would be on the loan balance determined in part *a.*

16. The vice president of finance for Global Supplies wishes to use financial futures to hedge her interest rate exposure. She will sell five Treasury futures contracts at $92,000 per contract. It is July and the contracts must be closed out in December of this year. Long-term interest rates are currently 10.5 percent. If they increase to 12 percent, assume the value of the contracts will go down by 10 percent. Also, if interest rates do increase by 1.5 percent, assume the firm will have additional interest expense on its business loans and other commitments of $49,500. This expense, of course, is separate from the futures contracts.

  a. What will be the profit or loss on the futures contract if interest rates go to 12 percent?

  b. Explain why a profit or loss took place on the futures contracts.

  c. After considering the hedging in part *a*, what is the net cost to the firm of the increased interest expense of $49,500? What percent of this increased cost did the treasurer effectively hedge away?

  d. Indicate whether there would be a profit or loss on the futures contracts if interest rates went down.

Selected References _____

Crane, Dwight B., and William L. White. "Who Benefits from a Floating Prime Rate." *Harvard Business Review* 50 (January–February 1972), pp. 121–29.

Dennon, Lester E. "The Security Agreement." *Journal of Commercial Bank Lending* 50 (February 1968), pp. 32–40.

Hawkins, Gregory D. "An Analysis of Revolving Credit Agreements." *Journal of Financial Economics* 59 (March 1982), pp. 59–81.

Hirt, Geoffrey A., and Stanley B. Block. *Fundamentals of Investment Management,* 2nd. ed. Homewood, Ill.: Richard D. Irwin, 1986.

James, Christopher. "An Analysis of Bank Loan Indexation." *Journal of Finance* 37 (June 1982), pp. 809–25.

Kolb, Robert W., and Raymond Chiang. "Improving Performance Using Interest-Rate Futures." *Financial Management* 10 (Autumn 1981), pp. 72–79.

Monroe, Ann. "Sales of Receivables by Big Firms Gain Respect in Public Offerings." *The Wall Street Journal*, December 2, 1985, p. 41.

Nadler, Paul S. "Compensating Balances and the Prime at Twilight." *Harvard Business Review* 50 (January–February 1972), pp. 112–20.

Peterik, Paul. "Getting by Your Banker: Tips on How to Come Away with the Loan." *Cash Flow* 8 (January 1987), pp. 31–35.

Schwartz, Robert A. "An Economic Model of Trade Credit." *Journal of Financial and Quantitative Analysis* 9 (September 1974), pp. 643–58.

Smith, Janet K. "Trade Credit and Information Asymmetry." *Journal of Finance* 42 (September 1987), pp. 863–72.

P A R T

4

The Capital Budgeting Process

9 The Time Value of Money

10 Valuation and Rates of Return

11 Cost of Capital

12 The Capital Budgeting Decision

13 Risk and Capital Budgeting

Introduction _____

A capital budgeting decision is one that involves the allocation of funds to projects that will have a life of at least one year and usually much longer. Examples might include the development of a major new product, a plant site location, or an equipment replacement decision. Because we may be locked into our decision for 10–20 years and large sums of money are usually involved, the capital budgeting decision must be approached with great care. Basic capital budgeting decisions determine whether there is under- or overcapacity in a given firm or within an industry. The problem has been complicated by the introduction of nonprofitable, but at times necessary, government regulations for pollution control and safety provisions.

The capital budgeting decision is of interest not only to students of finance, but also to those who desire careers in accounting, marketing, production management, and a number of other areas. Whether the marketing manager gets a new product approved for production and distribution may be a function of how well he or she provides data into the capital budgeting process and understands the analysis.

Because the capital budgeting process is long term in nature, we must develop a methodology for translating future inflows and outflows to the present. Thus, our first step will be to consider the time value of money in Chapter 9. Our understanding of compound sum, present value, annuities, and yields allows us to move back and forth between the future and the present. The student may be particularly interested in the extensive summary and review material at the end of the chapter.

We then move to the topic of valuation of sources of financing in Chapter 10. By understanding what measures investors use to determine required rates of return and current values for bonds, preferred stock, and common stock, we are also considering what the corporation must pay for these funds. The chapter on valuation thus naturally extends into the next chapter on cost of capital (financing) to the firm. As described in Chapter 11, the cost of capital represents the weighted cost of the various sources of financing to the firm and is generally a minimum standard for accepting an investment. The capital asset pricing model, an analytical approach to relating individual asset returns to market returns, is considered briefly in Chapter 11 and is also covered on an optional basis in Appendix 11A.

In Chapter 12 we bring together the concepts of time value of money and cost of capital to develop actual investment decisions. Though a number of methods of evaluating capital investments are discussed, such as the payback method and the internal rate of return method, the primary emphasis is on the net present value method. Here we discount future flows from an investment at the cost of capital to see whether they equal or exceed the required investment. If the answer is positive, we know that we have earned the cost of financing the project. Because these investment decisions depend upon the aftertax cash flow-generating capability of a project, the tax impact is carefully considered (particularly the effect of the Tax Reform Act of 1986).

In Chapter 13 we study risk in the capital budgeting decision process. Most managers and investors are risk averse—that is, all things being equal, they would prefer a certain predictable outcome of 10 percent, rather than a 50–50 chance of going broke or doubling their money (this is an extreme case). To reflect these preferences we incorporate a penalty for large risk in our decision-making process. A more risky investment may have to provide a higher return than a less risky investment. Since the objective of financial management is to maximize the market value of the firm and the wealth of its shareholders, we must determine the appropriate mix of profitability and risk to achieve this objective. As part of the analytical procedures introduced in the chapter, simulation techniques to approximate future outcomes are considered.

9

The Time Value of Money

In 1624, the Indians sold Manhattan Island at the ridiculously low figure of $24. But wait, was it really ridiculous? If the Indians had merely taken the $24 and reinvested it at 6 percent annual interest up to 1989, they would have had $42 billion, an amount sufficient to repurchase most of New York City. If the Indians had been slightly more astute and had invested the $24 at 7.5 percent compounded annually, they would now have close to $7,000,000,000,000 ($7 trillion)—and tribal chiefs would now rival oil sheikhs and Japanese tycoons as the richest people in the world. Another popular example is that $1 received 1,989 years ago, invested at 6 percent, could now be used to purchase all the wealth in the world.

While not all examples are this dramatic, the time value of money figures in many day-to-day decisions. Understanding the effective rate on a business loan, the mortgage payment in a real estate transaction, or the true return on an investment is dependent on understanding the time value of money. As long as an investor is able to garner a positive return on idle dollars, distinctions must be made between money received today and money received in the future. The investor/lender essentially demands that a financial "rent" be paid on his or her funds as current dollars are set aside today in anticipation of higher returns in the future.

Relationship to the Capital Outlay Decision _____

The decision to purchase new plant and equipment or to introduce a new product in the market requires using capital allocating or capital budgeting techniques. Essentially, we must determine whether future benefits are sufficiently large to justify current outlays. It is important that we develop the mathematical tools of the time value of money as the first step toward making capital allocating decisions. Let us now examine the basic terminology of "time value of money."

Compound Sum—Single Amount _____

In determining the compound sum, we measure the future value of an amount that is allowed to grow at a given interest rate over a period of time. Assume that an investor has $1,000 and wishes to know its worth after four years if it grows at 10 percent per year. At the end of the first year, he will have $1,000 × 1.10, or $1,100. By the end of year two, the $1,100 will have grown to $1,210 ($1,100 × 1.10). The four-year pattern is indicated below.

$$
\begin{array}{ll}
\text{Ist year} & \$1,000 \times 1.10 = \$1,100 \\
\text{2nd year} & \$1,100 \times 1.10 = \$1,210 \\
\text{3rd year} & \$1,210 \times 1.10 = \$1,331 \\
\text{4th year} & \$1,331 \times 1.10 = \$1,464
\end{array}
$$

After the fourth year, the investor has accumulated $1,464. Because compounding problems often cover a long period of time, a more generalized formula is necessary to describe the compounding procedure. We shall let:

S = Compound sum
P = Principal or present value
i = Interest rate
n = Number of periods

The simple formula is:

$$ S = P(1 + i)^n $$

In the present case, P = $1,000, i = 10 percent, n = 4, so we have:

$$ S = \$1,000(1.10)^4, \text{ or } \$1,000 \times 1.464 = \$1,464 $$

The term $(1.10)^4$ is found to equal 1.464 by multiplying 1.10 four times itself (the fourth power) or by using logarithms. An even quicker process is using an interest rate table, such as Table 9–1 for the com-

Table 9–1
Compound sum
of $1 ($IF_s$)

Periods	1%	2%	3%	4%	6%	8%	10%
1	1.010	1.020	1.030	1.040	1.060	1.080	1.100
2	1.020	1.040	1.061	1.082	1.124	1.166	1.210
3	1.030	1.061	1.093	1.125	1.191	1.260	1.331
4	1.041	1.082	1.126	1.170	1.262	1.360	1.464
5	1.051	1.104	1.159	1.217	1.338	1.469	1.611
10	1.105	1.219	1.344	1.480	1.791	2.159	2.594
20	1.220	1.486	1.806	2.191	3.207	4.661	6.727

pound sum of a dollar. With $n = 4$ and $i = 10$ percent, the value is also found to be 1.464.

The table tells us the amount that $1 would grow to if it were invested for any number of periods at a given interest rate. We multiply this factor times any other amount to determine the compound sum. An expanded version of Table 9–1 is presented at the back of the text in Appendix A.

In determining the compound sum, we will shorten our formula from $S = P(1 + i)^n$ to:

$$S = P \times IF_s \qquad (9\text{--}1)$$

where IF_s equals the interest factor found in the table.

If $10,000 were invested for 10 years at 8 percent, the compound sum, based on Table 9–1, would be:

$$S = P \times IF_s \, (n = 10, i = 8\%)$$
$$S = \$10,000 \times 2.159 = \$21,590$$

Present Value—Single Amount

In recent years, the sports pages have been filled with stories of athletes who receive multimillion dollar contracts for signing with sports organizations. Perhaps you have wondered how the Lakers or Yankees can afford to pay such fantastic sums. The answer may lie in the concept of present value—a sum payable in the future is worth less today than the stated amount.

The present value is the exact opposite of the compound sum. For example, earlier we determined that the compound sum of $1,000 for four periods at 10 percent was $1,464. We could reverse the process to state that $1,464 received four years into the future, with a 10 percent interest or discount rate, is worth only $1,000 today—its present value. The relationship is depicted in Figure 9–1.

**Figure 9–1
Relationship of
present value and
compound sum**

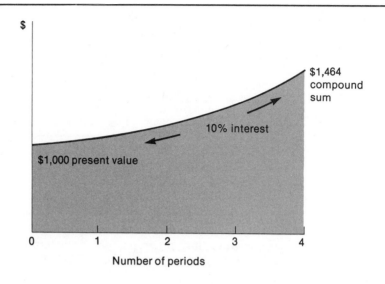

The formula for present value is derived from the original formula for the compound sum.

$$S = P(1 + i)^n \text{ Compound sum}$$

$$P = S\left[\frac{1}{(1 + i)^n}\right] \text{ Present value}$$

The present value can be determined by solving for a mathematical solution to the above formula, or by using Table 9–2, the present value of a dollar. In the latter instance, we restate the formula for present value as:

$$P = S \times IF_{pv} \qquad\qquad (9\text{–}2)$$

Once again, IF_{pv} represents the interest factor found in appropriate Table 9–2.

Let's demonstrate that the present value of $1,464, based on our assumptions, is $1,000 today.

$$P = S \times IF_{pv} (n = 4, i = 10\%) \text{ [Table 9–2]}$$
$$P = \$1,464 \times 0.683 = \$1,000$$

Compound Sum—Annuity

Our calculations up to now have dealt with single amounts rather than annuity values, which may be defined as a series of consecutive payments

**Table 9–2
Present value
of $1 ($IF_{pv}$)**

Periods	1%	2%	3%	4%	6%	8%	10%
1	0.990	0.980	0.971	0.962	0.943	0.926	0.909
2	0.980	0.961	0.943	0.925	0.890	0.857	0.826
3	0.971	0.942	0.915	0.889	0.840	0.794	0.751
4	0.961	0.924	0.888	0.855	0.792	0.735	0.683
5	0.951	0.906	0.863	0.822	0.747	0.681	0.621
10	0.905	0.820	0.744	0.676	0.558	0.463	0.386
20	0.820	0.673	0.554	0.456	0.312	0.215	0.149

An expanded table is presented in Appendix B.

or receipts of equal amount. The annuity values are generally assumed to occur at the end of each period. If we invest $1,000 at the end of each year for four years and our funds grow at 10 percent, what is the compound sum of this annuity? We may find the compound sum for each payment and then total to find the compound sum of an annuity (Figure 9–2).

The compound sum for the annuity in Figure 9–2 is $4,641. Although this is a four-period annuity, the first $1,000 comes at the *end* of the first period and has but three periods to run, the second $1,000 at the end of the second period, with two periods remaining—and so on down to the

**Figure 9–2
Compounding
process for annuity**

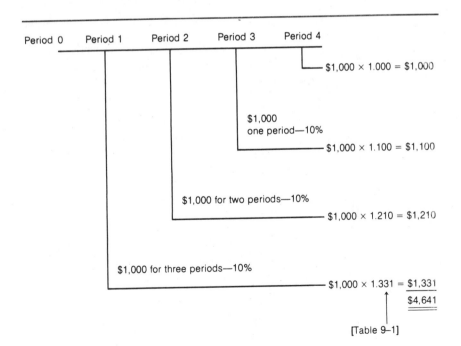

Table 9–3
Compound sum of an
annuity of $1 ($IF_{sa}$)

Periods	1%	2%	3%	4%	6%	8%	10%
1	1.000	1.000	1.000	1.000	1.000	1.000	1.000
2	2.010	2.020	2.030	2.040	2.060	2.080	2.100
3	3.030	3.060	3.091	3.122	3.184	3.246	3.310
4	4.060	4.122	4.184	4.246	4.375	4.506	4.641
5	5.101	5.204	5.309	5.416	5.637	5.867	6.105
10	10.462	10.950	11.464	12.006	13.181	14.487	15.937
20	22.019	24.297	26.870	29.778	36.786	45.762	57.275
30	34.785	40.588	47.575	56.085	79.058	113.280	164.490

An expanded table is presented in Appendix C.

last $1,000 at the end of the fourth period. The final payment (period 4) is not compounded at all.

Because the process of compounding the individual values is quite tedious, special tables are also available for annuity computations. We shall refer to Table 9–3, the compound sum of an annuity of $1. Let us define R as the annuity value and use Formula 9–3 for the compound sum of an annuity.[1] Note that in the IF term the first subscript, s, indicates compound sum and the second subscript, a, indicates that we are dealing with an annuity.

$$S = R \times IF_{sa} \ (n = 4, i = 10\%) \tag{9-3}$$
$$S = \$1,000 \times 4.641 = \$4,641$$

If a wealthy relative offered to set aside $2,500 a year for you for the next 20 years, how much would you have to your credit after 20 years if the funds grew at 8 percent?

$$S = R \times IF_{sa} \ (n = 20, i = 8\%)$$
$$S = \$2,500 \times 45.762 = \$114,405$$

A rather tidy sum considering that only a total of $50,000 has been invested over the 20 years.

Present Value—Annuity

To find the present value of an annuity, the process is reversed. In theory, each individual payment is discounted back to the present and then all

---

[1] $S = R(1 + i)^{n-1} + R(1 + i)^{n-2} + \ldots R(1 + i)^1 + R(1 + i)^0$

$$= R\left[\frac{(1 + i)^n - 1}{i}\right] = R \times IF_{sa}$$

Table 9–4
Present value of an annuity of $1 ($IF_{pva}$)

Periods	1%	2%	3%	4%	6%	8%	10%
1	0.990	0.980	0.971	0.962	0.943	0.926	0.909
2	1.970	1.942	1.913	1.886	1.833	1.783	1.736
3	2.941	2.884	2.829	2.775	2.673	2.577	2.487
4	3.902	3.808	3.717	3.630	3.465	3.312	3.170
5	4.853	4.713	4.580	4.452	4.212	3.993	3.791
8	7.652	7.325	7.020	6.773	6.210	5.747	5.335
10	9.471	8.983	8.530	8.111	7.360	6.710	6.145
20	18.046	16.351	14.877	13.590	11.470	9.818	8.514
30	25.808	22.396	19.600	17.292	13.765	11.258	9.427

An expanded table is presented in Appendix D.

of the discounted payments are added up, yielding the present value of the annuity. Table 9–4 allows us to eliminate extensive calculations and to find our answer directly. In Formula 9–4 the term A refers to the present value of the annuity.[2] Once again, assume that $R = \$1,000$, $n = 4$, and $i = 10$ percent—only now we want to know the present value of the annuity. Note that in the IF term the first subscript, $_{pv}$, represents present value and that the second subscript, $_a$, indicates an annuity.

$$A = R \times IF_{pva} \ (n = 4, i = 10\%) \qquad (9\text{–}4)$$
$$A = \$1,000 \times 3.170 = \$3,170$$

Determining the Annuity Value

In our prior discussion of annuities, we assumed that the unknown value was the compound sum or the present value—with specific information available on the annuity value (R), the interest rate, and the number of periods or years. In certain cases our emphasis may shift to solving for one of these other values (on the assumption that compound sum or present value is given). For now, we will concentrate on determining an unknown annuity value.

---

[2]
$$A = R\left[\frac{1}{(1+i)}\right]^1 + R\left[\frac{1}{(1+i)}\right]^2 + \ldots R\left[\frac{1}{(1+i)}\right]^n = R\left[\frac{1 - \dfrac{1}{(1+i)^n}}{i}\right]$$
$$= R \times IF_{pva}$$

Annuity Equaling a Compound Sum

Assuming that we wish to accumulate $4,641 after four years at a 10 percent interest rate, how much must be set aside at the end of each of the four periods? We take the previously developed statement for the compound sum of an annuity and solve for R.

$$S = R \times IF_{sa} \qquad\qquad (9\text{--}5)$$

$$R = \frac{S}{IF_{sa}}$$

S is given as $4,641, and IF_{sa} (interest factor) may be determined from Table 9–3 (compound sum of an annuity). Whenever you are working with an annuity problem relating to compound sum, you employ Table 9–3, regardless of the variable that is unknown. For $n = 4$ and $i = 10$ percent, IF_{sa} is 4.641. Thus R equals $1,000.

$$R = \frac{S}{IF_{sa}} = \frac{\$4,641}{4.641} = \$1,000$$

The solution is the exact reverse of that previously presented under the discussion of the compound sum of an annuity. As a second example, assume that the director of the Women's Tennis Association must set aside an equal amount for each of the next 10 years in order to accumulate $100,000 in retirement funds and that the return on deposited funds is 6 percent. Solve for the annual contribution, R.

$$R = \frac{S}{IF_{sa}} \ (n = 10, i = 6\%)$$

$$R = \frac{\$100,000}{13.181} = \$7,587$$

Annuity Equaling a Present Value

In this instance, we assume that you know the present value and that you wish to determine what size annuity can be equated to that amount. Suppose that your wealthy uncle presents you with $10,000 now to help you get through the next four years of college. If you are able to earn 6 percent on deposited funds, how much can you withdraw at the end of each year for four years? We need to know the value of an annuity equal to a given present value. We take the previously developed statement for the present value of an annuity and reverse it to solve for R.

$$A = R \times IF_{pva} \qquad\qquad (9\text{--}6)$$

$$R = \frac{A}{IF_{pva}}$$

The appropriate table is Table 9–4 (present value of an annuity). We determine an answer of $2,886.

$$R = \frac{A}{IF_{pva}}(n = 4, i = 6\%)$$

$$R = \frac{\$10,000}{3.465} = \$2,886$$

The flow of funds would follow the pattern in Table 9–5. Annual interest is based on the beginning balance for each year.

Table 9–5
Relationship of present value to annuity

Year	Beginning Balance	Annual Interest (6 percent)	Annual Withdrawal	Ending Balance
1	$10,000.00	$600.00	$2,886.00	$7,714.00
2	7,714.00	462.84	2,886.00	5,290.84
3	5,290.84	317.45	2,886.00	2,722.29
4	2,722.29	163.71	2,886.00	0

The same process can be used to indicate necessary repayments on a loan. Suppose that a homeowner signs a $40,000 mortgage to be repaid over 20 years at 8 percent interest. How much must he or she pay annually to eventually liquidate the loan? In other words, what annuity paid over 20 years is the equivalent of a $40,000 present value with an 8 percent interest rate?

$$R = \frac{A}{IF_{pva}} \ (n = 20, i = 8\%)$$

$$R = \frac{\$40,000}{9.818} = \$4,074^{[3]}$$

---

[3] The actual mortgage could be further refined into monthly payments of approximately $340.

Part of the payments to the mortgage company will go toward the payment of interest, with the remainder applied to debt reduction, as indicated in Table 9–6.

Table 9–6
Payoff table for loan (amortization table)

Period	Beginning Balance	Annual Payment	Annual Interest (8 percent)	Repayment on Principal	Ending Balance
1	$40,000	$4,074	$3,200	$ 874	$39,126
2	39,126	4,074	3,130	944	38,182
3	38,182	4,074	3,055	1,019	37,163

If this same process is followed over 20 years, the balance will be reduced to zero. The student might note that the homeowner will pay over $41,000 of *interest* during the term of the loan, as indicated below.

Total payments ($4,074 for 20 years)	$81,480
Repayment of principal	−40,000
Payments applied to interest	$41,480

Determining the Yield on an Investment

In our discussion thus far, we have considered the following time value of money problems.

		Formula		Table	Appendix
Compound sum—single amount . . .	(9–1)	$S = P \times IF_s$		9–1	A
Present value—single amount	(9–2)	$P = S \times IF_{pv}$		9–2	B
Compound sum—annuity	(9–3)	$S = R \times IF_{sa}$		9–3	C
Present value—annuity	(9–4)	$A = R \times IF_{pva}$		9–4	D
Annuity equaling a compound sum . .	(9–5)	$R = \dfrac{S}{IF_{sa}}$		9–3	C
Annuity equaling a present value . . .	(9–6)	$R = \dfrac{A}{IF_{pva}}$		9–4	D

In each case, we knew three out of the four variables and solved for the fourth. We will follow the same procedure once again, but now the unknown variable will be i, the interest rate, or yield on the investment.

Yield—Present Value of a Single Amount

An investment producing $1,464 after four years has a present value of $1,000. What is the interest rate, or yield on the investment?

We take the basic formula for the present value of a single amount and rearrange the terms.

$$P = S \times IF_{pv} \tag{9-7}$$

$$IF_{pv} = \frac{P}{S} = \frac{\$1,000}{\$1,464} = 0.683$$

The determination of IF_{pv} does not give us the final answer—but in effect, it scales down the problem so that we may ascertain the answer from Table 9–2, the present value of $1. A portion of Table 9–2 is presented below.

Periods	1%	2%	3%	4%	5%	6%	8%	10%
2	0.980	0.961	0.943	0.925	0.907	0.890	0.857	0.826
3	0.971	0.942	0.815	0.889	0.864	0.840	0.794	0.751
4	0.961	0.924	0.888	0.855	0.823	0.792	0.735	0.683

Read down the left-hand column of the table until you have located the number of periods in question (in this case $n = 4$), and read across the table for $n = 4$ until you have located the computed value of IF_{pv}. We see that for $n = 4$ and IF_{pv} equal to 0.683, the interest rate, or yield, is 10 percent. This is the rate that will equate $1,464 received in four years to $1,000 today.

If an IF_{pv} value does not fall under a given interest rate, an approximation is possible. For example, with $n = 3$ and $IF_{pv} = 0.861$, 5 percent may be suggested as an approximate answer.

Interpolation may also be used to find a more precise answer. In the above example, we write out the two IF_{pv} values that the designated IF_{pv} (0.861) falls between and take the difference between the two.

$$
\begin{array}{llr}
IF_{pv} \text{ at } 5\% & \ldots \ldots & 0.864 \\
IF_{pv} \text{ at } 6\% & \ldots \ldots & \underline{0.840} \\
& & 0.024
\end{array}
$$

We then find the difference between the IF_{pv} value at the lowest interest rate and the designated IF_{pv} value.

$$
\begin{array}{llr}
IF_{pv} \text{ at } 5\% & \ldots \ldots \ldots & 0.864 \\
IF_{pv} \text{ designated} & \ldots \ldots & \underline{0.861} \\
& & 0.003
\end{array}
$$

We next express this value (0.003) as a fraction of the preceding value (0.024) and multiply by the difference between the two interest rates (6 percent minus 5 percent). The value is added to the lower interest rate (5 percent) to get a more exact answer of 5.125 percent rather than the estimated 5 percent.

$$5\% + \frac{0.003}{0.024}(1\%) =$$
$$5\% + 0.125(1\%) =$$
$$5\% + 0.125\% \quad = 5.125\%$$

Yield—Present Value of an Annuity

We may also find the yield related to any other problem. Let's look at the present value of an annuity. Take the basic formula for the present value of an annuity, and rearrange the terms.

$$A = R \times IF_{pva} \qquad (9\text{–}8)$$

$$IF_{pva} = \frac{A}{R}$$

The appropriate table is Table 9–4 (the present value of an annuity of \$1). Assuming that a \$10,000 investment will produce \$1,490 a year for the next 10 years, what is the yield on the investment?

$$IF_{pva} = \frac{A}{R} = \frac{\$10,000}{\$1,490} = 6.710$$

If the student will flip back to Table 9–4 and read across the columns for $n = 10$ periods, he will see that the yield is 8 percent.

The same type of approximated or interpolated yield that applied to a single amount can also be applied to an annuity when necessary.

Special Considerations in Time Value Analysis

We have assumed that interest was compounded or discounted on an annual basis. This assumption will now be relaxed. Contractual arrangements, such as an installment purchase agreement or a corporate bond contract, may call for semiannual, quarterly, or monthly compounding periods. The adjustment to the normal formula is quite simple. To determine n, multiply the number of years by the number of compounding periods during the year. The factor for i is then determined by dividing the quoted annual interest rate by the number of compounding periods.

Case 1—Find the compound sum of a \$1,000 investment after five years at 8 percent annual interest, compounded semiannually.

$$n = 5 \times 2 = 10 \quad i = 8 \text{ percent} \div 2 = 4 \text{ percent}$$

Since the problem calls for the compound sum of a single amount, the formula is $S = P \times IF_s$. Using Table 9–1 for $n = 10$ and $i = 4$ percent, the answer is $1,480.

$$S = P \times IF_s$$
$$S = \$1,000 \times 1.480 = \$1,480$$

Case 2—Find the present value of 20 quarterly payments of $2,000 each to be received over the next five years. The stated interest rate is 8 percent per annum. The problem calls for the present value of an annuity.

$$A = R \times IF_{pva} \ (n = 20, \ i = 2\%)[\text{Table 9–4}]$$
$$A = \$2,000 \times 16.351 = \$32,702$$

Patterns of Payment

Time value of money problems may evolve around a number of different payment or receipt patterns. Not every situation will involve a single amount or an annuity. For example, a contract may call for the payment of a different amount each year over a three-year period. To determine present value, each payment is discounted (Table 9–2) to the present and then summed.

(Assume 8% discount rate)

1.	1,000 × 0.926 =	$ 926
2.	2,000 × 0.857 =	1,714
3.	3,000 × 0.794 =	2,382
		$5,022

A more involved problem might include a combination of single amounts and an annuity. If the annuity will be paid at some time in the future, it is referred to as a deferred annuity and it requires special treatment. Assume the same problem as above, but with an annuity of $1,000 that will be paid at the end of each year from the fourth through the eighth year. With a discount rate of 8 percent, what is the present value of the cash flows?

1.	$1,000	
2.	2,000	Present value = $5,022
3.	3,000	
4.	1,000	
5.	1,000	
6.	1,000	Five-year annuity
7.	1,000	
8.	1,000	

We know that the present value of the first three payments is $5,022, but what about the annuity? Let's diagram the five annuity payments.

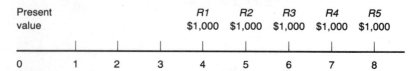

The information source is Table 9–4, the present value of an annuity of $1. For $n = 5$, $i = 8$ percent, the discount factor is 3.993—leaving a "present value" of the annuity of $3,993. However, tabular values only discount to the beginning of the first stated period of an annuity—in this case the beginning of the fourth year, as diagramed below.

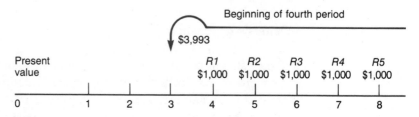

Each number represents the end of the period; that is, 4 represents the end of the fourth period.

The $3,993 must finally be discounted back to the present. Since this single amount falls at the beginning of the fourth period—in effect, the equivalent of the end of the third period—we discount back for three periods at the stated 8 percent interest rate. Using Table 9–2, we have:

$$P = S \times IF_{pv} \, (n = 3, i = 8\%)$$
$$P = \$3,993 \times 0.794 = \$3,170 \text{ (actual present value)}$$

The last step in the discounting process is shown below.

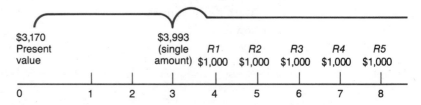

A *second method* for finding the present value of a deferred annuity is to:

1. Find the present value factor of an annuity for the total time period. In this case, where $n = 8$, $i = 8\%$, the IF_{pva} is 5.747.
2. Find the present value factor of an annuity for the total time period (8) minus the deferred annuity period (5).

$$8 - 5 = 3$$
$$n = 3, i = 8\%$$

The IF_{pva} value is 2.577.

3. Subtract the value in step 2 from the value in step 1, and multiply by R.

$$
\begin{array}{r}
5.747 \\
- \ 2.577 \\
\hline
3.170 \\
\end{array}
$$

$3.170 \times \$1,000 = \$3,170$ (present value of the annuity)

$3.170 is precisely the same answer for the present value of the annuity as that reached by the first method. The present value of the five-year annuity may now be added to the present value of the inflows over the first three years to arrive at the total value.

$5,022	First three period flows
+3,170	Five-year annuity
$8,192	Total present value

Special Review of the Chapter

In working a time value of money problem, the student should determine, first, whether the problem deals with compound sum or present value and, second, whether a single sum or an annuity is involved. The major calculations in Chapter 9 are summarized below.

1. *Compound sum of a single amount.*
   Formula: $S = P \times IF_s$
   Table: 9–1 or Appendix A.
   When to use: In determining the future value of a single amount.
   Sample problem: You invest $1,000 for four years at 10 percent interest. What is the value at the end of the fourth year?

2. *Present value of a single amount.*
   Formula: $P = S \times IF_{pv}$
   Table: 9–2 or Appendix B.

When to use: In determining the present value of an amount to be received in the future.

Sample problem: You will receive $1,000 after four years at a discount rate of 10 percent. How much is this worth today?

3. *Compound sum of an annuity.*
   Formula: $S = R \times IF_{sa}$
   Table: 9–3 or Appendix C.
   When to use: In determining the future value of a series of consecutive, equal payments (an annuity).
   Sample problem: You will receive $1,000 at the end of each period for four periods. What is the accumulated value (future worth) at the end of the fourth period if money grows at 10 percent?

4. *Present value of an annuity.*
   Formula: $A = R \times IF_{pva}$
   Table: 9–4 or Appendix D.
   When to use: In determining the present worth of an annuity.
   Sample problem: You will receive $1,000 at the end of each period for four years. At a discount rate of 10 percent, what is the current worth?

5. *Annuity equaling a compound sum.*

$$Formula: R = \frac{S}{IF_{sa}}$$

   Table: 9–3 or Appendix C.
   When to use: In determining the size of an annuity that will equal a future value.
   Sample problem: You need $1,000 after four periods. With an interest rate of 10 percent, how much must be set aside at the end of each period to accumulate this amount?

6. *Annuity equaling a present value.*

$$Formula: R = \frac{A}{IF_{pua}}$$

   Table: 9–4 or Appendix D.
   When to use: In determining the size of an annuity equal to a given present value.
   Sample problems:
   a. What four-year annuity is the equivalent of $1,000 today with an interest rate of 10 percent?

b. You deposit $1,000 today and wish to withdraw funds equally over four years. How much can you withdraw at the end of each year if funds earn 10 percent?

c. You borrow $1,000 for four years at 10 percent interest. How much must be repaid at the end of each year?

7. *Determining the yield on an investment.*

Formulas	Tables	
a. $IF_{pv} = \dfrac{P}{S}$	9–2, Appendix B	Yield—present value of a single amount
b. $IF_{pva} = \dfrac{A}{R}$	9–4, Appendix D	Yield—present value of an annuity

When to use: In determining the interest rate (i) that will equate an investment with future benefits.

Sample problem: You invest $1,000 now, and the funds are expected to increase to $1,360 after four periods.

What is the yield on the investment:

$$\text{Use } IF_{pv} = \frac{P}{S}.$$

8. *Less than annual compounding periods.*

Semiannual	Multiply $n \times 2$	Divide i by 2	then use
Quarterly	Multiply $n \times 4$	Divide i by 4	normal
Monthly	Multiply $n \times 12$	Divide i by 12	formula

When to use: If the compounding period is more (or perhaps less) frequent than once a year.

Sample problem: You invest $1,000 compounded semiannually at 8 percent per annum over four years. Determine the future sum.

9. *Patterns of payment—deferred annuity.*

Formulas	Tables	
$A = R \times IF_{pva}$	9–4, Appendix D	Method 1
$P = S \times IF_{pv}$	9–2, Appendix B	

When to use: If an annuity begins in the future.

Sample problem: You will receive $1,000 per period, starting at the end of the fourth period and running through the end of the eighth period. With a discount rate of 8 percent, determine the present value.

The student is encouraged to work the many problems found at the end of the chapter.

List of Terms

compound sum   compound sum of annuity
present value   semiannual compounding
interest factor (*IF*)   annuity
discount rate   yield

Discussion Questions

1. How is the compound sum (Appendix A) related to the present value of a single sum (Appendix B)?

2. How is the present value of a single sum (Appendix B) related to the present value of an annuity (Appendix D)?

3. Why does money have a time value?

4. Does inflation have anything to do with making a dollar today worth more than a dollar tomorrow?

5. Adjust the annual formula for a compound sum of a single amount at 12 percent for 10 years to a semiannual compounding formula. What are the interest factors (IF_s) for the two assumptions? Why are they different?

6. If, as an investor, you had a choice of daily, monthly, or quarterly compounding, which would you choose? Why?

7. What is a deferred annuity?

8. List five different financial applications of the time value of money.

Problems

1. What is the present value of:
   a. $6,000 in 10 years at 8 percent?
   b. $15,000 in 4 years at 10 percent?
   c. $10,000 in 25 years at 6 percent?
   d. $1,000 in 50 years at 14 percent?

2. If you invest $7,000 today, how much will you have:
   a. In 2 years at 9 percent?
   b. In 7 years at 10 percent?
   c. In 25 years at 12 percent?
   d. In 25 years at 12 percent (compounded semiannually)?

3. How much will you have to invest to receive:
   a. $20,000 in 5 years at 5 percent?
   b. $30,000 in 8 years at 20 percent?
   c. $5,000 each year for 10 years at 7 percent?
   d. $9,200 each year for 25 years at 13 percent?

4. Mr. Applebee will receive $4,400 a year for the next 16 years from a trust. If a 9 percent interest rate is applied, what is the current value of the future payments?

5. Mr. Elite invests $80,000 in an old, classic Rolls-Royce. He expects it to increase 12 percent per year for the next five years. How much will his car be worth after five years?

6. Ms. Michaels has been depositing $1,800 a year in her savings account every December, starting in 1981. Her account earns 6 percent, compounded annually. How much will she have on December of 1990? (Assume that a deposit is made in 1990). Make sure to carefully count the years.

7. If you owe $10,000 payable at the end of seven years, what amount would your creditor be willing to accept today if she can earn 8 percent on the funds?

8. At a growth rate (interest rate) of 9 percent annually, how long will it take for a sum to double? to triple? Select the year that is closest to the correct answer.

9. Cousin Bertha invested $100,000 10 years ago at 12 percent, compounded quarterly. How much has she accumulated?

10. Determine the amount of money in a savings account at the end of 5 years, given an initial deposit of $3,000 and an 8 percent annual interest rate when interest is compounded (a) annually, (b) semiannually, and (c) quarterly.

11. Mr. Flint retired as president of the Color Tile Company but is currently on a consulting contract for $45,000 per year for the next 10 years.

a. If Mr. Flint's opportunity cost (potential return) is 10 percent, what is the present value of his consulting contract?

b. Assuming that Mr. Flint will not retire for two more years and will not start to receive his 10 payments until the end of the third year, what would be the value of his deferred annuity?

12. Your rich uncle has offered you a choice of one of the three following alternatives: $10,000 now; $2,000 a year for eight years; or $24,000 at the end of eight years. Assuming you could earn 11 percent annually, which alternative should you choose? If you could earn 12 percent, would you still choose the same alternative?

13. You need $28,974 at the end of 10 years, and your only investment outlet is an 8 percent long-term certificate of deposit (compounded annually). With the certificate of deposit, you make an initial investment at the beginning of the first year.

a. What single payment could be made at the beginning of the first year to achieve this objective?

b. What amount could you pay at the end of each year annually for 10 years to achieve this same objective?

14. Amy Hirt started a paper route on January 1, 1982. Every three months, she deposits $300 in her bank account, which earns 8 percent annually but is compounded quarterly. On December 31, 1985, she used the entire balance in her bank account to invest in a certificate of deposit at 14 percent annually. How much will she have on December 31, 1988?

15. On January 1, 1987, Mr. Strong bought 100 shares of stock for $10 per share. On December 31, 1989, he sold the stock for $15 per share.

What is his annual rate of return? Interpolate to find the exact answer.

16. Dr. Emily Smart bought 1,000 shares of Quality Steel Products stock for $5 per share on January 1, 1987. Using interpolation, find her exact annual rate of return if she sells the stock:

a. On December 31, 1988, for $6 per share.

b. On December 31, 1991, for $7.85 per share.

c. On December 31, 1994, for $11 per share.

17. Robert Hunter has just invested $6,424 for his daughter (age one). This money will be needed for his daughter's education 17 years from now. He calculates that he will need $44,000 for his daughter's education by the time she goes to school.

What rate of return will Mr. Hunter need to achieve this goal?

18. Donald Johnson has just given an insurance company $20,000. In return, he will receive an annuity of $1,800 for 20 years.

    At what rate of return must the insurance company invest this $20,000 in order to make the annual payments? Interpolate.

19. Mary Mills has retired after 35 years with the Electric Company. Her total pension funds have an accumulated value of $300,000, and her life expectancy is 18 more years. Her pension fund manager assumes that she can earn an 8 percent return on her assets.

    What will her yearly annuity be for the next 18 years?

20. Dr. Cal Q. Later, an engineering professor, invests $60,000 in a parcel of land that is expected to increase in value by 12 percent per year for the next five years. He will take the proceeds and provide himself with a 10-year annuity.

    Assuming a 12 percent interest rate, how much will this annuity be?

21. You wish to retire after 18 years, at which time you want to have accumulated enough money to receive an annuity of $14,000 a year for 20 years of retirement. During the period before retirement you can earn 11 percent annually, while after retirement you can earn 8 percent on your money.

    What annual contributions to the retirement fund will allow you to receive the $14,000 annually?

22. If you borrow a principal amount of $6,489 and are required to repay the loan in five equal annual installments of $1,800, what is the interest rate associated with the loan?

23. If your father borrows $30,000 from the bank at 10 percent interest over the 10-year life of the loan, what equal annual payments must be made to discharge the loan, plus pay the bank its required rate of interest? (Round to the nearest dollar.) How much of his first payment will be applied to interest? To principal? Answer the same questions for the second payment.

24. Darla Lewis has purchased an annuity to begin payment at the end of 1991 (that is the date of the first payment). The annuity is for $12,000 per year and is designed to last eight years. Assume it is now the end of 1988.

    If the discount rate for this problem is 11 percent, what is the most she should have paid for this annuity?

25. Jacob Fox borrows $52,000 at 10 percent interest toward the purchase of a home. His mortgage is for 25 years.

    a. How much will his annual payments be? (Although home payments are usually on a monthly basis, we shall do our analysis on an annual basis for ease of computation. We get a reasonably accurate picture.)

    b. How much interest will he pay over the life of the loan?

    c. How much should he be willing to pay to get out of a 10 percent mortgage into an 8 percent mortgage with 25 years remaining on the mortgage? Assume that current interest rates are 8 percent. Disregard taxes.

26. Your younger sister, Veronica, will start college in six years. She has just informed your parents she wants to go to Western U., which will cost $10,000 per year for four years (assumed to come at the end of each year). Anticipating Veronica's ambitions, your parents started investing $1,200 per year six years ago and will continue to do so for six more years.

    How much more will your parents have to invest for the next six years to have the funds for Veronica's education? Use 9 percent as the appropriate interest rate throughout this problem (for discounting or compounding).

27. Veronica (from problem 26) is now 18 years old (six years have passed), and she wants to get married instead of going to school. Your parents have accumulated the necessary funds for her education.

    Instead of going to school, your parents are paying $4,658 for her current wedding and plan to take a year-end vacation costing $2,000 per year for the next three years.

    How much will your parents have at the end of three years to help you with graduate school, which you will start then? You plan to work on a master's and perhaps a Ph.D. If graduate school costs $7,000 per year, approximately how long will you be able to stay in school based on these funds? Use 9 percent as the appropriate interest rate throughout this problem.

28. You are chairperson of the investment fund for the Pacific Coast Baseball League. You are asked to set up a fund of semiannual payments to be compounded semiannually to accumulate a sum of $100,000 after ten years at a 10 percent annual rate (20 payments). The first payment into the fund is to take place six months from today, and the last payment is to take place at the end of the tenth year.

a. Determine how much the semiannual payment should be. (Round to whole numbers.)

On the day after the fourth payment is made (the beginning of the third year) the interest rate goes up to a 12 percent annual rate, and you can earn a 12 percent annual rate on funds that have been accumulated as well as all future payments into the fund. Interest is to be compounded semiannually on all funds.

b. Determine how much the revised semiannual payments should be after this rate change (there are 16 payments and compounding dates). The next payment will be in the middle of the third year. (Round all values to whole numbers.)

Selected References

Bierman, Harold, Jr.; Charles P. Bonini; and Warren H. Hausman. *Quantitative Analysis for Business Decisions.* 7th ed. Homewood, Ill.: Richard D. Irwin, 1986.

———; **and Seymour Smidt.** *The Capital Budgeting Decision.* 6th ed. New York: Macmillan, 1984.

Cissel, Robert, and Hellen Cissel. *Mathematics in Finance.* 4th ed. Boston: Houghton Mifflin, 1972.

Howell, James E., and Daniel Teichroew. *Mathematical Analysis for Business Decisions.* Rev. ed. Homewood, Ill.: Richard D. Irwin, 1971.

Solomon, Ezra. "The Arithmetic of Capital-Budget Decisions." *Journal of Business* 29 (April 1965), pp. 124–29.

10

Valuation and Rates of Return

In Chapter 9 we considered the basic principles of the time value of money. In this chapter, we will use many of those concepts to determine how financial assets (bonds, preferred stock, and common stock) are valued and how investors establish the rates of return they demand. In the next chapter we will use material from this chapter to determine the overall cost of financing to the firm. We merely turn the coin over. Once we know how much bondholders and stockholders demand in the way of rates of return, we then observe what the corporation is required to pay them in order to attract their funds. The cost of corporate financing (capital) is subsequently used in analyzing whether a project is acceptable for investment or not. These relationships are depicted in Figure 10–1.

Valuation Concepts

The valuation of a financial asset is based on determining the present value of future cash flows. Thus, we need to know the value of future cash flows and the discount rate to be applied to the future cash flows to determine the current value.

The market-determined required rate of return, which is the discount rate, depends on the market's perceived level of risk associated with the

Figure 10–1
The relationship between time value of money, required return, cost of financing, and investment decisions

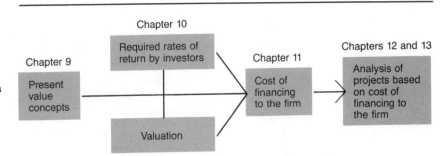

individual security. Also important is the idea that required rates of return are competitively determined among the many companies seeking financial capital. For example, IBM, due to its low financial risk, relatively high return, and strong market position in computers, is likely to raise debt capital at a significantly lower cost than can Armco Steel or LTV, two financially troubled firms. This implies that investors are willing to accept low return for low risk, and vice versa. In the way described above, the market allocates capital to companies based on risk, efficiency, and expected returns—which are based to a large degree on past performance. The reward to the financial manager for efficient use of capital in the past is a lower required return for investors than that of competing companies that did not manage their financial resources as well.

Throughout the balance of this chapter, we apply concepts of valuation to corporate bonds, preferred stock, and common stock. Although we describe the basic characteristics of each form of security as part of the valuation process, extended discussion of each security is deferred until later chapters.

Valuation of Bonds

As previously stated, the value of a financial asset is based on the concept of the present value of future cash flows. Let's apply this approach to bond valuation. A bond provides an annuity stream of interest payments and a $1,000 principal payment at maturity.[1] These cash flows are discounted at Y, the yield to maturity. The value of Y is determined in the bond markets and represents the required rate of return for bonds of a

---

[1]The assumption is that the bond has a $1,000 par value. If the par value is higher or lower, then this value would be discounted to the present from the maturity date.

given risk and maturity. More will be said about the concept of yield to maturity in the next section.

The price of a bond is thus equal to the present value of regular interest payments discounted by the yield to maturity added to the present value of the principal (also discounted by the yield to maturity).

This relationship can be expressed mathematically as follows.

$$P_b = \sum_{t=1}^{n} \frac{I_t}{(1 + Y)^t} + \frac{P_n}{(1 + Y)^n} \qquad (10\text{--}1)$$

where

$\quad P_b$ = Price of the bond

$\quad I_t$ = Interest payments

$\quad P_n$ = Principal payment at maturity

$\quad t$ = Number corresponding to a period; running from 1 to n

$\quad n$ = Total number of periods

$\quad Y$ = Yield to maturity (or required rate of return)

The first term in the equation says to take the sum of the present values of the interest payments (I_t); the second term directs you to take the present value of the principal payment at maturity (P_n). The discount rate used throughout the analysis is the yield to maturity (Y). The answer derived is referred to as P_b (the price of the bond). The analysis is carried out for n periods.

Let's assume that I_t (interest payments) equals $100; P_n (principal payment at maturity) equals $1,000; Y (yield to maturity) is 10 percent; and n (total number of periods) equals 20. We could say that P_b (the price of the bond) equals:

$$P_b = \sum_{t=1}^{20} \frac{\$100}{(1 + 0.10)^t} + \frac{\$1,000}{(1 + 0.10)^{20}}$$

Although the price of the bond could be determined with logarithms, it is much simpler to use present value tables. We take the present value of the interest payments and then add this value to the present value of the principal payment at maturity.

Present value of interest payments   In this case, we determine the present value of a $100 annuity for 20 years.[2] The discount rate is 10

---

[2]For now we are using *annual* interest payments for simplicity. Later in the discussion, we will shift to semiannual payments, and more appropriately determine the value of a bond.

percent. Using Appendix D, the present value of an annuity, we find the following:

$$A = R \times IF_{pva} \ (n = 20, \ i = 10\%)$$
$$A = \$100 \times 8.514 = \$851.40$$

Present value of principal payment (par value) at maturity   This single value of $1,000 will be received after 20 years. Note the term *principal payment at maturity* is used interchangeably with *par value* or *face value* of the bond. We discount $1,000 back to the present at 10 percent. Using Appendix B, the present value of a single amount, we find the following:

$$P = S \times IF_{pv} \ (n = 20, \ i = 10\%)$$
$$P = \$1,000 \times .149 = \$149$$

The current price of the bond, based on the present value of interest payments and the present value of the principal payment at maturity, is $1,000.40.

Present value of interest payments	$ 851.40
Present value of principal payment at maturity	149.00
Total present value, or price, of the bond	$1,000.40

The price of the bond in this case is essentially the same as its par, or stated, value to be received at maturity of $1,000.[3] This is because the annual interest rate is 10 percent (the annual interest payment of $100 divided by $1,000) and the yield to maturity, or discount rate, is also 10 percent. When the interest rate on the bond and the yield to maturity are equal, the bond will trade at par value. Later, we shall examine the mathematical effects of varying the yield to maturity above or below the interest rate on the bond. But first, let's more fully examine the concept of yield to maturity.

Concept of Yield to Maturity

In the previous example the yield to maturity that was used as the discount rate was 10 percent. The yield to maturity, or discount rate, is the required rate of return by bondholders. The bondholder, or any investor for that matter, will allow *three* factors to influence his or her required rate of return.

---

[3]The slight difference is due to the rounding procedures in the tables.

1. *The required Real Rate of Return*—This is the rate of return that the investor demands for giving up current use of the funds on a noninflation-adjusted basis. It is the financial "rent" that the investor charges for using his or her funds for one year, five years, or any given time period. Historically, the real rate of return demanded by investors has been about 2 to 3 percent. Throughout the 1980s the real rate of return has been much higher; that is, 5 to 7 percent.

2. *Inflation Premium*—In addition to the real rate of return discussed above, the investor requires a premium to compensate for the eroding effect of inflation on the value of the dollar. It would hardly satisfy an investor to have a 3 percent total rate of return in a 5 percent inflationary economy. Under such circumstances, the lender (investor) would be paying the borrower 2 percent (in purchasing power) for use of the funds. This would represent an irrational course of action. No one wishes to *pay* another party to use his or her funds. The inflation premium added to the real rate of return ensures that this will not happen. The size of the inflation premium will be based on the investor's expectations about future inflation. In the 1980s, the inflation premium has been of the magnitude of 3 to 4 percent. In the late 1970s, it was in excess of 10 percent.

   If one combines the real rate of return (part *a*) and the inflation premium (part *b*), the *risk-free rate of return* is determined. This is the rate that compensates the investor for the current use of his or her funds and for the loss in purchasing power due to inflation, but not for taking risks. As an example, if the real rate of return were 3 percent and the inflation premium were 4 percent, we would say the risk-free rate of return is 7 percent.[4]

3. *Risk Premium*—We must now add the risk premium to the risk-free rate of return. This is a premium associated with the special risks of a given investment. Of primary interest to us are two types of risks: *business risk* and *financial risk*. Business risk relates to the inability of the firm to hold its competitive position and maintain stability and growth in its earnings. Financial risk relates to the inability of the firm to meet its debt obligations as they come due. In addition to the two forms of risk mentioned above, the risk premium will be greater or less for different types of investments. For example, because bonds possess a contractual obligation for the firm to pay interest to bond-

---

[4]Actually, a slightly more accurate representation would be: Risk-free rate = (1 + real rate of return) (1 + inflation premium) − 1. We would show: (1.03) (1.04) − 1 = 1.0712 − 1 = .0712 = 7.12 percent.

holders, they are considered less risky than common stock where no such obligation exists.[5]

The risk premium of an investment may range from as low as zero on a very short-term U.S. government-backed security to 10 to 15 percent on a gold mining expedition. The typical risk premium is 2 to 6 percent. We shall assume that in the investment we are examining that the risk premium is 3 percent. If we add this risk premium to the two components of the risk-free rate of return developed in parts *a* and *b*, we arrive at an overall required rate of return of 10 percent.

```
+ Real rate of return  . . . . . .   3%
+ Inflation premium . . . . . . .    4
= Risk-free rate . . . . . . . . .   7%
+ Risk premium . . . . . . . . .     3
= Required rate of return  . . . .  10%
```

In this instance, we assume we are evaluating the required return on a bond issued by a firm. If the security had been the common stock of the same firm, the risk premium might be 5 to 6 percent and the required rate of return 12 to 13 percent.

Finally, in concluding this section, you should recall that the required rate of return on a bond is effectively the same concept as required yield to maturity.

Changing the Yield to Maturity and the Impact on Bond Valuation

In the earlier bond value calculation, we assumed the interest rate was 10 percent ($100 annual interest on a $1,000 par value bond) and the yield to maturity was also 10 percent. Under those circumstances, the price of the bond was basically equal to par value. Now let's assume that conditions in the market cause the yield to maturity to change.

Increase in inflation premium   For example, assume the inflation premium goes up from 4 to 6 percent. All else remains constant. The required rate of return would now be 12 percent.

```
+ Real rate of return  . . . . . .   3%
+ Inflation premium . . . . . . .   ⑥
= Risk-free rate . . . . . . . . .   9%
+ Risk premium . . . . . . . . .     3
= Required rate of return  . . . .  12%
```

---

[5]On the other hand, common stock carries the potential for unlimited return when the corporation is very profitable.

With the required rate of return, or yield to maturity, now at 12 percent, the price of the bond will change.[6] A bond that only pays 10 percent interest when the required rate of return (yield to maturity) is 12 percent will fall below its current value of approximately $1,000. The new price of the bond, as computed below, is $850.90.

Present value of interest payments—We take the present value of a $100 annuity for 20 years. The discount rate is 12 percent. Using Appendix D:

$$A = R \times IF_{pva} (n = 20, i = 12\%)$$
$$A = \$100 \times 7.469 = \$746.90$$

Present value of principal payment at maturity—We take the present value of $1,000 after 20 years. The discount rate is 12 percent. Using Appendix B:

$$P = S \times IF_{pv} (n = 20, i = 12\%)$$
$$P = \$1,000 \times .104 = \$104$$

Total present value—

Present value of interest payments	$746.90
Present value of principal payment at maturity	104.00
Total present value, or price, of the bond	$850.90

In this example, we assumed that increasing inflation caused the required rate of return (yield to maturity) to go up and the bond price to fall by approximately $150. The same effect would take place if the business risk increased or the demanded level for the *real* rate of return became higher.

Decrease in inflation premium   Of course, the opposite effect would happen if the required rate of return went down because of lower inflation, less risk, or other factors. Let's assume the inflation premium declines and the required rate of return (yield to maturity) goes down to 8 percent.

The 20-year bond with the 10 percent interest rate would now sell for $1,196.80.

Present value of interest payments—

$$A = R \times IF_{pva} (n = 20, i = 8\%) \qquad \text{[Appendix D]}$$
$$A = \$100 \times 9.818 = \$981.80$$

---

[6]Of course, the required rate of return on all other financial assets will also go up proportionally.

Present value of principal payment at maturity—

$$P = S \times IF_{pv} \ (n = 20, \ i = 8\%) \qquad \text{[Appendix B]}$$
$$P = \$1,000 \times .215 = \$215$$

Total present value—

Present value of interest payments . . . . $ 981.80
Present value of principal payment at maturity 215.00
Total present value, or price, of the bond $1,196.80

The price of the bond is now trading at $196.80 over par value. This is certainly the expected result because the bond is paying 10 percent interest when the yield in the market is only 8 percent. The 2 percent differential on a $1,000 par value bond represents $20 per year. The investor will receive this differential for the next 20 years. The present value of $20 for the next 20 years at the current market rate of interest of 8 percent is approximately $196.80. This explains why the bond is trading at $196.80 over its stated, or par, value.

The further the yield to maturity on a bond falls away from the stated interest rate on the bond, the greater the price change effect will be. This is illustrated in Table 10–1 for the 10 percent interest rate, 20-year bonds discussed in this chapter.

Table 10–1
Bond price table

(10 Percent Interest Payment 20 Years to Maturity)

Yield to Maturity	Bond Price
2%	$2,308.10
4	1,825.00
6	1,459.00
7	1,317.40
8	1,196.80
9	1,090.90
10	1,000.00*
11	920.30
12	850.90
13	789.50
14	735.30
16	643.90
20	513.00
25	407.40

*This value was computed earlier as $1,000.40 due to rounding. The correct value is $1,000.

We clearly see the impact that different yields to maturity have on the price of a bond.[7]

Time to Maturity

The impact of a change in yield to maturity on valuation is also affected by the remaining time to maturity. The effect of a bond paying 2 percent more or less than the going rate of interest is quite different for a 20-year bond than it is for a 1-year bond. In the latter case, the investor will only be gaining or giving up $20 for one year. That is certainly not the same as having this differential for an extended period of time. Let's once again return to the 10 percent interest rate bond and show the impact of a 2 percent decrease or increase in yield to maturity for varying *times* to maturity. The values are shown in Table 10–2 and graphed in Figure 10–2. The upper part of Figure 10–2 shows how the amount (premium) above par value is reduced as the number of years to maturity becomes smaller and smaller. Figure 10–2 should be read from left to right. The lower part of the figure shows how the amount (discount) below par value is reduced with progressively fewer years to maturity. Clearly, the longer the maturity, the greater the impact of changes in yield.

Table 10–2 **Impact of time to** **maturity on bond** **prices**	Time Period in Years (of 10 percent bond)	Bond Price with 8 Percent Yield to Maturity	Bond Price with 12 Percent Yield to Maturity
	0	$1,000.00	$1,000.00
	1	1,018.60	982.30
	5	1,080.30	927.50
	10	1,134.00	887.00
	15	1,170.90	864.11
	20	1,196.80	850.90
	25	1,213.50	843.30
	30	1,224.80	838.50

---

[7]The reader may observe that the impact of a decrease or increase in interest rates is not equal. For example, a 2 percent decrease in interest rates will produce a $196.80 gain in the bond price and an increase of 2 percent causes a $149.10 loss. While price movements are not symmetrical around the price of the bond when the time dimension is the maturity date of the bond, they are symmetrical around the duration of the bond. The duration represents the weighted average time period to recapture the interest and principal on the bond. While these concepts go beyond that appropriate for an introductory finance text, the interested reader may wish to consult Geoffrey A. Hirt and Stanley B. Block, *Fundamentals of Investment Management*, 2nd ed. (Homewood, Ill.: Richard D. Irwin, 1986) or Frank K. Reilly, *Investments*, 2nd ed. (Hinsdale, Ill.: Dryden Press, 1985).

**Figure 10–2
Relationship between
time to maturity and
bond price***

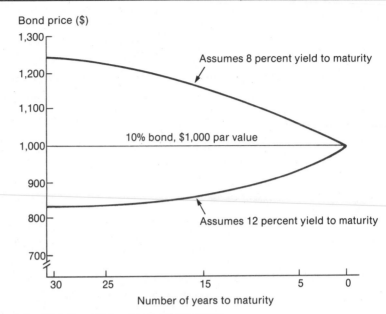

Bond price ($)

Assumes 8 percent yield to maturity

10% bond, $1,000 par value

Assumes 12 percent yield to maturity

Number of years to maturity

*The relationship in the graph is not symmetrical in nature.

Determining Yield to Maturity from the Bond Price

Up until now, we have used yield to maturity as well as other factors, such as the interest rate on the bond and number of years to maturity, to determine the price of the bond. We shall now assume that we know the price of the bond, the interest rate on the bond, and the years to maturity, and we wish to determine the yield to maturity. Once we have computed this value, we have determined the rate of return that investors are demanding in the marketplace to provide for inflation, risk, and other factors.

Let's once again present Formula 10–1:

$$P_b = \sum_{t=1}^{n} \frac{I_t}{(1 + Y)^t} + \frac{P_n}{(1 + Y)^n}$$

We now try to determine the value of Y, the yield to maturity, that will equate the interest payments (I_t) and the principal payment (P_n) to the price of the bond (P_b). This is similar to the calculations to determine yield in the prior chapter.

Assume a 15-year bond pays $110 per year (11 percent) in interest and $1,000 after 15 years in principal repayment. The current price of the bond is $932.21. We wish to determine the yield to maturity, or discount rate, that equates future flows with the current price.

In this trial and error process, the first step is to choose an initial percentage in the tables to try as the discount rate. Since the bond is trading below the par value of $1,000, we can assume the yield to maturity (discount rate) must be above the quoted interest rate of 11 percent. Let's begin the trial and error process.

A 13 percent discount rate   As a first approximation, we might try 13 percent and compute the present value of the bond as follows:

Present value of interest payments—

$$A = R \times IF_{pva} \ (n = 15, i = 13\%) \quad \text{[Appendix D]}$$
$$A = \$110 \times 6.462 = \$710.82$$

Present value of principal payment at maturity—

$$P = S \times IF_{pv} \ (n = 15, i = 13\%) \quad \text{[Appendix B]}$$
$$P = \$1,000 \times .160 = \$160$$

Total present value—

Present value of interest payments	$710.82
Present value of principal payment at maturity	160.00
Total present value or price of the bond	$870.82

The answer of $870.82 is below the current bond price of $932.21. This indicates we have used too high a discount rate in creating too low a value.

A 12 percent discount rate   As a next step in the trial and error process, we will try 12 percent.

Present value of interest payments—

$$A = R \times IF_{pva} \ (n = 15, i = 12\%) \quad \text{[Appendix D]}$$
$$A = \$110 \times 6.811 = \$749.21$$

Present value of principal payment at maturity—

$$P = S \times IF_{pv} \ (n = 15, i = 12\%) \quad \text{[Appendix B]}$$
$$P = \$1,000 \times .183 = \$183$$

Total present value—

Present value of interest payments	$749.21
Present value of principal payment at maturity	183.00
Total present value, or price, of the bond	$932.21

The answer precisely matches the bond price of $932.21 that we are evaluating. That indicates that the correct yield to maturity for the bond is 12 percent. Of course, if the computed value were slightly different from the price of the bond, we could use interpolation to arrive at the correct answer. An example of interpolating to derive yield to maturity is presented in Appendix 10A.

Formula for bond yield Because it is a tedious process to determine the bond yield to maturity through trial and error, an approximate answer can also be found by using Formula 10–2.[8]

Approximate yield to maturity $(Y') =$ (10–2)

$$\frac{\text{Annual interest payment} + \dfrac{\text{Principal payment} - \text{Price of the bond}}{\text{Number of years to maturity}}}{0.6 \text{ (Price of the bond)} + 0.4 \text{ (Principal payment)}}$$

Plugging in the values from the just completed analysis of yield to maturity, we show:

$$= \frac{\$110 + \dfrac{\$1,000 - 932.21}{15}}{0.6 \, (\$932.21) + 0.4 \, (\$1,000)}$$

$$= \frac{\$110 + \dfrac{\$67.79}{15}}{\$559.33 + \$400}$$

$$= \frac{\$110 + \$4.52}{\$959.33}$$

$$= \frac{\$114.52}{\$959.33}$$

$$= 11.94\%.$$

---

[8]This formula is recommended by Gabriel A. Hawawini and Ashok Vora, "Yield Approximations: A Historical Perspective," *Journal of Finance* 37 (March 1982), pp. 145–56. It tends to provide the best approximation.

The answer of 11.94 percent is a reasonably good approximation of the exact yield to maturity of 12 percent.[9] We use the prime (') symbol after Y to indicate the answer based on Formula 10–2 is only an approximation.

Note the numerator of Formula 10–2 represents the average annual income over the life of the bond and the denominator represents the average investment. That is, in the numerator, we take the annual interest payment of $110 and add that to the average annual change in the bond value over 15 years, which is computed as $4.52. This provides average annual income of $114.52. In the denominator, we take a *weighted* average of the original price of $932.21 and the final value of $1,000 that we will receive at maturity to get the average investment over the 15-year holding period.[10]

It should be pointed out that, in computing yield to maturity on a bond, financially oriented hand-held calculators[11] and software programs[12] for microcomputers can be extremely helpful. There are also useful bond tables in libraries. Nevertheless, it is important that students also understand the mechanics that go into the calculations.

As we have discussed throughout, the yield to maturity is the required rate of return that bondholders demand. More importantly for our purposes here, it also indicates the current cost to the corporation to issue bonds. In the prior example, the corporation had issued bonds at 11 percent, but market conditions changed and the current price of the bond fell to $932.21. At this current price, the ongoing yield to maturity increased to 12 percent (11.94 percent, using the approximation method). If the corporate treasurer were to issue new bonds today, he would have to respond to the current market-demanded rate of 12 percent rather than the initial yield of 11 percent. Only by understanding how investors value bonds in the marketplace can the corporate financial officer properly assess the cost of that source of financing to the corporation.

---

[9]The greater the premium or discount and the longer the period to maturity, the less accurate the approximation.

[10]As indicated by the Hawawini and Vora study (cited in footnote 8), this weighting procedure gives a better approximation than the simple arithmetic mean of the two values.

[11]See Appendix E as an example.

[12]See the Lotus 1–2–3 or Scratchpad Plus software packages that go with this text as an example.

Semiannual Interest and Bond Prices

We have been assuming that interest was paid annually in our bond analysis. In actuality, most bonds pay interest semiannually. Thus, a 10 percent interest rate bond may actually pay $50 twice a year instead of $100 annually. To make the conversion from an annual to semiannual analysis, we follow three steps.

1. Divide the annual interest rate by two.
2. Multiply the number of years by two.
3. Divide the annual yield to maturity by two.

Assume a 10 percent, $1,000 par value bond has a maturity of 20 years. The annual yield to maturity is 12 percent. In following the three steps above, we would show:

1. 10 % / 2 = 5% semiannual interest rate; therefore, 5% × $1,000 = $50 semiannual interest.
2. 20 × 2 = 40 periods to maturity.
3. 12 % / 2 = 6% yield to maturity, expressed on a semiannual basis.

In computing the price of the bond issued, on a semiannual analysis, we show:

Present value of interest payments—We take the present value of a $50 annuity for 40 periods. The semiannual discount rate is 6 percent. Using Appendix D:

$$A = R \times IF_{pva} (n = 40, i = 6\%)$$
$$A = \$50 \times 15.046 = \$752.30$$

Present value of principal payment at maturity—We take the present value of $1,000 after 40 periods, using a 6 percent discount rate. Note that once we go to a semiannual analysis with the interest payments, we consistently follow the same approach in discounting back the principal payment; otherwise, we would be using semiannual and annual calculations on the same bond. Using Appendix B:

$$P = S \times IF_{pv} (n = 40, i = 6\%)$$
$$P = \$1,000 \times .097 = \$97$$

Total present value—

Present value of interest payments	$752.30
Present value of principal payment at maturity	97.00
Total present value, or price, of the bond	$849.30

The answer of $849.30 is slightly below that which we found previously for the same bond, assuming an annual interest rate ($850.90). In terms of accuracy, the semiannual analysis is a more acceptable method. It is the method used in most bond tables, for example. As is true in many finance texts, the annual interest rate approach is given first for ease of presentation, and then the semiannual basis is given. In the problems at the back of the chapter, you will be asked to do problems on both an annual and semiannual interest payment basis.

Valuation and Preferred Stock

Preferred stock usually represents a perpetuity or, in other words, has no maturity date. It is valued in the market without any principal payment since it has no ending life. If preferred stock had a maturity date, the analysis would be similar to that of the preceding bond example. Preferred stock has a fixed dividend payment carrying a higher order of precedence than common stock dividends, but not the binding contractual obligation of interest on debt. Preferred stock, being a hybrid security, has neither the ownership privilege of common stock nor the legally enforceable provisions of debt. To value a perpetuity such as preferred stock, we first consider the formula:

$$P_p = \frac{D_p}{(1 + k_p)^1} + \frac{D_p}{(1 + k_p)^2} + \frac{D_p}{(1 + k_p)^3} + \ldots + \frac{D_p}{(1 + k_p)^\infty} \quad (10\text{--}3)$$

where

P_p = the price of preferred stock
D_p = the annual dividend for preferred stock. It is a constant value
K_p = the required rate of return, or discount rate, applied to preferred stock dividends

Note the formula calls for taking the present value of an infinite stream of constant dividend payments at a discount rate equal to K_p. Because we are dealing with an infinite stream of payments, Formula 10–3 can be reduced to a much more usable form as indicated in Formula 10–4.

$$P_p = \frac{D_p}{K_p} \quad (10\text{--}4)$$

According to Formula 10–4, all we have to do to find the price of preferred stock (P_p) is to divide the constant annual dividend payment (D_p) by the required rate of return that preferred stockholders are demanding (K_p). For example, if the annual dividend were $10 and the stockholder required a 10 percent rate of return, the price of preferred stock would be $100.

$$P_p = \frac{D_p}{K_p} = \frac{\$10}{.10} = \$100$$

As was true in our bond valuation analysis, if the rate of return required by security holders changes, the value of the financial asset (in this case, preferred stock) will change. You may also recall that the longer the life of an investment, the greater the impact of a change in required rate of return. It is one thing to be locked into a low-paying security for one year when the rate goes up; it is quite another to be locked in for 10 or 20 years. With preferred stock, you have a *perpetual* security, so the impact is at a maximum. Assume in the prior example that because of higher inflation or increased business risk that K_p (the required rate of return) increases to 12 percent. The new value for the preferred stock shares is:

$$P_p = \frac{D_p}{K_p} = \frac{\$10}{.12} = \$83.33$$

Of course, if the required rate of return were reduced to 8 percent, the opposite effect would take place. The preferred stock price would be computed as:

$$P_p = \frac{D_p}{K_p} = \frac{\$10}{.08} = \$125$$

It is not surprising that preferred stock is now trading well above its original price of $100. It is still offering a $10 dividend (10 percent of original offering price of $100), and the market is only demanding an 8 percent yield. In order to match the $10 dividend with the 8 percent rate of return, the market price will advance to $125.

Determining the Required Rate of Return (Yield) from the Market Price

In our analysis of preferred stock, we have used the value of the annual dividend (D_p) and the required rate of return (K_p) to solve for the price of preferred stock (P_p). We could change our analysis to solve for the required rate of return (K_p) as the unknown, given that we knew the annual dividend (D_p) and the preferred stock price (P_p). We take Formula 10–4 and rewrite it as Formula 10–5, where the unknown is the required rate of return (K_p).

$$P_p = \frac{D_p}{K_p} \text{ (reverse the position of } K_p \text{ and } P_p\text{)} \qquad (10\text{–}4)$$

$$K_p = \frac{D_p}{P_p} \qquad (10\text{–}5)$$

Using Formula 10–5, if the annual preferred dividend (D_p) is $10 and the price of preferred stock (P_p) is $100, the required rate of return (yield) would be 10 percent.

$$K_p = \frac{D_p}{P_p} = \frac{\$10}{\$100} = 10\%$$

If the price goes up to $130, the yield will only be 7.69 percent.

$$K_p = \frac{\$10}{\$130} = 7.69\%$$

We see the higher market price provides quite a decline in the yield.

Valuation of Common Stock

The value of a share of common stock may be interpreted by the shareholder as the *present value* of an expected stream of *future dividends*. Although in the short run stockholders may be influenced by a change in earnings or other variables, the ultimate value of any holding rests with the distribution of earnings in the form of dividend payments. Though the stockholder may benefit from the retention and reinvestment of earnings by the corporation, at some point the earnings must be translated into cash flow for the stockholder. A stock valuation model based on future expected dividends can be stated as:

$$P_o = \frac{D_1}{(1 + K_e)^1} + \frac{D_2}{(1 + K_e)^2} + \frac{D_3}{(1 + K_e)^3} + \cdots + \frac{D^\infty}{(1 + K_e)^\infty} \qquad (10\text{–}6)$$

where

P_0 = Price of the stock today
D = Dividend for each year
K_e = the required rate of return for common stock (discount rate)

This formula, with modification, is generally applied to three different circumstances.

1. No growth in dividends.
2. Constant growth in dividends.
3. Variable growth in dividends.

No Growth in Dividends

Under the no-growth circumstance, common stock is very similar to preferred stock. The common stock pays a constant dividend each year. For that reason, we merely translate the terms in Formula 10–5, which applies to preferred stock, to apply to common stock. This is shown as new Formula 10–7.

$$P_0 = \frac{D_0}{K_e} \qquad (10\text{–}7)$$

P_0 = Price of common stock today
D_0 = Current annual common stock dividend (a constant value)
K_e = Required rate of return for common stock

Assume D_0 = \$1.86 and K_e = 12 percent; the price of the stock would be \$15.50:

$$P_0 = \frac{\$1.86}{0.12} = \$15.50$$

A no-growth policy for common stock dividends does not hold much appeal for investors and so is seen infrequently in the real world.

Constant Growth in Dividends

A firm that increases dividends at a constant rate is a more likely circumstance. Perhaps a firm decides to increase its dividends by 5 or 7 percent per year. The general valuation approach is shown in Formula 10–8.

$$P_0 = \frac{D_0(1 + g)^1}{(1 + K_e)^1} + \frac{D_0(1 + g)^2}{(1 + K_e)^2} + \frac{D_0(1 + g)^3}{(1 + K_e)^3} + \ldots + \frac{D_0(1 + g)^\infty}{(1 + K_e)^\infty} \qquad (10\text{–}8)$$

where

$$P_0 = \text{Price of common stock today}$$
$$D_0(1 + g)^1 = \text{Dividend in year 1, } D_1$$
$$D_0(1 + g)^2 = \text{Dividend in year 2, } D_2 \text{, and so on}$$
$$g = \text{Constant growth rate in dividends}$$
$$K_e = \text{Required rate of return}$$
$$\text{for common stock (discount rate)}$$

In other words, the current price of the stock is the present value of the future stream of dividends growing at a constant rate. If we can anticipate the growth pattern of future dividends and determine the discount rate, we can ascertain the price of the stock.

For example, assume the following information:

$D_0 = $ Latest 12-month dividend (assume $1.87)
$D_1 = $ First year, $2.00 (growth rate, 7%)
$D_2 = $ Second year, $2.14 (growth rate, 7%)
$D_3 = $ Third year, $2.29 (growth rate, 7%)
etc., etc.
$K_e = $ Required rate of return (discount rate), 12%

then:

$$P_0 = \frac{\$2.00}{(1.12)^1} + \frac{\$2.14}{(1.12)^2} + \frac{\$2.29}{(1.12)^3} + \ldots + \frac{\text{Infinite dividend}}{(1.12)^\infty}$$

To find the price of the stock, we take the present value of each year's dividend. This is no small task when the formula calls for us to take the present value of an *infinite* stream of growing dividends. Fortunately, Formula 10–8 can be compressed into a much more usable form if two circumstances are satisfied.

1. The firm must have a constant dividend growth rate (*g*).
2. The discount rate (K_e) must exceed the growth rate (*g*).

For most introductory courses in finance, these assumptions are usually made to reduce the complications in the analytical process. This then allows us to reduce or rewrite Formula 10–8 as Formula 10–9. Formula 10–9 is the basic equation for finding the value of common stock and is referred to as the constant growth dividend valuation model.

$$P_0 = \frac{D_1}{K_e - g} \qquad (10\text{–}9)$$

This is an extremely easy formula to use in which:

$$P_0 = \text{Price of the stock today}$$
$$D_1 = \text{Dividend at the end of the first year (or period)}$$
$$K_e = \text{Required rate of return (discount rate)}$$
$$g = \text{Constant growth rate in dividends}$$

Based on the current example:

$$D_1 = \$2.00$$
$$K_e = .12$$
$$g = .07$$

and P_0 is computed as:

$$P_0 = \frac{D_1}{K_e - g} = \frac{\$2.00}{0.12 - 0.07} = \frac{\$2.00}{0.05} = \$40$$

Thus, given that the stock has a $2 dividend at the end of the first period, a discount rate of 12 percent, and a constant growth rate of 7 percent, the current price of the stock is $40.

Let's take a closer look at Formula 10–9 and the factors that influence valuation. For example, what is the anticipated effect on valuation if K_e (the required rate of return, or discount rate) increases as a result of inflation or increased risk? Intuitively, we would expect the stock price to decline if investors demand a higher return and the dividend and growth rate remain the same. This is precisely what happens.

If D_1 remains at $2.00 and the growth rate (g) is 7 percent, but K_e increases from 12 percent to 14 percent, using Formula 10–9, the price of the common stock will now be $28.57. This is considerably lower than its earlier value of $40.

$$P_0 = \frac{D_1}{K_e - g} = \frac{\$2.00}{0.14 - 0.07} = \frac{\$2.00}{0.07} = \$28.57$$

Similarly, if the growth rate (g) increases while D_1 and K_e remain constant, the stock price can be expected to increase. Assume $D_1 = \$2.00$, K_e is set at its earlier level of 12 percent, and g increases from 7 percent to 9 percent. Using Formula 10–9 once again, the new price of the stock would be $66.67.

$$P_0 = \frac{D_1}{K_e - g} = \frac{\$2.00}{0.12 - 0.09} = \frac{\$2.00}{0.03} = \$66.67$$

We should not be surprised to see that an increasing growth rate has enhanced the value of the stock.

Stock valuation based on future stock value   The discussion of stock valuation to this point has related to the concept of the present value of future dividends. This is a valid concept, but suppose we wish to approach the issue from a slightly different viewpoint. Assume we are going to buy a stock and hold it for three years and then sell it. We wish to know the present value of our investment. This is somewhat like the bond valuation analysis. We will receive a dividend for three years (D_1, D_2, D_3) and then a price (payment) for the stock at the end of three years (P_3). What is the present value of the benefits? What we do is add the present value of three years of dividends and the present value of the stock price after three years. Assuming a constant-growth dividend analysis, the stock price after three years is simply the present value of all future dividends after the third year (from the fourth year on). Thus, the current price of the stock in this case is nothing other than the present value of the first three dividends, plus the present value of all future dividends (which is equivalent to the stock price after the third year). Saying the price of the stock is the present value of all future dividends is also the equivalent of saying it is the present value of a dividend stream for a number of years, plus the present value of the price of the stock after that time period. The appropriate formula is still $P_0 = D_1/(K_e - g)$, which we have been using throughout this part of the chapter. This point is demonstrated in Problem 22 at the back of the chapter.

Determining the Required Rate of Return from the Market Price

In our analysis of common stock, we have used the first year's dividend (D_1), the required rate of return (K_e), and the growth rate (g) to solve for the stock price (P_0) based on Formula 10–9.

$$P_0 = \frac{D_1}{K_e - g} \quad \text{(previously presented Formula 10–9)}$$

We could change the analysis to solve for the required rate of return (K_e) as the unknown, given that we know the first year's dividend (D_1), the stock price (P_0), and the growth rate (g). We take the formula above and algebraically change it to provide Formula 10–10.

$$P_0 = \frac{D_1}{K_e - g} \qquad\qquad (10\text{–}9)$$

$$K_e = \frac{D_1}{P_0} + g \qquad\qquad (10\text{–}10)$$

Formula 10–10 allows us to compute the required return (K_e) from the investment. Returning to the basic data, from the common stock example:

K_e = Required rate of return (to be solved)
D_1 = Dividend at the end of the first year $2.00
P_0 = Price of the stock today, $40
g = Constant growth rate .07

$$K_e = \frac{\$2.00}{\$40} + 7\% = 5\% + 7\% = 12\%$$

In this instance, we would say the stockholder demands a 12 percent return on his common stock investment. Of particular interest are the individual parts of the formula for K_e that we have been discussing. Let's write out Formula 10–10 again.

$$K_e = \frac{\text{First year's dividend}}{\text{Common stock price}} \left(\frac{D_1}{P_0}\right) + \text{Growth } (g)$$

The first term represents the dividend yield that the stockholder will receive, and the second term represents the anticipated growth in dividends, earnings, and stock price. While we have been describing the growth rate primarily in terms of dividends, it is assumed that the earnings and stock price will also grow at that same rate over the long term if all else holds constant. You should also observe that the formula above represents a total return concept. The stockholder is receiving a current dividend plus anticipated growth in the future. If the dividend yield is low, the growth rate must be high to provide the necessary return. Conversely, if the growth rate is low, a high dividend yield will be expected. The concepts of dividend yield and growth are clearly interrelated.

The Price–Earnings Ratio Concept and Valuation

In Chapter 2 we introduced the concept of the price–earnings ratio. The price–earnings ratio represents a multiplier applied to current earnings to determine the value of a share of stock in the market. It is considered a pragmatic, everyday approach to valuation. If a stock has earnings per share of $3 and a price–earnings (P/E) ratio of 12 times, it will carry a market value of $36. Another company with the same earnings but a P/E ratio of 15 times will enjoy a market price of $45.

The price–earnings ratio is influenced by the earnings and sales growth of the firm, the risk (or volatility in performance), the debt–equity structure of the firm, the dividend policy, the quality of management, and a number of other factors. Firms that have bright expectations for the future tend to trade at high P/E ratios while the opposite is true of low P/E firms.

For example, the average P/E for all New York Stock Exchange firms was 15 in early 1988, but Capital Cities Communication Corporation traded at a P/E of 22 because of unusually bright prospects for the broadcasting/publishing industry. At the same time, General Motors traded at a relatively low P/E of seven because of less than favorable factors influencing the automobile industry.

Actually, P/E ratios can be looked up in *The Wall Street Journal* or the business section of most newspapers. Quotations from *The Wall Street Journal* are presented in Table 10–3. The first column (Div.) after the company name shows the annual dividend, and the second column (Yld) shows the dividend yield. This represents the annual dividend divided by the closing stock price. The third column after the company name (PE) is of primary interest in that it shows the current price–earnings ratio. For Texas Instruments, it is 17, indicating that the current stock price of 40¾ represents 17 times annual earnings.[13] The remaining columns show the daily sales and the high, low, and closing prices for the day, plus any changes from the previous day. The dividend valuation approach (based on the present value of dividends) that we have been using throughout the chapter is more theoretically sound and likely to be used by sophisticated financial analysts. Actually, to some extent, the two concepts can be brought together. A stock that has a high required rate of return (K_e) because of its risky nature will generally have a low P/E ratio. Similarly, a stock with a low required rate of return (K_e) because of the likelihood of positive future performance will normally have a high P/E ratio. In the first example, both methods provide a low valuation, while in the latter case, both methods provide a high valuation.

---

[13]The price–earnings ratio is not shown for some companies because they do not have positive earnings on which to base the calculation, or because it is the preferred stock of the company which is shown, in which case, the P/E ratio is not relevant because preferred stock does not have earnings per share as such.

Table 10–3
Quotations from *The Wall Street Journal*

Source: Reprinted by permission of *The Wall Street Journal.* © Dow Jones & Company, Inc. (November 23, 1987), p. 47. All rights reserved.

Variable Growth in Dividends

In the discussion of common stock valuation, we have considered procedures for firms that had no growth in dividends and for firms that had a constant growth. Most of the discussion and literature in finance assumes a constant growth dividend model. However, there is also a third case, and that is one of variable growth in dividends. The most common variable growth model is one in which the firm experiences supernormal (very rapid) growth for a number of years and then levels off to more normal, constant growth. The supernormal growth pattern is often experienced by firms in emerging industries, such as in the early days of electronics or microcomputers.

In evaluating a firm with an initial pattern of supernormal growth, we first take the present value of dividends during the exceptional growth period. We then determine the price of the stock at the end of the supernormal growth period by taking the present value of the normal, constant dividends that follow the supernormal growth period. We discount this price to the present and add it to the present value of the supernormal dividends. This gives us the current price of the stock.

A numerical example of a supernormal growth rate evaluation model is presented in Appendix 10B at the end of this chapter. (The appendix is optional and not essential to the continued development of the material in the text.)

Finally, in the discussion of common stock valuation models, readers may ask about the valuation of companies that currently pay no dividends. Since virtually all our discussion has been based on values associated with dividends, how can this "no dividend" circumstance be handled? One approach is to assume that even for the firm that pays no current dividends, at some point in the future, stockholders will be rewarded with cash dividends. We then take the present value of their deferred dividends.

A second approach to valuing a firm that pays no cash dividend is to take the present value of earnings per share for a number of periods and add that to the present value of a future anticipated stock price. The discount rate applied to future earnings is generally higher than the discount rate applied to future dividends.

Summary and Review of Formulas

The primary emphasis in this chapter is on valuation of financial assets: bonds, preferred stock, and common stock. Regardless of the security being analyzed, valuation is normally based on the concept of determining the present value of future cash flows. Thus, we draw on many of the time-value-of-money techniques developed in Chapter 9. Inherent in the valuation process is a determination of rate of return that investors demand. When we have computed this value, we have also identified what it will cost the corporation to raise new capital. Let's specifically review the valuation techniques associated with bonds, preferred stock, and common stock.

Bonds

The price, or current value, of a bond is equal to the present value of interest payments (I_t) over the life of the bond plus the present value of the principal payment (P_n) at maturity. The discount rate used in the analytical process is the yield to maturity (Y). The yield to maturity (required rate of return) is determined in the marketplace by such factors as the *real* rate of return, an inflation premium, and a risk premium.

The equation for bond valuation was presented as Formula 10–1.

$$P_b = \sum_{t=1}^{n} \frac{I_t}{(1 + Y)^t} + \frac{P_n}{(1 + Y)^n} \qquad [10\text{--}1]$$

The actual terms in the equation are solved by the use of present value tables. We say the present value of interest payments is:

$$A = R \times IF_{pva} \ (n = \underline{\ \ }; i = \underline{\ \ }) \qquad [\text{Appendix D}]$$

the present value of the principal payment at maturity is:

$$P = S \times IF_{pv} \ (n = \underline{\ \ }; i = \underline{\ \ }) \qquad [\text{Appendix B}]$$

We add these two values together to determine the price of the bond. We use both annual or semiannual analysis.

The value of the bond will be strongly influenced by the relationship of the yield to maturity in the market to the interest rate on the bond and also the length of time to maturity.

If you know the price of the bond, the size of the interest payments, and the maturity of the bond, you can solve for the yield to maturity through a trial and error approach (discussed in the chapter and expanded in Appendix 10A), by an approximation approach as presented in Formula 10–2, or by using financially oriented calculators (in Appendix E) or appropriate computer software.

Preferred Stock

In determining the value of preferred stock, we are taking the present value of an infinite stream of level dividend payments. This would be a tedious process if it were not for the fact that the mathematical calculations can be compressed into a simple formula. The appropriate equation is Formula 10–4.

$$P_p = \frac{D_p}{K_p} \qquad [10\text{--}4]$$

According to Formula 10–4, to find the preferred stock price (P_p) we take the constant annual dividend payment (D_p) and divide this value by the rate of return that preferred stockholders are demanding (K_p).

If, on the other hand, we know the price of the preferred stock and the constant annual dividend payment, we can solve for the required rate of return on preferred stock as:

$$K_p = \frac{D_p}{P_p} \qquad \text{[10–5]}$$

Common Stock

The value of common stock is also based on the concept of the present value of an expected stream of future dividends. Unlike preferred stock, the dividends are not necessarily level. The firm and shareholders may experience:

1. No growth in dividends.
2. Constant growth in dividends.
3. Variable or supernormal growth in dividends.

It is the second circumstance that receives most of the attention in the financial literature. If a firm has constant growth (g) in dividends (D) and the required rate of return (K_e) exceeds the growth rate, Formula 10–9 can be utilized.

$$P_0 = \frac{D_1}{K_e - g} \qquad \text{[10–9]}$$

In using Formula 10–9, all we need to know is the value of the dividend at the end of the first year, the required rate of return, and the discount rate. Most of our valuation calculations with common stock utilize Formula 10–9.

If we need to know the required rate of return (K_e) for common stock, Formula 10–10 can be employed.

$$K_e = \frac{D_1}{P_0} + g \qquad \text{[10–10]}$$

The first term represents the dividend yield on the stock and the second term the growth rate. Together they provide the total return demanded by the investor.

List of Terms

yield to maturity
real rate of return
inflation premium
risk premium
perpetuity
dividend valuation model

dividend yield
price–earnings ratio (P/E)
supernormal growth
discount rate
required rate of return

Discussion Questions

1. How is valuation of financial assets by investors related to the cost of financing (cost of capital) for the firm?

2. How is valuation of any financial asset related to future cash flows?

3. Why might investors demand a lower rate of return for an investment in IBM as compared to Armco Steel or LTV?

4. What are the three factors that influence the demanded rate of return by investors?

5. If inflationary expectations increase, what is likely to happen to yield to maturity on bonds in the marketplace? What is also likely to happen to the price of bonds?

6. Why is the remaining time to maturity an important factor in evaluating the impact of a change in yield to maturity on bond prices?

7. What are the three adjustments that have to be made in going from annual to semiannual bond analysis?

8. Why is a change in required yield for preferred stock likely to have a greater impact on price than a change in required yield for bonds?

9. What type of dividend pattern for common stock is similar to the dividend payment for preferred stock?

10. What two conditions must be met to go from Formula 10–8 to Formula 10–9 in using the dividend valuation model?

$$P_0 = \frac{D_1}{K_e - g} \qquad [10\text{--}9]$$

11. What are the two components that make up the required rate of return on common stock?

12. What are some factors that might influence a firm's price–earnings ratio?

13. How is the supernormal growth pattern likely to vary from the more normal, constant growth pattern?

14. What approaches can be taken in valuing a firm's stock when there is no cash dividend payment?

Problems

(For the first nine bond problems, assume interest payments are on an annual basis.)

1. Vanna Whitewall Tires, Inc., has $1,000 par value bonds outstanding at 11 percent interest. The bonds will mature in 20 years. Compute the current price of the bonds if the present yield to maturity is:
   a. 8 percent.
   b. 10 percent.
   c. 14 percent.

2. The Fortune Casino and Hotel Chain has a $1,000 par value bond outstanding that pays 9 percent annual interest. The current yield to maturity on such bonds in the market is 12 percent. Compute the price of the bonds for these maturity dates:
   a. 30 years.
   b. 15 years.
   c. 1 year.

3. For problem 2, graph the relationship in a manner similar to the bottom half of Figure 10–2 in the chapter. Also explain why the pattern of price change takes place.

4. Ken Keltner calls his broker to inquire about purchasing a bond of Northeast Airlines. His broker quotes a price of $1,250. Ken is concerned that the bond might be overpriced, based on the facts involved. The $1,000 par value bond pays 13 percent interest, and it has 16 years remaining until maturity. The current yield to maturity on similar bonds is 10 percent.

   Compute the new price of the bond and comment on whether you think it is overpriced in the marketplace.

5. Frazier Aluminum Company issued bonds in 1984 at $1,000 per bond. The bonds had a 25-year life when issued and the annual interest payment was then 12 percent. This return was in line with required returns by bondholders at that point in time as described below:

Real rate of return	3%
Inflation premium	6
Risk premium	3
Total return	12%

Assume that in 1989 the inflation premium is only 4 percent and is appropriately reflected in the required return (or yield to maturity) of the bonds. The bonds have 20 years remaining until maturity.

Compute the new price of the bond.

6. Lance Whittingham IV specializes in buying deep discount bonds. These represent bonds that are trading at well below par value. He has his eye on a bond issued by the Leisure Time Corporation. The $1,000 par value bond pays 4 percent annual interest and has 16 years remaining to maturity. The current yield to maturity on similar bonds is 10 percent.

   a. What is the current price of the bonds?
   b. By what percent will the price of the bonds increase between now and maturity?
   c. What is the annual compound rate of growth in the value of the bonds? (An approximate answer is acceptable.)

7. Bonds issued by the Marcos Shoe Company have a par value of $1,000, which, of course, is also the amount of principal to be paid at maturity. The bonds are currently selling for $850. They have 10 years remaining to maturity. The annual interest payment is 9 percent ($90).

   Compute the approximate yield to maturity, using Formula 10–2.

8. Bonds issued by the West Motel Corporation have a par value of $1,000, are selling for $1,100, and have 20 years remaining to maturity. The annual interest payment is 13.5 percent ($135).

   Compute the approximate yield to maturity, using Formula 10–2.

9. Optional—for problem 8, use the techniques in Appendix 10A to combine a trial-and-error approach with interpolation to find a more exact answer. You may choose to use a hand-held calculator instead.

(For the next two problems, assume interest payments are on a semi-annual basis.)

10. Albert Gray is considering a bond investment in the McFarlane Trust Company. The $1,000 bonds have a quoted annual interest rate of 8 percent and the interest is paid semiannually. The yield to maturity on the bonds is 10 percent annual interest. There are 15 years to maturity.

    Compute the price of the bonds based on semiannual analysis.

11. You are called in as a financial analyst to appraise the bonds of the Knight Corporation, the largest manufacturer of portable chairs in the Midwest. The $1,000 par value bonds have a quoted annual interest rate of 10 percent, which is paid semiannually. The yield to maturity on the bonds is 12 percent annual interest. There are 25 years to maturity.

    a. Compute the price of the bonds based on semiannual analysis.
    b. With 25 years remaining to maturity, if yield to maturity goes down to 8 percent, what will be the new price of the bonds?

12. The preferred stock of the Mitchell Publishing Company pays a dividend of $6.50. It has a required return of 8 percent.

    Compute the price of the preferred stock.

13. X-Tech Company issued preferred stock many years ago. It carries a fixed dividend of $5 per share. With the passage of time, yields have soared from the original 5 percent to 12 percent (yield is the same as required rate of return).

    a. What was the original issue price?
    b. What is the current value of this preferred stock?
    c. If the yield on the Standard & Poor's Preferred Stock Index declines, how will the price of the preferred stock be affected?

14. Brian's Video Corporation has preferred stock outstanding that pays an annual dividend of $8.40 per share. It has a price of $105. What is the required return (yield) on the preferred stock?

(All of the following problems pertain to the common stock section of the chapter.)

15. The Tri-State Motor Corporation pays a $3.50 cash dividend (D_o). They plan to maintain the dividend at this level for the foreseeable future as no growth is anticipated.

    If the required rate of return by common stockholders (K_e) is 14 percent, what is the price of the common stock?

16. Taylor Metals will pay a common stock dividend of $2.80 at the end of the year (D_1). The required return on common stock (K_e) is 12 percent. The firm has a constant growth rate (g) of 8 percent.
    Compute the current price of the stock (P_o).

17. Friedman Steel Company will pay a dividend of $1.50 per share in the next 12 months (D_1). The required rate of return (K_e) is 10 percent and the constant growth rate is 5 percent.
    a.   Compute P_0.

    (In the remaining questions in this problem all variables remain the same except the one specifically changed. Each question is independent of the others.)

    b.   Assume K_e, the required rate of return, goes up to 12 percent, what will be the new value of P_0?
    c.   Assume the growth rate (g) goes up to 7 percent, what will be the new value of P_0?
    d.   Assume D_1 is $2, what will be the new value of P_0?

18. The Hodges Corporation paid a dividend of $5 last year. Over the next 12 months, the dividend is expected to grow at 8 percent, which is the constant growth rate for the firm (g). The new dividend after 12 months will represent D_1. The required rate of return (K_e) is 14 percent.
    Compute the price of the stock (P_0).

19. Haltom Electronics has had the following pattern of earnings per share over the last five years:

Year	Earnings per Share
1984	$3.00
1985	3.18
1986	3.37
1987	3.57
1988	3.78

The earnings per share have grown at a constant rate (on a rounded basis) and will continue to do so in the future. Dividends represent 30 percent of earnings.

Project earnings and dividends for the next year (1989). Round all values in this problem to two places to the right of the decimal point.

If the required rate of return (K_e) is 10 percent, what is the anticipated stock price at the beginning of 1989?

20. A firm pays a $4.20 dividend at the end of year one (D_1), has a stock price of $60 ($P_0$), and a constant growth rate (g) of 6 percent. Compute the required rate of return (K_e).

21. A firm pays a $1.50 dividend at the end of year one (D_1), has a stock price of $60 ($P_0$), and a constant growth rate (g) of 9 percent.
   a. Compute the required rate of return (K_e).
   Indicate whether each of the following changes would make the required rate of return (K_e) go up or down. (Each question is separate from the others. No actual numbers are necessary.)
   b. The dividend payment increases.
   c. The expected growth rate increases.
   d. The stock price increases.

22. Royal Data Systems paid a $3 dividend last year. The dividend is expected to grow at a constant rate of 5 percent over the next three years. The required rate of return is 10 percent (this will also serve as the discount rate in this problem). Round all values to two places to the right of the decimal point where appropriate.
   a. Compute the anticipated value of the dividends for the next three years. That is, compute D_1, D_2, and D_3; for example, D_1 is $3.15 ($3.00 × 1.05). Round all values throughout this problem to two places to the right of the decimal point.
   b. Discount each of these dividends back to the present at a discount rate of 10 percent and then sum them.
   c. Compute the price of the stock at the end of the third year (P_3).

$$P_3 = \frac{D_4}{K_e - g}$$

(D_4 is equal to D_3 times 1.05)

   d. After you have computed P_3, discount it back to the present at a discount rate of 10 percent for three years.
   e. Add together the answers in part *b* and part *d* to get P_0, the current value of the stock. This answer represents the present value of the first three periods of dividends, plus the present value of the price of the stock after three periods (which, in turn, represents the value of all future dividends).
   f. Use Formula 10–9 to show that it will provide approximately the same answer as part *e*.

$$P_0 = \frac{D_1}{K_e - g} \qquad \text{[10–9]}$$

For Formula 10–9, use $D_1 = \$3.15$, $K_e = 10$ percent, and $g = 5$ percent. (The slight difference between the answers to part *e* and part *f* is due to rounding.)

Selected References

Barnes, Amir, and Dennis E. Logue. "The Evaluation Forecasts of a Security Analyst." *Financial Management* 2 (Summer 1975), pp. 38–45.

Bierwag, Gerald O. "Bond Returns, Discrete Stochastic Processes, and Duration." *Journal of Financial Research* 43 (Fall 1987), pp. 191–210.

Friend, Irwin, and Marshall Blume. "The Demand for Risky Assets." *American Economic Review* 75 (December 1975), pp. 900.

Gooding, Arthur E. "Qualification of Investors' Perceptions of Common Stocks: Risks and Return Dimensions." *Journal of Finance* 29 (December 1975), pp. 1,301–16.

Hirt, Geoffrey A., and Stanley B. Block. *Fundamentals of Investment Management.* 2nd ed. Homewood, Ill.: Richard D. Irwin, 1986.

McEnally, Richard W. "A Note on the Return of High Risk Common Stock." *Journal of Finance* 29 (March 1974), pp. 199–202.

Nelson, Charles R. "Inflation and Rates of Return on Common Stock." *Journal of Finance* 31. (May 1976), pp. 471–83.

Norgaard, Richard L. "An examination of the Yields of Corporate Bonds and Stocks." *Journal of Finance* 29 (September 1974), pp. 1,275–86.

Olsen, I. J. "Valuation of a Closely Held Corporation." *Journal of Accounting* 128 (August 1969), pp. 35–47.

Reilly, Frank K. *Investments.* 2nd ed. Hinsdale, Ill.: Dryden Press, 1985.

Spudeck, Raymond E., and R. Charles Moyer. "Reverse Splits and Shareholder Wealth: The Impact of Commissions." *Financial Management* 14 (Winter 1985), pp. 52–57.

Vandell, Robert F., and Jerry L. Stevens. "Personal Taxes and Equity Security Pricing." *Financial Management* 11 (Spring 1984), pp. 31–40.

Zivney, Terry L., and Donald J. Thompson, II. "Relative Stock Prices and the Firm Size Effect." *Journal of Financial Research* 43 (Summer 1987), pp. 99–110.

Appendix 10A: The Bond Yield to Maturity Using Interpolation

We will use a numerical example to demonstrate this process. Assume a 20-year bond pays $118 per year (11.8 percent) in interest and $1,000 after 20 years in principal repayment. The current price of the bond is $1,085. We wish to determine the yield to maturity or discount rate that equates the future flows with the current price.

Since the bond is trading above par value at $1,085, we can assume the yield to maturity must be below the quoted interest rate of 12 percent (the yield to maturity would be the full 12 percent at a bond price of $1,000). As a first approximation, we will try 10 percent. Annual analysis is used.

Present value of interest payments—

$$A = R \times IF_{pva} \ (n = 20, \ i = 10\%) \quad \text{[Appendix D]}$$
$$A = \$118 \times 8.514 \ = \$1,004.65$$

Present value of principal payment at maturity—

$$P = S \times IF_{pv} \ (n = 20, \ i = 10\%) \quad \text{[Appendix B]}$$
$$P = \$1,000 \times .149 = \$149$$

Total present value—

Present value of interest payments	$1,004.65
Present value of principal payment at maturity	149.00
Total present value, or price, of the bond	$1,153.65

The discount rate of 10 percent gives us too high a present value in comparison to the current bond price of $1,085. Let's try a higher discount rate to get a lower rate. We will use 11 percent.

Present value of interest payments—

$$A = R \times IF_{pva} \ (n = 20, \ i = 11\%) \quad \text{[Appendix D]}$$
$$A = \$118 \times 7.963 = \$939.63$$

Present value of principal payment at maturity—

$$P = S \times IF_{pv} \ (n = 20, \ i = 11\%) \quad \text{[Appendix B]}$$
$$P = \$1,000 \times .124 = \$124.00$$

Total present value—

Present value of interest payments	$ 939.63
Present value of principal payment at maturity	124.00
Total present value, or price, of the bond	$1,063.63

The discount rate of 11 percent gives us a value slightly lower than the bond price of $1,085. The rate for the bond must fall between 10 and 11 percent. Using linear interpolation, the answer is 10.76 percent.

$1,153.65 PV @ 10%	$1,153.65 PV @ 10%
1,163.63 PV @ 11%	1,085.00 bond price
$ 90.02	$ 68.65

$$10\% + \frac{\$68.65}{\$90.02}(1\%) = 10\% + .76(1\%) = 10.76\%$$

Problem

10A–1. Bonds issued by the Medford Corporation have a par value of $1,000, are selling for $865, and have 25 years to maturity. The annual interest payment is 8 percent.

Find yield to maturity by combining the trial-and-error approach with interpolation, as shown in this appendix. (Use an assumption of annual interest payments.)

Appendix 10B: Valuation of a Supernormal Growth Firm

The equation for the valuation of a supernormal growth firm is:

$$P_0 = \sum_{t=1}^{n}\frac{D_t}{(1 + K_e)^t} + P_n\left(\frac{1}{1 + K_e}\right)^n \qquad (10B\text{–}1)$$

(Supernormal (After supernormal
growth   growth period)
period)

Actually, the formula is not difficult to use. The first term calls for determining the present value of the dividends using the supernormal growth period. The second term calls for computing the present value of the future stock price as determined at the end of the supernormal growth period. If we add the two together, we arrive at the current stock price. We are adding together the two benefits the stockholder will receive: a future stream of dividends during the supernormal growth period and the future stock price.

Let's assume the firm paid a dividend over the last 12 months of $1.67; this represents the current dividend rate. Dividends are expected to grow by 20 percent per year over the supernormal growth period (n) of three years. They will then grow at a normal constant growth rate (g) of 5 percent. The required rate of return (discount rate) as represented by K_e is 9 percent. We first find the present value of the dividends during the supernormal growth period.

(1) *Present value of supernormal dividends—*

D_0 = $1.67. We allow this value to grow at 20 percent per year over the three years of supernormal growth.

$$D_1 = D_0 \, (1 \, + \, .20) = \$1.67 \, (1.20) = \$2.00$$
$$D_2 = D_1 \, (1 \, + \, .20) = \$2.00 \, (1.20) = \$2.40$$
$$D_3 = D_2 \, (1 \, + \, .20) = \$2.40 \, (1.20) = \$2.88$$

We then discount these values back at 9 percent to find the present value of dividends during the supernormal growth period.

	Supernormal Dividends	Discount Rate $K_e = 9\%$	Present Value of Dividends during the Supernormal Period
D_1	$2.00	.917	$1.83
D_2	2.40	.842	2.02
D_3	2.88	.772	2.22
			$6.07

The present value of the supernormal dividends is $6.07. We now turn to the future stock price.

(2) *Present value of future stock price—*

We first find the future stock price at the end of the supernormal growth period. This is found by taking the present value of the dividends that will be growing at a normal, constant rate after the supernormal period. This will begin *after* the third (and last) period of supernormal growth.

Since after the supernormal growth period the firm is growing at a normal, constant rate ($g = 5$ percent) and K_e (the discount rate) of 9 percent exceeds the new, constant growth rate of 5 percent, we have fulfilled the two conditions for using the constant dividend growth model after three years. That is, we can apply Formula 10–9 (without subscripts for now).

$$P = \frac{D}{K_e - g}$$

In this case, however, D is really the dividend at the end of the fourth period because this phase of the analysis starts at the beginning of the fourth period and D is supposed to fall at the *end* of the first period of analysis in the formula. Also, the price we are solving for now is the price at the beginning of the fourth period which, of course, is the same concept as the price at the end of the third period (P_3).

We thus say:

$$P_3 = \frac{D_4}{K_e - g} \tag{10B-2}$$

D_4 is equal to the previously determined value for D_3 of $2.88 moved forward one period at the constant growth rate of 5 percent.

$$D_4 = \$2.88 \,(1.05) = \$3.02$$

Also:

$$K_e = .09 \text{ discount rate (required rate of return)}$$
$$g = .05 \text{ constant growth rate}$$

$$P_3 = \frac{D_4}{K_e - g} = \frac{\$3.02}{.09 - .05} = \frac{\$3.02}{.04} = \$75.50$$

This is the value of the stock at the end of the third period. We discount this value back to the present.

Stock Price after Three Years	Discount Rate* $K_e = 9\%$	Present Value of Future Price
$75.50	.772	$58.29

*Note: n is equal to 3.

The present value of the future stock price (P_3) of $75.50 is $58.29.

By adding together the answers in part (1) and part (2) of this appendix, we arrive at the total present value, or price, of the supernormal growth stock.

(1) Present value of dividends during the normal growth period . . . . $ 6.07
(2) Present value of the future stock price 58.29
       Total present value, or price $64.36

The process we have just completed is presented in Figure 10B–1. The student who wishes to develop skills in growth analysis should work Problem 10B–1.

Problem

10B–1. The Selby Corporation paid a dividend of $1.40 over the last 12 months. The dividend is expected to grow at a rate of 25 percent over the next three years (supernormal growth). It will then grow at a normal, constant rate of 7 percent for the foreseeable future.

Figure 10B–1
Stock valuation under supernormal growth analysis

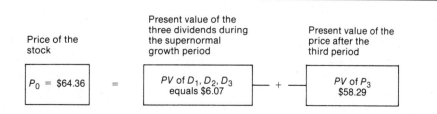

The required rate of return is 12 percent (this will also serve as the discount rate).

a.   Compute the anticipated value of the dividends for the next three years (D_1, D_2, and D_3). Round all values throughout this problem to two places to the right of the decimal point.

b.   Discount each of these dividends back to the present at a discount rate of 12 percent and then sum them.

c.   Compute the price of the stock at the end of the third year (P_3).

$$P_3 = \frac{D_4}{K_e - g}$$ [review Appendix 10B–1 for the definition of D_4]

d.   After you have computed P_3, discount it back to the present at a discount rate of 12 percent for three years.

e.   Add together the answers in part *b* and part *d* to get the current value of the stock. (This answer represents the present value of the first three periods of dividends plus the present value of the price of the stock after three periods.)

11

Cost of Capital

Throughout the previous two chapters, a number of references were made to discounting future cash flows in solving for the present value. How do you determine the appropriate interest rate or discount rate in a problem situation? Suppose that a young doctor is rendered incapable of practicing medicine due to an auto accident in the last year of his residency. The court determines that he could have made $100,000 a year for the next 30 years. What is the present value of these inflows? We must know the appropriate discount rate. If 10 percent is used, the value is $942,700; with 5 percent, the answer is $1,537,300—over half a million dollars is at stake.

In the corporate finance setting, the more likely circumstance is that an investment will be made today—promising a set of inflows in the future and we need to know the appropriate discount rate. The purpose of this chapter is to set down the methods and procedures for making such a determination.

First of all, the student should observe that if we invest money today to receive benefits in the future, we must be absolutely certain we are earning at least as much as it costs us to acquire the funds for investment—that, in essence, is the minimum acceptable return. If funds cost the firm 10 percent, then all projects must be tested to make sure they earn at least 10 percent. By using this as the discount rate, we can ascertain whether we have earned the financial cost of doing business.

The Overall Concept

How does the firm determine the cost of its funds or, more properly stated, the *cost of capital?* Suppose the plant superintendent wishes to borrow money at 6 percent to purchase a conveyor system, while a division manager suggests stock be sold at an effective cost of 12 percent to develop a new product. Not only would it be foolish indeed for each investment to be judged against the specific means of financing used to implement it, but this would also make investment selection decisions inconsistent. For example, picture financing a conveyor system having an 8 percent return with 6 percent debt and also evaluating a new product having an 11 percent return but financed with 12 percent common stock. If projects and financing are matched in this way, the project with the lower return would be accepted and the project with the higher return would be rejected. In reality, if stock and debt are sold in equal proportions, the average cost of financing would be 9 percent (one half debt at 6 percent and one half stock at 12 percent). With a 9 percent average cost of financing, we would now reject the 8 percent conveyor system and accept the 11 percent new product. This would be a rational and consistent decision. Though an investment financed by low-cost debt might appear acceptable at first glance, the use of debt might increase the overall risk of the firm and eventually make all forms of financing more expensive. Each project must be measured against the overall cost of funds to the firm. We now consider cost of capital in a broader context.

The determination of cost of capital can best be understood by examining the capital structure of a hypothetical firm, the Baker Corporation, in Table 11–1. Note that the aftertax costs of the individual sources

Table 11–1 Cost of capital— Baker Corporation		(1) Cost (aftertax)	(2) Weights	(3) Weighted Cost
Debt	K_d	7.05%	30%	2.12%
Preferred stock	K_p	10.94	10	1.09
Common equity (retained earnings)	K_e	12.00	60	7.20
Weighted average cost of capital	K_a			10.41%

of financing are shown, then weights are assigned to each, and finally a weighted average cost is determined. (The costs under consideration are those related to new funds which can be used for future financing, rather than historical costs.) In the remainder of the chapter, each of these procedural steps is examined.

Each element in the capital structure has an explicit or opportunity cost associated with it, herein referred to by the symbol K. These costs are directly related to the valuation concepts developed in the previous chapter. If a reader understands how a security is valued, then there is little problem in determining its cost. The mathematics involved in the cost of capital are not difficult. We begin our analysis with a consideration of the cost of debt.

Cost of Debt

The cost of debt is measured by the interest rate, or yield, paid to bond-holders. The simplest case would be a $1,000 bond paying $100 annual interest, thus providing a 10 percent yield. The computation may be more difficult if the bond is priced at a discount or premium from par value. Techniques for computing such bond yields were presented in Chapter 10, Valuation and Rates of Return.

For example, assume the firm is preparing to issue new debt. To determine the likely cost of the new debt in the marketplace, the firm will compute the yield on its currently outstanding debt. This is not the rate at which the old debt was issued, but the rate that investors are demanding today. Assume the debt issue pays $100 per year in interest, has a 20-year life, and is currently selling for $940. In order to find the current yield to maturity on the debt, we could use the trial-and-error process described in the previous chapter. That is, we would experiment with discount rates until we found the rate that would equate interest payments of $100 for 20 years and a maturity payment of $1,000 with $940 today. A simpler process would be to use Formula 10–2 from the prior chapter which gives us the approximate yield to maturity. We reproduce the formula below and relabel it Formula 11–1 to fit the numbering system in this chapter.

$$\text{Approximate yield to maturity } (Y') = \frac{\text{Annual interest payment} + \dfrac{\text{Principal payment} - \text{Price of the bond}}{\text{Number of years to maturity}}}{0.6(\text{Price of the bond}) + 0.4(\text{Principal payment})} \qquad (11\text{–}1)$$

For the bond under discussion, the approximate yield to maturity (Y') would be:

$$= \frac{\$100 + \dfrac{\$1,000 - \$940}{20}}{.6(\$940) + .4(\$1,000)}$$

$$= \frac{\$100 + \dfrac{60}{20}}{\$564 + \$400}$$

$$= \frac{\$100 + \$3}{\$964} = \frac{\$103}{\$964} = 10.68\%$$

In many cases, you will not have to compute the yield to maturity. It will simply be given to you. The practicing corporate financial manager also can normally consult a source such as Standard & Poor's Bond Guide to determine the yield to maturity on his firm's outstanding debt. An excerpt from this bond guide is presented in Table 11–2. If the firm

Table 11–2
Excerpt from Standard & Poor's Bond Guide

110 Ohi-ONE   STANDARD & POOR'S CORPORATION

Title-Industry Code & Co. Finances (In Italics)	I n d	Caps. 1984	Times Earn. 1985	Yr. 1986 End	Cash &Eqv	Current Assets Liabs Date Million $		L. Term Debt (Mil $)	Debt % Prop		Price Range					Mo. End Price		Yield to
Individual Issue Statistics	S&P		Eligible	Legality	Redemption Provisions		Out-			1972-85		1986		1987		Sale(s) Curr	to
Exchange Interest Dates	Qual- ity rating		Bond Form	M N N a H Y	Refund Earliest/ Other	Call Price For S.F.	Reg- ular	st'd'g (Mil $)	Underwriter Firm Year	High Low		High Low		High	Low or Bid	Yield	Mat.
Ohio Ed 1st 7⅝s 2002	fA	BBB-	F2 R	· · √	· · · ·	‡100.81	‡103.78	34.3	F2 '72	101⅜ 46¾	83½ 73¾	85½	74½ 74½	10.02 10.96		
1st 8⅜s 2003	mS	BBB-	X R	· · √	· · · ·	‡101.03	‡104.49	61.6	MB '73	101⅜ 49½	88⅜ 77½	90½	78¾ 78⅜	10.33 10.99		
· 1st('76) 9½s 2006	J	BBB-	X R	· · √	‡100¾	‡105.98	58.5	MB '76	108	54½ 100¾	86½ 102½	86¾	86½ 86¾	10.94 11.18		
· 1N('76) 8½s 2006	jD	BBB-	X R	· · √	· · · ·	‡100.97	‡105.99	47.6	MB '76	102	50 92½	78¾ 95¾	78¾	80	10.63 11.02		
· 1st('78) 9½s 2008	Mn15	BBB-	X R	· · √	100%	‡106.67	111	F2 '78	103½	54½ 100	85¼ 102	84	85½	11.16 11.38		
· 1st('80) 13¾s 2010	Ao15	BBB-	X R	· · √	110.34 100	‡111.49	90.0	MB '80	119	88 123½	113	113	122½	13.75 13.92		
· 1st('80) 11⅜s 2010	Jd15	BBB-	X R	· · √	100	‡108.62	100	MB '80	105	67½ 109	99½	109⅜	100 s100	11.88 11.88		
· 1st('84) 14½s 2014	Ms	BBB-	X R	· · · ·	‡111.60 □100	‡112.76	50.0	MB '84	112½	86½ 116¾	111½	113¾	96½ 96½	15.01 15.01		
· 1st('86) 10¾s '96	Jj15	BBB-	X R	· · √	‡102.97 □100	‡108.90	100	MB '86	· · · ·	107½	99½	108	97½ 100	10.86 10.85		
Ohio Power Co	sO	BBB-	X R	· · · ·	‡108.30	‡109.96	125	MB '86	· · · ·	104½	99½	105½	90½ 90½	11.62 11.66		
1st 4⅜s '87	72s		3.04	3.01	3.22 De	39.7 547	413	1264 45.4		1264							
1st 4⅜s '89	mN	A-	X CR	√ √	□100	100	'57	93	52½ 97¾	92½ 100	97¾	100	4.88 Mat		
1st 9s '94	Ao	A-	X CR	√ √	□100.30	‡100.30	22.0	'59	87	47½ 93¾	86½ 94½	92¾	93½	4.95 9.46		
	jD	A-	X R	√ √	□101.02	‡103.14	22.2	'69	109½	60½ 100¾	91½ 101¾	93	93	9.68 10.41		
1st 5s '96	Jj	A-	X R	√ √ √	□100.87	‡101.87	80.0 L4	38.8	F2 '67	74¼ 37½	76¼ 66¾	77¼	70½ 70½	7.10 10.44	
1st 6½s '97	fA	A-	X R	√ √	□101¼	‡102.72	46.6	F2 '66	89½ 44	83½ 73¾	84½	76 76	8.55 10.46		
1st 6⅝s '98	Ms	A-	X R	√ √	□101.17	‡103	55.7	F2 '68	92¾ 44½	84½ 74¾	85½	76½ 76½	8.82 10.51		
1st 7¾s '99	Ms	A-	X R	√ √	□101.57	‡103.84	67.8	F2 '69	102¾ 49½	90¾ 80¾	91½	81½ 81½	9.49 10.55		
1st 7¾s 2002	Ao	A-	X R	√ √	□101.12	‡103.42	16.9	F2 '72	101½ 47	88 76¾	89½	78½ 78½	9.76 10.61		
1st 7¾s 2002	sO	A-	X R	√ √	□100.89	‡103.35	24.0	'72	102¾ 47½	88¾ 77½	90	78½ 78½	9.87 10.65		
1st 8⅜s 2003	fA	A-	X R	√ √	□100.66	‡103.84	40.0	B9 '73	101¾ 51	93¾ 81¼	95	82¾ 82¾	10.12 10.65		
1st 10s 2006	Mn	A-	X R	√ √	□100	‡105.42	47.0	M4 '76	108¾ 51	107½ 97¼	109	94¾ 94¾	10.60 10.70		
1st 9¾s 2006	mN	A-	X R	√ √	□101.35	‡105.85	80.0	S1 '76	105¾ 53½	100½ 87¼	102¾	88¾ 88½	10.50 10.72		
1st 9s 2007	Ao	A-	X R	√ √	□101.40	‡106.17	40.0	B9 '77	103¾ 53½	98½ 93¼	99½	86 86	10.47 10.72		
1st 7¾s 2008	Ms	A-	X R	√ √	□100.47	‡106.10	38.0 L4	'78	100¾ 55	100¾ 87	101¾	87½ 87¾	10.54 10.74		
1st 12¾s 2013	Jd	A-	X R	√	‡110.20 □100	‡110.73	68.6 S1	'83	120¾ 66½	134¾ 117½	136½	104¾ 104¾	12.28 12.24		
SF Deb 5⅜s '96	Jj	BBB+	X R	· · √	□100.90	‡101.95	10.6	B9 '66	73¾ 37½	75½ 66¼	77	70 70	7.32 10.68		
SF Deb 6¾s '97	fA	BBB+	X R	· · √	□101.28	‡102.78	6.65	'67	88¾ 43½	82¼ 73½	84	75½ 75½	8.77 10.71		
SF Deb 7⅜s '99	Ms	BBB+	X R	· · √	□101.36	‡103.76	7.62 E1	'69	101	49½ 89¼	79¾	91½	81½ 81½	9.71 10.79		
Oklahoma Gas & Electric	72s		3.66	3.80	4.55 De	12.3 168	313	6-87	812	36.9							
· 1st 3⅜s '88	Jd	AA	X CR	√ √ √	100	100	15.0	M4 '58	89¼ 52	97 90	97¾	96.65 97	3.99 8.64		
· 1st 4⅜s '93	Ms	AA	X CR	√ √ √	‡100.11	‡100.78	15.0	M4 '63	71	44 83½	71	87½	81	77½ 77½	5.48 9.65	
· 1st 4¾s '95	Ms	AA	X CR	√ √ √	100	‡101.09	25.0	E5 '65	69½ 42	77¾ 67	82	70½ 71¾	6.30 10.07		
1st 5¾s '97	Jj	AA	X R	√ √	‡100.54	‡101.95	15.0	S1 '67	75½ 38½	76¾ 67¼	78½	70½ 70½	7.27 10.10		
1st 6⅞s '98	Jj	AA	X R	√ √ √	100	‡102.20	25.0	'68	90¾ 44½	83¾ 74	85½	76½ 76½	8.37 10.18		
1st 7¾s '99	Jj	AA	X R	√ √ √	‡100.57	‡103.06	12.5	'69	98½ 47¾	88¾ 78½	89½	79½ 79½	8.93 10.19		
1st 8¾s 2000	Jj	AA	X R	√ √ √	100	‡103.87	30.0	M4 '69	108¾ 55¼	99 88¼	100¾	89 89	9.69 10.21		
1st 7¾s 2002	Jj	AA	X R	√ √ √	‡100.67	‡103.90	40.0	S1 '72	100¾ 45½	86¼ 75¾	87½	76¾ 76¾	9.28 10.26		
1st 8½s 2004	Jj	AA	X R	√ √ √	‡101.14	‡105.39	75.0	M8 '74	104	52½ 95½	84	97½	84½ 84½	9.87 10.31	
1st 9¾s 2005	Jj	AA	X R	√ √ √	‡101.08	‡106.11	60.0	M4 '75	110¾ 58	107½ 92	109	87¾ 87¾	10.11 10.34		
1st 8⅜s 2006	Jj	AA	X R	√ √ √	‡101.17	‡106.20	55.0	S1 '76	106½ 53¾	98 85½	99½	86 86	10.03 10.34		
1st 8⅜s 2007	Jj	AA	X R	√ √ √	‡101.42	‡106.54	75.0	B9 '77	106½ 53½	95½ 82¾	96¾	83½ 83½	10.03 10.37		
1st 8¾s 2007	mN	AA	X R	√ √ √	‡101.29	‡106.54	35.0	M4 '77	101½ 52½	97½ 84¼	98½	85½ 85½	10.13 10.40		
1st 8½s 2016	fA15	AA	X R	· √	‡101.31	100	‡101.66	100	K1 '86	· · · ·	97½ 89½	99½	78½ 78½	10.49 10.64	
Olin Corp	14		3.95	d6.78	4.45 De	42.3 741	379	6-87	394	55.2							
Sub Nts 9⅜s '97	Jd15	BBB-	X R	· · · ·	· · · ·	NC	125	M8 '87	· · · ·	99½	92½ 92½	10.23 10.69				
ONEOK Inc	73b		2.95	2.74	2.71 Au	35.4 182	96.6	5-87	302	45.0							
Nts 15¾s '91	jD	BBB+	X R	· · · ·	□100	B10 '81	117½	95½ 117½	113	116	106½ 106½	14.47 13.36				

Uniform Footnote Explanations—See Page 1. Other: ¹Fr 7-1-91. ²Red rest'n(15 1/2%)to 4-15-90. ³Red rest'n(14 1/2%)to 3-1-89. ⁴Red rest'n(10.96%)to 1-15-91. ⁵Red rest'n(10.52%)to 10-1-91. ⁶Contr. by Amer Elec Pwr. ⁷Call $33M on 6-1-87 at 100. ⁸Red rest'n(12.94%)to 6-1-88. ⁹Red rest'n(8.94%)to 8-15-91. ¹⁰Fr 12-1-88.

Source: Standard & Poor's Bond Guide, October 1987, p. 110.

involved is Ohio Edison, for example, the financial manager could observe that debt maturing in 2008 would have a yield to maturity of 11.38 percent. This is true in spite of the fact that the debt was originally issued at 9.5 percent (because the current bond price is approximately $850).

Once the bond yield is determined through the formula or the tables (or is given to you), you must adjust the yield for tax considerations. In other words, yield to maturity indicates how much the corporation has to pay on a *before tax* basis. But keep in mind the interest payment on debt is a tax-deductible expense. Since interest is tax deductible, its true cost is less than its stated cost, because the government is picking up part of the tab by allowing the firm to pay less taxes. The aftertax cost of debt is actually the yield to maturity times one minus the tax rate.[1] This is presented as Formula 11–2.

$$K_d \text{ (Cost of debt)} = Y \text{ (Yield)} (1 - T) \qquad (11\text{--}2)$$

The term *yield* in the formula is interchangeable with yield to maturity or approximate yield to maturity. In using the approximate-yield-to-maturity formula earlier in this section, we determined that the *current* yield on existing debt was 10.68 percent. We shall assume that new debt can be issued at the same going market rate,[2] and that the firm is in a 34 percent tax bracket. Applying the tax adjustment factor, the aftertax cost of debt would be 7.05 percent.

$$\begin{aligned} K_d \text{ (Cost of debt)} &= Y \text{ (Yield)} (1 - T) \\ &= 10.68\% (1 - .34) \\ &= 10.68\% (.66) \\ &= 7.05\% \end{aligned}$$

Please refer back to Table 11–1 and observe in column (*1*) that the aftertax cost of debt is the 7.05 percent that we have just computed.

---

[1]The yield may also be thought of as representing the interest cost to the firm after consideration of all selling and distribution costs, though no explicit representation is given to these costs in relationship to debt. These costs are usually quite small, and they are often bypassed entirely in some types of loans. For those who wish to explicitly include this factor in Formula 11–1, we would have:

$$K_d = [\text{Yield} / (1 - \text{Distribution costs})] (1 - T)$$

[2]Actually, the rate might be slightly higher to reflect that bonds trading at a discount from par ($940 in this case) generally pay a lower yield to maturity than par value bonds because of potential tax advantages and higher leverage potential. This is not really a major issue in this case.

Cost of Preferred Stock

The cost of preferred stock is similar to the cost of debt in that a constant annual payment is made, but dissimilar in that there is no maturity date in which a principal payment must be made. In truth, the determination of the yield on preferred stock is simpler than determining the yield on debt. All you have to do is divide the annual dividend by the current price (this process was discussed in Chapter 10). This represents the rate of return to preferred stockholders as well as the annual cost to the corporation for the preferred stock issue.

Actually, we need to make one slight alteration to this process by dividing the dividend payment by the *net* price or proceeds received by the firm. Since a new share of preferred stock has a selling cost (flotation cost), the proceeds to the firm are equal to the selling price in the market minus the flotation cost. The cost of preferred stock is presented as Formula 11–3.[3]

$$K_p \text{ (cost of preferred stock)} = \frac{D_p}{P_p - F} \qquad (11\text{--}3)$$

where

K_p = Cost of preferred stock
D_p = The annual dividend on preferred stock
P_p = The price of preferred stock
F = Flotation, or selling, cost

In the case of the Baker Corporation, we shall assume the annual dividend is $10.50, the preferred stock price is $100, and the flotation, or selling, cost is $4. The effective cost is:

$$K_p = \frac{D_p}{P_p - F} = \frac{\$10.50}{\$100 - 4} = \frac{\$10.50}{\$96} = 10.94\%$$

Because a preferred stock dividend is not a tax deductible expense, there is no downward tax adjustment.

Please refer back to Table 11–1 and observe in column (1) that 10.94 percent is the value we used for the cost of preferred stock.

---

[3]Note that in Chapter 10, K_p was presented without any adjustment for flotation costs. The instructor may wish to indicate that we have altered the definition slightly. Some may wish to formally add an additional subscript to K_p to indicate we are now talking about the cost of *new* preferred stock. The adjusted symbol would be K_{pn}.

Cost of Common Equity

Determining the cost of common stock in the capital structure is a more involved task. The out-of-pocket cost is the cash dividend, but is it prudent to assume that the percentage cost of common stock is simply the current year's dividend divided by the market price?

$$\frac{\text{Current dividend}}{\text{Market price}}$$

If such an approach were followed, the common stock costs for selected U.S. corporations in January 1988 would be Disney (.6 percent), Motorola (1.4 percent), Texas Instruments (1.6 percent), and CBS (1.8 percent). Ridiculous, you say! If new common stock were assumed to cost such low amounts, the firms would have no need to issue other securities and could profitably finance projects that earned only 1 or 2 percent. How, then, do we find the correct theoretical cost of common stock to the firm?

Valuation Approach

In determining the cost of common stock, the firm must be sensitive to the pricing and performance demands of current and future stockholders. An appropriate approach is to develop a model for valuing common stock and to extract from this model a formula for the required return on common stock.

In Chapter 10 we discussed the constant dividend growth model and said that the current price of common stock could be stated to equal:

$$P_0 = \frac{D_1}{K_e - g}$$

where

P_0 = Price of the stock today
D_1 = Dividend at the end of the first year (or period)
K_e = Required rate of return
g = Constant growth rate in dividends

We then stated that we could arrange the terms in the formula to solve for K_e instead of P_0. This was presented in Formula 10–10 in the prior chapter. We present the formula once again and relabel it Formula 11–4.

$$K_e = \frac{D_1}{P_0} + g \tag{11–4}$$

The required rate of return (K_e) is equal to the dividend at the end of the first year (D_1), divided by the price of the stock today (P_0), plus a constant growth rate (g). Although the growth rate basically applies to dividends, it is also assumed to apply to earnings and stock price over the long term.

If $D_1 = \$2$, $P_0 = \$40$, and $g = 7\%$, we would say K_e equals 12 percent.

$$K_e = \frac{D_1}{P_0} + g = \frac{\$2}{\$40} + 7\% = 5\% + 7\% = 12\%$$

This means that stockholders expect to receive a 5 percent dividend yield on the stock price plus a 7 percent growth in their investment, making a total return of 12 percent.

Alternate Calculation of the Required Return on Common Stock

The required return on common stock can also be calculated by an alternate approach called the capital asset pricing model (CAPM). This topic is covered in Appendix 11A, so only brief mention will be made at this point. Some accept the capital asset pricing model as an important approach to common stock valuation, while others suggest it is not a valid description of how the real world operates.

Under the capital asset pricing model, the required return for common stock (or other investments) can be described by the following formula:

$$K_j = R_f + \beta(K_m - R_f) \qquad (11\text{--}5)$$

where

K_j = Required return on common stock

R_f = Risk-free rate of return; usually the current rate on Treasury bill securities

β = Beta coefficient. The beta measures the historical volatility of an individual stock's return relative to a stock market index. A beta greater than 1 indicates greater volatility (price movements) than the market, while the reverse would be true for a beta less than 1.

K_m = Return in the market as measured by an appropriate index

For the Baker Corporation example, we might assume the following values:

$$R_f = 5.5\%$$
$$K_m = 12\%$$
$$\beta = 1.0$$

K_j, based on Formula 11–5, would then equal:

$$K_j = 5.5\% + 1(12\% - 5.5\%) = 5.5\% + 1(6.5\%)$$
$$= 5.5\% + 6.5\% = 12\%$$

In this case, we have assumed that K_j (the required return under the capital asset pricing model) would equal K_e (the required return under the dividend valuation model). They are both computed to equal 12 percent. Under this equilibrium circumstance, the dividend valuation model and the capital asset pricing model would produce the same answer.

For now, we shall use the dividend valuation model exclusively; that is, we shall use $K_e = D_1/P_0 + g$ in preference to $K_j = R_f + \beta(K_m - R_f)$.

Those who wish to study the capital asset pricing model further are referred to Appendix 11A. This appendix is optional and not required for further reading in the text.

Cost of Retained Earnings

Up to this point, we have discussed the cost (required return) on common stock in a general sense. We have not really specified who is supplying the funds. One obvious supplier of common stock equity capital is the purchaser of new shares of common stock. But this is not the only source. For many corporations, the most important source of ownership or equity capital is in the form of retained earnings, an internal source of funds.

Accumulated retained earnings represent the past and present earnings of the firm minus previously distributed dividends. Retained earnings, by law, belong to the current stockholders. They can either be paid out to the current stockholders in the form of dividends or reinvested in the firm. As current funds are retained in the firm for reinvestment, they represent a source of equity capital to the firm that is being supplied by the current stockholders. They, however, should not be considered as free in nature. There is an opportunity cost involved. Why? As previously indicated, the funds could be paid out to the current stockholders in the form of dividends, and then redeployed by the stockholders in other stocks, bonds, real estate, etc. What is the expected rate of return on these alternative investments? That is, what is the opportunity cost? We assume that stockholders could at least earn an equivalent return to that provided by their present investment in the firm (on an equal risk basis). This represents $D_1/P_0 + g$. In the security markets, there are literally thousands of investments from which to choose, so that it is not implausible to assume that the stockholder can take dividend payments and reinvest them for a comparable yield.

Thus, when we compute the cost of retained earnings, this takes us back to the point at which we began our discussion of the cost of common stock. The cost of retained earnings is equivalent to the rate of return on the firm's common stock. This is the opportunity cost. Thus, we say the cost of common equity in the form of retained earnings is equal to the required rate of return on the firm's stock.[4]

$$K_e \text{ (Cost of common equity in the form of retained earnings)} = \frac{D_1}{P_0} + g \qquad (11\text{–}6)$$

Thus, K_e not only represents the required return on common stock as previously defined, but is also represents the cost of equity in the form of retained earnings. It is a symbol that has double significance.

For ease of reference, the terms in Formula 11–6 are reproduced in the box. They are based on prior values presented in this section on the cost of common stock.

---

[4]One could logically suggest that this is not a perfectly equivalent relationship. For example, if stockholders receive a distribution of retained earnings in the form of dividends, they will have to pay taxes on the dividends before they can reinvest them in equivalent yield investments. Also, the stockholder may incur brokerage costs in the process. For these reasons, one might suggest that the opportunity cost of retained earnings is less than the rate of return on the firm's common stock. The authors have generally supported this position in the past. However, the current predominant view is probably that the appropriate cost for retained earnings is equal to the rate of return on the firm's common stock. The strongest argument for this equality position is that, in a publicly traded company, a firm always has the option of buying back its stock in the market. Given that this is the case, it is assured a return of K_e. Thus, the firm should not make a physical asset investment that has an expected equity return of less than K_e. Having presented both sides of the argument, the authors have adopted the equality position in recent editions and have used it throughout this chapter. Nevertheless, some instructors may wish to discuss both sides of the issue. In the event a tax adjustment is made, the cost of retained earnings can be shown as $K_r = K_e(1 - tr)$; where K_r equals the cost of retained earnings, K_e equals the required rate of return on common stock, and tr equals the average stockholder marginal tax rate.

K_e = Cost of common equity in the form of retained earnings
D_1 = Dividend at the end of the first year, \$2
P_0 = Price of the stock today, \$40
g = Constant growth rate in dividends, 7%

We arrive at the value of 12%.

$$K_e = \frac{D_1}{P_0} + g = \frac{\$2}{\$40} + 7\% = 5\% + 7\% = 12\%$$

The cost of common equity in the form of retained earnings is equal to 12 percent. Please refer back to Table 11–1 and observe in column (*1*) that 12 percent is the value we have used for common equity.

Cost of New Common Stock

Let's now consider the other source of equity capital, new common stock. If we are issuing *new* common stock, we must earn a slightly higher return than K_e, which represents the required rate of return of *present* stockholders. The higher return is needed to cover the distribution costs of the new securities. Assume that the required return for present stockholders is 12 percent and that shares are quoted to the public at \$40. A new distribution of securities must earn slightly more than 12 percent to compensate the corporation for not receiving the full \$40 because of sales commissions and other expenses. The formula for K_e is restated as K_n (the cost of new common stock) to reflect this requirement.

Common stock $$K_e = \frac{D_1}{P_0} + g$$

New common stock $$K_n = \frac{D_1}{P_0 - F} + g \qquad (11\text{–}7)$$

The only new term is F (flotation, or selling, costs).
  Assume:

$$D_1 = \$2$$
$$P_0 = \$40$$
$$F = \$4$$
$$g = 7\%$$

then

$$K_n = \frac{\$2}{\$40 - \$4} + 7\%$$

$$= \frac{\$2}{\$36} + 7\%$$

$$= 5.6\% + 7\% = 12.6\%$$

The cost of new common stock to the Baker Corporation is 12.6 percent. This value will be used more extensively later in the chapter. New common stock is not assumed to be in the original capital structure for the Baker Corporation presented in Table 11–1.

Overview of Common Stock Costs

For those of you who are suffering from an overexposure to Ks in the computation of cost of common stock, let us boil down the information to the only two common stock formulas that you will be using in the rest of the chapter and in the problems at the back of the chapter.

$$K_e \text{ (Cost of common equity in the form of retained earnings)} = \frac{D_1}{P_0} + g$$

$$K_n \text{ (Cost of new common stock)} = \frac{D_1}{P_0 - F} + g$$

The primary emphasis will be on K_e for now, but later in the chapter we will also use K_n when we discuss the marginal cost of capital.

Optimal Capital Structure—Weighting Costs

Having established the techniques for computing the cost of the various elements in the capital structure, we must now discuss methods of assigning weights to these costs. We will attempt to weight capital components in accordance with our desire to achieve a minimum overall cost of capital. For the purpose of this discussion, Table 11–1 (Cost of Capital for the Baker Corporation) is *reproduced* at the top of page 313.

		Cost (aftertax)	Weights	Weighted Cost
Debt	K_d	7.05%	30%	2.12%
Preferred stock	K_p	10.94	10	1.09
Common equity (retained earnings)	K_e	12.00	60	7.20
Weighted average cost of capital	K_a			10.41%

How does the firm decide on the appropriate weights for debt, preferred stock, and common stock financing? Though debt is the cheapest form of financing, it should be used only within reasonable limits. In the Baker Corporation example, debt carried an aftertax cost of 7.05 percent, while other sources of financing cost at least 10.94 percent. Why not more debt? The answer is that the use of debt beyond a reasonable point may greatly increase the firm's financial risk and thereby drive up the costs of all sources of financing. For a more complete discussion of the theory related to this point, please see Appendix 11B: Capital Structure Theory and Modigliani and Miller.

Assume you are going to start your own company and are considering three different capital structures. For ease of presentation, only debt and equity (common stock) are being considered. The costs of the components in the capital structure change each time we vary the debt–equity mix (weights).

	Cost (aftertax)	Weights	Weighted Cost
Financial Plan A:			
Debt	6.5%	20%	1.3%
Equity	12.0	80	9.6
			10.9%
Financial Plan B:			
Debt	7.0%	40%	2.8%
Equity	12.5	60	7.5
			10.3%
Financial Plan C:			
Debt	9.0%	60%	5.4%
Equity	15.0	40	6.0
			11.4%

The firm is able to initially reduce the cost of capital with debt financing, but beyond Plan B the continued use of debt becomes unattractive and greatly increases the costs of the sources of financing. Traditional financial theory maintains that there is a U-shaped cost-of-capital curve relative to debt-equity mixes for the firm, as illustrated in Figure 11–1. In this

Figure 11–1
Cost of capital curve

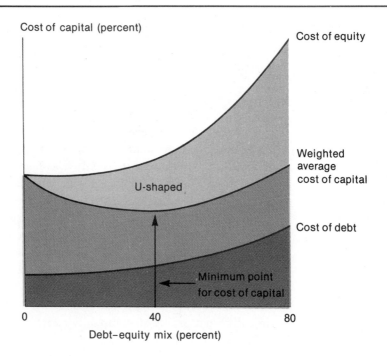

Cost of capital (percent)

Cost of equity

Weighted average cost of capital

U-shaped

Cost of debt

Minimum point for cost of capital

0   40   80

Debt–equity mix (percent)

example, the optimum capital structure occurs at a 40 percent debt-to-equity ratio.

Most firms are able to use 30–50 percent debt in their capital structure without exceeding norms acceptable to creditors and investors. Distinctions should be made, however, between firms that carry high or low business risks. As discussed in Chapter 5, Operating and Financial Leverage, a growth firm in a reasonably stable industry can afford to absorb more debt than its counterpart in cyclical industries. Examples of debt use by companies in various industries are presented in Table 11–3.

In determining the appropriate capital mix, the firm generally begins with its present capital structure and ascertains whether its current position is optimal.[5] If not, subsequent financing should carry the firm toward a mix that is deemed more desirable. Only the costs of new or incremental financing should be considered.

---

[5]Market value rather than book value should be used—though in practice book value is commonly used.

Table 11–3
Debt as a percentage
of total assets

Selected Companies, with Industry Designation	*Percent*
American Home Products (drugs and food)	24%
Quaker State (petroleum refining)	26
Polaroid (photographic equipment and film)	33
Lilly (Eli) & Co. (ethical drugs)	34
Weyerhauser (lumber and wood products)	38
General Motors (motor vehicles)	44
American Brands (tobacco and food)	46
American Standard (heating and plumbing equipment)	47
Gulf and Western Industries (conglomerate)	48
Gannett (newspaper and publishing)	49
Dow Chemical (chemicals)	51
Bethlehem Steel (blast furnaces and steelworks)	54
DiGiorgio (wholesale groceries)	63
Phillips Petroleum (integrated oil)	65
U.S. Home (home building)	70
Trans World Airlines (air transport)	86

Sources: annual reports, Standard & Poor's *Compustat* tapes, and *Moody's Industrial Manual.*

Capital Acquisition and Investment Decision Making

So far, the various costs of financial capital and the optimum capital structure have been discussed. Financial capital, as you may have figured out, consists of bonds, preferred stock, and common equity. These forms of financial capital appear on the corporate balance sheet under liabilities and equity. The money raised by selling these securities and retaining earnings is invested in the real capital of the firm, the long-term productive assets of plant and equipment.

Long-term funds are usually invested in long-term assets, with several asset–financing mixes possible over the business cycle. Obviously, a firm wants to provide all of the necessary financing at the lowest possible cost. This means selling common stock when prices are relatively high to minimize the cost of equity. The financial manager also wants to sell debt at low interest rates. Since there is short-term and long-term debt, he needs to know how interest rates move over the business cycle and when to use short-term versus long-term debt.

A firm has to find a balance between debt and equity to achieve its minimum cost of capital. Although we discussed minimizing the overall cost of capital (K_a) at a single debt-to-equity ratio, in reality a firm operates within a relevant range of debt to equity before it becomes penalized with a higher overall cost because of increased risk.

Figure 11–2 shows a theoretical cost-of-capital curve at three different points in time. As we move from time period t to time period $t + 2$, falling interest rates and rising stock prices cause a downward shift in K_a. This graph illuminates two basic points: (1) the firm wants to keep its debt-to-equity ratio between x and y at all times; and (2) the firm would rather finance its long-term needs at $K_at + 2$ than at K_at. Corporations are allowed some leeway in the money and capital markets, and it is not uncommon for the debt-to-equity ratio to fluctuate between x and y over a business cycle. The firm that is at point y has lost the flexibility of increasing its debt-to-equity ratio without incurring the penalty of higher capital costs.

Figure 11–2
Cost of capital over time

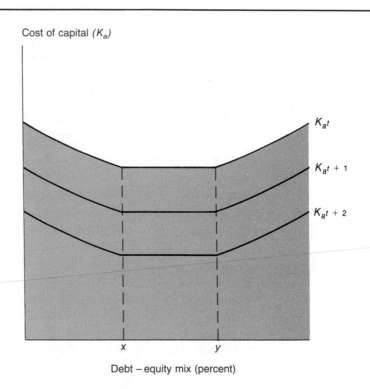

Cost of Capital in the Capital Budgeting Decision

It is always the current cost of capital for each source of funds that is important when making a capital budgeting decision. Historical costs for past fundings may have very little to do with current costs against which present returns must be measured. When raising new financial capital, a company will tap the various sources of financing over a reasonable period of time. Regardless of the particular source of funds that the company is using for the purchase of an asset, the required rate of return or discount rate will be the weighted average cost of capital. As long as the company earns its cost of capital, the common stock value of the firm will be maintained, since stockholder expectations are being met. For example, assume the Baker Corporation was considering making an investment in eight projects with the returns and costs shown in Table 11–4.

Table 11–4
Investment projects available to the Baker Corporation

Projects	Expected Returns	Cost ($ millions)
A	16.00%	$10
B	14.00	5
C	13.50	4
D	11.80	20
E	10.65	11
F	9.50	20
G	8.60	15
H	7.00	10
		$95 million

These projects could be viewed graphically and merged with the weighted average cost of capital in order to make a capital budgeting decision, as indicated in Figure 11–3.

Notice that the Baker Corporation is facing a total of $95 million in projects, but given the weighted average cost of capital of 10.41 percent it will choose only projects A through E, or $50 million in new assets. Selecting assets F, G, and H would probably reduce the market value of the common stock because these projects do not provide a return equal to the overall costs of raising funds. We cannot forget that the use of the weighted average cost of capital assumes that the Baker Corporation is in its optimum capital structure range.

The Marginal Cost of Capital

Nothing guarantees the Baker Corporation that its cost of capital will stay constant for as much money as it wants to raise even if a given capital structure is maintained. If a large amount of financing is desired, the market may demand a higher cost of capital for each amount of funds desired. The point is analogous to the fact that you may be able to go to your relatives and best friends and raise funds for an investment at 10

Figure 11–3
**Cost of capital and
investment projects
for the Baker
Corporation**

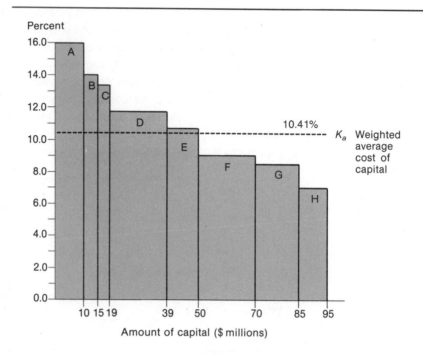

percent. After you have exhausted the lending or investing power of those closest to you, you will have to look to other sources and the marginal cost of your capital will go up.

As a background for this discussion, the cost of capital table for the Baker Corporation is reproduced again.

		Cost (aftertax)	Weights	Weighted Cost
Debt	K_d	7.05%	30%	2.12%
Preferred stock	K_p	10.94	10	1.09
Common equity (retained earnings)	K_e	12.00	60	7.20
Weighted average (cost of capital)	K_a			10.41%

We need to review the nature of the firm's capital structure in order to explain the concept of marginal cost of capital as it applies to the firm. Note the firm has 60 percent of the capital structure in the form of equity capital. The equity (ownership) capital is represented by retained earnings. It is assumed that 60 percent is the amount of equity capital that the firm must maintain to keep a balance between fixed income securities and ownership interest. But equity capital in the form of retained earnings can not grow indefinitely as the firm's capital needs expand. Retained earnings is limited to the amount of past and present earnings that can be redeployed into the investment projects of the firm. Let's assume the Baker Corporation has $23.40 million of retained earnings available for investment. Since retained earnings is to represent 60 percent of the capital structure, there is adequate retained earnings to support a capital structure of up to $39 million. More formally, we say that:

$$X = \frac{\text{Retained earnings}}{\text{Percent of retained earnings in the capital structure}} \quad (11\text{--}8)$$

(Where X represents the size of the capital structure that retained earnings will support.)

$$X = \frac{\$23.40 \text{ million}}{.60}$$

$$= \$39 \text{ million}$$

After the first $39 million of capital is raised, retained earnings will no longer be available to provide the 60 percent equity position in the capital structure. Nevertheless, lenders and investors will still require that 60 percent of the capital structure be in the form of common equity (ownership) capital. Because of this, *new* common stock will replace retained earnings to provide the 60 percent common equity component for the firm. That is, after $39 million, common equity capital will be in the form of new common stock rather than retained earnings.

In the left-hand portion of Table 11–5, we see the original cost of capital that we have been discussing throughout the chapter. This applies up to $39 million. After $39 million, the concept of marginal cost of capital becomes important. The cost of capital goes up as shown on the right-hand portion of the table.

Table 11–5   Cost of capital for different amounts of financing

First $39 Million				Next $11 Million			
	A/T Cost	Wts.	Weighted Cost		A/T Cost	Wts.	Weighted Cost
Debt . . . . . . K_d	7.05%	.30	2.12%	Debt . . . . . . K_d	7.05%	.30	2.12%
Preferred . . . . K_p	10.94	.10	1.09	Preferred . . . . K_p	10.94	.10	1.09
Common equity* . . . . K_e	12.00	.60	7.20	Common equity† . . . . K_n	12.60	.60	7.56
			$K_a = 10.41\%$				$K_{mc} = 10.77\%$

*Retained earnings.

†New common stock.

K_{mc}, in the bottom right-hand portion of the table, represents the *marginal* cost of capital, and it is 10.77 percent after \$39 million. What has happened is that the cost of capital has increased after \$39 million because common equity is now in the form of new common stock rather than retained earnings. The aftertax (A/T) cost of new common stock is slightly more expensive than retained earnings because of flotation costs (F). The equation for the cost of new common stock was shown earlier in the chapter as Formula 11–7. For the example we are doing:

$$K_n = \frac{D_1}{P_0 - F} + g = \frac{\$2}{\$40 - \$4} + 7\%$$

$$= \frac{\$2}{\$36} + 7\% = 5.6\% + 7\% = 12.6\%$$

The flotation cost (F) is \$4 and the cost of new common stock is 12.60 percent.

This is higher than the 12 percent cost of retained earnings that we have been using and causes the increase in the marginal cost of capital.

To carry the example a bit further, we will assume that the cost of debt of 7.05 percent applies to the first \$15 million of debt that the firm raises. After that, the aftertax cost of debt will rise to 8.60 percent. Since debt represents 30 percent of the capital structure for the Baker Corporation, the cheaper form of debt can be used to support the capital structure up to \$50 million. We derive the \$50 million by using Formula 11–9.

$$Z = \frac{\text{Amount of lower-cost debt}}{\text{Percent of debt in the capital structure}} \qquad (11\text{–}9)$$

(Where Z represents the size of the capital structure in which lower-cost debt can be utilized.)

$$Z = \frac{\$15 \text{ million}}{.30}$$

$$= \$50 \text{ million}$$

After the first \$50 million of capital is raised, lower-cost debt will no longer be available to provide 30 percent of the capital structure. After \$50 million in total financing, the aftertax cost of debt will go up to the previously specified 8.60 percent. The marginal cost of capital for over \$50 million in financing is shown in Table 11–6.

The change in the cost of debt gives way to a new marginal cost of capital (K_{mc}) of 11.23 percent after \$50 million of financing. You should

Table 11–6
Cost of capital for increasing amounts of financing

		Over $50 million		
		Cost (aftertax)	Weights	Weighted Cost
Debt (higher cost)	K_d	8.60%	.30	2.58%
Preferred stock	K_p	10.94	.10	1.09
Common equity (new common stock) . . .	K_n	12.60	.60	7.56
				$K_{mc} = 11.23\%$

observe that the capital structure with over $50 million of financing reflects not only the change in the cost of debt, but also the continued exclusive use of new common stock to represent common equity capital. Of course, this change took place at $39 million, but must be carried on indefinitely as the capital structure expands.

We could carry on this process by next indicating a change in the cost of preferred stock, or continually increasing the cost of debt or new common stock as more and more capital is used. For now, it is sufficient that you merely observe the basic process. To summarize, we have said that the Baker Corporation has a basic weighted average cost of capital of 10.41 percent. This value was developed throughout the chapter and was originally presented in Table 11–1. However, as the firm began to substantially expand its capital structure, the weighted average cost of capital increased. This gave way to the concept of marginal cost of capital. The first increase or break point was at $39 million in which the marginal cost of capital went up to 10.77 percent as a result of replacing retained earnings with new common stock. The second increase or break point was at $50 million in which the marginal cost of capital increased to 11.23 percent as a result of the utilization of more expensive debt. The changes are summarized below.

Amount of Financing	Marginal Cost of Capital
0–$39 million	10.41%
$39–50 million	10.77%
Over $50 million	11.23%

In the previously presented Figure 11–3, we showed returns from investments A through H. In Figure 11–4, we reproduce the returns originally shown in Figure 11–3, but now include the concept of marginal cost of capital. Observe the increasing cost of capital (dotted lines) in relationship to the decreasing returns (straight lines).

**Figure 11–4
Marginal cost of
capital and Baker
Corporation projects**

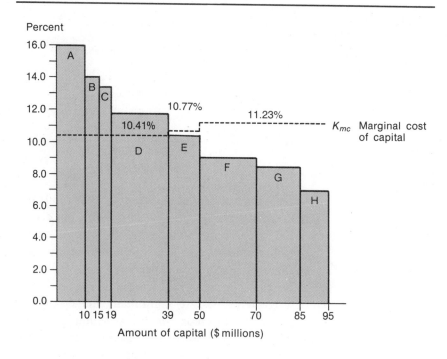

In the earlier presentation in Figure 11–3, the Baker Corporation was justified in choosing projects A through E for a capital expenditure of $50 million. This is no longer the case in Figure 11–4. Because of the increasing marginal cost of capital, the returns exceed the cost of capital only up to $39 million and now only projects A through D are acceptable.

Although the concept of marginal cost of capital is very important, for most of our capital budgeting decisions in the next chapter, we will assume we are operating on the initial flat part of the marginal cost of capital curve in Figure 11–4, and that most of our decisions can be made based on the initial weighted average cost of capital.

Summary

The cost of capital for the firm is determined by computing the costs of various sources of financing and weighting them in proportion to their representation in the capital structure. The cost of each component in the capital structure is closely associated with the valuation of that source. For debt and preferred stock, the cost is directly related to the current yield, with debt adjusted downward to reflect the tax deductible nature of interest.

For common stock, the cost of retained earnings (K_e) is the current dividend yield on the security plus an anticipated rate of growth for the future. Minor adjustments are made to the formula to determine the cost of new common stock. A summary of the Baker Corporation's capital costs is presented in Table 11–7.

Table 11–7   **Cost of components in the capital structure**

1. Cost of debt	$K_d = \text{Yield}\ (1 - T) = 7.05\%$	Yield $= 10.68\%$ $T\ =$ Corporate tax rate, 34%
2. Cost of preferred stock	$K_p = \dfrac{D_p}{P_p - F} = 10.94\%$	$D_p =$ Preferred dividend, \$10.50 $P_p =$ Price of preferred stock, \$100 $F\ =$ Flotation costs, \$4
3. Cost of common equity (retained earnings)	$K_e = \dfrac{D_1}{P_0} + g = 12\%$	$D_1 =$ First year common dividend, \$2 $P_0 =$ Price of common stock, \$40 $g\ =$ Growth rate, 7%
4. Cost of new common stock . . .	$K_n = \dfrac{D_1}{P_0 - F} + g = 12.60\%$	Same as above, with $F =$ flotation costs, \$4

We weigh the elements in the capital structure in accordance with our desire to achieve a minimum overall cost. While debt is usually the "cheapest" form of financing, excessive debt use may increase the financial risk of the firm and drive up the costs of all sources of financing. The wise financial manager attempts to ascertain what debt component will result in the lowest overall cost of capital. Once this has been determined, the weighted average cost of capital is the discount rate we use in present-valuing future flows to ensure we are earning at least the cost of financing.

The marginal cost of capital is also introduced to explain what happens to a company's cost of capital as it tries to finance a large amount of funds. First, the company will use up retained earnings, and the cost of financing will rise as higher-cost new common stock is substituted for retained earnings in order to maintain the optimum capital structure with the appropriate debt-to-equity ratio. Larger amounts of financial capital can also cause the individual means of financing to rise by raising interest rates or by depressing the price of the stock because more is sold than the market wants to absorb.

Review of Formulas

1. K_d (cost of debt) $= Y(1 - T)$ (11–2)
  Y is yield
  T is corporate tax rate

2. K_p (cost of preferred stock) $= \dfrac{D_p}{P_p - F}$ (11–3)

D_p is the annual dividend on preferred stock
P_p is the price of preferred stock
F is flotation, or selling, cost

3. K_e (cost of common equity) $= \dfrac{D_1}{P_0} + g$ (11–4)

D_1 is dividend at the end of first year (or period)
P_0 is the price of the stock today
g is growth rate in dividends

4. K_j (required return on common stock)

$$= R_f + \beta(K_m - R_f)$$ (11–5)

R_f is risk-free rate of return
β is beta coefficient
K_m is return in the market as measured by the appropriate index

5. K_e (cost of common equity in the form   (11–6)

of retained earnings) $= \dfrac{D_1}{P_0} + g$

D_1 is dividend at the end of the first year (or period)
P_0 is price of the stock today
g is growth rate in dividends

6. K_n (cost of new common stock) $= \dfrac{D_1}{P_0 - F} + g$ (11–7)

Same as above with:
F as flotation, or selling, cost

7. X (size of capital
structure that retained $= \dfrac{\text{Retained earnings}}{\text{\% of retained earnings in the capital structure}}$ (11–8)
earnings will support)

8. Z (size of capital
structure that lower-cost $= \dfrac{\text{Amount of lower-cost debt}}{\text{\% of lower cost debt in the capital structure}}$ (11–9)
debt will support)

List of Terms

financial capital
optimum capital structure
common equity
cost of capital
weighted average cost of capital

marginal cost of capital
dividend valuation model
flotation costs
capital asset pricing model
  (CAPM)

Discussion Questions

1. Why do we use the overall cost of capital for investment decisions even when only one source of capital will be used (e.g., debt)?

2. How does the cost of a source of capital relate to the valuation concepts presented in Chapter 10?

3. In computing the cost of capital, do we use the historical costs of existing debt and equity or the current costs as determined in the market? Why?

4. Why is the cost of debt less than the cost of preferred stock if both securities are priced to yield 10 percent in the market?

5. What are the two sources of equity (ownership) capital for the firm?

6. Explain why retained earnings has an opportunity cost associated with it?

7. Why is the cost of retained earnings the equivalent of the firm's own required rate of return on common stock (K_e)?

8. Why is the cost of new common stock (K_n) higher than the cost of retained earnings? (K_e)?

9. How are the weights determined to arrive at the optimal weighted average cost of capital?

10. Explain the traditional, U-shaped approach to the cost of capital.

11. Identify other variables (ratios) besides the debt-to-equity ratio that you think will influence a company's cost of capital. You may wish to refer to Chapter 3 for possibilities.

12. It has often been said that if the company can't earn a rate of return greater than the cost of capital it should not make investments. Explain.

13. What effect would inflation have on a company's cost of capital? (Hint: Think about how inflation influences interest rates, stock prices, corporate profits, and growth.)

14. What is the concept of marginal cost of capital?

Problems

1. Roberts Oral and Dental Supplies can issue debt yielding 11 percent. The company is in a 34 percent tax bracket. What is the aftertax cost of debt?

2. Calculate the aftertax cost of debt under each of the following conditions.

	Yield	Corporate Tax Rate
a.	7.6%	20%
b.	14.0	34
c.	12.0	15

3. Calculate the aftertax cost of debt on a bond yielding 10 percent. The issuing company pays tax at a rate of 30 percent and will incur distribution costs of 1 percent on this bond issue. (See text footnote 1.)

4. The Hudson Distributing Company has a $1,000 par value bond outstanding with 25 years to maturity. The bond carries an annual interest payment of $84 and is currently selling for $920. Hudson is in a 25 percent tax bracket. The firm wishes to know what the aftertax cost of a new bond issue is likely to be. The yield to maturity on the new issue will be the same as the yield to maturity on the old issue because the risk and maturity date will be similar.
   a. Compute the approximate yield to maturity on the old issue and use this as the yield for the new issue.
   b. Make the appropriate tax adjustment to determine the aftertax cost of debt.

5. For the Hudson Distributing Company described in problem number 4, assume that the yield on the bonds goes up by one percentage point and that the tax rate is now 34 percent.

a. What is the new aftertax cost of debt?

b. Has the aftertax cost of debt gone up or down from problem number four? Explain why.

6. Oklahoma Gas and Electric Company is planning to issue debt that will mature in the year 2005. In many respects the issue is similar to currently outstanding debt of the corporation. Using Table 11–2 in the chapter, identify:

a. The yield to maturity on similarly outstanding debt for the firm, in terms of maturity.

b. Assume that, because the new debt will be issued at par, the required yield to maturity will be 0.15 percent higher than the value determined in part *a*. Add this factor to the answer in *a*. (New issues at par sometimes require a slightly higher yield than old issues that are trading below par.)

c. If the firm is in a 34 percent tax bracket, what is the aftertax cost of debt? Use the required yield computed in part *b* in determining your answer.

7. Rollins Auto Parts, Inc., can sell preferred stock for $80 with an estimated flotation cost of $2. The preferred stock is expected to pay $8 per share in dividends.

a. Compute the cost of preferred stock.

b. Do we need to make a tax adjustment for the issuing firm?

8. The Holtz Corporation issued $100 par value stock 10 years ago. The stock provided a 9 percent preferred stock yield at the time of issue. The preferred stock is now selling for $85.

a. What is the current yield or cost of preferred stock? (Disregard flotation costs.)

b. If a 5 percent flotation (selling) cost is presently involved in issuing new preferred stock, what is the current cost to issue preferred stock? [Hint: divide the answer in part *a* by (1 − flotation percentage).]

9. Lincoln Enterprises wants you to calculate its cost of common stock. During the next 12 months, the company expects to pay dividends (D_1) of $2.40 per share, and the current price of its common stock is $40 per share. The expected growth rate is 8 percent.

a. Compute the cost of retained earnings (K_e). Use Formula 11–6.

b. If a $2 flotation cost is involved, compute the cost of new common stock (K_n). Use Formula 11–7.

10. Compute K_e and K_n under the following circumstances:
  a. $D_1 = \$4.20$, $P_0 = \$55$, $g = 5\%$, $F = \$3.80$.
  b. $D_1 = \$0.40$, $P_0 = \$15$, $g = 8\%$, $F = \$1$.
  c. E_1 (earnings at the end of period one) = $8, payout ratio equals 25 percent, $P_0 = \$32$, $g = 5\%$, $F = \$2$.
  d. D_0 (dividend at the beginning of the first period) = $3, growth rate for dividends and earnings $(g) = 9\%$, $P_0 = \$60$, $F = \$3.50$.

11. Business has been good for Modern Home Magazine, as indicated by the four-year growth in earnings per share. The earnings have grown from $1.00 to $1.63.
  a. Use Appendix A at the back of the text to determine the compound annual rate of growth in earnings $(n = 4)$.
  b. Based on the growth rate determined in part *a*, project earnings for next year (E_1). Round to two places to the right of the decimal point.
  c. Assume the dividend payout ratio is 30 percent. Compute (D_1). Round to two places to the right of the decimal point.
  d. The current price of the stock is $20. Using the growth rate (g) from part *a* and D_1 from part *c*, compute K_e.
  e. If the flotation cost is $1.10, compute the cost of new common stock (K_n).

12. Global Technology's capital structure is as follows:

Debt	35%
Preferred stock	15
Common equity	50

    The aftertax cost of debt is 6.5 percent; the cost of preferred stock is 10 percent; and the cost of common equity (in the form of retained earnings) is 13.5 percent.
    Calculate Global Technology's weighted average cost of capital in a manner similar to Table 11–1.

13. As an alternative to the capital structure shown in problem 12 for Global Technology, an outside consultant has suggested the following modifications:

Debt	60%
Preferred stock	5
Common equity	35

Under this new and more debt-oriented arrangement, the aftertax cost of debt is 8.8 percent, the cost of preferred stock is 11 percent, and the cost of common equity (in the form of retained earnings) is 15.6 percent. Recalculate Global's weighted average cost of capital.

Which plan is optimal in terms of minimizing the weighted average cost of capital?

14. Given the following information, calculate the weighted average cost of capital for Genex Corporation. Line up the calculations in the order shown in Table 11–1.

Percent of capital structure:

Debt	35%
Preferred stock . . .	10
Common equity . . .	55

Additional information:

Bond coupon rate	13%
Bond yield	11%
Dividend, expected common . . .	$3.00
Dividend, preferred	$10.00
Price, common	$50.00
Price, preferred	$98.00
Flotation cost, preferred	$5.50
Growth rate	8%
Corporate tax rate	30%

15. Given the following information, calculate the weighted average cost of capital for the Tower Corporation. Line up the calculations in the order shown in Table 11–1.

Percent of capital structure:

Preferred stock	10%
Common equity	60
Debt	30

Corporate tax rate	34%
Dividend, preferred	$8
Dividend, expected common	$3
Price, preferred	$102
Growth rate	6%
Bond yield	9%
Flotation cost, preferred . .	$4
Price, common	$60

16. Tasty Foods, a major grower of okra and spinach, is trying to calculate its cost of capital for use in a capital budgeting decision. Mr. Clark, the vice president of finance, has given you the following information and has asked you to compute the weighted average cost of capital.

The company currently has outstanding a bond, with a 10 percent coupon rate and a convertible bond with a 6.8 percent rate. The firm has been informed by its investment banker, Morgan Fairchild and Company, that bonds of equal risk and credit rating are *now* selling to yield 12.2 percent. The common stock has a price of $45 and an expected dividend (D_1) of $1.26 per share. The firm's historical growth rate of earnings and dividends per share has been 12 percent, but security analysts on Wall Street expect this growth to slow to 10 percent in future years. The preferred stock is selling at $50 per share and carries a dividend of $5 per share. The corporate tax rate is 34 percent. The flotation costs are 4 percent of the selling price for preferred stock. The optimum capital structure for Tasty Foods seems to be 35 percent debt, 10 percent preferred stock, and 55 percent common equity in the form of retained earnings.

Compute the cost of capital for the individual components in the capital structure and then calculate the weighted average cost of capital (similar to Table 11–1).

17. First Tennessee Utility Company faces increasing needs for capital. Fortunately, it has an Aa2 credit rating. The corporate tax rate is 34 percent. First Tennessee's treasurer is trying to determine the corporation's current weighted average cost of capital to assess the profitability of capital budgeting projects. Historically, the corporation's earnings and dividends per share have increased at about a 6 percent annual rate.

First Tennessee's common stock is selling at $60 per share, and the company will pay a $4.50 per share dividend (D_1). The company's $100 preferred stock has been yielding 9 percent in the current market. Flotation costs for the company have been estimated by its investment banker to be $1.50 for preferred stock. The company's optimum capital structure is 40 percent debt, 10 percent preferred stock, and 50 percent common equity in the form of retained earnings. Refer to the table on page 331 on bond issues for comparative yields on bonds of equal risks to First Tennessee. Compute the answer to questions *a, b, c* and *d* from the information given.

Data on Bond Issues

Issue	Moody's Rating	Price	Yield to Maturity
Utilities:			
Balt. G&E 8-3/8s 2006	Aa1	$975.25	8.60%
New York Tel. Co. 7½s 2009	Aa2	850.75	9.11
Miss. Pow. 9.62s 2008	A1	960.50	9.67
Industrials:			
IBM 9-3/8s 2004	Aaa	$1,050.50	8.50%
May Department St. 7.95s 2002	Aa3	940.00	11.81
General Mills 9-3/8s 2009	A2	1,030.75	9.05

a. Cost of debt, K_d. (Use the table above—relate to the utility bond credit rating for yield.)

b. Cost of preferred stock, K_p.

c. Cost of common equity in the form of retained earnings, K_e.

d. Weighted average cost of capital.

18. The Evans Corporation finds it is necessary to determine its marginal cost of capital. Evans current capital structure calls for 45 percent debt, 15 percent preferred stock, and 40 percent common equity. Initially, common equity will be in the form of retained earnings (K_e) and then new common stock (K_n). The costs of the various sources of financing are as follows: debt, 6.2 percent; preferred stock, 9.4 percent; retained earnings, 12.0 percent; and new common stock, 13.4 percent.

    a. What is the initial weighted average cost of capital? (Include debt, preferred stock, and common equity in the form of retained earnings, K_e.)

    b. If the firm has $20 million in retained earnings, at what size capital structure will the firm run out of retained earnings?

    c. What will the marginal cost of capital be immediately after that point? (Equity will remain at 40 percent of the capital structure, but will all be in the form of new common stock, K_n.)

    d. The 6.2 percent cost of debt referred to above applies only to the first $36 million of debt. After that the cost of debt will be 7.8 percent. At what size capital structure will there be a change in the cost of debt?

    e. What will the marginal cost of capital be immediately after that point? (Consider the facts in both parts c and d.)

19. Medical Research Corporation is in the process of expanding its research and production capacity to introduce a new line of

products. Current plans call for the expenditure of $100 million on four projects of equal size ($25 million), but different returns. Project A is in blood clotting proteins and has an expected return of 18 percent. Project B relates to a hepatitis vaccine and carries a potential return of 14 percent. Project C, dealing with a cardiovascular compound, is expected to earn 11.8 percent and Project D, an investment in orthopedic implants, is expected to show a 10.9 percent return.

The firm has $15 million in retained earnings. After a capital structure with $15 million in retained earnings is reached (in which retained earnings represent 60 percent of the financing), all additional equity financing must come in the form of new common stock.

Common stock is selling for $25 per share and underwriting costs are estimated at $3 if new shares are issued. Dividends for the next year will be $.90 per share ($D_1$), and earnings and dividends have grown consistently at 11 percent per year.

The yield on comparative bonds has been hovering at 11 percent. The investment banker feels that the first $20 million of bonds could be sold to yield 11 percent while additional debt might require a 2 percent premium and be marketed to yield 13 percent. The corporate tax rate is 34 percent. Debt represents 40 percent of the capital structure.

a. Based on the two sources of financing, what is the initial weighted average cost of capital? (Use K_d and K_e.)

b. At what size capital structure will the firm run out of retained earnings?

c. What will the marginal cost of capital be immediately after that point?

d. At what size capital structure will there be a change in the cost of debt?

e. What will the marginal cost of capital be immediately after that point?

f. Based on the information about potential returns on investments in the first paragraph and information on marginal cost of capital (in parts *a*, *c*, and *e*), how large a capital investment budget should the firm use?

g. Graph the answer determined in part *f*.

20. (Comprehensive problem.)

Milam Manufacturing is a very large company with common stock listed on the New York Stock Exchange and bonds traded over-the-counter. As of the current balance sheet, it has three bond issues outstanding:

$150 million of 9.5 percent series 2001
$ 50 million of 6 percent series 1994
$100 million of 4 percent series 1990

The vice president of finance is planning to sell $100 million of bonds next year to replace the debt due to expire in 1990. At present, market yields on similar Aaa bonds are 10.1 percent.

Milam also has $100 million of 5.5 percent noncallable preferred stock outstanding, and it has no intentions of selling any preferred stock at any time in the future. The preferred stock is currently priced at $58 per share, and its dividend per share is $5.50.

The company has had very volatile earnings, but its dividends per share have had a very stable growth rate of 6 percent and this will continue. The expected dividend (D_1) is $2.60 per share, and the common stock is selling for $50 per share. The company's investment banker has quoted Milam the following flotation costs: $2.40 per share for preferred stock and $1.80 per share for common stock.

On the advice of its investment banker, Milam will keep its debt at 50 percent and its equity at 50 percent. Milam sees no need to sell either common or preferred stock in the foreseeable future, because it generates enough internal funds for its investment needs when these funds are combined with debt financing. Milam's corporate tax rate is 34 percent.

Compute the cost of capital for the following:

a. Bond (debt) (K_d).
b. Preferred stock (K_p).
c. Common equity in the form of retained earnings (K_e).
d. New common stock (K_n).
e. Weighted average cost of capital.

Selected References

Alberts, W. W., and S. H. Archer. "Some Evidence on the Effects of Company Size on the Cost of Equity Capital." *Journal of Financial and Quantitative Analysis* 8 (March 1973), pp. 229–42.

Arditti, F. D. "The Weighted Average Cost of Capital: Some Questions on Its Definition, Interpretation, and Use." *Journal of Finance* 28 (September 1973), pp. 1,001–8.

Beranek, William. "The Cost of Capital, Capital Budgeting, and Maximization of Shareholder Wealth." *Journal of Finance and Quantitative Analysis* 10 (March 1975), pp. 1–21.

Bierman, Harold, Jr., and Jerome E. Hass. "Capital Budgeting under Uncertainty: A Reformulation." *Journal of Finance* 28 (March 1973), pp. 119–20.

Billingsley, Randall S.; Robert E. Lamy; M. Wayne Marr; and G. Rodney Thompson. "Split Ratings and Bond Reoffering Yields." *Financial Management* 14 (Summer 1985), pp. 59–66.

Brennan, Michael J. "A New Look at the Weighted Average Cost of Capital." *Journal of Business Finance* 5, no. 1 (1973), pp. 24–30.

Brigham, Eugene F., and Keith V. Smith. "The Cost of Capital to the Small Firm." *Engineering Economics* 13 (Fall 1967), pp. 1–26.

Conine, Thomas E., Jr., and Maury Tamarkin. "Divisional Cost of Capital Estimation: Adjusting for Leverage." *Financial Management* 14 (Spring 1986), pp. 54–58.

Durand, David. *Costs of Debt and Equity Funds for Business: Trends and Problems of Measurement.* Conference on Research in Business Finance. New York: National Bureau of Economic Research, New York, 1952.

Harris, Robert S. "Using Analyst's Growth Forecasts to Estimate Shareholder Required Rate of Return." *Financial Management* 15 (Spring 1986), pp. 58–67.

Howe, Keith M., and James H. Patterson. "Capital Investment Decisions under Economies of Scale in Flotation Costs." *Financial Management* 14 (Autumn 1985), pp. 61–69.

Long, Susan W. "Risk-Premium Curve vs. Capital Market Line: Differences Explained." *Financial Management* 7 (Spring 1978), pp. 60–64.

Miller, Merton H. "Debt and Taxes." *Journal of Finance* 32 (May 1977), pp. 261–73.

Modigliani, Franco, and Merton H. Miller. "The Cost of Capital, Corporation Finance and the Theory of Investment." *American Economic Review* 48 (June 1958), pp. 261–96.

————. "Taxes and the Cost of Capital: A Correction." *American Economic Review* 53 (June 1963), pp. 433–43.

Murphy, J. Austin. "The Effect of Portfolio Insurance on the Probability Distribution of Return." *Journal of Financial Education* 16 (Fall 1987), pp. 6–11.

Nantell, Timothy J., and C. Robert Carlson. "The Cost of Capital as a Weighted Average." *Journal of Finance* 30 (December 1975), pp. 1,343–55.

Ofer, Aharon R. "Investors' Expectations of Earnings Growth, Their Accuracy, and Effects on the Structure of Realized Rates of Return." *Journal of Finance* 30 (May 1975), pp. 509–23.

Roll, Richard. "A Critique of the Asset Pricing Theory's Test. Part 1: On the Past and Potential Testability of the Theory." *Journal of Financial Economics* 4 (March 1977), pp. 129–76.

————. "Ambiguity When Performance Is Measured by the Securities Market Line." *Journal of Finance* 33 (September 1978), pp. 1,051–70.

Sharpe, William F. "Capital Asset Prices: A Theory of Market Equilibrium under Conditions of Risk." *Journal of Finance* 19 (September 1964), pp. 425–42.

Siegel, Jeremy J. "The Application of the DCF Methodology for Determining the Costs of Equity Capital." *Financial Management* 14 (Spring 1985), pp. 46–53.

Appendix 11A: Cost of Capital and the Capital Asset Pricing Model (Optional)

The Capital Asset Pricing Model

The capital asset pricing model (CAPM) relates the risk–return trade-offs of individual assets to market returns. Common stock returns over time have generally been used to test this model since stock prices are widely available and efficiently priced, as are market indexes of stock performance. In theory the CAPM encompasses all assets, but in practice it is difficult to measure returns on all types of assets or to find an all-encompassing market index. For our purposes, we will use common stock returns to explain the model and occasionally we will generalize to other assets.

The basic form of the CAPM is a linear relationship between returns on individual stocks and stock market returns over time. By using least squares regression analysis, the return on an individual stock, K_j, is expressed in Formula 11A–1.

$$K_j = \alpha + \beta K_m + e \qquad (11A\text{--}1)$$

where

K_j = Return on individual common stock of a company
α = Alpha, the intercept on the y-axis
β = Beta, the coefficient
K_m = Return on the stock market (an index of stock returns is used, usually the Standard & Poor's 500 Index)
e = Error term of the regression equation

As indicated in Table 11A–1 and Figure 11A–1, this equation uses historical data to generate the beta coefficient (β), a measurement of the

Table 11A–1
Performance of PAI and the market

Year	Rate of Return on Stock	
	PAI	Market
1	12.0%	10.0%
2	16.0	18.0
3	20.0	16.0
4	16.0	10.0
5	6.0	8.0
Mean return	14.0%	12.4%
Standard deviation	4.73%	3.87%

Figure 11A–1
Linear regression of
returns between PAI
and the market

Year	K_j	K_m	$\Sigma K_j K_m$	$\Sigma K_j \Sigma K_m$	ΣK_m^2	$(\Sigma K_m)^2$
			936	4,340	844	3,844
1.......12%		10%				
2.......16		18				
3.......20		16				
4.......16		10				
5....... 6		8				
70%		62%				

$$\beta = \frac{n\Sigma K_j K_m - \Sigma K_j \Sigma K_m}{n\Sigma K_m^2 - (\Sigma K_m)^2} = \frac{5(936) - 4,340}{5(844) - 3,844} = 0.9$$

$$\alpha = \frac{\Sigma K_j - \text{B}\Sigma K_m}{n} = \frac{70 - 0.9(62)}{5} = 2.8$$

return performance of a given stock versus the return performance of the market. Assume that we want to calculate a beta for Parts Associates, Inc. (PAI), and that we have the performance data for that company and the market shown in Table 11A–1. The relationship between PAI and the market appears graphically in Figure 11A–1.

The alpha term in Figure 11A–1 of 2.8 percent is the y-intercept of the linear regression. It is the expected return on PAI stock if returns on the market are zero. However, if the returns on the market are expected to approximate the historical rate of 12.4 percent, the expected return on PAI would be $K_j = 2.8 + 0.9(12.4) = 14.0$ percent. This maintains the historical relationship. If the returns on the market are expected to rise to 18 percent next year, expected return on PAI would be $K_j = 2.8 + 0.9(18.0) = 19$ percent.

Notice that we are talking in terms of expectations. The CAPM is an expectational (ex ante) model, and there is no guarantee that historical data will reoccur. One area of empirical testing involves the stability and predictability of the beta coefficient based on historical data. Research has indicated that betas are more useful in a portfolio context (for groupings of stocks) because the betas of individual stocks are less stable from period to period than portfolio betas. In addition, research indicates that betas of individual common stocks have the tendency to approach 1.0 over time.

The Security Market Line

The capital asset pricing model evolved from Formula 11A–1 into a risk premium model where the basic assumption is that in order for investors to take more risk they must be compensated by larger expected returns. Investors should also not accept returns that are less than they can get from a riskless asset. For CAPM purposes it is assumed that short-term U.S. Treasury bills may be considered a riskless asset.[1] When viewed in this context, an investor must achieve an extra return above that obtainable from a Treasury bill in order to induce the assumption of more risk. This brings us to the more common and theoretically useful model:

$$K_j = R_f + \beta(K_m - R_f) \qquad (11A\text{--}2)$$

where

$$
\begin{aligned}
R_f &= \text{Risk-free rate of return} \\
\beta &= \text{Beta coefficient from Formula 11A--1} \\
K_m &= \text{Return on the market index} \\
K_m - R_f &= \text{Premium or excess return of the market versus the} \\
&\quad \text{risk-free rate (since the market is riskier than } R_f, \text{ the}} \\
&\quad \text{assumption is that the expected } K_m \text{ will be greater than} \\
&\quad R_f) \\
\beta(K_m - R_f) &= \text{Expected return above the risk-free rate for the stock} \\
&\quad \text{of Company } j, \text{ given the level of risk}
\end{aligned}
$$

The model centers on "beta," the coefficient of the premium demanded by an investor to invest in an individual stock. For each individual security, beta measures the sensitivity (volatility) of the security's return to the market. By definition, the market has a beta of 1.0, so that if an individual company's beta is 1.0, it can expect to have returns as volatile

---

[1]A number of studies have also indicated that longer-term government securities may appropriately represent R_f (the risk-free rate).

as the market and total returns equal to the market. A company with a beta of 2.0 would be twice as volatile as the market and would be expected to generate more returns, whereas a company with a beta of 0.5 would be half as volatile as the market.

The term $(K_m - R_f)$ indicates that common stock is expected to generate a rate of return higher than the return on a U.S. Treasury bill. This makes sense since common stock has more risk. In fact, research by Roger Ibbottson shows that this risk premium over the last 60 years is close to 6.5 percent on average but exhibits a wide standard deviation.[2] In the actual application of the CAPM to cost of capital, companies often will use this historical risk premium in their calculations. In our example, we use 6.5 percent to represent the expected $(K_m - R_f)$.

For example, assuming that the risk-free rate is 5.5 percent and that the market risk premium $(K_m - R_f)$ is 6.5 percent, the following returns would occur with betas of 2.0, 1.0, and 0.5:

$$K_2 = 5.5\% + 2.0\ (6.5\%) = 5.5\% + 13.0\% = 18.5\%$$
$$K_1 = 5.5\% + 1.0\ (6.5\%) = 5.5\% + 6.5\% = 12.0\%$$
$$K_{.5} = 5.5\% + 0.5\ (6.5\%) = 5.5\% + 3.25\% = 8.75\%$$

The beta term measures the riskiness of an investment relative to the market. In order to outperform the market, one would have to assume more risk by selecting assets with betas greater than 1.0. Another way of looking at the risk-return trade-off would be that if less risk than the market is desired, an investor would choose assets with a beta of less than 1.0. Beta is a good measure of a stock's risk when the stock is combined into a portfolio, and therefore it has some bearing on the assets that a company acquires for its portfolio of real capital.

In Figure 11A–1, individual stock returns were compared to market returns and the beta from Formula 11A–1 was shown. From Formula 11A–2, the risk-premium model, a generalized risk–return graph called the security market line (SML) can be constructed that identifies the risk-return trade-off of any common stock (asset) relative to the company's beta. This is shown in Figure 11A–2.

The required return for all securities can be expressed as the risk-free rate plus a premium for risk. Thus we see that a stock with a beta of 1.0 would have a risk premium of 6.5 percent added to the risk-free rate of 5.5 percent to provide a required return of 12 percent. Since a beta of

---

[2]Ibbotson Associates, *Stocks, Bonds, Bills and Inflation: 1986 Yearbook*, (Chicago, Ill.: Ibbotson Associates and Capital Market Research Center, 1987).

Figure 11A–2
The security market line (SML)

Required rates of return

Percent

$$SML = R_f + \beta (K_m - R_f)$$

6.5% Market risk premium

Beta (risk)

1.0 implies risk equal to the stock market, the return is also at the overall market rate. If the beta is 2.0, twice the market risk premium of 6.5 percent must be earned and we add 13 percent to the risk-free rate of 5.5 percent to determine the required return of 18.5 percent. For a beta of 0.5, the required return is 8.75 percent.

Cost of Capital Considerations

When calculating the cost of capital for common stock, remember that K_e is equal to the expected total return from the dividend yield and capital gains.

$$K_e = \frac{D_1}{P_0} + g$$

K_e is the return required by investors based on expectations of future dividends and growth. The SML provides the same information, but in a market-related risk-return model. As required returns rise, prices must fall to adjust to the new equilibrium return level, and as required returns fall, prices rise. Stock markets are generally efficient and when stock prices are in equilibrium, the K_e derived from the dividend model will be equal to K_j derived from the SML.

The SML helps us to identify several circumstances that can cause the cost of capital to change. Figure 11–2 in Chapter 11 examined required rates of returns over time with changing interest rates and stock prices. Figure 11A–3 does basically the same thing, only through the SML format.

When interest rates increase from the initial period (R_{f1} versus R_{f0}), the security market line in the next period is parallel to SML_0, but higher. What this means is that required rates of return have risen for every level of risk, as investors desire to maintain their risk premium over the risk-free rate.

One very important variable influencing interest rates is the rate of inflation. As inflation increases, lenders try to maintain their real dollar purchasing power, so they increase the required interest rates to offset inflation. The risk-free rate can be thought of as:

$$R_f = RR + IP$$

where

    RR is the real rate of return on a riskless government security when inflation is zero.

    IP is an inflation premium that compensates lenders (investors) for loss of purchasing power.

Figure 11A–3
The security market line and changing interest rates

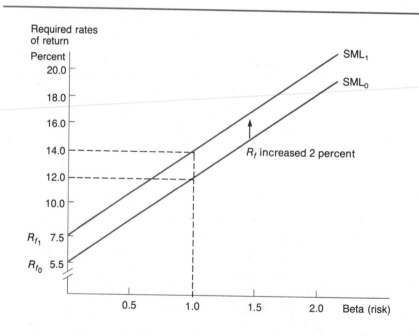

An upward shift in the SML indicates that the prices of all assets will shift downward as interest rates move up. In Chapter 10, Valuation and Rates of Return, this was demonstrated in the discussion which showed that when market interest rates went up, bond prices adjusted downward to make up for the lower coupon rate (interest payment) on the old bonds.

Another factor affecting the cost of capital is a change in risk preferences by investors. As investors become more pessimistic about the economy, they require larger premiums for assuming risks. Even though the historical average market risk premium may be close to 6.5 percent, this is not stable and investors' changing attitudes can have a big impact on the market risk premium. For example, the 1987 stock market crash on October 19 (a 22.6 percent decline in one day) had to be somewhat influenced by investors' quick move to a more risk-averse attitude. This risk aversion shows up in higher required stock returns and lower stock prices. For example, if investors raise their market risk premium to 8 percent, the rates of return from the original equations will increase as follows:

$$K_2 = 5.5\% + 2.0\,(8.0\%) = 5.5\% + 16.0\% = 21.5\%$$
$$K_1 = 5.5\% + 1.0\,(8.0\%) = 5.5\% + 8.0\% = 13.5\%$$
$$K_{.5} = 5.5\% + 0.5\,(8.0\%) = 5.5\% + 4.0\% = 9.5\%$$

The change in the market risk premium will cause the required market return (beta = 1.00) to be 13.5 percent instead of the 12 percent from Figure 11A–2. Any asset riskier than the market would have a larger increase in the required return. For example, a stock with a beta of 2.0 would need to generate a 21.5 percent return, instead of the 18.5 percent in Figure 11A–2. The overall shape of the new security market line (SML$_1$) is shown in Figure 11A–4. Note the higher slope for SML, in comparison to SML$_0$.

In many instances, rising interest rates and pessimistic investors go hand in hand, so that the SML may change its slope and intercept at the same time. This combined effect would cause severe drops in the prices of risky assets and much larger required rates of return for such assets.

The capital asset pricing model and the security market line have been presented to further your understanding of market-related events that impact the firm's cost of capital, such as market returns and risk, changing interest rates, and changing risk preferences.

While the capital asset pricing model has received criticism because of the difficulties of dealing with the betas of individual securities and because of the problems involved in consistently constructing the appro-

Figure 11A–4
The security market
line and changing
investor expectations

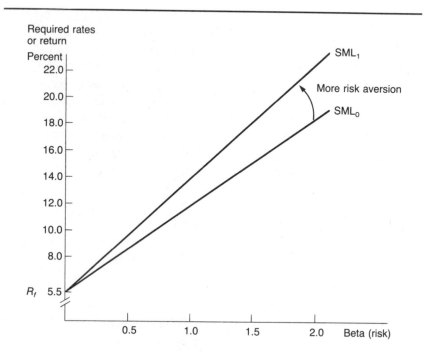

priate slope of the SML to represent reality, it provides some interesting insights into risk–return measurement.

List of Terms

capital asset pricing model   risk-free rate of interest
security market line   market risk premium

Discussion Questions

11A–1. How does the capital asset pricing model help explain changing costs of capital?

11A–2. Why does K_e approximate K_j, or why does $D_1/(P_0 - g)$ approximate $R_f + \beta (K_m - R_f)$?

11A–3. How does the SML react to changes in the rate of interest, changes in the rate of inflation, and changing investor expectations?

Problems

11A–1. Assume that $R_f = 6$ percent and $K_m = 11$ percent. Compute K_j for the following betas, using Formula 11A–2.

   a.   0.6

   b.   1.5

   c.   2.0

11A–2. In the preceding problem, R_f increases to 8.5 percent, and the market risk premium $(K_m - R_f)$ is 6.5 percent. Compute K_j for the three betas of 0.6, 1.5, and 2.0.

Appendix 11B: Capital Structure Theory and Modigliani and Miller

The foundation supporting cost of capital theories was primarily developed by Professors Modigliani and Miller in the late 1950s and mid 1960s.[1] They actually went through an evolutionary process in which they proposed many different theories and conclusions about cost of capital.

However, before we discuss Modigliani and Miller, we will briefly touch upon the work of David Durand in the early 1950s, which was the first written attempt to describe the effect of financial leverage on cost of capital and valuation. Professor Durand described three different theories of cost of capital: the net income (NI) approach, the net operating income (NOI) approach, and the traditional approach.[2]

Net Income (NI) Approach

Under the net income approach, it is assumed that the firm can raise all the funds it desires at a constant cost of equity and debt. Since debt tends to have a lower cost than equity, the more debt utilized the lower the overall cost of capital and the higher the evaluation of the firm as indicated in Figure 11B–1.

---

[1]Franco Modigliani and Merton H. Miller, "The Cost of Capital, Corporation Finance and the Theory of Investment," *American Economic Review,* June 1958, and "Taxes and the Cost of Capital: A Correction," *American Economic Review,* June 1963, pp. 433–43.

[2]See David Durand, "Costs of Debt and Equity Funds for Business: Trends and Problems of Measurement," *Conference on Research in Business Finance,* National Bureau of Economic Research, New York, 1952.

Figure 11B–1
Net income (NI)
approach

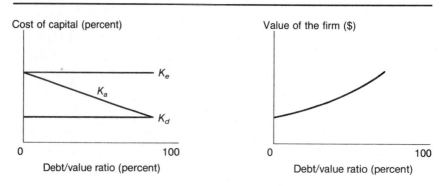

K_e = Cost of equity; K_d = Cost of debt; K_a = Cost of capital

Under the net income (NI) approach, the firm would indeed be foolish not to use 100 percent debt in order to minimize cost of capital and maximize valuation. However, the assumption of constant cost of all forms of financing regardless of the level of utilization was severely challenged by practitioners.

Net Operating Income (NOI) Approach

A second approach covered by Professor Durand was the net operating income (NOI) approach. Under this proposition, the low cost of debt is assumed to remain constant with greater debt utilization, but the cost of equity increases to such an extent that the cost of capital remains unchanged. Essentially, only operating income matters, and how you finance it makes no difference in terms of cost of capital or valuation. In Figure 11B–2, we see the effects of the net operating income (NOI) approach.

Figure 11B–2
Net operating income
(NOI) approach

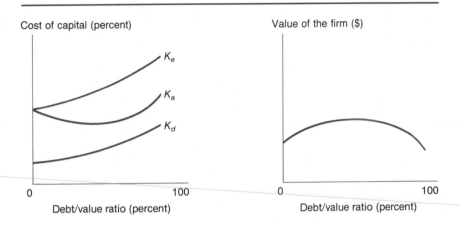

**Figure 11B–3
Traditional approach
as described by
Durand**

Finally, Professor Durand described the traditional approach. This falls somewhere between the net income (NI) approach and the net operating income (NOI) approach, in which there are benefits from increased debt utilization, but only up to a point. After that point, the cost of capital begins to turn up and the valuation of the firm begins to turn down. A graphic presentation of the traditional approach is seen in Figure 11B–3.

The student will perhaps realize that the traditional approach described by Durand in 1952 is very similar to what is accepted today (as described in the main body of the chapter), but the many theories of Modigliani and Miller had a major impact as we went from 1952 to the currently existing theory.

Modigliani and Miller's Initial Approach

The approaches described by Durand were largely unsupported by theories and mathematical proofs. The major contribution by Modigliani and Miller (M&M) was to add economic and financial theories to naive assumptions. Although it is beyond the scope of this text to go through all the various mathematical proofs of M&M, their basic positions will be presented.

Under the initial Modigliani and Miller approach, it is assumed that the value of the firm and its cost of capital is independent of the means of financing that takes place. This is very similar to the NOI approach described by Durand, but the rationale or mechanism for arriving at this conclusion is different.

M&M stipulate that the value of the firm equals the following:

$$V = \frac{EBIT}{K_a}$$
(11B–1)

where

$$V = \text{Value}$$
$$EBIT = \text{Earnings before interest and taxes}$$
$$K_a = \text{Cost of capital}$$

They further stipulate that:

$$K_a = K_{eu}$$
(11B–2)

K_{eu} represents the cost of equity for an unlevered firm (one with no debt).

But what if a firm decides to include debt in its capital structure? Then the cost of equity for this levered firm will increase by a risk premium to compensate for the additional risk associated with the debt.

$$K_{eL} = K_{eu} + \text{Risk premium}$$
$$K_{eL} = K_{eu} + (K_{eu} - I)\,(D/S)$$
(11B–3)

K_{eL} represents the cost of equity to the levered firm, I is the interest rate on the debt, D is the amount of debt financing, and S is the amount of stock (equity) financing. The actual symbols aren't really very important for our purposes. The important point to observe in Formula 11B–3 is that there is a risk premium associated with the cost of equity financing (K_e) when there is leverage involved.

M&M thus say a firm cannot reduce the cost of capital or increase the valuation of the firm, because any benefits from cheaper debt are offset by the increased cost of equity financing. That is:

$$K_{eL} = K_{eu} + \text{Risk premium}$$

M&M then go on to demonstrate that, if a leveraged firm could increase its value over another firm not using leverage (when all else is equal in terms of operating performance), then investors would simply sell off the overpriced leveraged firm and use *homemade leverage* (borrow on their own) to buy the underpriced, unleveraged firm's stock. Since both firms are equal in terms of operating performance, investors would simply arbitrage between the values of the two to bring them into equilibrium (sell the overpriced firm and buy the underpriced one using their own personally borrowed funds as part of the process).

In summary, under the initial M&M hypothesis, the value of a firm and its cost of capital are completely unaffected by the firm's capital structure.

Modigliani and Miller with the Introduction of Corporate Taxes

As is true of many economic models, M&M made a number of assumptions in their initial theory of cost of capital that tended to simplify the analysis. The most critical simplifying assumption was to ignore the impact of corporate taxes on the cost of capital to the firm (Durand made similar simplifying assumptions). Once M&M began to consider the effect of taxes, their whole outlook changed. Because interest on debt is a tax deductible expense, the tax effect greatly reduces the cost of debt and the associated cost of capital. Furthermore, with a reduced cost of capital, there is an increased valuation for the firm.

A key adjustment to a basic valuation formula is that:

$$V_L = V_U + TD \qquad \text{(11B–4)}$$

Formula 11B–4 says that the value of a leveraged firm (V_L) is equal to the value of an unleveraged firm (V_U), plus an amount equal to the corporate tax rate (T) times the amount of debt (D) the firm has. If an unleveraged firm has a value of \$1,000,000 (V_U), then a leveraged firm with \$400,000 in debt and a tax rate of 34 percent will have a value of \$1,136,000.

$$
\begin{aligned}
V_L &= V_U + TD \\
&= \$1,000,000 + 0.34\,(\$400,000) \\
&= \$1,000,000 + 136,000 \\
&= \$1,136,000
\end{aligned}
$$

A firm with \$600,000 in debt will have a value of \$1,204,000 and so on.

$$
\begin{aligned}
V_L &= V_U + TD \\
&= \$1,000,000 + 0.34\,(\$600,000) \\
&= \$1,000,000 + \$204,000 \\
&= \$1,204,000
\end{aligned}
$$

Graphically, we are led to the positions presented in Figure 11B–4.

As can be viewed in Figure 11B–4, once corporate taxes are introduced, it is assumed that every increment of debt will reduce the cost of capital,

Figure 11B–4
Modigliani and Miller
with corporate taxes

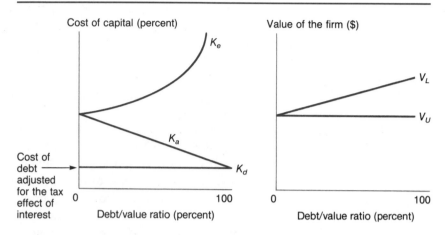

eventually down to the cost of debt itself. Furthermore, the more debt a firm has, the higher its valuation will be.[3]

Under the second version of M&M, every firm should be 100 percent (perhaps 99.9 percent) financed by debt to lower its cost of capital and increase its valuation.

Modigliani and Miller with bankruptcy considerations

Since no firm or investor in the real world operates on the basis of the just described M&M hypothesis, there must be some missing variables. One of the disadvantages of heavy borrowing is that the firm may eventually go bankrupt (a topic discussed in Appendix 16A). Clearly, a firm which does not borrow at all has *no* such threat. All things being equal, the threat of bankruptcy increases as the amount of borrowing increases.

When bankruptcy occurs, the firm may be forced to sell off assets at a fraction of their value. Furthermore, there is likely to be substantial legal fees, court costs, and administrative expenses. Even if a firm does not go bankrupt, but is on the verge of bankruptcy, customers may be hesitant to do business with the firm. Suppliers may demand advanced payments and so on.

Also, as a firm increases the amount of debt it has, there are likely to be restrictive covenants or provisions in debt agreements that hinder the

---

[3]The only constraint to this proposition is that the amount of debt cannot exceed the amount of assets.

normal operations of the firm (the current ratio must be at a given level or no new projects can be undertaken without lender approval).

All of these bankruptcy-related considerations have an implicit cost. If the potential cost of bankruptcy were $10 million, then the probability of that bankruptcy must also be considered. Of course, if the firm has no debt, then the probability of bankruptcy is zero and the obvious cost is zero. If the firm has 50 percent debt, there may be a 10 percent probability of bankruptcy and the expected cost is $1 million ($10 million × 10 percent). Finally, with 90 percent debt, there may be a 25 percent probability of bankruptcy and the expected cost is $2,500,000 ($10,000,000 × 25 percent). Once these expected costs of bankruptcy are present valued, they must be deducted from the current, unadjusted value of the firm to determine true value. Similarly, the expected value of the threat of future bankruptcy also tends to increase the cost of capital to the firm as progressively more debt is utilized.

In Figure 11B–5, we combine the effect of the corporate tax advantage (M&M II) with the effect of the bankruptcy threat (M&M III) to show the impact of financial leverage on the cost of capital and valuation of the firm.

As you can see in panel (a) of Figure 11B–5, the black line, which combines the tax effect with the bankruptcy effect, takes us all the way back to the initial proposition first discussed in the main body of the chapter, which is that cost of capital tends to be U-shaped in nature. We have simply added some additional theory to support this proposition. In panel (b) of Figure 11B–5, we also see from the black line that the combined effect of taxation and bankruptcy allows the firm to maximize valuation at a given debt level and then the valuation begins to diminish.

The Miller Model

As if to temporarily confuse an already settled issue, Professor Miller announced at the annual meeting of the American Finance Association in 1976 that he was rejecting his own latest version of the M&M hypothesis (M&M III, as indicated by the black lines in Figure 11B–5).[4] His new premise was that he had considered corporate taxes but not personal taxes in the earlier M&M models. He suggested that, when one began considering personal taxes in the process, stock ownership had substantial ad-

[4]Merton H. Miller, "Debt and Taxes," *Journal of Finance*, May 1977, pp. 261–75.

**Figure 11B–5
Combined impact of
the corporate tax
effect and bankruptcy
effect on valuation
and cost of capital**

(a)

Cost of capital (percent)

K_a (M+M with tax effect and bankruptcy effect)

K_a (original M+M)

K_a (M+M with tax effect)

0   100

Debt/value ratio (percent)

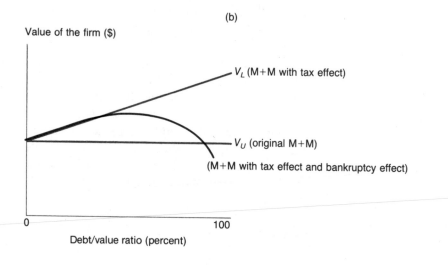

(b)

Value of the firm ($)

V_L (M+M with tax effect)

V_U (original M+M)

(M+M with tax effect and bankruptcy effect)

0   100

Debt/value ratio (percent)

vantages over debt ownership. Why? Because, at the time, gains from
stock ownership were potentially taxed at a much lower rate than interest
income, due to the capital gains component that was part of the anticipated
return to stockholders. Long-term capital gains have traditionally been
taxed at a rate 40–60 percent lower than other income. Miller said that
once you factored all tax considerations (corporate and personal) into the
analysis, there was not an overall advantage to debt utilization to the firm
and, therefore, the cost of capital was unaffected by the capital structure
of the firm.

Subsequent research has partially taken issue with Professor Miller. Fortunately, from a theoretical viewpoint, the Tax Reform Act of 1986 has made the tax treatment of capital gains exactly equal to other forms of income. Therefore, the personal tax effect enunciated by Professor Miller in 1976 has now been negated and we can somewhat safely return to the U-shaped approach generally described in this chapter and in the appendix.

List of Terms

net income (NI) approach	traditional approach
net operating income (NOI) approach	homemade leverage

Discussion Questions

11B–1. What is the difference between the net income (NI) approach, the net operating income (NOI) approach, and the traditional approach?

11B–2. Under the initial Modigliani and Miller approach, does the use of debt affect the cost of capital? Explain.

11B–3. How do corporate taxes and bankruptcy considerations change the initial Modigliani and Miller approach? What is the net effect?

12 The Capital Budgeting Decision

The decision on capital outlays is among the most significant that a firm will have to make. A decision to build a new plant or expand into a foreign market may influence the performance of the firm over the next decade. The airline industry has shown a tendency to expand in excess of its needs, while other industries have insufficient capacity. The auto industry has often miscalculated its product mix and has had to shift down from one car size to another at an enormous expense.

The capital budgeting decision involves the planning of expenditures for a project with a life of at least one year, and usually a considerably longer period. In the public utilities sector, a time horizon of 25 years is not unusual. The capital expenditure decision requires extensive planning to ensure that engineering and marketing information is available, product design is completed, necessary patents are acquired, and the capital markets are tapped for the necessary funds. Throughout this chapter, we will use techniques developed under the discussion of the time value of money to equate future flows to the present, while using the cost of capital as the basic discount rate.

A problem a manager faces is that as the time horizon moves farther into the future, uncertainty becomes a greater hazard. The manager is uncertain about annual costs and inflows, product life, interest rates, economic conditions, and technological change. A good example of the vagueness of the marketplace can be observed in the hand calculator industry in the mid-1970s. A number of firms tooled up in the early 1970s in the hope of being first to break through the $100 price range for pocket calculators, assuming that penetration of the $100 barrier would bring a larger market share and high profitability. However, technological advancement, price cutting, and the appearance of Texas Instruments in the consumer market drove prices down by 60–90 percent and made the $100 pocket calculator a museum piece. Rapid Data Systems, the first entry into the under-$100 market, went into bankruptcy. Of course, not all new developments are quite so perilous, and a number of techniques, which will be treated in the next chapter, have been devised to cope with the impact of uncertainty on decision making.

In this chapter, capital budgeting will be studied under the following major topical headings: administrative considerations, accounting flows versus cash flows, methods of ranking investment proposals, selection strategy, combining cash flow and selection strategy, and the replacement decision. Later in the chapter, emphasis is placed on tax laws and their impact on depreciation and capital budgeting decisions.

Administrative Considerations

A good capital budgeting program requires that a number of steps be taken in the decision-making process.

1. Search and discovery of investment opportunities.
2. Collection of data.
3. Evaluation and decision making.
4. Reevaluation and adjustment.

The search for new opportunities is the least emphasized, though perhaps the most important, of the four steps. Although it is outside the scope of this book to suggest procedures for developing an organization that is conducive to innovation and creative thinking, the marginal return of such an organization is likely to be high (and a high marginal return is the essence of capital budgeting).

The collection of data should go beyond engineering data and market surveys and should attempt to capture the relative likelihood of the occurrence of various events. The probabilities of increases or slumps in product demand may be evaluated from statistical analysis, while other outcomes may be estimated subjectively.

Figure 12–1
Capital budgeting
procedures

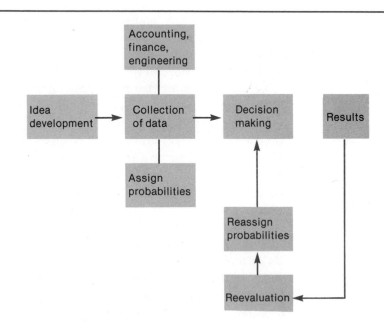

After all data have been collected and evaluated, the final decision must be made. Generally, determinations involving relatively small amounts will be made at the department or division level, while major expenditures can only be approved by top management. A constant monitoring of the results of a given decision may indicate that a whole new set of probabilities must be developed, based on first-year experience, and the initial decision to choose Product A over Product B must be reevaluated and perhaps reversed. The preceding factors are delineated in Figure 12–1.

Accounting Flows versus Cash Flows

In most capital budgeting decisions the emphasis is on cash flow, rather than reported income. Let us consider the logic of using cash flow in the capital budgeting process. Because depreciation does not represent an actual expenditure of funds in arriving at profit, it is added back to profit to determine the amount of cash flow generated.[1] Assume that the Alston Corporation has $50,000 of new equipment to be depreciated at $5,000

---

[1]As explained in Chapter 2, depreciation is not a new source of funds (except in tax savings), but represents a noncash outlay to be added back.

per year. The firm has $20,000 in earnings before depreciation and taxes and is in a 34 percent tax bracket. The information is presented in Table 12–1.

Table 12–1
Cash flow for Alston Corporation

Earnings before depreciation and taxes (cash inflow)	$20,000
Depreciation (noncash expense) . . .	5,000
Earnings before taxes	15,000
Taxes (cash outflow)	5,100
Earnings after taxes	9,900
Depreciation	+5,000
Cash flow	$14,900

Alternative method of cash flow calculation

Cash inflow (EBDT)	$20,000
Cash outflow (taxes)	−5,100
Cash flow	$14,900

The firm shows $9,900 in earnings after taxes, but it adds back the noncash deduction of $5,000 in depreciation to arrive at a cash flow figure of $14,900. The logic of adding back depreciation becomes even greater if we consider the impact of *$20,000* in depreciation for the Alston Corp. (Table 12–2). Net earnings before and after taxes are zero, but the company has $20,000 cash in the bank.

Table 12–2
Revised cash flow for Alston Corporation

Earnings before depreciation and taxes	$20,000
Depreciation	20,000
Earnings before taxes	0
Taxes	0
Earnings after taxes	0
Depreciation	+20,000
Cash flow	$20,000

To the capital budgeting specialist, the use of cash flow figures is well accepted. However, top management does not always take a similar viewpoint. Assume you are the president of a firm listed on the New York Stock Exchange and must select between two alternatives. Proposal A will provide zero in aftertax earnings and $100,000 in cash flow, while Proposal B, calling for no depreciation, will provide $50,000 in aftertax earnings and cash flow. As president of a publicly traded firm, you have security analysts constantly penciling in their projections of your earnings for the next quarter and you fear your stock may drop dramatically if earnings are too low by even a small amount. Although Proposal A is superior, you may be more sensitive to aftertax earnings than to cash flow and you may therefore select Proposal B. Perhaps you are also overly concerned about the short-term impact of a decision rather than the long-term economic benefits that might accrue.

The student must be sensitive to the concessions to short-term pressures that are sometimes made by top executives. Nevertheless, in the material that follows, the emphasis is on the use of proper evaluation techniques to make the best economic choice and assure long-term wealth maximization.

Methods of Ranking Investment Proposals

Three widely used methods for evaluating capital expenditures will be considered, along with the shortcomings and advantages of each.

1. Payback method.
2. Internal rate of return.
3. Net present value.

The first method, while not conceptually sound, is often used. Approaches 2 and 3 are more acceptable, and one or the other should be applied to most situations.

Payback Method

Under the payback method, we compute the time required to recoup the initial investment. Assume that we are called upon to select between Investment A and Investment B in Table 12–3.

The payback period for Investment A is 2 years, while Investment B requires 3.8 years. In the latter case, we recover $6,000 in the first three

Table 12–3 Investment alternatives		Cash Inflows (of $10,000 investment)	
	Year	Investment A	Investment B
	1	$5,000	$1,500
	2	5,000	2,000
	3	2,000	2,500
	4		5,000
	5		5,000

years, leaving us with the need for another $4,000 to recoup the full $10,000 investment. Since the fourth year has a total inflow of $5,000, $4,000 represents 0.8 of that value. Thus, the payback period for Investment B is 3.8 years.

In using the payback method to select Investment A, two important considerations are ignored. First of all, there is no consideration of inflows after the cutoff period. The $2,000 in year 3 for Investment A is ignored, as is the $5,000 in year 5 for Investment B. Even if the $5,000 were $50,000, it would have no impact on the decision.

Second, the method fails to consider the concept of the time value of money. If we had two $10,000 investments with the following inflow patterns, the payback method would rank them equally.

Year	Early Returns	Late Returns
1	$9,000	$1,000
2	1,000	9,000
3	1,000	1,000

Although both investments have a payback period of two years, the first alternative is clearly superior because the $9,000 comes in the first year rather than the second.

The payback method does have some features that help to explain its use by U.S. corporations. It is easy to understand, and it places a heavy emphasis on liquidity. An investment must recoup the initial investment quickly or it will not qualify (most corporations use a maximum time horizon of three to five years). A rapid payback may be particularly important to firms in industries characterized by rapid technological developments.

Nevertheless, the payback method, concentrating as it does on only the initial years of investment, fails to discern the optimum or most economic solution to a capital budgeting problem. The analyst is therefore required to consider the more theoretically correct methods.

Internal Rate of Return

The internal rate of return (IRR) calls for determining the yield on an investment, that is, calculating the interest rate that equates the cash outflows (cost) of an investment with the subsequent cash inflows. The simplest case would be an investment of $100 which provides $120 after one year, or a 20 percent internal rate of return. For more complicated situations, we use Appendix B (present value of a single amount) and

Appendix D (present value of an annuity) and the techniques described in Chapter 9, The Time Value of Money. For example, a $1,000 investment returning an annuity of $244 per year for five years provides an internal rate of return of 7 percent, as indicated by the following calculations.

1. First divide the investment (present value) by the annuity.

$$\frac{(Investment)}{(Annuity)} = \frac{\$1,000}{\$244} = 4.1 \ (IF_{pva})$$

2. Then proceed to Appendix D (present value of an annuity). The factor of 4.1 for five years indicates a yield of 7 percent.

Whenever an annuity is being evaluated, annuity interest factors (IF_{pva}) can be used to find the final IRR solution. If an uneven cash inflow is involved, we are not so lucky. We need to use a trial and error method. The first question is, Where do we start? What interest rate should we pick for our first trial? Assume that we are once again called upon to evaluate the two investment alternatives in Table 12–3, only this time using the internal rate of return to rank the two projects. Because neither proposal represents a precise annuity stream, we must use the trial and error approach to determine an answer. We begin with Investment A.

	Cash Inflows (of $10,000 investment)	
Year	Investment A	Investment B
1	$5,000	$1,500
2	5,000	2,000
3	2,000	2,500
4		5,000
5		5,000

1. In order to find a beginning value to start our first trial, average the inflows as if we were really getting an annuity.

$$
\begin{array}{r}
\$\ 5,000 \\
5,000 \\
\underline{2,000} \\
\$12,000 \div 3 = \$4,000
\end{array}
$$

2. Then divide the investment by the "assumed" annuity value in step 1.

$$\frac{\text{(Investment)}}{\text{(Annuity)}} = \frac{\$10,000}{\$4,000} = 2.5 \ (IF_{pva})$$

3. Proceed to Appendix D to arrive at a *first approximation* of the internal rate of return, using:

$$IF_{pva} \text{ factor} = 2.5$$
$$n \text{ (period)} = 3$$

The factor falls between 9 and 10 percent. This is only a first approximation—our actual answer will be closer to 10 percent or higher because our method of averaging cash flows theoretically moved receipts from the first two years into the last year. This averaging understates the actual internal rate of return. The same method would overstate the IRR for Investment B because it would move cash from the last two years into the first three years. Since we know that cash flows in the early years are worth more and increase our return, we can usually gauge whether our first approximation is overstated or understated.

4. We now enter into a trial and error process to arrive at an answer. Because these cash flows are uneven rather than an annuity, we need to use Appendix B. We will begin with 10 percent and then try 12 percent.

Year	10 percent		Year	12 percent	
1	$5,000 × 0.909 =	$ 4,545	1	$5,000 × 0.893 =	$4,465
2	5,000 × 0.826 =	4,130	2	5,000 × 0.797 =	3,985
3	2,000 × 0.751 =	1,502	3	2,000 × 0.712 =	1,424
		$10,177			$9,874

At 10 percent, the present value of the inflows exceeds $10,000—we therefore use a higher discount rate.

At 12 percent, the present value of the inflows is less than $10,000—thus the discount rate is too high.

The answer must fall between 10 percent and 12 percent, indicating an approximate answer of 11 percent.

If we want to be more accurate, the results can be *interpolated*. Because the internal rate of return is determined when the present value of the inflows (PV_I) equals the present value of the outflows (PV_O), we need to find a discount rate that equates the PV_I to the cost of $10,000 ($PV_O$). The total difference in present values between 10 percent and 12 percent is $303.

$10,177	. . . . .	PV_1 @ 10%	$10,177	. . . . . PV_1 @ 10%
9,874	. . . . .	PV_1 @ 12%	10,000	. . . . . (cost)
$ 303			$ 177	

The solution at 10 percent is $177 away from $10,000. Actually the solution is ($177/$303) percent of the way between 10 and 12 percent. Since there is a 2 percent difference between the two rates used to evaluate the cash inflows, we need to multiply the fraction by 2 percent and then add our answer to 10 percent for the final answer of:

$$10\% + (\$177/\$303)(2\%) = 11.17\% \text{ IRR}$$

In Investment B, the same process will yield an answer of 14.33 percent (you may wish to confirm this).

The use of the internal rate of return calls for the prudent selection of Investment B in preference to Investment A, the exact opposite of the conclusion reached under the payback method.

	Investment A	Investment B	Selection
Payback method	2 years	3.8 years	Quicker payback: Investment A
Internal rate of return . . .	11.17%	14.33%	Higher yield: Investment B

The final selection of any project under the internal rate-of-return method will also depend upon the yield exceeding some minimum cost standard, such as the cost of capital to the firm.

Net Present Value

The final method of investment selection is to determine the net present value of an investment. This is done by discounting back the inflows over the life of the investment to determine whether they equal or exceed the required investment. The basic discount rate is usually the cost of capital to the firm. Thus, inflows that arrive in later years must provide a return that at least equals the cost of financing those returns. If we once again evaluate Investments A and B—using an assumed cost of capital or a discount rate of 10 percent—we arrive at the following figures for net present value.

$10,000 investment, 10 percent discount rate

Year	Investment A	Year	Investment B
1	. . . $5,000 × 0.909 = $ 4,545	1	. . . $1,500 × 0.909 = $ 1,364
2	. . . 5,000 × 0.826 = 4,130	2	. . . 2,000 × 0.826 = 1,652
3	. . . 2,000 × 0.751 = 1,502	3	. . . 2,500 × 0.751 = 1,878
	$10,177	4	. . . 5,000 × 0.683 = 3,415
		5	. . . 5,000 × 0.621 = 3,105
			$11,414

Present value of inflows $10,177		Present value of inflows $11,414
Present value of outflows . . . 10,000		Present value of outflows . . . 10,000
Net present value . . . . . . $ 177		Net present value . . . . . . $ 1,414

While both proposals appear to be acceptable, Investment B has a considerably higher net present value than Investment A.[2] Under most circumstances the net present value and internal rate of return methods give theoretically correct answers, and the subsequent discussion will be restricted to these two approaches. A summary of the various conclusions reached under the three methods is presented in Table 12–4.

**Table 12–4
Capital budgeting
results**

	Investment A	Investment B	Selection
Payback method	2 years	3.8 years	Quicker payout: Investment A
Internal rate of return . . .	11.17%	14.33%	Higher yield: Investment B
Net present value	$177	$1,414	Higher net present value: Investment B

Selection Strategy

In both the internal rate of return and net present value methods, the profitability must equal or exceed the cost of capital for the project to be potentially acceptable. However, other distinctions are necessary—namely,

---

[2]A further possible refinement under the net present value method is to compute a profitability index.

$$\text{Profitability index} = \frac{\text{Present value of the inflows}}{\text{Present value of the outflows}}$$

For Investment A the profitability index is 1.0177 ($10,177/$10,000) and for Investment B it is 1.1414 ($11,414/$10,000). The profitability index can be helpful in comparing returns from different size investments by placing them on a common measuring standard. This, of course, was not necessary in this example.

whether the projects are *mutually exclusive or not*. If investments are mutually exclusive, the selection of one alternative will preclude the selection of any other alternative. Assume we are going to build a specialized assembly plant in the Midwest and four major cities are under consideration, only one of which will be picked. In this situation, we select the alternative with the highest acceptable yield or the highest net present value and disregard all others. Even if certain locations provide a marginal return in excess of the cost of capital, assumed to be 10 percent, they will be rejected. In the table below, the possible alternatives are presented.

Mutually exclusive alternatives

	IRR	Net present value
Dayton	15%	$ 300
Columbus	12	200
St. Paul	11	100
Cost of capital . . .	10	—
Gary	9	(100)

Among the mutually exclusive alternatives, only Dayton would be selected. Of course, if the alternatives were not mutually exclusive (much-needed multiple retail outlets), we would accept all of the alternatives that provide a return in excess of our cost of capital, and only Gary would be rejected.

Applying this logic to Investments A and B in the prior discussion and assuming a cost of capital of 10 percent, only Investment B would be accepted if the alternatives were mutually exclusive, while both would clearly qualify if they were not mutually exclusive.

	Investment A	Investment B	Accepted if Mutually Exclusive	Accepted if Not Mutually Exclusive
Internal rate of return . . .	11.17%	14.33%	B	A, B
Net present value	$177	$1,414	B	A, B

The discussion to this point has assumed that the internal rate of return and net present value methods will call for the same decision. Although this is generally true, there are exceptions. Two rules may be stated:

1. Both methods will accept or reject the same investments based on minimum return or cost of capital criteria. If an investment has a positive net present value, it will also have a yield in excess of the cost of capital.

2. In certain limited cases, however, the two methods may give different answers in selecting the best investment from a range of acceptable alternatives.

Reinvestment Assumption

It is only under this second state of events that a preference for one method over the other must be established. A prime characteristic of the internal rate of return is the assumption that all inflows can be reinvested at the yield from a given investment. For example, in the case of the aforementioned Investment A yielding 11.17 percent, the assumption is made that the dollar amounts coming in each year can, in fact, be reinvested at that rate. For Investment B, with a 14.33 percent internal rate of return, the new funds are assumed to be reinvested at this high rate. The relationships are presented in Table 12–5.

For investments with a very high IRR, it may be unrealistic to assume that reinvestment can take place at an equally high rate. The net present value method, depicted in Table 12–6, makes the more conservative assumption that each inflow can be reinvested at the cost of capital or discount rate.

The reinvestment assumption under the net present value method allows for a certain consistency. Inflows from each project are assumed to

Table 12–5
The reinvestment assumption—internal rate of return ($10,000 investment)

Investment A (11.17% IRR)			Investment B (14.33% IRR)		
Year	Cash Flow		Year	Cash Flow	
1	$5,000 →		1	$1,500 →	
2	5,000 →		2	2,000 →	
3	2,000 →	reinvested at 11.17%	3	2,500 →	reinvested at 14.33%
			4	5,000 →	
			5	5,000 →	

Table 12–6
The reinvestment assumption—net present value ($10,000 investment)

Investment A			Investment B		
Year	Cash Flow		Year	Cash Flow	
1	$5,000 →		1	$1,500 →	
2	5,000 →		2	2,000 →	
3	2,000 →	reinvested at 10% (cost of capital)	3	2,500 →	reinvested at 10% (cost of capital)
			4	5,000 →	
			5	5,000 →	

have the same (though conservative) investment opportunity. Although this may not be an accurate picture for all firms, net present value is generally the preferred method.

Capital Rationing

At times, management may place an artificial constraint on the amount of funds that can be invested in a given period. The executive planning committee may emerge from a lengthy capital budgeting session to announce that only $5 million may be spent on new capital projects this year. Although $5 million may represent a large sum, it is still an artificially determined constraint and not the product of marginal analysis, in which the return for each proposal is related to the cost of capital for the firm, and projects with positive net present values are accepted.

A firm may adopt a posture of capital rationing because it is fearful of growth or hesitant to use external sources of financing (perhaps debt). In a strictly economic sense, capital rationing hinders a firm from achieving maximum profitability. With capital rationing as indicated in Table 12–7, acceptable projects must be ranked, and only those with the highest positive net present value are accepted.

Table 12–7
Capital rationing

	Project	Investment	Total Investment	Net Present Value
Capital	A	$2,000,000		$400,000
rationing	B	2,000,000		380,000
solution →	C	1,000,000	$5,000,000	150,000
	D	1,000,000		100,000
Best	E	800,000	6,800,000	40,000
solution →	F	800,000		(30,000)

Under capital rationing, only Projects A through C, calling for $5 million in investment, will be accepted. Although Projects D and E have returns exceeding the cost of funds, as evidenced by a positive net present value, they will not be accepted with the capital rationing assumption.

Net Present Value Profile

An interesting way to summarize the characteristics of an investment is through the use of the net present value profile. The profile allows us to graphically portray the net present value of a project at different discount rates. Let's apply the profile to the investments that we have been discussing. The projects are summarized again below.

	Cash Inflows (of $10,000 investment)	
	---	---
Year	Investment A	Investment B
1	$5,000	$1,500
2	5,000	2,000
3	2,000	2,500
4		5,000
5		5,000

To apply the net present value profile, you need to know *three* characteristics about an investment:

1. *The net present value at a zero discount rate.* Actually, that is easy to determine. A zero discount rate means no discount rate at all. The values simply retain their original value. For Investment A, the net present value would be $2,000 ($5,000 + $5,000 + $2,000 − $10,000). For Investment B, the answer is $6,000 ($1,500 + $2,000 + $2,500 + $5,000 + $5,000 − $10,000).
2. *The net present value as determined by a normal discount rate* (such as the cost of capital). For these two investments, we use a discount rate of 10 percent. As previously summarized in Table 12–4, the net present values for the two investments at that discount rate are $177 for Investment A, and $1,414 for Investment B.
3. *The internal rate of return for the investments.* Once again referring to Table 12–4, we see the internal rate of return is 11.17 percent for Investment A, and 14.33 percent for Investment B. The reader should also realize that the internal rate of return is the discount rate that allows the project to have a net present value of zero. This characteristic will become more important when we present our graphic display.

We summarize the information about discount rates and net present values for each investment here, and graphically in Figure 12–2.

Investment A	
Discount Rate	Net Present Value
0	$2,000
10%	177
11.17% (IRR)	0

Investment B	
Discount Rate	*Net Present Value*
0	$6,000
10%	1,414
14.33% (IRR)	0

Note that in Figure 12–2 we have graphed the three points for each investment. For example, for Investment A, we showed a $2,000 net present value at a zero discount rate, a $177 net present value at a 10 percent discount rate, and a zero net present value at an 11.17 percent discount rate. We then connected the points. The same procedure was applied to Investment B. The reader can also visually approximate what the net present value for the investment projects would be at other discount rates (such as 5 percent).

In the current example, the net present value of Investment B was superior to Investment A at every point. This is not always the case in comparing projects. To illustrate, let's introduce a new project, Investment C, and then compare it with Investment B.

Figure 12–2
Net present value profile

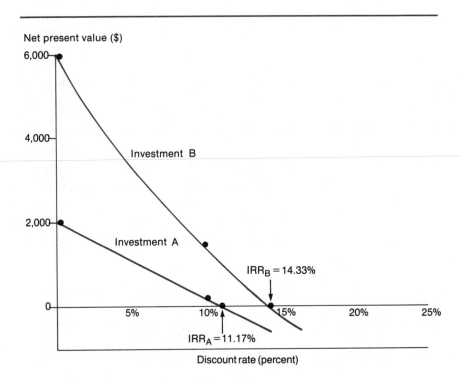

Invest C	
($10,000 Investment)	
Year	Cash Inflows
1	$9,000
2	3,000
3	1,200

Characteristics of Investment C

1. The net present value at a zero discount rate for this project is $3,200 ($9,000 + $3,000 + $1,200 − $10,000).
2. The net present value at a 10 percent discount rate is $1,560.
3. The internal rate of return is 22.51 percent.

You could compute these values for yourself, but that is really not necessary at this point.

Comparing Investment B to Investment C in Figure 12–3, we observe that at low discount rates, Investment B has a higher net present value

Figure 12–3
Net present value
profile with crossover

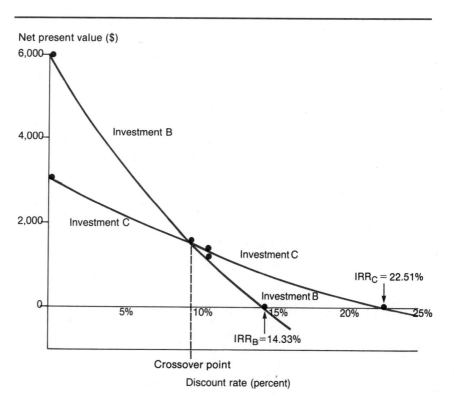

than Investment C. However, at high discount rates, Investment C has a higher net present value than Investment B. The actual crossover point can be viewed at approximately 8.7 percent. That is to say, if you had to choose between Investment B and Investment C, your answers would be dependent on the discount rate. At low rates (below 8.7 percent), you would opt for Investment B. At higher rates (above 8.7 percent), you would select Investment C. Since the cost of capital is presumed to be 10 percent, you would probably prefer Investment C, but keep in mind the cost of capital can change.

Why does Investment B do well compared to Investment C at low discount rates and relatively poorly compared to Investment C at high discount rates? This difference is related to the timing of inflows. Let's examine the inflows.

	Cash Inflows (of $10,000 investment)	
Year	Investment B	Investment C
1	$1,500	$9,000
2	2,000	3,000
3	2,500	1,200
4	5,000	
5	5,000	

Investment B has heavy late inflows ($5,000 in both the fourth and fifth years) and these are more strongly penalized by high discount rates. Investment C has extremely high early inflows and these hold up well with high discount rates.

As previously mentioned in the chapter, if the investments are non-mutually exclusive or there is not capital rationing, we would probably accept both Investment B and Investment C at discount rates below 14.33 percent, because they both would have positive net present values. On the other hand, if we can only select one, the decision may well turn on the discount rate. Observe in Figure 12–3, at a discount rate of 5 percent, we would select Investment B, at 10 percent we would select Investment C, and so on. The net present value profile helps us to make such decisions. Now back to basic capital budgeting issues.

Combining Cash Flow Analysis and Selection Strategy _____

Many of the points that we have covered thus far will be reviewed in the context of a capital budgeting decision, in which we determine the annual cash flows from an investment and compare them to the initial outlay. In order to be able to analyze a wide variety of cash flow patterns, we shall first consider the types of depreciation that are allowable under the Tax Reform Act of 1986.

The New Rules for Depreciation

Under the Tax Reform Act of 1986, assets are classified according to eight different categories which determine the allowable rate of depreciation write-off. Each class is referred to as an "ACRS category." ACRS stands for "Accelerated Cost Recovery System" and is a carryover term from the 1981 tax legislation. Some references are also made to ADR, which stands for "Asset Depreciation Range," or the expected physical life of the asset or class of assets. For example, an asset may have a midpoint of its ADR of four years, which means that the middle of its expected useful life is four years. Most assets can still be written off more rapidly than the midpoint of their ADR (Asset Depreciation Range). An asset with a midpoint of its ADR of four years might be written off over three years. Table 12–8 shows the various categories for depreciation.

Table 12–8
Categories for depreciation write-off

Class	
3-year ACRS	All property with ADR midpoints of four years or less. Autos and light trucks are *excluded* from this category.
5-year ACRS	Property with ADR midpoints of more than four, but less than 10 years. Key assets in this category include automobiles, light trucks, and technological equipment such as computers and research related properties.
7-year ACRS	Property with ADR midpoints of 10 years or more, but less than 16 years. Most types of manufacturing equipment would fall into this category, as would office furniture and fixtures.
10-year ACRS	Property with ADR midpoints of 16 years or more, but less than 20 years. Petroleum refining products, railroad tank cars, and manufactured homes fall into this group.
15-year ACRS	Property with ADR midpoints of 20 years or more, but less than 25 years. Land improvement, pipeline distribution, telephone distribution, and sewage treatment plants all belong in this category.
20-year ACRS	Property with ADR midpoints of 25 years or more (with the exception of real estate, which is treated separately). Key investments in this category include electric gas utility property and sewer pipes.
27½-year write-off	This is the first of two categories for real estate (real property). Investments in residential real estate fall into this category.
31½-year write-off	This is the second real estate category and includes all nonresidential real estate. Examples include office buildings, warehouses, and shopping centers.

It is not necessary that you become an expert in determining the category in which an asset belongs. In problems at the end of this material you will be given enough information to easily make a determination.

Each of the eight categories in Table 12–8 has its own rate of depreciation that you apply to the initial purchase price of the asset. The rates will be presented to you shortly, but let's talk briefly about the development of the rates.

For the first four categories the assumed method of depreciation is 200 percent declining balance with an ability to switch over to straight-line at the optimum point. For the next two categories the method is 150 percent declining balance with the same switchover provision. In the last two categories only straight-line depreciation can be used.[3]

Here is a summary of the depreciation methods for each category.

Category	Depreciation Method
3-year ACRS	200 percent declining balance—switch to straight-line
5-year ACRS	
7-year ACRS	
10-year ACRS	
15-year ACRS	150 percent declining balance—switch to straight-line
20-year ACRS	
27½-year category	straight-line
31½-year category	

Let's demonstrate how the rates are developed for the tax tables using the five-year ACRS category. The method in this case is 200 percent declining balance, with a switchover to straight-line. The rates in the tax tables are further developed with the use of the half-year convention, which treats all property as if it were placed in service in mid-year. The half-year convention is also extended to the sale or retirement of an asset. Thus for five-year ACRS depreciation, it is assumed that the asset was purchased in the middle of the first year, so you get a half year's depreciation for that year; then it is assumed you hold the asset for four complete years (the second through the fifth); and finally it is assumed you sell the asset in the middle of the sixth year.

Year 1 . . . 1/2 year
Year 2 . . . 1 year
Year 3 . . . 1 year
Year 4 . . . 1 year
Year 5 . . . 1 year
Year 6 . . . 1/2 year
                    5-year ACRS depreciation

---

[3]Corporations may also elect to use straight-line depreciation for the other ACRS categories. This is usually not advisable.

Using 200 percent declining balance, you first determine the straight-line rate and multiply the rate by two. For a five-year asset, straight-line depreciation would be 20 percent per year. With 200 percent declining balance, you can take 40 percent per year.

How much depreciation would you take in the first year? With the half-year convention, you can take 20 percent (½ of 40 percent). In the second year, 80 percent of the asset will still be undepreciated. You deduct 40 percent of that value for the full year. This amounts to 40 percent times 80 percent or 32 percent depreciation for the year. Complicating the calculation slightly is the switchover to straight-line depreciation after 2½ years. The actual depreciation rates are:

Year	Depreciation Rates
1 (1/2 year)	.200
2	.320
3	.192
4	.115
5	.115
6 (1/2 year)	.058

These rates are all applied to the initial purchase price and they fully accomplish the same objective as going through the process of working out the 200 percent declining balance rates with a switchover to straight-line depreciation. Only a very foolish person would go through the process of computing these annual rates for each of the eight ACRS depreciation categories. The IRS and tax preparation services provide them for you in tabular form. The rates are presented in Table 12–9.[4]

Using Table 12–9, assume you purchase a $50,000 asset that falls in the five-year ACRS category. How much would your depreciation be for the next six years? (Don't forget that we get an extra year because of the half-year convention.) The depreciation schedule is shown in Table 12–10.

One of the few simplifying features of the new tax law is that investment tax credits (ITC's) are no longer available on the purchase of a new asset. An investment tax credit represents a percentage of the purchase price that may be deducted from tax obligations. Because there is no longer an adjustment for the ITC, the depreciation base seen in Table 12–10 is always the same as the purchase price of the asset.

---

[4]The rates for the last two categories are omitted since they merely represent straight-line depreciation.

Table 12–9   Depreciation percentages (expressed in decimals)

Depreciation Year	3-Year ACRS	5-Year ACRS	7-Year ACRS	10-Year ACRS	15-Year ACRS	20-Year ACRS
1	.333	.200	.143	.100	.050	.038
2	.445	.320	.245	.180	.095	.072
3	.148	.192	.175	.144	.086	.067
4	.074	.115	.125	.115	.077	.062
5		.115	.089	.092	.069	.057
6		.058	.089	.074	.062	.053
7			.089	.066	.059	.045
8			.045	.066	.059	.045
9				.065	.059	.045
10				.065	.059	.045
11				.033	.059	.045
12					.059	.045
13					.059	.045
14					.059	.045
15					.059	.045
16					.030	.045
17						.045
18						.045
19						.045
20						.045
21						.017
	1.000	1.000	1.000	1.000	1.000	1.000

Table 12–10 Depreciation schedule

(1) Year	(2) Depreciation Base	(3) Percentage Depreciation (Table 12–9)	(4) Annual Depreciation
1	$50,000	.200	$10,000
2	50,000	.320	16,000
3	50,000	.192	9,600
4	50,000	.115	5,750
5	50,000	.115	5,750
6	50,000	.058	2,900
		Total Depreciation	$50,000

Actual Investment Decision

Assume in the $50,000 depreciation analysis shown in Table 12–10 that
we are given additional facts and asked to make an investment decision
about whether this asset should be purchased or not. We shall assume
that we are purchasing a piece of machinery that will have a six-year

productive life. It will produce income of $18,500 before deductions for depreciation and taxes for the first three years. In the last three years, the income before depreciation and taxes will be $12,000. Furthermore, we will assume a corporate tax rate of 34 percent and a cost of capital of 10 percent for the analysis. The annual cash flow related to the machinery is presented in Table 12–11. For each year, we subtract depreciation from "earnings before depreciation and taxes" to arrive at earnings before taxes. We then subtract out the taxes to determine earnings after taxes. Finally, depreciation is added back in to arrive at cash flow. The cash flow starts at $15,610 in the first year and ends at $8,960 in the last year.

Table 12–11　　Cash flow related to the purchase of machinery

	Year 1	Year 2	Year 3	Year 4	Year 5	Year 6
Earnings before depreciation and taxes (EBDT)	$18,500	$18,500	$18,500	$12,000	$12,000	$12,000
Depreciation (from Table 12–10)	10,000	16,000	9,600	5,750	5,750	2,900
Earnings before taxes	8,500	2,500	8,900	6,250	6,250	9,100
Taxes (34%)	2,890	850	3,026	2,125	2,125	3,094
Earnings after taxes	5,610	1,650	5,874	4,125	4,125	6,006
+ Depreciation	10,000	16,000	9,600	5,750	5,750	2,900
Cash flow	$15,610	$17,650	$15,474	$ 9,875	$ 9,875	$ 8,906

Having determined the annual cash flows, we now are in a position to discount the values back to the present at the previously specified cost of capital, 10 percent. The analysis is presented in Table 12–12. At the bottom of the same table, the present value of the inflows is compared to the present value of the outflows (simply the cost of the asset) to arrive at a new present value of $8,289. On the basis of the analysis, it appears that the asset should be purchased.

Table 12–12
Net present value
analysis

Year	Cash Flow (inflows)	Present Value Factor (10%)	Present Value
1	$15,610	.909%	$14,189
2	17,650	.826	14,579
3	15,474	.751	11,621
4	9,875	.683	6,745
5	9,875	.621	6,132
6	8,906	.564	5,023
		Present value of inflows	$58,289

Present value of inflows	$58,289
Present value of outflows (cost)	50,000
Net present value	$ 8,289

The Replacement Decision

So far, our analysis has centered on an investment that is being considered as a net addition to the present plant and equipment. However, many investment decisions occur because of new technology, and these are considered replacement decisions. The financial manager often needs to determine whether a new machine with advanced technology can do the job better than the machine being used at present.

These replacement decisions include several additions to the basic investment situation. For example, we need to include the sale of the old machine in our analysis. This sale will produce a cash inflow that partially offsets the purchase price of the new machine. In addition, the sale of the old machine will usually have tax consequences. Some of the cash inflow from the sale will be taxable if the old machine is sold for more than book value. If it is sold for less than book value, this will be considered a loss and will provide a tax benefit.

The replacement decision can be analyzed by using a total analysis of both the old and new machine or by using an incremental analysis which emphasizes the changes in cash flows between the old and the new machine. We will emphasize the incremental approach.

Assume the Bradley Corporation purchased a computer two years ago for $120,000. The asset is being depreciated under the five-year ACRS schedule shown in Table 12–9, which implies a six-year write-off because of the half-year convention. We will assume the old computer can be sold for $37,600. A new computer will cost $180,000 and will also be written off using the five-year ACRS schedule in Table 12–9.

The new computer will provide cost savings and operating benefits over the old computer of $42,000 per year for the next six years. These cost savings and operating benefits are the equivalent of increased earnings before depreciation and taxes. The firm is in a 34 percent tax bracket and has a 10 percent cost of capital.

First of all, we need to determine the net cost of the new computer. We will take the purchase price of the new computer ($180,000) and subtract the cash inflow from the sale of the old computer.

Sale of Old Asset

The cash inflow from the sale of the old computer is based on the sale price as well as the related tax factors. In order to determine these tax factors, we first compute the book value of the old computer and compare this figure to the sale price to determine if there is a taxable gain or loss. The book value of the old computer is shown in Table 12–13.

Table 12–13
Book value of old computer

Year	Depreciation Base	Percentage Depreciation (Table 12–9)	Annual Depreciation
1	$120,000	.200	$24,000
2	120,000	.320	38,400
Total depreciation to date			$62,400

Purchase price	$120,000
Total depreciation to date	62,400
Book value	$ 57,600

Since the book value of the old computer is $57,600 and the sale price (previously given) is $37,600, there will be a $20,000 loss.

Book value	$57,600
Sales price	37,600
Tax loss on sale	$20,000

This loss can be written off against other income for the corporation.[5] The Bradley Corporation is in a 34 percent tax bracket, so the tax write-off is worth $6,800.

Tax loss on sale	$20,000
Tax rate	34%
Tax benefit	$ 6,800

We now add the tax benefit to the sale price to arrive at the cash inflow from the sale of the old computer.

Sale price of old computer	$37,600
Tax benefit from sale	6,800
Cash inflow from sale of old computer	$44,400

The computation of the cash inflow figure allows us to compute the net cost of the new computer. The purchase price of $180,000, minus the cash inflow from the sale of the old computer, provides a value of $135,600 as indicated in Table 12–14.

Table 12–14
Net cost of new computer

Price of new computer	$180,000
− Cash flow from sale of old computer	44,400
Net cost of new computer	$135,600

[5]Note that had there been a capital gain instead of a loss, it is automatically taxed at the corporation's normal tax rate. Under the Tax Reform Act of 1986, there no longer is a different long-term capital gains tax rate for *corporations* or individuals.

The question then becomes: Are the incremental gains from the new computer compared to the old computer large enough to justify the net cost of $135,600? We will assume that both will be operative over the next six years, although the old computer will run out of depreciation in four more years. We will base our cash flow analysis on (a) the incremental gain in depreciation and the related tax shield benefits and (b) cost savings.

Incremental Depreciation

The annual depreciation on the new computer will be:

Year	Depreciation Base	Percentage Depreciation (Table 12–9)	Annual Depreciation
1	$180,000	.200	$ 36,000
2	180,000	.320	57,600
3	180,000	.192	34,560
4	180,000	.115	20,700
5	180,000	.115	20,700
6	180,000	.058	10,440
			$180,000

The annual depreciation on the old computer for the remaining four years would be:

Year*	Depreciation Base	Percentage Depreciation (Table 12–9)	Annual Depreciation
1	$120,000	.192	$23,040
2	120,000	.115	13,800
3	120,000	.115	13,800
4	120,000	.058	6,960

*The next four years represent the last four years for the old computer, which is already two years old.

Table 12–15   Analysis of incremental depreciation benefits

(1) Year	(2) Depreciation on New Computer	(3) Depreciation on Old Computer	(4) Incremental Depreciation	(5) Tax Rate	(6) Tax Shield Benefits
1	$36,000	$23,040	$12,960	.34	$ 4,406
2	57,600	13,800	43,800	.34	14,892
3	34,560	13,800	20,760	.34	7,058
4	20,700	6,960	13,740	.34	4,672
5	20,700		20,700	.34	7,038
6	10,440		10,440	.34	3,550

In Table 12–15, we bring together the depreciation on the old and new computers to determine incremental depreciation and the related tax shield benefits. Since depreciation shields other income from being taxed, it is worth the amount being depreciated times the tax rate. For example, in year one, $12,960 in incremental depreciation will stop $12,960 from being taxed, and with the firm in a 34 percent tax bracket, this represents a tax savings of $4,406. The same type of analysis applies to each subsequent year.

Cost Savings

The second type of benefit relates to cost savings from the new computer. As previously stated, these savings are assumed to be $42,000 for the next six years. The aftertax benefits are shown in Table 12–16.

As indicated in Table 12–16, we take the cost savings in column 2 and multiply by one minus the tax rate. This indicates the value of the savings on an aftertax basis.

Table 12–16 Analysis of incremental cost savings benefits	(1) Year	(2) Cost Savings	(3) 1 − Tax Rate	(4) Aftertax Savings
	1	$42,000	.66	$27,720
	2	42,000	.66	27,720
	3	42,000	.66	27,720
	4	42,000	.66	27,720
	5	42,000	.66	27,720
	6	42,000	.66	27,720

We now combine the incremental tax shield benefits from depreciation (Table 12–15) and the aftertax cost savings (Table 12–16) to arrive at total annual benefits in table 12–17 on page 378 (column 4). These benefits are discounted to the present at a 10 percent cost of capital. The present value of the inflows is $151,864 as indicated at the bottom of column 6 in Table 12–17.

We now are in a position to compare the present value of incremental benefits of $151,864 from Table 12–17 to the net cost of the new computer of $135,600 from Table 12–14.

Present value of incremental benefits	$151,864
Net cost of new computer	135,600
Net present value	$ 16,264

Table 12–17   Present value of the total incremental benefits

(1) Year	(2) Tax Shield Benefits from Depreciation (from Table 12–15)	(3) Aftertax Cost Savings (from Table 12–16)	(4) Total Annual Benefits	(5) Present Value Factor (10%)	(6) Present Value
1	$ 4,406	$27,720	$32,126	.909	$ 29,203
2	14,892	27,720	42,612	.826	35,198
3	7,058	27,720	34,778	.751	26,118
4	4,672	27,720	32,392	.683	22,124
5	7,038	27,720	34,758	.621	21,585
6	3,550	27,720	31,270	.564	17,636
		Present value of incremental benefits			$151,864

Clearly, there is a positive net present value, and the purchase of the computer should be recommended on the basis of the financial analysis. Of course, there may be other subjective factors to consider as well.

Summary

The capital budgeting decision involves the planning of expenditures for a project with a life of at least one year and usually a considerably longer time. Although top management is often anxious about the impact of decisions on short-term reported income, the planning of capital expenditures dictates a longer time horizon. Three primary methods are used to analyze capital investment proposals: the payback method, the internal rate of return, and the net present value. The first method is unsound, while the last two are acceptable, with net present value deserving our greatest attention.

Investment alternatives may be classified as either mutually exclusive or nonmutually exclusive. If they are mutually exclusive, the selection of one alternative will preclude the selection of all other alternatives, and projects with a positive net present value may be eliminated in favor of projects with an even higher net present value. The same is also true under capital rationing, a less than desirable method in which management arbitrarily determines the maximum amount that can be invested in any time period. The student must carefully define each situation and apply the appropriate capital budgeting technique. Tax considerations are also a major factor in capital budgeting decisions. In this chapter, the impact of the 1986 tax legislation on depreciation and related factors is considered in the analysis. In Chapter 13 we will examine how risk fits into the capital budgeting decision-making process.

List of Terms

planning horizon	capital rationing
payback	cash flow
internal rate of return	accelerated cost recovery system (ACRS)
net present value	net present value profile
mutually exclusive	asset depreciation range (ADR)
reinvestment assumption	depreciation base

Discussion Questions

1. What are the important administrative considerations in the capital budgeting process?

2. Why does capital budgeting rely for analysis on cash flows rather than on net income?

3. What are the weaknesses of the payback method?

4. What is normally used as the discount rate in the net present value method?

5. What does the term *mutually exclusive investments* mean?

6. If a corporation has projects that will earn more than the cost of capital, should it ration capital? Shouldn't it be able to find external funds and thus increase its wealth?

7. What is the net present value profile? What three points (characteristics) should be determined to compute the profile?

8. How does an asset's ADR (asset depreciation range) relate to its ACRS category?

9. What type of asset must be written off over the longest period under the depreciation provisions of the Tax Reform Act of 1986?

Problems

1. Assume that a corporation has earnings before depreciation and taxes of $90,000 and depreciation of $40,000, and that it is in the 34 percent tax bracket. Compute its cash flow.

2. Assume a $40,000 investment and the following cash flows for two alternatives:

Year	Investment X	Investment Y
1	$ 6,000	$15,000
2	8,000	20,000
3	10,000	10,000
4	20,000	—
5	30,000	—

Which of the alternatives would you select under the payback method?

3. Referring back to problem 2, if the inflow in the fifth year for Investment X were $30,000,000 instead of $30,000, would your answer change under the payback method?

4. A firm buys a new piece of equipment for $11,778 and will receive a cash flow of $2,000 per year for 10 years. What is the internal rate of return?

5. Ned Worth invests $31,782 in a business and will receive a cash inflow of $3,000 per year for 20 years. What is the internal rate of return?

6. Aerospace Dynamics will invest $110,000 in a project that will produce the following cash flows. The cost of capital is 11 percent. Should the project be undertaken? (Note: the fourth year's cash flow is negative.)

Year	Cash Flow
1	$36,000
2	44,000
3	38,000
4	(44,000)
5	81,000

7. The Horizon Corporation will invest $60,000 in a temporary project that will generate the following cash inflows for the next three years.

Year	Cash Flow
1	$15,000
2	25,000
3	40,000

The firm will also be required to spend $10,000 to close down the project at the end of the three years. If the cost of capital is 10 percent, should the investment be undertaken?

8. The Ogden Corporation makes an investment of $25,000, which yields the following cash flows:

Year	Cash Flow
1	$ 5,000
2	5,000
3	8,000
4	9,000
5	10,000

a. What is the present value with a 9 percent discount rate (cost of capital)?

b. What is the internal rate of return? Use the interpolation procedure shown in this chapter.

c. In this problem would you make the same decision in parts *a* and *b?*

9. The Green Goddess Salad Oil Company is considering the purchase of a new machine that would increase the speed of bottling and save money. The net cost of this machine is $45,000. The annual cash flows have the following projections.

Year	Cash Flow
1	$15,000
2	20,000
3	25,000
4	10,000
5	5,000

a. If the cost of capital is 10 percent, what is the net present value of selecting the new machine?

b. What is the internal rate of return?

c. Should the project be accepted? Why?

10. You are asked to evaluate the following two projects for Adventures Club, Inc. Using the net present value method, combined with the profitability index approach described in footnote 2 of this chapter, which project would you select? Use a discount rate of 12 percent.

Project X (trips to Disneyland)		Project Y (International Film Festivals)	
($10,000 investment)		($22,000 investment)	
Year	Cash Flow	Year	Cash Flow
1	$4,000	1	$10,800
2	5,000	2	9,600
3	4,200	3	6,000
4	3,600	4	7,000

11. The Waste Disposal Corporation will invest $50,000 in a project. The firm's discount rate (cost of capital) is 9 percent. The investment will provide the following inflows:

1	$10,000
2	10,000
3	16,000
4	18,000
5	20,000

The internal rate of return is 12.8 percent.

a. If the reinvestment assumption of the net present value method is used, what will be the total value of the inflows after five years? (Assume the inflows come at the end of each year.)

b. If the reinvestment assumption of the internal rate of return method is used, what will be the total value of the inflows after five years?

c. Generally, is one investment assumption likely to be better than another?

12. Noncreative Toys uses a process of capital rationing in its decision making. The firm's cost of capital is 12 percent. It will only invest $80,000 this year. It has determined the internal rate of return for each of the following projects:

Project	Project Size	Percent of Internal Rate of Return
A	$15,000	14%
B	25,000	19
C	30,000	10
D	25,000	16.5
E	20,000	21
F	15,000	11
G	25,000	18
H	10,000	17.5

a. Pick out the projects that the firm should accept.

b. If projects B and G are mutually exclusive, how would that affect your overall answer? That is, which projects would you accept in spending the $80,000?

13. Miller Electronics is considering two new investments. Project C calls for the purchase of a coolant recovery system. Project H represents the investment in a heat recovery system. The firm wishes to use a net present value profile in comparing the projects. The investment and cash flow patterns are as follows:

Project C ($25,000 investment)		Project H ($25,000 investment)	
Year	Cash Flow	Year	Cash Flow
1	$ 6,000	1	$20,000
2	7,000	2	6,000
3	9,000	3	5,000
4	13,000		

a. Determine the net present value of the projects based on a zero-discount rate.
b. Determine the net present value of the projects based on a 9 percent discount rate.
c. The internal rate of return on Project C is 13.01 percent, and the internal rate of return on Project H is 15.68 percent. Graph a net present value profile for the two investments similar to Figure 12–3. (Use a scale up to $10,000 on the vertical axis, with $2,000 increments. Use a scale up to 20 percent on the horizontal axis, with 5 percent increments.)
d. If the two projects are not mutually exclusive, what would your acceptance or rejection decision be if the cost of capital (discount rate) is 8 percent? (Use the net present value profile for your decision; no actual numbers are necessary.)
e. If the two projects are mutually exclusive (the selection of one precludes the selection of the other), what would be your decision if the cost of capital is (1) 5 percent, (2) 13 percent, (3) 19 percent? Once again, use the net present value profile for your answer.

14. Software Systems is considering an investment of $20,000, which produces the following inflows:

Year	Cash Flow
1	$11,000
2	9,000
3	5,800

You are going to use the net present value profile to approximate the value for the internal rate of return. Please follow these steps:
a. Determine the net present value of the project based on a zero-discount rate.
b. Determine the net present value of the project based on a 10 percent discount rate.
c. Determine the net present value of the project based on a 20 percent discount rate (it will be negative).

d. Draw a net present value profile for the investment (use a scale up to $6,000 on the vertical axis, with $2,000 increments. Use a scale up to 20 percent on the horizontal axis, with 5 percent increments.) Observe the discount rate at which the net present value is zero. This is an approximation of the internal rate of return on the project.

e. Actually compute the internal rate of return based on the interpolation procedure presented in this chapter. Compare your answers in parts *d* and *e*.

15. The Cry-Slur Corporation is going to purchase an asset for $200,000 that will produce $95,000 per year for the next four years in earnings before depreciation and taxes. The asset will be depreciated using the three-year ACRS depreciation schedule in Table 12–9. (This represents four years of depreciation based on the half-year convention.) The firm is in a 34 percent tax bracket. Fill in the schedule below for the next four years.

Earnings before depreciation and taxes	_____
Depreciation	_____
Earnings before taxes	_____
Taxes	_____
Earnings after taxes	_____
+ Depreciation	_____
Cash flow	_____

16. Assume a $50,000 investment is going to be made in each of the following assets. Using Table 12–8 and Table 12–9, indicate the dollar amount of the first year's depreciation.
    a. Electric and gas utility property.
    b. Petroleum refining products.
    c. Automobiles.
    d. Office furniture.

17. (Basic investment decision.)
    The Keystone Corporation will purchase an asset that qualifies for three-year ACRS depreciation. The cost is $60,000 and the asset will provide the following stream of earnings before depreciation and taxes for the next four years:

Year 1	$27,000
Year 2	30,000
Year 3	23,000
Year 4	15,000

The firm is in a 34 percent tax bracket and has an 11 percent cost of capital. Should they purchase the asset?

18. (Basic investment decision.)

    Bemis Labs will acquire new equipment that falls under the five-year ACRS category. The cost is $200,000. If the equipment is purchased, the following earnings before depreciation and taxes will be generated for the next six years:

Year 1	$80,000
Year 2	70,000
Year 3	50,000
Year 4	31,000
Year 5	27,000
Year 6	20,000

    The firm is in a 25 percent tax bracket and has a 15 percent cost of capital. Should Bemis Labs buy the equipment?

19. (Basic investment decision.)

    The Thorpe Corporation is considering the purchase of manufacturing equipment with a 10-year midpoint in its asset depreciation range (ADR). Carefully refer to Table 12–8 to determine in what depreciation category the asset falls. (Hint: it is not 10 years.) The asset will cost $80,000 and it will produce earnings before depreciation and taxes of $28,000 per year for three years, and then $12,000 a year for seven more years. The firm has a tax rate of 34 percent. With a cost of capital of 12 percent, should it purchase the asset? In doing your analysis, if you have years in which there is no depreciation, merely enter a zero for depreciation.

20. (Basic investment decision.)

    The Mattingly Ball Bearing Company has a proposed contract with the First Military Base Facility of Georgia. The initial investment in land and equipment will be $90,000. Of this amount, $60,000 is subject to five-year ACRS depreciation. The balance is in nondepreciable property. The contract covers a six-year period. At the end of six years the nondepreciable assets will be sold for $30,000. The depreciated assets will have zero resale value.

    The contract will require an investment of $40,000 in working capital at the beginning of the first year and, of this amount, $20,000 will be returned to the Mattingly Ball Bearing Company after six years.

    The investment will produce $32,000 in income before depreciation and taxes for each of the six years. The corporation is in a 34 percent tax bracket and has a 10 percent cost of capital.

    Should the investment be undertaken?

21. (Taxable losses and gains on the sale of an asset.)

An asset was purchased three years ago for $140,000. It falls into the five-year category for ACRS depreciation. The firm is in a 34 percent tax bracket. Compute the:

a.   Tax loss on the sale and the related tax benefit if the asset is sold for $15,320.

b.   Gain and related tax on the sale if the asset is sold for $58,820. (Refer to footnote 5.)

22. (Replacement decision.)

Graphic Systems purchased a computerized graphing device two years ago for $80,000. It falls into the five-year category for ACRS depreciation. The equipment can be currently sold for $28,400.

A new piece of equipment will cost $210,000. It falls into the five-year category for ACRS depreciation.

Assume the new equipment would provide the following stream of added cost savings for the next six years:

Year	Cost Savings
1	$76,000
2	66,000
3	62,000
4	60,000
5	56,000
6	42,000

The tax rate is 34 percent and the cost of capital is 12 percent.

a.   What is the book value of the old equipment?

b.   What is the tax loss on the sale of the old equipment?

c.   What is the tax benefit from the sale?

d.   What is the cash inflow from the sale of the old equipment?

e.   What is the net cost of the new equipment? (Include the inflow from the sale of the old equipment.)

f.   Determine the depreciation schedule for the new equipment.

g.   Determine the depreciation schedule for the remaining years of the old equipment.

h.   Determine the incremental depreciation between the old and new equipment and the related tax shield benefits.

i.   Compute the aftertax benefits of the cost savings.

j.   Add the depreciation tax shield benefits and the aftertax cost savings, and determine the present value. (See Table 12–17 as an example.)

k.   Compare the present value of the incremental benefits (*j*) to the net cost of the new equipment (*e*). Should the replacement be undertaken?

23. (Replacement decision.)

The Woodruff Corporation purchased a piece of equipment three years ago for $230,000. It has an asset depreciation range (ADR) midpoint of eight years. The equipment currently can be sold for $90,000.

A new piece of equipment will cost $320,000. It also has an ADR of eight years.

Assume the old and new equipment would provide the following operating gains (or losses) over the next six years:

	New Equipment	Old Equipment
1	$80,000	$25,000
2	76,000	16,000
3	70,000	9,000
4	60,000	8,000
5	50,000	6,000
6	45,000	(7,000)

The firm has a 36 percent tax rate and a 9 percent cost of capital. Should the new equipment be purchased to replace the old equipment?

Selected References

Bacon, Peter W. "The Evaluation of Mutually Exclusive Investments." *Financial Management* 6 (Summer 1977), pp. 55–58.

Bernard, Richard H. "Mathematical Programming Models for Capital Budgeting—A Survey, Generalization, and Critique." *Journal of Financial and Quantitative Analysis* 4 (June 1969), pp. 111–58.

Brick, Ivan, and Daniel G. Weaver. "A Comparison of Capital Budgeting Techniques in Identifying Profitable Investments." *Financial Management* 13 (Winter 1984), pp. 29–39.

Brigham, Eugene F., and T. Craig Tapley. "Financial Leverage and the Use of the Net Present Value Investment Criterion: A Reexamination." *Financial Management* 14 (Summer 1985), pp. 48–52.

Dorfman, Robert. "The Meaning of Internal Rates of Return." *Journal of Finance* 36 (December 1981), pp. 1,010–21.

Durand, David. "Comprehensiveness in Capital Budgeting." *Financial Management* 10 (Winter 1981), pp. 7–13.

Golbe, Devra L., and Barry Schacter. "The Net Present Value Rule and an Algorithm for Maintaining a Constant Debt–Equity Ratio." *Financial Management* 14 (Summer 1985), pp. 53–58.

Howe, Keith M. "Does Inflationary Change Affect Capital Asset Life?" *Financial Management* 16 (Summer 1987), pp. 63–67.

Klommer, Thomas. "Empirical Evidence on the Adoption of Sophisticated Capital Budgeting Techniques." *Journal of Business* 45 (July 1972), pp. 387–97.

Lipscomb, Joseph. "Real Estate Capital Budgeting." *The Real Estate Appraiser and Analyst* 48 (Summer 1982), pp. 23–31.

Petty, J. William; David F. Scott, Jr.; and Monroe M. Bird. "The Capital Expenditure Decision-Making Process of Large Corporations." *Engineering Economist* 20 (Spring 1975), pp. 159–72.

Pruitt, Stephen W., and Lawrence J. Gitman. "Capital Budgeting Forecasts Biases: Evidence From the Fortune 500." *Financial Management* 16 (Winter 1986), pp. 15–22.

Rappaport, Alfred, and Robert A. Taggart, Jr. "The Evaluation of Capital Expenditure Proposals under Inflation." *Financial Management* 11 (Spring 1982), pp. 5–13.

Ross, Marc. "Capital Budgeting Practices of Twelve Large Manufactures." *Financial Management* 15 (1986), pp. 15–22.

Van Horne, James C. "A Note of Biases in Capital Budgeting Introduced by Inflation." *Journal of Financial and Quantitative Analysis* 6 (January 1971), pp. 653–58.

Weaver, James B. "Organizing and Maintaining a Capital Expenditure Program." *Engineering Economist* 20 (Fall 1974), pp. 1–36.

13

Risk and Capital Budgeting

No one area is more essential to financial decision making than the evaluation and management of risk. The price of a firm's stock is, to a large degree, influenced by the amount of risk that investors perceive to be inherent in the firm. A company is constantly trying to achieve the appropriate mix between profitability and risk to satisfy those with a stake in its affairs and to achieve the goal of wealth maximization for shareholders.

The difficulty is not in finding viable investment alternatives but in determining an appropriate position on the risk–return scale. Would a firm prefer a 25 percent potential return on a new product in oil-sensitive Western Europe or a safe 8 percent return on an extension of its current product line in its home territory? The question can only be answered in terms of profitability, the risk position of the firm, and management and stockholder disposition toward risk. In this chapter, we examine additional definitions of risk, its measurement and its incorporation into the *capital budgeting* process, and the basic tenets of portfolio theory.

Definition of Risk in Capital Budgeting

Risk may be defined in terms of the variability of possible outcomes from a given investment. If funds are invested in a 30-day U.S. government obligation, the outcome is certain and there is no variability—hence no risk. On the other hand, if we invest the same funds in a gold-mining expedition to the deepest wilds of Africa, the variability of possible outcomes is great and we say the project is replete with risk.

The student should observe that risk is measured not only in terms of losses but also in terms of uncertainty.[1] We say that gold mining carries a high degree of risk not just because you may lose your money but because there is a wide range of possible outcomes. Observe in Figure 13–1 examples of three investments with different risk characteristics. Note that in each case the distributions are centered on the same expected value ($20,000) but that the variability (risk) increases as we move from Investment A to Investment C. Because you may *gain* or *lose* the most in Investment C, it is clearly the riskiest of the three.

The Concept of Risk Averse

A basic assumption in financial theory is that most investors and managers are risk averse—that is, for a given situation they would prefer relative certainty to uncertainty. In Figure 13–1, they would prefer Investment A over Investments B and C, although all three investments have the same expected value of $20,000. You are probably risk averse, too. Assume you have saved $1,000 toward your last year in college and are challenged to flip a coin, double or nothing. Heads, you end up with $2,000—tails, you are broke. Given that you are not enrolled at the University of Nevada at Las Vegas or that you are not an inveterate gambler, you will probably stay with your certain $1,000.

This is not to say that investors or businessmen are unwilling to take risks—but rather that they will require a higher expected value or return for risky investments. In Figure 13–2, we compare a low-risk proposal with an expected value of $20,000 to a high-risk proposal with an expected value of $30,000. The higher expected return may well compensate for absorbing greater risk.

Throughout the chapter, we will develop methods for incorporating a higher demanded return for risky investments. For Evel Knievel, back in the 1970s, it was $7 million to jump over the Snake River Canyon— for a corporation, it may be a bonus return of 5 percent over the cost of capital.

---

[1]We use the term *uncertainty* in its normal sense, rather than in the more formalized sense in which it is sometimes used in decision theory to indicate that insufficient evidence is available to estimate a probability distribution.

Figure 13–1
Variability and risk

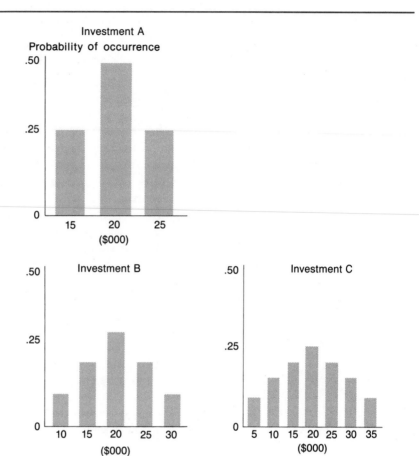

Investment A
Probability of occurrence

Investment B

Investment C

Figure 13–2
Risk–return trade-off

Actual Measurement of Risk

A number of basic statistical devices may be employed to measure the extent of risk inherent in any given situation. Assume that we are examining an investment with the possible outcomes and probability of outcomes shown in Table 13–1.

The probabilities in Table 13–1 may be based on past experience, industry ratios and trends, interviews with company executives, and sophisticated simulation techniques. The probability values may be quite easy to determine for the introduction of a mechanical stamping process in which the manufacturer has 10 years of past data, but difficult to assess for a new product in a foreign market. In any event, we force ourselves into a valuable analytical process.

With the data before us, we compute two important statistical measures—the expected value and the standard deviation. The expected value is a weighted average of the outcomes (D) times their probabilities (P).

$$\bar{D}(\text{expected value}) = \Sigma DP \qquad (13\text{–}1)$$

$$
\begin{array}{rcl}
D & P & DP \\
300 \times .2 & = & \$\ 60 \\
600 \times .6 & = & 360 \\
900 \times .2 & = & \underline{180} \\
& \$600 & = \Sigma DP
\end{array}
$$

The expected value is \$600. We then compute the standard deviation— the measure of dispersion or variability around the expected value:

$$\sigma\ (\text{standard deviation}) = \sqrt{\Sigma (D - \bar{D})^2 P} \qquad (13\text{–}2)$$

The following steps should be followed:

Step 1:	Step 2:	Step 3:	Step 4:
Subtract the Expected Value $(\bar{D})$ from Each Outcome (D)	Square $(D - \bar{D})$	Multiply by P and Sum	Determine the Square Root

D	$\bar{D}$	$(D - \bar{D})$	$(D - \bar{D})^2$	P	$(D - \bar{D})^2 P$	
$300 - 600 =$		$- 300$	90,000	$\times$ .20 $=$	18,000	
$600 - 600 =$		0	0	$\times$ .60 $=$	0	
$900 - 600 =$		$+ 300$	90,000	$\times$ .20 $=$	$\underline{18,000}$	
					36,000	$\sqrt{36,000} = \$190$

The standard deviation of \$190 gives us a rough average measure of how far each of the three outcomes falls away from the expected value. Generally, the larger the standard deviation (or spread of outcomes), the greater is the risk, as indicated in Figure 13–3.

Table 13–1
Probability distribution of outcomes

	Outcome	Probability of Outcome	Assumptions
	$300	.2	Pessimistic
	600	.6	Moderately successful
	900	.2	Optimistic

Figure 13–3
Probability distribution with differing degrees of risk

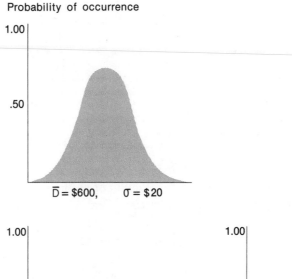

$\overline{D} = \$600, \qquad \sigma = \$20$

$\overline{D} = \$600, \qquad \sigma = \$190$

$\overline{D} = \$600, \qquad \sigma = \$300$

The student will note that in Figure 13–3 we compare the standard deviation of three investments with the same expected value of $600. If the expected values of the investments were quite different (such as $600 versus $6,000), a direct comparison of the standard deviations for each distribution would not be very helpful in measuring risk. In Figure 13–4 we show such an occurrence.

Note that the investment in Panel A of Figure 13–4 appears to have a high standard deviation—but not when related to the expected value of

Figure 13–4

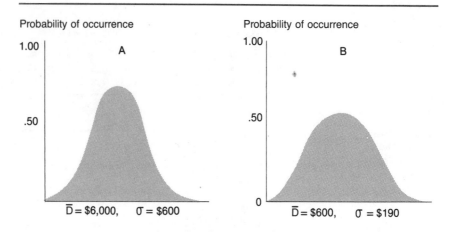

Probability of occurrence

1.00   A

.50

$\bar{D} = \$6,000, \quad \sigma = \$600$

Probability of occurrence

1.00   B

.50

0

$\bar{D} = \$600, \quad \sigma = \$190$

the distribution. A standard deviation of $600 on an investment with an expected value of $6,000 may indicate less risk than a standard deviation of $190 on an investment with an expected value of only $600.

We can eliminate the size difficulty by developing a third measure, the coefficient of variation (V). This term calls for nothing more difficult than dividing the standard deviation of an investment by the expected value. Generally, the larger the coefficient of variation, the greater is the risk.

$$\text{Coefficient of variation } (V) = \frac{\sigma}{\bar{D}} \qquad (13\text{–}3)$$

For the investments in Panels A and B of Figure 13–4, we show:

$$
\begin{array}{cc}
A & B \\
\dfrac{600}{6,000} = .10 & \dfrac{190}{600} = .317
\end{array}
$$

We have correctly identified the second investment as carrying the greater risk.

Another risk measure, the beta (β), is widely used with portfolios of common stock. Beta measures the volatility of returns on an individual stock relative to the stock market index of returns, such as the Standard & Poor's 500-stock index.[2] A common stock with a beta of 1.0 is said to be of equal risk with the market. Stocks with betas greater than 1.0 are riskier than the market, while stocks with betas of less than 1.0 are less risky than the market. Table 13–2 presents a sample of betas for several well-known companies from 1982–87.

---

[2]Other market measures may also be utilized.

Table 13–2
Betas for a five-year
period (1982–1987)

Company Name	Beta
Baltimore Gas and Electric	0.75
Gordon Jewelry	0.80
Southern California Edison	0.85
Syntex	0.95
Standard & Poor's 500 Stock Index	1.00
Gulf & Western	1.05
General Dynamics	1.10
Citicorp	1.25
Lowe's Companies	1.50
Paine Webber	1.75

Risk and the Capital Budgeting Process

How can risk analysis be used effectively in the capital budgeting process? In Chapter 12, The Capital Budgeting Decision, we made no explicit distinction between risky and nonrisky events.[3] We showed the amount of the investment and the annual returns—making no comment about the riskiness or likelihood of achieving these returns. We know that enlightened investors and managers need further information. A $1,400 investment that produces "certain" returns of $600 a year for three years is not the same as a $1,400 investment that produces returns with an expected value of $600 for three years—but a high coefficient of variation. Investors, being risk averse by nature, will apply a stiffer test to the second investment. How can this new criterion be applied to the capital budgeting process?

Risk-Adjusted Discount Rate

A favored approach to adjusting for risk is to use different discount rates for proposals with different risk levels. A project that carries a normal amount of risk and does not change the overall risk composure of the firm should be discounted at the cost of capital. Investments carrying greater than normal risk will be discounted at a higher rate; and so on. In Figure 13–5, we show a possible risk-discount rate trade-off scheme. Risk is assumed to be measured by the coefficient of variation (V).

The normal risk for the firm is represented by a coefficient of variation of 0.30. An investment with this risk would be discounted at the firm's

---

[3]Our assumption was that the risk factor could be considered as constant for various investments.

**Figure 13–5
Relationship of risk
to discount rate**

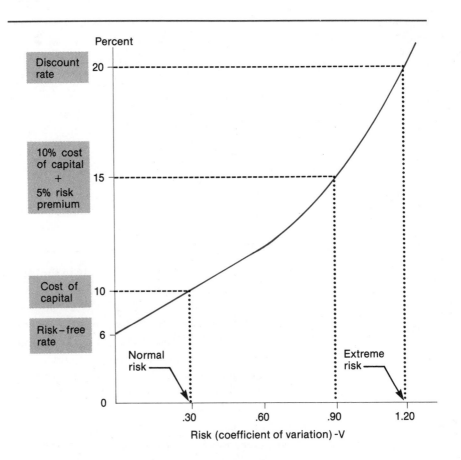

normal cost of capital of 10 percent. As the firm selects riskier projects
with, for example, a *V* of 0.90, a risk premium of 5 percent is added for
an increase in *V* of 0.60. If the company selects a project with a coefficient
of variation of 1.20, it will now add another 5 percent risk premium for
this additional *V* of 0.30. Notice that the same risk premium of 5 percent
was added for a smaller increase in risk. This is an example of being
increasingly risk averse at higher levels of risk and potential return.

Increasing Risk over Time

It seems that our ability to forecast accurately diminishes as we forecast
farther out in time. As the time horizon becomes longer, more uncertainty
enters the forecast. The decline in oil prices sharply curtailed the search
for petroleum and left many drillers in serious financial condition in the

Figure 13–6
Risk over time

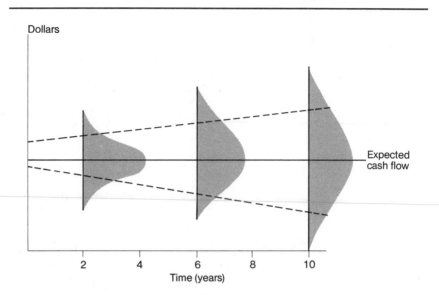

1980s after years of expanding drilling activity. The downfall of real estate investments in many sectors of the country in the late 1980s is another example. Only a few years before, investors in the Sun Belt states were fighting over opportunities to get into hot deals. Many of these deals went sour when office and shopping center vacancy rates climbed to 20–25 percent in Dallas, Houston, Atlanta, and elsewhere. These unexpected events create a higher standard deviation in cash flows and increase the risk associated with long-lived projects. Figure 13–6 depicts the relationship between risk and time.

Even though a forecast of cash flows shows a constant expected value, Figure 13–6 shows that the range of outcomes and probabilities increase as we move from year 2 to 10. The standard deviations increase for each forecast of cash flow. If cash flows were forecast as easily for each period, all distributions would look like the first one for year 2. Using progressively higher discount rates to compensate for risk tends to penalize late flows more than early flows, and this is consistent with the notion that risk is greater for longer-term cash flows than for near-term cash flows.

Qualitative Measures

Rather than relate the discount rate—or required return—to the coefficient of variation or possibly the beta, management may wish to set up

Table 13–3
Risk categories and
associated discount
rates

	Discount rate
Low or no risk (repair to old machinery)	6%
Moderate risk (new equipment)	8
Normal risk (addition to normal product line)	10
Risky (new product in related market)	12
High risk (completely new market)	16
Highest risk (new product in foreign market)	20

risk classes based on qualitative considerations. Examples are presented in Table 13–3. Once again, we are equating the discount rate to the perceived risk.

Example—risk-adjusted discount rate In Chapter 12 we compared two $10,000 investment alternatives and indicated that each had a positive net present value (at a 10 percent cost of capital). The analysis is reproduced in Table 13–4.

Though both proposals are acceptable, if they were mutually exclusive, only Investment B would be undertaken. But what if we add a risk dimension to the problem? Assume that Investment A calls for an addition to the normal product line and is assigned a discount rate of 10 percent. Further assume that Investment B represents a new product in a foreign market and must carry a 20 percent discount to adjust for the large risk component. As indicated in Table 13–5 our answers are reversed and Investment A is now the only acceptable alternative.

Other methods besides the risk-adjusted discount rate approach are also used to evaluate risk in the capital budgeting process. The spectrum runs from a seat-of-the-pants "executive preference" approach to so-

Table 13–4
Capital budgeting
analysis

Investment A	Investment B
Year (10% discount rate)	Year (10% discount rate)
1 . . . . $5,000 × 0.909 = $ 4,545	1 . . . . $1,500 × 0.909 = $ 1,364
2 . . . . 5,000 × 0.826 = 4,130	2 . . . . 2,000 × 0.826 = 1,652
3 . . . . 2,000 × 0.751 = 1,502	3 . . . . 2,500 × 0.751 = 1,878
$10,177	4 . . . . 5,000 × 0.683 = 3,415
	5 . . . . 5,000 × 0.621 = 3,105
	$11,414
Present value of inflows $10,177	Present value of inflows $11,414
Investment 10,000	Investment 10,000
Net present value . . . . . . $ 177	Net present value . . . . $ 1,414

Table 13–5
Capital budgeting
decision adjusted for
risk

	Investment A (10% discount rate)		Investment B (20% discount rate)
Year		Year	
1	$5,000 × 0.909 = $ 4,545	1	$1,500 × 0.833 = $ 1,250
2	5,000 × 0.826 = 4,130	2	2,000 × 0.694 = 1,388
3	2,000 × 0.751 = 1,502	3	2,500 × 0.579 = 1,448
	$10,177	4	5,000 × 0.482 = 2,410
		5	5,000 × 0.402 = 2,010
			$ 8,506

Present value of inflows $10,177		Present value of inflows . . . . $ 8,506	
Investment 10,000		Investment 10,000	
Net present value . . . . $ 177		Net present value . . . . $ (1,494)	

phisticated computer-based statistical analysis. All methods, however, include a common approach—that is, they must give recognition to the riskiness of a given investment proposal and an appropriate adjustment for risk.[4]

Simulation Models

Computers make it possible to simulate various economic and financial outcomes, using a large number of variables. Thus simulation is one way of dealing with the uncertainty involved in forecasting the outcomes of capital budgeting projects or other types of decisions. A Monte Carlo simulation model uses random variables for inputs. By programming the computer to randomly select inputs from probability distributions, the outcomes generated by a simulation are distributed about a mean, and instead of generating one return or net present value, a range of outcomes with standard deviations is provided. A simulation model relies on repetition of the same random process as many as several hundred times. Since the inputs are representative of what one might encounter in the real world, many possible combinations of returns are generated.

One of the benefits of simulation is its ability to test various possible combinations of events. This sensitivity testing allows the planner to ask

---

[4]As an example, each value might be penalized for lack of certainty (adjusted for risk) and then a risk-free discount rate might be applied to the resultant values. This is termed the *certainty equivalent approach*. In practice, the expected value for a given year is multiplied by a percentage figure indicating the degree of certainty and then translated back to the present at a risk-free discount rate (less than the cost of capital). Items with a high degree of certainty are multiplied by 100 percent, less certain items by 75 percent, and so on down the scale.

"what if" questions, such as: What will happen to the returns on this project if oil prices go up? go down? What effect will a 5 percent increase in interest rates have on the net present value of this project? The analyst can use the simulation process to test out possible changes in economic policy, sales levels, inflation, or any other variable that is included in the modeling process. Some simulation models are driven by sales forecasts with assumptions to derive income statements and balance sheets. Others generate probability acceptance curves for capital budgeting decisions by informing the analyst about the probabilities of having a positive net present value.

For example, each distribution in Figure 13–7 will have a value picked randomly and used for one simulation. The simulation will be run many

Figure 13–7
Simulation flow chart

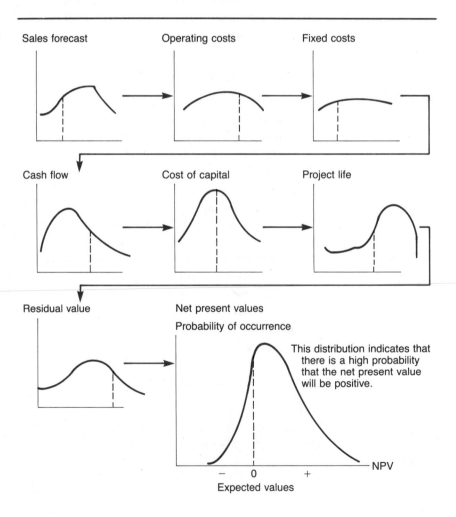

times, each time selecting a new random variable to generate the final probability distribution for the net present value (at the bottom). For that probability distribution, the expected values are on the horizontal axis and the probability of occurrence is on the vertical axis. The outcomes also indicate something about the riskiness of the project, which is indicated by the overall dispersion.

Decision Trees

Decision trees help lay out the sequence of decisions that can be made and present a tabular or graphical comparison resembling the branches of a tree, which highlight the differences between investment choices. In Figure 13–8 we examine a semiconductor firm considering two choices: (A) expanding the production of semiconductors for sale to end users of these tiny chips or (B) entering the highly competitive home computer market by using the firm's technology. The cost of both projects is the same $60 million, but the net present value (NPV) and risk are different.

If the firm expands its semiconductor capacity (Project A), it is assured of some demand so that a high likelihood of a positive rate of return exists. The market demand for these products is volatile over time, but long-run growth seems to be a reasonable expectation as the United States increases the emphasis on technology. If the firm expands into the home

Figure 13–8
Decision trees

	(1) Expected Sales	(2) Probability	(3) Present Value of Cash Flow from Sales ($ millions)	(4) Initial Cost ($ millions)	(5) NPV (3) − (4) ($ millions)	(6) Expected NPV (2) × (5) ($ millions)
Expand semiconductor capacity	High	.50	$100	$60	$40	$20.00
	Moderate	.25	75	60	15	3.75
	Low	.25	40	60	(20)	(5.00)
A					Expected NPV	= $18.75
Start						
B Enter home computer market	High	.20	$200	$60	$140	$28.00
	Moderate	.50	75	60	15	7.50
	Low	.30	25	60	(35)	(10.50)
					Expected NPV	= $25.00

computer market (Project B), it faces stiff competition from many existing firms. It stands to lose more money if expected sales are low than it would under option A; but it will make more if sales are high. Even though project B has a higher expected NPV than project A, its extra risk does not make for an easy choice. Clearly, more analysis would have to be done before management made the final decision between these two projects. Nevertheless, the decision tree provides for an important analytical process.

The Portfolio Effect

Up to this point, we have been primarily concerned with the risk inherent in an *individual* investment proposal. While this approach is quite useful, we also need to consider the impact of a given investment on the overall risk of the firm—the "portfolio effect."[5] For example, we might undertake an investment in the building products industry that appears to carry a high degree of risk—but if our primary business is the manufacture of electronic components for industrial use, we may actually diminish the overall risk exposure of the firm. Why? Because electronic component sales expand when the economy does well and falter in a recession. The building products industry reacts in the opposite fashion—performing poorly in boom periods and generally reacting well in recessionary periods. By investing in the building products industry, an electronic components manufacturer could actually smooth out the cyclical fluctuations inherent in its business and reduce overall risk exposure, as indicated in Figure 13–9.

The risk reduction phenomenon is demonstrated by a less dispersed probability distribution. We say the standard deviation for the entire company (the portfolio of investments) has been reduced.

Portfolio Risk

Whether or not a given investment will change the overall risk of the firm depends on its relationships to other investments. If one airline purchases another, there is very little risk reduction. Highly correlated investments—that is, projects which move in the same direction in good times as well as bad—do little or nothing to diversify away risk. Projects moving

---

[5]Here the portfolio of investments refers to plant, equipment, new products, and so forth, rather than stocks and bonds.

**Figure 13–9
Portfolio
considerations in
evaluating risk**

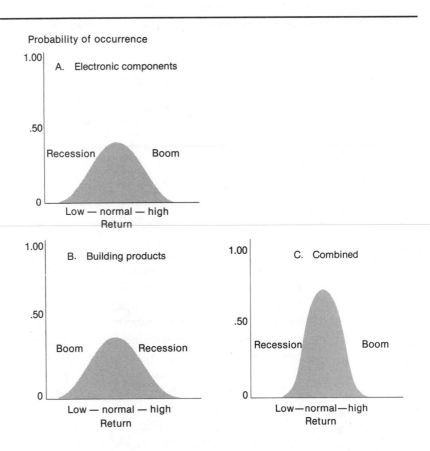

in opposite directions (building products and electronic components) are referred to as being negatively correlated and provide a high degree of risk reduction.

Finally, projects which are totally uncorrelated provide some overall reduction in portfolio risk—though not as much as negatively correlated investments. For example, if a beer manufacturer purchases a textile firm, the projects are neither positively nor negatively correlated; but the purchase will reduce the overall risk of the firm simply through the "law of large numbers." If you have enough unrelated projects going on at one time, good and bad events will probably even out.

The extent of correlation among projects is represented by a new term called the *coefficient of correlation*—a measure that may take on values anywhere from − 1 to + 1.[6] Examples are presented in Table 13–6.

[6]Coefficient of correlation is not to be confused with coefficient of variation—a term used earlier in the chapter.

Table 13–6
Measures of
correlation

Coefficient of Correlation	Condition	Example	Impact on Risk
−1	Negative correlation	Electronic components, building products	Large risk reduction
0	No correlation	Beer, textile	Some risk reduction
+1	Positive correlation	Two airlines	No risk reduction

In the real world, very few investment combinations take on values as extreme as − 1 or + 1, or for that matter exactly 0. The more likely case is a point somewhere between, such as − .2 negative correlation or + .3 positive correlation, as indicated along the continuum in Figure 13–10.

The fact that risk can be reduced by combining risky assets with low or negatively correlated assets can be seen by the example of Conglomerate, Inc. Conglomerate has fairly average returns and standard deviations of returns. The company is considering the purchase of two separate but large companies with sales and assets equal to its own. Management is struggling with the decision since both companies have a 14 percent rate of return, which is 2 percent higher than that of Conglomerate, and they have the same standard deviation of returns as that of Conglomerate, at 2.82 percent. This information is presented in the first three columns of Table 13–7.

Since management desires to reduce risk (σ) and to increase returns at the same time, it decides to analyze the results of each combination.[7] These are shown in the last two columns in Table 13–7. A combination with Positive Correlation, Inc., increases the mean return for Conglomerate, Inc., to 13 percent but maintains the exact same standard deviation of returns (no risk reduction). Why? Because the coefficient of correlation

Figure 13–10
Levels of risk
reduction as
measured by the
coefficient of
correlation

	Significant Risk Reduction	Some Risk Reduction	Minor Risk Reduction	
Extreme risk reduction	−1 −.5 −.2	0 +.3	+.5 +1	No reduction

[7]In Chapter 20, you will evaluate a merger situation in which there is no increase in earnings, only a reduction in the standard deviation. Because the lower risk may mean a higher price-earnings ratio, this could be beneficial.

Table 13–7 Rates of return for Conglomerate, Inc., and two merger candidates

Year	(1) Conglomerate, Inc.	(2) Positive Correlation, Inc. + 1.0	(3) Negative Correlation, Inc. − .9	(1) + (2) Conglomerate, Inc. + Positive Correlation, Inc.	(1) + (3) Conglomerate, Inc. + Negative Correlation, Inc.
1	14%	16%	10%	15%	12%
2	10	12	16	11	13
3	8	10	18	9	13
4	12	14	14	13	13
5	16	18	12	17	14
Mean return	12%	14%	14%	13%	13%
Standard deviation of returns (σ)	2.82%	2.82%	2.82%	2.82%	.63%
Correlation coefficients with Conglomerate, Inc.				+1.0	−.9

is + 1.0 and no diversification benefits are achieved. A combination with Negative Correlation, Inc., also increases the mean return to 13 percent; but it reduces the standard deviation of returns to 0.63 percent, a significant reduction in risk. This occurs because of the offsetting relationship of returns between the two companies, as evidenced by the coefficient of correlation of − .9. When one company has high returns, the other has low returns, and vice versa.

Evaluation of Combinations

The firm should evaluate all possible combinations of projects, determining which will provide the best trade-off between risk and return. In Figure 13–11, we see a number of alternatives that might be available to a given firm. Each point represents a combination of different possible investments. For example, point *F* might represent a semiconductor manufacturer combining three different types of semiconductors, plus two types of calculators, and two products in totally unrelated fields. In choosing between the various points or combinations, management should have two primary objectives:

1. Achieve the highest possible return at a given risk level.
2. Provide the lowest possible risk at a given return level.

Figure 13–11
Risk–return trade-
offs

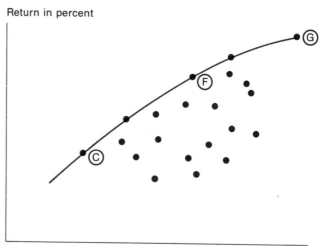

Figure 13–11
Risk–return trade-offs

All the best opportunities will fall along the leftmost sector of the diagram (line *C–F–G*). Each point on the line satisfies the two objectives of the firm. Any point to the right is less desirable.

After we have developed our best risk–return line, known in the financial literature as the "efficient frontier," we must determine where on the line our firm should be. There is no universally correct answer. To the extent we are willing to take large risks for superior returns, we will opt for some point on the upper portion of the line—such as *G*. A more conservative selection might be *C or F*.

The Share Price Effect

The firm must be sensitive to the wishes and demands of shareholders. To the extent that unnecessary or undesirable risks are taken, a higher discount rate and lower valuation may be assigned to the stock in the market. Higher profits, resulting from risky ventures, could have a result opposite from that intended. In raising the coefficient of variation, or beta, we could be lowering the overall valuation of the firm.

The aversion of investors to nonpredictability (and the associated risk) is confirmed by observing the relative valuation given to cyclical stocks versus highly predictable growth stocks in the market. Metals, autos, and housing stocks generally trade at an earnings multiplier well below that for industries with level, predictable performance, such as drugs, soft drinks, and even alcohol or cigarettes. Each company must carefully analyze its own situation to determine the appropriate trade-off between risk and return. The changing desires and objectives of investors tend to make the task somewhat more difficult.

Summary

Risk may be defined as the potential variability of the outcomes from an investment. The less predictable the outcomes, the greater is the risk. Both management and investors tend to be risk averse—that is, all things being equal, they would prefer to take less risk, rather than greater risk.

The most commonly employed method to adjust for risk in the capital budgeting process is to alter the discount rate based on the perceived risk level. High-risk projects will carry a risk premium, producing a discount rate well in excess of the cost of capital.

In assessing the risk components in a given project, management may rely on simulation techniques to generate probabilities of possible outcomes, and decision trees to help isolate the key variables to be evaluated.

Management must consider not only the risk inherent in a given project, but also the impact of a new project on the overall risk of the firm (the portfolio effect). Negatively correlated projects have the most favorable effect on smoothing out business cycle fluctuations. The firm may wish to consider all combinations and variations of possible projects and to select only those that provide a total risk–return trade-off consistent with its goals.

Review of Formulas

1. $\bar{D}$ (expected value) $= \Sigma DP$ (13–1)

D is outcome
P is probability of outcome

2. σ (standard deviation) $= \sqrt{\Sigma(D - \bar{D})^2 P}$ (13–2)

D is outcome
$\bar{D}$ is expected value
P is probability of outcome

3. V (coefficient of variation) $= \dfrac{\sigma}{\bar{D}}$ (13–3)

σ is standard deviation
$\bar{D}$ is expected value

List of Terms

risk
risk averse
expected value
standard deviation
coefficient of variation
risk-adjusted discount rate

portfolio effect
coefficient of correlation
efficient frontier
beta
simulation
decision tree

Discussion Questions

1. If corporate managers are risk averse, does this mean that they will not take risks? Explain.

2. Discuss the concept of risk and how it might be measured.

3. When is the coefficient of variation a better measure of risk than the standard deviation?

4. Explain how the concept of risk can be incorporated into the capital budgeting process.

5. If risk is to be analyzed in a qualitative way, place the following investment decisions in order from the lowest risk to the highest risk:
   a.   New equipment.
   b.   Completely new market.
   c.   Repair old machinery.
   d.   New product in a foreign market.
   e.   New product in a related market.
   f.   Addition to a new product line.

6. Assume that a company, correlated with the economy, is evaluating six projects, of which two are positively correlated with the economy, two are negatively correlated, and two are not correlated with it at all. Which two projects would you select to minimize the company's overall risk?

7. Assume that a firm has several hundred possible investments and that it wants to analyze the risk–return trade-off for portfolios of 20 projects. How should it proceed with the evaluation?

8. Explain the effect of the risk–return trade-off on the market value of common stock.

9. What is the purpose of using simulation analysis?

10. Why might an analyst set up a decision tree in attempting to make a decision?

Problems

1. Tucker Chemicals is evaluating the introduction of a new product. The possible levels of unit sales and the probabilities of occurrence are given.

Possible Market Reaction	Sales in Units	Probabilities
Low response	10	.10
Moderate response	30	.30
High response	45	.40
Very high response	60	.20

   a. What is the expected value of unit sales for the new product?
   b. What is the standard deviation of unit sales?

2. Five investment alternatives have the following returns and standard deviations of returns.

Alternative	Returns: Expected Value	Standard Deviation
A	$ 1,000	$200
B	3,000	300
C	3,000	400
D	5,000	700
E	10,000	900

   a. Using the coefficient of variation, rank the five alternatives from lowest risk to highest risk.
   b. If you were to choose between alternatives B and C only, would you need to use the coefficient of variation? Why?

3. Possible outcomes for three investment alternatives and their probabilities of occurrence are given below.

	Alternative 1		Alternative 2		Alternative 3	
	Outcomes	Probability	Outcomes	Probability	Outcomes	Probability
Failure	50	.2	90	.3	80	.4
Acceptable . . .	80	.4	160	.5	200	.5
Successful . . .	120	.4	200	.2	400	.1

Rank the three alternatives in terms of risk (compute the coefficient of variation).

4. Donna Rice Modeling Studios is considering opening in a new location in Denver, Colorado. An aftertax cash flow of $120 per day (expected value) is projected for each of the two locations that are being evaluated.

   Which of these sites would you select based on the distribution of these cash flows (use the coefficient of variation as your measure of risk):

Site A		Site B	
Probability	Cash Flows	Probability	Cash Flows
.15	$ 80	.10	$ 50
.50	110	.20	80
.30	140	.40	120
.05	220	.20	160
		.10	190
Expected value	$120	Expected value	$120

5. Dixie Dynamite Company is evaluating two different methods of blowing up old buildings for commercial purposes over the next five years. Method one (implosion) is relatively low in risk for this business and will carry a 12 percent discount rate. Method two (explosion) is less expensive to perform, but more dangerous, and will call for a higher discount rate of 16 percent. Either method will require an initial capital outlay of $75,000. The inflows from projected business over the next five years are given below. Which method should be selected using net present value analysis?

Years	Method 1	Method 2
1	$18,000	$20,000
2	24,000	25,000
3	34,000	35,000
4	26,000	28,000
5	14,000	15,000

6. Larry's Athletic Lounge is planning an expansion program to increase the sophistication of the exercise equipment. Larry is considering some new equipment priced at $20,000 with an estimated life of five years. Larry is not sure how many members the new equipment will attract, but he estimates that his increased yearly cash flows for the next five years will have the following probability distribution. Larry's cost of capital is 14 percent.

P (probability)	Cash Flow
.2 . . .	$2,400
.4 . . .	4,800
.3 . . .	6,000
.1 . . .	7,200

a. What is the expected cash flow?

b. What is the expected net present value and internal rate of return?

c. Should Larry buy the new equipment?

7. Cole Coal Company is analyzing the purchase of two different coal mines in Wyoming. Only one investment will be made. The Cheyenne Mine will cost $1,000,000 and will produce $200,000 per year in years 5 through 15 and $400,000 per year in years 16 through 25. The Laramie Mine will cost $1,200,000 and will produce $150,000 per year for the next 25 years. The cost of capital is 10 percent.

a. Which investment should be made? (Note: in looking up present value factors for this problem, you need to work with the concept of a deferred annuity for the Cheyenne Mine. The returns in years 5 through 15 actually represent 11 years; the returns in years 16 through 25 represent 10 years.)

b. If the Cheyenne Mine justifies an extra 5 percent premium over the normal cost of capital because of its riskiness and relative uncertainty of flows, does the investment decision change?

8. Mr. Monty Terry, a real estate investor, is trying to make a decision about two potential small shopping center purchases. His choices are the Wrigley Village and Crosley Square. The anticipated annual cash inflows from each are as follows:

Wrigley Village		Crosley Square	
Yearly Aftertax Cash Inflow (in 000s)	Probability	Yearly Aftertax Cash Inflow (in 000s)	Probability
10	.1	20	.1
30	.2	30	.3
40	.3	35	.4
50	.3	50	.2
60	.1		

a. Find the expected value of the cash flow for each shopping center.

b. What is the coefficient of variation for each shopping center?

c. Which shopping center has more risk?

9. Referring to problem 8, Mr. Terry is likely to hold the shopping center of his choice for 25 years and will use this period for decision-

making purposes. Either shopping center can be purchased for $300,000. Mr. Terry uses a risk-adjusted discount rate approach when evaluating investments. His scale is related to the coefficient of variation (for other types of investments, he also considers other measures).

Coefficient of Variation	Discount Rate
0–0.30	8%
0.31–0.60	11 (cost of capital)
0.61–0.90	14
Over 0.90	18

a. Compute the risk-adjusted net present value for Wrigley Village and Crosley Square using cash flow figures (in 000s) from the previous problem.

b. Which investment should Mr. Terry accept if the two investments are mutually exclusive. If the investments are not mutually exclusive and no capital rationing is involved, how would your decision be affected?

10. Roper Fashions is preparing a strategy for the fall season. One option is to go to a highly imaginative new, four gold button sport coat with special emblems on the front pocket. The all-wool product will be available for males and females alike. A second option would be to produce a traditional blue blazer line. The marketing research department has determined that the new, four gold button coat and traditional blue blazer line offer the following probabilities of outcomes and related cash flows.

Expected Sales	New Coat		Blazer	
	Probability	Present Value of Cash Flows from Sales	Probability	Present Value of Cash Flows from Sales
Fantastic . . .	.5	$130,000	.3	$65,000
Moderate . . .	.2	70,000	.4	50,000
Dismal	.3	0	.3	35,000

The initial cost to get into the new coat line is $50,000 in designs, equipment and inventory. The blazer line would carry an initial cost of $30,000.

a. Diagram a complete decision tree of the possible outcomes similar to Figure 13–8. Take the analysis all the way through the process of computing expected NPV (last column) for each investment.

b. Given the analysis in part *a,* would you automatically make the investment indicated?

11. When returns from a project can be assumed to be normally distributed, such as those shown in Figure 13–6 (represented by a symmetrical, bell-shaped curve), the areas under the curve can be determined from statistical tables based on standard deviations. For example, 68.26 percent of the distribution will fall within one standard deviation of the expected value ($\bar{D} \pm 1\sigma$). Similarly, 95.44 percent will fall within two standard deviations ($\bar{D} \pm 2\sigma$), and so on. An abbreviated table of areas under the normal curve is shown here.

Number of σ's from Expected Value	+ or −	+ and −
0.5	0.1915	0.3830
1.0	0.3413	0.6826
1.5	0.4332	0.8664
1.96	0.4750	0.9500
2.0	0.4772	0.9544

Assume Project A has an expected value of $20,000 and a standard deviation (σ) of $4,000.

a. What is the probability that the outcome will be between $16,000 and $24,000?

b. What is the probability that the outcome will be between $14,000 and $26,000?

c. What is the probability that the outcome will be at least $12,000?

d. What is the probability that the outcome will be less than $27,840?

e. What is the probability that the outcome will be less than $16,000 or greater than $26,000?

12. The Palo Alto Microchip Corporation projects the following pattern of inflows from an investment. The inflows are spread over time to reflect delayed benefits. Each year is independent of the others.

Year 1		Year 5		Year 10	
Cash Inflow	Probability	Cash Inflow	Probability	Cash Inflow	Probability
50	.20	40	.25	30	.30
60	.60	60	.50	60	.40
70	.20	80	.25	90	.30

The expected value for all three years is $60.

a. Compute the standard deviation for each of the three years.

b. Diagram the expected values and standard deviations for each of the three years in a manner similar to Figure 13–6.

c. Assuming a 5 percent and 10 percent discount rate, complete the table on page 414 for present value factors.

Year	IF_{PV} 5 Percent	IF_{PV} 10 Percent	Difference
1	0.952	0.909	0.043
5	_____	_____	_____
10	_____	_____	_____

d. Is the increasing risk over time, as diagrammed in part *b*, consistent with the larger differences in $IF_{PV}s$ over time as computed in part *c*?

e. Assume the initial investment is $110. What is the net present value of the investment at a 10 percent discount rate? Should the investment be accepted?

13. General Munchies is a food company specializing in snack foods. It is seeking to diversify its business and lower its risk. Currently, it is examining three companies—a toy company, a fast-food chain, and a lumber company. Each of these companies can be bought at the same multiple of earnings. The following represents information about the companies.

Company	Correlation with General Munchies	Sales ($ millions)	Average Earnings ($ millions)	Standard Deviation in Earnings ($ millions)
General Munchies	+1.0	$100	$10	$2
Toy Company	+.3	100	10	5
Fast Food Company . . .	+.8	100	10	3
Lumber Company	−.5	100	10	6

a. Discuss what would happen to GM's portfolio risk–return if it bought Toy Company? Fast Food Company? Lumber Company?

b. If you were going to buy one company, which would you choose? Why?

c. If you wanted to buy two companies, which would you choose? Why?

14. Mrs. Markowitz is looking at a number of different types of investments for her portfolio. She has just retired after 40 years of service in the library at U.C.L.A. She identifies eight possible investments.

	Return	Risk			Return	Risk
(a)	11%	1.5%		(e)	14	5.0
(b)	11	2.1		(f)	15	5.0
(c)	13	3.0		(g)	15	5.8
(d)	13	4.2		(h)	16	7.0

a. Graph the data in a manner similar to Figure 13–11. Use the following axes for your data.

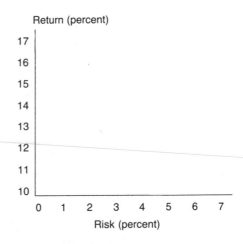

b. Draw a curved line representing the efficient frontier.
c. What two objectives do points on the efficient frontier satisfy?
d. Is there one point on the efficient frontier that is best for all investors?

15. (Comprehensive problem.)

Tobacco Company of America is a very stable billion dollar company with sales growth of about 5 percent per year in good or bad economic conditions. Because of this stability (a correlation coefficient with the economy of + .3 and a standard deviation of sales of about 5 percent from the mean), Mr. Weed, the vice president of finance, thinks the company can absorb some small risky company that could add quite a bit of return without increasing the company's risk very much. He is currently trying to decide which of two companies he will buy. Tobacco Company of America's cost of capital is 10 percent.

Computer Whiz Company (cost $75 million)		American Micro-Technology (cost $75 million)	
Probability	Aftertax Cash Flows for 10 Years ($ millions)	Probability	Aftertax Cash Flows for 10 Years ($ millions)
.3	$ 6	.2	$ (1)
.3	10	.2	3
.2	16	.2	10
.2	25	.3	25
		.1	31

a.   What is the expected cash flow from both companies?
b.   Which company has the lower coefficient of variation?
c.   Compute the net present value of each company.
d.   Which company would you pick, based on net present values?
e.   Would you change your mind if you added the risk dimensions to the problem? Explain.
f.   What if Computer Whiz had a correlation coefficient with the economy of + .5 and AMT had one of − .1? Which of the companies would give you the best portfolio effects for risk reduction?
g.   What might be the effect of the acquisitions on the market value of Tobacco Company's stock?

16. Virgil Trucking Company is considering the purchase of 50 new diesel trucks that are 15 percent more fuel efficient than the ones the firm is now using. Mr. George R. Kell, the president, has found that the company uses an average of 10 million gallons of diesel fuel per year at a price of $1.20 per gallon. If he can cut fuel consumption by 15 percent, he will save $1,800,000 per year (1,500,000 gallons times $1.20).

Mr. Kell assumes that the price of diesel fuel is an external market force that he cannot control and that any increased costs of fuel will be passed on to the shipper through higher rates endorsed by the Interstate Commerce Commission. If this is true, then fuel efficiency would save more money as the price of diesel fuel rose (at $1.30 per gallon, he would save $1,950,000 in total if he buys the new trucks). Mr. Kell has come up with two possible forecasts as shown below— each of which he feels has about a 50 percent chance of coming true. Under assumption number one, diesel prices will stay relatively low; under assumption number two, diesel prices will rise considerably.

Fifty new trucks will cost Virgil Trucking $4 million. Under a special provision from the Interstate Commerce Commission, the allowable depreciation will be 25 percent in year 1, 38 percent in year 2, and 37 percent in year 3. The firm has a tax rate of 40 percent and a cost of capital of 16 percent.

a.   First compute the yearly expected costs of diesel fuel for both assumption one (relatively low prices) and assumption two (high prices) from the forecasts below.

Forecast for assumption one:

Probability (same for each year)	Price of Diesel Fuel per Gallon		
	Year 1	Year 2	Year 3
.1	$0.90	$1.00	$1.10
.2	1.00	1.15	1.20
.3	1.20	1.30	1.50
.2	1.35	1.50	1.65
.2	1.50	1.60	1.75

Forecast for assumption two:

Probability (same for each year)	Price of Diesel Fuel per Gallon		
	Year 1	Year 2	Year 3
.1	$1.25	$1.40	$1.50
.3	1.30	1.70	2.00
.4	1.60	2.00	2.20
.2	1.80	2.20	2.60

b. What will be the dollar savings in diesel expenses each year for assumption one and for assumption two?

c. Find the cash flow after taxes for both forecasts.

d. Compute the net present value of the truck purchases for each fuel forecast assumption and the combined net present value (that is, weigh the NPVs by .5).

e. If you were Mr. Kell, would you go ahead with this capital investment?

f. How sensitive to fuel prices is this capital investment?

Selected References

Blume, M. E. "On the Assessment of Risk." *Journal of Finance* 26 (March 1971), pp. 95–117.

Brigham, Eugene F.; Dilip K. Shome; and Steve R. Vinson. "The Risk Premium Approach to Measuring a Utility's Cost of Equity." *Financial Management* 14 (Spring 1985), pp. 33–45.

Chen, Son-Nan, and William T. Moore. "Investment Decisions under Uncertainty: Application and Estimation Risk in the Hiller Approach." *Journal of Financial and Quantitative Analysis* 17 (September 1982), pp. 425–37.

Fabozzi, Frank J. "The Use of Operations Research Techniques for Capital Budgeting Decisions: A Sample Survey." *Journal of Operations Research Society* 29 (1978), pp. 39–42.

Green, Richard C., and Sanjay Stivastava. "Risk Aversion and Arbitrage." *Journal of Finance* 40 (March 1985), pp. 39–42.

Hayes, Robert H. "Incorporating Risk Aversion into Risk Analysis." *Engineering Economist* 20 (Winter 1975), pp. 99–121.

Hertz, David B. "Investment Policies That Pay Off." *Harvard Business Review* 46 (January–February 1968), pp. 96–108.

——— . "Risk Analysis in Capital Investment." *Harvard Business Review* 22 (January–February 1964), pp. 95–106.

Hillier, Fredrick S. "A Basic Model for Capital Budgeting of Risky Interrelated Projects." *Engineering Economist* 17 (Fall 1971), pp. 1–30.

Lessard, Donald R., and Richard S. Bower. "Risk-Screening in Capital Budgeting." *Journal of Finance* 28 (May 1973), pp. 331–38.

Levy, Haim, and Marshall Sarnat. "The Portfolio Analysis of Multiperiod Capital Investment under Conditions of Risk." *Engineering Economist* 16 (Fall 1970), pp. 1–19.

Lewellen, Wilbur G., and Michael E. Long. "Simulation versus Single-Value Estimates in Capital Expenditure Analysis." *Decision Sciences* 3 (1972), pp. 19–33.

Logue, Dennis E., and T. Craig Tapley. "Performance Monitoring and the Timing of Cash Flows." *Financial Management* 14 (Autumn 1986), pp. 34–39.

Markowitz, Harry. "Portfolio Selection." *Journal of Finance* 7 (March 1952), pp. 77–91.

Osteryoung, Jerome S.; Elton Scott; and Gordon S. Roberts. "Selecting Capital Projects with the Coefficient of Variation." *Financial Management* 6 (Summer 1977), pp. 65–70.

Richardson, L. K. "Do High Risks Lead to High Returns?" *Financial Analysts Journal* 26 (March–April 1970), pp. 88–99.

Sick, Gordon A. "A Certainty-Equivalent Approach to Capital Budgeting Forecasts." *Financial Management* 15 (Winter 1986), pp. 22–32.

P A R T

5

Long-Term Financing

14 Capital Markets

15 Investment Banking: Public and Private Placement

16 Long-Term Debt and Lease Financing

17 Common and Preferred Stock Financing

18 Dividend Policy and Retained Earnings

19 Convertibles and Warrants

Introduction

The methods of long-term financing that are available to the firm are diverse and constantly changing. At times, there appears to be a battleground in which the government, large corporations, and small businesses are fighting one another for a shrinking amount of available funds. There has been much talk of a shortage of capital for investment in the United States, particularly as the government runs up large deficits and draws funds out of the private sector. Whether such a shortage really exists is a debatable point.

Fortunately during the 1980s, foreign investors have been supplying a large amount of the capital needed by the U.S. government and American businesses. The historic stock market decline of over 22 percent (508 points on the Dow Jones Industrial Average) on October 19, 1987, was a temporary blow to capital markets worldwide. Only time will tell whether financial capital will be readily available during the rest of the 1980s and early 1990s. As a result of the international collapse of common stock prices, there is more uncertainty about long-term capital markets than is normal. One thing is certain: the supply and demand for financial capital is taking place in an international market, and most of the following chapters have an increased amount of material on the international impact of this trend.

In Chapter 14 we take a close look at the security markets, with an eye toward major changes that are taking place. In the next chapter, we examine the actual process of selling securities to the public through an investment banker. The investment banker is responsible for the analysis, pricing, and distribution of stocks or bonds and serves as the middleman between the corporation and the public. As part of our discussion of investment banking, we also consider the advantages and disadvantages of going public—that is, of selling corporate stock to the general public in the over-the-counter market or through an organized exchange—rather than maintaining ownership in private hands. H. Ross Perot, at one time depicted by *Fortune* magazine as the "Fastest Richest Texan Ever," is studied in the context of going public during the market hysteria of an earlier time period. Rockefeller Center Properties, Inc., is presented as a recent example of going public.

In Chapters 16 and 17, we study the advantages, disadvantages, and limitations of long-term debt, preferred stock, and common stock. Although the analysis is developed primarily from the corporate viewpoint (should the issue take place or not?), the investor's viewpoint is also considered. Under long-term debt financing, we also consider the lease alternative to "borrowing funds and purchasing the asset outright." Significant changes in accounting requirements for leasing dramatize the close parallel between borrowing and leasing.

In Chapter 18, we examine a critically important decision for a corporation: whether it should pay out retained earnings in the form of dividends or hold the funds in the corporation for financing future projects. Retained earnings represent an important form of internal long-term financing and must be related to the growth and the life cycle of the firm. In each case, the impact of dividend policy on stockholder expectations and market value maximization must be considered.

Corporate securities that may be converted into common stock or that have special provisions for the purchase of common stock are considered in Chapter 19. The investment features of convertibles and warrants are evaluated along with their potential usage in corporate finance. The related accounting implications of these securities also receive attention.

14

Capital Markets

Security markets are generally separated into short-term and long-term markets. The short-term markets comprise securities with maturities of one year or less and are referred to as *money markets*. The securities most commonly traded in these markets, such as Treasury bills, commercial paper, and negotiable certificates of deposit, were previously discussed under working capital and cash management and will not be covered again.

The long-term markets are called *capital markets* and consist of securities having maturities greater than one year. The most common corporate securities in this category are bonds, common stock, preferred stock, and convertible securities. These securities are found on the firm's balance sheet under the designation long-term liabilities and equities. Taken together, these long-term securities comprise the firm's capital structure.

In this chapter, we will be looking at how the capital markets are organized and integrated into the corporate and economic system of the United States. Capital markets are becoming increasingly international as suppliers of financial capital seek out the best risk–return opportunities from among the major industrialized countries in the global economy. The globalization of the capital markets is highlighted in this chapter, but first we look at U.S. capital markets.

Competition for Funds in the Capital Markets _____

In order to put corporate securities into perspective, it is necessary to look at other securities that are available in the capital markets. The federal government, government agencies, state governments, and local municipalities all compete with one another for a limited supply of financial capital. The capital markets serve as a way of allocating the available capital to the most efficient user. Therefore, the ultimate investor must choose among many kinds of securities, both corporate and noncorporate. Before investors part with their money, they desire to maximize their return for any given level of risk, and thus the expected return from the universe of securities acts as an allocating mechanism in the markets.

The size of the corporate and noncorporate capital markets is large. The total dollar amount of new security issues with maturities of more than one year rose from $76 billion in 1970 to $738 billion by 1986. This does not include the tremendous amount of funds raised in the short-term money markets. Over this time period, new issues of corporate securities averaged closed to 40 percent of the total, while all forms of government securities made up the other 60 percent. Figure 14–1 depicts the specific composition of long-term funds raised from 1970 through 1986.

**Figure 14–1
Composition of long–
term funds raised**

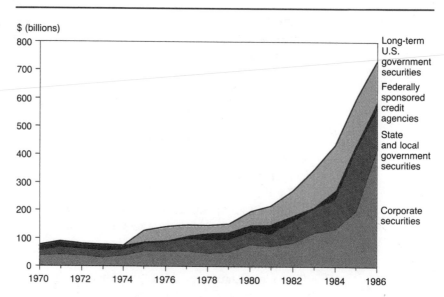

Government Securities

U.S. government securities   In accordance with government fiscal policy, the U.S. Treasury manages the federal government's debt in order to balance the inflows and outflows. When deficits are incurred, the Treasury can sell short-term or long-term securities to finance the shortfall. In Figure 14–1 only long-term financing is depicted.

Over the total 17-year period shown, long-term U.S. government financing averaged 26.5 percent of the total. From 1970 through 1975, however, long-term financing by the Treasury averaged only about 2 percent of the total as the Treasury primarily used short-term Treasury bills for its cash needs during this period. Since 1976, the use of long-term U.S. government financing has averaged close to 30 percent as the U.S. government ran up large deficits. The recessions of the early 1980s and a string of $100 to $200 billion-plus deficits from years from 1982 through the present caused the U.S. government to be the biggest demander of long-term capital, particularly in 1984 and 1985, averaging almost 39 percent of total long-term funds raised for those two years.[1]

It remains to be seen how effective the Gramm-Rudman "balanced budget bill" will be in reducing deficits and, ultimately, government borrowing. The legislation calls for the government to have its budget in balance by the mid-1990s.

Foreign governments, notably Japan and West Germany, have been helpful in supplying capital to finance the U.S. deficit. By the end of 1986, the total gross public debt of the United States was $2.214 trillion, and 11.4 percent or $252.5 billion was held by foreigners. In 1986 alone, foreigners bought $39 billion of U.S. government debt or 14.5 percent of the total U.S. debt sold in 1986 of $268.9 billion. Foreign investors, including foreign governments, have preferred the higher relative interest rates in the United States, compared to other industrial countries, as well as the political stability and economic strength of the U.S. economy. Additionally, such countries as Japan and West Germany have a large trade surplus of dollars that need to be invested.

Federally sponsored credit agencies   Most of the federally sponsored credit agencies are involved in making loans to the housing market or to

---

[1]When short-term U.S. government financing is added to long-term U.S. government financing, the amounts greatly increase.

rural farm areas. The Federal National Mortgage Association (Fannie Mae) has the most debt outstanding, followed by the Federal Home Loan Banks (FHLB). Both of these agencies are involved in the housing market. Fannie Mae is included as a government-sponsored agency, even though it is currently a privately run corporation. It still maintains a quasi-agency relationship with the United States, based on its original government charter. The third largest agency is the group of 37 Farm Credit Banks. The depressed farm economy has created many problems for farm lenders as farmers have defaulted on their loans. The Farm Credit System sustained losses of $2.7 billion in 1985 and $1.9 billion in 1986. With record losses, the Farm Credit System moves closer to insolvency and a government bailout.

Over the period 1970–86, federally sponsored agencies averaged 7.1 percent of the long-term financing shown in Figure 14–1. Long-term financing for government-sponsored agencies has been rather inconsistent, rising from 1.5 percent in 1975 to 16.4 percent in 1978 and accounting for only 1.8 percent of total long-term financing in 1986.

State and local issues   These issues are sometimes referred to as municipal securities or tax exempt offerings, because the interest on them is normally exempt from federal income taxes and from state taxes in the state of issue. During the 1970–86 period, state and local municipalities accounted for about the same percentage of long-term funds raised (26.4 percent) as the U.S. government. This is illustrated in Figure 14–1. When huge federal deficits began to mushroom in 1980, long-term municipal financing fell into third place, behind U.S. Treasury and corporate financing. In 1985, federal income tax reform was considered in Congress, which threatened to eliminate the tax exclusion for interest on municipal bonds beginning in 1986. This caused a swell of new municipal offerings to lock in favored tax treatment in 1985. The total volume of funds raised by state and municipal governments amounted to $214 billion, or 35.5 percent of the total long-term funds raised in 1985. The tax law revisions in 1986 maintained the deductibility of interest on municipal bonds; but the lower marginal tax rates removed a large incentive for individual and corporations to purchase these "tax free" bonds, and they accounted for only 19.9 percent of total long-term funds raised in 1986.

Corporate Securities

Corporate bonds   One misconception held by many investors is that corporate bond markets are dominated in size by the market for common stocks. This is far from the truth. In the new issues market, bonds averaged 74 percent of all long-term corporate securities sold from 1970 through 1986. Bonds as a percentage of total corporate issues have ranged from highs of 83.9 percent in 1986 and 83.7 percent in 1974 to a low of 57 percent in 1983. Stock prices reached their low prices of the decade in 1974, and bonds were the dominant source of external corporate financing. On the other hand, the low point of bond financing was reached in 1983. Stock prices soared after having been low for quite some time, and corporations rushed to increase equity financing before stock prices decreased. At other times, such as 1986, bond offerings became especially sensitive to the level of interest rates and the expectation of their future levels. From 1984 through 1986, long-term interest rates declined, and financial managers were concerned that interest rates might return to the former high levels of the early 1980s. New bond offerings set records in all three years, rising from $110 billion in 1984 to $355 billion in 1986. When interest rates are expected to rise, financial managers try to lock in long-term financing at low costs and balance the company's debt structure towards more long-term debt and away from short-term debt.

Preferred stock Preferred stock is the least used of all long-term securities. It has averaged only 5.7 percent of long-term corporate financing for the period from 1970 to 1986. The major reason for the small amount of financing by preferred stock is that the dividend is not deductible to the corporation before income taxes, as is bond interest. Given a choice between selling bonds and preferred stock, which are both fixed-income securities, most financial managers would choose bonds because they have a lower aftertax cost of capital.

Common stock The sale of common stock during the period 1970–86 averaged 20.3 percent of total corporate long-term financing. When total long-term funds, including government financing, are considered, common stock only accounted for about 8 percent of all long-term financing. This small percentage of new common stock financing illustrates that corporations do not regularly rely upon common stocks as a major source of funds. Even though new issues of common stock set records in 1986 of $56.9 billion, the total sources of all corporate long-term funds had grown to $424 billion, and common stock financing accounted for much less than its 17-year average of 20.3 percent. Figure 14–2 provides comparative data on the use of various financing alternatives by U.S. corporations.

**Figure 14–2
Long-term corporate
financing, 1970–1986**

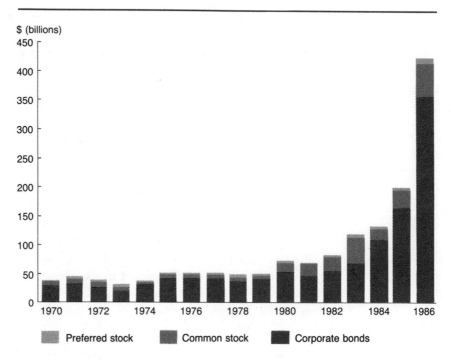

$ (billions)

Preferred stock   Common stock   Corporate bonds

Equity financing, in general When financing by common stock and preferred stock is combined, one industry has historically stood out, at least until recently. Stock financing of any significance from 1970 through 1982 was done by utility companies. Utilities accounted for an average of 41.7 percent of the stock financing during this time period. In 1974, utilities sold 61 percent of all stock offerings and, in the following five years, averaged over 50 percent of the total stock financing.

The pattern began to change in 1983. From 1983 to 1986, other firms besides public utilities were also heavy users of equity capital, and utilities only accounted for 7 percent of total stock issues. Manufacturing companies accounted for almost 22 percent of equity financing during this period and other industries were also important. However, real estate and financial companies were by far the largest users of new equity, accounting for 22 percent of equity raised in 1982 and rising steadily to 50 percent by 1986. The increased dependence upon equity financing for the financial segment of the economy can be expected to continue. Banks, investment bankers, and retail stockbrokers all need more equity capital to compete in global financial markets dominated by large financial companies. The new tax law has also made debt less advantageous to the real estate industry and has increased the need for equity capital in this industry segment.

Internal versus External Sources of Funds

So far we have discussed how corporations raise funds externally through long-term financing, using bonds, common stock, and preferred stock. Another extremely important source of funds to the corporation is internally generated funds as represented by retained earnings and cash flow added back from depreciation. In our previous discussions of cost of capital (Chapter 11), the cost of retained earnings was considered, and our capital budgeting decisions (Chapter 12) also included cash flow from depreciation.

A look at Figure 14–3 shows that the ratio of external funds to total funds (external plus internal funds) peaked at 34 percent in 1971 and continued on a downward slide to 16 percent in 1979. During the rising bull market for stocks and bonds from 1982 to 1987, corporations took advantage of high security prices, and the ratio of external funds reached a high of 53 percent in 1986.

What about the composition of internal funds that make up the balance of the financing in Figure 14–3? A surprising thing for many people is that retained earnings do not account for the majority of internal funds. Figure 14–4 shows that, on average, retained earnings made up around 40 percent of internal funds generated between 1964–1979. The balance is in depreciation. Corporate earnings did not fully recover from the 1980–81 recession until 1987, and during 1980–86 earnings were relatively low. Low earnings, coupled with accelerated depreciation methods and higher dividends, created an internal funds flow derived mainly from depreciation benefits. Retained earnings accounted for only about 11 percent of

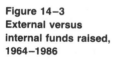

**Figure 14–3
External versus
internal funds raised,
1964–1986**

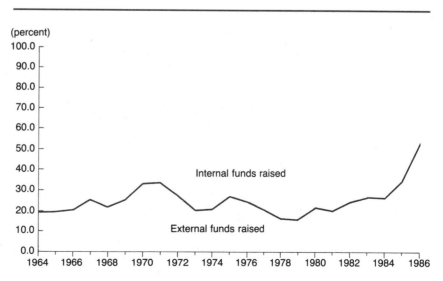

**Figure 14–4
Retained earnings as
a percentage of
internal funds, 1964–
1986**

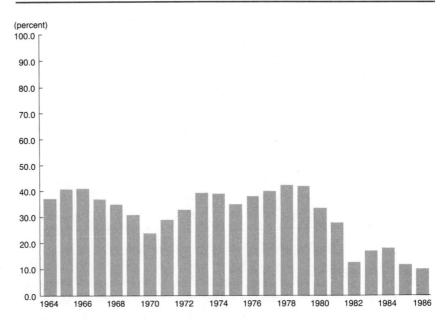

all internal funds in 1986. The decline in retained earnings exerted a large influence on corporations, increasing the need for external funds during the 1980s.

The Supply of Capital Funds

Having discussed the major users of capital in the U.S. economy, we turn our attention to the suppliers of capital. In a three-sector economy, consisting of business, government, and households, the major supplier of funds for investment is the household sector. Corporations and the federal government have traditionally been net demanders of funds. Figure 14–5 diagrams the flow of funds through our basic three-sector economy.

As households receive wages and transfer payments from the government and wages and dividends from corporations, they generally save some portion of their income. These savings are usually funneled to financial intermediaries that, in turn, make investments in the capital markets with the funds received from the household sector. This is known as indirect investment. The types of financial institutions that channel funds into the capital markets are specialized and diverse. Funds may flow into commercial banks, savings and loans, mutual savings banks, and credit unions. Households may also purchase mutual fund shares,

Figure 14–5
Flow of funds
through the economy

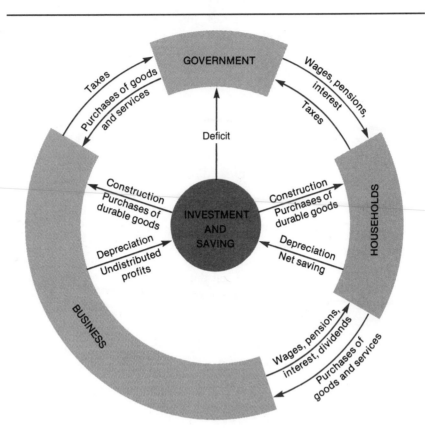

invest in life insurance, or participate in some form of private pension plan or profit sharing. All these financial institutions act as intermediaries; they help make the flow of funds from one sector of the economy to another very efficient and competitive. Without intermediaries, the cost of funds would be higher, and the efficient allocation of funds to the best users at the lowest cost would not take place.

The international saver and investor has also become a critical supplier to the U.S. capital markets, as previously pointed out. Of the gross public debt owed by the U.S. government, a quarter of a trillion dollars is held by foreigners (approximately 11 percent).

The Role of the Security Markets

Security markets exist to aid the allocation of capital among households, corporations, and governmental units, with financial institutions acting as intermediaries. Just as financial institutions specialize in their services and investments, so are the capital markets divided into many functional subsets, with each specific market serving a certain type of security. For example, the common stocks of some of the largest corporations are traded on the New York Stock Exchange, whereas government securities are traded by government security dealers in the over-the-counter markets.

Once a security is sold for the first time as an original offering, the security trades in its appropriate market among all kinds of investors. This trading activity is known as *secondary trading,* since funds flow among investors, rather than to the corporation. The purpose of secondary trading is to provide liquidity to investors and to keep prices competitive among alternative security investments.

Security markets provide liquidity in two ways. First, they enable corporations to raise funds by selling new issues of securities rapidly and at fair, competitive prices. Second, they allow the investor who purchases securities to sell them with relative ease and speed and thereby to turn a paper asset into cash. Ask yourself the question, "Would I buy securities if there were no place to sell them?" You would probably think twice before committing funds to an illiquid investment. Without markets, corporations and governmental units would not be able to raise the large amounts of capital necessary for economic growth.

The Organization of the Security Markets

The competitive structure and organization of the security markets have changed considerably since the early 1970s. In this section, we present the current organization of the markets, and provide an update of significant events of the last few years. The most common division of security markets is between organized exchanges and over-the-counter markets. Each will be examined separately.

The Organized Exchanges

Organized exchanges are either national or regional in scope. Each exchange has a central location where all buyers and sellers meet in an auction market to transact purchases and sales. Buyers and sellers are not actually present on the floor of the exchange but are represented by brokers who act as their agents. These brokers are registered members of the exchange. On the New York Stock Exchange, the number of members has been fixed at 1,366 since 1953, while the American Stock Exchange has a fixed limit of 650 members.

The New York Stock Exchange (NYSE) and the American Stock Exchange (AMEX) are national exchanges, and each is governed by an elected board of directors, of whom half are public directors and the other half industry representatives. Although the Midwest and Pacific Coast exchanges are the largest of the so-called regional exchanges, they trade primarily issues of large national companies. Some of the smaller exchanges, such as the Detroit, Boston, Cincinnati, and PBW,[2] are more regional in the sense that most of the companies listed on them are headquartered or do their principal business in the region in which the exchange is located. These smaller exchanges account for a very small percentage of trading in listed securities.

Securities can only be listed and traded on an exchange with the approval of the board of governors. Until October 1976, the NYSE and AMEX were mutually exclusive and did not allow shares of stock to be listed on both exchanges. Under prodding from the Securities and Exchange Commission (SEC), both exchanges agreed to allow dual listing so securities could be traded on both exchanges simultaneously. Currently no companies maintain dual listing on the NYSE and AMEX. Dual listing has long been common between the NYSE and the regional exchanges. Approximately 90 percent of the stocks traded on the Midwest and Pacific exchanges are also traded on the NYSE. This means that the shares of many large companies can be purchased on several different exchanges, which helps to make prices more competitive and the markets more efficient in establishing prices.

Although dual trading has been a common practice for many years, brokers on the floor of an exchange did not have immediate price information from the other markets. In order to make prices of all competitive trades in the same stock available to all market participants at the same time, the Securities and Exchange Commission applied pressure for creation of a consolidated tape, which became reality on June 16, 1975. The consolidated tape presents the prices and volume of all shares traded on the regional exchanges and the NYSE. This information is visible to all brokers on the floor of each exchange and allows traders on each exchange to follow the activity and prices on all other exchanges, as well as any over-the-counter trades in listed securities. Because of the consolidated tape, prices are more competitive and efficient.

---

[2]The PBW was formed by a merger of the Philadelphia, Baltimore, and Washington exchanges.

The New York Stock Exchange

Size and liquidity The NYSE is the largest and most important of all
the exchanges. In 1987, it accounted for over 80 percent of the dollar
volume of all listed stocks. Liquidity provided by the NYSE is also evident
by the fact that the normal daily share-trading volume during 1987 was
150–200 million shares. By the end of 1987, companies listed on the
NYSE had over 50 billion shares of stock listed on the exchange, their
worth being close to $2.5 trillion. We can see that the NYSE is certainly
an important mechanism in the flow of funds among investors of all types.

Listing requirements Each organized exchange has some minimum
requirement that a company must meet before the exchange will agree
to trade its securities. Most of the largest U.S. companies are traded on
the NYSE, as its listing requirements are more stringent than those of
the AMEX or the regionals.

   Although each case is decided on its own merits, according to the *NYSE
Fact Book*, the minimum requirements for a company to be listed on the
New York Stock Exchange for the first time are as follows:

1. Demonstrated earning power under competitive conditions of: *either*
   $2.5 million before federal income taxes for the most recent year and
   $2 million pre-tax for each of the preceding two years, *or* an aggregate
   for the last three fiscal years of $6.5 million *together with* a minimum
   in the most recent fiscal year of $4.5 million. (All three years must be
   profitable.)
2. Net tangible assets of $16 million, but greater emphasis is placed on
   the aggregate market value of the common stock.
3. Market value of publicly held shares, at least equal to $18 million.
4. A total of 1,100,000 common shares publicly held.
5. *Either* 2,000 holders of 100 shares or more, *or* 2,200 total stockholders
   together with average monthly trading volume (for the most recent six
   months) of 100,000 shares.

   Corporations desiring to be listed on exchanges have made the decision
that public availability of the stock on an exchange will benefit their
shareholders. The benefits will occur either by providing liquidity to
owners or by allowing the company a more viable means for raising
external capital for growth and expansion. The company must pay annual
listing fees to the exchange and additional fees based on the number of
shares traded each year.

The New York Stock Exchange also has the authority to remove (delist) or suspend a security from trading when the security fails to meet certain criteria. There is much latitude in these decisions, but generally a company's security may be considered for delisting if there are fewer than 1,200 round-lot (100 share) owners, 600,000 shares or fewer in public hands, and market value of the security is less than $5 million. A company that easily exceeded these standards on first being listed may fall below them during hard times.

Foreign Exchanges

As the industrialized world has grown, capital markets around the world have increased in size and importance. The decline of the U.S. dollar relative to other currencies has made other world stock markets more important relative to U.S. exchanges. Actually, the Tokyo Stock Exchange is now the largest in the world, with the dollar value of its securities exceeding that of the New York Stock Exchange.

As a sign of the international capital markets, large U.S. international companies—such as IBM, Sears, and McDonald's—trade on the Tokyo and Frankfurt stock exchanges; and many foreign companies trade on the New York Stock Exchange—such as Sony and TDK of Japan; British Petroleum, Royal Dutch Petroleum and Phillips G.N.V. of the Netherlands; and BMW and Siemens of Germany.

Table 14–1 lists the major global stock markets by country, alphabetically. Not all are large but most are flourishing, with growing volume, new listings, and increased interest by investors worldwide.

As more companies have their common stock listed on exchanges around the world, the easier it will be for trading to be continuous for 24 hours per day. Already several exchanges have linked their trading floors so

Table 14–1
Global stock markets

Australia	Mexico
Austria	Netherlands
Belgium	Norway
Canada	Singapore/Malaysia
Denmark	Spain
France	Sweden
Germany	Switzerland
Hong Kong	United Kingdom
Italy	United States
Japan	

trading can be maintained at all hours of the day. For example, the Chicago Mercantile Exchange, which specializes in metals, foreign exchange currencies, and interest rate futures contracts, has instituted 24-hour computer trading by linking with Reuters Holding PLC. This new system will enable customers around the world to trade financial futures products when their own exchange is closed. Other systems patterned after this could begin to show up in stock and bond markets during the next five years.

The Over-the-Counter Markets

Corporations trading in the over-the-counter market (OTC) are referred to as unlisted. This is primarily a domestic market. There is no central location for the OTC market; instead, a network of dealers all over the country is linked by computer display terminals, telephones, and teletypes. The difference between *dealers* in the OTC markets and *brokers* on exchanges is that dealers own the securities they trade, while brokers act as agents for the buyers and sellers. Dealers are much like any wholesaler or retailer who possesses an inventory of goods. They price the goods to reflect their cost and to manage their inventory by seeking a balance between supply and demand.

Many dealers make markets in the same security, and this creates very competitive prices. With the advent of a centralized computer to keep track of all trades and prices, dealers have up-to-the-minute price information on all competing dealers. Many people currently think that the structure of the OTC market is more competitive and cost efficient than organized exchanges.

At least 5,000 stocks are actively traded over-the-counter, but the average price of the securities is low, so the dollar volume of the stocks traded is not as great as that of the organized exchanges. The OTC markets are supervised by the National Association of Securities Dealers (NASD). In recent years the NASD has divided the OTC market into various groupings based on size and trading requirements. The segment with the biggest companies is the National Market List, followed by the National List and Supplemental List. These categories make it easier to distinguish between various-sized companies. The National Market List would include such companies as Apple Computer, MCI Communications, Intel, Coors, Lotus Development, and so on, while the National List would include smaller companies centered in one city or state, such as Bancorp Mississippi. The Supplemental List would include very small developmental companies, with stock priced as low as 25¢ per share, or companies that are closely held by the founders, with very few shares available for trading. The NASD estimates that at least 600 companies trading on the National Market List would meet the listing requirements of the New York Stock Exchange.

Although the AMEX and NYSE both trade corporate bonds and a small number of government securities, the bulk of all bond trading is done over-the-counter. Trading in government bonds, notes, and Treasury bills through government security dealers makes the OTC the largest market of all for security transactions in total dollars (though the NYSE is clearly the largest for just stocks).

Market Efficiency

We have mentioned competitive and efficient markets in this chapter, but so far we have not given any criteria to judge whether the U.S. securities markets are indeed competitive and efficient.

Criteria of Efficiency

There are several concepts of market efficiency and there are many degrees of efficiency, depending on which market we are talking about. Markets in general are efficient when: (1) prices adjust rapidly to new information; (2) there is a continuous market, in which each successive trade is made at a price close to the previous price (the faster that the price responds to new information and the smaller the differences in price changes, the more efficient the market); and (3) the market can absorb large dollar amounts of securities without destabilizing the price.

A key variable affecting efficiency is the certainty of the income stream. The more certain the expected income, the less volatile price movements will be. Fixed-income securities, with known maturities, have reasonably efficient markets. The most efficient market is that for U.S. government securities, with the short-term Treasury bill market being exemplary. Corporate bond markets are somewhat efficient, but less so than government bond markets. A question that is still widely debated and researched by academics is the degree of efficiency for common stock.

The Efficient Market Hypothesis

If stock markets are efficient, it is very difficult for investors to select portfolios of common stocks that can outperform the stock market in general. The efficient market hypothesis is stated in three forms—the weak, semistrong, and strong.

The weak form simply states that past price information is unrelated to future prices, and that trends cannot be predicted and taken advantage of by investors. The semistrong form states that prices currently reflect all *public* information. Most of the research in this area focuses on changes in public information and on the measurement of how rapidly prices converge to a new equilibrium after new information has been released. The strong form states that all information, *both private and public,* is immediately reflected in stock prices.

Generally researchers have indicated that markets are efficient in the weak and semistrong sense (with some exceptions), but not in the strong sense (private, insider information is valuable—though generally illegal to use for quick profits).

Our objective in bringing up this subject is to make you aware that much current research is focused on the measurement of market efficiency. As communications systems advance, information gets disseminated faster and more accurately. Furthermore, securities laws are forcing fuller disclosure of corporate data. It would appear that our security markets are generally efficient, but not perfect, in digesting information and adjusting stock prices.

Regulation of the Security Markets

Organized securities markets are regulated by the Securities and Exchange Commission (SEC) and by the self-regulation of the exchanges. The OTC market is controlled by the National Association of Securities Dealers. Three major laws govern the sale and subsequent trading of securities. The Securities Act of 1933 pertains to new issues of securities, while the Securities Exchange Act of 1934 deals with trading in the securities markets. The latest legislation is the Securities Acts amendments of 1975, whose main emphasis is on a national securities market. The primary purpose of these laws is to protect unwary investors from fraud and manipulation and to make the markets more competitive and efficient by forcing corporations to make relevant investment information public.

Securities Act of 1933

The Securities Act of 1933 was enacted after congressional investigations of the abuses present in the securities markets during the 1929 crash. Its primary purpose was to provide full disclosure of all pertinent investment information whenever a corporation sold a new issue of securities. For this reason, it is sometimes referred to as the truth-in-securities act. The Securities Act of 1933 has several important features, which follow:

1. All offerings except government bonds and bank stocks that are to be sold in more than one state must be registered with the SEC.[3]
2. The registration statement must be filed 20 days in advance of the date of sale and must include detailed corporate information.[4] If the SEC finds the information misleading, incomplete, or inaccurate, it will delay the offering until the registration statement is corrected. The SEC in no way certifies that the security is fairly priced, but only that the information seems to be accurate.
3. All new issues of securities must be accompanied by a prospectus containing the same information appearing in the registration statement. Usually included in the prospectus are a list of directors and officers; their salaries, stock options, and shareholdings; financial reports certified by a CPA; a list of the underwriters; the purpose and use of the funds to be provided from the sales of securities; and any other reasonable information that investors may need before they can wisely invest their money. A preliminary prospectus may be distributed to potential buyers before the offering date, but it will not contain the offering price or the underwriting fees. It is called a "red herring" because stamped on the front in red letters are the words *preliminary prospectus*.
4. For the first time, officers of the company and other experts preparing the prospectus or the registration statement could be sued for penalties and recovery of realized losses if any information presented was fraudulent, factually wrong, or omitted.

Securities Exchange Act of 1934

This act created the Securities and Exchange Commission to enforce the securities laws. The SEC was empowered to regulate the securities markets

---

[3]Actually the SEC was not established until 1934. References to the SEC in this section refer to 1934 to the present. The FTC performed these functions in 1933.

[4]Shelf registration, which was initiated by the SEC in 1982, changes this provision somewhat. Shelf registration is discussed in Chapter 15.

and those companies listed on the exchanges. Specifically, the major points of the Securities Exchange Act of 1934 are:

1. Guidelines for inside trading were established. Insiders must hold securities for at least six months before they can sell them. This is to prevent them from taking quick advantage of information, which could result in a short-term profit. All short-term profits are payable to the corporation.[5] Insiders were at first generally thought to be officers, directors, employees, or relatives. In the late 1960s, however, the SEC widened its interpretation to include anyone having information that was not public knowledge. This could include security analysts, loan officers, large institutional holders, and many others who had business dealings with the firm.
2. The Federal Reserve's Board of Governors became responsible for setting margin requirements to determine how much credit would be available to purchasers of securities.
3. Manipulation of securities by conspiracies among investors was prohibited.
4. The SEC was given control over the proxy procedures of corporations (a proxy is an absent stockholder's vote).
5. In its regulation of companies traded on the markets, the SEC required that certain reports be filed periodically. Corporations must file quarterly financial statements and annual 10K reports with the SEC and send annual reports to stockholders. The 10K report has more financial data than the annual report and can be very useful to an investor or a loan officer. Most companies will now send 10K reports to stockholders on request.
6. The act required all security exchanges to register with the SEC. In this capacity, the SEC supervises and regulates many pertinent organizational aspects of exchanges, such as the mechanics of listing and trading.

The Securities Acts Amendments of 1975

The major focus of the Securities Acts amendments of 1975 was to direct the SEC to supervise the development of a national securities market.

---

[5] In the mid-1980s, Congress and the SEC passed legislation to make the penalty three times the size of the gain.

No exact structure was put forth, but the law did assume that any national market would make extensive use of computers and electronic communication devices. In addition, the law prohibited fixed commissions on public transactions and also prohibited banks, insurance companies, and other financial institutions from buying stock exchange memberships to save commission costs for their own institutional transactions. This act is a worthwhile addition to the securities laws, since it fosters greater competition and more efficient prices. Much progress has already been made on the national market system as mandated by this act.

Current Legislative Issues

In the late 1980s, a wave of new legislation is also being considered to further deal with the abuses of insider trading. The scandals surrounding the massive profits accumulated by Wall Street traders Ivan Boesky, Dennis Levine, and others, as a result of using improperly acquired information, has triggered the congressional interest. While most of these people have been successfully prosecuted, a fear remains that the small trader may be at a competitive disadvantage when it comes to privileged information. It is anticipated that broader interpretations and tougher rules against insider trading may be forthcoming.

Another development of the late 1980s has been the use of program trading by large institutional investors (such as mutual funds, pension funds, and bank trust departments). Program trading means that computer-based trigger points in the market are established by these traders for unusually big orders to buy or sell securities. If a large number of institutional investors engage in program trading at the same time (and all are either buying or selling), there is the potential for a market crash (such as on October 19, 1987) or an incredible market rise. Many government regulators are looking into the process of program trading, with an eye toward future legislation. Perhaps appropriate industry cooperation will head off new laws in this area—only time will tell.

Summary

In this chapter we presented the concept of a capital market, in which corporations compete for funds not only among themselves but with governmental units of all kinds. Corporations only account for about 40 percent of all funds raised in the capital market, and most of that is obtained through the sale of corporate debt. We also depicted a three-sector economy, consisting of households, corporations, and governmental units, and showed how funds flow through the capital markets from suppliers of funds to the ultimate users. This process is highly dependent upon the efficiency of the financial institutions that act as intermediaries in channeling the funds to the most productive users.

Security markets are divided into organized exchanges and over-the-counter markets. Brokers act as agents for stock exchange transactions, and dealers make markets over-the-counter at their own risk as owners of the securities they trade. The New York Stock Exchange is the largest of the organized exchanges. We explored some of its major characteristics, such as its relative size, the liquidity it provides corporations and investors, and its requirements for listing securities. Although the OTC market for stock is not as large as that of the organized exchanges, a majority of corporate bond trades and almost all trades in municipal and federal government securities are transacted over-the-counter.

Throughout this chapter we have tried to present the concept of efficient markets doing an important job in allocating financial capital. We find that the existing markets provide liquidity for both the corporation and the investor, and that they are efficient in adjusting to new information. Because of the laws governing the markets, much information is available for investors, and this in itself creates more competitive prices. In the future, we expect even more efficient markets, with a national market system using the best of both the NYSE and OTC trading systems.

List of Terms

money markets	dual trading
capital markets	listing requirements
U.S. Treasury securities	regional stock exchanges
municipal securities	over-the-counter (OTC)
federally sponsored	markets
agency securities	National Market List
internal corporate funds	brokers
external corporate funds	dealers
financial intermediaries	market efficiency
three-sector economy	Securities Act of 1933
secondary trading	Securities Exchange Act of 1934
New York Stock Exchange	Securities Acts amendments of
National Association	1975
of Securities Dealers	Securities and Exchange Com-
(NASD)	mission (SEC)
American Stock Exchange	

Discussion Questions

1. Name the major competitors for funds in the capital markets.

2. Why has the use of long-term financing by the government been so high since 1976? How might the Gramm-Rudman legislation potentially affect this, in the late 1980s and 1990s?

3. What are two key areas in which federally sponsored credit agencies make loans?

4. What has been the percentage composition of long-term financing by corporations from 1970 through 1986?

5. Historically, what industry has had the largest user of stock offerings? What segment of the economy became particularly important to stock offerings in the 1980s and reached 50 percent of the market in 1986?

6. As an internal source of funds, are retained earnings the most important item?

7. Explain the role of financial intermediaries in the flow of funds through the economy.

8. Discuss the importance of security markets for both the corporation and the stockholder or bondholder.

9. What is the difference between organized exchanges and over-the-counter markets?

10. Why does the New York Stock Exchange have listing requirements? What are the major requirements? How do they compare with the listing requirements of the other exchanges?

11. What is the largest security exchange in the world? Suggest three U.S. companies that trade on foreign exchanges.

12. Into what three groupings has the OTC market been divided by the National Association of Security Dealers (NASD)?

13. How would you define efficient security markets?

14. The efficient market hypothesis is interpreted in a weak form, a semistrong form, and a strong form. How can we differentiate its various forms?

15. Why is the 24-hour trading day becoming progressively more important?

16. Discuss the major implications of the Securities Act of 1933 and the Securities Exchange Act of 1934.

17. Why has there been a renewed interest in regulating insider trading in the 1980s?

Problem

1. Go to the latest issue of the *Federal Reserve Bulletin* and see whether you can update Figures 14–1 and 14–2.

Selected References

Dann, Larry Y.; David Myers; and Robert J. Raab. "Trading Rules, Large Blocks, and the Speed of Price Adjustment." *Journal of Financial Economics* 4 (January 1977), pp. 3–22.

Hempel, George; Bill Marshall; and Jess Yawitz. "The Use of Average Maturity as a Risk Proxy in Investment Portfolios." *Journal of Finance* 30 (May 1975), pp. 325–33.

Howe, John S., and Kathryn Kelm. "The Stock Price Impacts of Overseas Listings." *Financial Management* 16 (Autumn 1987), pp. 51–56.

Jensen, Michael C. "Some Anomalous Evidence Regarding Market Efficiency." *Journal of Financial Economics* 5 (June/September 1978).

Lease, Ronald C.; Wilbur G. Lewellen; and Gary G. Schlarbaum. "The Individual Investor: Attributes and Attitudes." In *Issues in Managerial Finance.* Hinsdale, Ill.: Dryden, 1976, pp. 175–98.

Marsh, Paul. "The Choice between Equity and Debt: An Empirical Study." *Journal of Finance* 37 (March 1982), pp. 121–44.

Oppenheimer, Henry, and Gary Schlarbaum. "Investing with Ben Graham: An Ex Ante Test of the Efficient Markets Hypothesis." *Journal of Financial and Quantitative Analysis* 16 (September 1981), pp. 341–60.

Ritter, Lawrence S. *The Flow of Funds Accounts: A Framework for Financial Analysis.* New York: Institute of Finance, New York University, 1968.

———. **and William L. Silber.** *Principles of Money, Banking, and Financial Markets.* New York: Basic Books, 1974.

Selected issues of the *Federal Reserve Bulletin.*

Sweeney, Richard J., and Arthur D. Worga. "The Pricing of Interest Rate Risk: Evidence from the Stock Market." *Journal of Finance* 41 (June 1986), pp. 393–410.

15

Investment Banking: Public and Private Placement

In Chapter 15 we will examine the role of the investment banker, the advantages and disadvantages of selling securities to the public, and the private placement of securities with insurance companies, pension funds, and other lenders. Illustrative material is presented about many companies involved in financing issues.

The Role of Investment Banking

The investment banker is the great link between the corporation in need of funds and the investor. As a middleman, the investment banker is responsible for designing and packaging a security offering and selling the securities to the public. The investment banking fraternity has long been thought of as an elite group—with appropriate memberships in the country club, the yacht club, and other such venerable institutions. Several changes have taken place in the investment banking industry over the last 10 years.

Competition has become the new way of doing business, in which the fittest survive and prosper, while others drop out of the game. Raising capital has become an international proposition, and firms need to be very large to compete. Salomon Brothers has been the biggest U.S. investment banker for many years, and its growth reflects the trends in the whole industry. In 1983, Salomon was the lead underwriter for $15.76 billion of security offerings and, four years later, in 1987, it was the lead underwriter for over $50 billion. This extreme growth is a result of the longest peacetime economic growth since the 1930s and of the need of corporations to finance the modernization and expansion of their plant and equipment. In the next section we look at the many functions an investment banker performs.

Enumeration of Functions

As a middleman in the distribution of securities, the investment banker plays a number of key roles.

Underwriter   In most cases the investment banker is a risk taker. He will contract to buy securities from the corporation and resell them to other security dealers and the public. By giving a "firm commitment" to purchase the securities from the corporation, he is said to *underwrite* any risks that might be associated with a new issue. While the risk may be fairly low in handling a bond offering for Exxon or General Electric in a stable market, such may not be the case in selling the shares of a less-known firm in a very volatile market environment.

Though most large, well-established investment bankers would not consider managing a public offering without assuming the risk of distribution, smaller investment houses may handle distributions for relatively unknown corporations on a "best-efforts" or commission basis. Some issuing companies even choose to sell their own securities directly. Both the "best efforts" and "direct" methods account for a relatively small portion of total offerings. Table 15–1 shows the distribution of corporate securities by method of sale for registered securities.

Table 15–1   Corporate securities issues by method of distribution ($ millions)

	Underwritten			Best Efforts Offering			Direct by Issuer		
	Debt	*Preferred Stock*	*Common Stock*	*Debt*	*Preferred Stock*	*Common Stock*	*Debt*	*Preferred Stock*	*Common Stock*
1986	45,340	9,724	29,736	420	11	10,839	1,753	8	2,773
1985	32,288	5,009	17,103	480	5	9,289	308	49	2,322
1984	21,770	3,258	6,128	218	9	8,227	520	167	2,253
1983	16,110	4,742	20,053	153	16	8,448	342	33	2,182
1982	21,874	4,530	10,696	1,346	13	8,644	2,591	13	1,566

Source: Securities and Exchange Commission.

Market maker During distribution and in later time periods, the investment banker may make a market in a given security—that is, engage in the buying and selling of the security to ensure a liquid market. He may also provide research on the firm to encourage active investor interest.

Adviser The investment banker may advise clients on a continuing basis about the types of securities to be sold, the number of shares or units for distribution, and the timing of the sale. A company considering a stock issuance to the public may be persuaded, in counsel with an investment banker, to borrow the funds from an insurance company or, if stock is to be sold, to wait for two more quarters of earnings before going to the market. The investment banker also provides important advisory services in the area of mergers and acquisitions, leveraged buy-outs, and corporate restructuring.

Agency functions The investment banker may act as an agent for a corporation that wishes to place its securities privately with an insurance company, a pension fund, or a wealthy individual. In this instance, the investment banker will shop around among potential investors and negotiate the best possible deal for the corporation. He may also serve as an agent in merger and acquisition transactions. Because of the many critical roles that the investment banker plays, he may be requested to sit on the board of directors of the client company.

The Distribution Process

The actual distribution process requires the active participation of a number of parties. The principal or managing investment banker will call upon other investment banking houses to share the burden of risk and to aid in the distribution. To this end, they will form an underwriting syndicate comprising as few as 2 or as many as 100 investment banking houses. In Figure 15–1, we see a typical case in which a hypothetical firm, the Maxwell Corporation, wishes to issue 250,000 additional shares of stock with Merrill Lynch as the managing underwriter and an underwriting syndicate of 15 firms.

The underwriting syndicate will purchase shares from the Maxwell Corporation and distribute them through the channels of distribution. Syndicate members will act as wholesalers in distributing the shares to brokers and dealers who will eventually sell the shares to the public. Large investment banking houses may be vertically integrated, acting as underwriter-dealer-broker and capturing all fees and commissions.

**Figure 15–1
Distribution process
in investment
banking**

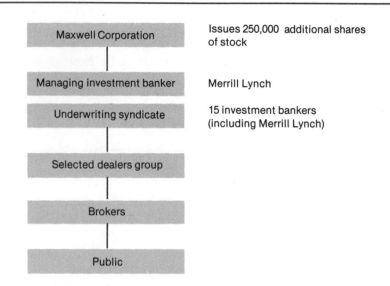

Issues 250,000 additional shares
of stock

Merrill Lynch

15 investment bankers
(including Merrill Lynch)

The spread   The spread represents the total compensation for those who
participate in the distribution process. If the public or retail price is $21.50
and the managing investment banker pays a price of $20.00 to the issuing
company, we say there is a total spread of $1.50. The $1.50 may be
divided up among the participants, as indicated in Figure 15–2.

Note that the lower a party falls in the distribution process, the higher
the price for shares. The managing investment banker pays $20, while
dealers pay $20.75. Also, the farther down the line the securities are
resold, the higher is the potential profit. If the managing investment
banker resells to dealers, he makes 75 cents per share; if he resells to the
public, he makes $1.50.

**Figure 15–2
Allocation of
underwriting spread**

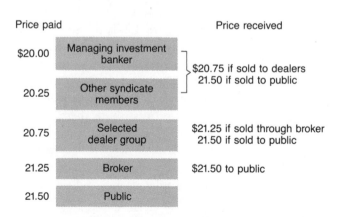

The total spread of $1.50 in the present case represents 7 percent of the offering price ($1.50/$21.50). Generally, the larger the dollar value of an issue, the smaller the spread is as a percentage of the offering price. Percentage figures on underwriting spreads for U.S. corporations are presented in Table 15–2. Because there is more uncertainty in the market reaction to common stock, a larger spread often exists for common stock than for other types of offerings.

**Table 15–2
Underwriting compensation as a percentage of proceeds**

Size of Issue ($ millions)	Spread	
	Common Stock	Debt
Under 0.5	11.3%	7.4%
0.5–0.9	9.7	7.2
1.0–1.9	8.6	7.0
2.0–4.9	7.4	4.2
5.0–9.9	6.7	1.5
10.0–19.9	6.2	1.0
20.0–49.9	4.9	1.0
50.0 and over . . .	2.3	0.8

Source: Securities and Exchange Commission data.

Since the Maxwell Corporation stock issue is for $5.375 million (250,000 shares × $21.50), the 7 percent spread is in line with SEC figures in Table 15–2. It should be noted that the issuer bears not only the "give-up" expense of the spread in the underwriting process but also out-of-pocket costs related to legal and accounting fees, printing expenses, and so forth. On a small issue, these may represent 6–8 percent of the value of the issue. As indicated in Table 15–3, when the spread plus the out-

**Table 15–3
Total costs to issue stock (percentage of total proceeds)**

Size of Issue ($ millions)	Common Stock		
	Spread	Out-of-Pocket Cost*	Total Expense
Under 0.5	11.3%	7.3%	18.6%
0.5–0.9	9.7	4.9	14.6
1.0–1.9	8.6	3.0	11.6
2.0–4.9	7.4	1.7	9.1
5.0–9.9	6.7	1.0	7.7
10.0–19.9	6.2	0.6	6.8
20.0–49.9	4.9	0.8	5.7
50.0 and over	2.3	0.3	2.6

*Out-of-pocket cost of debts is approximately the same.

Source: Securities and Exchange Commission data.

of-pocket costs are considered, the total cost of a new issue is rather high. Of course, substantial benefits may be received in return.

Pricing the Security

Because the syndicate members purchase the stock for redistribution in the marketing channels, they must be careful about the pricing of the stock. When a stock is sold to the public for the first time (i.e., the firm is going public), the managing investment banker will do an in-depth analysis of the company to determine its value. The study will include an analysis of the firm's industry, financial characteristics, and anticipated earnings and dividend-paying capability. Based on appropriate valuation techniques, a price will be tentatively assigned and will be compared to that enjoyed by similar firms in a given industry. If the industry's average price–earnings ratio is 12, the firm should not stray too far from this norm. Anticipated public demand will also be a major factor in pricing a new issue.

The great majority of the issues handled by investment bankers are, however, additional issues of stocks or bonds for companies already trading publicly. When additional shares are to be issued, the investment bankers will generally set the price at slightly below the current market value. This process, known as underpricing, will help ensure a receptive market for the securities.

At times an investment banker will also handle large blocks of securities for existing stockholders. Because the number of shares may be too large to trade in normal channels, the investment banker will manage the issue and underprice the stock below current prices to the public. Such a process is known as a secondary offering, in contrast to a primary offering, in which new corporate securities are sold.

Dilution

A problem a company faces when issuing additional securities is the actual or perceived dilutive effect on shares currently outstanding. In the case of the Maxwell Corporation, the 250,000 new shares may represent a 10 percent increment to shares currently in existence. Perhaps the firm had earnings of $5 million on 2,500,000 shares prior to the offering, indicating earnings per share of $2. With 250,000 new shares to be issued, earnings per share will temporarily slip to $1.82.

Of course, the proceeds from the sale of new shares may well be expected to provide the increased earnings necessary to bring earnings back to at least $2. While financial theory dictates that a new equity issue should not be undertaken if it diminishes the overall wealth of current stockholders, there may be a perceived time lag in the recovery of earnings per share as a result of the increased shares outstanding. For this reason, there may be a temporary weakness in a stock when an issue of additional shares is proposed. In most cases, this is overcome with the passage of time.

Market Stabilization

Another problem may set in when the actual public distribution begins—namely, unanticipated weakness in the stock or bond market. Since the sales group normally has made a firm commitment to purchase stock at a given price for redistribution, it is essential that the price of the stock remain relatively strong. Syndicate members, committed to purchasing the stock at $20 or better, could be in trouble if the sales price fell to $19 or $18. The managing investment banker is generally responsible for stabilizing the offering during the distribution period and may accomplish this by repurchasing securities as the market price moves below the initial public offering price of $21.50.

The period of stabilization usually lasts two or three days after the initial offering, but it may extend up to 30 days for difficult-to-distribute securities. In a very poor market environment, stabilization may be virtually impossible to achieve. As a classic example, when Federal Reserve Board Chairman Paul Volcker announced an extreme credit-tightening policy in October 1979, newly underwritten, high-quality IBM bond prices fell dramatically and Salomon Brothers and other investment bankers got trapped into approximately $10 million in losses. The bonds later recovered in value, but the investment bankers had already taken their losses.

Aftermarket

The investment banker is also interested in how well the underwritten security behaves after the distribution period—for his ultimate reputation rests on bringing strong securities to the market. This is particularly true of initial public offerings.

Research has indicated that initial public offerings often do well in the immediate aftermarket. For example, one study examined approximately 500 firms and determined that there were 10.9 percent excess returns one week after issue (excess returns refers to movement in the price of the stock above and beyond the market). There were also positive excess returns of 11.6 percent for a full month after issue, but a negative market-adjusted performance of -3.0 percent one full year after issue.[1] Because the managing underwriter may underprice the issue initially to ensure a successful offering, quite often there is a jump in value after the issue first goes public. However, the efficiency of the market eventually takes hold, and sustained long-term performance is very much dependent on the quality of the issue and the market conditions at play.

Changes in the Investment Banking Industry

The investment banking function has been rapidly expanding. The growth in investment banking revenue has not been predominantly in the under-writing area, but rather in other functions performed. Major increases have taken place in corporate finance and merger/acquisition advisory services. Additionally, investment banking is becoming more internationally oriented, causing many firms (such as First Boston) to become global in nature.

The investment banking industry has remained fiercely competitive on the basis of performance. Furthermore, there has been a tremendous move toward vertical integration. Firms that were at one time primarily investment bankers, specializing in underwriting and corporate client services, have moved into more broadly based brokerage distribution services. Even more significant is the backward vertical integration that has taken place, as retail brokerage firms have acquired investment banking houses. As an example of the latter, in the late 1970s Merrill Lynch acquired White Weld & Company, a firm prominent in the investment banking industry.

In the early 1980s, nonbrokerage firms moved into the brokerage area through acquisitions. Since the acquired brokerage houses were also engaged in investment banking activities, acquiring firms obtained investment banking capabilities as well. The merger of Prudential Insurance Company with Bache Halsey Stuart Shields was the first of these types of mergers. In retrospect, as of year-end 1987, Prudential and Sears (who acquired Dean Witter Reynolds) are both having problems generating significant profits from their brokerage and investment banking acquisitions. Only American Express, which acquired the retail brokers Shear-

---

[1]Frank K. Reilly, "New Issues Revisited," *Financial Management* 6 (Winter 1977), pp. 28–42.

son Loeb Rhoades and E. F. Hutton and the investment banker Lehman Brothers, is having some success with the merged firms. However, these acquisitions spurred traditional securities firms, such as Merrill Lynch, First Boston, and others to accelerate their expansion plans and expand their staffs over the last 10 years.

As previously mentioned, a major change occurring during the 1980s in the investment banking industry is the shift in emphasis from underwriting new security issues to mergers and acquisitions. By the end of 1987, mergers and acquisition work created more profits for investment bankers than underwriting.

Perhaps the biggest change encompassing the investment banking industry is the consolidation of large financial resources among a few very large investment bankers. Table 15–4 shows the consolidation of capital and clout with a few houses. Salomon Brothers was the lead manager of $53.6 billion in public securities issues in 1986, but First Boston was close behind. The next four places were almost a dead heat, with Morgan Stanley, Merrill Lynch, Goldman Sachs, and Drexel Burnham separated by "only" $2.8 billion. Salomon Brothers did almost 12 times more business than the tenth place firm, Prudential-Bache. Table 15–4 shows that the firms specialize in certain areas of underwriting. For example, Goldman Sachs was in first place in the sale of common stock, and Drexel Burnham dominated the high-yield junk bond market. Salomon Brothers had a wide lead in the sale of mortgage-backed securities, and First Boston was far out in front in the asset-backed securities area (see Chapter 8 for examples of asset-backed securities).

Table 15–4
Leading underwriters for U.S. issuers in 1986 ($ billions)

Lead Manager	Total Amount	Common Stock	Preferred Stock and Debt			
			Mortgage Backed	Asset Backed	Junk Bonds	Other
Salomon Brothers . . .	$53.6	$4.1	$18.0	$0.8	$ 2.4	$28.3
First Boston	47.0	2.3	12.3	9.0	1.5	21.9
Morgan Stanley	33.2	3.1	4.3	—	2.3	23.6
Merrill Lynch	31.4	4.4	8.0	—	3.2	16.1
Goldman Sachs	31.0	4.9	2.8	—	1.5	22.3
Drexel Burnham	30.4	2.7	1.4	0.2	14.6	11.5
Shearson Lehman . . .	19.9	3.2	4.1	—	2.0	10.6
Kidder Peabody	10.5	1.8	3.1	—	0.8	4.8
Paine Webber	5.1	1.4	1.2	—	0.5	2.0
Prudential-Bache . . .	4.5	1.9	1.5	—	0.5	0.6

Source: *The Wall Street Journal,* January 5, 1987.

Shelf Registration

In February of 1982, the Securities and Exchange Commission began allowing a new filing process, called shelf registration, under SEC Rule 415. Shelf registration permits large companies, such as Exxon or Polaroid, to file one comprehensive registration statement, which outlines the firm's financing plans for up to the next two years. Then, when market conditions seem appropriate, the firm can issue the securities without further SEC approval. Future issues are thought to be sitting on the shelf, waiting for the appropriate time to appear.

Shelf registration is at variance with the traditional requirement that security issuers file a detailed registration statement for SEC review and approval each and every time they plan a sale. Whether investors are deprived of important "current" information as a result of shelf registration is difficult to judge. While shelf registration was started on an experimental basis by the SEC in 1982, it has now become a permanent part of the underwriting process. Shelf registration has been most frequently used with debt issues, with relatively less utilization in the equity markets (corporations do not wish to announce equity dilution in advance).

Shelf registration has contributed to the concentrated nature of the investment banking business, previously discussed. The strong firms are acquiring more and more business, and, in some cases, are less dependent on large syndications to handle debt issues. Only investment banking firms with a big capital base and substantial expertise are in a position to benefit from this new registration process.

Public versus Private Financing

Our discussion to this point has assumed that the firm was distributing stocks or bonds in the public markets (through the organized exchanges or over-the-counter, as explained in Chapter 14). However, many companies, by choice or circumstance, prefer to remain private in nature—restricting their financial activities to direct negotiations with bankers, insurance companies, and so forth. Let us evaluate the advantages and the disadvantages of public versus private financing and then explore the avenues open to a privately financed firm.

Advantages of Being Public

First of all, the corporation may tap the security markets for a greater amount of funds by selling securities directly to the public. With over

45 million individual stockholders in the country, combined with thousands of institutional investors, the greatest pool of funds is channeled toward publicly traded securities. Furthermore, the attendant prestige of a public security may be helpful in bank negotiations, executive recruitment, and the marketing of products. Some corporations listed on the New York Stock Exchange actually allow stockholders a discount on the purchase of their product lines.

Stockholders of a heretofore private corporation may also sell part of their holdings if the corporation decides to go public. A million-share offering may contain 500,000 authorized but unissued corporate shares (a primary offering) and 500,000 existing stockholder shares (a secondary offering). The stockholder is able to achieve a higher degree of liquidity and to diversify his or her portfolio. A publicly traded stock with an established price may also be helpful for estate planning purposes.

Finally, going public allows the firm to play the merger game, using marketable securities for the purchase of other firms. The high visibility of a public offering may even make the firm a potential recipient of attractive offers for its own securities. (This, of course, may not be viewed as an advantage by some firms that do not wish to be acquired.)

Disadvantages of Being Public

The company must make all information available to the public through SEC and state filings. Not only is this tedious, time consuming, and expensive, but important corporate information on profit margins and product lines must be divulged. The president must adapt himself to being a public relations representative to all interested members of the securities industry.

Another disadvantage of being public is the tremendous pressure for short-term performance placed on the firm by security analysts and large institutional investors. Quarter-to-quarter earnings reports can become more important to top management than providing a long-run stewardship for the company. A capital budgeting decision calling for the selection of Alternative A—carrying a million dollars higher net present value than Alternative B—may be discarded in favor of the latter because Alternative B adds two cents more to next quarter's earnings per share.

In a number of cases, the blessings of having a publicly quoted security may become quite the opposite. Although a security may have had an enthusiastic reception in a strong "new-issues" market, such as that of 1961–62, 1967–68, or 1981–83, a dramatic erosion in value may later take place, causing embarrassment and anxiety for stockholders and employers.

A final disadvantage is the high cost of going public. As indicated in Table 15–3, for issues under a million dollars the underwriting spread plus the out-of-pocket cost may run in the 15 to 18 percent range.

Public Offerings

A Classic Example of Instant Wealth—EDS Goes Public

Some people are probably more familiar with Apple Computer and Steven Jobs's millionaire status than they are with Electronic Data Systems (EDS) and H. Ross Perot. Perot's success story makes Jobs's pale by comparison. In September 1968, Perot took EDS public, and within one month he found himself worth $300 million. This was no small accomplishment for a man who, six years earlier, had been an IBM salesman with only a few thousand dollars in the bank and a degree from the Naval Academy.

The original EDS offering—managed by P. W. Presprich, a New York investment banker—was at 118 times current earnings (the norm was 10 to 12 times earnings). After one month in the hot new-issues market of 1967–68, the stock was trading at over 200 times earnings. A company with earnings of only $1.5 million had a market value well over $300 million, exceeding many of Fortune's 500 largest companies. By 1970, EDS had a quoted market value of $1.5 billion. All of this was accomplished by a firm with a few hundred employees.

It is interesting to note that Perot's main concern in the initial pricing of his stock was not to set too low a value. In the strong new-issues market of the period, too many computer issues, which had been underpriced when they first crossed the tape, quickly doubled or tripled in price. Perot considered this an irrevocable loss to original shareholders, who initially sold large blocks of their holdings. He was determined to avoid this by fully pricing his stock and only trading a small percentage of the total capitalization on the initial offering (only 650,000 shares out of 11.5 million). Even at a price–earnings ratio of 118 at initial trading, the stock jumped from $16.50 to $23 in one day.[2]

In the bear markets of the 1970s, EDS suffered more than most companies, and its stock price declined from a high of $161 per share in 1970 to a low of $12 ½ in 1974. Total market value retreated from a high of $1.5 billion to about $200 million. After recovering to $50 per share in

---

[2]A. M. Louis, "Fastest Richest Texan Ever," *Fortune*, November 1968, pp. 168–70.

1983, Perot sold EDS to General Motors Corporation in 1984 for $2.5 billion, and stockholders received Class E common stock of General Motors (discussed more fully in Chapter 17). Perot became the largest single shareholder of General Motors through his ownership of Class E shares and was elected to the board of directors. By 1986, GM tired of Perot's criticism of corporate policy and, in a very controversial move, it bought out his shares of stock and he resigned from the board.

Rockefeller Center Properties, Inc.

The offering of Rockefeller Center Properties, Inc., is one of the biggest initial public offerings of common stock to date and gave the world an inside look at the Rockefeller family's real estate empire, which was largely tied up in New York's Rockefeller Center. On September 13, 1985, an offering of 37.5 million shares of Rockefeller Center Properties took place at $20 per share for a grand total of $750 million. The offering set up public ownership (60 percent) along with the Rockefeller family (40 percent) of a public real estate investment trust stock traded on the New York Stock Exchange.

The Rockefeller example is in contrast to the EDS example in several ways. The primary reason for the offering was the Rockefeller family's need for money. There are 79 living descendants of John D. Rockefeller, Jr., and most of their assets (especially the younger generation) had been tied up in the 1934 trusts set up by John D. Rockefeller. Unfortunately, the cash flow from these trusts was very small, compared to the $1.6 billion size of the underlying assets. EDS, in contrast, raised money for corporate expansion, rather than family needs. Second, Rockefeller Properties has $1.6 billion of marketable assets as collateral, whereas EDS only had growth prospects with very few assets. Nevertheless, the EDS stock soared to new highs after the stock offering while Rockefeller Properties, in a raging bull market, only hit a high of $20 ⅜ (recall the offering price was $20) and only traded at 18 ¾ a year and a half later. In the Rockefeller case, it seems that the underwriters priced the initial offering of stock at a fully valued price of $20 per share.

Table 15–5 is the advertisement of the Rockefeller Center Properties, Inc., stock offering and depicts many of the characteristics of the distribution process discussed early in the chapter. The lead underwriters, Goldman, Sachs & Company and Shearson Lehman Brothers, Inc., are listed on line one. On the following lines the syndicate of investment bankers responsible for the selling and distribution of the common stock

Table 15-5

Source: An ad that appeared in *The Wall Street Journal*, September 13, 1985, p. 39.

are listed by size of their position. For example, Lazard Frères & Company, First Boston Corporation, Merrill Lynch Capital Markets, and Salomon Brothers, Inc., are responsible for millions of shares, while those companies listed on the last line, such as Stifel, Nicolaus & Company and Wood Gundy Corporation, would be responsible for only thousands of shares. Also, there is an international nature to the offering, with such firms as Deutsche Bank Capital, EuroPartners Securities Corporation, Swiss Bank Corporation International Securities, Inc., and Yamaichi International participating.

Private Placement

Private placement refers to the selling of securities directly to insurance companies, pension funds, and wealthy individuals, rather than through the security markets. This financing device may be employed by a growing firm that wishes to avoid or defer an initial public stock offering or by a publicly traded company that wishes to incorporate private funds into its financing package. Private placement usually takes the form of a debt instrument.

Figure 15–3 presents the history of publicly and privately placed bonds since 1964. We can see that publicly placed bonds are by far the most popular method of raising debt capital; but, as new bond issues increased during the 1984–86 period, the volume of privately placed issues was a significant amount ($61 billion dollars in 1986).

The advantages of private placement are worthy of note. First of all, there is no lengthy, expensive registration process with the SEC. Second, the firm has greater flexibility in negotiating with one or a handful of insurance companies, pension funds, or bankers than is possible in a public offering. Because there is no SEC registration or underwriting, the initial costs of a private placement may be considerably lower than those of a public issue. However, the interest rate is usually higher to compensate the investor for holding a less liquid obligation.

Going Private and Leveraged Buy-Outs

Throughout the years, there have always been some firms going from being public to being private. In the 1970s, a number of firms gave up their public listings to go private, but these were usually small firms.

**Figure 15–3
Public versus private
placement of bonds**

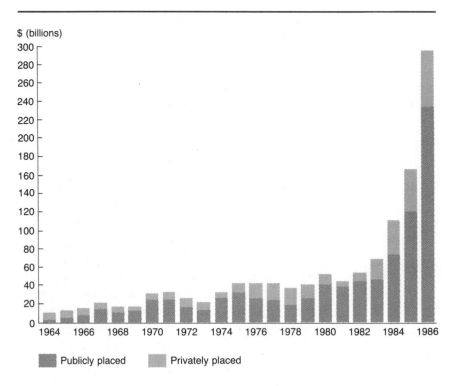

Management figured that it could save several hundred thousand dollars a year in annual report expenses, legal and auditing fees, and security analysts meetings—a significant amount for a small company.

In the 1980s, however, very large corporations have been going private and not just to save several hundred thousand dollars. More likely, they have a long-term strategy in mind.

There are basically two ways to accomplish going private. First, a publicly owned company can be purchased by a private company or, secondly, the company can repurchase all publicly traded shares from the stockholders. Both methods have been in vogue and are accomplished through the use of a leveraged buy-out. In a leveraged buy-out, either the management or some other investor group borrows the needed cash to repurchase all the shares of the company. After the repurchase, the company exists with a lot of debt and heavy interest expense. What worries many analysts is that the borrowing is done at banks, rather than through the securities markets. This may cause a misdirection of capital into nonproductive activities (leveraged buy-outs) instead of capital formation for new ventures and products. An additional fallout when a large firm goes private is that common stock outstanding tends to disappear, leaving fewer investment choices for investors.

Usually, management of the private company must sell off assets to reduce the debt load, and a corporate restructuring occurs, wherein divisions and products are sold and assets redeployed into new, higher-return areas. Over the long run, these strategies could be rewarding, and these companies could again become publicly owned. Table 15–6 lists nine firms going private in 1985, with prices in excess of one half billion dollars and a total value of over $14 billion.

By 1987, many of the companies that had gone private in 1985 or earlier could now be resold to the public at handsome profits. Table 15–7 presents a list of firms that had successfully managed leveraged buy-outs only to go public one or two years later. Two firms (Beatrice and Uniroyal) also appear in Table 15–6 as companies that went private in 1985. Notice that Beatrice sold the various parts of its company in pieces—Avis, Coke Bottling, International Playtex, and other businesses. In the case of Beatrice, the sum of the parts was worth more than the whole company all together.

Restructuring is one area that has attracted the expertise of investment bankers. As specialists in the valuation of assets, investment bankers try to determine the "breakup value" of a large company. This is its value if all its divisions were divided up and sold separately. When investors try to buy a company to take advantage of the breakup value, they bid the common stock price higher, creating more wealth for existing stockholders. While the existing stockholders all received prices for their shares higher than those that existed in the market before the buy-out, it is clear from Table 15–7 that there was extra profit available for the buy-out team when the firms were actually divided up and sold.

Table 15–6
Large firms going
private in 1985

	($ millions)
Beatrice Corporation	$ 6,200
Storer Communications, Inc.	2,510
Levi Strauss & Co.	1,450
Northwest Industries, Inc.	1,000
Uniroyal, Inc.	836
Denny's, Inc.	734
SCOA Industries	637
Scovill, Inc.	523
Parsons Corp.	518
Total value	$14,408

Table 15–7

Miraculous Changes in Market Value

COMPANY	*LBO PRICE DATE	VALUE WHEN TAKEN PUBLIC OR SOLD	PERCENTAGE INCREASE
BEATRICE	$6.2 billion 4/86	$10 billion (est.) Assets sold: Avis for $1.6 billion; Coke bottling unit for $1 billion; 80% of International Playtex for $1.25 billion; other businesses for $2.15 billion	61%
BLUE BELL	$470 billion 11/84	$792 million Sold to VF Corp. for $378 million in cash and stock plus assumption of $414 million in long-term debt	69%
DR PEPPER	$650 million 2/84	$866 million Assets sold: Canada Dry for $175 million; bottling plants and other businesses sold for $215 million; Dr Pepper sold for $416 million	33%
LESLIE FAY	$58 million 4/82	$360 million Taken public again 8/86	521%
LILY TULIP	$180 million 3/81	$326 million Sold to Owens-Illinois 4/86	81%
METROMEDIA	$1.1 billion 6/84	$6.5 billion (est.) Assets sold: seven TV stations for $2 billion; cellular radio business for $1.1 billion; other businesses worth $2.4 billion	490%
FRED MEYER	$420 million 12/81	$900 million (est.) Retailing operation worth $380 million when taken public 4/86; real estate estimated at over $500 million	114%
SFN	$450 million 2/85	$1.1 billion (est.) Assets sold: Scott Foresman for $520 million; South-Western Publishing for $270 million; TV and radio stations for $154 million	144%
UNIROYAL	$900 million 9/85	$1.4 billion (est.) Assets sales pending; chemicals business for $750 million; other businesses for $350 million; estimated net worth of the rest of the company is $422 million	55%

Since 1981, 260 public companies have gone private. Of those, some 30 or so have been taken public again or broken up and the assets sold off. The average increase in value for the 30 between being bought and being sold again is about 150%. Managers made out like gangbusters.

*LBO price stands for leveraged buy-out price or the price that was paid when the firm went private.

Source: *Fortune*, January 19, 1987, p. 104.

Summary

The role of the investment banker is critical to the distribution of securities in the U.S. economy. The investment banker serves as an underwriter or risk taker by purchasing the securities from the issuing corporation and redistributing them to the public, and he or she may continue to maintain a market in the distributed securities long after they have been sold to the public. The investment banking firm can also help a company sell a new issue on a "best efforts" basis. Investment bankers also serve as advisers to corporations and have become more important to corporations in the 1980s in providing advice on mergers, acquisitions, and leveraged buy-outs, and on resisting hostile takeover attempts.

The advantages of selling securities in the public markets must be weighed against the disadvantages. While going public may give the corporation and major stockholders greater access to funds as well as additional prestige, these advantages quickly disappear in a down market. Furthermore, the corporation must open its books to the public and orient itself to the short-term emphasis of investors.

Investment bankers have become larger and consolidated into fewer firms. The industry has become dominated by five to eight large investment bankers able to take down large blocks of securities and compete in a more international market. Shelf registration has also become an alternative to public syndications, particularly with debt issues, and is advantageous to the larger investment bankers.

Private placement—or the direct distribution of securities to large insurance companies, pension funds, and wealthy individuals—may bypass the rigors of SEC registration and allow more flexibility in terms. A number of corporations actually changed their structure from public to private during the bear market of 1973–74. This trend had become evident again in 1984 and 1985, with many large companies going private through leveraged buy-outs. However, a number of these companies publicly distributed their shares a year or two later.

List of Terms

investment banker	public placement
underwriting	private placement
market maker	going private
underwriting syndicate	bull market
managing underwriter	bear market
underwriting spread	secondary offering
dilution of earnings	shelf registration
market stabilization	leveraged buy-out

Discussion Questions

1. In what way is an investment banker a risk taker?

2. What is the purpose of market stabilization activities during the distribution process?

3. Discuss how an underwriting syndicate decreases risk for each under-writer and at the same time facilitates the distribution process.

4. Discuss the reason for the differences between underwriting spreads for stocks and bonds.

5. Explain how the price–earnings ratio is related to the pricing of a new security issue and the dilution effect.

6. What is a shelf registration? How does it differ from the traditional requirements for security offerings?

7. Comment on the market performance of companies going public, both immediately after the offering has been made and some time later. Relate this to research that has been done in this area.

8. Discuss key changes that have been going on in the investment bank-ing-brokerage community in terms of vertical integration. Also, who are some of the new participants in the industry?

9. Discuss the benefits accruing to a company that is traded in the public securities markets.

10. What are some reasons why a corporation may prefer to remain privately held?

11. If a company were looking for capital by way of a private placement, where would it look for funds?

12. How does a leveraged buy-out work? What does the debt structure of the firm normally look like after a leveraged buy-out? What might be done to reduce the debt?

13. How might a leveraged buy-out eventually lead to high returns to the investors?

Problems

1. Midas and Company is the managing investment banker for a new major underwriting. The price of the stock to the managing invest-ment banker is $15 per share. Other syndicate members may buy at $15.25. The price to the selected dealer group is $15.60, with a price to the brokers of $16. Finally, the price to the public is $16.50.
   a. If Midas and Company sells its shares to the dealer group, what will its percentage return be?

    b. If Midas and Company performs the dealers' function, also, and sells to brokers, what will its percentage return be?

    c. If Midas and Company fully integrates its operation and sells directly to the public, what will its percentage return be?

2. The Hamilton Corporation currently has 4 million shares of stock outstanding and will report earnings of $6 million in the current year. The company is considering the issuance of one million additional shares that will net $30 per share to the corporation.

    a. What is the immediate dilution potential for this new stock issue?

    b. Assume the Hamilton Corporation can earn 10.5 percent on the proceeds of the stock issue in time to include it in the current year's results. Should the new issue be undertaken based on earnings per share?

3. Winston Sporting Goods is considering a public offering of common stock. Its investment banker has informed the company that the retail price will be $18 per share for 600,000 shares. The company will receive $16.50 per share and will incur $150,000 in registration, accounting, and printing fees.

    a. What is the spread on this issue in percentage terms? What are the total expenses of the issue as a percentage of total value (at retail)?

    b. If the firm wanted to net $18 million from this issue, how many shares must be sold?

4. Becker Brothers is the managing underwriter for a 1 million share issue by Jay's Hamburger Heaven. Becker Brothers is "handling" 10 percent of the issue. Its price is $25 and the price to the public is $26.40.

    Becker also provides the market stabilization function. During the issuance, the market for the stock turned soft, and Becker was forced to purchase 40,000 shares in the open market at an average price of $25.75. It later sold the shares at an average value of $23.

    Compute Becker Brothers *overall* gain or loss from managing this issue.

5. Ward Door Company is about to go public. The investment banking firm of Peabody and Company is attempting to price the issue. The home furnishing industry generally trades at a 25 percent discount below the P/E ratio on the Standard & Poor's 500 Stock Index. Assume that index currently has a P/E ratio of 16. Ward Door Company can be compared to the home furnishing industry as follows:

	Ashley	Homebuilding Industry
Growth rate in earnings per share . . .	10 percent	8 percent
Consistency of performance	Increased earnings 4 out of 5 years	Increased earnings 3 out of 5 years
Debt to total assets	55 percent	45 percent
Turnover of product	Slightly below average	Average
Quality of management	High	Average

Assume, in assessing the initial P/E ratio, the investment banker will first determine the appropriate industry P/E based on the Standard & Poor's 500 Index. Then a half point will be added to the P/E ratio for each case in which Ward Door Company is superior to the industry norm, and a half point will be deducted for an inferior comparison. On this basis, what should the initial P/E be for Ward?

6. The investment banking firm of Drexel Burns and Company uses a dividend valuation model to appraise the shares of Lambert Aerospace Company. Dividends (D_1) at the end of the current period will be $1.20. The growth rate ($g$) is 7 percent and the discount rate (K_e) is 12 percent.

  a. Using Formula 10–9 from Chapter 10, what should be the price of the stock to the public?

  b. If there is a 6 percent total underwriting spread on the stock, how much will the issuing corporation receive?

  c. If the issuing corporation requires a net price of $23.50 (proceeds to the corporation) and there is a 6 percent underwriting spread, what should be the price of the stock to the public?

7. The Foster Corporation needs to raise $1 million of debt on a 20-year issue. If it places the bonds privately, the interest rate will be 11 percent. Twenty thousand in out-of-pocket costs will be incurred. For a public issue the interest rate will be 10 percent and the underwriting spread will be 5 percent. There also will be $80,000 of out-of-pocket costs.

Assume interest on the debt is paid semiannually, and that the debt will remain outstanding for the full 20-year period, at which time it will be repaid. Which plan offers the higher net present value? For each plan, compare the net amount of funds initially available (inflow) to the present value of future payments to determine net present value. Assume the appropriate discount rate is 12 percent (use 6 percent semiannually throughout the analysis). Disregard taxes.

8. Electron Corporation has net income of $10 million and 4 million shares outstanding. Its common stock is currently selling for $30 per share. Electron plans to sell common stock in order to set up a major new production facility costing $12,600,000. This production facility will not produce a profit for one year, and then is expected to earn an 18 percent return on the investment. Morgan Goldman, an investment banking firm, plans to sell the issue to the public for $28 per share with a spread of 10 percent.

   a. How many shares of stock must be sold to net $12,600,000? (Note: no out-of-pocket costs must be taken into consideration in this problem.)

   b. Why is the investment banker selling the stock at less than its current market price?

   c. What were the earnings per share (EPS) and the price–earnings ratio before the issue (based on a stock price of $30)? What will be the price per share immediately after the sale of stock if the P/E stays constant?

   d. Compute the EPS and the price (P/E stays constant) after the new production facility begins to produce a profit.

   e. Are the shareholders better off because of the sale of stock and the resultant investment? What other financing strategies could the company have tried in order to increase earnings per share?

9. The Presley Corporation is about to go public. It currently has aftertax earnings of $7,500,000 and 2,500,000 shares are owned by the present stockholders (the Presley family). The new public issue will represent 600,000 new shares. The new shares will be priced to the public at $20 per share, with a 5 percent spread on the offering price. There will also be $200,000 in out-of-pocket costs to the corporation.

   a. Compute the net proceeds to the Presley Corporation.

   b. Compute the earnings per share immediately before the stock issue.

   c. Compute the earnings per share immediately after the stock issue.

   d. Determine what rate of return must be earned on the net proceeds to the corporation so that there will not be a dilution in earnings per share during the year of going public.

   e. Determine what rate of return must be earned on the proceeds to the corporation so that there will be a 5 percent increase in earnings per share during the year of going public.

10. I. B. Michaels has a chance to participate in a new public offering by Hi-Tech Microcomputers. His broker informs him that there is

a very strong demand for the 500,000 shares to be issued. His broker's firm is assigned 15,000 shares in the distribution and will allow Michaels, a relatively good customer, 1.5 percent of their 15,000 share allocation.

The initial offering price is $30 per share. There is a strong after-market, and the stock goes to $33 one week after issue. After the first full month after issue, Mr. Michaels is quite pleased to observe his shares are selling for $34.75. He is content to place his shares in a lockbox and eventually use their anticipated increased value to help send his son to college many years in the future. However, one year after the distribution, he looks up the shares in *The Wall Street Journal* and finds they are trading at $28.75.

a. Compute the total dollar profit or loss on Mr. Michaels' shares one week, one month, and one year after the purchase. In each case, compute the profit or loss against the initial purchase price.

b. Also compute this percentage gain or loss from the initial $30 price and compare this to the results that might be expected in an investment of this nature based on prior research. Assume the overall stock market was basically unchanged during the period of observation.

c. Why might a new public issue be expected to have a strong aftermarket?

11. The management of Quantum Labs decided to go private in 1987 by buying in all 2 million shares at $24.25 per share. By 1989, management had restructured the company by selling off the chemical division for $9 million, the petroleum research division for $12 million, and the synthetic coating division for $14.5 million. Because these divisions had only been marginally profitable, Quantum Labs is a stronger company after the restructuring. Quantum is now able to concentrate exclusively on contract research and will generate a profit of $1.60 per share this year. Investment bankers have contacted the firm and indicated that, if it reentered the public market, the 2 million shares it purchased to go private could now be reissued to the public at a P/E ratio of 18 times earnings per share.

a. What was the initial total cost to Quantum Labs to go private?

b. What is the total value to the company from (1) the proceeds from the divisions that were sold as well as (2) the current value of the 2 million shares (based on current earnings and an anticipated P/E ratio of 18)?

c. What is the percentage return to the management of Quantum

Labs from the restructuring? Use answers from parts *a* and *b* to help determine this value.

12. (*Comprehensive problem—impact of new public offering.*)

The Anton Corporation, a manufacturer of radar control equipment, is planning to sell its shares to the general public for the first time. The firm's investment banker, E. F. Sutton and Company, is working with the Anton Corporation in determining a number of items. Information on the Anton Corporation follows.

ANTON CORPORATION
Income Statement
For the Year 198X

Sales (all on credit)	$22,428,000
Cost of goods sold	16,228,000
Gross profit	6,200,000
Selling and administrative expenses	2,659,400
Operating profit	3,540,600
Interest expense	370,600
Net income before tax	3,170,000
Taxes	1,442,000
Net income	$ 1,728,000

Balance Sheet
As of December 31, 198X

Assets

Cash	$ 150,000
Marketable securities	100,000
Accounts receivable	2,000,000
Inventory	3,800,000
Total current assets	6,050,000
Net plant and equipment	6,750,000
Total assets	$12,800,000

Liabilities and Stockholders' Equity

Accounts payable	$ 1,000,000
Notes payable	1,200,000
Total current liabilities	2,200,000
Long-term liabilities	2,380,000
Total liabilities	4,580,000
Common stock (1,200,000 shares at $1 par)	1,200,000
Capital paid in excess of par	2,800,000
Retained earnings	4,220,000
Total stockholders' equity	8,220,000
Total liabilities and stockholders' equity	$12,800,000

The new public offering will be at 10 times the earnings per share.

a. Assume that 500,000 new corporate shares will be issued to the general public. What will earnings per share immediately after the public offering be? (Round to two places to the right of the decimal point.) Based on the price–earnings ratio of 10, what will the initial price of the stock be? Use earnings per share after the distribution in the calculation.

b. Assuming an underwriting spread of 7 percent and out-of-pocket costs of $150,000, what will net proceeds to the corporation be?

c. What return must the corporation earn on the net proceeds to equal the earnings per share before the offering? How does this compare with current return on the total assets on the balance sheet?

d. Now assume that, of the initial 500,000 share distribution 250,000 shares belong to current stockholders and 250,000 are new corporate shares, and these will be added to the 1,200,000 corporate shares currently outstanding. What will earnings per share immediately after the public offering be? What will the initial market price of the stock be? Assume a price–earnings ratio of 10 and use earnings per share after the distribution in the calculation.

e. Assuming an underwriting spread of 7 percent and out-of-pocket costs of $150,000, what will net proceeds to the corporation be?

f. What return must the corporation now earn on the net proceeds to equal earnings per share before the offering? How does this compare with current return on the total assets on the balance sheet?

Selected References

Block, Stanley, B., and Marjorie T. Stanley. "The Price Movement Pattern and Financial Characteristics of Companies Approaching the Unseasoned Securities Market in the Late 1970s." *Financial Management* 9 (Winter 1980), pp. 30–36.

Friend, Irwin, et al. *Investment Banking and the New Issues Markets.* Cleveland: World, 1967.

Hayes, Samuel L., III. "Investment Banking: Power Structure in Flux." *Harvard Business Review* 49 (March-April 1971), pp. 136–52.

———. "The Transformation of Investment Banking." *Harvard Business Review* 57 (January-February 1979), pp. 153–70.

Hess, Alan C., and Peter A. Frost. "Tests for Price Effects of New Issues of Seasoned Securities." *Journal of Finance* 37 (March 1982), pp. 11–25.

Ibbotson, Roger G. "Price Performance of Common Stock New Issues." *Journal of Financial Economics* 2 (September 1975), pp. 253–72.

Johnson, Keith B.; T. Gregory Morton; and M. Chapman Findlay III. "An Empirical Analysis of the Flotation Costs of Corporate Securities, 1971–1972." *Journal of Finance* 30 (September 1975), pp. 1129–33.

Logue, Dennis E. "On the Pricing of Unseasoned New Issues, 1965–1969." *Journal of Financial and Quantitative Analysis* 8 (January 1973), pp. 91–103.

Louis, A. M. "Fastest Richest Texan Ever." *Fortune*, November 1968, pp. 168–70.

McDonald, J. G., and A. K. Fisher. "New Issue Stock Price Behavior." *Journal of Finance* 27 (March 1972), pp. 97–102.

Moore, Nathan H.; David R. Peterson; and Pamela P. Peterson. Shelf Registration and Stockholder Wealth: A Comparison of Shelf and Traditional Equity Offerings." *Journal of Finance* 41 (June 1986), pp. 451–63.

Reilly, Frank K. "New Issues Revisited." *Financial Management* 6 (Winter 1977), pp. 28–42.

Rogowski, Robert J., and Eric H. Sórensen. "Deregulation in Investment Banking: Shelf Registration, Structure, and Performance." *Financial Management* 14 (Spring 1985), pp. 5–15.

16

Long-Term Debt and Lease Financing

The Shakespearean quote of "Neither a borrower nor a lender be" hardly applies to corporate financial management. The virtues and drawbacks of debt usage were considered in Chapter 5, Operating and Financial Leverage, and in Chapter 11, The Cost of Capital. One can only surmise that today's financial managers, many of whom were educated in the 1950s and 1960s, remember the advantages a bit better than the disadvantages. Debt usage has been at unprecedented levels in the late 1970s and 1980s. In Chapter 16 we will consider the importance of debt in the U.S. economy, the nature of long-term debt instruments, the mechanics of bond yields and pricing, and the decision to call back or refund an existing bond issue. Finally, lease financing will be considered as a special case of long-term debt financing. We give particular attention to accounting rules that affect leasing.

The Expanding Role of Debt

Corporate debt has increased more than tenfold since World War II. This growth is related to rapid business expansion, the inflationary impact on the economy, and, at times, inadequate funds generated from the internal operations of business firms. The rapid expansion of the U.S. economy

Figure 16–1
Times interest earned

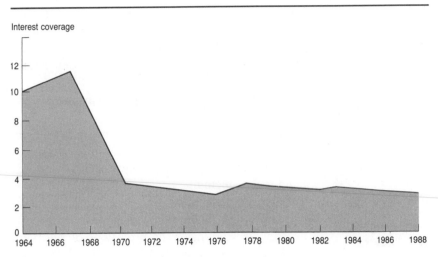

Interest coverage

has placed pressure on U.S. corporations to raise capital and will continue to do so in the future. In this context, a whole new set of rules has been developed for evaluating corporate bond issues. Much deterioration in borrowing qualifications has taken place. In 1967, the average U.S. manufacturing corporation had its interest payments covered by operating earnings at a rate of 11.7 times (operating earnings were more than 11 times as great as interest). By the late 1980s the ratio had diminished to approximately three times. Nor has this been a short-term, cyclical phenomenon, but rather a slow, steady decline with only short-term reversals, as indicated in Figure 16–1.

Even with a decline in the interest-paying capability of corporate borrowers, relatively few corporations actually default on their obligations, and an even smaller number are liquidated. Nevertheless, a debt contract dictates the lender's potential influence over a corporation and its relative bargaining position in the event the worst comes to pass.

The Debt Contract

The corporate bond represents the basic long-term debt instrument for most large U.S. corporations. The bond agreement specifies such basic items as the par value, the coupon rate, and the maturity date.

Par Value The initial value of the bond. The par value is sometimes referred to as the principal or face value. Most corporate bonds are initially traded in $1,000 units.

Coupon Rate   The actual interest rate on the bond, usually payable in semiannual installments. To the extent that interest rates in the market go above or below the coupon rate after the bond has been issued, the market price of the bond will change from the par value.

Maturity Date   The final date on which repayment of the bond principal is due.

The bond agreement is supplemented by a much longer document termed a bond indenture. The indenture, often containing over 100 pages of complicated legal wording, covers every minute detail surrounding the bond issue—including collateral pledged, methods of repayment, restrictions on the corporation, and procedures for initiating claims against the corporation. A financially independent trustee is appointed by the corporation to administer the provisions of the bond indenture under the guidelines of the Trust Indenture Act of 1939. Let's examine two items of interest in any bond agreement: the security provisions of the bond and the methods of repayment.

Security Provisions

A secured claim is one in which specific assets are pledged to bondholders in the event of default. Only infrequently are pledged assets actually sold off and the proceeds distributed to bondholders. Typically, the defaulting corporation is reorganized and existing claims are partially satisfied by issuing new securities to the participating parties. Of course, the stronger and better secured the initial claim, the higher the quality of the new security to be received in exchange. When a defaulting corporation is reorganized for failure to meet obligations, existing management may be terminated and, in extreme cases, held legally responsible for any imprudent actions.

A number of terms are used to denote collateralized or secured debt. Under a *mortgage agreement,* real property (plant and equipment) is pledged as security for the loan. A mortgage may be *senior* or *junior* in nature, with the former requiring satisfaction of claims before payment is given to the latter. Bondholders may also attach an *after-acquired property clause,* requiring that any new property be placed under the original mortgage.

The student should realize that not all secured debt will carry every protective feature, but rather a carefully negotiated position including some safeguards and rejecting others. Generally, the greater the protection offered a given class of bondholders, the lower is the interest rate on the bond. Bondholders are willing to assume some degree of risk to receive a higher yield.

Unsecured Debt

A number of corporations issue debt that is not secured by a specific claim to assets. In Wall Street jargon, the name *debenture* refers to a long-term, unsecured corporate bond. Among the major participants in debenture offerings are such prestigious firms as American Telephone & Telegraph, Exxon, International Paper, and Dow Chemical. Because of the legal problems associated with "specific" asset claims in a secured bond offering, the trend is to unsecured debt—allowing the bondholder a general claim against the corporation, rather than a specific lien against an asset.

Even unsecured debt may be divided between high-ranking and subordinated debt. A *subordinated debenture* is an unsecured bond in which payment to the holder will take place only after designated senior debenture holders are satisfied. The hierarchy of creditor obligations for secured as well as unsecured debt is presented in Figure 16–2, along with consideration of the position of stockholders. For a further discussion of payment of claims and the hierarchy of obligations, the reader should see Appendix 16A, Financial Alternatives for Distressed Firms, which also covers bankruptcy considerations.

Methods of Repayment

The method of repayment for bond issues may not always call for one lump-sum disbursement at the maturity date. Some Canadian and British government bonds are perpetual in nature. More interestingly, West Shore Railroad 4 percent bonds are not scheduled to mature until 2361 (almost 400 years in the future). Nevertheless, most bonds have some orderly or preplanned system of repayment. In addition to the simplest arrangement—a single-sum payment at maturity—bonds may be retired by serial payments, through sinking-fund provisions, through conversion, or by a call feature.

Serial payments　The bonds are paid off in installments over the life of the issue. Each bond has its own predetermined date of maturity and receives interest only to that point. Although the total issue may span

Figure 16–2
Priority of claims

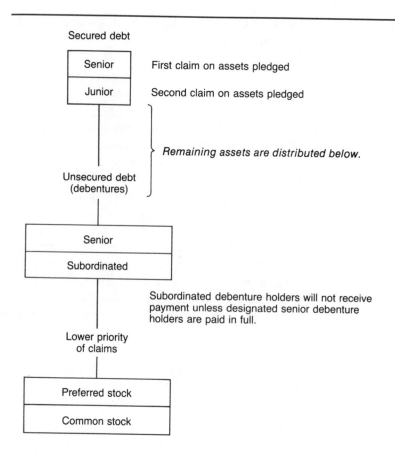

over 20 years, 15 or 20 different maturity dates may be assigned specific dollar amounts.

Sinking-fund provision   A less structured but more popular method of debt retirement is through the use of a sinking fund. Under this arrangement, semiannual or annual contributions are made by the corporation into a fund administered by a trustee for purposes of debt retirement. The trustee takes the proceeds and goes into the market to purchase bonds from willing sellers. If no willing sellers are available, a lottery system may be used among outstanding bondholders.

Conversion   A more subtle method of reducing debt outstanding is to provide for debt conversion into common stock. Although this feature is exercised at the option of the bondholder, a number of incentives or penalties may be utilized to encourage conversion. The mechanics of convertible bond trading are discussed at length in Chapter 19, Convertibles and Warrants.

Call feature A call provision allows the corporation to call in or force in the debt issue prior to maturity. The corporation will pay a premium over par value of 5 to 10 percent—a bargain value to the corporation if bond prices are up. Modern call provisions usually do not take effect until the bond has been outstanding at least 5 to 10 years. Often the call provision declines over time, usually by 0.5–1 percent per year after the call period begins. A corporation may decide to call in outstanding debt issues when interest rates on new securities are considerably lower than those on previously issued debt (let's get the high cost, old debt off the books).

Now that we have covered the key features of the bond indenture, let us examine an existing bond. Table 16–1 presents a page from Moody's Bond Record. We find that Pfizer Incorporated has two bond issues: an 8.5 percent sinking fund (S.F.) debenture due in 1999 and a 9.25 percent sinking fund (S.F.) debenture due in the year 2000. More specific features of the 9.25 percent bond are found in Table 16–2 from the Standard & Poor's Corporate Records.

As we can see in Table 16–2, the 9.25 percent bond was sold on August 19, 1975, and had an original authorized offering of $100 million. As of December 1986, $28.2 million were still outstanding. A check of the sinking-fund requirements indicates that retirement was required beginning in 1987 and ending in 1999. Actually, Pfizer decided to use its option to retire a portion of the bonds earlier than specified in the bond indenture. The information in Table 16–2 also provides other pertinent information found in the indenture, such as the interest payment dates, trustees, registrars, denominations of each bond, call features (listed under "redeemable otherwise"), redemption restrictions, security provisions, and a price listing on the NYSE Bond Exchange over the prior four years.

Bond Prices, Yields, and Ratings

The financial manager must be sensitive to interest rate changes and price movements in the bond market. The treasurer's interpretation of market conditions will influence the timing of new issues, the coupon rate offered, the maturity date, and the necessity for a call provision. Lest the student of finance think that bonds maintain stable long-term price patterns, he or she need merely examine bond pricing during the five-year period 1967–72. When the market interest rate on outstanding 30-year, Aaa

Table 16-1 Moody's Bond Record

Issue	Interest Dates	Current Call Price	Moody's Rating	Current Price	Yield to Mat.	1987 High	1987 Low	1946-86 High	1946-86 Low	Amt. Outst. Mil.$	Sink. Fund Prov.	Legal Status	Fed. Tax	Issued	Price	Yld.
Pennsylvania Railroad gen. 4.25 D 1981 [1]	+10-170	N.C.	N.R.		flat	---	---	135½	7¾	43.6	No		N	1931	96.50	4.42
do gen. 4.25 E 1984	+7-170	100.00	N.R.		flat	---	---	135½	8	36.1	Yes		N	1930	97.50	4.37
do gen. 3.125 F 1985	+7-170	100.00	N.R.		flat	---	---	130	8	45.3	100.25		N	1-10-45	100.68	3.10
•Pennwalt Corp. deb. 9.125 1995	F&A 1	101.29ᵃ	Baa1r	95	sale 10.06	102	94	112	62½	13.84	Yes	13	N	7-30-70	99.50	9.18
•Pennzoil Co. deb. 14.00 1991	F&A 1	[2]100.00	A2 r	101	bid 13.60	111	102¾	110¾	92	200	No	13	N	1-28-81	100.00	14.00
do nts. 8.25 1991	F&A 1	N.C.	A2 r		-----	---	---	99¾	99¾	150	No		N	8-21-86	99.80	8.35
do deb. 14.625 1991	F&A 1	100.00	A2 r		-----	---	---	183		100	No		N	1-28-81	100.00	14.63
do deb. 15.00 1992	M&N 1	[1]100.00	A2 r	105½	bid 13.33	116	110	117	96¾	150	No	13	N	5-12-82	100.00	15.00
do deb. 12.125 2007	J&D1	§108.94ᵃ	A2 r	108⅜	bid 11.04	113¾	110⅜	111¼	86	100	Yes	1	N	Ref. fr. 12-1-92@ 105.59		
do deb. 10.00 2011	M&S 1	§107.78ᵃ	A2 r		-----	---	---	100	98¼	200	Yes		N	Ref. fr. 3-1-96@ 104.09		
do deb. 10.125 2011	F&A 1	§108.55ᵃ	A2 r		-----	---	---	101	98⅞	150	Yes		N	Ref. fr. 8-1-96@ 104.50		
do deb. 9.00 2017	A&O 1	§109.00ᵃ	A2 r		-----	100	100	---	---	100	Yes		N	Ref. fr. 4-1-97@ 104.50		
• do s.f.deb. 7.50 1988	J&D 1	100.00	A2 r	98¼	bid 10.68	100⅝	99¾	105⅞	65	27.54	100.35	13	N	6-18-68	101.035	7.40
• do s.f.deb. 7.375 1988	A&O 1	100.00	A2 r	98⅜	sale 8.68	101⅛	98⅞	102½	63⅜	27.63	100.00	13	N	10-15-68	100.00	7.375
• do s.f.deb. 8.375 1996	M&S 1	101.73ᵃ	A2 r	90	bid 10.18	100⅝	97¾	105½	57¾	39.45	Yes	13	N	3-23-71	100.25	8.35
• do s.f.deb. 8.75 2001	J30&D31	104.38ᵃ	A2 r	85½	bid 10.76	99	97½	104	60¼	70.37	Yes	13	N	11-13-77	100.00	8.75
do nts. 9.125 1996	M&S 1	[4]100.00	A2 r		-----	---	---	99½	99½	100	No		N	3-11-86	99.50	9.20
do eurounts. 9.00 1993	MAY 7		A2 r	90⅜	bid 11.26	100	90⅞	99⅜	96	100	No		F	4-15-86	99.50	9.00
Pennzoil O/S Fin NV eurodeb. 15.25 1990 [1]	APR 1	101.00ᵃ	A2 r		-----	100¾	100¾	107	103¾	75.0	No		F	3-15-82	99.50	15.35
•Penril Corp. sr.sub.nts. 10.875 1993	F&A1	100.00	Caa r	51	bid	---	---	50	43½	18.0	Yes		N	1-28-83		
•People Express Airlines sec.eq.ctf. 13.50 A 1990	J&D 15		B3 r		-----	100	100	100	100	25.0	No		N	6-13-85	100.00	13.50
do sec.eq.ctf. 14.00 B 1995	J&D 15		B3 r		-----	99¾	99¾	99¾	99¾	100	Yes		N	6-13-85	99.75	14.05
do sec.eq.ctf. 14.375 1996	A&O 15	[7]102.00ᵃ	B3 r		-----	100	100	100	100	125	No		N	4-17-86	100.00	14.38
do sec.eq.ctf. 14.75 1999	A&O 15	[5]105.54ᵃ	B3 r	84	bid 18.10	95	84	97¼	84	67.1	Yes		N	4-18-84	97.25	15.22
do nts. 16.50 1991	J&J 15	N.C.	Caa r	86	bid	---	104	86	99	99	40.0	Yes		N	7-11-84	99.05	16.73
do exten. 14.375 1995 [1]	M&N15	[10]102.00ᵃ	Caa r		-----	---	---	100	100	125	No		N	11-7-85	100.00	14.375
Peoples Gas L. & C. 1st&ref. 6.25 L 1992	F&A15	101.21ᵃ	Aa3 r	86½	bid 9.85	91	85½	103¾	52	34.4	100.55	13	N	8-24-67	101.00	6.17
do 1st&ref. 8.875 M 1995	M&S15	102.81ᵃ	Aa3 r	92¼	bid 10.33	99¼	92¼	109⅜	60½	18.7	Yes	13	N	9-16-70	100.75	8.80
do 1st&ref. 7.625 N 1997	A&O15	102.97ᵃ	Aa3 r	82¾	bid 10.55	96¾	81	102¾	52½	31.2	Yes	13	N	4-12-72	100.277	7.60
do 8.25 O 1998	J&J15	103.44ᵃ	Aa3 r	85¼	bid 10.58	95½	85¼	101⅜	54¾	24.3	Yes	13	N	7-25-73	100.00	8.25
PepsiCo Cap Res Inc. zero cpn.eurodeb. 1988-12 [1]	[12]N.P.	100.00	Aa3		-----	---	---	---	---	59.3	No	13	F	3-31-82	---	---
PEPSICO CAP CORP NV eurounts. 1992 [1]	[14]N.P.	100.00	Aa3	k 65	bid 10.37	69¾	65	68¼	26	49.1	No		F	1-82	26.00	
do eurounts. 1994 [1]	[14]N.P.	100.00	Aa3	k 52	bid	58¾	52	57¾	20¾	47.1	No		F	2-82	20.75	
PepsiCo Inc. nts. 13.50 1990 [17]	J&J 22	N.C.	Aa3 r		-----	101	101	---	---	50.0	No		N	7-8-87	101.00	13.50
• do nts. 7.625 1998	J&D 18	N.C.	Aa3 r		-----	100	83	---	---	163.4	No		N	12-4-86	99.73	7.66
do eurounts. 18.50 1989	JUN 15		Aa3 r	101⅜	bid 17.49	102½	101¼	---	---	60.0	No		F	6-15-87	101.25	17.73
Pepsico O/S Fin. gtd.eurobonds 7.25 1994 [18]	FEB 26	[15]101.25ᵃ	Aa3 r	k101⅜	bid 6.92	105⅜	101¼	106½	100	250	No		F	2-84	100.00	7.25
do gtd.eurounts. 1994 [11]	[14]N.P.	100.00	Aa3 r		-----	53⅜	53	20¾	20¾	125	No		F	2-82	20.75	
PepsiCo Cap Res Inc. zero cpn.deb. 2012 [21]	APR 1	0100.00	Aa3		-----	---	---	---	---	59.3	No		N	3-31-82		
Pernambuco (Braz) 2.125 2008 [21]	M&S 1	100.00	N.R.		flat	---	---	88⅜	21¼	0.24	Yes		F	Mar 1927	97.75	2.18
•Peru (Rep) ext. 6.00 1960	+6-132		N.R.		flat	---	---	125	14⅜	0.66	Yes		F	Dec 1927	91.50	8.32
Pet Inc. s.f.deb. 5.875 1992	J&D 1	100.00	N.R.	82	bid 10.98	95	81	99	50	10.0	100.00		N	6-20-67	99.00	5.95
Petro-Canada deb. 7.25 1996 [32]	MAY 15	N.C.	Aaa r	k 79½	bid 11.01	95½	79½	100¼	91½	200	No		F	4-18-86	100.25	7.21
Petro-Canada deb. 8.25 2016 [21]	J&D 15	N.C.	Aaa r		-----	97	95½	98¼	98¼	200	No		F	12-4-86	98.18	8.42
Petro-Lewis Corp. sr.nts. 15.25 1992 [34]	JAJ&O1	110.00ᵃ	Ca r		flat	98¾	49	100	49	114.6	Yes		N	MAY 1985		
do sub.nts. 13.75 1993 [21]	A&O1	100.00	Ca r		flat	64½	14¾	69	14¾	95.7	Yes		N	MAY 1985		
do sr.sub.deb. 12.625 2003	F&A15	100.00	Ca r		flat	62½	26	95	26	47.3	Yes		N	8-12-81	69.83	18.25
do sub.deb. 11.00 1997	J30&D31	[16]101.10ᵃ	Ca r		flat	66¾	19	99¾	19	16.2	Yes		N	1-12-78		
do sub.deb. 12.25 1998	F&A 1	[17]101.23ᵃ	Ca r		flat	63½	21	68½	21	24.3	Yes		N	7-25-78		
do var.rt.sub.deb. 14.00 2000 [1]	J&J 1	[18]104.13ᵃ	Ca r		flat	66¾	22	96	22	24.3	Yes		N	6-25-80		
do zero cpn.nts. 1988	[14]N.P.	100.00	Ca r		flat	64⅝	20	64⅝	20	13.68	No		N	8-2-82		
do zero cpn.nts. 1989	[14]N.P.	100.00	Ca r		flat	61	15	61	15	20.6	No		N	8-12-81	25.65	17.75
do sr.sub.nts. 11.50 1993	F&A15	100.00	Ca r		flat	69	30	88¼	30	22.2	Yes		N	2-9-83	89.47	13.44
Petro. Heat & Power Co. sub.nts. 9.85 1994 [32]	JAJ&O1	102.00ᵃ	B2 r		-----	---	---	99¼	98¼	20.0	No		N	6-22-84	99.25	14.64
do sub.nts. 13.875 1995	A&O1	[15]105.20ᵃ	B2 r		-----	---	---	98⅜	98¾	25.0	Yes		N	10-1-85	98.68	14.13
PETTIBONE CORP. sub.deb. 12.375 2000	M&S 1	[6]100.00	Ca r	102⅜	bid	102⅜	102¾	225½	65	17.5	Yes		N	8-29-80		
➤PFIZER INC. s.f.deb. 8.50 1999	A&O15	102.71ᵃ	Aaa r	87¼	sale 10.43	101¾	87¼	104¾	58	50.1	Yes	123	N	4-18-74	99.25	
➤ do s.f.deb. 9.25 2000	F&A15	103.50ᵃ	Aaa r	95¼	bid 9.93	104½	100.91½	111	61½	28.2	Yes	123	N	8-19-75	99.50	
•Phelps Dodge Corp. s.f.deb. 8.10 1996	J&D15	101.62ᵃ	Baa3r	90	bid 9.84	92¼	89	106½	50	64.2	Yes		N	7-16-71	100.00	8.10
Phila. Balt. & Wash. gen. 5.00 B 1974 [21]	+8-170	N.C.	N.R.		flat	---	---	120	23	10.0	No		N	2-1-1924		
do gen. 4.50 C 1977 [21]	+7-170	N.C.	N.R.		flat	---	---	135	16	11.3	No		N	Jan 1931	102.00	4.40
•Phila. Elect. Co. 1st&ref. 3.75 1988 [21]	M&N 1	100.30ᵃ	Baa3	96¼	bid 11.75	100	95½	100	47¼	40.0	No	1	N	3-30-58	99.75	3.77
• do 1st&ref. 5.00 1989	A&O 1	100.30ᵃ	Baa3	93	bid 9.06	94¾	92	108⅛	51⅜	50.0	No	1	N	10-15-59	101.00	4.93
• do 1st&ref. 3.75 1989	A&O15	103.00ᵃ	Baa3	104¾	bid 12.43	109¼	107	110½	86	125	No	1	N	10-6-80	100.00	13.75
• do 1st&ref. 6.50 1993	M&S 1	101.40ᵃ	Baa3	89¾	ask 9.05	92½	86¼	104½	49	60.0	No	1	N	3-11-68	100.00	6.50
• do 1st&ref. 4.50 1994	M&N 1	101.30ᵃ	Baa3	69	bid 11.38	107½	79	102½	39¼	50.0	No	1	N	5-13-64	100.823	4.45
• do 1st&ref. 8.75 1994	M&N 1	N.C.	Baa3	94	bid 9.96	---	103	103	103	100	No	1	N	10-29-86	99.72	8.80
• do 1st&ref. 9.00 1995	F&A1	103.30ᵃ	Baa3	90⅞	sale 10.84	103	90¼	114¾	57⅞	55.9	101.70	1	N	2-3-70	100.225	8.78
• do 1st&ref. 10.875 1995	M&N15	§107.57ᵃ	Baa3	94	bid 12.06	109⅝	109⅝	107	103	150	No	1	N	Ref. fr. 11-15-90@ 103.03		
• do 1st&ref. 8.25 1996	J&J 1	103.00ᵃ	Baa3	80¾	bid 11.84	99	75¾	108⅝	52¾	80.0	No	1	N	Ref. fr. 4-1-92@ 100.527	8.20
• do 1st&ref. 6.125 1997	A&O 1	102.10ᵃ	Baa3r	69¾	bid 11.24	83	73¾	102	41¾	75.0	No	1	N	10-10-67	100.342	6.10
• do 1st&ref. 10.00 1997	J&J 15	§110.00ᵃ	Baa3r	94	bid 11.02	100	96½	---	---	100	No		N	Ref. fr. 7-15-92@ 104.45		
• do 1st&ref. 11.00 1997	A&O 15	[13]103.15ᵃ	Baa3r		-----	100	100	---	---	100	No	1	N	10-7-87	100.00	11.00
• do 1st&ref. 7.50 1998	A&O15	103.30ᵃ	Baa3r	75	bid 11.66	92	75	103¾	47¼	100	No	1	N	6-15-72	100.57	7.45
• do 1st&ref. 7.50 1999	J&J15	103.30ᵃ	Baa3r	69	bid 12.77	91¼	74¼	101¾	46¼	100	No	1	N	1-22-73	100.00	7.50
• do 1st&ref. 11.00 2000	F&A 1	104.40ᵃ	Baa3r	97½	bid 11.37	107	100	115	66	54.4	Yes	1	N	4-23-75	101.00	11.00
• do 1st&ref. 7.75 2000	J&J15	103.50ᵃ	Baa3r	75¾	bid 11.34	92½	79	107	48	6.800	Yes	1	N	12-10-70	100.00	7.75
• do 1st&ref. 11.625 2000	A&O15	106.40ᵃ	Baa3r	100⅜	sale 11.52	107¼	100	119⅞	66	65.0	No	12	N	4-23-75	101.00	11.49
• do 1st&ref. 7.375 2001	J&D15	104.00ᵃ	Baa3r	73¼	bid 11.21	88¼	73¼	102½	44¾	65.0	No	1	N	12-13-71	100.907	7.30
• do 1st&ref. 9.625 2002	F&A 1	105.39ᵃ	Baa3r	85	bid 11.79	103¾	86	110¾	55	100	No	1	N	7-28-76	100.00	9.625
• do 1st&ref. 8.625 2003	J&J15	105.33ᵃ	Baa3r	79	bid 11.55	97¼	78	102¼	51½	100	No	1	N	7-6-77	100.26	8.60
• do 1st&ref. 8.50 2004	J&J15	105.20ᵃ	Baa3r	78	bid 11.52	92¼	69½	101⅛	50½	125	No	1	N	1-16-74	100.875	8.42
• do 1st&ref. 12.50 2005	A&O15	108.50ᵃ	Baa3r	100¼	bid 12.46	113¾	103	111	72	100	No	1	N	10-1-79	100.00	12.50
• do 1st&ref. 9.125 2006	M&S 1	105.11ᵃ	Baa3r	83	bid 11.34	100	83	106¼	53½	100	No	1	N	2-25-76	100.00	9.13
• do 1st&ref. 8.625 2007	M&S15	105.70ᵃ	Baa3r	80½	bid 11.09	96¾	75	102¾	51¼	75.0	No	1	N	3-8-77	100.00	8.63
• do 1st&ref. 9.125 2008	M&S15	106.83ᵃ	Baa3r	86¼	bid 10.80	100⅞	81⅞	100⅝	52½	100	No	1	N	3-7-78	100.77	9.05
• do 1st&ref. 13.375 2013	J&D15	§110.75ᵃ	Baa3r	108	bid 12.34	116¾	114¼	115½	79½	8.000	No		N	Ref. fr. 6-15-88@ 110.32		
• do 1st&ref. 11.75 2014	M&N15	§110.34ᵃ	Baa3r		-----	100	96¾	110⅜	96¾	250	No		N	Ref. fr. 11-15-90@ 108.23		
• do 1st&ref. 10.25 2016	M&N 1	§109.66ᵃ	Baa3r		-----	100	96½	100½	96½	250	No		N	Ref. fr. 11-1-91@ 108.28		
• do 1st&ref. 11.00 2016	J&J 15	§110.50ᵃ	Baa3r	86¾	bid 12.79	98	92	103¼	102	125	No		N	Ref. fr. 7-15-92@ 108.63		
• do 1st&ref. 12.125 2016 [1]	A&O 15	§111.53ᵃ	Baa3r		-----	99¾	99¾	---	---	100	No		N	Ref. fr. 10-15-92@ 108.65		
• do 1st&ref. 9.375 2017	A&O 1	§109.31ᵃ	Baa3r	76	bid 12.45	---	---	100	100	100	No		N	Ref. fr. 4-1-92@ 107.30		

[1]Now Penn. Central. [2]Fr. 2-1-88. [3]Fr. 5-1-89. [4]Gtd. by Pennzoil Co. [5]Fr. 6-15-92. [6]Fr. 4-15-93. [7]Fr. 4-15-91. [8]Joint Exten. Term Sec. [9]Fr. 11-15-92, may be redeemed by holder fr. 11-15-90. [10]Gtd. by Pepsico, Inc. [11]Due ser. ea. April 1 fr. 1988-2012. [12]Zero coupon gtd. nts., Gtd. by Pepsico Inc. [13]Due 2-4-92. [14]Gtd. by Pepsico Inc., zero coupon gtd. nts. [15]Due 3-2-94. [16]Australian Dollar Nts;Amt. outstg in Australian dollars. [17]Gtd. by Pepsico Inc., Bearer Bonds. [18]Fr. 2-26-89. [19]Gtd. by Pepsico Inc., zero coupon. [20]Stamped. [21]Gtd. by Canada. [22]Gtd by Gvt. of Canada. [23]Sr. sec. nts. Exchange offer. [24]Exchange offer. Co.may extend maturity thru 4-1-2000. [25]Non-Ref.at int cost less than 11%. [26]Non-Ref.at int.cost less than

12.25%. [27]Int. rt. fr. 7-1-87 thru 7-1-88. [28]Non-Ref.at int.cost less than 13%. [29]Sub. serial.,due 3-15. [30]Due 8-15-89. [31]Sub. exch. var. rt. nts., int. thru 12-31-87. [32]Fr. 10-1-90. [33]Non-Ref.at int.cost less than 14.94%. [34]Fr. 10-15-92.

Notes: Moody's ratings are subject to change. Because of the possible time lapse before Moody's assignment or change of a rating and your use of this monthly publication, we suggest you verify the current rating of any security or issuer in which you are interested. For standard abbreviations and symbols, see page 3.

Table 16–2
Pfizer Incorporated
bonds

9¼% SINKING FUND DEBS.; Due Aug. 15, 2000
Authorized $100,000,000
Outstg. (Dec. 31, 1986)............................. 28,200,000
Retired or in treas. 71,800,000
   INDENTURE DATED (Aug. 15, 1975.) INTEREST
PAYABLE Feb. & Aug. 15, to holders registered the
preceding Feb. & Aug. 1, respectively. PRINCIPAL &
INTEREST PAYABLE at trustee's office. INTEREST
GRACE PERIOD- 30 days.
   TRUSTEE & REGISTRAR- Chase Manhattan
Bank (N.A.), NYC.
   DENOMINATIONS- Fully registered, $1,000 and
multiples thereof.
   SINKING FUND requires retirement on 30 days'
notice at 100 & int. of $6,500,000 Debs. each Aug.
15, 1987-99, Co. having non-cumulative option to
retire up to like amount more each year. Optional
redemptions may be used to reduce mandatory
requirements. Credit may be taken for Debs. otherwise acquired.
   REDEEMABLE OTHERWISE on 30 days' notice at
the following prices & int. thru each Aug. 14, with the
price declining annually after until Aug. 15, 1995,
when the price of 100 is reached:
1987 ... 103.938   1988 ... 103.500   1989 ... 103.063
   SECURITY- Same as 8½% Debs. due 1999.
   LISTED- NYSE.

1986	105⅞	92⅜	1985	92	78½
1984	81½	71½	1983	86¾	76¾

Source: *Standard & Poor's Corporate Records*, June 1987, p. 8,702.

corporate bonds went from 5.10 percent to 8.10 percent, the average price of existing bonds dropped 36 percent. A conservative investor would be quite disillusioned to see a $1,000, 5.10 percent bond now quoted at $640.[1] A similar pattern of bond price declines occurred in 1979–81. Though most bonds are virtually certain to be redeemed at their face value at maturity ($1,000 in this case), this is small consolation to the bondholder who has many decades to wait. Of course, at times, bonds also greatly increase in value, such as in 1984–85.

As indicated above and in Chapter 10, the price of a bond is intimately tied to current interest rates. A bond paying 5.10 percent ($51 a year) will fare quite poorly when the going market rate is 8.10 percent ($81 a year). In order to maintain a market in the older issue, the price is adjusted downward to reflect current market demands. The longer the life of the issue, the greater the influence of interest rate changes on the price of

---

[1] Bond prices are generally quoted as a percentage of original par value. In this case, the quote would read 64.

Table 16–3
Interest rates and
bond prices (the
bond pays 12 percent
interest)

Years to Maturity	Rate in the Market (percent)—Yield to Maturity*				
	8%	10%	12%	14%	16%
1　. . . .	$1,038.16	$1,018.54	$1,000	$981.48	$963.98
15　. . . .	1,345.52	1,153.32	1,000	875.54	774.48
25　. . . .	1,429.92	1,182.36	1,000	862.06	754.98

*This table is based on semiannual interest, but you enter it with annual values.

the bond.[2] The same process will work in reverse if interest rates go down. A 30-year, $1,000 bond initially issued to yield 8.10 percent would go up to $1,500 if interest rates declined to 5.10 percent (assuming the bond is not callable). A further illustration of interest rate effects on bond prices is presented in Table 16–3 for a bond paying 12 percent interest. Observe that not only interest rates in the market but years to maturity have a strong influence on bond prices.

For the last four decades, the pattern has been long-term interest rates to move upward (Figure 16–3). However, there has been a meaningful decline in long-term interest rates in the mid to late 1980s.

Bond Yields

Bond yields are quoted on three different bases: coupon rate, current yield, and yield to maturity. We will apply each to a $1,000 par value bond paying $100 per year interest for 10 years. The bond is currently selling in the market for $900.

Coupon Rate (*nominal yield*) Stated interest payment divided by the par value.

$$\frac{\$100}{\$1,000} = 10\%$$

Current Yield Stated interest payment divided by the current price of the bond.

$$\frac{\$100}{\$900} = 11.11\%$$

---

[2]This is known as Malkiel's second theory of bonds. In fact, it is only completely true when the coupon rate of the bond equals or is greater than the original discount rate.

Figure 16–3
Long-term yields
on debt

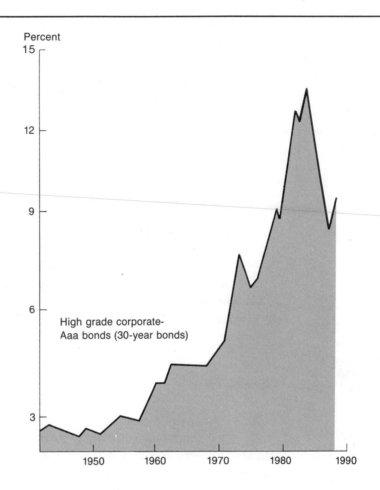

Percent

High grade corporate-
Aaa bonds (30-year bonds)

Yield to Maturity The interest rate that will equate future interest payments and the payment at maturity to the current market price. This represents the concept of the internal rate of return. In the present case, an interest rate of approximately 11.70 percent will equate interest payments of $100 for 10 years and a final payment of $1,000 to the current price of $900. A simple formula may be used to approximate yield to maturity.[3] This formula was initially presented in Chapter 10.

---

[3]The exact answer can be found through Appendix E at the back of the text.

$$\text{Approximate Yield to Maturity } (Y') = \frac{\text{Annual interest payment} + \dfrac{\text{Principal payment} - \text{Price of the bond}}{\text{Number of years to maturity}}}{0.6 \text{ (Price of the bond)} + 0.4 \text{ (Principal payment)}} \qquad (16\text{--}1)$$

$$= \frac{\$100 + \dfrac{\$1{,}000 - 900}{10}}{0.6\ (\$900) + 0.4\ (\$1{,}000)}$$

$$= \frac{\$100 + \dfrac{\$100}{10}}{\$540 + \$400}$$

$$= \frac{\$100 + \$10}{\$940} = \frac{\$110}{\$940} = 11.70\%$$

Extensive bond tables indicating yield to maturity are also available. When financial analysts speak of bond yields, the general assumption is that they are speaking of yield to maturity. This is deemed to be the most significant measure of return.

Bond Ratings

Both the issuing corporation and the investor are concerned about the rating their bond is assigned by the two major bond rating agencies—Moody's Investor Service and Standard & Poor's Corporation. The higher the rating assigned a given issue, the lower the required interest payments are to satisfy potential investors. This is because highly rated bonds carry lower risk. A major industrial corporation may be able to issue a 30-year bond at 9.5 percent yield to maturity because it is rated Aaa, whereas a smaller, regional firm may only qualify for a B rating and be forced to pay 12 or 13 percent.

As an example of rating systems, Moody's Investor Service provides the following nine categories of ranking:

Aaa   Aa   A   Baa   Ba   B   Caa   Ca   C

The first two categories represent the highest quality (for example, IBM and Procter & Gamble); the next two, medium to high quality; and so on. Beginning in 1982, Moody's began applying numerical modifiers to categories Aa through B: 1 is the highest in a category, 2 is the mid-range, and 3 is the lowest. Thus, a Aa2 rating means the bond is in the mid-range of Aa. Standard & Poor's has a similar letter system with + and − modifiers.

Bonds receive ratings based on the corporation's ability to make interest payments, its consistency of performance, its size, its debt–equity ratio, its working capital position, and a number of other factors. The yield spread between higher- and lower-rated bonds changes with the economy. If investors are pessimistic about economic events, they will accept as much as 3 percent less return to go into securities of very high quality, whereas in more normal times the spread may be only 1.5 percent.

Examining Actual Bond Ratings

Three actual bond offerings are presented in Table 16–4 to illustrate the various terms we have used.

Table 16–4
Outstanding bond issues

		Rating	Price	Yield Maturity
Exxon 6's	Sinking-fund debentures due 1997	Aaa	$780	9.50%
Duke Power Co. 10⅛ s . . .	Senior mortgage bonds due 2009	Aa2	$997	10.19%
Pier I 11½ s	Subordinated debentures due 2003	B1	$905	12.93%

The student will recall first of all that the true return on a bond issue is measured by yield to maturity (the last column of Table 16–4). Directing our attention to the Exxon bonds, we note that the oil bonds are unsecured, as indicated by the term *debentures*. Furthermore, they have a sinking-fund provision for retirement of debt. Because of the extremely high quality of the company and the sinking-fund retirement plan, the bonds are accorded a Aaa rating. Nevertheless, the bonds carry a market price of $780 because the interest rate at time of issue (6 percent) is below the demanded rate of interest of 9.5 percent in early 1988 for bonds of equal quality and maturity. Similar observations may be made for the other two bond issues.

The Refunding Decision

Assume you are the financial vice president for a corporation that has issued bonds at 11.75 percent, only to witness a drop in interest rates to

9.5 percent. If you do not believe interest rates will go down further, and in fact believe that they will go back up, you may wish to redeem the expensive 11.75 percent bonds and to issue new debt at the prevailing 9.5 percent rate. This process is labeled a "refunding operation." It is made feasible by the call provision that enables a corporation to buy back bonds at close to par, rather than at high market values, when interest rates are declining. Although long-term interest rates tended to move up in the 50s, 60s, 70s, and 80s, there were periods of decline in interest rates that provided an excellent environment for refunding. The mid- to late-1980s was one such period.

A Capital Budgeting Problem

The refunding decision involves outflows in the form of financing costs related to redeeming and reissuing securities, and inflows represented by savings in annual interest costs and some tax savings. In the present case, we shall assume that the corporation issued $10 million worth of 11.75 percent debt with a 25-year maturity and that the debt has been on the books for five years. The corporation now has the opportunity to buy back the old debt at 10 percent above par (the call premium) and to issue new debt at 9.5 percent interest with a 20-year life. The underwriting cost for the old issue was $125,000, and the underwriting cost for the new issue is $200,000. We shall also assume that the corporation is in the 34 percent tax bracket and uses a 6 percent discount rate for refunding decisions. Since the savings from a refunding decision are certain—unlike the savings from most other capital budgeting decisions—we use the aftertax cost of new debt as the discount rate, rather than the more generalized cost of capital.[4] Actually, in this case, the aftertax cost of new debt is 9.5 percent × (1 − Tax rate), or 9.5% × 0.66 = 6.27%. We round to 6 percent. The facts in this example are restated at the top of page 485.

---

[4] A minority opinion would be that there is sufficient similarity between the bond refunding decision and other capital budgeting decisions to disallow any specialized treatment. Also, note that although the bondholders must still bear some risk of default, for which they are compensated, the corporation assumes no risk.

Restatement of facts

	Old Issue	New Issue
Size	$10,000,000	$10,000,000
Interest rate	11.75%	9.5%
Total life	25 years	20 years
Remaining life	20 years	20 years
Call premium	10%	—
Underwriting costs	$125,000	$200,000
Tax bracket	34%	
Discount rate	6%	

Let's go through the capital budgeting process of defining our outflows and inflows and determining the net percent value.

Step A—Outflow considerations

1. *Payment of call premium*—The first outflow is the 10 percent call premium on $10 million, or $1 million. This prepayment penalty is necessary to call in the original issue. Being an *out-of-pocket* tax-deductible expense, the $1 million cash expenditure will cost us only $660,000 on an aftertax basis. We multiply the expense by $(1 - \text{Tax rate})$ to get the aftertax cost.

$$\$1,000,000 \ (1 - T) = \$1,000,000 \ (1 - 0.34) = \$660,000$$

Net cost of call premium = $660,000

2. *Underwriting cost on new issue*—The second outflow is the $200,000 underwriting cost on the new issue. The actual cost is somewhat less because the payment is tax deductible, though the write-off must be spread over the life of the bond. While the actual $200,000 is being spent now, equal tax deductions of $10,000 a year will take place over the next 20 years (in a manner similar to depreciation).

The tax savings from a *noncash* write-off equal the amount times the tax rate. For a company in the 34 percent tax bracket, $10,000 of annual tax deductions will provide $3,400 of tax savings each year for the next 20 years. The present value of these savings is the present value of a $3,400 annuity for 20 years at 6 percent interest:

$$\$3,400 \times 11.470 \ (n = 20, i = 6\%) = \$38,998$$

The net cost of underwriting the new issue is the actual expenditure now, minus the present value of future tax savings:

```
Actual expenditure  . . . . . . . .  $200,000
 − PV of future tax savings   . . . .    38,998
Net cost of underwriting
    expense on the new issue . . . .  $161,002
```

Step B—Inflow Considerations

The major inflows in the refunding decision are related to the reduction of annual interest expense and the immediate write-off of the underwriting cost on the old issue.

3. *Cost savings in lower interest rates*—The corporation will enjoy a 2.25 percent drop in interest rates, from 11.75 percent to 9.50 percent, on $10 million of bonds.

```
11.75% × $10,000,000 . . . .  $1,175,000
 9.50% × $10,000,000 . . . .     950,000
Savings . . . . . . . . . .   $ 225,000
```

Since we are in the 34 percent tax bracket, this is equivalent to $148,500 of aftertax benefits per year for 20 years. We have taken the savings and multiplied by one minus the tax rate to get the aftertax benefits.

$$\$225,000 \ (1 - T)$$
$$\$225,000 \ (1 - 0.34)$$
$$\$148,500$$

Applying a 6 percent discount rate for a 20-year annuity:

$$\$148,500 \times 11.470 \ (n = 20, i = 6\%) = \$1,703,295$$

```
Cost savings in lower interest rates . . . . $1,703,295
```

4. *Underwriting cost on old issue*—There is a further cost savings related to immediately writing off the remaining underwriting costs on the old bonds. Note that the initial amount of $125,000 was spent five years ago and was to be written off for tax purposes over 25 years at $5,000 per year. Since five years have passed, $100,000 of old underwriting costs have not been amortized.

```
Original amount  . . . . . . . . . . . .  $125,000
Written off over five years . . . . . . . .    25,000
Unamortized old underwriting costs . . . .  $100,000
```

There is a tax benefit associated with the immediate write-off of old underwriting costs, which we shall consider shortly.

Note, however, that this is not a total gain. We would have gotten the $100,000 additional write-off eventually if we had not called in the old bonds. By calling them in now, we simply take the write-off sooner. If we extended the write-off over the remaining life, we would have taken $5,000 a year for 20 years. Discounting this value, we show:

$$\$5,000 \times 11.470 \ (n = 20, i = 6\%) = \$57,350$$

Thus, we are getting a write-off of $100,000 now, rather than a present value of future write-offs of $57,350. The gain in immediate tax write-offs is $42,650. The tax savings from a *noncash* tax write-off equal the amount times the tax rate. Since we are in the 34 percent tax bracket, our savings from this write-off are $14,501.

Immediate write-off	$100,000
− PV of future write-off	57,350
Gain from immediate write-off	$42,650

$$\$42,650(T)$$
$$42,650(.34) = \$14,501$$

Net gain from the underwriting on the old issue . . . $14,501

Step C—Net Present Value

We now compare our outflows and our inflows.

Outflows		Inflows	
1. Net cost of call premium	$660,000	3. Cost savings in lower interest rates	$1,703,295
2. Net cost of under-writing expense on new issue	161,002	4. Net gain from under-writing cost on old issue	14,501
	$821,002		$1,717,796

Present value of inflows	$1,717,796
Present value of outflows	821,002
Net present value	$ 896,794

The refunding decision has a positive net present value, suggesting that interest rates have dropped to a sufficiently low level to indicate refunding is in order. The only question is, Will interest rates go lower—indicating an even better time for refunding? This is a consideration that all firms must face, and there is no easy answer.

A number of other factors could be plugged into the problem. For example, there could be overlapping time periods in the refunding procedure when both issues are outstanding and the firm is paying double interest (hopefully for less than a month). The dollar amount, however, tends to be quite small and is not included in the analysis.

In working problems, the student should have minimum difficulty if he or she follows the four suggested calculations. Note, by way of review, that in each of the four calculations we had the following tax implications:

1. Payment of call premium—the cost equals the amount times (1 − Tax rate) for this *cash tax-deductible expense*.
2. Underwriting costs on new issue—we pay an amount now and then amortize it over the life of the bond for tax purposes. This subsequent amortization is similar to depreciation and represents a *noncash write-off* of a tax-deductible expense. The tax saving from the amortization is equal to the amount times the tax rate.
3. Cost savings in lower interest rates—cost savings are like any form of income, and we will retain the cost savings times (1 − Tax rate).
4. Underwriting cost on old issue—once again, the writing off of underwriting costs represents a *noncash write-off* of a tax-deductible expense. The tax savings from the amortization are equal to the amount times the tax rate.

Innovative Forms of Bond Financing

As interest rates continued to show increasing volatility in the 1980s, two innovative forms of bond financing became very popular. We shall examine the zero-coupon rate bond and the floating rate bond.

The zero-coupon rate bond, as the name implies, does not pay interest. It is, however, sold at a deep discount from face value. The return to the investor is the difference between the investor's cost and the face value received at the end of the life of the bond. For example, in early 1982, BankAmerica Corporation offered $1,000 zero-coupon rate bonds with maturities of 5, 8, and 10 years. The 5-year bonds were sold for $500, the 8-year bonds for $333.33, and the 10-year bonds for $250. All three provided an initial yield to maturity (through gain in value) of approximately 14.75 percent. A dramatic case of a zero-coupon bond was an issue offered by PepsiCo, Inc., in 1982, in which the maturities ranged from 6 to 30 years. The 30-year $1,000 par value issue could be purchased for $26.43, providing a yield of approximately 12.75 percent. The purchase price per bond of $26.43 represents only 2.643 percent of the par value. A million dollars worth of these 30-year bonds could be initially purchased for a mere $26,430.

The advantage to the corporation is that there is immediate cash inflow to the corporation, without any outflow until the bonds mature. Furthermore, the difference between the initial bond price and the maturity value may be amortized for tax purposes by the corporation over the life of the bond. This means that the corporation will be taking annual deductions without current cash outflow.

From the investor's viewpoint, the zero-coupon bonds allow him or her to lock in a multiplier of the initial investment. For example, an investor may know that he will get four times his investment in 10 (or perhaps 12) years. The major drawback is that the annual increase in the value of bonds is taxable as ordinary income as it accrues, even though the bondholder does not have his return until maturity. For this reason, most investors in zero-coupon rate bonds have tax-exempt or deferred status (pension funds, foundations, charitable organizations, Individual Retirement Accounts, and the like).

The prices of the bonds tend to be highly volatile because of changes in interest rates. Even though the bonds provide no annual interest payment, there is still an initial yield to maturity that may prove to be too high or too low with changes in the marketplace.

In the 1980s, Merrill Lynch and Salomon Brothers and other brokerage houses began offering a variation of the zero-coupon rate bond through selling future interests in government securities. The securities, which are held in custody for the benefit of investors, are sold at a fraction of face value and ultimately redeemed at full value. The investor receives a multiple of the original investment and no interest. These securities tend to be long term (20–30 years).

A second type of innovative bond issue is the floating rate bond (already quite popular in European capital markets). In this case, instead of a change in the price of the bond, the interest rate paid on the bond changes with market conditions (usually monthly or quarterly). Thus, a bond that was initially issued to pay 13 percent may lower the interest payments to 10 percent during some years and raise them to 16 percent in others. The interest rate is usually tied to some overall market rate, such as the yield on Treasury bonds (perhaps 120 percent of the going yield on long-term Treasury bonds).

The advantage to the investor is that he or she has a constant (or almost constant) market value for the security, even though interest rates vary. The one exception that can cause a change to this principle is that floating rate bonds often have broad limits that interest payments cannot exceed.

For example, the interest rate on a 13 percent initial offering may not be allowed to go over 20 percent or below 6 percent. If long-term interest rates dictated an interest payment of 22 percent, the payment would still remain at 20 percent. This could cause some short-term loss in market value. To date, floating rate bonds have been relatively free of this problem.

To keep matters in perspective, zero-coupon rate bonds and floating rate bonds still represent a relatively small percentage of the total market of new debt offerings. Nevertheless, they are gaining in importance and should be part of a basic understanding of long-term debt instruments.

Advantages and Disadvantages of Debt

The financial manager must consider whether debt will contribute to or detract from the firm's operations. In certain industries, such as the airlines, very heavy debt utilization is a way of life, whereas in other industries (drugs, photographic equipment) reliance is placed on other forms of capital.

Benefits of Debt

The advantages of debt may be enumerated as:

1. Interest payments are tax deductible. Because the maximum corporate tax rate is 34 percent, the effective aftertax cost of interest is approximately two-thirds of the dollar amount expended.
2. The financial obligation is clearly specified and of a fixed nature (with the exception of floating rate bonds). Contrast this with selling an ownership interest in which stockholders have open-end participation in the sharing of profits.
3. In an inflationary economy, debt may be paid back with "cheaper dollars." A $1,000 bond obligation may be repaid in 10 or 20 years with dollars that have shrunk in value by 50 or 60 percent. In terms of "real dollars," or purchasing power equivalents, one might argue that the corporation should be asked to repay something in excess of $2,000. Presumably, high interest rates in inflationary periods compensate the lender for loss in purchasing power, but this is not always the case.
4. The use of debt, up to a prudent point, may lower the cost of capital to the firm. To the extent that debt does not strain the risk position of the firm, its low aftertax cost may aid in reducing the weighted overall cost of financing to the firm.

Drawbacks of Debt

Finally, we must consider the disadvantages of debt:

1. Interest and principal payment obligations are set by contract and must be met, regardless of the economic position of the firm.
2. Both indenture agreements may place burdensome restrictions on the firm, such as maintenance of working capital at a given level, limits on future debt offerings, and guidelines for dividend policy. Although bondholders generally do not have the right to vote, they may take virtual control of the firm if important indenture provisions are not met.
3. Utilized beyond a given point, debt may serve as a depressant on outstanding common stock values.

Eurobond Market

A final item of interest in the bond market is the Eurobond. A Eurobond takes us out of the purely domestic framework and into foreign markets. It may be defined as a bond payable in the borrower's currency but sold outside the borrower's country, usually by an international syndicate. An example might be a bond of a U.S. corporation, payable in dollars and sold in London, Paris, or Frankfurt. Disclosure requirements in the Eurobond market are less demanding than those of the Securities and Exchange Commission or other domestic regulatory agencies. Investors in Eurobonds are generally not able to rely on bond-rating agencies, though Moody's and Standard & Poor's have been rating selected Eurobond issues for a fee.

Leasing as a Form of Debt

When a corporation contracts to lease an oil tanker or a computer and signs a noncancelable, long-term agreement, the transaction has all the characteristics of a debt obligation. Long-term leasing was not recognized as a debt obligation in the early post-World War II period, but since the mid-60s there has been a strong movement by the accounting profession to force companies to fully divulge all information about leasing obligations and to indicate the equivalent debt characteristics.

This position was made official for financial reporting purposes as a result of Statement 13, issued by the Financial Accounting Standard Board (FASB) in November 1976. In essence, this statement said that certain types of leases must be shown as long-term obligations on the financial statements of the firm. Prior to FASB Statement 13, lease obligations could merely be divulged in footnotes to financial statements, and large lease obligations did not have to be included in the debt structure (except for the upcoming payment). Consider the case of firm ABC, whose balance sheet is shown in Table 16–5.

Table 16–5
Balance sheet
($ millions)

Current assets	$ 50	Current liabilities	$ 50
Fixed assets	150	Long-term liabilities	50
		Total liabilities	100
		Stockholders' equity	100
		Total liabilities and stockholders'	
Total assets	$200	equity	$200

Prior to the issuance of FASB Statement 13, a footnote to the financial statements might have indicated a lease obligation of $12 million a year for the next 15 years, with a present value of $100 million dollars. With the issuance of FASB Statement 13, this information has, of necessity, been moved directly to the balance sheet, as indicated in Table 16–6.

Table 16–6
Revised balance
sheet ($ millions)

Current assets	$ 50	Current liabilities	$ 50
Fixed assets	150	Long-term liabilities	50
*Leased property		*Obligation under	
under capital lease	100	capital lease	100
		Total liabilities	200
		Stockholders' equity	100
		Total liabilities and stockholders'	
Total assets	$300	equity	$300

*See text, below.

We see that both a new asset and a new liability have been created, as indicated by the asterisks. The essence of this treatment is that a long-term, noncancelable lease is tantamount to purchasing the asset with borrowed funds, and this should be reflected on the balance sheet. Note that between the original balance sheet (Table 16–5) and the revised balance sheet (Table 16–6), the total-debt-to-total-assets ratio has gone from 50 percent to 66.7 percent.

$$\text{Original:} \quad \frac{\text{Total debt}}{\text{Total assets}} = \frac{\$100 \text{ million}}{\$200 \text{ million}} = 50\%$$

$$\text{Revised:} \quad \frac{\text{Total debt}}{\text{Total assets}} = \frac{\$200 \text{ million}}{\$300 \text{ million}} = 66.7\%$$

Though this represents a substantial increase in the ratio, the impact on the firm's credit rating or stock price may be minimal. To the extent that the financial markets are efficient, the information was *already* known by analysts who took the data from footnotes or other sources and made their own adjustments. Nevertheless, corporate financial officers fought long, hard, and unsuccessfully to keep the lease obligation off the balance sheet. They tend to be much less convinced about the efficiency of the marketplace.

Capital Lease versus Operating Lease

Actually, not all leases must be capitalized (present-valued) and placed on the balance sheet. It is only under circumstances in which substantially all the benefits and risks of ownership are transferred in a lease that this treatment is necessary. Under these circumstances, we have a *capital* (or financing) lease. Identification as a capital lease and the attendant financial treatment are required whenever any *one* of the four following conditions is present:

1. The arrangement transfers ownership of the property to the lessee (the leasing party) by the end of the lease term.
2. The lease contains a bargain purchase price at the end of the lease. The option price will have to be sufficiently low so exercise of the option appears reasonably certain.
3. The lease term is equal to 75 percent or more of the estimated life of the leased property.
4. The present value of the minimum lease payments equals 90 percent or more of the fair value of the leased property at the inception of the lease.[5]

A lease that does not meet any of these four criteria is not regarded as a *capital* lease, but as an *operating* lease. An operating lease is usually short term and is often cancelable at the option of the lessee. Furthermore, the lessor (the owner of the asset) may provide for the maintenance and upkeep of the asset, since he or she is likely to get it back. An operating lease does not require the *capitalization*, or presentation, of the full ob-

---

[5]The discount rate used for this test is the leasing firm's new cost of borrowing or the lessor's (the firm that owns the asset) implied rate of return under the lease. The lower of the two must be used when both are known.

ligation on the balance sheet. Operating leases are used most frequently with such assets as automobiles and office equipment, while capital leases are used with oil drilling equipment, airplanes and rail equipment, certain forms of real estate, and other long-term assets. The greatest volume of leasing obligations is represented by capital leases.

Income Statement Effect

The capital lease calls not only for present-valuing the lease obligation on the balance sheet but also for treating the arrangement for income statement purposes as if it were somewhat similar to a purchase-borrowing arrangement. Thus, under a capital lease the intangible asset account shown in Table 16–6 as "Leased property under capital lease" is amortized or written off over the life of the lease with an annual expense deduction. Also, the liability account shown in Table 16–6 as "Obligation under capital lease" is written off through regular amortization, with an implied interest expense on the remaining balance. Thus, for financial reporting purposes the annual deductions are amortization of the asset, plus the implied interest expense on the remaining present value of the liability. Though the actual development of these values and accounting rules is best deferred to an accounting course, the finance student should understand the close similarity between a capital lease and borrowing to purchase an asset, for financial reporting purposes.

An operating lease, on the other hand, usually calls for an annual expense deduction equal to the lease payment, with no specific amortization, as is indicated in Appendix 16B (Lease versus Purchase Decision) at the end of this chapter.

Advantages of Leasing

Why is leasing so popular? It has emerged as a $100 billion industry, with such firms as Clark Equipment, Citicorp, and U.S. Leasing International providing an enormous amount of financing. Major reasons for the popularity of leasing include the following:

1. The lessee may lack sufficient funds or the credit capability to purchase the asset from a manufacturer, who is willing, however, to accept a lease arrangement or to arrange a lease obligation with a third party.

2. The provisions of a lease obligation may be substantially less restrictive than those of a bond indenture.
3. There may be no down payment requirement, as would generally be the case in the purchase of an asset (leasing allows for a larger indirect loan).
4. The lessor may possess particular expertise in a given industry—allowing for expert product selection, maintenance, and eventual resale. Through this process, the negative effects of obsolescence may be reduced.
5. Creditor claims on certain types of leases, such as real estate, are restricted in bankruptcy and reorganization proceedings. Leases on chattels (non-real estate items) have no such limitation.

There are also some tax factors to be considered. Where one party to a lease is in a higher tax bracket than the other party, certain tax advantages, such as depreciation write-off or research-related tax credits, may be better utilized. For example, a wealthy party may purchase an asset for tax purposes, then lease the asset to another party in a lower tax bracket for actual use. Also, lease payments on the use of land are tax-deductible, whereas landownership does not allow a similar deduction for depreciation. It should be pointed out that tax advantages related to leasing were reduced somewhat with the passage of the Tax Reform Act of 1986.

Finally, a firm may wish to engage in a sale-leaseback arrangement, in which assets already owned by the lessee are sold to the lessor and then leased back. This process provides the lessee with an infusion of capital, while allowing the lessee to continue to use the asset. Even though the dollar costs of a leasing arrangement are often higher than the dollar costs of owning an asset, the advantages cited above may outweigh the direct cost factors.

Summary

The use of debt financing by corporations has grown very rapidly since the end of World War II, and the quality of corporate debt coverage has deteriorated.

Corporate bonds may be secured by a lien on a specific asset or may carry an unsecured designation, indicating that the bondholder possesses a general claim against the corporation. A special discussion of the hierarchy of claims for firms in financial distress is presented in Appendix 16A.

Bond prices have been in a steady decline for the last four decades, due to rising interest rates. Nevertheless, cyclical downturns in interest rates have afforded an excellent opportunity for refunding—that is, replacing high-interest-rate bonds with lower-interest-rate bonds. This was particularly true in the mid- to late-1980s. The financial manager must consider whether the savings in interest will compensate for the additional cost of calling in the old issue and selling a new one.

Finally, the long-term, noncancelable lease should be considered as a special debt form available to the corporation. It is capitalized on the balance sheet to represent both a debt and an asset account and is amortized on a regular basis. Leasing offers a means of financing in which lessor expertise and other financial benefits can be imparted to the lessee (leasing party).

A lease versus purchase decision for an operating lease is presented in Appendix 16B.

List of Terms

par value	coupon rate
maturity date	current yield
indenture	yield to maturity
secured debt	bond ratings
mortgage agreement	refunding
unsecured debt	capital lease
debenture	operating lease
subordinated debenture	Eurobond
serial payments	zero-coupon rate bond
sinking fund	floating rate bond
call feature	

Discussion Questions

1. Corporate debt has been expanding very dramatically since World War II. What has been the impact on interest coverage, particularly since 1967?

2. What are some of the basic features of bond agreements?

3. What is the difference between a bond agreement and a bond indenture?

4. Discuss the relationship between the coupon rate (original interest rate at time of issue) on a bond and its security provisions.

5. Take the following list of securities and arrange them in order of their priority of claims:

Preferred stock	Senior debenture
Subordinated debenture	Senior secured debt
Common stock	Junior secured debt

6. What method of "bond repayment" reduces debt and increases the amount of common stock outstanding?

7. What is the purpose of serial repayments and sinking funds?

8. Under what circumstances would a call on a bond be exercised by a corporation? What is the purpose of a deferred call?

9. Discuss the relationship between bond prices and interest rates. What impact do changing interest rates have on the price of long-term bonds versus short-term bonds?

10. What is the difference between the following yields: coupon rate, current yield, yield to maturity?

11. How does the bond rating affect the interest rate paid by a corporation on its bonds?

12. Bonds of different risk classes will have a spread between their interest rates. Is this spread always the same? Why?

13. Explain how the bond refunding problem is similar to a capital budgeting decision?

14. What cost of capital is generally used in evaluating a bond refunding decision? Why?

15. Discuss the advantages and disadvantages of debt.

16. Explain how the zero-coupon rate bond provides return to the investor. What are the advantages to the corporation?

17. Explain how floating rate bonds can save the investor from potential embarrassments in portfolio valuation.

18. What do we mean by capitalizing lease payments?

19. Explain the close parallel between a capital lease and the borrow-purchase decision from the viewpoint of both the balance sheet and the income statement.

Problems

1. The Archer Corporation has a bond outstanding with a $110 annual interest payment, a market price of $800, and a maturity date in 10 years. (Assume that the par value of bonds in all the following problems is $1,000 unless otherwise specified.) Find the following:
   a. The coupon rate.
   b. The current yield.
   c. The approximate yield to maturity.

2. The Lincoln Investment Fund buys 900 bonds of the Nichols Corporation through its broker. The bonds pay 11 percent annual interest. The yield to maturity (market rate of interest) is 14 percent. The bonds have a 25-year maturity. Using an assumption of semiannual interest payments:
   a. Compute the price of a bond (refer to "semiannual interest and bond prices" in Chapter 10 for review if necessary).
   b. Compute the total value of the 900 bonds.

3. Marvin Gardens pays a 12 percent coupon rate on debentures that are due in 20 years. The current yield to maturity on bonds of similar risk is 10 percent. The bonds are currently callable at $1,060. The theoretical value of the bonds will be equal to the present value of the expected cash flow from the bonds. This is the normal definition we use.
   a. Find the theoretical market value of the bonds using semiannual analysis.
   b. Do you think the bonds will sell for the price you arrived at in part *a?* Why?

4. The yield to maturity for 15-year bonds is as follows for four different bond rating categories.

Aaa	9.4%	Aa2	10.0%
Aa1	9.6	Aa3	10.2

   The bonds of Falter Corporation were rated as Aa1 and issued at par a few weeks ago. The bonds have just been downgraded to Aa2. Determine the new price of the bonds, assuming a 15-year maturity and semiannual interest payments.

5. A previously issued Aa1, 20-year industrial bond provides a return one fourth higher than the prime interest rate of 9 percent. Previously

issued public utility bonds provide a yield of one half of a percentage point higher than previously issued industrial bonds. Finally, new issues of Aa1 public utility bonds pay ⅜ths of a percentage point more than previously issued public utility bonds.

What should the interest rate be on a newly issued Aa1 public utility bond?

6. A 15-year, $1,000 par value zero-coupon rate bond is to be issued to yield 12 percent.

    a. What should be the initial price of the bond? (Take the present value of $1,000 for 15 years at 12 percent using Appendix B.)

    b. If immediately upon issue, interest rates dropped to 10 percent, what would be the value of the zero-coupon rate bond?

    c. If immediately upon issue, interest rates increased to 14 percent, what would be the value of the zero-coupon rate bond?

7. Ten years ago, the Citicorpse Corporation borrowed $7,650,000. Since then, cumulative inflation has been 70 percent (approximately 5.5 percent per year).

    a. When the firm repays the original $7,650,000 loan this year, what will be the effective purchasing power of the $7,650,000? (Hint: divide the loan amount by one plus cumulative inflation.)

    b. To maintain the original $7,650,000 purchasing power, how much should the lender be repaid?

    c. If the lender knows he will only receive $7,650,000 in payment after 10 years, how might he be compensated for the loss in purchasing power?

8. A $1,000 par value bond was issued 25 years ago at a 12 percent coupon rate. It currently has 15 years remaining to maturity. Interest rates on similar debt obligations are now 8 percent.

    a. What is the current price of the bond? (Look up the answer in Table 16–3.)

    b. Assume Mr. Sharp bought the bond three years ago, when it had a price of $1,070. He paid 30 percent of the purchase price in cash and borrowed the rest (known as buying on margin). He used the interest payments from the bond to cover the interest costs on the loan. By what percentage did the bond price increase from the time it was purchased by Mr. Sharp to the present (value computed in part *a*).

    c. What is Mr. Sharp's percentage gain on his cash investment?

9. The Delta Corporation has a $20 million bond obligation outstanding, which it is considering refunding. Though the bonds were initially issued at 13 percent, the interest rates on similar issues have declined to 11.5 percent. The bonds were originally issued for 20 years and have 16 years remaining. The new issue would be for 16 years. There is a 9 percent call premium on the old issue. The underwriting cost on the new $20,000,000 issue is $560,000 and the underwriting cost on the old issue was $400,000. The company is in a 40 percent tax bracket, and it will use a 7 percent discount rate (rounded aftertax cost of debt) to analyze the refunding decision.

   Should the old issue be refunded with new debt?

10. The Harding Corporation has $50 million of bonds outstanding which were issued at a coupon rate of 13⅞ percent seven years ago. Interest rates have fallen to 13 percent. Mr. Warren, the vice president of finance, does not expect rates to fall any further. The bonds have 18 years left to maturity, and Mr. Warren would like to refund the bonds with a new issue of equal amount also having 18 years to maturity. The Harding Corporation has a tax rate of 34 percent. The underwriting cost on the old issue was 2.5 percent of the total bond value. The underwriting cost on the new issue will be 1.8 percent of the total bond value. The original bond indenture contained a five-year protection against a call, with an 8 percent call premium starting in the sixth year and scheduled to decline by one-half percent each year thereafter (consider the bond to be seven years old for purposes of computing the premium). Assume the discount rate is equal to the aftertax cost of new debt rounded to the nearest whole number. Should the Harding Corporation refund the old issue?

11. In problem 10, what would be the aftertax cost of the call premium at the end of the year 13 (in dollar value)?

12. The Richmond Corporation has just signed a 144-month lease on an asset with an 18-year life. The minimum lease payments are $3,000 per month ($36,000 per year) and are to be discounted back to the present at an 8 percent annual discount rate. The estimated fair value of the property is $290,000. Should the lease be recorded as a capital lease or an operating lease?

13. The Bradley Corporation has heavy lease commitments. Prior to FASB Statement No. 13, it merely footnoted lease obligations in the balance sheet, which appeared as follows:

BRADLEY CORPORATION

($ millions)

Current assets $150	Current liabilities . . . . $ 50
Fixed assets 250	Long-term liabilities 100
	Total liabilities 150
	Stockholders' equity 250
	Total liabilities and
Total assets $400	stockholders' equity $400

The footnotes stated that the company had $22 million in annual capital lease obligations over the next 20 years.

a. Discount these annual lease obligations back to the present at a 7 percent discount rate (round to the nearest million dollars).

b. Construct a revised balance sheet that includes lease obligations, as in Table 16–6.

c. Compute total debt to total assets on the original and revised balance sheets.

d. Compute total debt to equity on the original and revised balance sheets.

e. In an efficient capital market environment, should FASB Statement 13 consequences, as viewed in the answers to parts *c* and *d*, change stock prices and credit ratings?

f. Comment on management's perception of market efficiency (the viewpoint of the financial officer).

14. The Rosen Corporation plans to lease an $800,000 asset to the Boone Corporation. The lease will be for 12 years.

a. If the Rosen Corporation desires a 10 percent return on its investment, how much should the lease payments be?

b. If the Rosen Corporation is able to generate $120,000 in immediate tax shield benefits from the asset to be purchased for the lease arrangement, and will pass the benefits along to the Boone Corporation in the form of lower lease payments, how much should the revised lease payments be? Continue to assume the Rosen Corporation desires a 10 percent return on the 12-year lease.

Selected References

Boot, John C. G., and George M. Frankfurter. "The Dynamics of Corporate Debt Management." *Journal of Financial and Quantitative Analysis* 7 (September 1972), pp. 1957–66.

Brennan, Michael J., and Eduardo S. Schwartz. "Bond Pricing and Market Efficiency." *Financial Analysts Journal* 38 (September–October 1982), pp. 49–56.

Brick, Ivan; William Fung; and Marti Subrahmanyam. "Leasing and Financial Intermediation: Comparative Tax Advantages." *Financial Management* 16 (Spring 1987), pp. 55–59.

Cason, Roger L. "Leasing, Asset Lives, and Uncertainty: A Practitioner's Comments." *Financial Management* 16 (Summer 1987), pp. 13–16.

Collins, Robert A. "An Empirical Comparison of Bankruptcy Prediction Models." *Financial Management* 9 (Summer 1980), pp. 52–57.

Ederington, Louis H. "Why Split Ratings Occur." *Financial Management* 15 (Spring 1986), pp. 37–47.

Ferri, Michael G. "An Empirical Examination of Determinants of Bond Yield Spreads." *Financial Management* 7 (August 1978), pp. 40–46.

Hawkins, David M., and Mary M. Wehle. *Accounting for Leases.* New York: Financial Executive Research Foundation, 1973.

Kolodny, Richard. "The Refunding Decision in the Near Perfect Markets." *Journal of Finance* 29 (December 1974), pp. 1467–78.

Lindvall, John R. "New Issue Corporate Bonds, Seasoned Market Efficiency, and Yield Spreads." *Journal of Finance* 32 (September 1977), pp. 1057–67.

Livingston, Miles. "Measuring the Benefit of a Bond Refunding: The Problem of Nonmarketable Call Options." *Financial Management* 16 (Spring 1987), pp. 38–40.

Ogden, Joseph P. "Determinants of the Relative Interest Rate Sensitivities of Corporate Bonds." *Financial Management* 16 (Spring 1987), pp. 22–30.

Pinches, George E., and Kent A. Mingo. "The Role of Subordination and Industrial Bond Ratings." *Journal of Finance* 30 (March 1975), pp. 201–6.

Rao, Ramesh K. S. "The Impact of Yield Changes on the Systematic Risk of Bonds." *Journal of Financial and Quantitative Analysis* 17 (March 1982), pp. 115–27.

Schall, Lawrence D. "Analytic Issues in Lease vs. Purchase Decisions." *Financial Management* 16 (Summer 1987), pp. 17–22.

Sibly, A. M. "Some Evidence on the Cash Flow Effects of Bond Refunding." *Financial Management* 3 (Autumn 1974), pp. 50–53.

Turnbull, Stuart M. "Swaps: A Zero Sum Game?" *Financial Management* 16 (Spring 1987), pp. 15–21.

Weingartner, H. Martin. "Leasing, Assets Lives and Uncertainty: Guides to Decision Making." *Financial Management* 16 (Summer 1987), pp. 5–12.

Appendix 16A: Financial Alternatives for Distressed Firms

A firm may be in financial distress because of *technical insolvency* or *bankruptcy*. The first term refers to a firm's inability to pay its bills as they come due. Thus, a firm may be technically insolvent, even though it has a positive net worth; there simply may not be sufficient liquid assets to meet current obligations. The second term, bankruptcy, indicates that the market value of a firm's assets are less than its liabilities and the firm has a negative net worth. Under the law, either technical insolvency or bankruptcy may be adjudged as a financial failure of the business firm.

There are also many firms that do not fall into either category but are still suffering from extreme financial difficulties. Perhaps they are rapidly approaching a situation in which they cannot pay their bills or their net worth will soon be negative.

Firms in the types of financial difficulty discussed in the first two paragraphs may participate in out-of-court settlements or in-court settlements through formal bankruptcy proceedings under the National Bankruptcy Act.

Out-of-court settlements, where possible, allow the firm and its creditors to bypass certain lengthy and expensive legal procedures. Of course, if an agreement cannot be reached on a voluntary basis between a firm and its creditors, in-court procedures will be necessary.

Out-of-Court Settlement

Out-of-court settlements may take many forms. Four alternatives will be examined. The first is an *extension,* in which creditors agree to allow the firm more time to meet its financial obligations. A new repayment schedule will be developed, subject to the acceptance of the creditors.

A second alternative is a *composition,* under which creditors agree to accept a fractional settlement of their original claim. They may be willing to do this because they believe the firm is unable to meet its total obligations and they wish to avoid formal bankruptcy procedures. In the case of either a proposed extension or a composition, some creditors may not agree to go along with the arrangements. If their claims are relatively small, major creditors may allow them to be paid off immediately and in full to hold the agreement together. If their claims are large, no out-of-court settlement may be possible, and formal bankruptcy proceedings may be necessary.

A third type of out-of-court settlement may take the form of a *creditor committee* established to run the business. Here the parties involved assume that management can no longer effectively conduct the affairs of the firm. Once the creditors' claims have been partially or fully settled, a new management team may be brought in to replace the creditor committee. Of course, the outgoing management may be willing to accept the imposition of a creditor committee only when formal bankruptcy proceedings appear likely and they wish to avoid that stigma. There are also circumstances in which creditors are unwilling to form such a committee because they fear lawsuits from other dissatisfied creditors or from common or preferred stockholders.

A fourth type of out-of-court settlement is an *assignment*, in which liquidation of assets takes place without going through formal court action. To effect an assignment, creditors must agree on liquidation values and the relative priority of claims. This is not an easy task.

In actuality, there may be combinations of two or more of the above-described out-of-court procedures. For example, there may be an extension as well as a composition, or a creditor committee may help to establish one or more of the alternatives.

In-Court Settlements—Formal Bankruptcy

When it is apparent that an out-of-court settlement cannot be reached, the next step is formal bankruptcy. Bankruptcy proceedings may be initiated voluntarily by the company or, alternatively, by creditors.

Once the firm falls under formal bankruptcy proceedings, a referee is appointed by the court to oversee the activities. The referee becomes the arbitrator of the proceedings, whose actions and decisions are final, subject only to review by the court. A trustee will also be selected to properly determine the assets and liabilities of the firm and to carry out a plan of reorganization or liquidation for the firm.

Reorganization

If the firm is to be reorganized (under the Bankruptcy Act's Chapter 11 restructuring), the plan must prove to be fair and feasible. An *internal reorganization* calls for an evaluation of current management and their operating policies. If current management is shown to be incompetent, they will probably be discharged and replaced by new management. An evaluation and possible redesign of the current capital structure is also necessary. If the firm is top-heavy with debt (as is normally the case), alternate securities, such as preferred or common stock, may replace part of the debt.[1] Of course, it is imperative that any restructuring be fair to all parties involved.

An *external reorganization*, in which a merger partner is found for the firm, may also be considered. The surviving firm must be deemed strong enough to carry out the financial and management obligations of the joint

---

[1]Another possibility is income bonds, in which interest is payable only if earned.

entities. Old creditors and stockholders may be asked to make concessions to ensure that a feasible arrangement is established. Their motivation is that they hope to come out further ahead than if such a reorganization were not undertaken. Ideally, the firm should be merged with a strong firm in its own industry, although this is not always possible. The savings and loan and banking industries have been particularly adept at merging weaker firms with stronger firms within the industry.

Liquidation

A liquidation or sell-off of assets may be recommended when an internal or external reorganization does not appear possible, and a determination is made that the assets of the firm are worth more in liquidation than through a reorganization. Priority of claims becomes extremely important in a liquidation, because it is unlikely that all parties will be fully satisfied in their demands.

The priority of claims in a bankruptcy liquidation is as follows:

1. Cost of administering the bankruptcy procedures (lawyers get in line first).
2. Wages due workers if earned within three months of filing the bankruptcy petition. The maximum amount is $600 per worker.
3. Taxes due at the federal, state, or local level.
4. Secured creditors to the extent that designated assets are sold off to meet their claims. Secured claims that exceed the sales value of the pledged assets are placed in the same category as other general creditor claims.
5. General or unsecured creditors are next in line. Examples of claims in this category are those held by debenture (unsecured bond) holders, trade creditors, and bankers who have made unsecured loans.

   There may be senior and subordinated positions within category 5, indicating that subordinated debt holders must turn over their claims to senior debt holders until complete restitution is made to the higher-ranked category. Subordinated debenture holders may keep the balance if anything is left over after that payment.
6. Preferred stockholders.
7. Common stockholders.

The priority of claims 4 through 7 is similar to that presented in Figure 16–2 of this chapter.

Let us examine a typical situation to determine "who" should receive "what" under a liquidation in bankruptcy. Assume the Mitchell Corporation has a book value and liquidation value as shown in Table 16A–1. Liabilities and stockholders' claims are also presented.

Table 16A–1
Financial data for the Mitchell Corporation

Assets

	Book Value	Liquidation Value
Accounts receivable	$ 200,000	$ 160,000
Inventory	410,000	240,000
Machinery and equipment	240,000	100,000
Building and plant	450,000	200,000
	$1,300,000	$700,000

Liabilities and Stockholders' Claims

Liabilities:	
Accounts payable	$ 300,000
First lien, secured by machinery and equipment*	200,000
Senior unsecured debt	400,000
Subordinated debentures	200,000
Total liabilities	1,100,000
Stockholders' claims:	
Preferred stock	50,000
Common stock	150,000
Total stockholders' claims	200,000
Total liabilities and stockholders' claims	$1,300,000

*A lien represents a potential claim against property. The lien holder has a secured interest in the property.

We see that the liquidation value of the assets is far less than the book value ($700,000 versus $1,300,000). Also, the liquidation value of the assets will not cover the total value of liabilities ($700,000 compared to $1,100,000). Since all liability claims will not be met, it is evident that lower-ranked preferred stockholders and common stockholders will receive nothing.

Before a specific allocation is made to the creditors (those with liability claims), the three highest priority levels in bankruptcy must first be covered. That would include the cost of administering the proceedings, allowable past wages due to workers, and overdue taxes. For the Mitchell Corporation, we shall assume these total $100,000. Since the liquidation value of assets was $700,000, that would leave $600,000 to cover creditor demands, as indicated in the left-hand column of Table 16A–2.

Table 16A–2   Asset values and claims

Assets		Creditor Claims	
Asset values in liquidation	$700,000	Accounts payable	$ 300,000
Administrative costs, wages,		First lien, secured by	
and taxes	– 100,000	machinery and equipment	200,000
Remaining asset values	$600,000	Senior unsecured debt	400,000
		Subordinated debentures	200,000
		Total liabilities	$1,100,000

Before we attempt to allocate the values in the left-hand column of Table 16A–2 to the right-hand column, we must first identify any creditor claims that are secured by the pledge of a specific asset. In the present case, there is a first lien on the machinery and equipment of $200,000. Referring back to Table 16A–1, we observe that the machinery and equipment has a liquidation value of only $100,000. The secured debt holders will receive $100,000, with the balance of their claim placed in the same category as the unsecured debt holders. In Table 16A–3, we show asset values available for unsatisfied secured claims and unsecured debt (top portion) and the extent of the remaining claims (bottom portion).

**Table 16A–3
Asset values
available for
unsatisfied secured
claims and
unsecured debt
holders—and their
remaining claims**

Asset values:	
Asset values in liquidation	$700,000
Administrative costs, wages, and taxes	100,000
Remaining asset values	600,000
Payment to secured creditors	– 100,000
Amount available to unsatisfied	
secured claims and unsecured debt	$500,000
Remaining claims of unsatisfied	
secured debt and unsecured debt:	
Secured debt (unsatisfied first lien)	$ 100,000
Accounts payable	300,000
Senior unsecured debt	400,000
Subordinated debentures	200,000
	$1,000,000

In comparing the available asset values and claims in Table 16A–3, it appears that the settlement on the remaining claims should be at a 50 percent rate ($500,000/$1,000,000). The allocation will take place in the manner presented in Table 16A–4.

Each category receives 50 percent as an initial allocation. However, the subordinated debenture holders must transfer their $100,000 initial al-

Table 16A-4
Allocation
procedures for
unsatisfied secured
claims and
unsecured debt

(1) Category	(2) Amount of Claim	(3) Initial Allocation (50%)	(4) Amount Received
Secured debt (unsatisfied 1st lien) . . .	$ 100,000	$ 50,000	$ 50,000
Accounts payable	300,000	150,000	150,000
Senior unsecured debt	400,000	200,000	300,000
Subordinated debentures	200,000	100,000	0
	$1,000,000	$500,000	$500,000

location to the senior debt holders in recognition of their preferential position. The secured debt holders and those having accounts payable claims are not part of the senior-subordinated arrangement and, thus, hold their initial allocation position.

Finally, in Table 16A–5, we show the total amounts of claims, the amount received, and the percent of the claim that was satisfied.

Table 16A-5
Payments and
percent of claims

(1) Category	(2) Total Amount of Claim	(3) Amount Received	(4) Percent of Claim Satisfied
Secured debt (1st lien)	$200,000	$150,000	75%
Accounts payable	300,000	150,000	50
Senior unsecured debt	400,000	300,000	75
Subordinated debentures	200,000	0	0

The $150,000 in column (3) for secured debt represents the $100,000 from the sale of machinery and equipment, and $50,000 from the allocation process in Table 16A–4. The secured debt holders and senior-unsecured debt holders come out on top (it is coincidental that they are equal). Furthermore, the subordinated debt holders and, as previously mentioned, the preferred and common stockholders receive nothing. Naturally, allocations in bankruptcy will vary from circumstance to circumstance. Working problem 16A–1 will help to reinforce many of the liquidation procedure concepts discussed in this section.

List of Terms

technical insolvency   assignment
bankruptcy   internal reorganization
extension   external reorganization
composition   liquidation

Discussion Questions

16A–1. What is the difference between technical insolvency and bankruptcy?

16A–2. What are four types of out-of-court settlements? Briefly describe each.

16A–3. What is the difference between an internal reorganization and an external reorganization under formal bankruptcy procedures?

16A–4. What are the first three priority items under liquidation in bankruptcy?

Problem

16A–1. The trustee in the bankruptcy settlement for Immobil Corporation lists the following book values and liquidation values for the assets of the corporation. Liabilities and stockholders' claims are also shown below.

	Book Value	*Liquidation Value*
Assets		
Accounts receivable	$1,000,000	$ 700,000
Inventory	1,100,000	600,000
Machinery and equipment	800,000	400,000
Building and plant	3,000,000	1,800,000
	$5,900,000	$3,500,000
Liabilities and Stockholders' Claims		
Liabilities:		
Accounts payable	$2,000,000	
First lien, secured by machinery and equipment	650,000	
Senior unsecured debt	1,300,000	
Subordinated debentures	1,450,000	
Total liabilities	5,400,000	
Stockholders' claims:		
Preferred stock	100,000	
Common stock	400,000	
Total stockholders' claims	500,000	
Total liabilities and stockholders' claims	$5,900,000	

a. Compute the difference between the liquidation value of the assets and the liabilities.

b. Based on the answer to part *a*, will preferred stock or common stock participate in the distribution?

c. Assuming that the administrative costs of bankruptcy, workers' allowable wages, and unpaid taxes add up to $300,000, what is the total of remaining asset value available to cover secured and unsecured claims?

d. After the machinery and equipment is sold to partially cover the first lien secured claim, how much will be available from the remaining asset liquidation values to cover unsatisfied secured claims and unsecured debt?

e. List the remaining asset claims of unsatisfied secured debt holders and unsecured debt holders in a manner similar to that shown at the bottom portion of Table 16A–3.

f. Compute a ratio of your answers in part *d* and part *e*. This will indicate the initial allocation ratio.

g. List the remaining claims (unsatisfied secured and unsecured) and make an initial allocation and final allocation similar to that shown in Table 16A–4. Subordinated debenture holders may keep the balance after full payment is made to senior debt holders.

h. Show the relationship of amount received to total amount of claim in a similar fashion to that of Table 16A–5. (Remember to use the sales [liquidation] value for machinery and equipment plus the allocation amount in part *g* to arrive at the total received on secured debt.)

Appendix 16B: Lease versus Purchase Decision

The classic lease versus purchase decision does not fit a *capital* leasing decision given the passage of FASB Statement 13 and the similar financial accounting and tax treatment accorded to a capital lease and borrowing to purchase. Nevertheless, the classic lease versus purchase decision is still appropriate for the short-term *operating* lease.

Assume a firm is considering the purchase of a $6,000 asset in the three year ACRS category (with a four-year write-off) or entering into two sequential operating leases, for two years each. Under the operating leases, the annual payments would be $1,400 on the first lease and $2,600 on the second lease. If a firm purchased the asset, it would pay $1,893 annually to amortize a $6,000 loan over four years at 10 percent interest. This is based on the use of Appendix D for the present value of an annuity.

$$R = \frac{A}{IF_{pva}} = \frac{\$6,000}{3.170} = \$1,893 \ (n = 4, \ i = 10\%)$$

The firm is in a 30 percent tax bracket. In doing our analysis, we look first of all at the aftertax costs of the operating lease arrangements in Table 16B–1. The tax shield in column (2) indicates the amount that the lease payments will save us in taxes. In column (3) we see the net aftertax cost of the lease arrangement.

Table 16B–1
Aftertax cost of operating leases

Year	(1) Payment	(2) Tax Shield 30% of (1)	(3) Aftertax Cost
1	$1,400	$420	$ 980
2	1,400	420	980
3	2,600	780	1,820
4	2,600	780	1,820

For the borrowing and purchasing decision, we must consider not only the amount of the payment but also separate out those items that are tax deductible. First we consider interest and then depreciation.

In Table 16B–2, we show an amortization table to pay off a $6,000 loan over four years at 10 percent interest with $1,893 annual payments. In column (1) we show the beginning balance for each year. This is followed by the annual payment in column (2). We then show the amount of interest we will pay on the beginning balance at a 10 percent rate in column (3). In column (4) we subtract the interest payment from the annual payment to determine how much is applied directly to the repayment of principal. In column (5) we subtract the repayment of principal from the beginning balance to get the year-end balance.

Table 16B–2
Amortization Table

Year	(1) Beginning Balance	(2) Annual Payment	(3) Annual Interest 10% of (1)	(4) Repayment on Principal (2) − (3)	(5) Ending Balance (1) − (4)
1	$6,000	$1,893	$600	$1,293	$4,707
2	4,707	1,893	471	1,422	3,285
3	3,285	1,893	329	1,564	1,721
4	1,721	1,893	172	1,721	0

After determining our interest payment schedule, we look at the depreciation schedule that would apply to the borrow–purchase decision. Using the three-year ACRS depreciation category (with the associated four year write-off), the asset is depreciated at the rates indicated in Table 16B–3.

**Table 16B–3
Depreciation
schedule**

Year	Depreciation Base	Depreciation Percentage	Depreciation
1	$6,000	.333	$1,998
2	6,000	.445	2,670
3 . . . . : . . .	6,000	.148	888
4	6,000	.074	444
			$6,000

We now bring our interest and depreciation schedules together in Table 16B–4 to determine the aftertax cost, or cash outflow, associated with the borrow–purchase decision.

**Table 16B–4
Aftertax cost of
borrow-purchase**

Year	(1) Payment	(2) Interest	(3) Depreciation	(4) Total tax Deductions	(5) Tax Shield 30% × (4)	(6) Net After-tax Cost (1) − (5)
1	$1,893	$600	$1,998	$2,598	$779	$1,114
2	1,893	471	2,670	3,141	942	951
3	1,893	329	888	1,217	365	1,528
4	1,893	172	444	616	185	1,708

The interest and depreciation charges are tax-deductible expenses and provide a tax shield against other income. The total deductions in column (4) are multiplied by the tax rate of 30 percent to show the tax shield benefits in column (5). In column (6), we subtract the tax shield from the payments to get the net aftertax cost, or cash outflow.

Finally, we compare the cash outflows from leasing to the cash outflows from borrowing and purchasing. To consider the time value of money, we discount the annual values at an interest rate of 7 percent. This is the aftertax cost of debt to the firm, and it is computed by multiplying the interest rate of 10 percent by (1 − Tax rate). Because the costs associated with both leasing and borrowing are contractual and certain, we use the aftertax cost of debt as the discount rate, rather than the normal cost of capital. The overall analysis is presented in Table 16B–5.

The borrow–purchase alternative has a lower present value of aftertax costs ($4,422 versus $4,646), which would appear to make it the more desirable alternative. However, many of the previously discussed qualitative factors that support leasing must also be considered in the decision-making process.

Table 16B–5
Net present-value
comparison

Year	Aftertax Cost of Leasing	Present-value Factor at 7%	Present Value	Aftertax Cost of Borrow-Purchase	Present-value Factor at 7%	Present Value
1 . . .	$ 980	0.935	916	$1,114	0.935	$1,042
2 . . .	980	0.873	856	951	0.873	830
3 . . .	1,820	0.816	1,485	1,528	0.816	1,247
4 . . .	1,820	0.763	1,389	1,708	0.763	1,303
			4,646			4,422

Problem

Problem 16B–1. The Piedmont Corporation is considering whether to borrow funds and purchase an asset or to lease the asset under an operating lease arrangement. If it purchases the asset, the cost will be $20,000. It can borrow funds for four years at 12 percent interest. The firm will use the three-year ACRS depreciation category (with the associated four-year write-off). Assume a tax rate of 34 percent.

The other alternative is to sign two operating leases, one with $5,200 for the first two years and the other with payments of $8,800 for the last two years. In your analysis, round all values to the nearest dollar.

a. Compute the aftertax cost of the leases for the four years.

b. Compute the annual payment for the loan (round to the nearest dollar).

c. Compute the amortization schedule for the loan. (Disregard a small difference from a zero balance at the end of the loan—due to rounding.)

d. Determine the depreciation schedule.

e. Compute the aftertax cost of the borrow–purchase alternative.

f. Compute the present value of the aftertax cost of the two alternatives. The aftertax cost of debt should be rounded to the nearest whole number to determine the discount rate.

g. Which alternative should be selected, based on minimizing the present value of aftertax costs?

17

Common and Preferred Stock Financing

The ultimate ownership of the firm resides in common stock, whether it is in the form of all outstanding shares of a closely held corporation or one share of IBM. In terms of legal distinctions, it is the common stockholder alone who directly controls the business. While control of the company is legally in the shareholders' hands, it is practically wielded by management on an everyday basis. It is also important to realize that large creditors may exert tremendous pressure on a firm to meet certain standards of performance, even though the creditor has no voting power.

Although there are over 45 million common stockholders in the United States, increasingly this ownership is being held by large institutional interests, rather than the individual investor. As would be expected, management has become increasingly sensitive to these large stockholders who may side with corporate raiders in voting their shares for or against merger offers or takeover attempts (these topics are covered in Chapter 20). Mutual funds, pension funds, insurance companies, and bank trust accounts are all examples of institutional investors. For example, Table 17–1 presents a list of companies with the 25 largest institutional ownerships by dollar value at the end of June 1987. Institutional investors owned 49.4 percent of IBM, worth $48.621 billion. The highest per-

514

**Table 17–1
Institutional
ownership of U.S.
companies**

Stock	Number of Institutions	Percent Owned	Ownership ($ millions)
IBM	717	49.4%	$48,621.4
General Electric	640	46.7	23,200.3
Exxon Corp.	612	34.7	23,046.6
Ford Motor	426	59.7	15,872.3
Digital Equipment	480	74.4	15,829.2
Merck & Co.	529	58.1	13,529.2
Philip Morris	534	58.4	12,460.5
Du Pont Co.	492	38.0	10,961.1
General Motors	503	40.9	10,799.9
Eastman Kodak	527	52.6	10,231.2
Sears Roebuck	474	52.8	10,063.8
Johnson & Johnson	497	62.6	9,946.3
Minnesota Min. & Mfg.	500	59.4	9,614.1
Mobil Corp.	533	45.0	9,329.0
Amoco Corp.	511	41.6	9,275.6
Atlantic Richfield	506	54.4	9,229.7
Lilly (Eli) & Co.	422	67.2	8,768.3
Chevron Corp.	499	39.9	8,472.0
Coca-Cola Co.	477	50.2	8,451.5
Royal Dutch ADR	404	23.6	8,355.4
American Express	499	55.7	8,211.3
Dow Chemical	482	46.9	7,717.9
Hewlett-Packard	455	48.3	7,560.8
Procter & Gamble Co.	455	45.1	7,430.5
Bristol-Myers	524	49.7	7,082.0

Source: *Barron's*, August 31, 1987, p. 26.

centage ownership was of Digital Equipment, at 74.4. At the time this list was compiled, the stock market was near its all-time high. The values will change with the ups and downs of the stock market.

Preferred stock plays a secondary role in financing the corporate enterprise. It represents a hybrid security, combining some of the features of debt and common stock. Though the preferred stockholder does not have an ownership interest in the firm, he or she does have a priority of claims to dividends that is superior to that of the common stockholder.

In order to understand the rights and characteristics of the different means of financing, we shall examine the powers accorded to shareholders under each arrangement. In the case of common stock everything revolves around three key rights; namely, the residual claim to income, the voting right, and the right to purchase new shares. We shall examine each of these in detail and then consider the rights of preferred stockholders.

Common Stockholders' Claim to Income _____

All income that is not paid out to creditors or preferred stockholders automatically belongs to common stockholders. Thus, we say they have a residual claim to income. This is true regardless of whether these residual funds are actually paid out in dividends or retained in the corporation. A firm that earns $10 million before capital costs and pays $1 million in interest to bondholders and a like amount in dividends to preferred stockholders will have $8 million available for common stockholders.[1] Perhaps half of that will be paid out as common stock dividends and the balance will be reinvested in the business for the benefit of stockholders, with the hope of providing even greater income, dividends, and price appreciation in the future.

Of course, it should be pointed out that the common stockholder does not have a legal or enforceable claim to dividends. Whereas a bondholder may force the corporation into bankruptcy for failure to make interest payments, the common stockholder must accept circumstances as they are or attempt to change management if a new dividend policy is desired.

Occasionally, a company will have several classes of common stock outstanding that carry different rights to dividends and income. For example, Wang Laboratories, a manufacturer of word processors and office computer systems, has Class B and Class C common stock outstanding, where the Class B stock is entitled to 5 cents per share per year more in dividends than the Class C Stock. A more recent innovation, however, has come from General Motors Corporation through two acquisitions. In October of 1984, GM acquired Electronic Data Systems (EDS) for cash and General Motors Class E common stock (total value $2.5 billion), and, in 1985, GM acquired Hughes Aircraft for cash and Class H common stock (total value $5.8 billion).

Both Class E and Class H common stock are distinct from the regular GM common shares in both voting rights and dividend rights. The dividends on the Class E stock are based on the income generated by EDS, and the dividends on the Class H stock are based on the earnings of Hughes Aircraft. Both of these companies are now subsidiaries of General Motors. However, General Motors has distributed stock dividends of Class E and Class H shares to its regular GM stockholders and has thus created a minority-owned public group of shareholders for these subsidiaries. Both General Motors Class E and H shares are listed on the New York Stock Exchange.

_____

[1] Tax consequences related to interest payments are ignored for the present.

The Voting Right

Because the common stockholders are the owners of the firm, they are accorded the right to vote in the election of the board of directors and on all other major issues. Common stockholders may cast their ballots as they see fit on a given issue, or assign a proxy, or "power to cast their ballot," to management or some outside contesting group. As mentioned in the previous section, some corporations have different classes of common stock with unequal voting rights. In the case of the Wang Laboratories' Class B and C stock and General Motors' Class E and H stock, not only are dividends unequal but voting rights are also unequal. Regular General Motors common stock is entitled to one vote per share, while each GM Class E share is entitled to 0.25 votes per share and each Class H share is entitled to 0.50 vote per share. At future designated time periods, both Class E and H shares will be exchangeable for GM common shares at exchange rates based on future earnings.

In the case of Wang Laboratories, Class B and C shares were used to differentiate the original founders' shares and those shares sold to the public. The founders wanted to preserve their control of the company and assure their continuing management while at the same time raise new capital for expansion. To ensure this result the Class B common stock was sold to the public and carried a higher dividend but had inferior voting rights to the Class C founders' shares. The Class B shares as a group have 1/10 of one vote per share and elect 25 percent of the directors. The Class C shareholders have one vote per share and elect 75 percent of the board of directors. In this way the Wang family is able to maintain control of the company as founders.

Perhaps the Ford Motor Company is the biggest and best example of "founders" stock. The regular common stock (no class) has one vote and is entitled to elect 60 percent of the board of directors, and the Class B shares have one vote but are entitled as a class of shareholders to elect 40 percent of the board of directors as long as there are at least 30,375,000 Class B shares outstanding. There are currently 129 owners of Class B stock, which is solely reserved for Ford family members or their descendants, trusts, or appointed interests. As of March 31, 1988, there were 472,400,000 shares of Ford common and 38,600,000 shares of Class B. In this way the Ford family has a very important position in Henry Ford's company without owning more than about 8 percent of the current outstanding stock. Both common and Class B stock share in dividends equally, and no stock dividends may be given unless to both common and Class B in proportion to their ownership. Class B is convertible into common on a share-for-share basis.

While common stockholders and the different classes of common stock that they own may, at times, have different voting rights, they do have a vote. Bondholders and preferred stockholders may vote only when a violation of their corporate agreement exists and a subsequent acceleration of their rights takes place. For example, Continental Illinois Corporation, the Chicago banking giant on the edge of bankruptcy in 1984, failed to pay dividends on one series of preferred stock for five quarters from July 1, 1984, to September 30, 1985. The preferred stockholder agreement stated that failure to pay dividends for six consecutive quarters would result in the preferred stockholders being able to elect two directors to the board to represent their interests. Continental Illinois declared a preferred dividend in November of 1985 to pay all current and past dividends on two classes of preferred stock, thus avoiding the voting issue for preferred stockholders.

Cumulative Voting

The most important voting matter is the election of the board of directors. As indicated in Chapter 1, the board has primary responsibility for the stewardship of the corporation. If illegal or imprudent decisions are made, the board can be held legally accountable. Furthermore, members of the board of directors normally serve on a number of important subcommittees of the corporation, such as the audit committee, the long-range financial planning committee, and the salary and compensation committee. The board election process may take place through the familiar majority rule system or by cumulative voting. Under majority voting, any group of stockholders owning over 50 percent of the common stock may elect all of the directors. Under cumulative voting, it is possible for those who hold less than a 50 percent interest to elect some of the directors. The provision for some minority interests on the board is important to those who, at times, wish to challenge the prerogatives of management.

How does this cumulative voting process work? A stockholder gets one vote for each share of stock he or she owns times one vote for each director to be elected. The stockholder may then accumulate votes in favor of a specified number of directors.

Assume there are 10,000 shares outstanding, you own 1,001, and nine directors are to be elected. Your total number of votes under a cumulative election system is:

Number of shares owned	1,001
Number of directors to be elected	9
Number of votes	9,009

Let us assume you cast all your votes for the one director of your choice. With nine directors to be elected, there is no way for the owners of the remaining shares to exclude you from electing a person to one of the top nine positions. If you own 1,001 shares, the majority interest could control a maximum of 8,999 shares. This would entitle them to 80,991 votes.

Number of shares owned (majority)	8,999
Number of directors to be elected	9
Number of votes (majority)	80,991

These 80,991 votes cannot be spread thinly enough over nine candidates to stop you from electing your one director. If they are spread evenly, each of the majority's nine choices will receive 8,999 votes (80,991/9). Your choice is assured 9,009 votes. Because the nine top vote-getters win, you will claim one position. Note that candidates do not run head-on against each other (such as Place A or Place B on the ballot), but rather that the top nine candidates are accorded directorships.

To determine the number of shares needed to elect a given number of directors under cumulative voting, the following formula is used:

$$\frac{\text{Shares}}{\text{required}} = \frac{\begin{array}{c}\text{Number of directors desired} \times\\ \text{Total number of shares outstanding}\end{array}}{\begin{array}{c}\text{Total number of directors to be}\\ \text{elected} + 1\end{array}} + 1 \quad (17\text{--}1)$$

The formula reaffirms that in the previous instance 1,001 shares would elect one director.

$$\frac{1 \times 10,000}{9 + 1} + 1 = \frac{10,000}{10} + 1 = 1,001$$

If three director positions out of nine are desired, 3,001 shares are necessary.

$$\frac{3 \times 10,000}{9 + 1} + 1 = \frac{30,000}{10} + 1 = 3,001$$

Note that, with approximately 30 percent of the shares outstanding, a minority interest can control one third of the board. If instead of cumulative voting a majority rule system were utilized, a minority interest could elect no one. The group that controlled 5,001 or more shares out of 10,000 would elect each and every director.

As a restatement of the problem: If we know the number of minority shares outstanding under cumulative voting and wish to determine how many directors that can be elected, we use the formula:

Number of directors that can be elected

$$= \frac{(\text{Shares owned} - 1) \times (\text{Total number of directors to be elected} + 1)}{(\text{Total number of shares outstanding})} \qquad (17\text{--}2)$$

Plugging 3,001 shares into the formula, we show:

$$\frac{(3,001 - 1)(9 + 1)}{10,000} = \frac{3,000(10)}{10,000} = 3$$

If the formula yields an uneven number of directors, such as 3.3 or 3.8, you always round down to the nearest whole number (i.e., 3).

It is not surprising that 22 states require cumulative voting in preference to majority rule, that 18 consider it permissible as part of the corporate charter, and that only 10 make no provision for its use. Such consumer-oriented states as California, Illinois, and Michigan require cumulative voting procedures.

The Right to Purchase New Shares

In addition to a claim to residual income and the right to vote for directors, the common stockholders may also enjoy a privileged position in the offering of new securities. If the corporate charter contains a *preemptive right* provision, holders of common stock must be given the first option to purchase new shares. While only two states specifically require the use of preemptive rights, most other states allow for its inclusion in the corporation charter.

The preemptive right provision ensures that management cannot subvert the position of present stockholders by selling shares to outside interests without first offering them to current shareholders. If such protection were not afforded, a 20 percent stockholder might find his or her interest reduced to 10 percent through the distribution of new shares to outsiders. Not only would voting rights be diluted, but proportionate claims to earnings per share would be reduced.

The Use of Rights in Financing

Many corporations also engage in a preemptive rights offering to tap this built-in market for new securities—the current investors. Let us assume that the Walton Corporation has 9 million shares outstanding and that the current market price is $40 a share (the total market value is $360 million). Walton needs to raise $30 million for new plant and equipment and will sell 1 million new shares at $30 per share.[2] As part of the process, it will use a rights offering in which each old shareholder receives a first option to participate in the purchase of new shares.

Each old shareholder will receive one right for each share of stock owned and may combine a specified number of rights plus $30 cash to buy a new share of stock. Let us consider these questions:

1. How many rights should be necessary to purchase one new share of stock?
2. What is the monetary value of these rights?

Rights required   Since 9 million shares are currently outstanding and 1 million new shares will be issued, the ratio of old to new shares is 9 to 1. On this basis, the old stockholder may combine nine rights plus $30 cash to purchase one new share of stock.

A stockholder with 90 shares of stock would receive an equivalent number of rights, which could be applied toward the purchase of 10 shares of stock at $30 per share. As indicated later in the chapter, stockholders may choose to sell their rights, rather than exercise them in the purchase of new shares.

Monetary value of a right   Anything that contributes toward the privilege of purchasing a considerably higher priced stock for $30 per share must have some market value. Consider the following two-step analysis.

Nine old shares sold at $40 per share, or for $360; now one new share will be introduced for $30. Thus, we have a total market value of $390 spread over 10 shares. After the rights offering has been completed, the average value of a share is theoretically equal to $39.[3]

Nine old shares sold at $40 per share $360
One new share will sell at $30 per share   30
Total value of 10 shares $390
Average value of one share   . . . . $ 39

The rights offering thus entitles the holder to buy a stock that should carry a value of $39 (after the transactions have been completed) for $30. With a differential between the anticipated price and the subscription

[2]If this were not a rights offering, the discount from the current market price would be much smaller. The new shares might sell for $38 or $39.

[3]A number of variables may intervene to change the value. This is a "best" approximation.

price of $9 and nine rights required to participate in the purchase of one share, the value of a right in this case is $1.

Average value of one share	$39
Subscription price	30
Differential	$ 9
Rights required to buy one share	9

Formulas have been developed to determine the value of a right under any circumstance. Before they are presented, let us examine two new terms that will be part of the calculations—*rights-on* and *ex-rights*. When a rights offering is announced, a stock initially trades rights-on; that is, if you buy the stock, you will also acquire a right toward a future purchase of the stock. After a certain period (say four weeks) the stock goes ex-rights—when you buy the stock you no longer get a right toward future purchase of stock. Consider the following:

Date	Value of Stock	Value of Right
March 1: Stock trades rights-on	$40	$1 (part of $40)
April 1: Stock trades ex-rights	39	$1
April 30: End of subscription period	39	—

Once the ex-rights period is reached, the stock will go down by the theoretical value of the right. The remaining value ($39) is the ex-rights value. Though there is a time period remaining between the ex-right date (April 1) and the end of the subscription period (April 30), the market assumes the dilution has already taken place. Thus, the ex-rights value reflects precisely the same value as can be expected when the new, underpriced $30 stock issue is sold. In effect, it projects the future impact of the cheaper shares on the stock price.

The formula for the value of the right when the stock is trading rights-on is:

$$R = \frac{M_o - S}{N + 1} \qquad (17\text{--}3)$$

where

M_o = Market value—rights-on, $40

S = Subscription price, $30

N = Number of rights required to purchase a new share of stock; in this case, 9

$$\frac{\$40 - \$30}{9 + 1} = \frac{\$10}{10} = \$1$$

Using Formula 17–3, we determine that the value of a right in the Walton Corporation offering is $1. An alternative formula giving precisely the same answer is:

$$R = \frac{M_e - S}{N} \qquad (17\text{--}4)$$

The only new term is M_e, the market value of the stock when the shares are trading ex-rights. We show:

$$R = \frac{\$39 - \$30}{9} = \frac{\$9}{9} = \$1$$

These are all theoretical relationships, which may be altered somewhat in reality. If there is great enthusiasm for the new issue, the market value of the right may exceed the initial theoretical value (perhaps the right will trade for $1⅜).

Effect of Rights on Stockholder's Position

At first glance, a rights offering appears to bring great benefits to stockholders. But is this really the case? Does a shareholder really benefit from being able to buy a stock that is initially $40 (and later $39) for $30. Don't answer too quickly!

Think of it this way: Assume 100 people own shares of stock in a corporation and one day decide to sell new shares to themselves at 25 percent below current value. They cannot really enhance their wealth by selling their own product more cheaply to themselves. What is gained by purchasing inexpensive new shares is lost by diluting existing outstanding shares.

Take the case of Stockholder A, who owns nine shares before the rights offering and also has $30 in cash. His holdings would appear as follows:

Nine old shares at $40	$360
Cash	30
Total value	$390

If he receives and exercises nine rights to buy one new share at $30, his portfolio will contain:

Ten shares at $39 (diluted value)	$390
Cash	0
Total value	$390

Clearly, he is no better off. A second alternative would be for him to sell his rights in the market and stay with his position of owning only nine shares and holding cash.

Nine shares at $39 (diluted value) $351
Proceeds from sale of nine rights   9
Cash . . . . :   30
        Total value $390

As indicated above, whether he chooses to exercise his rights or not, the stock will still go down to a lower value (others are still diluting). Once again, his overall value remains constant. The value received for the rights ($9) exactly equals the extent of dilution in the value of the original nine shares.

The only foolish action would be for the stockholder to throw away the rights as worthless securities. He would then suffer the pains of dilution without the offset from the sale of the rights.

Nine shares at $39 (diluted value) $351
Cash   30
        Total value $381

Empirical evidence indicates that this careless activity takes place 1 to 2 percent of the time.

Desirable Features of Rights Offerings

The student may ask, If the stockholder is no better off in terms of total valuation, why undertake a rights offering? There are a number of possible advantages.

As previously indicated, by giving current stockholders a first option to purchase new shares, we protect their current position in regard to voting rights and claims to earnings. Of equal importance, the use of a rights offering gives the firm a built-in market for new security issues. Because of this built-in base, distribution costs are likely to be considerably lower than under a straight public issue in which investment bankers must underwrite the full risk of distribution.[4]

Also, a rights offering may generate more interest in the market than would a straight public issue. There is a market not only for the stock

---

[4]Though investment bankers generally participate in a rights offering as well, their fees are less because of the smaller risk factor.

but also for the rights. Because the subscription price is normally set 15–25 percent below current value, there is the "nonreal" appearance of a bargain, creating further interest in the offering.

A last advantage of a rights offering over a straight stock issue is that stock purchased through a rights offering carries lower margin requirements. The margin requirement specifies the amount of cash or equity that must be deposited with a brokerage house or a bank, with the balance of funds eligible for borrowing. Though not all investors wish to purchase on margin, those who do so prefer to put down a minimum amount. While normal stock purchases may require a 50 percent margin (half cash, half borrowed), stock purchased under a rights offering may be bought with as little as 25 percent down, depending on the current requirements of the Federal Reserve Board.

Poison Pills

During the 1980s, a new wrinkle was added to the meaning of rights when firms began receiving merger and acquisition proposals from companies interested in acquiring voting control of the firm. Many firms (managements) did not want to give up control of the company, and so they devised a method of making the firm very unattractive to a potential acquisition-minded company. As you can tell from our discussion of voting provisions, a company using majority voting only needs to control over 50 percent of the voting shares to exercise total control. Management of companies considered potential takeover targets began to develop defensive tactics in fending off these unwanted mergers. One widely used strategy was called the *poison pill*.

A poison pill is a rights offer made to existing shareholders of Company X with the sole purpose of making it more difficult for another firm to acquire Company X. Most poison pills have a trigger point. When a potential buyer accumulates a given percentage of the common stock (for example, 25 percent), the other shareholders receive rights to purchase additional shares from the company, generally at very low prices. If the rights are exercised by shareholders, this increases the total shares outstanding and dilutes the potential buyer's ownership percentage. Poison pill strategies often do not have to be voted on by shareholders to be put into place. At International Paper Company, however, the poison pill issue was put on the proxy ballot and 76 percent of the voting shareholders sided with management to maintain the poison pill defense. This was surprising, because many institutional investors are opposed to the pill.

They feel that it lowers the potential for maximizing shareholder value by discouraging potential high takeover bids.

Preferred Stock Financing

Having discussed bonds (in Chapter 16) and common stock, we are prepared to look at this intermediate or hybrid form of security known as preferred stock. You may question the validity of the term *preferred*, for preferred stock does not possess any of the most desirable characteristics of debt or common stock. In the case of debt, bondholders have a contractual claim against the corporation for the payment of interest and may throw the corporation into bankruptcy if payment is not forthcoming. Common stockholders, of course, are the owners of the firm and have a residual claim to all income not paid out to others. Preferred stockholders, on the other hand, are merely entitled to receive a stipulated dividend and, generally, must receive the dividend prior to the payment of dividends to common stockholders. However, their right to annual dividends is not compelling to the corporation, as is true of interest on debt, and the corporation may forgo preferred dividends when this is deemed necessary.

For example, XYZ Corporation might issue 12 percent preferred stock with a $100 par value. Under normal circumstances, the corporation would pay the $12 per share dividend. Let us also assume that it has $1,000 bonds carrying 12.2 percent interest and shares of common stock with a market value of $50, normally paying a $1 cash dividend. The 12.2 percent interest *must* be paid on the bonds. The $12 preferred dividend has to be paid before the $1 dividend on common, but both may be waived without threat of bankruptcy. The common stockholder is the last in line to receive payment, but his potential participation is unlimited. Instead of getting a $1 dividend, he may someday receive many times that much.

Justification for Preferred Stock

Because preferred stock has few unique characteristics, why might the corporation choose to issue it and, equally important, why are investors willing to purchase the security?

Most corporations that issue preferred stock do so to achieve a balance in their capital structure. It is a means of expanding the capital base of the firm without diluting the common stock ownership position or incurring contractual debt obligations. Firms that are heavy users of debt, such as public utilities and capital goods producers, may go to preferred stock to balance their sources of financing.

Even here, there may be a drawback. While interest payments on debt are tax deductible, preferred stock dividends are not. Thus, the interest cost on 10 percent debt may be only 6.5 to 7 percent on an aftertax cost basis, while the aftertax cost on 10 percent preferred stock would be the stated amount. A firm issuing the preferred stock may be willing to pay the higher aftertax cost to assure investors that it has a balanced capital structure and because preferred stock may have a positive effect on the costs of the other sources of funds in the capital structure.

Investor interest Primary purchasers of preferred stock are corporate investors, insurance companies, and pension funds. To the corporate investor, preferred stock offers a very attractive advantage over bonds. The tax law provides that any corporation receiving *either preferred or common* dividends from another corporation must add only 30 percent of such dividends to its taxable income. Thus, 70 percent of such dividends are exempt from taxation. On a preferred stock issue paying a 10 percent dividend, only 3 percent would be taxable. By contrast, the interest on bonds is usually taxable to the recipient, except for municipal bond interest.

For example, if we take the 1987 figures for Aa bond yields and high-grade preferred stock yields in Table 17–2 on page 528, and adjust them to aftertax yields to a corporation, the advantage of preferred stock ownership to these investors is evident. Since interest on bonds receives no tax reduction, the aftertax bond yield must be adjusted by the corporation's marginal tax rate of 34 percent.

$$\text{Aftertax bond yield} = \text{Before-tax bond yield} \times (1 - \text{tax rate})$$
$$= 9.68\% \times (1 - .34)$$
$$= 6.39\%$$

For preferred stock, the adjustment also includes the advantageous 30 percent taxing provision.

$$\begin{aligned} \text{Aftertax preferred} \\ \text{yield} &= \text{Before-tax stock yield} \times [1 - (\text{tax rate})(.30)] \\ &= 8.37\% \times [1 - (0.34)(0.30)] \\ &= 8.37\% \times (1 - 0.102) \\ &= 8.37\% \times 0.898 \\ &= 7.52\% \end{aligned}$$

The aftertax yield on preferred stock is higher than the aftertax bond yield, even though the bond has the higher before-tax yield. Because of

Table 17–2
Before-tax yields on
corporate bonds and
on high-grade
preferred stock

Year*	Aa Bond Yields	High-grade Preferred Stock Yields	Yield Spread Bonds – Preferred
1947	2.70	3.79	−1.09
1952	3.04	4.13	−1.09
1957	4.03	4.63	−0.60
1962	4.47	4.50	−0.03
1967	5.66	5.46	0.20
1972	7.49	6.85	0.64
1977	8.24	7.60	0.64
1978	8.92	8.25	0.67
1979	10.46	9.50	0.96
1980	12.50	10.57	1.93
1981	14.75	12.36	2.39
1982	14.41	12.53	1.88
1983	12.42	11.02	1.40
1984	13.31	11.59	1.72
1985	11.82	10.49	1.33
1986	9.47	8.76	0.71
1987	9.68	8.37	1.31

Source: Selected issues of the *Federal Reserve Bulletin.*

this tax consideration, it is not surprising that corporations are able to issue preferred stock at a slightly lower yield than debt. As indicated in Table 17–2, since the late 1960s, preferred stock has been trading at a 0.20 to 2.5 percent lower yield than comparable bonds.

Summary of tax considerations   Tax considerations work in two opposite directions. First, they make the aftertax cost of debt cheaper than preferred stock to the issuing corporation, because interest is deductible to the payer. (This is true, in spite of the fact the quoted rate may be higher.) Second, tax considerations generally make the receipt of preferred dividends more valuable than corporate bond interest to corporate investors, because 70 percent of the dividend is exempt from taxation.

Provisions Associated with Preferred Stock

A preferred stock issue contains a number of stipulations and provisions that define the stockholder's claim to income and assets.

1. Cumulative dividends   Most preferred stock issues have a cumulative claim to dividends. That is, if preferred stock dividends are not paid in any one year, they accumulate and must be paid in total before common stockholders can receive dividends. If preferred stock carries a $12 cash dividend and the company does not pay dividends for three years, preferred stockholders must receive the full $36 before common stockholders can receive anything.

The cumulative dividend feature makes a corporation very aware of its obligation to preferred stockholders. When a financially troubled corporation has missed a number of dividend payments under a cumulative arrangement, there may be a financial recapitalization of the corporation in which preferred stockholders receive new securities in place of the dividend arrearage. Assume that the corporation has now missed five years of dividends under a $12 a year obligation and still remains in a poor cash position. Preferred stockholders may be offered $60 or more in new common stock for forgiveness of the missed dividend payments. Preferred stockholders may be willing to cooperate in order to receive some potential benefit for the future.

2. Conversion feature Like certain forms of debt, preferred stock may be convertible into common shares. Thus, $100 in preferred stock may be convertible into X number of shares of common stock at the option of the holder. The topic of convertibility is discussed at length in Chapter 19, Convertibles and Warrants. Approximately 40 percent of preferred stock issues have this conversion feature.

3. Call feature Also, preferred stock, like debt, may be callable; that is, the corporation may retire the security prior to maturity at some small premium over par. This, of course, accrues to the advantage of the corporation and to the disadvantage of the preferred stockholder. A preferred issue carrying a call provision will be accorded a slightly higher yield than a similar issue without this feature. The same type of refunding decision applied to debt obligations in Chapter 16 could also be applied to preferred stock.

4. Participation provision A *small* percentage of preferred stock issues are participating; that is, they may participate over and above the quoted yield when the corporation is enjoying a particularly good year. Once the common stock dividend equals the preferred stock dividend, the two classes of securities may share equally in additional payouts.

5. Floating rate Beginning in 1982, a few preferred stock issuers made the dividend floating in nature. These issuers include such firms as Alcoa, U.S. Steel, and BankAmerica Corporation. Typically, the dividend is changed on a quarterly basis, based on current market conditions. Because the dividend rate only changes quarterly, there is still some small price change possibility between dividend adjustment dates. Nevertheless, it is less than the price change for regular preferred stock.

6. Par value   A final important feature associated with preferred stock is par value. Unlike the par value of common stock, which is often only a small percentage of the actual value, the par value of preferred stock is set at the anticipated market value at the time of issue. The par value establishes the amount due to preferred stockholders in the event of liquidation. Also, the par value of preferred stock determines the base against which the percentage or dollar return on preferred stock is computed. Thus, 12 percent preferred stock would indicate $12 a year in preferred dividends if the par value were $100, but only $6 annually if the par value were $50.

Comparing Features of Common and Preferred Stock and Debt

In Table 17–3, we compare the characteristics of common stock, preferred stock, and bonds. The student should carefully consider the comparative advantages and disadvantages of each.

In terms of the risk–return features of these three classes of securities and also of the other investments discussed in Chapter 7, we might expect the risk–return patterns depicted in Figure 17–1 on page 532. The lowest return is obtained from savings accounts, and the highest return and risk are generally associated with common stock. In between, we note that short-term instruments generally, though not always, provide lower returns than longer-term instruments. We also observe that government securities pay lower returns than issues originated by corporations, because of the lower risk involved. Next on the scale after government issues is preferred stock. This hybrid form of security generally pays a lower return than even well-secured corporate debt instruments, because of the 70 percent tax-exempt status of preferred stock dividends to corporate purchasers. Thus, the focus on preferred stock is not just on risk–return trade-offs but also on aftertax return.[5]

Next, we observe increasingly high return requirements on debt, based on the presence or absence of security provisions and the priority of claims

---

[5]In a strict sense, preferred stock does not belong on the straight line because of its unique tax characteristics.

Table 17–3 Features of alternative security issues

	Common Stock	Preferred Stock	Bonds
1. Ownership and control of the firm	Belongs to common stockholders through voting right and residual claim to income	Limited rights when dividends are missed	Limited rights under default in interest payments
2. Obligation to provide return	None	Must receive payment before common stockholder	Contractual obligation
3. Claim to assets in bankruptcy	Lowest claim of any security holder	Bondholders and creditors must be satisfied first	Highest claim
4. Cost of distribution	Highest	Moderate	Lowest
5. Risk–return trade-off	Highest risk, highest return (at least in theory)	Moderate risk, moderate return	Lowest risk, moderate return
6. Tax status of payment by corporation	Not deductible	Not deductible	Tax deductible Cost = Interest payment × (1 − Tax rate)
7. Tax status of payment to recipient	70 percent of dividend to other corporation is tax exempt.	Same as common stock	Municipal bond interest is tax exempt

on unsecured debt. Finally, at the top of the scale is common stock. Because of its lowest priority of claim in the corporation and its volatile price movement, it has the highest demanded return.

While extensive research studies have tended to validate these general patterns,[6] short-term or even intermediate-term reversals have taken place, in which investments with lower risk have outperformed investments at the higher end of the risk scale.

[6]Roger G. Ibbotson and Rex A. Sinquefield, "Stocks, Bonds, Bills and Inflation: Year by Year Historical Returns (1926–1974)," *Journal of Business* 49, no. 1 (January 1976). Also Lawrence Fisher and James H. Lorie, *A Half Century of Returns on Common Stocks and Bonds* (Chicago: University of Chicago Graduate School of Business, 1977). Followup studies by these authors confirmed the same results.

Figure 17–1
Risk and expected
return for various
security classes

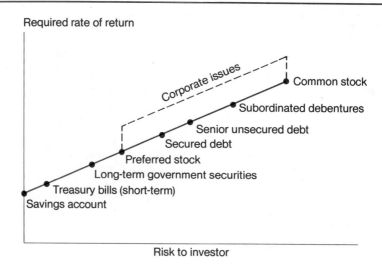

Required rate of return

Corporate issues

Common stock

Subordinated debentures

Senior unsecured debt

Secured debt

Preferred stock

Long-term government securities

Treasury bills (short-term)

Savings account

Risk to investor

Summary

While common stock is still owned by over 45 million individual investors, institutional ownership through mutual funds, pension funds, insurance companies, and bank trusts is increasing every year.

Common stock ownership carries three primary rights or privileges. First, there is a residual claim to income. All funds not paid out to other classes of securities automatically belong to the common stockholder; the firm may then choose to pay out these residual funds in dividends or to reinvest them for the benefit of common stockholders. Different classes of stock, such as the Wang Class B and Class C stock, may carry different dividends. There are also cases, such as the new GM Class E and H stock, where dividends are tied to the performance of a subsidiary company.

Because common stockholders are the ultimate owners of the firm, they alone have the privilege of voting (except under default or other unusual conditions). There may be more than one class of stock, having differing voting rights. The key example where voting rights are not equal is usually founders' stock, such as in Ford Motor Company's Class B stock and Wang Laboratories' Class C common stock. The General Motors' Class E and H stock also have different rights as a result of acquisitions by General Motors.

To expand the role of minority stockholders, many corporations use a system of cumulative voting, in which each stockholder has voting power equal to the number of shares owned times the number of directors to be elected. By cumulating votes for a small number of selected directors, minority stockholders are able to have representation on the board.

Common stockholders may also enjoy a first option to purchase new shares. This privilege is extended through the procedure known as a rights offering. A shareholder receives one right for each share of stock owned and may combine a certain number of rights, plus cash, to purchase a new share. While the cash or subscription price is usually somewhat below the current market price, the stockholder neither gains nor loses through the process.

A hybrid, or intermediate, security, falling between debt and common stock, is preferred stock. Preferred stockholders are entitled to receive a stipulated dividend and must receive this dividend before any payment is made to common stockholders. Preferred dividends usually accumulate if they are not paid in a given year, though preferred stockholders cannot initiate bankruptcy proceedings or seek legal redress if nonpayment occurs.

Finally, common stock, preferred stock, bonds, and other securities tend to receive returns over the long run in accordance with risk, with corporate issues generally paying a higher return than government securities.

Review of Formulas

$$1. \quad \frac{\text{Shares}}{\text{required}} = \frac{\begin{array}{c}\text{Number of directors desired} \times \\ \text{Total number of shares outstanding}\end{array}}{\begin{array}{c}\text{Total number of directors to be} \\ \text{elected} + 1\end{array}} + 1 \qquad (17\text{--}1)$$

2. Number of directors that can be elected   (17–2)

$$= \frac{\begin{array}{c}(\text{Shares owned} - 1) \times \\ (\text{Total number of directors to be elected} + 1)\end{array}}{(\text{Total number of shares outstanding})}$$

3. $R = \dfrac{M_o - S}{N + 1}$ (17–3)

R is the value of a right

M_o is the market value of the stock—rights-on (stock carries a right)

S is the subscription price

N is the number of rights required to purchase a new share of stock

4. $R = \dfrac{M_e - S}{N}$ (17–4)

   R is the value of a right

   M_e is the market value of stock—ex-rights (stock no
        longer carries a right)

   S is the subscription price

   N is number of rights required to purchase a new
        share of stock

List of Terms

common stockholder	floating rate preferred stock
cumulative voting	preferred stock
preemptive right	cumulative preferred stock
rights offering	participating preferred stock
rights-on	majority vote
ex-rights	poison pill
founders' stock	
margin requirement	

Discussion Questions

1. Why has corporate management become increasingly sensitive to the desires of large institutional investors?

2. What determines the dividend payments on General Motors' Class E and Class H shares?

3. Why might a corporation use a special category such as founders' stock in issuing common stock?

4. What is the purpose of cumulative voting? Are there any disadvantages to management?

5. Why has preferred stock not been particularly popular as a source of funds for corporations?

6. What is the most likely explanation for the use of preferred stock?

7. How does the preemptive right protect stockholders from dilution?

8. If common stockholders are the *owners* of the company, why do they have the last claim on assets and a residual claim on income?

9. During a rights offering, the underlying stock is said to sell "rights-on" and "ex-rights." Explain the meaning of these terms and their significance to current stockholders and potential stockholders.

10. Why might management use a poison pill strategy?

11. Preferred stock is often referred to as a hybrid security. What is meant by this term?

12. If preferred stock is riskier than bonds, why has preferred stock had lower yields than bonds in recent years?

13. A small amount of preferred stock is participating. What would your reaction be if someone said common stock is also participating?

14. What is an advantage of floating rate preferred stock for the risk-averse investor?

Problems

1. Mr. Jack Robinson owns 5,001 shares of Preston Trucking Company common stock. There are nine seats on the Preston Company board of directors, and the company has a total of 50,000 shares of common stock outstanding. Preston Company uses cumulative voting. Can Mr. Robinson elect himself to the board when the vote to elect nine directors is held next week?

2. The Lindsey Corporation has been experiencing declining earnings but has just announced a 50 percent salary increase for top executives. A dissident group of stockholders wants to oust the existing board of directors. There are currently 11 directors and 60,000 shares of stock outstanding. Mr. Perk, the president of the company, has the full support of the existing board. The dissident stockholders control proxies for 20,001 shares. Mr. Perk is worried about losing his job.
   a. Under cumulative voting procedures, how many directors can the dissident stockholders elect with the proxies they now hold? How many directors could they elect under majority rule with these proxies?
   b. How many shares (or proxies) are needed to elect six directors under cumulative voting?

3. Quantum Corporation is holding a stockholders meeting next week. Mr. Kinsey is the president of the company and has the support of the existing board of directors. All nine members of the board are

up for reelection. Mr. Allen is a dissident stockholder. He controls proxies for 30,001 shares. Mr. Kinsey and his friends on the board control 50,001 shares. Other stockholders, whose loyalties are unknown, will be voting the remaining 19,998 shares. The company uses cumulative voting.

a. How many directors can Mr. Allen be sure of electing?
b. How many directors can Mr. Kinsey and his friends be sure of electing?
c. How many directors could Mr. Allen elect if he obtains all the proxies for the uncommitted votes? (Uneven values must be rounded *down* to the nearest whole number regardless of the amount.)

4. In problem 3, if 12 directors were to be elected, and Mr. Kinsey and his friends had 50,001 shares and Mr. Allen had 30,001 shares plus half the uncommited votes, how many directors could Mr. Allen elect?

5. Mr. Rogers controls proxies for 38,000 of the 70,000 outstanding shares of Ingot Industrial Company. Mr. Kermit heads a dissident group which controls the remaining 32,000 shares. There are seven board members to be elected and cumulative voting rules apply. Mr. Rogers does not understand cumulative voting and plans to cast 100,000 of his 266,000 (38,000 × 7) votes for his brother-in-law, Mel. The remaining votes will be spread evenly over three other candidates.

a. How many directors can Mr. Kermit elect if Mr. Rogers acts as described above? Use logical analysis rather than a set formula to answer part *a*.
b. How many directors can Mr. Kermit elect if Mr. Rogers acts in an optimal manner? (Round down to the nearest whole number.)
c. If Mr. Rogers spreads his votes evenly over seven candidates, trying to get all his people on the board, how many directors could Mr. Kermit elect? Use logical analysis rather than a set formula to answer part *c*.

6. Daily Planet Newspapers, Inc., has issued rights to its shareholders. The subscription price is $35 and four rights are needed along with the subscription price to buy one of the new shares. The stock is selling for $45 rights-on.

a. What would be the value of one right?
b. If the stock goes ex-rights, what would the new stock price be?

7. Green Acres Farm, Inc., has announced a rights offering for its

shareholders. Edna Kelly owns 500 shares of Green Acres stock. Five rights plus $72 are needed to buy one of the new shares. The stock is currently selling for $80 rights-on.

    a. What is the value of a right?

    b. How many of the new shares could Edna buy if she exercised all her rights? How much cash would this require?

    c. Edna doesn't know if she wants to exercise her rights or sell them. Which alternative would have the most beneficial effect on her wealth?

8. Kevin Gallagher has $1,000 to invest. He has been looking at Treynor Machine Tool Company common stock. Treynor has issued a rights offering to its current stockholders. Ten rights plus $35 will buy one new share. Treynor stock is selling for $40 ex-rights.

    a. How many rights could Kevin buy with his $1,000? Alternatively, how many shares of stock could he buy with the same $1,000 at $40 per share.

    b. If Kevin invests his $1,000 in Treynor rights and the price of Treynor stock rises to $50 per share ex-rights, what would his dollar profit on the rights be?

    c. If Kevin invests his $1,000 in Treynor stock and the price of the stock rises to $50 per share ex-rights, what would his dollar profit be?

    d. What would the answer to part *b* be if the price of Treynor stock falls to $30 per share ex-rights instead of rising to $50?

    e. What would the answer to part *c* be if the price of Treynor stock falls to $30 per share ex-rights?

9. Mr. and Mrs. Anderson own five shares of Magic Tricks Corporation common stock. The market value of the stock is $60. They also have $48 in cash. They have just received word of a rights offering. One new share of stock can be purchased at $48 for each five shares currently owned (based on five rights).

    a. What is the value of a right?

    b. What is the value of the Andersons' portfolio before the rights offering? (Portfolio in this question represents stock plus cash.)

    c. If the Andersons participate in the rights offering, what will be the value of their portfolio, based on the diluted value (ex-rights) of the stock?

    d. If they sell their five rights but keep their stock at its diluted value and hold onto their cash, what will be the value of their portfolio?

10. Kristy Fashions, Inc., has 4.5 million shares of common stock outstanding. The current market price of Kristy Fashions common stock is $60 per share rights-on. The company's net income this year is $18 million. A rights offering has been announced in which 450,000 new shares will be sold at $55 per share. The subscription price of $55 plus 10 rights is needed to buy one of the new shares.

   a. What are the earnings per share and price–earnings ratios before the new shares are sold via the rights offering?

   b. What would the earnings per share be immediately after the rights offering? What would the price–earnings ratio be immediately after the rights offering? (Assume there is no change in the market value of the common stock, except for the change which occurs when the stock begins trading ex-rights.) Round all answers to two places to the right of the decimal point.

11. The Jefferson Corporation has some excess cash that it would like to invest in marketable securities for a long-term hold. Its vice president of finance is considering three investments (Jefferson is in a 34 percent tax bracket). Which should he select based on aftertax return: (*a*) Treasury bonds at a 10 percent yield, (*b*) corporate bonds at a 13 percent yield, or (*c*) preferred stock at an 11 percent yield.

12. Ace Tools Corporation has a cumulative preferred stock issue outstanding, which has a stated annual dividend of $10 per share. The company has been losing money and has not paid the preferred dividends for the last four years. There are 275,000 shares of preferred stock outstanding and 600,000 shares of common stock.

   a. How much is the company behind in preferred dividends?

   b. If Ace Tools earns $9,500,000 in the coming year after taxes and before dividends, and this is all paid out to the preferred stockholders, how much will the company be in arrears (behind in payments)? Keep in mind that the coming year would represent the fifth year.

   c. How much would be available for common stock dividends in the coming year if $9,500,000 is earned as explained in part *b?*

13. Franklin Kite Company is four years in arrears on cumulative preferred stock dividends. There are 650,000 preferred shares outstanding and the annual dividend is $7 per share. The vice president of finance sees no real hope of paying the dividends in arrears. He is devising a plan to compensate the preferred stockholders for 90 percent of the dividends in arrears.

a. How much should the compensation be?

b. Franklin will compensate the preferred stockholders in the form of bonds paying 12 percent interest in a market environment in which the going rate of interest is 14 percent. The bonds will have a 25-year maturity. Using the bond valuation table in Chapter 16 (Table 16–3), indicate the market value of a $1,000 par value bond.

c. Based on market value, how many bonds must be issued to provide the compensation determined in part *a?* (Round to the nearest whole number.)

14. The treasurer of Petroco Resources (a corporation) currently has $100,000 invested in preferred stock yielding 9.5 percent. He appreciates the tax advantages of preferred stock and is considering buying $100,000 more with borrowed funds. The cost of the borrowed funds is 11.5 percent. He suggests this proposal to his board of directors. They are somewhat concerned by the fact that the treasurer is paying 2 percent more for funds than he is earning. Petroco Resources is in a 34 percent tax bracket.

a. Compute the amount of the aftertax income from the additional preferred stock if it is purchased.

b. Compute the aftertax borrowing cost to purchase the additional preferred stock. That is, multiply the interest cost times $(1 - T)$.

c. Should the treasurer proceed with his proposal?

d. If interest rates and dividend yields in the market go up six months after a decision to purchase is made, what impact will this have on the outcome?

15. Referring back to the original information in problem 14, if the yield on the $100,000 of preferred stock is still 9.5 percent and the borrowing cost remains 11.5 percent, but the tax rate is only 15 percent, is this a feasible investment?

16. The Crandall Corporation currently has 100,000 shares outstanding, which are selling at $50 per share. It needs to raise $900,000. Net income after taxes is $500,000. Its vice president of finance and its outside investment banker have decided on a rights offering but are not sure how much to discount the subscription price from the current market value. Discounts of 10 percent, 20 percent, and 40 percent have been suggested. Common stock is the sole means of financing for the Crandall Corporation.

a. For each discount, determine the subscription price, the number of shares to be issued, and the number of rights required to purchase one share. (Round to one place after the decimal point where necessary.)

b. Determine the value of one right under each of the plans. (Round to two places after the decimal point.)

c. Compute the earnings per share before and immediately after the rights offering under a 10 percent discount from the subscription price.

d. By what percentage has the number of shares outstanding increased?

e. Stockholder X has 100 shares before the rights offering and participated by buying 20 new shares. Compute his total claim to earnings both before and after the rights offering (that is, multiply shares by the earnings per share figures computed in part *c*).

f. Should Stockholder X be satisfied with this claim over a longer time?

17. (Comprehensive problem.)

Hoffman Bike Parts, Inc., is a small firm that has been very profitable over the past five years and has also exhibited a strong earnings growth trend. Mr. Hoffman owns 35 percent of the 2 million shares of common stock outstanding, but he is nevertheless worried about being taken over by a larger firm some time in the future. He has read some articles in *The Wall Street Journal* about techniques used to discourage forced mergers and takeovers. Hoffman Bike Parts, Inc., currently uses majority voting for nine directors. Mr. Hoffman wonders which of the following proposals would make it easier for him to reject a takeover bid.

a. What would be the effect of cumulative voting?

b. What would be accomplished if shareholders could only vote for one third of the directors every year (staggered terms)?

c. Should Mr. Hoffman reduce or increase the number of directors? Is the answer to this question dependent on majority rule or cumulative voting?

Selected References

Alderson, Michael J.; Keith C. Brown; and Scott L. Lummer. "Dutch Auction Rate Preferred Stock." *Financial Management* 16 (Summer 1987), pp. 68–73.

Bacon, P. W. "The Subscription Price in Rights Offerings." *Financial Management* 1 (September 1972), pp. 59–64.

Bear, Robert M., and Anthony J. Curley. "Unseasoned Financing." *Journal of Financial and Quantitative Analysis* 10 (June 1975), pp. 311–26.

Bhagat, Sanjai; James A. Brickley; and Ronald C. Lease. "The Authorization of Additional Common Stock: An Empirical Investigation." *Financial Management* 15 (Autumn 1986), pp. 45–53.

Davidson, Wallace N. III, and John L. Glascock. "The Announcement Effects of Preferred Stock Re-Ratings." *Journal of Financial Research* 36 (Winter 1985), pp. 317–26.

Donaldson, Gordon. "In Defense of Preferred Stock." *Harvard Business Review* 40 (July–August 1962), pp. 132–36.

Ederington, Louis H. "Uncertainty, Competition, and Costs in Corporate Bond Underwriting." *Journal of Financial Economics* 2 (March 1975), pp. 71–94.

Edmister, Robert O. "Commission Costs Structure: Shifts and Scale Economies." *Journal of Finance* 33 (May 1978), pp. 447–86.

Eibott, Peter. "Trends in the Value of Individual Stockholdings." *Journal of Business* 47 (July 1974), pp. 339–48.

Fisher, Lawrence, and James H. Lorie. *A Half Century of Returns on Common Stocks and Bonds.* Chicago: University of Chicago Graduate School of Business, 1977.

Ibbotson Associates. *Stocks, Bonds, Bills and Inflation: 1987 Yearbook.* Chicago: Ibbotson Associates Capital Management Research Center, 1987.

Ibbotson, Roger G., and Rex A. Sinquefield. "Stocks, Bonds, Bills, and Inflation: Year by Year Historical Returns (1926–1974)." *Journal of Business* 49 (January 1976), pp. 11–47.

Keane, S. M. "The Significance of Issue Price in Rights Issues." *Journal of Business Finance* 4 (September 1972), pp. 40–45.

Levy, Haim, and Marshall Sarnat. "Risk, Dividend Policy, and the Optimal Pricing of Rights Offering." *Journal of Money, Credit, and Banking* 3 (November 1971), pp. 840–9.

Mikkelson, Wayne H., and Megan Patch. "Stock Price Effects and Costs of Secondary Distributions." *Journal of Financial Economics* 14 (June 1985), pp. 165–94.

Pinches, George E. "Financing with Convertible Preferred Stock, 1960–1967." *Journal of Finance* 25 (March 1970), pp. 53–63.

Soldofsky, Robert M., and Craig R. Johnson. "Rights Timing." *Financial Analysts Journal* 23 (July–August 1967), pp. 101–4.

Winger, Berhard J.; Carl R. Chen; John D. Martin; J. William Petty; and Steven Hayden. "Adjustable Rate Preferred Stock." *Financial Management* 15 (Spring 1986), pp. 48–57.

18

Dividend Policy and Retained Earnings

A successful owner of a small business must continually decide what to do with the profits his or her firm has generated. One option is to reinvest in the business—purchasing new plant and equipment, expanding inventory, and perhaps hiring new employees. Another alternative, however, is to withdraw the funds from the business and invest them elsewhere. Prospective uses might include buying other stocks and bonds, purchasing a second business, or perhaps spending a lost weekend in Las Vegas.

A corporation and its stockholders must face exactly the same type of decision. Should funds associated with profits be retained in the business, or paid out to stockholders in the form of dividends?

The Marginal Principle of Retained Earnings

In theory, corporate directors should ask, "How can the best use of the funds be made?" The rate of return that the corporation can achieve on retained earnings for the benefit of stockholders must be compared to what stockholders could earn if the funds were paid out to them in dividends. This is known as the marginal principle of retained earnings. Each potential project to be financed by internally generated funds must provide a higher rate of return than the stockholder could achieve for himself. We speak of this as the opportunity cost of using stockholder funds.

Life Cycle Growth and Dividends

One of the major influences on dividends is the corporate growth rate in sales and the subsequent return on assets. Figure 18–1 shows a corporate life cycle and the corresponding dividend policy that is most likely to be found at each stage. A small firm in the initial stages of development (Stage I) pays no dividends because it needs all of its profits (if there are any) for reinvestment in new productive assets. If the firm is successful in the marketplace, the demand for its products will create growth in sales, earnings, and assets, and the firm will move into Stage II. At this stage, sales and returns on assets will be growing at an increasing rate, and earnings will still be reinvested. In the early part of Stage II, stock dividends (distribution of additional shares) may be instituted, and, in

Figure 18–1
Life cycle growth and dividend policy

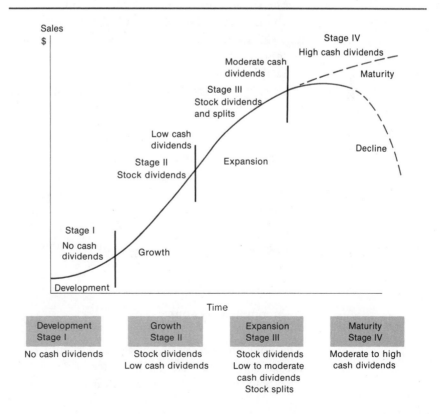

the latter part of Stage II, *low* cash dividends may be started, to inform investors that the firm is profitable but that cash is needed for internal acquisition.

After the growth period the firm enters Stage III. The expansion of sales continues, but at a decreasing rate, and returns on investment may decline as more competition enters the market and tries to take away the firm's market share. During this period the firm is more and more capable of paying cash dividends, as the asset expansion rate slows and external funds become more readily available. Stock dividends and stock splits are still common in the expansion phase, and the dividend payout ratio usually increases from a low level of 5 to 15 percent of earnings to a moderate level of 25 to 40 percent of earnings. Finally, at Stage IV, maturity, the firm maintains a stable growth rate in sales similar to that of the economy as a whole; and, when risk premiums are considered, its returns on assets level out to those of the industry and the economy. In unfortunate cases, firms suffer declines in sales if product innovation and diversification have not taken place over the years. In Stage IV, assuming maturity rather than decline, dividends might range from 40 to 60 percent of earnings. These percentages will be different from industry to industry, depending on the individual characteristics of the company, such as operating and financial leverage and the volatility of sales and earnings over the business cycle.

As the chapter continues, more will be said about stock dividends, stock splits, the availability of external funds, and other variables that affect the dividend policy of the firm.

Dividends as a Passive Variable

In the preceding analysis, dividends were used as a passive decision variable: They are only to be paid out if the corporation cannot make better use of the funds for the benefit of stockholders. The active decision variable is retained earnings: We decide how much to retain, and then the *residual is paid out in dividends*.

An Incomplete Theory

The only problem with the residual theory is that we have not given recognition to how stockholders feel about receiving dividends. If the stockholders' only concern is with achieving the highest return on their investment, either in the form of *corporate retained earnings remaining in the business* or as *current dividends paid out,* then there is no issue. But if stockholders have a preference for current funds, for example, over retained earnings, then our theory is incomplete. The issue is not only whether reinvestment of retained earnings or dividends provides the highest return but also how stockholders react to the two alternatives.

While some researchers maintain that stockholders are indifferent to the division of funds between retained earnings and dividends[1] (holding investment opportunities constant), others disagree.[2] Though there is no conclusive proof one way or the other, the judgment of most researchers is that investors do have some preference between dividends and retained earnings.

Arguments for the Relevance of Dividends

A strong case can be made for the relevance of dividends because they *resolve uncertainty* in the minds of investors. Though retained earnings reinvested in the business theoretically belong to common stockholders, there is still an air of uncertainty about their eventual translation into dividends. Thus, it can be hypothesized that stockholders might apply a higher discount rate (K_e) and assign a lower valuation to funds that are retained in the business as opposed to those that are paid out.[3]

It is also argued that dividends may be viewed more favorably than retained earnings because of the *information content* they contain. In essence, the corporation is telling the stockholder, "We are having a good year, and we wish to share the benefits with you." Though the corporation may be able to do just as well with the funds and perhaps provide even greater dividends in the future, some researchers find that "in an uncertain world in which verbal statements can be ignored or misinterpreted, div-

---

[1]Merton H. Miller and Franco Modigliani, "Dividend Policy, Growth and Valuation of Shares," *Journal of Business* 34 (October 1961), pp. 411–33. Under conditions of perfect capital markets with an absence of taxes and flotation costs, it is argued that the sum of discounted value per share after dividend payments equals the total valuation before dividend payments.

[2]Myron J. Gordon, "Optimum Investment and Financing Policy," *Journal of Finance* 18 (May 1963), pp. 264–72; and John Lintner, "Dividends, Earnings, Leverage, Stock Prices, and the Supply of Capital to the Corporation," *Review of Economics and Statistics* 44 (August 1962), pp. 243–69.

[3]Ibid.

idend action does provide a clear-cut means of making a statement that speaks louder than a thousand words."[4]

The relevance of dividends in policy determination can also be argued from the viewpoint that the optimum dividend payout rate should be low. Because certain stockholders may be in high tax brackets, retention of funds in excess of investment needs might be recommended in order to defer the potential tax obligation. This argument is less important with the passage of the Tax Reform Act of 1986, as is indicated later in the chapter.

The primary contention in arguing for the relevance of dividend policy is that stockholders' needs and preferences go beyond the *marginal principle of retained earnings*. The issue is not only who can best utilize the funds (the corporation or the stockholder) but also what are the stockholders' preferences. In practice, it appears that most corporations adhere to the following logic. First, a determination is made of the investment opportunities of the corporation relative to a required return (marginal analysis). This is then tempered by some subjective notion of stockholders' desires. It is not surprising that corporations with unusual growth prospects and high rates of return on internal investments generally pay a relatively low dividend (the small amount may be paid out only for its informational content). For the more mature firm, an analysis of both investment opportunities and stockholder preferences may indicate that a higher rate of payout is necessary. Examples of dividend policies of selected major U.S. corporations are presented in Table 18–1. The normal payout has been approximately 50 percent of aftertax earnings in the post–World War II period.

Dividend Stability

In considering stockholder desires in dividend policy, a primary factor is the maintenance of stability in dividend payments. Thus, corporate management must not only ask, "How many profitable investments do we have this year?" It must also ask, "What has been the pattern of dividend payments in the last few years?" Though earnings may change from year to year, the dollar amount of cash dividends tends to be much more stable, increasing in value only as new permanent levels of income are achieved. Note in Figure 18–2 the considerably greater volatility of earn-

---

[4]Ezra Solomon, *The Theory of Financial Management* (New York: Columbia University Press, 1963), p. 142.

Table 18–1
Corporate dividend policy

	Four-Year Growth Rate in Earnings per Share (1983–87)	Dividend Payout as Percentage of Aftertax Earnings (1987)
Category 1— rapid growth:		
Aston-Tate (software)	56.2%	0.0%
Digital Equipment (computers)	34.2	0.0
Genentech (biotech research)	51.0	0.0
Research-Cottrell (engineering)	39.9	13.9
Category 2— slow growth:		
Allegheny Power System	3.8	69.9
Carolina Power	4.5	68.9
Pacific Gas and Electric	0.9	75.8
Tuscon Electric	3.7	72.2

Figure 18–2
Corporate profits (seasonally adjusted annual rates, quarterly)

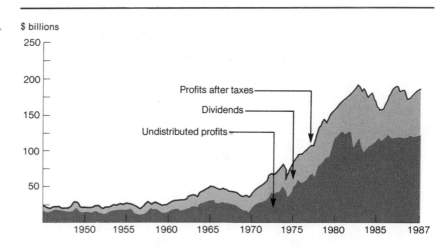

ings compared to dividends for U.S. corporations in the post–World War II period.

By maintaining a record of relatively stable dividends, corporate management hopes to lower the discount rate (K_e) applied to future dividends of the firm, thus raising the value of the firm. The operative rule appears to be that a stockholder would much prefer to receive $1 a year for three years, rather than 75 cents for the first year, $1.50 for the second year, and 75 cents for the third year—for the same total of $3. Once again, we temper our policy of marginal analysis of retained earnings to include a notion of stockholder preference, with the emphasis on stability of dividends.

Other Factors Influencing Dividend Policy ————————————

Corporate management must also consider the legal basis of dividends, the cash flow position of the firm, and the corporation's access to capital markets. Other factors that must be considered include management's desire for control and the tax and financial position of shareholders. Each is briefly discussed.

Legal Rules

Most states forbid firms to pay dividends that would impair the initial capital contributions to the firm. For this reason, dividends may only be distributed from past and current earnings. To pay dividends in excess of this amount would mean that the corporation is returning to investors their original capital contribution (raiding the capital). If the ABC Company has the following statement of net worth, the maximum dividend payment would be $20 million.

Common stock (1 million shares at $10 par value)*	$10,000,000
Retained earnings	20,000,000
Net worth	$30,000,000

*If there is a "paid-in capital in excess of par" account, some states will allow additional dividend payments against capital, while others will not. To simplify the problem for now, paid-in capital in excess of par is not considered.

Why all the concern about impairing permanent capital? Since the firm is going to pay dividends only to those who contributed capital in the first place, what is the problem? Clearly, there is no abuse to the stockholders, but what about the creditors? They have extended credit on the assumption that a given capital base would remain intact throughout the life of the loan. While they may not object to the payment of dividends from past and current earnings, they must have the protection of keeping contributed capital in place.[5]

---

[5]Of course, on liquidation of the corporation, the contributed capital to the firm may be returned to common stockholders after creditor obligations are met. Normally, stockholders who need to recoup all or part of their contributed capital sell their shares to someone else.

Even the laws against having dividends exceed the total of past and current earnings (retained earnings) may be inadequate to protect creditors. Because retained earnings is merely an accounting concept and in no way certifies the current liquidity of the firm, a company paying dividends equal to retained earnings may, in certain cases, jeopardize the operation of the firm. Let us examine Table 18–2.

Table 18–2
Dividend policy
considerations

Cash . . . . $ 1,000,000	Debt $10,000,000
Accounts receivable . . . 4,000,000	Common stock 10,000,000
Inventory 15,000,000	Retained earnings 15,000,000
Plant and equipment . . . 15,000,000	$35,000,000
$35,000,000	

Current earnings . . . . . $ 1,500,000
Potential dividends 15,000,000

Theoretically, management could pay up to $15,000,000 in dividends by selling off assets even though current earnings are only $1,500,000. In most cases, such frivolous action would not be taken; but the mere possibility encourages creditors to closely watch the balance sheets of corporate debtors and, at times, to impose additional limits on dividend payments as a condition for the granting of credit.

Cash Position of the Firm

Not only do retained earnings fail to portray the liquidity position of the firm, but there are also limitations to the use of current earnings to indicate liquidity. As described in Chapter 4, Financial Forecasting, a growth firm producing the greatest gains in earnings may be in the poorest cash position. As sales and earnings expand rapidly, there is an accompanying buildup in receivables and inventory that may far outstrip cash flow generated through earnings. Note that the cash balance in Table 18–2 represents only two thirds of current earnings of $1,500,000. A firm must do a complete funds flow analysis before establishing a dividend policy.

Access to Capital Markets

The medium-to-large-size firm with a good record of performance may have relatively easy access to the financial markets. A company in such a position may be willing to pay dividends now, knowing that it can sell new common stock or bonds in the future if funds are needed. Some corporations may even issue debt or stock *now* and use part of the proceeds to ensure the maintenance of current dividends. Though this policy seems at variance with the concept of a dividend as a reward, management may justify its action on the basis of maintaining stable dividends. It should be clear that, in the era of the 1970s and 80s, only a relatively small percentage of firms had sufficient ease of entry to the capital markets to modify their dividend policy in this regard. Many firms may actually defer the payment of dividends, because they know that they will have difficulty in going to the capital markets for more funds.

Desire for Control

Management must also consider the effect of the dividend policy on its collective ability to maintain control. The directors and officers of a small, closely held firm may be hesitant to pay any dividends at all for fear of diluting the cash position of the firm and forcing the owners to look to outside investors for financing. The funds may be available only through venture capital sources that wish to have a large say in corporate operations.

A larger firm with a broad base of shareholders may face a different type of threat in regard to dividend policy. Stockholders, spoiled by a past record of dividend payments, may demand the ouster of management if dividends are withheld.

Tax Position of Shareholders

While the payment of a cash dividend is generally taxable to the recipient, some feel the burden much more heavily than others. To the wealthy doctor or lawyer, dividend income can be taxed up to 33 percent under the Tax Reform Act of 1986. Even the average taxpayer will probably pay a 15–20 percent tax. Contrast this with the corporate recipient (such as General Motors owning Xerox stock), in which 70 percent of the dividend payment is tax exempt, and only a maximum tax of 34 percent is paid against the 30 percent balance (the overall rate is 10.2 percent). Furthermore, many large institutional investors, such as pension funds and charitable organizations, are tax exempt.

Because of differences among investors' tax rates, certain investor preferences for dividends versus capital gains have been observed in the market. This investor behavior is called the *clientele effect*. Investors in high marginal tax brackets usually prefer companies that reinvest most of their earnings, thus creating more growth in earnings and stock prices and enabling them to pay taxes sometimes *well into the future*. Companies following these dividend policies will most probably be found in the growth and expansion stages (see Figure 18–1). Investors in lower marginal tax brackets will have a greater preference for dividends, since the tax penalty is less at lower marginal tax rates. The clientele effect is also used to explain the advantages of a stable dividend policy that makes investors more certain about the type of return they will receive.

One additional point is of importance. With the passage of the Tax Reform Act of 1986, dividends are now taxed at the same rate as long-term capital gains; that is, gains on securities that are held for at least six months. Prior to tax reform, long-term capital gains were taxed at only 40 percent of the rate applied to dividends or other forms of income. This, of course, means that dividends have increased attractiveness, because a dollar of dividends produces just as much aftertax income as a dollar of capital gains. The only advantage of the latter is that the tax is deferred into the future when the stock is actually sold.

Because of the changing tax laws, some corporations that traditionally paid no cash dividends decided to change their policy. An example is the Tandy Corporation, a major producer and seller of consumer electronics and personal computers. For the first time in the history of the corporation, Tandy began paying a cash dividend in 1987. The $0.50 per share dividend represented a $44.5 million payout on the 89 million shares outstanding.

Dividend Payment Procedures

Now that we have examined the many factors that influence dividend policy, let us track the actual procedures for announcing and paying a dividend. Though dividends are quoted on an annual basis, the payments actually take place over four quarters during the year. For example, in 1987, Monsanto Company (the chemical firm) paid $2.80 a year in cash dividends. This meant stockholders could expect to receive 70 cents a quarter in dividends. Because the stock was selling at $72 per share in December of 1987, we say the annual dividend yield is 3.89 percent ($2.80/$72).

There are actually three key dates associated with the declaration of a quarterly dividend: the ex-dividend date, the holder-of-record date, and the payment date.

We must begin with the holder-of-record date. On this date, the firm examines its books to determine who is entitled to a cash dividend. In order to have your name included on the corporate books, you must have bought or owned the stock before the ex-dividend date, which is four business days before the holder-of-record date. If you bought the stock on the ex-dividend date or later, your name will eventually be transferred to the corporate books, but you will have bought the stock without the quarterly dividend privilege. Thus, we say you bought the stock ex-dividend.[6] As an example, a stock with a holder-of-record date of March 5 will go ex-dividend on March 1. You must buy the stock by the last day of February to get the dividend. Investors are very conscious of the date on which the stock goes ex-dividend, and the value of the stock may go down by the value of the quarterly dividend on the ex-dividend date (all other things being equal). Finally, in our example, we might assume the payment date is April 2 and checks will go out to entitled stockholders on or about this time.

Stock Dividend

A stock dividend represents a distribution of additional shares to common stockholders. The typical size of such dividends is in the 10 percent range, so that a stockholder with 10 shares might receive 1 new share in the form of a stock dividend. Larger distributions of 20–25 percent or more are usually considered to have the characteristics of a stock split, a topic to be discussed later in the chapter.

Accounting Considerations for a Stock Dividend

Assume that prior to the declaration of a stock dividend the XYZ Corporation has the net worth position indicated in Table 18–3.

If a 10 percent stock dividend is declared, shares outstanding will increase by 100,000 (10 percent times 1,000,000 shares). An accounting transfer will take place between retained earnings and the two capital stock accounts based on the market value of the stock dividend. If the stock is selling at $15 a share, we will assign $1,000,000 to common stock (100,000 shares times $10 par) and $500,000 to capital in excess of par. The net worth position of XYZ after the transfer is shown in Table 18–4.

---

[6]In this case, the old stockholder will receive the dividend.

Table 18-3 XYZ Corporation's financial position before stock dividend	Capital accounts	Common stock (1,000,000 shares at $10 par)	$10,000,000
		Capital in excess of par	5,000,000
		Retained earnings	15,000,000
		Net worth	$30,000,000

Table 18-4 XYZ Corporation's financial position after stock dividend	Capital accounts	Common stock (1,000,000 shares at $10)	$11,000,000
		Capital in excess of par	5,500,000
		Retained earnings	13,500,000
		Net worth	$30,000,000

Value to the Investor

An appropriate question might be: Is a stock dividend of real value to the investor? Suppose that your finance class collectively purchased $1,000 worth of assets and issued 10 shares of stock to each class member. Three days later, it is announced that each stockholder will receive an extra share. Has anyone benefited from the stock dividend? Of course not! The asset base remains the same ($1,000), and your proportionate ownership in the business is unchanged (everyone got the same new share). You merely have more paper to tell you what you already knew.

The same logic is essentially true in the corporate setting. In the case of the XYZ Corporation, shown in Tables 18–3 and 18–4, we assumed that 1 million shares were outstanding before the stock dividend and 1.1 million shares afterward. Now let us assume that the corporation had aftertax earnings of $6.6 million. Without the stock dividend, earnings per share would be $6.60, and with the dividend $6.00.

$$\text{Earnings per share} = \frac{\text{Earnings after taxes}}{\text{Shares outstanding}}$$

Without stock dividend:

$$= \frac{\$6.6 \text{ million}}{1 \text{ million shares}} = \$6.60$$

With stock dividend:

$$= \frac{\$6.6 \text{ million}}{1.1 \text{ million shares}} = \$6.00 \\ (10\% \text{ decline})$$

Earnings per share have gone down by exactly the same percentage that shares outstanding increased. For further illustration, assuming that Stockholder A had 10 shares before the stock dividend and 11 afterward, what are his or her total claims to earnings? As expected, they remain the same, at $66.

$$\text{Claims to earnings} = \text{Shares} \times \text{Earnings per share}$$

Without stock dividend:

$$10 \times \$6.60 = \$66$$

With stock dividend:

$$11 \times \$6.00 = \$66$$

Taking the analogy one step further, assuming the stock sold at 20 times earnings before and after the stock dividend, what is the total market value of the portfolio in each case?

$$\text{Total market value} = \text{Shares} \times \left(\frac{\text{Price/earnings}}{\text{ratio}} \times \frac{\text{Earnings per}}{\text{share}} \right)$$

Without stock dividend:

$$10 \times (20 \times \$6.60)$$
$$10 \times \$132 = \$1,320$$

With stock dividend:

$$11 \times (20 \times \$6.00)$$
$$11 \times \$120 = \$1,320$$

The total market value is unchanged. Note that, if the stockholder sells off the 11th share to acquire cash, his or her stock portfolio will be worth $120 less than it was worth before the stock dividend.

Possible Value of Stock Dividends

There are limited circumstances under which a stock dividend may be more than a financial sleight of hand. If, at the time a stock dividend is declared, the cash dividend per share remains constant, the stockholder will receive greater total cash dividends. Assume that the annual cash dividend for the XYZ Corporation will remain $1 per share even though earnings per share decline from $6.60 to $6.00. In this instance, a stockholder moving from 10 to 11 shares as the result of a stock dividend has a $1 increase in total dividends. The overall value of his portfolio may then increase in response to larger dividends.

Use of Stock Dividends

Stock dividends are most frequently used by growth companies as a form of "informational content" in explaining the retention of funds for reinvestment purposes. This was indicated in the discussion of the life cycle of the firm earlier in the chapter. A corporation president may state that "instead of doing more in the way of cash dividends, we are providing a stock dividend. The funds remaining in the corporation will be used for highly profitable investment opportunities." The market reaction to such an approach may be neutral or slightly positive.

A second use of stock dividends may be to camouflage the inability of the corporation to pay cash dividends and to cover up the ineffectiveness of management in generating cash flow. The president may proclaim, "Though we are unable to pay cash dividends, we wish to reward you with a 15 percent stock dividend." Well-informed investors are likely to react very negatively.

Stock Splits

A stock split is similar to a stock dividend, only more shares are distributed. For example, a two-for-one stock split would double the number of shares outstanding. In general, the rules of the New York Stock Exchange and the Financial Accounting Standards Board encourage distributions in excess of 20–25 percent to be handled as stock splits.

The accounting treatment for a stock split is somewhat different from that for a stock dividend, in that there is no transfer of funds from retained earnings to the capital accounts but merely a reduction in par value and a proportionate increase in the number of shares outstanding. For example, a two-for-one stock split for the XYZ Corporation would necessitate the accounting adjustments shown in Table 18–5.

In this case, all adjustments are in the common stock account. Because the number of shares are doubled and the par value halved, the market price of the stock should drop proportionately. There has been much discussion in the financial literature about the impact of a split on overall stock value. While there might be some positive benefit, that benefit is virtually impossible to capture after the announcement of a split has taken

Table 18–5
XYZ Corporation
before and after
stock split

Before	
Common stock (1 million shares at $10 par)	$10,000,000
Capital in excess of par	5,000,000
Retained earnings	15,000,000
	$30,000,000
After	
Common stock (2 million shares at $5 par)	$10,000,000
Capital in excess of par	5,000,000
Retained earnings	15,000,000
	$30,000,000

place. Perhaps a $66 stock will drop only to $36 after a two-for-one split, but one must act very early in the process to benefit.

The primary purpose of a stock split is to lower the price of a security into a more popular trading range. A stock selling for over $50 per share may be excluded from consideration by many small investors. Splits are popular because only the stronger companies that have witnessed substantial growth in market price are in a position to participate in them.

Repurchase of Stock as an Alternative to Dividends _____

A firm with excess cash and inadequate investment opportunities may choose to repurchase its own shares in the market, rather than pay a cash dividend. For this reason, the stock repurchase decision may be thought of as an alternative to the payment of cash dividends.

We will show that the benefits of the stockholder are equal under either alternative, at least in theory. For purposes of study, assume that the Morgan Corporation's financial position may be described by the data in Table 18–6.

The firm has $2 million in excess cash, and it wishes to compare the value to stockholders of a $2 cash dividend (on the million shares outstanding) as opposed to spending the funds to repurchase shares in the market. If the cash dividend is paid, the shareholder will have $30 in stock and the $2 cash dividend. On the other hand, the $2 million may be used to repurchase shares at slightly over market value (to induce sale).[7] The overall benefit to stockholders is that earnings per share will go up as the number of shares outstanding is decreased. If the price–earnings ratio of the stock remains constant, then the price of the stock

---

[7]In order to derive the desired equality between the two alternatives, the purchase price for the new shares should equal the current market price plus the proposed cash dividend under the first alternative ($30 + $2 = $32).

Table 18–6
Financial data of
Morgan Corporation

Earnings after taxes	$3,000,000
Shares	1,000,000
Earnings per share	$3
Price–earnings ratio	10
Market price per share	$30
Excess cash	$2,000,000

should also go up. If a purchase price of $32 is used to induce sale, then 62,500 shares will be purchased.

$$\frac{\text{Excess funds}}{\text{Purchase price per share}} = \frac{\$2,000,000}{\$32} = 62,500 \text{ shares}$$

Total shares outstanding are reduced to 937,500 (1,000,000 − 62,500). Revised earnings per share for the Morgan Corporation become:

$$\frac{\text{Earnings after taxes}}{\text{Shares}} = \frac{\$3,000,000}{937,500} = \$3.20$$

Since the price–earnings ratio for the stock is 10, the market value of the stock should go to $32. Thus, we see that the consequences of the two alternatives are presumed to be the same.

(1) *Funds Used for Cash Dividend*	(2) *Funds Used to Repurchase Stock*
Market value per share $30	
Cash dividend per share 2	Market value per share $32
$32	

In either instance, the total value is presumed to be $32. Theoretically, the stockholder would be indifferent with respect to the two alternatives.

Prior to the passage of the Tax Reform Act of 1986, there would have been a clear tax advantage associated with the repurchase decision, because the $2 gain could possibly qualify as a long-term capital gain. As previously mentioned, such gains were taxed at 40 percent of the normal rate. Since capital gains no longer receive preferential tax treatment, the aftertax consequences of a $2 dividend or $2 increase in value are now the same. Nevertheless, there are valid reasons for stock repurchases.

Other Reasons for Repurchase

In addition to using the repurchase decision as an alternative to cash dividends, corporate management may acquire its own shares in the market, because it believes they are selling at a low price. A corporation president who sees his firm's stock decline by 25–30 percent over a six-month period may determine that the stock is the best investment available to the corporation.

By repurchasing shares, the corporation is able to maintain a constant demand for its own securities and, perhaps, to stave off further decline. Stock repurchases by corporations were partially credited with stabilizing the stock market after the 508-point crash on October 19, 1987. Reacquired shares may also be used for employee stock options or as part of a tender offer in a merger or an acquisition. Firms may also reacquire part of their shares as a protective device against being taken over as a merger candidate. In Table 18–7, we see some enormous stock repurchases conducted by major U.S. corporations in 1987.

There is one caveat for firms that continually repurchase their own shares. Some analysts may view the action as a noncreative use of funds. The analysts may say, "Why aren't the funds being used to develop new products or to modernize plant and equipment?" Thus, it is important

Table 18–7
Stock repurchases

Biggest Announced Stock Buybacks of 1987

COMPANY	COMMON SHARES (in millions)	VALUE	COMPANY	COMMON SHARES (in millions)	VALUE
General Motors	64.0	$4.72 billion	Procter & Gamble	10.0	810.0 million
Santa Fe Southern Pacific	60.0	3.38 billion	Salomon	21.3	808.7 million
Ford	27.9	2.00 billion	Hewlett-Packard	15.3	750.0 million
Coca-Cola	40.0	1.80 billion	Nynex	10.0	736.3 million
Henley Group	64.5	1.76 billion	Chrysler	27.0	729.0 million
Gencorp	12.5	1.63 billion	Burlington Industries	8.0	640.0 million
IBM	12.9	1.57 billion	Monsanto	8.0	627.0 million
American Express	40.0	1.35 billion	ITT	10.0	625.0 million
Allied-Signal	25.0	1.11 billion	Hospital Corp. of America	12.0	612.0 million
Owens-Illinois	20.0	1.11 billion	Atlantic Richfield	8.3	600.0 million
J.C. Penney	20.0	1.04 billion	Schlumberger	20.0	595.0 million
Hercules	15.0	1.02 billion	Tektronix	15.6	593.2 million
IC Industries	30.8	1.00 billion	Boeing	15.0	592.5 million
Merck	5.4	1.00 billion	Kimberly-Clark	9.0	547.5 million
Philip Morris	10.0	933.5 million	Kraft	10.0	547.5 million
Bristol-Myers	25.0	925.0 million	Eaton	8.5	500.0 million
NCR	14.0	825.3 million	K mart	17.9	500.0 million

NOTE: Figures represent announcements, not actual purchases, and may include more than one announcement. Values are actual dollar amounts when available or estimates based on closing prices before announcements.
Source: Merrill Lynch & Co.

that the corporation carefully communicate the reason(s) for the repurchase decision to analysts and shareholders—such as the fact that the stock is a great bargain at its current price.

Dividend Reinvestment Plans

During the 1970s, many companies started dividend reinvestment plans for their shareholders. These plans take various forms, but basically they provide the investor with an opportunity to buy additional shares of stock with the cash dividend paid by the company. Some plans, such as that of American Telephone & Telegraph, will sell treasury stock or authorized but unissued shares to the stockholders. With this type of plan, the company is the beneficiary of increased cash flow, since dividends paid are returned to the company for reinvestment in common stock. These types of plans have been very popular with cash-short utilities, and very often utilities will allow shareholders a 5 percent discount from market value at the time of purchase. This is justified, because no investment banking or underwriting fees need be paid.

Under a second popular dividend reinvestment plan, the company's transfer agent, usually a bank, buys shares of stock in the market for the stockholder. This plan provides no cash flow for the company; but it is a service to the shareholder, who benefits from much lower transaction costs, the right to own fractional shares, and more flexibility in choosing between cash and common stock. Usually, a shareholder can also add cash payments of up to $1,000 per month to his or her dividend payments and receive the same lower transaction costs. Shareholder accounts are kept at the bank, and quarterly statements are provided. Shares will be sent out to stockholders on request or will be sold on request for a commission that is usually lower than that charged by a broker.

Summary

The first consideration in the establishment of a dividend policy is the firm's ability to reinvest the funds versus that of the stockholder. To the extent that the firm is able to earn a higher return, reinvestment of retained earnings may be justified. However, we must temper this "highest return theory" with a consideration of stockholder preferences and the firm's need for earnings retention and growth as presented in the life cycle growth curve.

Stockholders may be given a greater payout than the optimum determined by rational analysis in order to resolve their uncertainty about the future and for informational content purposes. Conversely, stockholders may prefer a greater than normal retention in order to defer the income tax obligation associated with cash dividends. Another important consideration in establishing a dividend policy may be the stockholders' desire for steady dividend payments.

Lesser factors influencing dividend policy are legal rules relating to maximum payment, the cash position of the firm, and the firm's access to capital markets. One must also consider the desire for control by corporate management and stockholders.

An alternative (or a supplement) to cash dividends may be the use of stock dividends and stock splits. While neither of these financing devices directly changes the intrinsic value of the stockholders' position, they may provide communication to stockholders and bring the stock price into a more acceptable trading range. A stock dividend may take on some actual value when total cash dividends are allowed to increase. Nevertheless, the alert investor will watch for abuses of stock dividends—situations in which the corporation indicates that something of great value is taking place when, in fact, the new shares that are created merely represent the same proportionate interest for each shareholder.

The decision to repurchase shares may be thought of as an alternative to the payment of a cash dividend. Decreasing shares outstanding will cause earnings per share, and perhaps the market price, to go up. The increase in the market price may be equated to the size of the cash dividend forgone.

Many firms are now offering stockholders the option of reinvesting cash dividends in the company's common stock. Cash-short companies have been using dividend reinvestment plans in order to raise external funds. Other companies simply provide a service to stockholders by allowing them to purchase shares in the market for low transaction costs.

List of Terms

marginal principle of retained earnings	life cycle curve
residual dividends	clientele effect
declaration date	dividend payment date
ex-dividend date	stock dividends
dividend record date	stock split
dividend information content	dividend reinvestment plans
dividend payout	corporate stock repurchase
dividend yield	

Discussion Questions

1. How does the marginal principle of retained earnings relate to the returns that a stockholder may make in other investments?

2. Discuss the difference between a passive and an active dividend policy.

3. How does the stockholder, in general, feel about the relevance of dividends?

4. Explain the relationship between a company's growth possibilities and its dividend policy.

5. Discuss the major factors that may influence the firm's willingness and ability to pay dividends.

6. If you buy a stock on the ex-dividend date, will you receive the upcoming quarterly dividend?

7. Why did the Tax Reform Act of 1986 make cash dividend payments more popular to investors?

8. How is a stock split (versus a stock dividend) treated on the financial statements of a corporation?

9. Why might a stock dividend or a stock split be of limited value to an investor?

10. Does it make sense for a corporation to repurchase its own stock? Explain.

11. How does the life cycle curve explain the relationship between corporate growth and residual dividend theory?

12. What advantages to the corporation and the stockholder do dividend reinvestment plans offer?

Problems

1. Webb Enterprises earned $120 million last year and retained $54 million. What is the payout ratio?

2. The stock of the Pills Berry Corporation is currently selling at $60 per share. The firm pays a dividend of $1.80 per share.
   a. What is the annual dividend yield?
   b. If the firm has a payout rate of 50 percent, what is the firm's P/E ratio?

3. In doing a five-year analysis of future dividends, the Spartan Corporation is considering the following two plans. The values represent dividends per share.

Year	Plan A	Plan B
1	$2.10	$0.50
2	2.10	2.80
3	2.10	0.30
4	2.20	5.60
5	2.20	2.40

   a. How much in total dividends per share will be paid under each plan over the five years?

   b. Mr. Craig, the vice president of finance, suggests that stockholders often prefer a stable dividend policy to a highly variable one. He will assume that stockholders apply a lower discount rate to dividends that are stable. The discount rate to be used for Plan A is 10 percent; the discount rate for Plan B is 12 percent. Which plan will provide the higher present value for the future dividends? (Round to two places to the right of the decimal point.)

4. The Pitney Bow and Arrow Corporation has two very important stockholders: Mr. Beasley, a wealthy individual, and the Dakota Corporation. Mr. Beasley is in a 33 percent marginal tax bracket, while the Dakota Corporation is in a 34 percent bracket.

   a. If Mr. Beasley receives $2.60 in cash dividends, how much in taxes will he pay?

   b. If the Dakota Corporation receives $2.60 in cash dividends, how much in taxes will it pay? (Please review the partial exemption accorded to corporate recipients of cash dividends.)

5. The following companies have different financial statistics. What dividend policies would you recommend for them? Explain your reasons.

	Turtle Co.	Hare Corp.
Growth rate in sales and earnings	5%	20%
Cash as a percentage of total assets	15%	2%

6. The Overseas Shipping Company's common stock is selling for $80 the day before the stock goes ex-dividend. The annual dividend yield is 6.25 percent, and dividends are distributed quarterly. Based solely on the impact of the cash dividend, by how much should the stock go down on the ex-dividend date? What will the new price of the stock be?

7. Below are the earnings per share and the dividends per share of three companies.

XYZ Co.		ABC Co.		Widget Co.	
EPS	DPS	EPS	DPS	EPS	DPS
$2.00	$1.00	$2.00	$1.00	$2.00	$1.00
2.10	1.05	2.10	1.00	2.10	.75
2.40	1.20	2.40	1.00	2.40	1.00
2.80	1.40	2.80	1.00	2.80	1.50
3.00	1.50	3.00	1.20	3.00	1.00

  a. What are the payout ratios for each company on an annual basis?
  b. Can you explain some of the reasons for such differences in payout patterns?
  c. Which company would you prefer to own as a stockholder? Why? What other kinds of information would you want before you invested your money?

8. The Western Pipe Company has the following capital section in its balance sheet. Its stock is currently selling for $5 per share.

Common stock (50,000 shares at $1 par)	$ 50,000
Capital in excess of par	50,000
Retained earnings	100,000
	$200,000

The firm intends to first declare a 10 percent stock dividend and then pay a 20-cent cash dividend (which also causes a reduction of retained earnings). Show the capital section of the balance sheet after the first transaction and then after the second transaction.

9. Rolex Discount Jewelers is trying to determine the maximum amount of cash dividends it can pay this year. Assume its balance sheet is as follows:

Assets

Cash	$ 350,000
Accounts receivable	900,000
Fixed assets	1,150,000
Total assets	$2,400,000

Liabilities and Stockholders' Equity

Accounts payable	$ 395,000
Long-term notes payable	330,000
Common stock (250,000 shares at $3 par)	750,000
Retained earnings	925,000
Total liabilities and stockholders' equity	$2,400,000

    a.   From a legal perspective, what is the maximum amount of dividends per share that the firm could pay? Is this realistic?

    b.   In terms of cash availability, what is the maximum amount of dividends per share the firm could pay?

    c.   Assume the firm earned an 18 percent return on stockholders' equity. If the board wishes to pay out 50 percent of earnings in the form of dividends, how much will dividends per share be?

10. The Wilson Corporation has earnings of $900,000, with 300,000 shares outstanding. Its P/E ratio is 18. The firm is holding $500,000 of funds to invest or pay out in dividends. If the funds are retained, the aftertax return on investment will be 15 percent, and this will add to present earnings. The 15 percent is the normal return anticipated for the corporation and the P/E ratio would remain unchanged. If the funds are paid out in the form of dividends, the P/E ratio will increase by 10 percent, because the stockholders in this corporation have a preference for dividends over retained earnings. Which plan will maximize the market value of the stock?

11. The Madison Corporation has done very well in the stock market during the last three years—its stock has risen from $20 per share to $50 per share. Its current statement of net worth is:

Common stock (2 million shares issued at a par value of $10 per share, 6 million shares authorized)	$20,000,000
Paid-in capital in excess of par	9,000,000
Retained earnings	50,000,000
Net worth	$79,000,000

    a.   What changes would occur in the statement of net worth after a two-for-one stock split?

    b.   What would the statement of net worth look like after a three-for-one stock split?

    c.   Assume that Madison earned $5 million. What would its earnings per share be before and after the two-for-one stock split and the three-for-one stock split?

    d.   What would the price per share be before and after the two-for-one and the three-for-one stock splits? (Assume that the price–earnings ratio stays the same.)

    e.   Should a stock split change the price–earnings ratio for Madison?

12. Slick Products sells marked playing cards to blackjack dealers. It has not paid a dividend in many years, but is currently contemplating some kind of dividend. The capital accounts for the firm are:

Common stock (150,000 shares at $1 par)	$150,000
Capital paid in excess of par	150,000
Retained earnings	400,000
Net worth	$700,000

The company's stock is selling for $6 per share and it earned $0.60 per share this year, indicating a P/E ratio of 10.

a. What adjustments would have to be made to the capital accounts for a 10 percent stock dividend?

b. What adjustments would be made to EPS and the stock price? (Assume the P/E ratio remains constant.)

c. How many shares would an investor end up with if he or she originally had 100 shares?

d. What is the investor's total investment worth before and after the stock dividend if the P/E ratio remains constant? (There may be a small difference due to rounding.)

e. Has Slick Products pulled a magic trick, or has it given the investor something of value? Explain.

13. The Lomax Corporation has $4 million in earnings after taxes and 1 million shares outstanding. The stock trades at a P/E of 10. The firm has $3 million in excess cash.

a. Compute the current price of the stock.

b. If the $3 million is used to pay dividends, how much will dividends per share be?

c. If the $3 million is used to repurchase shares in the market at a premium price of $43 per share, how many shares will be reacquired? (Round to the nearest share.)

d. What will the new earnings per share be? (Round to the nearest cent.)

e. If the P/E remains constant, what will the new price of the securities be? By how much, in terms of dollars, did the repurchase increase the stock price?

f. Given the passage of the Tax Reform Act of 1986, is there any tax advantage to capital appreciation versus the receipt of cash dividends?

g. What are some other reasons a corporation may wish to repurchase its own shares in the market?

14. The Majestic Corporation has the following pattern of net income each year, and associated capital expenditure projects for which the firm can earn a higher return than the stockholders could earn if the funds were paid out in the form of dividends.

Year	Net Income	Profitable Capital Expenditure
1	$ 5 million	$4 million
2	8 million	6 million
3	10 million	8 million
4	7 million	7 million
5	12 million	5 million

The Majestic Corporation has 1 million shares outstanding (the following questions are separate from each other).

a. If the marginal principle of retained earnings is applied, how much in total cash dividends will be paid over the five years?

b. If the firm simply uses a payout ratio of 40 percent of net income, how much in total cash dividends will be paid?

c. If the firm pays a 10 percent stock dividend in years 2 through 5, and also pays a cash dividend of $2.50 per share for each of the five years, how much in total dividends will be paid?

d. Assume the payout ratio in each year is to be 30 percent of net income and the firm will pay a 20 percent stock dividend in years 2 through 5, how much will dividends per share for each year be?

Selected References

Ang, James S. "Do Dividends Matter? A Review of Corporate Dividend Theories and Evidence." *Monograph Series, in Finance and Economics* (1987), pp. 1–58.

Asquith, Paul, and David W. Mullins, Jr. "Signaling With Dividends, Stock Purchases, and Equity Issues." *Financial Management* 15 (Autumn 1986), p. 2,744.

Baker, H. Kent; Gail E. Farrelly; and Richard B. Edelman. "A Survey of Management Views on Dividend Policy." *Financial Management* 14 (Autumn 1985), pp. 78–84.

Barker, C. A. "Evaluation of Stock Dividends." *Harvard Business Review* 36 (July–August 1958), pp. 99–114.

Bierman, Harold, Jr., and Richard West. "The Acquisition of Common Stock by the Corporate Issuer." *Journal of Finance* 21 (December 1966), pp. 687–96.

Dielmen, T.; R. Wright; and T. Nantell. "Stock Effects of Stock Repurchasing: A Random Coefficient Regression Approach." *Journal of Financial and Quantitative Analysis* 15 (March 1980), pp. 175–89.

Elton, Edwin J., and Martin J. Gruber. "The Cost of Retained Earnings—Implications of Share Repurchase." *Industrial Management Review* 9 (Spring 1968), pp. 87–104.

Fama, Eugene F. "The Empirical Relationships between the Dividend and Investment Decision of Firms." *American Economic Review* 54 (September 1964), pp. 656–82.

Gordon, Myron J. "Optimum Investment and Financing Policy." *Journal of Finance* 18 (May 1963), pp. 264–72.

Grinblatt, Mark S.; Ronald W. Masulis; and Sheridan Titman. "The Valuation Effect of Stock Splits and Stock Dividends." *Journal of Financial Economics* 13 (December 1984), pp. 461–90.

Johnson, Keith B. "Stock Splits and Price Changes." *Journal of Finance* 21 (December 1966), pp. 675–86.

Kalay, Avner. "Stockholder–Bondholder Conflict and Dividend Constraints." *Journal of Financial Economics* 59 (July 1982), pp. 211–33.

———. "The Ex-dividend Day Behavior of Stock Prices: A Reexamination of the Clientele Effect." *Journal of Finance* 37 (September 1982), pp. 1,059–70.

Lintner, John. "Distribution of Income of Corporations Among Dividends, Retained Earnings, and Taxes." *American Economic Review* 46 (May 1956), pp. 97–113.

Miller, Merton H., and Franco Modigliani. "Dividend Policy, Growth, and the Valuation of Shares." *Journal of Business* 34 (October 1961), pp. 411–33.

Pettit, R. Richardson. "Dividend Announcements, Security Performance, and Capital Market Efficiency." *Journal of Finance* 27 (December 1972), pp. 993–1,007.

Solomon, Ezra. *The Theory of Financial Management.* New York: Columbia University Press, 1963.

19

Convertibles and Warrants

There are as many types of securities as there are innovative corporate treasurers or forward-looking portfolio managers. In the inflation–dis-inflation, volatile-interest-rate period of the 1970s and the 1980s, investors have looked to security features providing special downside protection as well as capital appreciation potential. Many of these securities also are an outgrowth of the wheeler-dealer, fast-buck period of the late 1960s. The particular emphasis in this chapter is on convertible securities and warrants.

Convertible Securities

A convertible security is a bond or share of preferred stock that can be converted, at the option of the holder, into common stock. Thus, the owner has a fixed-income security that can be transferred to a common stock interest if and when the affairs of the firm indicate that such a conversion is desirable. For purposes of discussion, we will refer to convertible bonds (debentures), although the same principles apply to convertible preferred stock.

When a convertible debenture is initially issued, a *conversion ratio* to common stock is specified. The ratio indicates the number of shares of common stock to which the debentures may be converted. Assume that in 1988 the Williams Company issued $10 million of 25-year, 6 percent convertible debentures, with each $1,000 bond convertible into 20 shares of common stock. The conversion ratio of 20 may also be expressed in terms of a *conversion price*. To arrive at the conversion price, we divide the par value of the bond by the conversion ratio of 20. In the case of the Williams Company, the conversion price is $50. Conversely, the conversion ratio may also be found by dividing the par value by the conversion price ($1,000/$50 = 20). The information given determines what procedure you follow.

Value of the Convertible Bond

As a first consideration in evaluating a convertible bond, we must examine the value of the conversion privilege. In the above case, we might assume that the common stock is selling at $45 per share, so the total conversion value is $900 ($45 × 20). Nevertheless, the bond may sell for par or face value ($1,000) in anticipation of future developments in the common stock and because interest payments are being received on the bonds. With the bond selling for $1,000 and a $900 conversion value, there is a $100 *conversion premium*, representing the dollar difference between market value and conversion value. The conversion premium generally will be influenced by the expectations of future performance of the common stock. If investors are optimistic about the prospects of the common stock, the premium may be large.

If the price of the common stock really takes off and goes to $60 per share, the conversion privilege becomes quite valuable. The bonds, which are convertible into 20 shares, will go up to at least $1,200, and perhaps more. Note that you do not have to convert to common immediately, but may enjoy the movement of the convertible in concert with the common.

What happens if the common stock goes in the opposite direction? Assume that instead of going from $45 to $60 the common stock simply drops from $45 to $25—what will happen to the value of the convertible debentures? We know the value of a convertible bond will go down in response to the drop in the common stock, but will it fall all the way to its conversion value of $500 (20 × $25 per share)? The answer is clearly no, because the debenture still has value as an interest-bearing security. If the going market rate of interest in straight debt issues of similar maturity (25 years) and quality is 8 percent, we would say the debenture

Figure 19–1
Price movement
pattern for a
convertible bond

has a pure bond value of $785.46.[1] Thus, a convertible bond has a floor value,[2] but no upside limitation. The price pattern for the convertible bond is depicted in Figure 19–1.

We see the effect on the convertible bond price as the common stock price, shown along the X-axis, is assumed to change. Note that the floor (pure bond) value for the convertible is well above the conversion value when the common stock price is very low. As the common stock price moves to higher levels, the convertible bond moves in concert with the conversion value. Representative information on outstanding convertible bonds is presented in Table 19–1.

The first two bonds in the table are good examples of what is meant by a floor value. Alliant Computer is in the volatile computer industry, and when the common stock declined to $9.50 per share the conversion

---

[1]Based on discounting procedures covered in Chapter 10, Valuation and Rates of Return. Semiannual interest payments are assumed.

[2]The floor value can change if interest rates in the market change. For ease of presentation, we shall assume they are constant for now.

Table 19–1   Pricing pattern for convertible bonds outstanding, October 1987

Issue, Coupon, and Maturity	(1) Conversion Value	(2) Market Value of Bond	(3) Pure Bond Value	(4) Yield to Maturity on Bond	(5) Market Rate for Bond of Similar Maturity and Quality
Alliant Comp.					
7.25, 2012	$ 239.00	$ 620.00	$ 620.00	12.3%	12.3%
Anacomp, Inc.					
13.875, 2002,	564.30	1,000.00	1,000.00	13.875	13.875
Bally Mfg.					
6, 98	784.80	945.00	610.00	6.7	12.8
IBM					
6.375, 96	1,486.25	1,361.25	821.55	1.74	9.5
Pfizer, Inc.					
8.75, 06	2,314.10	2,327.50	900.00	0.9	9.9
Sterling Software					
8, 2000	468.70	705.00	590.00	12.5	15.0

Source: Data from Value Line Convertibles, October 19, 1987, and Moody's Bond Record, October 1987.

value followed it to $239 (each share was convertible into 25.157 shares). Anacomp, Inc., had a series of bad years, and the common stock declined to a low of $3 per share before reaching $9.87. The conversion value reached a low of $171.25 before recovering to $564.30. Because Alliant and Anacomp were able to maintain their coupon payments, the bond prices sold in the market at their pure bond values. In other words, the pure bond value kept the market price of the bond from falling to the low conversion value levels.

In the case of Pfizer, the bond is trading well above the pure bond value of $900, indicating that the conversion privilege is very valuable and that interest payments are probably not a factor in establishing the bond price. Note that Bally Manufacturing is selling at a large premium over its conversion value. Since the conversion value is greater than the pure bond value, we can assume that the market price of the bond is being supported by the expectations of a rising stock price. At a market price of $945, the pure bond value of $610 does not act as much of a floor value. Instead, the stock price is the deciding factor in determining the bond's market price. The Sterling Software bond has a conversion value lower than the pure bond value and a market price higher than the pure bond value. In this case, the pure bond value acts as a partial floor value, and the expectation that the stock price might go up also helps to create a market price that is at a premium to both the pure bond value and conversion value. A decline in either the pure bond value or the stock price would cause the market value of the Sterling Software convertible bond to decrease.

Is This Fool's Gold?

Have we repealed the old risk–return trade-off principle—that in order to get superior returns we must take larger than normal risks? With convertible bonds, we appear to limit our risk while maximizing our return potential.

Although there is some truth to this statement, there are many qualifications. For example, once convertible debentures begin going up in value, say to $1,100 or $1,200, the downside protection becomes pretty meaningless. In the case of the Williams Company in our earlier example, the floor is at $785.46. If an investor were to buy the convertible bond at $1,200, he would be exposed to $414.54 in potential losses (hardly adequate protection for a true risk averter). Also, if interest rates in the market rise, the floor price, or pure bond value, could fall, creating more downside risk.

A second drawback with convertible bonds is that the purchaser is invariably asked to accept below-market rates of interest on the debt instrument. The interest rate on convertibles is generally one third below that for instruments in a similar risk class at time of issue. In the sophisticated environment of the bond and stock markets, one seldom gets an additional benefit without having to suffer a corresponding disadvantage.

The student will also recall that the purchaser of a convertible bond normally pays a premium over the conversion value. For example, if a $1,000 bond were convertible into 20 shares of common at $45 per share, a $100 conversion premium might be involved initially. If the same $1,000 were invested directly in common stock at $45 per share, 22.2 shares could be purchased. If the shares go up in value, we have 2.2 more shares on which to garner a profit.

Lastly, convertibles may suffer from the attachment of a call provision giving the corporation the option of redeeming the bonds at a specified price above par ($1,000) in the future. In a subsequent section, we will see how the corporation can use this device to force the conversion of the bonds into common stock.

None of these negatives is meant to detract from the fact that convertibles carry some inherently attractive features if they are purchased with investor objectives in mind. If the investor wants downside protection, he or she should search out convertible bonds trading below par, perhaps within 10–15 percent of the floor value. Though a fairly large move in the stock may be necessary to generate upside profit, the investor has the desired protection and some hope for capital appreciation.

Advantages and Disadvantages to the Corporation

Having established the fundamental characteristics of the convertible security from the *investor* viewpoint, let us now turn the coin over and examine the factors a corporate financial officer must consider in weighing the advisability of a convertible offer for the firm.

Not only has it been established that the interest rate paid on convertible issues is lower than that paid on a straight debt instrument, but the convertible feature may be the only device for allowing smaller corporations access to the bond market. In this day of debt-ridden corporate balance sheets, investor acceptance of new debt may be contingent upon a special sweetener, such as the ability to convert to common.

Convertible debentures are also attractive to a corporation that believes its stock is currently undervalued. You will recall that in the case of the Williams Company, $1,000 bonds were convertible into 20 shares of common stock at a conversion price of $50. Since the common stock had a current price of $45 and new shares of stock might be sold at only $44,[3] the corporation effectively received $6 over current market price, assuming future conversion. Of course, one can also argue that if the firm had delayed the issuance of common stock or convertibles for a year or two, the stock might have gone up from $45 to $60 and new common stock might have been sold at this lofty price.

To translate this to overall numbers for the firm, if a corporation needs $10 million in funds and offers straight stock now at a net price of $44, it must issue 227,273 shares ($10 million shares/$44). With convertibles, the number of shares potentially issued is only 200,000 shares ($10 million/$50). Finally, if no stock or convertible bonds are issued now and the stock goes up to a level at which new shares can be offered at a net price of $60, only 166,667 will be required ($10 million/$60).

Table 19–2 demonstrates the company's ability to sell stock at premium prices through the use of convertible bonds. The typical convertible bond, according to Value Line Convertibles, had a 20 percent conversion pre-

---

[3]There is always a bit of underpricing to ensure the success of a new offering.

Yield to maturity	8.5%
Years to maturity	22.9
Size	$50.4 million
Investment value grade	Ba Moody's Rating
Initial premium	
over conversion value	20.0%

mium at issue. The table also provides a composite picture of the yield to maturity, years to maturity, size, and investment rating. Notice that the average size of convertibles is quite small, with an average offering of only $50.4 million per issue. The typical nonconvertible issue is well in excess of $100 million. This is, partially, because many small companies with less than a top-grade credit rating are primary issuers of convertible bonds.

Another matter of concern to the corporation is the accounting treatment accorded to convertibles. In the funny-money days of the conglomerate merger movement of the 1960s, corporate management often chose convertible securities over common stock, because the convertibles had a nondilutive effect on earnings per share. As is indicated in a later section on reporting earnings for convertibles, the rules were changed in 1969, and this is no longer the case.

Inherent in a convertible issue is the presumed ability of the corporation to force the security holder to convert the present instrument to common stock. We will examine this process.

Forcing Conversion

How does a corporation, desirous of shifting outstanding debt to common stock, force conversion? The principal device is the call provision, as discussed in Chapter 16, Long-Term Debt and Lease Financing. We know that, when the value of the common stock goes up, the convertible security will move in a similar fashion. Table 19–3 indicates that convertible debentures may go up substantially in value. Some particularly successful convertibles have more than quadrupled in price.

Notice that the coupon rates of the convertible bonds in Table 19–3 were relatively low, compared to existing coupon rates of approximately 9.5 to 12.5 percent in October of 1987 for straight bonds of the same risk class. The companies were content to pay the tax-deductible interest

**Table 19–3
Successful
convertible bonds
not yet called as of
October 1987**

Issue, Coupon, Maturity	Market Price	Current Call Price	Current Yield	Dividend Yield
Crane Co.				
5.00%, 1993	$5,945.00	$1,000.00*	0.84%	2.73%
Pepsi Co, Inc.,				
4.75%, 1996	5,630.00	1,012.30	0.84	1.71
Ralston Purina Co.,				
5.75%, 2000	5,275.00	1,023.00	1.09	1.53
Rochester Telephone Corp.,				
4.75%, 1994	2,145.62	1,011.90	2.21	5.35
Saint Regis Corp.,				
4.875%, 1998	3,977.50	1,012.20	1.23	1.89
Sherwin-Williams,				
6.25%, 1995	5,890.00	1,007.40	1.06	1.65

*Initially $1,100.

expense and allow the bonds to trade in the market until maturity. Additionally, all the companies in the above table had very few bonds still trading in the market. Most of the bonds had been voluntarily converted into common stock by the owners. Because the current yields were so low, owners could get higher cash dividend yields from the underlying common stock, and it was to their advantage to convert to common stock. All call prices in Table 19–3 were low enough to "force" conversion if the company so desired; but there was no advantage to the company to do so in these particular situations, since common stock dividends were paid after taxes, while interest was paid before taxes.

If one of these companies wanted to call in the bonds for conversion, this is how it would work. As an example, we will use the Crane Company convertible bond from Table 19–3. At the time of issue, the corporation established a future privilege for calling in the bond at 10 percent above par value—thus, the $1,000 debenture was redeemable at $1,100. Most bonds have an initial 5 to 10 percent call premium, which declines over time. The Crane Company bond has risen in value to $5,945 per $1,000 bond. The call price has declined annually from its initial value of $1,100 to its current level of $1,000. An owner of this bond is entitled to 180.18 common shares per bond. If Crane wishes to force conversion, it announces that it is going to call the issue at $1,000. Bondholders now have the choice between converting to 180.18 shares of stock worth $5,945[4]

---

[4]The common stock shares were selling at $33. Thus, the conversion value was $5,945 (180.18 × $33). This is also the same as the pre-call market value of the bond.

or accepting a call price of $1,000. Any rational bondholder will take the shares and, thus, the higher value. This demonstrates the derivation of the term *forced* conversion. By calling the bond, Crane would force the conversion of debt to equity. This would change the composition of the balance sheet by decreasing the debt-to-asset ratio.

Conversion may also be encouraged through a step-up in the conversion price over time. When the bond is issued, the contract may specify the following conversion provisions:

	Conversion Price	Conversion Ratio
First five years . . .	$40	25.0 shares
Next three years . . .	45	22.2 shares
Next two years . . .	50	20.0 shares
Next five years . . .	55	18.2 shares

At the end of each time period, there is a strong inducement to convert rather than accept an adjustment to a higher conversion price and a lower conversion ratio.

Euro-Convertible Bonds

Over the past 20 years, many companies have been selling convertible bonds to foreign investors, particularly in Europe.[5] The Eurobonds are dollar denominated and sold primarily in Western European countries. Foreign investors like convertible Eurobonds because they have the safety of a bond but the chance to grow with U.S. stock prices since they are convertible into a U.S. firm's stock. U.S. companies like Eurobonds because they skirt U.S. capital transfer restrictions and allow companies to raise dollars outside of the United States. Table 19–4 presents some selected convertible Eurobonds.

Accounting Considerations with Convertibles ⸻

Prior to 1969, the full impact of the conversion privilege as it applied to convertible securities, warrants (long-term options to buy stock), and other dilutive securities was not adequately reflected in reported earnings

---

[5]Steve Dawson, "A Somber Fifteenth Euro-Convertible Bond Reunion," *Journal of Portfolio Management*, Winter 1985, pp. 85–87.

Table 19–4
Selected issues of
convertible
Eurobonds, October
1987

Issue, Coupon, and Maturity	Conversion Value	Market Value of Bond	Call Price (in percent)
American Brands			
cv. eurodeb., 7.75, 2002	$ 982.50	$1,101.25	105.43%
Southwest Airlines			
euro c.s.d., 6.75, 1998	517.50	867.50	102.00
Southern Cal. Ed. Fin			
euro c.s.d., 12.50, 1997	1,937.50	1,937.50	101.00
Texaco Cap. N.V.			
euro c.s.d., 11.875, 1994	810.00	1,038.75	105.00

Source: Moody's Bond Record, October 1987.

per share. Since all of these securities may generate additional common stock in the future, the potential effect of dilution should be considered. Let us examine the unadjusted (for conversion) financial statements of the XYZ Corporation in Table 19–5.

An analyst would hardly be satisfied in accepting the unadjusted earnings per share figure of $1 for the XYZ Corporation. In computing earnings per share, we have not accounted for the 400,000 additional shares of common stock that could be created by converting the bonds. How then do we make this full disclosure? According to Accounting Principles Board Opinion 15, issued by the American Institute of Certified Public

Table 19–5

XYZ CORPORATION

1. *Capital section of balance sheet:*
   Common stock (1 million shares at $10 par) $10,000,000
   4.5% convertible debentures (10,000 debentures of $1,000; convertible into 40 shares per bond, or a total of 400,000 shares) 10,000,000
   Retained earnings 20,000,000
       Net worth $40,000,000

2. *Condensed income statement:*
   Earnings before interest and taxes . . . . $ 2,450,000
   Interest (4.5% of $10 million) 450,000
   Earnings before taxes 2,000,000
   Taxes (50%) 1,000,000
   Earnings after taxes . . . . $ 1,000,000

3. *Earnings per share:*

$$\frac{\text{Earnings after taxes}}{\text{Shares of common outstanding}} = \frac{\$1,000,000}{1,000,000} = \$1$$

Accountants in 1969 and amended by the Financial Accounting Standards Board's Statement 55 in 1982, we need to compute earnings per share using two different methods when there is potential dilution of a material nature.

1. $$\text{Primary earnings per share} = \frac{\text{Adjusted earnings after taxes}}{\text{Shares outstanding} + \text{Common stock equivalents}} \qquad (19\text{--}1)$$

Common stock equivalents include warrants, other options, and any *convertible securities that paid less than two thirds of the average Aa bond yield at time of issue.*

2. $$\text{Fully diluted earnings per share} = \frac{\text{Adjusted earnings after taxes}}{\substack{\text{Shares outstanding} + \text{Common stock} \\ \text{equivalents} + \textit{All convertibles} \\ \textit{regardless of the interest rate}}} \qquad (19\text{--}2)$$

The intent in computing both primary and fully diluted earnings per share is to consider the effect of potential dilution. Common stock equivalents represent those securities that are capable of generating new shares of common stock in the future.[6] Note that convertible securities may or may not be required in computing primary earnings per share, depending on rates, but must be included in computing fully diluted earnings per share.

In the case of the XYZ Corporation in Table 19–5, the convertibles pay 4.5 percent interest. We assume that the average Aa bond yield at time of issue was 9 percent, so they are considered as common stock equivalents and are included in both primary and fully diluted earnings per share.

We get new earnings per share for the XYZ Corporation by assuming that 400,000 new shares will be created from potential conversion, while at the same time allowing for the reduction in interest payments that would take place as a result of the conversion of the debt to common stock. Since before-tax interest payments on the convertibles are $450,000 for the XYZ Corporation and a 50 percent tax rate is assumed, the aftertax cost is $225,000. The assumption is that this aftertax interest cost will

---

[6]Warrants and options are similar to convertibles in that they may be used to acquire common stock. Warrants are discussed in the next section.

be saved and can be added back to income. Making the appropriate adjustment to the numerator and denominator, we show adjusted earnings per share.

$$
\begin{array}{c}
\text{Primary} \\
\text{earnings} \\
\text{per share*}
\end{array}
=
\frac{\text{Adjusted earnings after taxes}}{\text{Shares outstanding} + \text{Common stock equivalents}}
$$

$$
=
\frac{
\begin{array}{cc}
\textit{Reported} & \textit{Interest} \\
\textit{earnings} & \textit{savings}
\end{array}
}{}
$$

$$
=
\frac{\$1,000,000 + \$225,000}{1,000,000 + 400,000}
=
\frac{\$1,225,000}{1,400,000}
= \$0.88
$$

*Same as fully diluted in this instance.

We see a 12 cent reduction from the earnings per share figure of $1 in Table 19–5. The new figure is the value that a sophisticated security analyst would use.

Financing through Warrants

A warrant is an option to buy a stated number of shares of stock at a specified price over a given time period. For example, the warrants of Cetus Corporation enable the holder to buy one share of stock at a price of $30 any time between now and June 30, 1993. If the value of Cetus Corporation common stock goes up to $40 or $50, the warrants will be quite valuable.

Warrants are sometimes issued as a sweetener to a bond offering, and they may enable the firm to issue debt when this would not be feasible otherwise. The warrants are usually detachable from the bond issue, have their own market price, and are generally traded on the New York Stock Exchange or American Stock Exchange. After warrants are exercised, the initial debt to which they are attached remains in existence.

Because a warrant is dependent on the market movement of the underlying common stock and has no "security value" as such, it is highly speculative in nature. If the common stock of the firm is volatile, the value of the warrants may change dramatically.

Tri-Continental Corporation warrants went from $\frac{1}{32}$ to $75\frac{3}{4}$ between 1942 and 1969, while United Airlines warrants moved from $4\frac{1}{2}$ to 126 between 1962 and 1966. Of course, this is not a one-way street, as holders of LTV warrants will attest as they saw their holdings dip from 83 to $2\frac{1}{4}$ in the 1968–70 bear market.

Valuation of Warrants

Because the value of a warrant is closely tied to the underlying stock price, we can develop a formula for the minimum value (intrinsic value) of a warrant.

$$3. \quad \begin{matrix}\text{Minimum value} \\ \text{of a warrant}\end{matrix} = \left(\begin{matrix}\text{Market value of} \\ \text{common stock}\end{matrix} - \begin{matrix}\text{Option price} \\ \text{of warrant}\end{matrix}\right) \qquad (19\text{–}3)$$

$$\times \begin{matrix}\text{Number of shares each warrant} \\ \text{entitles holder to purchase}\end{matrix}$$

Using the data from Table 19–6, we see that Navistar International common stock is trading at 6.50 in October of 1987.[7] Each warrant carries with it the option to purchase one share of Navistar International stock at $5 per share until December 15, 1993. Using Formula 19–3, the minimum value (intrinsic value) is $1.50 or (6.50 − 5.00) × 1. Since

Table 19–6   Relationships determining warrant prices, October 1987

(1) Firm: Place of Warrant Listing, and Stock Listing*	(2) Warrant Price	(3) Stock Price	(4) Option Price	(5) Number of Shares	(6) Intrinsic Value†	(7) Speculative Premium	(8) Due Date
Bristol Myers: NYSE, NYSE	$12.00	$47.38	$16.42	0.332	$10.28	$ 1.72	12/31/94
Cetus Corp: OTC, OTC	7.00	22.37	30.00	1.000	−7.63	14.63	06/30/93
Navistar Intl: NYSE, NYSE	3.38	6.50	5.00	1.000	1.50	1.88	12/15/93
Pan Am Corp.: NYSE, NYSE	1.50	4.50	8.00	1.000	−3.50	5.00	5/01/93
Public Service N.H.: OTC, NYSE	0.88	3.00	5.00	1.000	−2.00	2.88	10/15/91
Tri Star Pictures: OTC, OTC‡	3.00	14.62	12.00	0.500	1.31	1.69	12/31/93
Turner Broadcasting: OTC, ASE	8.25	13.12	11.25	2.000	3.74	4.51	12/15/91
Wickes Companies: OTC, NYSE	10.38	20.63	22.15	5.000	−7.60	17.98	6/15/93

*OTC = over-the-counter market; NYSE = New York Stock Exchange; AMEX = American Stock Exchange.
†Even though the intrinsic value is negative in several cases, a warrant may not have an actual value of less than zero. The negative values are given so the speculative premium may be calculated easily.
‡Tri Star Pictures' warrant is callable at $2.25 after 12/30/89.

---

[7]Navistar International is the new name for the firm formerly known as International Harvester.

the warrant has several years to run, and is an effective vehicle for speculative trading, it is trading at $3.38 per warrant. This is $1.88 more than its intrinsic value, or a speculative premium of over 100 percent. Investors are willing to pay a premium because a small percentage gain in the stock price may generate large percentage increases in the warrant price. Formula 19–4 demonstrates the calculation of the speculative premium.

$$\text{Speculative premium of a warrant} = \text{Warrant price} - \text{Intrinsic value} \quad (19\text{–}4)$$

For Navistar International, we use the formula to show the previously stipulated $1.88.

$$\$1.88 = \$3.38 - \$1.50$$

Even if Navistar International were trading at less than the $5 option price, the warrant might still have some value in the market. Speculators might purchase the warrant in the hope that the common stock would increase sufficiently in the future to make the option provision valuable. As an example of an extreme case, the warrants of Cetus Corporation in Table 19–6 are selling at $7 in spite of the fact the stock price is $7.63 below (not above) the option price. Cetus has been involved with medical biotechnology and is in the forefront in cancer research. In the minds of investors, Cetus has a bright future. If the company can just develop one big blockbuster drug, the stock price could soar.

Many warrants continue to trade on this kind of speculation. The typical relationship between the warrant price and intrinsic value of a warrant is depicted in Figure 19–2. We assume the warrant entitles the holder to purchase one new share of common at $20. Note that, although the intrinsic value of the warrant is negative at a common stock price between 0 and 20, the warrant still carries some value in the market. Also, observe that the difference between the market price of the warrant and its intrinsic value is diminished at the upper ranges of value. Two reasons may be offered for the declining premium.

First, the speculator loses the ability to use leverage to generate high returns as the price of the stock goes up. When the price of the stock is relatively low, say $25, and the warrant is in the $5 range, a 10-point movement in the stock could mean a 200 percent gain in the value of the warrant, as indicated in the left-hand panel of Table 19–7.

At the upper levels of stock value, much of this leverage is lost. At a stock value of $50 and a warrant value of approximately $30, a 10-point movement in the stock would produce only a 33 percent gain in the warrant as indicated in the right panel of Table 19–7.

Figure 19–2
Market price relation-
ships for a warrant

Another reason why speculators pay a very low premium at higher stock prices is that there is less downside protection. A warrant selling at $30 when the stock price is $50 is more vulnerable to downside movement than is a $5–$10 warrant when the stock is in the 20s.

Table 19–7
Leverage in valuing
warrants

Low Stock Price	*High Stock Price*
Stock price, $25; warrant price, $5* + 10-point movement in stock price New warrant price, $15 (10-point gain)	Stock price, $50; warrant price, $30 + 10-point movement in stock price New warrant price, $40 (10-point gain)
Percentage gain in warrant $= \dfrac{\$10}{\$5} \times 100 = 200\%$	Percentage gain in warrant $= \dfrac{\$10}{\$30} \times 100 = 33\%$

*The warrant price would, of course, be greater than $5, because of the speculative premium. Nevertheless, we use $5 for ease of computation.

Use of Warrants in Corporate Finance

Let us judge the suitability of warrants for corporate financing purposes. As previously indicated, warrants may allow for the issuance of debt under difficult circumstances. While a straight debt issue may not be acceptable or may be accepted only at extremely high rates, the same security may be well received because detachable warrants are included. Warrants may also be included as an add-on in a merger or acquisition agreement. A firm might offer $20 million in cash plus 10,000 warrants in exchange for all the outstanding shares of the acquisition candidate.

The use of warrants has traditionally been associated with such aggressive high-flying firms as real estate investment trusts, airlines, and conglomerates. However, in the 1970s staid and venerable American Telephone & Telegraph came out with a $1.57 billion debt offering, sweetened by the use of warrants.

As a financing device for creating new common stock, warrants may not be as desirable as convertible securities. A corporation with convertible debentures outstanding may force the conversion of debt to common stock through a call, while no similar device is available to the firm with warrants.[8] The only possible inducement might be a step-up in option price—whereby the warrant holder may pay a progressively higher option price if he does not exercise by a given date.

Accounting Considerations with Warrants

As with convertible securities, the potential dilutive effect of warrants must be considered. All warrants are included in computing both primary and fully diluted earnings per share.[9] The accountant must compute the number of new shares that could be created by the exercise of all warrants, with the provision that the total can be reduced by the assumed use of the cash proceeds to purchase a partially offsetting amount of shares at the market price. Assume that warrants to purchase 10,000 shares at $20 are outstanding and that the current price of the stock is $50. We show the following:

1. New shares created 10,000
2. Reduction of shares from cash proceeds (computed below) 4,000
   Cash proceeds—10,000 shares at $20 = $200,000
   Current price of stock—$50
   Assumed reduction in shares outstanding from
   cash proceeds = $200,000/$50 = 4,000
3. Assumed net increase in shares from exercise
   of warrants (10,000 − 4,000) 6,000

---

[8]It should be pointed out that a number of later financing devices can blur this distinction. See Jerry Miller, "Accounting for Warrants and Convertible Bonds," *Management Accounting*, January 1973, pp. 26–28.

[9]Under most circumstances, if the market price is below the option price, dilution need not be considered. APB Opinion 15, par. 35.

In computing earnings per share, we will add 6,000 shares to the denominator, with no adjustment to the numerator. This, of course will lead to some dilution in earnings per share. Its importance must be interpreted by the financial manager and security analyst.

Summary

A number of security devices related to the debt and common stock of the firm became popular in the 1960s and in subsequent decades. Each security offers downside protection or upside potential, or a combination of these features.

A convertible security is a bond or share of preferred stock that can be converted into common stock at the option of the holder. Thus, the holder has a fixed income security that will not go below a minimum amount because of the interest or dividend payment feature and, at the same time, he or she has a security that is potentially convertible to common stock. If the common stock goes up in value, the convertible security will appreciate as well. From a corporate viewpoint, the firm may force conversion to common stock through a call feature and, thus, achieve a balanced capital structure. Interest rates on convertibles are usually lower than those on straight debt issues.

A warrant is an option to buy a stated number of shares of stock at a specified price over a given time period. The warrant has a large potential for appreciation if the stock goes up in value. Warrants are used primarily as sweeteners for debt instruments or as add-ons in merger tender offers. When warrants are exercised, the basic debt instrument to which they may be attached is not eliminated, as is the case for a convertible debenture. The potential dilutive effect of warrants and convertible securities must be considered in computing earnings per share.

Review of Formulas

1. Primary earnings per share $=$

$$\frac{\text{Adjusted earnings after taxes}}{\text{Shares outstanding + Common stock equivalents}} \quad (19\text{--}1)$$

2. Fully diluted earnings per share $=$

$$\frac{\text{Adjusted earnings after taxes}}{\text{Shares outstanding + Common stock equivalents} + \textit{All convertibles regardless of the interest rate}} \quad (19\text{--}2)$$

3. $\text{Minimum value of a warrant} = \left(\begin{array}{c} \text{Market value of} \\ \text{common stock} \end{array} - \begin{array}{c} \text{Option price} \\ \text{of warrant} \end{array} \right)$ (19–3)

$\times \quad \begin{array}{l} \text{Number of shares each warrant} \\ \text{entitles holder to purchase} \end{array}$

4. $\text{Speculative premium of a warrant} = \text{Warrant price} - \text{Intrinsic value}$ (19–4)

List of Terms

convertible security	primary earnings per share
conversion ratio	fully diluted earnings per share
conversion price	warrant
conversion value	financial sweetener
conversion premium	minimum warrant value
pure bond value	speculative warrant premium
floor price	leverage
forced conversion	intrinsic value
step-up in conversion	

Discussion Questions

1. How can a company force conversion of a convertible bond?

2. What are the basic advantages to the corporation of issuing convertible securities?

3. Explain the difference between primary earnings per share and fully diluted earnings per share.

4. Why are investors willing to pay a premium over the theoretical value (pure bond value or conversion value)?

5. Why is it said that convertible securities have a floor price?

6. Find the prices of the following two convertible bonds in *The Wall Street Journal*: Automatic Data cv 6½ 2011 and Datapoint cv 8⅞ 2006.
   a. Explain what factors cause their prices to be different from their par value of $1,000.
   b. What will happen to the pure bond value if long-term interest rates decline?

7. What is meant by a step-up in the conversion price?

8. What adjustments to earnings after taxes are necessary in order to compute primary earnings per share for convertibles?

9. Explain how convertible bonds and warrants are similar and different.

10. Explain why warrants generally are issued (why are they used in corporate finance?).

11. What are the reasons that warrants sell above their intrinsic value?

Problems

1. Diet Food, Inc., has warrants outstanding which allow the holder to purchase 1.5 shares of stock per warrant at $25 per share (option price). The common stock is currently selling for $30, while the warrant is selling for $12.50 per share.
   a. What is the intrinsic (minimum) value of this warrant?
   b. What is the speculative premium on this warrant?
   c. What should happen to the speculative premium as the expiration date approaches?

2. Alberto Cosmetics, Inc., has a $1,000 par value convertible bond outstanding that can be converted into 25 shares of common stock. The common stock is currently selling for $34.50 a share and the convertible bond is selling for $950.
   a. What is the conversion value of the bond?
   b. What is the conversion premium?
   c. What is the conversion price?

3. H & B Brewing Company has a convertible bond quoted on the NYSE bond market at 85. (Bond quotes represent percentage of par value. Thus, 70 represents $700, 80 represents $800, and so on.) It matures in 10 years and carries a coupon rate of 4.5 percent. The conversion price is $20, and the common stock is currently selling for $10 per share on the NYSE.
   a. Compute the conversion premium.
   b. At what price does the common stock need to sell for the conversion value to be equal to the current bond price?

4. The Brown Shoe Company has a convertible bond outstanding, trading in the marketplace at $820. The par value is $1,000, the coupon rate is 6 percent, and the bond matures in 20 years. The conversion

price is $40 and the company's common stock is selling for $20 per share. Interest is paid semiannually.

a. What is the conversion value?

b. If similar bonds, which are not convertible, are currently yielding 10 percent, what is the pure bond value of this convertible bond? (Use semiannual present value analysis as described in Chapter 10.)

5. XIMIX, Inc., has a $1,000 par value convertible bond outstanding with a coupon rate of 7 percent and a maturity date of 10 years. It is rated Baa2, and competitive bonds of the same risk class carry an 8 percent return. The conversion price is $40. Currently, the common stock is selling for $30 per share on the New York Stock Exchange.

a. What is the conversion ratio?

b. What is the conversion value?

c. Compute the pure bond value. (Use semiannual analysis.)

d. Draw a graph that includes the floor price and the conversion value but not the convertible bond price.

e. Which will influence the current bond price more—the pure bond value or conversion value?

6. Alice Overland Truck Company has convertible bonds outstanding that are callable at $1,080. The bonds are convertible into 22 shares of common stock. The stock is currently selling for $58.75 per share.

a. If the firm announces that it is going to call the bonds at $1,080, what action are bondholders likely to take, and why?

b. Assume that instead of the call feature, the firm has the right to drop the conversion ratio from 22 down to 20 after 5 years and down to 18 after 10 years. If the bonds have been outstanding for four years and 11 months, what will the price of the bonds be if the stock price is $60? Assume the bonds carry no conversion premium.

c. Further assume you anticipate in two months that the common stock price will be up to $63. Considering the conversion feature, should you convert now or continue to hold the bond for at least two more months?

7. You can buy a warrant for $5, which gives you the option to buy one share of common stock at $18 per share. The stock is currently selling at $20 per share.

a. What is the intrinsic (minimum) value of the warrant?

b. What is the speculative premium on the warrant?

c. If the stock rises to $30 per share and the warrant sells at its theoretical value without a premium, what will be the percentage increase in the stock price and the warrant price if you bought the stock and the warrant at the prices stated above, $5 and $20? Explain this relationship.

8. Go Getum Investment Group bought 100 Growth Company warrants one year ago and would like to exercise them today. The warrants were purchased for $24 each and they expire when trading ends today (assume there is no speculative premium left). Growth Company common stock is selling today for $50 per share. The option price is $30 and each warrant entitles the holder to purchase two shares of stock each at the option price.

   a. If the warrants are exercised today, what would Go Getum's total dollar profit or loss be?

   b. What is Go Getum's percentage rate of return?

9. Assume, in problem 8, Growth Company common stock was selling for $40 per share when Go Getum bought the warrants.

   a. What was the intrinsic value of a warrant at that time?

   b. What was the speculative premium per warrant when the warrants were purchased?

   c. What would Go Getum's total dollar profit or loss have been had they invested the $2,400 directly in Growth Company's common stock one year ago at $40 per share and sold it today at $50 per share?

   d. What would the percentage rate of return be on this common stock investment? Compare this to the rate of return on the warrant investment computed in 8*b*.

10. Mr. Hymen Flyer has $1,000 to invest in the market. He is considering the purchase of 50 shares of Volatile Corporation at $20 per share. His broker suggests that he may wish to consider purchasing warrants instead. The warrants are selling for $5, and each warrant allows him to purchase one share of Volatile common stock at $18 per share.

   a. How many warrants can Mr. Flyer purchase for the same $1,000?

   b. If the price of the stock goes to $30, what would be his total dollar and percentage return on the stock?

   c. At the time the stock goes to $30, the speculative premium on the warrant goes to 0 (though the intrinsic value of the warrant goes up). What would be Mr. Flyer's total dollar and percentage return on the warrant?

    d. Assuming that the speculative premium remains $3.50 over the intrinsic value, how far would the price of the stock have to fall before the warrant has no value?

11. Baines Industries has net income of $350,000 in the current fiscal year. There are 100,000 shares of common stock outstanding along with convertible bonds, which have a total face value of $800,000. The $800,000 is represented by 800 different $1,000 bonds. Each $1,000 bond pays 5 percent interest and was issued when the average Aa bond yield was 9 percent. The conversion ratio is 20. The tax rate is 34 percent. Calculate Baines's primary earnings per share in accordance with APB Opinion No. 15. (Note: to get aftertax savings in interest, multiply the before-tax figure by 1 − T.)

12. Using the information from problem 11, assume the average Aa bond yield was 7 percent instead of 9 percent at the time the convertible bonds were issued. All other facts are the same.
    a. What are the primary earnings per share for Baines Industries?
    b. Indicate the value for fully diluted earnings per share.

13. The Ultralight Aircraft Company has 2 million shares of stock outstanding. It also has two convertible bond issues outstanding with terms as follows:

1.	9 percent convertible, 1998	$12,000,000
2.	10 percent convertible, 2006	$15,000,000

The issue with the 9 percent coupon rate was first sold when average Aa bonds were yielding 12 percent and is convertible into 300,000 shares. The issue with the 10 percent coupon rate was first sold when average Aa bonds were yielding 15.5 percent and is convertible into 400,000 shares. Earnings after taxes are $4 million and the tax rate is 50 percent.
    a. Compute both primary and fully diluted earnings per share for Ultra.
    b. Now assume Ultra also has warrants outstanding, which allow the holder to buy 100,000 shares of stock at $20 per share. The stock is currently selling for $40 per share. Compute primary earnings per share considering the possible impact of both the warrants and convertibles.

14. The Ryan Cement Company has $2.5 million in 9 percent convertible bonds outstanding. Each bond has a $1,000 par value. The conversion ratio is 60, the stock price is $22, and the bond matures in 10 years.

The bonds are currently selling at a conversion premium of $100 over their conversion value.

a. If the price of Ryan Cement Company common stock rises to $30 this date next year, what would your rate of return be if you bought a convertible bond today and sold it in one year? Assume that, on this date next year, the conversion premium has shrunk from $100 to $10.

b. Assume that the yield on similar nonconvertible bonds has declined to 8 percent at the time of sale. What would the pure bond value be at that point in time? (Use semiannual analysis.) Would the pure bond value have a significant effect on valuation then?

15. The Furgeson Corporation has 1,000 convertible bonds ($1,000 par value) outstanding, each of which may be converted to 50 shares ($20 conversion price). The $1 million worth of bonds has 15 years to maturity. The current price of the stock is $25 per share. Furgeson's net income in the most recent fiscal year was $300,000. The bonds pay 12 percent interest and were issued when the average Aa bond rate was 13 percent. The corporation has 150,000 shares of common stock outstanding. Current market interest rates on long-term bonds of equal quality are 14 percent. A 30 percent tax rate is assumed.

a. Compute fully diluted earnings per share.

b. Assume that the bonds currently sell at a 5 percent conversion premium over straight conversion value (based on a stock price of $25). However, as the price of the stock increases from $25 to $35 due to new events, there will be an increase in the bond price, but zero conversion premium. Under these circumstances, determine the rate of return on a convertible bond investment after this price change, based on appreciation in value.

c. Now assume that the stock price fell to $15 per share because a competitor introduced a new product. Would the straight conversion value be greater than the pure bond value, based on the interest rates stated above? (See Table 16–3 in Chapter 16 to get the bond value without having to go through the actual computation.)

d. In the case of part *c*, if the convertible traded at a 20 percent premium over the straight conversion value, would the convertible be priced above the pure bond value?

e. If long-term interest rates in the market go down to 10 percent, while the stock price is at $26, with a 4 percent conversion premium, what would the difference be between the market price of the convertible bond and the pure bond value. Assume 15 years to maturity, and once again use Table 16–3 for part of your answer.

f. If Furgeson were able to retire the convertibles and to replace them with 40,000 shares of common stock selling at $25 per share and paying a 6.5 percent dividend yield (dividend to price ratio), would the aftertax cash outflow related to the convertible be greater or less than the cash outflow related to the stock?

16. Schering Plough and Shovel (SPS) has $20 million of convertible bonds outstanding (20,000 bonds at $1,000 par value) with a coupon rate of 10 percent. Interest rates are currently 8 percent for bonds of equal risk. The bonds were originally sold when the average Aa rate was 12 percent, and they have 20 years left to maturity. The bonds may be called at a 10 percent premium over par, as well as converted into 30 shares of common stock. The tax rate for the company is 40 percent.

The firm's common stock is currently selling for $40 per share and it pays a dividend of $3.50. The expected income for the company is $34 million with 4 million shares of common stock currently outstanding.

Make a thorough analysis of this bond and determine whether SPS should call the bond at the 10 percent call premium. In your analysis, consider the following:

a. The impact of the call on primary and fully diluted earnings per share and the common stock price (assume that the call forces conversion).

b. The consequences of your decision on financing flexibility.

c. The net change in cash outflows to the company.

d. If the bond is called, will the stockholders take the call price or the 30 shares of common stock?

Selected References

Alexander, Gordon J., and Roger O. Stover. "Pricing in the New Issue Debt Market." *Financial Management* 6 (Fall 1977), pp. 35–39.

Baumol, William J.; Burton G. Malkiel; and Richard E. Quandt. "The Valuation of Convertible Securities." *Quarterly Journal of Economics* 80 (February 1966), pp. 48–59.

Billingsley, Randall S.; Robert E. Lamy; and G. Rodney Thompson. "Valuation of Primary Issue Convertible Bonds." *Journal of Financial Research* 39 (Fall 1986), pp. 251–60.

Black, Fischer, and Myron Scholes. "The Pricing of Options and Corporate Liabilities." *Journal of Political Economy* 81 (May–June 1973), pp. 637–54.

Brigham, Eugene F. "An Analysis of Convertible Debentures: Theory and Some Empirical Evidence." *Journal of Finance* 21 (March 1966), pp. 35–54.

Dawson, Steve. "A Somber Fifteenth Euro-Convertible Bond Reunion." *Journal of Portfolio Management,* (Winter 1985), pp. 85–87.

Finnerty, John D. "Stock-for-Debt Swaps and Shareholder Returns." *Financial Management* 14 (Autumn 1985), pp. 5–17.

King, Raymond. "Convertible Bond Valuation: An Empirical Test." *Journal of Financial Research* 37 (Spring 1986), pp. 53–70.

Lewellen, Wilbur G., and George A. Racette. "Convertible Debt Financing." *Journal of Financial and Quantitative Analysis* 7 (December 1973), pp. 777–92.

Marr, Wayne M., and G. Rodney Thompson. "The Pricing of New Convertible Bond Issues." *Financial Management* 13 (Summer 1984), pp. 38–40.

Mikkelson, Wayne H. "Convertible Calls and Stock Price Declines." *Financial Analysts Journal,* January–February 1985, pp. 63–69.

Miller, Jerry. "Accounting for Warrants and Convertible Bonds." *Management Accounting,* January 1973, pp. 26–28.

Rush, David F., and Ronald W. Melicher. "An Empirical Examination of Factors Which Influence Warrant Prices." *Journal of Finance* 29 (December 1974), pp. 1,449–66.

Schwartz, Eduardo S. "The Valuation of Warrants: Implementing a New Approach." *Journal of Financial Economics* 4 (January 1977), pp. 79–94.

Sinkey, Joseph F., and James A. Miles. "The Use of Warrants in the Bail Out of First Pennsylvania Bank: An Application of Option Pricing." *Financial Management* 27 (Autumn 1982), pp. 27–32.

Soldofsky, Robert M. "Yield-Risk Performance of Convertible Securities." *Financial Analysts Journal* 39 (March–April 1971), pp. 61–65.

P A R T

6

Expanding the Perspective of Corporate Finance

20 External Growth through Mergers

21 International Financial Management

The final two topics, mergers and international finance, are particularly appropriate for the current financial environment. Both have achieved increasing importance as financial managers have attempted to grow and diversify away from traditional product lines and across international borders.

Mergers have long been recognized as offering the potential for risk reduction by combining diversified firms under common control. However, the achievement of such risk reduction can be an elusive process, as overly optimistic planners often find obstacles in their way. The successful merger must be based on realistic expectations and a careful consideration of postmerger performance. We shall evaluate both of these factors in Chapter 20.

The latest merger wave is somewhat unique in that it is populated by such high-quality acquiring firms as Du Pont, General Electric, and Colgate Palmolive. It is also unusual in that many of the mergers of the mid-to-late 1980s are unfriendly in nature. That is, the acquired firm did not necessarily wish to be taken over by the acquiring firm.

In the merger chapter, we examine the significant financial and management variables that influence the merger decision, including the price paid, the accounting implications, the stock market effect, and the motivations of the participating parties. The chapter provides an overview of many topics discussed earlier in the text.

The importance of the multinational business firm is considered in Chapter 21. In an ever-shrinking world, the financial manager must be prepared to make decisions that have worldwide effects. In prior chapters, basic business decisions were considered primarily in terms of the direct "dollar" impact on profitability. As the business firm moves into foreign markets and deals in deutsche marks, Swiss francs, and Japanese yen, the foreign exchange implications of decisions must also be considered. A firm may suddenly have to receive a future payment in a currency that is rapidly declining in value. How is this circumstance to be handled? The international financial manager must understand his or her options.

Although foreign investments may carry unusual political and economic risks, they also allow for expanded market potential. Local customs and requirements in regard to taxation and payment of dividends must be carefully examined. A major example in Chapter 21 considers these factors.

Finally, international financing arrangements, such as the Eurodollar market and Eurobond market, which were touched on in Part 3 of the book, are now given expanded coverage. Also, the relationship of the multinational firm to foreign stock markets is considered.

20

External Growth through Mergers

Many of the previously discussed points regarding financial planning, risk–return analysis, valuation, capital budgeting, and portfolio management can be examined in the very meaningful context of mergers and acquisitions. To this extent, Chapter 20 may be thought of as an integrative chapter for much of the material discussed throughout the text.

There have been a number of major merger movements in the industrial history of the United States, beginning in the late 1890s with the development of the oil, railroad, tobacco, and steel industries and culminating with the merger mania of the late 1970s and 1980s. This last wave of mergers is of particular interest to us because it has significantly influenced the current corporate environment.

The major theme of this latest merger movement is that it is cheaper to acquire other companies than it is to expand through new product development or the purchase of new plant and equipment.

A second significant feature of the modern merger boom has been that the major participants are no longer the "urge to merge" gunslinger conglomerate giants of the 1960s, but are rather old and conservative corporations, such as Du Pont, General Electric, and Colgate Palmolive. In addition, foreign acquirers, such as British Petroleum, have come on the scene in a big way as foreign companies have opted for U.S. invest-

595

ments. Foreigners seem to be attracted to U.S. companies because of the relatively stable political climate and the fear that the United States will impose import restrictions. This has caused foreigners to either undertake joint ventures with U.S. companies, buy U.S. companies, or build U.S. facilities.

A final development of the latest merger movement has been the unfriendly buy-out, in which a major acquiring company identifies a target company and attempts to acquire it without management approval. At first this activity was centered in the oil industry, with unfriendly takeover attempts by T. Boone Pickens of Gulf Oil, Phillips Petroleum, and Union Oil of California (Unocal). Phillips Petroleum and Unocal fended off the takeover by restructuring their balance sheet with a heavy debt load and with strategies designed to reduce the value of the company if the takeover were successful. These self-emasculating strategies are also a form of poison pills. Gulf was bought by white knight Chevron for a record $13.3 billion. The next two largest mergers of the 1980s were also with oil companies: Mobil Corporation bought Superior Oil Company for $5.7 billion and Texaco bought Getty Oil Company for $10.125 right out from under Pennzoil Company. This merger resulted in a lawsuit by Pennzoil, in which the Texas courts ruled in favor of Pennzoil and declared a judgment against Texaco of $10.3 billion. This caused Texaco to file bankruptcy and eventually settle the suit for $3 billion (the largest such payment in U.S. history). Table 20–1 lists the 10 biggest acquisitions in the mid-1980s.

Table 20–1   Ten biggest acquisitions in the mid-1980s

Target	Buyer	Target's Stock Price 8/12/82	Acquisition Price Per Share	Acquisition Price Total ($ billions)	Closing Date
Gulf Oil Corp.	Chevron Corp.	24.25	$ 80.00	$13.3	6/15/84
Getty Oil Co.	Texaco, Inc.	43.50	128.00	10.1	2/17/84
Standard Oil Co.	British Petroleum Co.	28.50	71.50	7.6	6/29/87
Beatrice Cos.	Kohlberg Kravis Roberts	19.50	50.00	6.3	4/17/86
RCA Corp.	General Electric Co.	17.125	66.00	6.1	6/06/86
Superior Oil Co.	Mobil Corp.	22.00	45.00	5.7	9/28/84
Shell Oil Co.	Royal Dutch/Shell Group	29.50	60.00	5.7	6/07/85
General Foods	Philip Morris Cos.	34.00	120.00	5.6	11/01/85
Safeway Stores	Kohlberg Kravis Roberts	16.00	69.00	5.3	11/24/86
Hughes Aircraft	General Motors Corp.	N.A.*	N.A.*	5.0	12/20/85

*N.A. = not applicable.

After oil prices tended to drift lower, corporate raiders began looking for other targets with undervalued assets and found companies like MGM, ABC, and Prentice-Hall in movies, broadcasting, and publishing. Then the move was on to retail stores, where hidden real estate values were thought to exist. The wheel next turned to food companies with the acquisition of General Foods by Philip Morris. In 1986, Dart & Kraft led the acquirers with 18 acquisitions, followed by Macmillan, Inc., with 15 and McGraw-Hill with 12 acquisitions. Who knows what industry will be the target by the time you read this chapter. Given the stock market "Crash of 1987," it remains to be seen if the same corporate raiders still have the financial muscle to continue their acquisition binge. Table 20–2 presents a history of merger activity, showing the large increase in the number and size of acquisitions over a 10-year period. While 1984 had the biggest percentage increase in merger value, 1986 set new records partially because of the record stock market climb.

In the following sections of this chapter, we examine the motives for business combinations; the establishment of negotiated terms of exchange, with the associated accounting implications; and the stock market effect of mergers (including unfriendly takeovers). In the final section of the chapter, the structure and use of holding companies is presented.

Motives for Business Combinations

A business combination may take the form of either a *merger* or a *consolidation*. A merger is defined as a combination of two or more companies in which the resulting firm maintains the identity of the acquiring com-

Table 20–2
Ten-year merger completion record, 1977–1986

Year	No. of Transactions	% Change	Value ($ millions)	% Change
1977	1,209	+5.6%	*	—
1978	1,452	+20.1	*	—
1979	1,529	+5.3	$ 34,177.2	—
1980	1,565	+2.4	32,958.9	−3.6%
1981	2,326	+48.6	67,208.9	+103.9
1982	2,297	−1.2	60,402.3	−10.1
1983	2,385	+3.8	52,535.5	−13.0
1984	3,144	+31.8	125,693.0	+139.3
1985	3,397	+8.0	144,283.5	+14.8
1986	4,024	+18.4	190,512.3	+32.0

*Value data for these years are incomplete.

Source: *Mergers & Acquisitions, Almanac & Index,* May/June 1987.

pany. In a consolidation, two or more companies are combined to form an entirely new entity. A consolidation might be utilized when the firms are of equal size and market power. For purposes of our discussion, the primary emphasis will be on mergers, though virtually all of the principles presented could apply to consolidations as well.

Financial Motives

The motives for mergers and consolidations are both financial and non-financial in nature. We examine the financial motives first. As discussed in Chapter 13, a merger allows the acquiring firm to enjoy a potentially desirable *portfolio effect* by achieving risk reduction while perhaps maintaining the firm's rate of return. If two firms that benefit from opposite phases of the business cycle combine, their variability in performance may be reduced. Risk-averse investors may then discount the future performance of the merged firm at a lower rate and thus assign it a higher valuation than was assigned to the separate firms. The same point can be made in regard to multinational mergers. Through merger, a firm that has holdings in diverse economic and political climates can enjoy some reduction in the risks that derive from foreign exchange translation, government politics, military takeovers, and localized recessions.

While the portfolio diversification effect of a merger is intellectually appealing—with each firm becoming a mini-mutual fund unto itself—the practicalities of the situation can become quite complicated. No doubt, one of the major forces of the merger wave of the mid-to-late 1960s was the desire of the conglomerates for diversification. The lessons we have learned from the LTVs, the Littons, and others is that too much diversification can strain the operating capabilities of the firm. As one form of evidence on the lack of success of some of these earlier mergers, the ratio of divestitures[1] to new acquisitions was only 11 percent in 1967, but it rose to over 50 percent almost a decade later.[2]

A second financial motive is the *improved financing posture* that a merger can create as a result of expansion in size. Larger firms may enjoy greater access to financial markets and thus be in a better position to raise debt and equity capital. Such firms may also be able to attract larger and more prestigious investment bankers to handle future financing.

---

[1]A divestiture is a spin-off or a sell-off of a subsidiary or a division.

[2]James W. Bradley and Donald H. Korn, "Acquisition and Merger Trends Affecting the Portfolio Manager," *Financial Analysts Journal* 33 (November–December 1977), p. 66.

Greater financing capability may also be inherent in the merger itself. This is likely to be the case if the acquired firm has a strong cash position or a low debt–equity ratio that can be used to expand borrowing by the acquiring company.

A final financial motive is the *tax loss carry-forward* that might be available in a merger if one of the firms has previously sustained a tax loss. The Tax Reform Act of 1986 significantly changes the way companies may use tax-loss carry-forwards of companies acquired in mergers. Congress tried to reduce the occurrence of one company buying another solely to receive the tax-loss benefits. To support this reasoning, the Tax Reform Act of 1986 put in place several limitations on these tax-loss carry-forwards, which take effect when more than a 50 percent ownership change (in market value) has taken place. The tax law establishes a method for placing a dollar limit on the amount of net operating tax-loss carry-forwards that can be used in each succeeding year. While the full value of the loss may be used, the law limits how much can be taken each year.

In the following example, we assume that all the losses can be carried forward, and that they are within the limitations set by the tax act. Firm A acquires Firm B, which has a $220,000 tax-loss carry-forward. We look at Firm A's financial position before and after the merger. The assumption is that the firm has a 40 percent tax rate.

The tax shield value of a carry-forward is equal to the loss involved times the tax rate ($220,000 × 40 percent = $88,000). Based on the carry-forward, the company is able to reduce its total taxes $120,000 to $32,000, and thus it could pay $88,000 for the carry-forward alone (this is on a nondiscounted basis).

	1989	1990	1991	Total Values
Firm A (without merger):				
Before-tax income	$100,000	$100,000	$100,000	$300,000
Taxes (40%)	40,000	40,000	40,000	120,000
Income available				
to stockholders	$ 60,000	$ 60,000	$ 60,000	$180,000
Firm A (with merger and associated tax benefits):				
Before-tax income	$100,000	$100,000	$100,000	$300,000
Tax loss carry-forward . . .	100,000	100,000	20,000	220,000
Net taxable income	0	0	80,000	80,000
Taxes (40%)	0	0	32,000	32,000
Income available				
to stockholders	$100,000	$100,000	$ 68,000	$268,000

As would be expected, income available to stockholders also has gone up by $88,000 ($268,000 − $180,000 = $88,000). Of course, Firm B's anticipated operating gains and losses for future years must also be taken into consideration in analyzing the deal.

Nonfinancial Motives

The nonfinancial motives for mergers and consolidations include the desire to expand management and marketing capabilities as well as the acquisition of new products. Particularly popular industries in the latest merger movement—in addition to energy-related companies—have been companies in entertainment, retailing, food products, and financial services.

While mergers may be directed toward either horizontal integration (that is, the acquisition of competitors) or vertical integration (the acquisition of buyers or sellers of goods and services to the company), antitrust policy generally precludes the elimination of competition. For this reason, mergers are often directed toward companies in allied but not directly related fields. The pure conglomerate merger of firms in totally unrelated firms is still undertaken, but less frequently than in the past.

Perhaps the greatest management motive for a merger is the possible synergistic effect. Synergy is said to take place when the whole is greater than the sum of the parts. This "2 + 2 = 5" effect may be the result of eliminating overlapping functions in production and marketing as well as meshing together various engineering capabilities. In terms of planning related to mergers, there is often a tendency to overestimate the possible synergistic benefits that might accrue.[3]

Motives of Selling Stockholders

Most of our discussion has revolved around the motives of the acquiring firm that initiates a merger. Likewise, the selling stockholders may be motivated by a desire to receive the acquiring company's stock—which may have greater acceptability or activity in the marketplace than the stock they hold. Also, when cash is offered instead of stock, this gives the selling stockholders an opportunity to diversify their holdings into many new investments. As will be discussed later in the chapter, the

---

[3]T. Hogarty, "The Profitability of Corporate Mergers," *Journal of Business* 43 (July 1970), pp. 317–27.

selling stockholders generally receive an attractive price for their stock that may well exceed its current market or book value.

In addition, officers of the selling company may receive attractive post-merger management contracts as well as directorships in the acquiring firm. In some circumstances, they may be allowed to operate the company as a highly autonomous subsidiary after the merger (though this is probably the exception).[4]

A final motive of the selling stockholders may simply be the bias against smaller businesses that has developed in this country and around the world. Real clout in the financial markets may dictate being part of a larger organization. These motives should not be taken as evidence that all or even most officers or directors of smaller firms wish to sell out—a matter that we shall examine further when we discuss negotiated offers versus takeover attempts.

Terms of Exchange

In determining the price that will be paid for a potential acquisition, a number of factors are considered, including earnings, dividends, and growth potential. We shall divide our analysis between cash purchases and stock-for-stock exchanges, in which the acquiring company trades stock rather than paying cash for the acquired firm.

Cash Purchases

The cash purchase of another company can be viewed within the context of a capital budgeting decision. Instead of purchasing new plant or machinery, the purchaser has opted to acquire a *going concern*. For example, assume that the Invest Corporation is analyzing the acquisition of the Sell Corporation for $1 million. The Sell Corporation has expected cash flow (aftertax earnings plus depreciation) of $100,000 per year for the next 5 years and $150,000 per year for the 6th through the 20th year. Furthermore, the synergistic benefits of the merger (in this case, combining production facilities) will add $10,000 per year to cash flow. Finally, the Sell Corporation has a $50,000 tax loss carry-forward that can be used immediately by the Invest Corporation. Assuming a 40 percent tax rate, the $50,000 loss carry-forward will shield $20,000 of profit from taxes

---

[4]This is most likely to happen when the acquiring firm is a foreign company.

immediately. The Invest Corporation has a 10 percent cost of capital, and this is assumed to remain stable with the merger. Our analysis would be as follows:

```
Cash outflow:
    Purchase price . . . . . . . . . . . . . . . . . . . . . .   $1,000,000
        Less tax shield benefit
        from tax-loss carry-forward ($50,000 × 40%) . . . .         20,000
    Net cash outflow . . . . . . . . . . . . . . . . . . . .     $ 980,000


Cash inflows:
    Years 1–5:  $100,000   Cash inflow
                  10,000   Synergistic benefit

                $110,000   Total cash inflow
    Present value of $110,000 × 3.791  . . . . . . .         $  417,010


    Years 6–20:  $150,000   Cash inflow
                   10,000   Synergistic benefit
                 $160,000   Total cash inflow
    Present value of $160,000 × 4.723  . . . . . . .            755,680

        Total present value of inflows  . . . . . . . .      $1,172,690
```

The present value factor for the first five years (3.791) *is* based on $n = 5$, $i = 10$ percent, and can be found in Appendix D. For the 6th through the 20th year, we take the present value factor in Appendix D for $n = 20$, $i = 10$ percent, and subtract from this the present value factor for $n = 5$, $i = 10$ percent. This allows us to isolate the 6th through the 20th year with a factor of 4.723 (8.515 − 3.791).

The net present value of the investment is:

```
Total present value of inflows . . . .   $1,172,690
Net cash outflow  . . . . . . . . .         980,000
Net present value . . . . . . . . .      $  192,690
```

The acquisition appears to represent a desirable alternative for the expenditure of cash, with a positive net present value of $192,690. As previously indicated, in the market environment of the late 1970s and 1980s many firms could be purchased at a value below the replacement costs of their assets and, thus, represented a potentially desirable capital investment. As an extreme example, Anaconda Copper had an asset replacement value of $1.3 billion when the firm was purchased by Atlantic Richfield for $684 million.

Stock-for-Stock Exchange

On a stock-for-stock exchange, we use a somewhat different analytical approach, emphasizing the earnings per share impact of exchanging securities (and ultimately the market valuation of those earnings). The analysis is primarily from the viewpoint of the acquiring firm. The shareholders of the acquired firm are concerned mainly about the initial price they are paid for their shares and about the outlook for the acquiring firm.

Assume that Expand Corporation is considering the acquisition of Small Corporation. Significant financial information on the firms before the merger is provided in Table 20–3.

Table 20–3
Financial data on potential merging firms

	Small Corporation	Expand Corporation
Total earnings	$200,000	$500,000
Number of shares of stock outstanding	50,000	200,000
Earnings per share	$4.00	$2.50
Price–earnings ratio (P/E)	7.5×	12×
Market price per share	$30.00	$30.00

We begin our analysis with the assumption that one share of Expand Corporation ($30) will be traded for one share of Small Corporation ($30). (In actuality, Small Corporation will probably demand more than $30 per share because the acquired firm usually gets some premium over the current market value. We will later consider the impact of paying such a premium.)

If 50,000 new shares of Expand Corporation are traded in exchange for all the old shares of Small Corporation, Expand Corporation will then have 250,000 shares outstanding. At the same time, its claim to earnings will go to $700,000 when the two firms are combined. Postmerger earnings per share will be $2.80 for the Expand Corporation, as indicated in Table 20–4.

Table 20–4
Postmerger earnings per share

Total earnings: Small ($200,000) + Expand ($500,000) $700,000

Shares outstanding in surviving corporation:
Old (200,000) + New (50,000) 250,000

$$\text{New earnings per share for Expand Corporation} = \frac{\$700,000}{250,000} = \$2.80$$

A number of observations are worthy of note. First, the earnings per share of Expand Corporation have increased as a result of the merger, rising from $2.50 to $2.80. This has occurred because Expand Corporation's P/E ratio was higher than that of Small Corporation at the time of the merger (12.0 versus 7.5) as seen in Table 20–3. Whenever a firm acquires another entity whose P/E ratio is lower than its own, there is an immediate increase in earnings per share. The P/E ratio comparison is an important variable that we shall follow closely in our subsequent discussion.

As previously indicated, it is unlikely that Small Corporation will give up its shares at the current market value of $30 per share. We shall now assume that Expand Corporation is willing to pay 33 percent over market value. This would imply that the shareholders of Small Corporation would receive $40 worth of stock for each share of stock outstanding. Since Expand shares are trading at $30 per share, it must offer 1⅓ shares of Expand Corporation for each share of Small Corporation. This means that Expand Corporation will have to issue 66,667 new shares (50,000 old shares of Small Corporation × 1⅓). Postmerger earnings per share for Expand Corporation are now shown in Table 20–5 to be $2.62.

Table 20–5 **Adjusted postmerger earnings per share**	Total earnings: Small ($200,000) + Expand ($500,000) $700,000
	Shares outstanding in surviving corporation: Old (200,000) + New (66,667) 266,667
	New earnings per share for Expand Corporation $= \dfrac{\$700,000}{266,667} = \$2.62$

Even though Expand Corporation has paid the shareholders of Small Corporation a 33 percent premium over market value, it has still been able to increase its earnings per share from $2.50 premerger (Table 20–3) to $2.62 postmerger (Table 20–5). Why? Well, once again its P/E ratio was higher than that paid to Small Corporation in the exchange transaction. Expand Corporation enjoys a P/E of 12 times earnings, while Small Corporation was purchased at a 33 percent premium over its current P/E of 7.5, or at 10 times earnings. As previously stated, whenever a firm purchases another company at a lower P/E ratio than its own, there is an immediate increase in earnings per share.

One might also wish to determine whether the stockholders of Small Corporation have benefited from the latest suggested merger transaction. In terms of market values they have come out ahead, whereas in terms

**Table 20–6
Postmerger analysis
of the acquired firm's
shareholders**

A. Trade-in market value:
One share of Small Corporation ($30) traded for 1 1/3 shares of Expand
Corporation ($40 total value)

Gain for Small Corporation shareholders: $10

B. Trade-in earnings per share:
One share of Small Corporation previously represented $4.00 in earnings per share
(Table 20–2): 1 1/3 shares of Expand Corporation represents $3.48 in earnings per
share (the $2.62 postmerger value in Table 20–4 times 1.33)

Dilution in earnings per share for Small Corporation shareholders: $0.52

of earnings per share they have lost out. Both results are indicated in
Table 20–6.

Previous research has indicated that stockholders of the *acquired* company are more concerned with the market value exchanged than with the
earnings, dividends, or book value exchanged.[5] Thus the $10 increase in
market value will probably compensate for the decrease in the claims to
earnings per share.[6] The stockholders can always sell out after the merger
and take a $10 capital gain. At times, however, stockholders may be
concerned about trading or maintaining parity in dividends per share.
The acquiring company may offer fixed-income securities as well as common stock to maintain parity.

Long-Term Considerations

In Table 20–5 we showed the earnings per share for Expand Corporation
to be $2.62 as a result of the merger—a 12-cent gain over the premerger
figure of $2.50. Although Expand Corporation is enjoying an *immediate*
appreciation in earnings per share, we must still consider the long-run
impact of the merger and its influence on our ultimate objective of market
value maximization.

Consider this: The reason Expand Corporation was able to enjoy an
immediate appreciation in earnings per share as a result of the merger

---

[5]Frank K. Reilly, "What Determines the Ratio of Exchange in Corporate Mergers?" *Financial
Analysts Journal* 18 (November–December 1962), pp. 47–50. Also, Lynn E. Dellenbarger, "A
Study of Relative Common Stock Equity Values in Fifty Mergers of Listed Industrial Corpo-
rations, 1950–57," *Journal of Finance* 18 (September 1963), p. 565.

[6]Earnings-per-share parity would indicate an exchange ratio of 1.6 Expand Corporation shares
for each Small Corporation share ($4.00/2.50 = 1.6). The $4.00 represents Small Corporation's
premerger EPS, while the $2.50 is Expand Corporation's premerger EPS.

was that it had a higher P/E ratio than Small Corporation. The reason for Expand's higher P/E ratio may be that it had superior growth prospects, less risk, a better product in the marketplace, more rigorous accounting procedures, or a number of other factors.

We shall assume for now that the differential in the P/E ratios can be explained, in large measure, by differing growth prospects. Perhaps Expand Corporation, without the merger, could be expected to grow at 10 percent per year, while Small Corporation would only grow by 6 percent. Since Expand Corporation is initially contributing \$50,000 to earnings and Small Corporation \$20,000, the postmerger weighting on earnings is five-sevenths and two-sevenths, respectively. Without considering any postmerger operating benefits (synergy), the new weighted growth rate for Expand Corporation after the merger would be:

$$\tfrac{5}{7}\,(10\%) + \tfrac{2}{7}\,(6\%) = 7.14\% + 1.71\% = 8.85\%.$$

The net effect is that Expand Corporation will suffer a decline of 1.15 percent in its growth rate at the same time that it enjoys a 12-cent immediate increase in earnings per share (\$2.50 to \$2.62). We look at the combined effect of these two variables in Table 20–7 as we extend the time horizon to 10 years.

Although earnings per share will be 12 cents higher immediately as a result of the merger, the slower postmerger growth rate of 8.85 percent indicates that after four years there is an indifference point between

Table 20–7
Anticipated earnings per share for Expand Corporation with and without the merger over 10 years

Year	Without Merger			With Merger (Small Corporation)		
	Beginning Earnings per Share	Growth Rate	Anticipated Earnings per Share	Beginning Earnings per Share	Growth Rate	Anticipated Earnings per Share
1 . . .	\$2.50	10%	\$2.75	\$2.62	8.85%	\$2.85
2 . . .	2.75		3.03	2.85		3.10
3 . . .	3.03		3.33	3.10		3.37
4 . . .	3.33		3.66	3.37		3.66
5 . . .	3.66		4.03	3.66		3.98
6 . . .	4.03		4.43	3.98		4.33
7 . . .	4.43		4.87	4.33		4.71
8 . . .	4.87		5.36	4.71		5.13
9 . . .	5.36		5.90	5.13		5.58
10 . . .	5.90		6.49	5.58		6.07

earnings with and without the merger (at $3.66). After 10 years, *non-merging* would actually provide 42 cents more in earnings per share ($6.49 versus $6.07). The long-term dilutive effect on earnings is the result of the differential growth rates and the absence of synergy. If the merger produced synergy by increasing the operating effectiveness of the combined firms by 15 percent, the immediate effect would be to increase earnings per share to $3.01 ($2.62 × 1.15) and tenth-year earnings to $6.98 ($6.07 × 1.15). Nevertheless, as has been pointed out, synergistic benefits may be difficult to achieve.

Buying a Company at a Higher P/E Ratio

As an alternative strategy, assume that Expand Corporation is considering the acquisition of Growth Corporation. Although Growth Corporation is currently the same in size as Small Corporation, it enjoys a relatively high P/E ratio (14 ×) and a strong anticipated growth in earnings per share (18 percent). Financial information for Growth Corporation is presented in Table 20–8 along with data for Expand Corporation.

Table 20–8 Financial data for potential merging firms

	Growth Corporation	Expand Corporation
Total earnings	$200,000	$500,000
Number of shares of stock outstanding	50,000	200,000
Earnings per share	$4.00	$2.50
Price–earning ratio (P/E)	14X	12X
Market price per share	$56.00	$30.00
Growth rate in earnings per share	18%	10%

In order to effect a merger, we shall assume that Expand Corporation will pay the shareholders of Growth Corporation a 40 percent premium over market value. With each share of Growth Corporation currently selling at $56 per share, this would indicate a price of $78.40 per share ($56 × 1.4). To purchase 50,000 shares of Growth Corporation, the total value exchanged would be $3,920,000.

```
     $78.40   Price per share
  ×  50,000   Shares
 $3,920,000   Total price
```

Since $30 shares of Expand Corporation are to be traded in the merger, 130,667 shares must be given to the shareholders of Growth Corporation.

$$\frac{\text{Purchase price}}{\text{Value of Expand Corporation shares}} = \frac{\$3,920,000}{\$30} = 130,667 \text{ shares}$$

Postmerger earnings per share are $2.12, as indicated in Table 20–9.

**Table 20–9
Postmerger earnings
per share**

Total earnings: Growth ($200,000) + Expand ($500,000)	$700,000
Shares outstanding in surviving corporation: Old (200,000) + New (130,667)	330,667

$$\text{New earnings per share for Expand Corporation} = \frac{\$700,000}{330.667} = \$2.12$$

The earnings per share of Expand Corporation have been diluted from $2.50 to $2.12 as a result of the merger. Once again, the reason can be found in the relative P/E ratios. Growth Corporation is being purchased at a 40 percent premium over its current P/E ratio of 14, or at 19.6 times earnings. Since Expand Corporation's P/E ratio is only 12, dilution has set in. Nevertheless, a strong inducement factor for Expand Corporation is the high rate of increase in earnings per share of 18 percent for the Growth Corporation. On a weighted basis, this will increase the post-merger earnings per share growth rate of Expand Corporation to 12.28 percent.

$$\tfrac{5}{7}\,(10\%) + \tfrac{2}{7}\,(18\%) = 7.14\% + 5.14\% = 12.28\%$$

Rounding to 12.3 percent, the anticipated stream of future earnings for Expand Corporation with and without the Growth Corporation merger is indicated in Table 20–10.

In spite of the initial dilution in earnings per share, Expand Corporation will eventually benefit from the merger with 10th-year earnings per share at a level 30 cents higher than without merger. If the analysis is extended to 15 years, the difference between the two alternatives becomes approximately $1.70. Although it may take a dilutive, high-growth acquisition longer to show positive benefits, the eventual gains may be substantial. Of course, the presence of synergy would shorten the break-even period and expand the long-term positive benefits.

A comparison of the two merger plans with a nonmerger strategy for Expand Corporation is presented in Figure 20–1.

Table 20–10
Anticipated earnings for Expand Corporation with and without a merger with Growth Corporation, over 10 years

	Without Merger			With Merger (Growth Corporation)		
Year	Beginning Earnings per Share	Growth Rate	Anticipated Earnings per Share	Beginning Earnings per Share	Growth Rate	Anticipated Earnings per Share
1	$2.50	10%	$2.75	$2.12	12.3%	$2.38
2	2.75		3.03	2.38		2.67
3	3.03		3.33	2.67		3.00
4	3.33		3.66	3.00		3.37
5	3.66		4.03	3.37		3.79
6	4.03		4.43	3.79		4.26
7	4.43		4.87	4.26		4.79
8	4.87		5.36	4.79		5.38
9	5.36		5.90	5.38		6.04
10	5.90		6.49	6.04		6.79

Figure 20–1
Impact of alternative plans on Expand Corporation

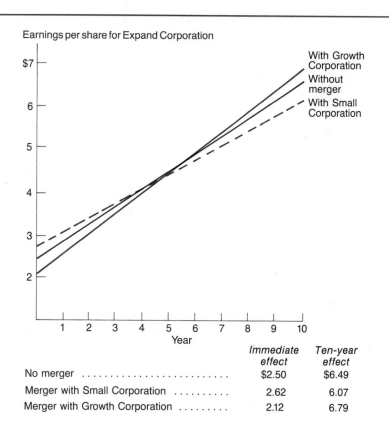

Earnings per share for Expand Corporation

	Immediate effect	Ten-year effect
No merger	$2.50	$6.49
Merger with Small Corporation	2.62	6.07
Merger with Growth Corporation	2.12	6.79

The earnings-per-share impact of a merger is influenced by the exchange ratio (relative price–earnings ratios as reflected in the terms of exchange), the relative growth rates of the firms, and the relative sizes of the firms. In regard to the last variable, if Growth Corporation had the same earnings as Expand Corporation, there would be a tremendous dilution in earnings per share down to $1.90, followed by an annual increase in earnings per share of 14 percent. Earnings per share would grow to over $7 after 10 years.

Market Value Maximization

The basic merger plans diagramed in Figure 20–1 indicate the possibilities in buying a slow-growth firm at a relatively low P/E ratio and a high-growth firm at a relatively high P/E ratio. There is no right or wrong decision as such. The ultimate answer lies in the concept of market value maximization. We must try to assess how shareholders (present and potential) will view the merger. Thus we must consider not only the immediate impact on earnings per share but also the effect on the surviving firm's postmerger P/E ratio. While the merger with Small Corporation will increase Expand Corporation's earnings per share from $2.50 to $2.62, will there be a decrease in Expand Corporation's postmerger P/E ratio because of the decrease in the corporate growth rate from 10 percent to 8.85 percent? Similarly, will the dilution in earning per share from $2.50 to $2.12 as a result of the Growth Corporation acquisition be more than offset by an increase in the corporate growth rate from 10 percent to 12.3 percent and a possible increase in the P/E ratio? In Table 20–11 we look at possible postmerger P/E ratios and stock prices for Expand Corporation, assuming a merger with *Growth Corporation.*

Undoubtedly, a corporate treasurer would like to study all of these possibilities in the context of a premerger price of $30 per share. Based

Table 20–11 Postmerger valuation based on increased level of P/E ratio (current level of 12)*	Potential Increase in P/E Ratio (percent)				
	1%	*10%*	*20%*	*30%*	*40%*
New P/E ratio	12.1×	13.2×	14.4×	15.6×	16.8×
Postmerger earnings	$2.12	$2.12	$2.12	$2.12	$2.12
Postmerger market value . . .	$25.65	$27.98	$30.53	$33.07	$35.62

*Additional analysis could also be done based on a declining P/E ratio.

on similar experiences of other companies in the industry or on past corporate history, relative probabilities of outcomes may be assigned and the expected value determined. (See problem 9 at the end of the chapter.)

Portfolio Effect

Inherent in all of our discussion is the importance of the merger's portfolio effect on the risk–return posture of the firm. The reduction or increase in risk may influence the P/E ratio as much as the change in the growth rate. To the extent that we are diminishing the overall risk of the firm in a merger, the P/E ratio may increase even if the potential earnings growth is unchanged. Business risk reduction may be achieved through acquiring another firm that is influenced by a set of factors in the business cycle opposite from those that influence our own firm, while financial risk reduction may be achieved by restructuring our postmerger financial arrangements to include less debt.

Perhaps Expand Corporation may be diversifying from a heavy manufacturing industry into the real estate/housing industry. While heavy manufacturing industries move with the business cycle, the real estate/housing industry tends to be countercyclical. Even though the expected value of earnings per share may remain relatively constant as a result of the merger, the standard deviation of possible outcomes may decline as a result of risk reduction through diversification, as is indicated in Figure 20–2.

We see that the expected value of the earnings per share has remained constant in this instance but that the standard deviation has gone down.

Figure 20–2
Risk-reduction
portfolio benefits

Because there is less risk in the corporation, the investor may be willing to assign a higher valuation, thus increasing the price–earnings ratio.

Accounting Considerations in Mergers and Acquisitions

The role of financial accounting probably has no greater significance than in the area of mergers and acquisitions. When a price substantially above book value is paid for a potential acquisition, goodwill may be created on the books of the acquiring firm and the writing off of this goodwill over time can have a negative impact on earnings per share. Many firms try to avoid the creation of goodwill. Let's see what the issues and the options are.

A merger can be treated on the books of the acquiring firm as either *a pooling of interests* or *a purchase of assets*. Under a pooling of interests, the financial statements of the firms are combined, subject to some minor adjustments, and no goodwill is created. In order to qualify for a pooling of interests, certain criteria must be met, such as:

1. The acquiring corporation issues only common stock, with rights identical to its old outstanding voting stock, in exchange for substantially all of the other company's voting stock.
2. The acquired firm's stockholders maintain an ownership position in the surviving firm.
3. The combined entity does not intend to dispose of a significant portion of the assets of the combined companies within two years.
4. The combination is effected in a single transaction.[7]

Goodwill may be created when the second type of merger recording—a purchase of assets—is used. Because of the criteria described above (particularly items 1 and 2), a purchase of assets treatment, rather than a pooling of interests treatment, is generally necessary when the tender offer is in cash, bonds, preferred stock, or common stock with restricted rights. Under a purchase of assets accounting treatment, any excess of purchase price over book value must be recorded as goodwill and written off over a maximum period of 40 years. If a company purchases a firm with a $4 million book value (net worth) for $6 million, $2 million of goodwill is created on the books of the acquiring company, and it must

---

[7]Accounting Principles Board, "Business Combinations," APB Opinion 16 (New York: AICPA, 1970. A number of lesser criteria are also involved.

be written off over a maximum period of 40 years. This would cause a $50,000-per-year reduction in reported earnings ($2 million/40 years). Because the writing off of goodwill is not a tax-deductible expense, the firm suffers the full amount of the deduction without any tax relief. Under a pooling of interests accounting treatment, you will recall, goodwill is not created.

The main reason we look at the pooling of interests versus the purchase of assets accounting treatment is to recognize the potentially beneficial effect to a corporation of exchanging common stock, rather than non-equity compensation (cash, bonds, preferred stock, and so on), and thus perhaps qualifying as a pooling of interests. Common stock also more readily qualifies a merger for a tax-free exchange under Section 368(a) of the Internal Revenue Code. Under a tax-free exchange, the stockholders of the acquired firm may defer a tax obligation until the newly acquired shares have actually been sold. Thus, there would be no immediate tax for trading a share of stock in Growth Corporation that was purchased 10 years ago at $5 for $78.40 in Expand Corporation stock. If and when the Expand Corporation stock is sold, the tax will be recognized. If the tender offer were $78.40 in cash, there would be an immediate tax obligation.

In analyzing accounting and tax considerations, we see that the acquiring corporation has some inducement to offer common stock to qualify as a pooling of interests when the exchange offer exceeds book value; also, that the stockholders of the acquired firm have some incentive to receive common stock when the exchange offer exceeds their initial cost basis in order to avoid immediate taxes. During the 1960s and part of the 1970s, common stock, often supplemented by convertible securities and warrants, was a frequently used mode of exchange.[8] In the merger movement of the late 1970s and in the 1980s, cash offers have come into vogue.

Why? First of all, stockholders of the acquired firms have become somewhat disenchanted with the postmerger performances of acquiring companies' common stock. For this reason they have been willing to take cash, pay a tax, and invest in a new and diversified set of investments. Acquiring corporations have gone along with the cash tender offer pattern, in spite of the requirement for purchase of assets accounting treatment,

---

[8]The popularity of the last two items was reduced somewhat by Accounting Principles Board Opinion 15, "Earnings per Share," issued by the AICPA in May 1969, which required tough standards for the dilutive effects of convertibles and warrants, as described in Chapter 19.

in order to satisfy the demands of selling stockholders.[9] Additionally acquiring corporations have found it easier to find cash in the 1980s. Investment bankers have been packaging junk (low rated) bond financing to raise cash for purchases; banks have been willing to lend money to companies with merger appetites; and venture capital and foreign investors have all been more than willing to finance companies' purchases of target companies.

Also, by using cash instead of stock, a corporation may diminish the perceived dilutive effect of a merger. If Small Corporation or Growth Corporation had been acquired for straight cash by Expand Corporation, no new shares would have been issued and earnings per share would have gone up proportionately by the amount of new aftertax earnings. This latter argument tends to be weakened by recognition of the fact that cash tendered in a merger has a substantial capital cost associated with it and, furthermore, that new shares of stock may later have to be authorized and sold to finance the cash drain.

Negotiated versus Tendered Offers

Traditionally, mergers have been negotiated in a friendly atmosphere between officers and directors of the participating corporations. Product lines, quality of assets, and future growth prospects are discussed, and eventually an exchange ratio is hammered out and represented to the investment community and the financial press.

As previously mentioned, the merger wave of the late 1970s and the 1980s has helped to create a wholly new atmosphere. The takeover *tender offer,* in which a company attempts to acquire a target firm against its will, has come into vogue. One of the most notorious examples was the announced intent of American Express to take over McGraw-Hill in early 1979. At that time McGraw-Hill was selling at $26 per share. The initial American Express offer was for $34, and eventually the offer went up to $40. McGraw-Hill fought off the offer by maintaining that American Express would obstruct the independent character required of a publisher. McGraw-Hill was able to discourage the unwelcome offer from American Express, but many small McGraw-Hill stockholders sued the publisher, claiming that the calling off of the merger caused them to lose an opportunity to advance the cash value of their holdings.

---

[9]Also where a substantial postmerger asset write-up is possible, the corporation may acquire a beneficial tax base for depreciation, rather than nontax-deductible goodwill.

Not all companies are able to fend off the unwanted advances of suitors. An entire vocabulary has developed on Wall Street around the concept of the target takeover. For example, the *Saturday Night Special* refers to a surprise offer that is made just before the market closes for the weekend and takes the target company's officers by surprise. By the time the officers can react, the impact of the offer has already taken place. Perhaps a stock is trading at $20 and an unfriendly offer comes in at $28. Though the offer may please the company's stockholders, its management faces the dangers of seeing the company going down the wrong path in a merger and perhaps of their being personally ousted.

In order to avoid an unfriendly takeover, management may turn to a *white knight* for salvation. A white knight represents a third firm that management calls upon to help it avoid the initial unwanted tender offer. For example, in 1978 Babcock and Wilcox received an unsolicited takeover bid from United Technologies to purchase its stock at $42 per share. Since the stock was currently selling at 34¾, this was not a bad offer. However, the company turned to J. Ray McDermott & Company as a friendly suitor. After a bidding war, Babcock and Wilcox was eventually purchased by McDermott for $65 a share. Under similar circumstances in the 1980s, Conoco turned to Du Pont as a suitor after being pursued on an unfriendly basis by Seagrams and others. Also, Marathon Oil merged with U.S. Steel to avoid an unfriendly tender offer from Mobil Oil. The biggest white knight was Chevron Corporation, who "saved" Gulf Oil from T. Boone Pickens at a cost of $13.3 billion.

Many firms that wish to avoid takeovers have moved their corporate offices to states that have tough prenotification and protection provisions in regard to takeover offers. Other companies have bought in portions of their own shares to restrict the amount of stock available for a takeover or have encouraged employees to buy stock under corporate pension plans. Other protective measures include increasing dividends to keep stockholders happy and staggering the election of members of the board of directors to make outside power plays more difficult to initiate. Possible target companies have also bought up other companies to increase their own size and make themselves more expensive and less vulnerable. One of the key rules for avoiding a targeted takeover is to never get caught with too large a cash position. A firm with large cash balances serves as an ideal target for a *leveraged* takeover. The acquiring company is able to negotiate a bank loan based on the target company's assets and then to go into the marketplace to make a cash tender offer. For example, CIT Financial left itself wide open in April 1979 when it sold off a banking subsidiary for $425 million. At that point CIT had cash balances equal to $20 per share for shares which had a market value in the $30–$40 range. RCA bought the company for $65 per share.

While a takeover bid may not appeal to management, it may be enticing to stockholders, as previously indicated. Herein lies the basic problem. The bidding may get so high that stockholders demand action. The desire of management to maintain the status quo can come into conflict with the objective of stockholder wealth maximization.

Premium Offers and Stock Price Movements

Until the latest merger wave, the average premium paid over market value in a merger or acquisition was of the magnitude of 20–25 percent.[10] In the merger movement of the late 1970s and 1980s, the average premium appears to have been closer to 50–60 percent.[11]

Many of the companies acquired in the latest merger movement have tended to be of unusually high quality and thus have commanded a high premium. The motivation of the acquiring company in making the purchase was often not to turn around a poor performance, but to take advantage of the superior market or product position of the acquired company.

Many acquisition candidates have represented some of the most interesting stock market performers of the decade. Often the daily volume leaders and outstanding price movers were acquisition candidates. Researchers have found that potential acquirees have superior price performance on a risk-adjusted basis.[12] It is not surprising that a company which is offered a large premium over its current market value has a major upside movement. The only problem for the investor is that much of this activity may take place before the public announcement of the merger offer. If a firm is selling at $25 per share when informal negotiations begin, it may be $34 by the time an announced offer of $40 is made. Still, there are good profits to be made if the merger goes through.

---

[10]William A. Alberts and Joel E. Segall, *The Corporate Merger* (Chicago: University of Chicago Press, 1966), pp. 117–18. Also George D. McCarthy, *Acquisitions and Mergers* (New York: Ronald, 1963), pp. 92–102.

[11]Selected issues of *Mergers and Acquisitions*, 1981–87.

[12]Gershon Mandelker, "Risk and Return: The Case of Merging Firms," *Journal of Financial Economics* 1 (December 1974), pp. 303–35. Mandelker found the merger effect beginning to influence the acquiree's stock seven months before consummation of the merger, with the cumulative average residual (excess returns) moving positively at that point. A number of later studies have confirmed this finding.

A group of investors who specialize in merger situations came into high visibility in the late 1970s and the 1980s. Known as ARBs (arbitrageurs), their strategy is to purchase the stock of the acquisition candidate in the hope of being bought out at the tender offer price. In the prior example, they would accumulate stock at between $34 and $38 in the hope of selling out at $40. The ARBs often become the allies of acquiring companies because their profits (and their avoidance of losses) are dependent on the merger's actual completion.

In a stock-for-stock exchange, an arbitrageur may attempt to protect his or her profit position by buying the stock of the acquisition candidate and, at the same time, short-selling the stock of the acquirer. A short sell is a current sale of stock that is not owned, with the intention of acquiring the stock in the future to close out the position. The arbitrageur buys the acquiree's stock at $34 and simultaneously short-sells the acquiring company's stock at $40. When the merger has been consummated, the arbitrageur will trade the acquiree's stock for a share of the acquiring company's stock and use the stock to cover the $40 short position. Thus the selling price is preestablished at $40, and the buy price at $34. Even if the acquiring company's stock goes up or *down* from $40 after the merger has been announced, the sale price and profit spread have been established.

The only problem with this strategy or of any merger-related investment strategy is that the merger may be called off. In that case the merger candidate's stock, which shot up from $25 to $34, may fall back to $25, and the Johnny-come-lately investor would lose $9 per share.[13] In Table 20–12, we consider the case of three canceled mergers. Of course, if a new suitor comes along shortly after cancellation (or, in fact, causes the original cancellation), the price may quickly rebound.

All this information on price movement patterns has significance to corporate financial managers, who must understand and react to the mo-

Table 20–12
Stock movement of potential acquirees

Acquirer—Potential Acquiree	Preannouncement	One Day after Announcement	One Day after Cancellation
Mead Corp.—Occidental Petroleum	20⅜	33¼	23¼
Olin Corp.—Celanese	16	23¾	16¾
Chicago Rivet—MITE	20¾	28⅛	20¾

[13]The arbitrageur also would not have new stock of the acquiring company to cover his short position, since there would be no exchange of shares.

tivations of investors. For example, once the ARBs have established their investment position, these arbitrageurs will do everything possible to see that the merger goes through. This, at a minimum, will include voting all their shares in favor of a merger. On a more active basis, it may encompass a strategy of influencing other large stockholders, and it could ultimately include an attempt to discredit the management of a target company in the eyes of shareholders.

Two-Step Buy-Out

Another merger ploy that has been undertaken in the recent merger movement is the two-step buy-out. Under this plan the acquiring company attempts to gain control by offering a very high cash price for 51 percent of the shares outstanding. At the same time, it announces a second, lower price that will be paid, either in cash, stock, or bonds, at a subsequent point in time. As an example, an acquiring company may offer stockholders of a takeover target company a $70 cash offer that can be executed in the next 20 days (for 51 percent of the shares outstanding). Subsequent to that time period, the selling stockholders will receive $57.50 in preferred stock for each share.

This buy-out procedure accomplishes two purposes. First, it provides a strong inducement to stockholders to quickly react to the offer. Those who delay must accept a lower price. Secondly, it allows the acquiring company to pay a lower total price than if a single offer is made. In the example above, a single offer may have been made for $68 a share. Assume 1 million shares are outstanding. The single offer has a total price tag of $68,000,000, while the two-step offer would have called for only $63,875,000.

Single offer:
    1,000,000 shares at $68 = $68,000,000

Two-step offer:
    510,000 shares (51%) at $70   = $35,700,000
    490,000 shares (49%) at $57.50 = <u>28,175,000</u>
                                   $63,875,000

An example of a two-step buy-out was the Mobil Oil attempt to acquire 51 percent of Marathon Oil shares at a price of $126 in cash, with a subsequent offer to buy the rest of the shares for $90 face value debentures. In this case, Marathon Oil decided to sell out to U.S. Steel, which also made a two-step offer of $125 in cash or $100 in notes to later subscribers. Incidentally, before the bidding began, Marathon Oil was selling for $60 a share.

The SEC has continued to keep a close eye on the two-step buy-out. Government regulators fear that smaller stockholders may not be sophisticated enough to compete with arbitrageurs or institutional investors in rapidly tendering shares to ensure receipt of the higher price. The SEC has emphasized the need for a pro rata processing of stockholder orders, in which each stockholder receives an equal percentage of shares tendered.

Holding Companies

The holding company achieved its greatest popularity in the early part of the 20th century, and it is still in evidence today in a number of industries, particularly in public utilities. A holding company is one that has control over one or more other firms. In order to establish voting control, the holding company may own less than a majority interest but is able to determine policy as a result of widely spread minority interests among the other stockholders.

The primary advantage of the holding company is that it affords unusual opportunities for leverage. Assume that Giant Holding Corporation has the investment interests in Companies A, B, and C that are shown in Table 20–13. All numbers are assumed to represent millions of dollars. Also assume that Giant Holding Corporation has effective voting control of the three companies because of the widely dispersed interests of these companies' other owners. It owns 20 percent of the equity of Company A, as indicated by Giant Holding Corporation's balance sheet holding of $10 million in Company A (an asset) and Company A's common stock equity account of $50 million. In the case of Company B, the ratio is 37.5 percent ($15 million/$40 million), while for Company C it is 25 percent ($20 million/$80 million). Through these interlocking positions, Giant Holding Corporation controls $420 million in assets (the combined assets of the three companies). Note that it is doing this with only $20 million of common stock equity in its own firm. Its equity to "assets controlled" ratio is 4.8 percent ($20 million/$420 million). If we really want to get creative, we can assume that another holding company has control of Giant Holding Corporation with only a small investment in it, thus creating additional levels of ownership.

The holding company device also benefits from the isolation of the "legal" risks of the firms. Theoretically, if Company C loses money, this will not *legally* affect the other firms, because Company C is a separate legal entity with separate shareholders.

Table 20–13
Assets, liabilities,
and stockholders'
equity of Giant
Holding Corporation
and related
companies (in $
millions)

GIANT HOLDING CORPORATION

Assets		Liabilities and Stockholders' Equity	
Common stockholdings:		Long-term debt	$15
Company A	$10	Preferred stock	10
Company B	15	Common stock equity	20
Company C	20		$45
	$45		

COMPANY A

Assets		Liabilities and Stockholders' Equity	
Current assets	$ 50	Current liabilities	$ 20
Plant and equipment	50	Long-term debt	30
	$100	Common stock equity	50
			$100

COMPANY B

Assets		Liabilities and Stockholders' Equity	
Current assets	$ 60	Current liabilities	$ 10
Plant and equipment	60	Long-term debt	70
	$120	Common stock equity	40
			$120

COMPANY C

Assets		Liabilities and Stockholders' Equity	
Current assets	$ 80	Current liabilities	$ 20
Plant and equipment	120	Long-term debt	100
	$200	Common stock equity	80
			$200

Drawbacks

The drawbacks are those inherent in any pyramiding arrangement.[14] Although Companies A, B, and C are separate legal entities, and one cannot force the bankruptcy of another, there can be an indirect chain effect that is disastrous. For example, if Company A has a bad year, it may be unable to pay dividends to the holding company, which, in turn, may be

---

[14]There are also many serious legal questions associated with holding companies.

unable to pay interest on the $15 million it has in long-term debt. The more complicated the arrangement, the more vulnerable the operation is to reversals.

The holding company also suffers from the problem of multiple taxation. For example, Company A must pay taxes on its profits and then declare dividends to the holding company, which are also partially taxable. Although there is a 70 percent exemption on dividends paid to another corporation, the 30 percent additional tax bite is still significant,[15] particularly when one considers that the stockholders of the holding company will have to pay a third tax on the dividends declared to them.

The administrative problems and procedures of a holding company are also worthy of note. With multiple managements, boards of directors, dividend policies, and reporting systems, the expenses are high and the opportunities for problems substantial.

Summary

Corporations may seek external growth through mergers in order to achieve risk reduction, to improve access to the financial markets through increased size, or to obtain tax carry-forward benefits. A merger may also expand the marketing and management capabilities of the firm and allow for new-product development. While some mergers promise synergistic benefits (the 2 + 2 = 5 effect), this can be an elusive feature, with initial expectations exceeding subsequent realities.

The *cash* purchase of another corporation takes on many of the characteristics of a classical capital budgeting decision. In a *stock-for-stock* exchange, there is often a trade-off between immediate gain or dilution in earnings per share and future growth. If a firm buys another firm with a P/E ratio lower than its own, there is an immediate increase in earnings per share, but the long-term earnings growth prospects must also be considered. The ultimate objective of a merger, as is true of any financial decision, is stockholder wealth maximization, and the immediate and delayed effects of the merger must be evaluated in this context.

The accounting considerations in a merger are also important. Where the purchase price exceeds the book value of the acquired firm (after postmerger asset value adjustments), goodwill may be created which must be written off directly against future earnings per share. In order to avoid

---

[15]Only if the holding company has an 80 percent or greater ownership interest can the second tax be avoided.

goodwill creation, the merger may be treated as a pooling of interests rather than a purchase of assets if certain restrictive conditions are met. For example, stock must be tendered rather than cash, debt, preferred stock, or other financial instruments.

In the merger wave of the late 1970s and the 1980s, the unsolicited tender offer for a target company gained in popularity. Offers were made at values well in excess of the current market price, and management of the target company became trapped in the dilemma of maintaining its current position versus agreeing to the wishes of the acquiring company, the arbitrageurs, and even the target company's own stockholders.

Finally, the holding company is viewed as a means of accumulating large asset control with a minimum equity investment through leveraging the investment. However, many tax, administrative, and legal problems are inherent in this form or organization.

List of Terms

merger	purchase of assets
consolidation	goodwill
portfolio effect	tender offer takeover
tax loss carry-forward	merger premium
synergy	merger arbitrageur
terms of exchange	two-step buy-out
market value maximization	holding company
pooling of interests	leveraged buy-out

Discussion Questions

1. Briefly discuss three significant features of the merger movement of the late 1970s and the 1980s.

2. Is risk reduction in the firm's portfolio of undertakings likely to be best achieved through horizontal integration, vertical integration, or conglomerate-type acquisitions?

3. If a firm wishes to achieve immediate appreciation in earnings per share as a result of a merger, how can this be best accomplished in terms of exchange variables? What is a possible drawback to this approach in terms of long-range considerations?

4. What is the essential difference between a pooling of interests and a purchase of assets accounting treatment of a merger? Is goodwill amortization a tax-deductible expense?

5. If Ford Motor Company were to merge with Chrysler Corporation, suggest three forms of synergy that might take place.

6. Generally, a stockholder of the selling corporation will demand a higher price if cash consideration is tendered. Explain why this might be the case.

7. Explain how the weak stock market of the late 1970s served as an impetus to the merger wave of the late 1970s and 1980s.

8. It is possible for the postmerger P/E ratio to move in a direction opposite to that of the immediate postmerger earnings per share. Explain why this could happen.

9. Explain why unusually high premiums have been paid in the latest merger movement.

10. Suggest some ways in which firms have tried to avoid being part of a target takeover.

11. Why do management and stockholders often have divergent viewpoints about the desirability of a takeover?

12. How does a merger arbitrageur benefit from a possible merger? What is the danger in being a merger arbitrageur? Explain.

13. Compare the use of leverage in a holding company to the concept of operating and financial leverage explained in Chapter 5. What tax problems related to dividends does a holding company have?

14. What is the purpose(s) of the two-step buy-out from the viewpoint of the acquiring company?

Problems

1. The Charles Corporation desires to expand. It is considering a cash purchase of the Atlas Corporation for $2 million. The Atlas Corporation has a $400,000 tax-loss carry-forward that could be used immediately by the Charles Corporation, which is paying taxes at the rate of 34 percent. The Atlas Corporation will provide $260,000 per year in cash flow (aftertax income plus depreciation) for the next 20

years. If the Charles Corporation has a cost of capital of 12 percent, should the Charles–Atlas merger be undertaken?

2. Kemp's Supply Sidemolding is considering a cash acquisition of Roth Homebuilding for $2,200,000. Roth will provide the following pattern of cash inflows and synergistic benefits for the next 20 years. There is no tax-loss carry-forward.

	Years		
	1–5	*6–15*	*6–20*
Cash inflow (aftertax)	$220,000	$240,000	$280,000
Synergistic benefits (aftertax)	$ 20,000	$ 22,000	$ 40,000

The cost of capital for the acquiring firm is 12 percent. Should the merger be undertaken? (If you have any difficulty with delayed time value of money problems, consult Chapter 9).

3. The Mobull Corporation is considering a two-step buy-out of Phillips Corporation. The latter firm has 2 million shares outstanding and its stock price is currently $40 per share. In the two-step buy-out Mobull will offer to buy 51 percent of Phillips's shares outstanding for $68 in cash, and the balance in a second offer of 980,000 convertible preferred stock shares; each share of preferred stock would be valued at 45 percent over Phillips's common stock current value. Mr. Hanson, a newcomer to the management team at Mobull, suggests that only one offer for all Phillips's shares be made at $65.25 per share. Compare the total costs of the two alternatives. Which is preferred in terms of minimizing costs?

4. Robert Sadler helped start Gulf Engineering Company in 1953. At the time, he purchased 100,000 shares of stock at 10 cents per share. In 1989, he has the opportunity to sell his interest in the company to Alpha Technology for $50 a share. His tax rate would be 33 percent.
   a. If he sells out his interest, what will be the value for before-tax profit, taxes, and aftertax profit?
   b. Assume, instead of cash, he accepts stock valued at $50 per share. He holds the stock for five years and then sells it for $90.50 (the stock pays no cash dividends). What will be the value for before-tax profit, taxes, and aftertax profit?
   c. Using a 10 percent discount rate, compare the aftertax profit figure in part *b* to part *a*. (That is, discount back the figure for five years.)

5. A merger between Pica Corporation and Elite Corporation is under consideration. The financial information for these firms is as follows:

	Elite Corporation	Pica Corporation
Total earnings	$300,000	$600,000
Number of shares of stock outstanding	100,000	300,000
Earnings per share	$3	$2
Price–earnings ratio	8×	12×
Market price per share	$24	$24

   a. On a share-for-share exchange basis, what will the postmerger earnings per share be?

   b. If Pica Corporation pays a 25 percent premium over the market value of Elite Corporation, how many shares will be issued?

   c. With the 25 percent premium, what will the postmerger earnings per share be? (Round to the nearest cent.)

   d. With a 50 percent premium, how many shares will be issued and what will be the postmerger earnings per share?

   e. With a 75 percent premium, how many shares will be issued and what will be the postmerger earnings per share?

   f. Explain what has happened in parts *a, c, d,* and *e* in terms of relative P/E ratios and the earnings per share impact of the acquisition.

6. In the case of the Pica and Elite merger described in problem 5, assume that a 100 percent premium will be paid, but that there is a 20 percent synergistic benefit to total earnings from the merger. Will the postmerger earnings go up or down, based on your calculations?

7. Median Corporation is considering a share-for-share exchange with Passive Corporation. The financial information for these firms is as follows:

	Passive Corporation	Median Corporation
Total earnings	$10,000,000	$15,000,000
Number of shares of stock outstanding	4,000,000	10,000,000
Earnings per share	$2.50	$1.50
Price–earnings ratio	4 ×	10 ×
Market price per share	$10.00	$15.00

Median Corporation has agreed to pay Passive Corporation a 20 percent premium over market value. Without the merger, Median

Corporation will grow at a 12 percent rate for the next 10 years. Passive Corporation is expected to grow by 2 percent per year.

a. Compute the postmerger earnings per share. (Round to the nearest cent.)
b. Compute the anticipated postmerger growth rate for the combined firms for the next 10 years. Weight the combined growth rate on the basis of relative earnings contributed to the merged firm.
c. Project earnings per share annually for the next 10 years for Median Corporation based on no merger and based on a merger with Passive Corporation.

8. As a second alternative, Median Corporation (in problem 7) is also considering a merger with Dynamo Corporation. The financial information for these firms is as follows:

	Dynamo Corporation	Median Corporation
Total earnings	$5,000,000	$15,000,000
Number of shares of stock		
outstanding	2,500,000	10,000,000
Earnings per share	$2.00	$1.50
Price–earnings ratio	12 ×	10 ×
Market price per share	$24.00	$15.00

Median Corporation has agreed to pay Dynamo Corporation a 50 percent premium over market value. As previously stated, without the merger Median would grow at a 12 percent rate for the next 10 years. Dynamo Corporation is expected to grow at a 24 percent rate for the next 10 years.

a. Compute the postmerger earnings per share. (Round to the nearest cent.)
b. Compute the anticipated postmerger growth rate for the combined firms for the next 10 years.
c. Project earnings per share annually for the next 10 years for Median Corporation based on no merger (already computed) and based on a merger with Dynamo Corporation.

9. Based on the answers developed to problems 7 and 8:
a. Briefly describe the characteristics of the Median Corporation merger with Passive Corporation in terms of initial dilution, break-even point, and impact after 10 years. Do the same for the Median Corporation–Dynamo Corporation merger. (No graphs are necessary.)

b. In the case of the merger between Median Corporation and Dynamo Corporation, assume the following possible immediate postmerger P/E ratios with the associated probabilities. Compute an expected value for the price of Median Corporation stock after the merger.

P/E	Probability
10	.20
12	.40
14	.30
16	.10

c. In regard to the Median Corporation–Dynamo Corporation merger, if the firms had wished to trade strictly on the basis of earnings per share, what would the exchange ratio be?

d. In regard to the Median Corporation–Dynamo Corporation merger, if 12 percent initial synergy were involved, what would the merger's break-even time period be? (That is, after how many years would earnings per share with and without the merger be approximately equal?)

10. Assume the Mason Corporation is considering the acquisition of the Dixon Corporation. The expected earnings per share for the Mason Corporation will be $4.00 with or without the merger. However, the standard deviation of the earnings will go from $2.00 to $1.40 with the merger because the two firms are negatively correlated.

a. Compute the coefficient of variation for the Mason Corporation before and after the merger.

b. Discuss the possible impact on the postmerger Mason P/E ratio, assuming that investors are risk averse.

11. Bork Construction Company is considering two mergers. The first is with Firm A in its own volatile industry, whereas the second is a merger with Firm B in an industry that moves in the opposite direction (and will tend to level out performance due to negative correlation).

Bork Construction Merger with Firm A		Bork Construction Merger with Firm B	
Possible Earnings ($ in millions)	Probability	Possible Earnings ($ in millions)	Probability
10	.30	$30	.25
40	.40	40	.50
70	.30	50	.25

    a. Compute the mean, standard deviation, and coefficient of variation for both investments (consult Chapter 13 to review statistical concepts if necessary).

    b. Assuming investors are risk averse, which alternatives can be expected to bring the higher valuation?

12. The Graham Corporation is considering the acquisition of the Dodd Corporation. The book value of the Dodd Corporation is $20 million, and the Graham Corporation is willing to pay $50 million in cash and preferred stock. No upward adjustment of assets is anticipated. The Graham Corporation has 1 million shares outstanding. A purchase of assets financial recording will be used, with a 40-year write-off of goodwill.

    a. How much will the annual amortization be?

    b. How much will the annual amortization be on a per share basis?

    c. Is any tax benefit involved?

    d. Explain how the recording of goodwill could have been avoided.

13. The Chicago Power Corporation, a holding company, has investments in three other firms. Values are expressed in millions of dollars.

TINKER CORPORATION

Assets		Liabilities and Stockholders' Equity	
Current assets	$100	Current liabilities	$ 50
Plant and equipment	200	Long-term debt	150
	$300	Common stock equity	100
			$300

EVERS CORPORATION

Assets		Liabilities and Stockholders' Equity	
Current assets	$150	Current liabilities	$150
Plant and equipment	250	Long-term debt	100
	$400	Common stock equity	150
			$400

CHANCE CORPORATION

Assets		Liabilities and Stockholders' Equity	
Current assets	$175	Current liabilities	$ 50
Plant and equipment	275	Long-term debt	200
	$450	Common stock equity	200
			$450

The Chicago Power Corporation has voting control of the three other corporations with the following investment interests in each: 20 percent of the equity in the Tinker Corporation, 30 percent of the equity in Evers Corporation, and 25 percent of the equity in the Chance Corporation.

a. Fill in the table below for the Chicago Power Company's investments in the three companies.

Assets

Common stockholdings:
Tinker Corporation . . .	————
Evers Corporation	————
Chance Corporation . . .	————
Total	————

b. Fill in the table below for the Chicago Power Corporation's liabilities and stockholders' equity. Liabilities are equal to 80 percent of the total assets in part *a*, with the balance in stockholders' equity.

Liabilities and Stockholders' Equity

Liabilities	————
Stockholders' equity	————
Total	————

c. Compute the ratio of the Chicago Power Corporation's stockholders' equity to the total holding company assets for the three corporations.

Selected References

Alberts, William A., and Joel E. Segall. *The Corporate Merger.* Chicago: University of Chicago Press, 1966 and 1974.

Bierman, Harold, Jr. "A Neglected Tax Incentive for Mergers." *Financial Management* 14 (Summer 1984), pp. 29–32.

Block, Stanley B. "The Effect of Mergers and Acquisitions on the Market Value of Common Stock." *Southern Journal of Business* 4 (October 1969), pp. 189–95.

Bloom, Bradley M. "Putting Takeover Madness in Perspective." *Financial Management* 15 (Summer 1986), pp. 59–61.

Bradley, James W., and Donald H. Korn. "Acquisition and Merger Trends Affecting the Portfolio Manager." *Financial Analysts Journal* 33 (November–December 1977), pp. 65–70.

Brown, Keith C., and Michael V. Raymond. "Risk Arbitrage and the Prediction of Successful Corporate Takeovers." *Financial Management* 15 (Autumn 1986), pp. 54–63.

Conn, Robert L., and James F. Nielson. "An Empirical Test of the Larson–Gonedes Exchange Ratio Determination Model." *Journal of Finance* 32 (June 1977), pp. 749–59.

Cummin, Robert I. "Unfriendly Corporate Takeovers—Old Style." *Financial Analysts Journal* 85 (June–August 1982), pp. 65–70.

Davidson, Wallace N. III; Sharon Hatten Garrison; and Glen V. Henderson, Jr. "Examining Merger Synergy With the Capital Asset Pricing Model." *Financial Review* 22 (May 1987), pp. 233–48.

Dodd, Peter, and Richard Ruback. "Tender Offers and Stockholder Returns." *Journal of Financial Economics* 5 (December 1977), pp. 351–73.

Hogarty, T. "The Profitability of Corporate Mergers." *Journal of Business* 43 (July 1970), pp. 317–27.

Larson, Kermit D., and Nicholas J. Gonedes. "Business Combinations: An Exchange Ratio Determination Model." *Accounting Review* 44 (October 1969), pp. 720–28.

Mandelker, Gershon. "Risk and Return: The Case of Merging Firms." *Journal of Financial Economics* 1 (December 1974), 303–35.

Melicher, Ronald W., and David F. Rush. "Evidence on the Acquisition Related Performance of Conglomerate Firms." *Journal of Finance* 29 (March 1974), pp. 141–49.

Merjos, Anna. "Costly Propositions—Some Big Mergers Have Lately Fallen Through." *Barron's,* May 14, 1979, pp. 9–13.

Reilly, Frank K. "What Determines the Ratio of Exchange in Corporate Mergers?" *Financial Analysts Journal* 18 (November–December 1962), pp. 47–50.

Scott, James H., Jr. "On the Theory of Conglomerate Mergers." *Journal of Finance* 32 (September 1977), pp. 1,235–49.

Shrieves, Ronald E., and Mary M. Pashly. "Evidence on the Association between Mergers and Capital Structure." *Financial Management* 13 (Autumn 1984), pp. 39–84.

21

International Financial Management

Introduction

During the post-World War II era, advances in communications and transportation systems brought people everywhere closer together. In this shrinking world, it became easier to interact with others through trade, regardless of geographic origin, location, or nationality. The political systems that emerged from World War II also contributed to the establishment of trade relations between nations. Under the Marshall Plan, the United States helped the war-torn nations of Western Europe rebuild their economies. Western Europe, Canada, and Japan experienced sustainable growth under the economic leadership of the United States. As the economies of Western nations grew in this manner, their trade relations were also strengthened. Concurrently, European nations formed the European Common Market in an effort to promote better trade relations among themselves. Technology and capital also started to flow from the United States to the allied countries. Thus, the United States became the dominant partner in the world economy.

Material for this chapter was developed by Professor G. N. Naidu in conjunction with the authors.

Today, the world economy is more integrated than ever, and nations are dependent on one another for many valuable and scarce resources. Just as the United States is dependent on Saudi Arabia for part of its oil, the Saudis are dependent on the United States for computers, aircraft, and military hardware. Even an arch rival of the United States like the USSR has been dependent on the United States and Canada for agricultural commodities and high technology goods for many years. This growing interdependence necessitates the development of sound international business relations, which, in turn, will enhance the prospects for future international cooperation and understanding. It is virtually impossible for any country to isolate itself from the impact of international developments in an integrated world economy.

The significance of international business operations becomes more apparent if we look at the size of foreign sales relative to the domestic sales for major American corporations. Table 21–1 shows that, in such companies as Dow Chemical, Exxon, Gillette, IBM, J.P. Morgan, and Mobil, foreign sales account for over 50 percent of total sales in 1987.

Table 21–1

	Foreign Sales (percent of total sales)	Foreign Operating Profit (percent of total operating profit)	Foreign Assets (percent of total assets)
Avon Products	35.7%	42.5%	26.0%
Chase Manhattan	46.0	58.5	43.2
Citcorp	46.4	49.3	46.8
Coca-Cola	46.4	62.5	24.7
Dow Chemical	53.5	53.2	49.4
Exxon	72.0	74.9	44.2
Ford Motor	31.8	25.1	49.7
Gillette	60.9	62.8	59.1
Hercules	36.4	71.3	31.4
Hewlett-Packard	46.3	46.2	32.5
H. J. Heinz	36.7	32.7	39.2
IBM	50.5	66.5	47.7
J. P. Morgan	54.8	48.7	47.9
Merck	49.0	36.9	36.4
Mobil	59.5	132.1*	47.2
Pfizer	44.5	33.3	37.1
Unisys	42.9	78.4	29.0
Warner-Lambert	43.7	40.4	45.0

*Foreign profit is over 100 percent due to domestic losses.

Also, you should note the importance of foreign profits and foreign assets. Just as foreign operations affect the performance of American business firms, developments in international financial markets also affect our lifestyles. If you took a summer trip to France or Germany in 1987, you might have been disappointed to find out how much more expensive hotels, food, and recreation were compared to a few short years ago. The primary reason was the precipitous drop in the dollar relative to many foreign currencies. Of course, many foreigners might be attracted to Disney World and other vacation spots in the United States, because their currencies would buy increasingly more due to the decline in the value of the dollar. This chapter deals with the international dimensions of corporate finance. We believe that this chapter provides a basis for understanding the complexities of international financial decisions. Such an understanding is important whether you work for a multinational manufacturing firm, a large commercial bank, a major brokerage firm, or any firm involved in international transactions.

International business operations, by their very nature, are complex, risky, and require special understanding. Many major U.S. banks have had to learn the lessons of international finance through painful experience. In the worldwide recession of 1981–83, many less-developed, third world countries found difficulty in repaying their debt obligations as their exports dropped. The ingenuity of world financial institutions was challenged (and continue to be challenged) to avoid disaster.

In the following section of this chapter a description of the international business firm and its environment is presented. Then foreign exchange rates and the variables influencing foreign currency values are explained, and strategies dealing with foreign exchange risk are examined. The foreign investment decision is then illustrated through an example, and finally, international financing sources, including the Eurodollar market, the Eurobond market, and foreign equity markets, are discussed.

The Multinational Corporation: Nature and Environment

The focus of international financial management has been the multinational corporation (MNC). One might ask, just what is a multinational corporation? Some definitions of a multinational corporation require that a minimum percentage (often 30 percent or more) of a firm's business activities be carried on outside its national borders. For our understanding, however, a firm doing business across its national borders is considered a multinational enterprise. There are several forms that multinational corporations can take. Four are briefly examined.

Exporter   An MNC could produce a product domestically and export some of that production to one or more foreign markets. This is, perhaps, the least risky method—reaping the benefits of foreign demand without committing any long-term investment to that foreign country.

Licensing agreement   A firm with exporting operations may get into trouble when a foreign government imposes or substantially raises an import tariff to a level at which the exporter cannot compete effectively with the local domestic manufacturers. The foreign government may even ban all imports into the country at times. When this happens, the exporting firm may grant a license to an independent local producer to use the firm's technology in return for a license fee or a royalty. In essence, then, the MNC will be exporting technology, rather than the product, to that foreign country.

Joint venture   As an alternative to licensing, the MNC may establish a joint venture with a local foreign manufacturer. The legal, political, and economic environments around the globe are more conducive to the joint venture arrangement than any of the other modes of operations. Historical evidence also suggests that a joint venture with a local entrepreneur exposes the firm to the least amount of political risk. Consequently, this position is preferred by most business firms and by foreign governments as well.

Fully owned foreign subsidiary   Although the joint venture form is desirable for many reasons, it may be hard to find a willing and cooperative local entrepreneur with sufficient capital to participate. Under these conditions, the MNC may have to go it alone. For political reasons, however, a wholly owned foreign subsidiary was becoming more of a rarity in the late-80s. The reader must keep in mind that whenever we mention a *foreign affiliate* in the ensuing discussion, it could be a joint venture or a fully owned subsidiary.

As the firm crosses its national borders, it faces an environment that is riskier and more complex than its domestic surroundings. Sometimes the social and political environment can be hostile. In spite of these difficult challenges, foreign affiliates often are more profitable than domestic businesses. A purely domestic firm faces several basic risks, such as the risk related to maintaining sales and market share, the financial risk of too much leverage, the risk of a poor equity market, and so on. In addition to these types of risks, the foreign affiliate is exposed to foreign-exchange risk and political risk. While the foreign affiliate experiences a larger amount of risk than a domestic firm, it actually lowers the portfolio risk of its parent corporation by stabilizing the combined operating cash flows for the MNC. This risk reduction occurs because foreign and domestic economies are less than perfectly correlated.

Foreign business operations are more complex because the host country's economy may be different from the domestic economy. The rate of inflation in many foreign countries is likely to be higher than in the United States. The rules of taxation are usually different. The structure and operation of financial markets and institutions also vary from country to country, as do financial policies and practices. The presence of a foreign affiliate benefits the host country's economy. Foreign affiliates have been a decisive factor in shaping the pattern of trade, investment, and the flow of technology between nations. They can have a significant positive impact on a host country's economic growth, employment, trade, and balance of payments. This positive contribution, however, is occasionally overshadowed by allegations of wrongdoing. For example, some host countries have charged that foreign affiliates subverted their governments and caused instability of their currencies in international money and foreign exchange markets. The less-developed countries (LDCs) have, at times, alleged that foreign businesses exploit their labor with low wages. The multinational companies are also under constant criticism in their home countries where labor unions charge the MNCs with exporting jobs, capital, and technology to foreign nations while avoiding their fair share of taxes. In spite of all these criticisms, the multinational companies have managed to survive and prosper. The MNC is well positioned to take advantage of imperfections in the global markets. Furthermore, since current global resource distribution favors the MNC's survival and growth, it may be concluded that the multinational corporation is here to stay.

Foreign Exchange Rates

Suppose you are planning to spend a semester in Paris studying the French culture. To put your plan into operation you will need French currency, that is, French francs (FF), so you can pay for your expenses during your stay in France. How many French francs you can obtain for $1,000 will depend on the exchange rate at that time. The relationship between the values of two currencies is known as the exchange rate. The exchange rate between U.S. dollars and French francs is stated as dollars per franc or francs per dollar. For example, the quotation of $0.16 per franc is the same as FF6.25 per dollar. At this exchange rate you can purchase 6,250 French francs with $1,000. *The Wall Street Journal* publishes exchange rates of major foreign currencies each day. The names of some countries' currencies and their exchange rates relative to the U.S. dollar are shown in Table 21–2. This table shows dollars (fractions of dollars) that one can exchange for each unit of foreign currency ($/currency). As you may notice from this table, the exchange rates change over time. By comparing exchange rates between August 1, 1985, and August 1, 1987, you will observe that most currencies increased in value relative to the dollar during that time period. That is, the foreign currency would buy more dollars (fractions of dollars) in 1987 than in 1985. For example, the German deutsche mark was the equivalent of 0.3506 dollars in August of 1985, but increased to 0.5393 dollars in August of 1987. By taking the reciprocal of these two values, we could also say the dollar was worth 2.85 $(1 \div 0.3506)$ deutsche marks in August of 1985 and only 1.85 $(1 \div .5393)$ deutsche marks in August of 1987.

Table 21–2
Selected currencies and exchange rates. Dollar (fractions of dollar) that one can exchange for each unit of foreign currency: $/currency.

Country	Currency	August 1, 1985	August 1, 1987
Austria	schilling	$0.0497	$0.0766
Belgium	franc	0.0175	0.0260
Denmark	krone	0.0945	0.1417
France	franc	0.1151	0.1620
Germany	deutsche mark	0.3506	0.5393
India	rupee	0.0850	0.0763
Italy	lira	0.0008	0.0005
Japan	yen	0.0042	0.0066
Mexico	peso	0.0029	0.0007
Netherlands	guilder	0.3122	0.4773
Portugal	escudo	0.0060	0.0069
South Africa	rand	0.4500	0.4835
Spain	peseta	0.0061	0.0079
Sweden	krona	0.1188	0.1544
Switzerland	franc	0.4235	0.6502
United Kingdom	pound	1.3465	1.6030

Of course, the dollar was not weaker against all currencies, as also indicated in Table 21–2. Examples of countries that had decreasing buying power relative to the dollar include India, Italy, and Mexico. Many of these countries had severe economic or political problems to overcome.

Factors Influencing Exchange Rates

The present international monetary system consists of a mixture of "freely" floating exchange rates and fixed rates. The currencies of the major trading partners of the United States are traded in free markets. In such a market the exchange rate between two currencies is determined by the supply of, and the demand for, those currencies. This activity, however, is subject to intervention by many countries' central banks. Factors that tend to increase the supply or decrease the demand schedule for a given currency will bring down the value of that currency in foreign exchange markets. Similarly, the factors that tend to decrease the supply or increase the demand for a currency will raise the value of that currency. Since fluctuations in currency values result in foreign exchange risk, the financial executive must understand the factors causing these changes in currency values. Although the value of a currency is determined by the aggregate supply and demand for that currency, this alone does not help our financial manager understand or predict the changes in exchange rates. Fundamental factors, such as inflation, interest rates, balance of payments, and government policies, are quite important in explaining both the short-term and long-term fluctuations of a currency value.

Inflation   A parity between the purchasing powers of two currencies establishes the rate of exchange between the two currencies. Suppose it takes $1.00 to buy one dozen apples in New York and 2.50 deutsche marks to buy the same apples in Frankfurt, Germany. Then the rate of exchange between the U.S. dollar and deutsche mark is DM2.50/$1.00 or $0.40/DM. If prices of apples double in New York while the prices in Frankfurt remain the same, you know that the purchasing power of a dollar in New York will drop 50 percent. Consequently, you will be able to exchange $1.00 for only DM 1.25 in foreign currency markets (or receive $0.80 per DM). Currency exchange rates, therefore, tend to vary inversely with their respective purchasing powers in order to provide the same or similar purchasing power in each country. This is called the *purchasing power parity theory.* When the inflation rate differential between two countries changes, the exchange rate also adjusts to correspond to the relative purchasing powers of the countries.

Interest rates   Another economic variable that has a significant influence on exchange rates is interest rates. As a student of finance, you should know that investment capital flows in the direction of higher yield for a given level of risk. This flow of short-term capital between money markets occurs because investors seek equilibrium through arbitrage buying and selling. If investors can earn 10 percent interest per year in the United States and 16 percent per year in Britain, they will prefer to invest in Britain, provided that the inflation rate and risk are the same in both countries. As investors buy British pounds with U.S. dollars, the value of the pound will appreciate relative to the dollar. At the same time, the increased demand for British securities also tends to reduce the interest rate differential between the United Kingdom and the United States. Thus, interest rates and exchange rates adjust until the foreign exchange market and the money market reach equilibrium. This interplay between interest rate differentials and exchange rates is called the *interest rate parity theory.*

Balance of payments   The term *balance of payments* refers to a system of government accounts that catalogs the flow of economic transactions between the residents of one country and the residents of other countries. (The balance of payments statement for the United States is prepared by the U.S. Department of Commerce quarterly and annually.) It resembles the funds statement presented in Chapter 2, and keeps track of the country's exports and imports as well as the flow of capital and gifts. When a country sells (exports) more goods and services to foreign countries than it purchases (imports) from abroad, it will have a surplus in its balance of trade. Japan, for example, through its aggressive competition in world markets, exports more goods than it imports and has been enjoying a trade surplus for quite some time. Since the foreigners who buy Japanese goods are expected to pay their bills in yen, the demand for yen and, consequently, its value increase in foreign currency markets. On the other hand, continuous deficits in the balance of payments is expected to depress the value of a currency, because such deficits would increase the supply of that currency relative to the demand. This has generally been the case with the U.S. dollar during the mid-to-late 1980s.

Government policies   A national government may, through its central bank, intervene in the foreign exchange market, buying and selling currencies as it sees fit to support the value of its currency relative to others. Sometimes a given country may deliberately pursue a policy of maintaining an undervalued currency in order to promote cheap exports. In Communist countries the currency values are set by government decree. Even in some free market countries, the central banks fix the exchange rates, subject to periodic review and adjustment. At times, some nations affect the foreign exchange rate indirectly by restricting the flow of funds into and out of the country. Monetary and fiscal policies also affect the currency value in foreign exchange markets. For example, expansionary monetary policy and excessive government spending are primary causes of inflation, and continual use of such policies eventually reduces the value of the country's currency.

Other factors   A pronounced and extended stock market rally in a country attracts investment capital from other countries, thus creating a huge demand by foreigners for that country's currency. This increased demand is expected to increase the value of that currency. Similarly, a significant drop in demand for a country's principal exports worldwide is expected to result in a corresponding decline in the value of its currency. The South African rand and British pound are two examples from recent history. A precipitous drop in gold prices and an apparent oil glut are cited as the reasons for the depreciation of these two currencies during the 1980s. Political turmoil in a country often drives capital out of the country into stable countries. A mass exodus of capital, due to the fear of political risk, undermines the value of a country's currency in the foreign exchange market. Also, widespread labor strikes which may appear to weaken the nation's economy will have a depressing influence on its currency value.

Although a wide variety of factors that can influence exchange rates have been discussed, a few words of caution are in order. All of these variables will not necessarily influence all currencies to the same degree. Some factors may have an overriding influence on one currency's value, while their influence on another currency may be negligible at that time.

Spot Rates and Forward Rates

When you look into a major financial newspaper (e.g., *The Wall Street Journal*), you will discover that two exchange rates exist simultaneously for most major currencies—the spot rate and the forward rate. The spot rate for a currency is the exchange rate at which the currency is traded for immediate delivery. For example, you walk into a local commercial bank and ask for French francs. The banker will indicate the rate at which the franc is selling, say FF 6.25/$. If you like the rate, you buy 6,250 francs with $1,000 and walk out the door. This is a spot market transaction at the retail level. The trading of currencies for future delivery is called a forward market transaction. To illustrate, suppose IBM Corporation expects to receive FF 70 million from a French customer 30 days from now. It is not certain, however, what these francs will be worth in dollars 30 days from today. In order to eliminate this uncertainty, IBM calls a bank and offers to sell FF 70 million for U.S. dollars 30 days from now.

In their negotiation, the two parties may agree on an exchange rate of FF 7/$. Since the exchange rate is established for future delivery, it is a forward rate. After 30 days, IBM delivers FF 70 million to the bank and receives $10 million. The difference between spot and forward exchange rates, expressed in dollars per unit of foreign currency, may be seen in the following values on August 1, 1987.

Rates	Deutsche Mark (DM) ($/DM)	British Pound (£) ($/£)
Spot	$0.5393	$1.6030
30-day forward	0.5406	1.6006
90-day forward	0.5431	1.5945
180-day forward	0.5478	1.5859

The forward exchange rate of a currency is slightly different from the spot rate prevailing at that time. Since the forward rate deals with a future time, the expectations regarding the future value of that currency are reflected in the forward rate. Forward rates may be greater than the current spot rate (premium) or less than the current spot rate (discount). On August 1, 1987, forward rates on the deutsche mark were at a premium in relation to the spot rate, while the forward rates for the British pound were at a discount from the spot rate. This means that, on that day, the participants in the foreign exchange market expected the deutsche mark to appreciate relative to the U.S. dollar in the future, and the British pound to depreciate against the dollar. The discount or premium is usually expressed as an annualized percentage deviation from the spot rate. The percentage discount or premium is computed with the following formula:

Forward premium
(or discount)

$$= \frac{\text{Forward rate} - \text{Spot rate}}{\text{Spot rate}} \times \frac{12}{\substack{\text{Length of} \\ \text{forward contract} \\ \text{(in months)}}} \times 100 \quad (21\text{--}1)$$

For example, on August 1, 1987, the 90-day forward contract in deutsche marks was selling at 2.82 percent premium:

$$\left(\frac{0.5431 - 0.5393}{0.5393} \right) \times \frac{12}{3} \times 100 = 2.8184\%$$

while the 90-day forward contract in pounds was trading at a 2.12 percent discount:

$$\left(\frac{1.5945 - 1.6030}{1.6030}\right) \times \frac{12}{3} \times 100 = 2.1210\% \text{ (discount)}$$

Normally, the forward premium or discount is between 0.5 percent and 10 percent.

The spot and forward transactions are said to take place in the over-the-counter market. Foreign currency dealers (usually large commercial banks) and their customers (importers, exporters, investors, multinational firms, and so on) negotiate the exchange rate, the length of the forward contract, and the commission in a mutually agreeable fashion. Although the length of a typical forward contract may generally vary between one month and six months, contracts for longer maturities are not uncommon. The dealers, however, may require higher returns for longer contracts.

Cross rates   Since all currencies are quoted against the U.S. dollar in *The Wall Street Journal*, sometimes it may be necessary to work out the cross rates for other currencies than the dollar. For example, on August 1, 1987, the Danish krone was selling for $0.1417 and the British pound was selling for $1.6030. The cross rate between the krone and the pound is 11.31 (krones/pounds). In determining this value, we show that one dollar will buy 7.057 krones (1 ÷ 0.1417) and a pound is equal to $1.6030 dollars. Thus, 7.057 Danish krones per *dollar* times 1.6030 *dollars* per pound equals 11.31 Danish krones per pound.

Managing Foreign Exchange Risk

When the parties associated with a commercial transaction are located in the same country, the transaction is denominated in a single currency. International transactions inevitably involve more than one currency (because the parties are domiciled residents of different countries). Since most foreign currency values fluctuate from time to time, the monetary value of an international transaction measured in either the seller's currency or the buyer's currency is likely to change when payment is delayed. As a result, the seller may receive less revenue than expected or the buyer may have to pay more than the expected amount for the merchandise. Thus the term *foreign exchange risk* refers to the possibility of a drop in revenue or an increase in cost in an international transaction due to a change in foreign exchange rates. Importers, exporters, investors, and multinational firms are all exposed to this foreign exchange risk.

The international monetary system has undergone a significant change over the last 15 years. The free trading Western nations basically went from a fixed exchange rate system to a "freely" floating rate system. For the most part, the new system proved its agility and resilience during the most turbulent years of oil price hikes and hyperinflation of the last decade. The free market exchange rates responded and adjusted well to these adverse conditions. Consequently, the exchange rates fluctuated over a much wider range than before. The increased volatility of exchange markets forced many multinational firms, importers, and exporters to pay more attention to the function of foreign exchange risk management.

The foreign exchange risk of a multinational company is divided into three types of exposure. They are: accounting or translation exposure; transaction exposure; and economic exposure. An MNC's foreign assets and liabilities, which are denominated in foreign currency units, are exposed to losses and gains due to changing exchange rates. This is called accounting, or translation, exposure. The amount of loss or gain resulting from this form of exposure and the treatment of it in the parent company's books, depends on the accounting rules established by the parent company's government. In the United States, the rules are spelled out in Financial Accounting Standards Board Statement 52 (FASB 52). Under FASB 52, all foreign currency denominated assets and liabilities are converted at the rate of exchange in effect on the date of balance sheet preparation. An unrealized translation gain or loss is held in an equity reserve account while the realized gain or loss is incorporated in the parent's consolidated income statement for that period. Thus, FASB 52 reduces the impact of accounting exposure resulting from the translation of a foreign subsidiary's balance sheet on reported earnings of multinational firms.

However, foreign exchange gains and losses resulting from international transactions, which are known as transaction gains and losses, are reflected in the income statement for the current period. As a consequence of these transactional gains and losses, the volatility of reported earnings per share increases. Three different strategies can be used to minimize this transaction exposure.

1. Hedging in the forward exchange market.
2. Hedging in the money market.
3. Hedging in the currency futures market.

Forward exchange market hedge   To see how the transaction exposure can be covered in forward markets, suppose Electricitie de France, an electric company in France, purchased a large generator from General Electric of the United States for FF 8.725 million on October 26, 1987, and GE was promised the payment in French francs in 90 days. Since GE is now exposed to exchange risk by agreeing to receive the payment in French francs in the future, it is up to GE to find a way to reduce this exposure. One simple method is to hedge the exposure in the forward exchange market. On October 26, 1987, to establish the forward cover, GE sells a forward contract to deliver the FF 8.725 million, 90 days from now in exchange for $1.405 million. On January 25, 1988, GE receives payment from Electricitie de France and delivers the FF 8.725 million to the bank that signed the contract. In return, the bank delivers $1.405 million to GE. Thus, through this international transaction, GE receives the same dollar amount it expected three months ago regardless of what happened to the value of French francs in the interim. In contrast, if the sale had been invoiced in U.S. dollars, Electricitie de France, not GE, would have been exposed to the exchange risk.

Money market hedge   A second way to have eliminated transaction exposure in the previous example would have been to borrow money in French francs and then convert it to U.S. dollars immediately. When the accounts receivable from the sale is collected three months later, the loan is cleared with the proceeds. In this case, GE's strategy consists of the following steps. On October 26, 1987:

1. Borrow FF 8,470,874 (FF 8,725,000 / 1.03 = FF 8,470,874) at the rate of 12 percent per year for three months. You borrow less than the full amount of FF 8,725,000 in recognition of the fact that interest must be paid on the loan. Twelve percent interest for 90 days translates into 3 percent. Thus, FF 8,725,000 is divided by 1.03 to arrive at the size of the loan prior to the interest payment.
2. Convert the French francs into the U.S. dollars in the spot market.

Then on January 25, 1988 (90 days later):

3. Receive the payment FF 8,725,000 from Electricitie de France.
4. Clear the loan with the proceeds received from Electricitie de France.

The money market hedge basically calls for matching the exposed asset (accounts receivable) with a liability (loan payable) in the same currency. Some firms prefer this money market hedge because of the early availability of funds possible with this method.

Currency futures market hedge   Transaction exposure associated with a foreign currency can also be covered in the currency futures market. The International Monetary Market (IMM) of the Chicago Mercantile Exchange began trading in futures contracts in foreign currencies on May 16, 1972. Trading in currency futures contracts also made a debut on the London International Financial Futures Exchange (LIFFE) in September 1982. Other markets have also developed around the world. Just as futures contracts are traded in corn, wheat, hogs, and beans, foreign currency futures contracts are traded in these markets. Although the futures market and forward market are similar in concept, they differ in their operations. To illustrate the hedging process in the currency futures market, suppose that, in June, the Chicago-based Continental Illinois National Bank considers lending 500,000 deutsche marks to a German subsidiary of a U.S. parent company for six months. The bank purchases the deutsche marks in the spot market, delivers them to the borrower, and simultaneously hedges its transaction exposure by selling December contracts in deutsche marks for the same amount. In December when the loan is cleared, the bank sells the deutsche marks in the spot market and buys back the December deutsche mark contracts. The transactions are illustrated as follows for the spot and futures market:[1]

Date	Spot Market	Futures Market
June 1	Buys 500,000 deutsche marks (DM) at $0.5380/DM = $269,000	Sells DM 500,000 for December delivery at $0.5370/DM = $268,500
December 1 . . .	Sells DM 500,000 at $0.5350/DM = $267,500 Loss $1,500	Buys DM 500,000 at $0.5350/DM = $267,500 Gain $1,000

While the loan was outstanding, the deutsche mark dropped its value in relation to the U.S. dollar. Had the bank remained unhedged, it would have lost $1,500 in the spot market. By hedging in the futures market, the bank reduced the loss to only $500. A $1,000 gain in the futures market was used to cancel out all but $500 of the $1,500 loss in the spot market.

Hedging is not the only means companies have for protecting themselves against foreign exchange risk. Over the years, multinational companies

---

[1] For purposes of this example, we assumed the deutsche mark was trading at a discount in the futures market. Had it been trading at a premium, the hedge would have been even more attractive.

have developed, for this purpose, elaborate foreign asset management programs, which involve such strategies as switching cash and other current assets into strong currencies, while piling up debt and other liabilities in depreciating currencies. Companies also encourage the quick collection of bills in weak currencies by offering sizable discounts, while extending liberal credit in strong currencies.

Foreign Investment Decisions

It is estimated from the *Directory of American Firms Operating in Foreign Countries* that there are more than 4,000 U.S. firms with one or more foreign affiliates. One might ask, What motivated the American firms to move their operations overseas? Several explanations are offered for the move to foreign soil. First, with the emergence of trading blocks like the common market in Europe, American firms feared that their goods might face import tariffs in those countries. To avoid such trade barriers, U.S. firms started manufacturing in foreign countries. The second factor was the lower production costs overseas. Firms were motivated by the significantly lower wage costs prevailing in foreign countries. Consequently, firms in labor-intensive industries, such as textiles and electronics, moved some of their operations to countries where labor was cheap. Third, superior American technology gave U.S. firms an easy access to oil exploration, mining, and manufacturing in many developing nations. A fourth advantage relates to taxes. The U.S.-based multinational firms are able to postpone payment of U.S. taxes on income earned abroad until such income is actually repatriated (forwarded) to the parent company. This tax deferral provision can be used by an MNC to minimize its tax liability. Some countries, like Israel, Ireland, and South Africa, offer special tax incentives for foreign firms that establish operations there. Although the benefits of lower taxes and lower wage costs and the technological gap have gradually diminished in recent years, the average rate of return on U.S. investment abroad continues to be higher than on U.S. domestic investments.

The decision to invest in a foreign country by a firm operating in an oligopolistic industry is also motivated by strategic considerations. When a competitor undertakes a direct foreign investment, other companies quickly follow with defensive investments in the same foreign country. Foreign investments undertaken by U.S. tire and rubber companies are classic examples of this competitive reaction. Wherever you find a Firestone subsidiary in a foreign country, you are likely to see a Goodyear affiliate also operating in that country.

Many academicians believe that international diversification of risks is also an important motivation for direct foreign investment. The basic premise of portfolio theory in finance is that an investor can reduce the risk level of a portfolio by combining those investments whose returns are less than perfectly positively correlated. In addition to domestic diversification, it is shown in Figure 21–1 that further reduction in investment risk can be achieved by diversifying across national boundaries. International stocks, in Figure 21–1, show a consistently lower percentage of risk compared to any given number of U.S. stocks in a portfolio. It is argued, however, that institutional and political constraints, language barriers, and lack of adequate information on foreign investments prevent investors from diversifying across nations. Multinational firms, on the other hand, through their unique position around the world, derive the benefits of international diversification. This argument has been weakened somewhat by the introduction of international mutual funds.

**Figure 21–1
Risk reduction from
international
diversification**

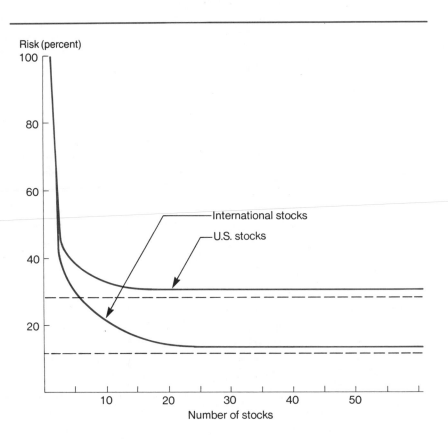

While the U.S.-based firms took the lead in establishing overseas subsidiaries during the 1950s and 1960s, the European and Japanese firms started this activity in the 1970s. The flow of foreign direct investment into the United States has proceeded at a rapid rate, particularly since 1975. These investments employ millions of people. It is quite evident that the United States is becoming an attractive site for foreign investment. In addition to the international diversification and strategic considerations, many other factors are responsible for this rapid inflow of foreign capital into the United States. Increased foreign labor costs in some countries and saturated overseas markets in others are partly responsible. In Japan, an acute shortage of land suitable for industrial development and a near total dependence on imported oil prompted some of their firms to locate in the United States. In Germany, a large number of paid holidays, restrictions limiting labor layoffs, and worker participation in management decision making caused many firms to look favorably at the United States. Political stability, large market size, and access to advanced technology are other primary motivating factors for firms to establish their operations in the United States. Also, large balance of payments deficits have spread hundreds of millions of dollars around the world for potential reinvestment in the United States, particularly by the Japanese.

To some extent, foreign investors in the U.S. Treasury bond market have been bankrolling enormous budget deficits that the government has been running up. When the U.S. government began falling $150–200 billion into the red on an annual basis in the 1980s, many analysts thought this would surely mean high inflation, high interest rates, and perhaps a recession. They also were sure that there would be a "shortage of capital" for investment purposes, because of large government borrowing to finance the deficits. For the most part, foreign investors from Japan, Western Europe, Canada, and elsewhere have bailed the government out by supplying the necessary capital. Of course, this now means the United States is more dependent on flows of foreign capital into the country. We must satisfy our "outside" investors or face the unpleasant consequences. Over the course of a decade, we have gone from being the largest lender in the world to the largest borrower.

Analysis of Political Risk

Business firms tend to make direct investments in foreign countries for a relatively long time. Because of the time necessary to recover the initial investment, they do not intend to liquidate their investments quickly. The government may change hands several times during the foreign firm's tenure in that country; and, when a new government takes over, it may not be as friendly or as cooperative as the previous administration. An unfriendly government can interfere with the foreign affiliates in many ways. It may impose foreign exchange restrictions, or the foreign ownership share may be limited to a set percentage of the total. Repatriation (transfer) of a subsidiary's profit to the parent company may be blocked, at least temporarily; and, in the extreme case, the government may even expropriate (take over) the foreign subsidiary's assets. The multinational company may experience a sizable loss of income or property, or both, as a result of this political interference. Many well-known U.S. firms, like Anaconda, ITT, and Occidental Petroleum, have lost hundreds of millions of dollars in politically unstable countries. Over the last decade, more than 60 percent of U.S. companies doing business abroad suffered some form of politically inflicted damage. Therefore, analysis of foreign political risk is gaining more attention in multinational firms.

The best approach to protection against political risk is to conduct a thorough investigation of the country's political stability long before the firm makes any investment in that country. Companies have been using different methods for assessing political risk. Some firms hire consultants to provide them with a report of political-risk analysis. Others form their own advisory committees (little state departments) consisting of top-level managers from headquarters and foreign subsidiaries. After ascertaining the country's political-risk level, the multinational firm can use one of the following strategies to guard against such risk:

1. One strategy is to establish a joint venture with a local entrepreneur. By bringing a local partner into the deal, the MNC not only limits its financial exposure but also minimizes antiforeign feelings.

2. Another risk-management tactic is to enter into a joint venture, preferably with firms from other countries. For example, Chevron may pursue its oil production operation in Zaire in association with Royal Dutch Petroleum and Nigerian National Petroleum as partners. The foreign government will be more hesitant to antagonize a number of partner-firms of many nationalities at the same time.

3. When the perceived political-risk level is high, insurance against such risks can be obtained in advance. Overseas Private Investment Corporation (OPIC), a federal government agency, sells insurance policies to qualified firms. This agency insures against losses due to inconvertibility into dollars of amounts invested in a foreign country. Policies are also available from OPIC to insure against expropriation and

against losses due to war or revolution. Many firms have made use of this service over the years. For example, Greenlaw, Inc., a Florida-based firm, insured its fruit-processing plant in the Dominican Republic through OPIC. Private insurance companies, such as Lloyds of London, American International Group Inc., CIGNA, and others, issue similar policies to cover political risk. Political-risk umbrella policies do not come cheaply. Coverage for projects in "fairly safe" countries can cost anywhere from 0.3 percent to 12 percent of the insured values per year. Needless to say, they are more expensive or unavailable in troubled countries. OPIC's rates are lower than those of private insurers, and its policies extend for 20 years, compared to three years or less for private insurance policies.

Cash Flow Analysis and the Foreign Investment Decision

Direct foreign investments are often relatively large in size. As we mentioned previously, these investments are exposed to some extraordinary risks, such as foreign exchange fluctuations and political interference, which are nonexistent for domestic investments. Therefore, the final decision is often made at the board of directors level after considering the financial feasibility and the strategic importance of the proposed investment. Financial feasibility analysis for foreign investments is basically conducted in the same manner as it is for domestic capital budgets. Certain important differences exist, however, in the treatment of foreign tax credits, foreign exchange risk, and remittance of cash flows. To see how these are handled in foreign investment analysis, let us consider a hypothetical illustration.

Tex Systems, Inc., a Texas-based manufacturer of word processing equipment, is considering the establishment of a manufacturing plant in Salaysia, a country in Southeast Asia. The Salaysian plant will be a wholly owned subsidiary of Tex Systems, and its estimated cost is 90 million ringgits (2 ringgits = $1). Based on the exchange rate between ringgits and dollars, the cost in dollars is $45 million. In addition to selling in the local Salaysian market, the proposed subsidiary is expected to export its word processors to the neighboring markets in Singapore, Hong Kong, and Thailand. Expected revenues and operating costs are as shown in Table 21–3. The country's investment climate, which reflects the foreign exchange and political risks, is rated BBB (considered fairly safe) by a leading Asian business journal. After considering the investment climate and the nature of the industry, Tex Systems has set a target rate of return of 20 percent for this foreign investment. Salaysia has a 25 percent cor-

Table 21–3   Cash flow analysis of a foreign investment

	Projected Cash Flows (million ringgits unless otherwise stated)					
	Year 1	Year 2	Year 3	Year 4	Year 5	Year 6
Revenues	45.00	50.00	55.00	60.00	65.00	70.00
− Operating expenses	28.00	30.00	30.00	32.00	35.00	35.00
− Depreciation	10.00	10.00	10.00	10.00	10.00	10.00
Earnings before Salaysian taxes	7.00	10.00	15.00	18.00	20.00	25.00
− Salaysian income tax (25%) . . .	1.75	2.50	3.75	4.50	5.00	6.25
Earnings after foreign income taxes	5.25	7.50	11.25	13.50	15.00	18.75
= Dividends repatriated	5.25	7.50	11.25	13.50	15.00	18.75
Gross U.S. taxes (30% of foreign earnings before taxes)	2.10	3.00	4.50	5.40	6.00	7.50
− Foreign tax credit	1.75	2.50	3.75	4.50	5.00	6.25
Net U.S. taxes payable	0.35	0.50	0.75	0.90	1.00	1.25
Aftertax dividend received by Tex Systems	4.90	7.00	10.50	12.60	14.00	17.50
Exchange rate (ringgits/$)	2.00	2.04	2.08	2.12	2.16	2.21
Aftertax dividend (U.S. $)	2.45	3.43	5.05	5.94	6.48	7.92
IF_{pv} (at 20%)	0.833	0.694	0.579	0.482	0.402	0.335
PV of dividends ($)	2.04 +	2.38 +	2.92 +	2.86 +	2.60 +	2.65 = $15.45

porate income tax rate, and has waived the withholding tax on dividends repatriated (forwarded) to the parent company. A dividend payout ratio of 100 percent is assumed for the foreign subsidiary. Tex Systems' marginal tax rate is 30 percent. It was agreed by Tex Systems and the Salaysian government that the subsidiary will be sold to a Salaysian entrepreneur after six years for an estimated 30 million ringgits. The plant will be depreciated over a period of six years using the straight-line method. The cash flows generated through depreciation cannot be remitted to the parent company until the subsidiary is sold to the local private entrepreneur six years from now. The Salaysian government requires the subsidiary to invest the depreciation-generated cash flows in local government bonds yielding an aftertax rate of 15 percent. The depreciation cash flows thus compounded and accumulated can be returned to Tex Systems when the project is terminated. Although the value of ringgits in the foreign exchange market has remained fairly stable for the past three years, the projected budget deficits and trade deficits of Salaysia may result in a gradual devaluation of ringgits against the U.S. dollar at the rate of 2 percent per year for the next six years.

Note: the analysis in Table 21–3 is primarily done in terms of ringgits. Expenses (operating, depreciation, and Salaysian income taxes) are subtracted from revenues to arrive at earnings after foreign income taxes. These earnings are then repatriated (forwarded) to Tex Systems in the form of dividends. Dividends repatriated thus begin at 5.25 ringgits (in millions) in year 1 and increase to 18.75 ringgits in year 6. The next item, gross U.S. taxes, refers to the unadjusted U.S. tax obligation. As specified, this is equal to 30 percent of foreign earnings before taxes (earnings before Salaysian taxes).[2] For example, gross U.S. taxes in the first year are equal to:

Earnings before Salaysian taxes	7.00
30% of foreign earnings before taxes	30%
Gross U.S. taxes	2.10

From gross U.S. taxes, Tex Systems may take a foreign tax credit equal to the amount of Salaysian income tax paid. Gross U.S. taxes minus this foreign tax credit are equal to net U.S. taxes payable. Finally, aftertax dividends received by Tex Systems are equal to dividends repatriated minus U.S. taxes payable. In the first year, the values are:

Dividends repatriated	5.25
Net U.S. taxes payable	−0.35
Aftertax dividends received by Tex Systems	4.90

The figures for aftertax dividends received by Tex Systems are all stated in ringgits (the analysis up to this point has been in ringgits). These ringgits will now be converted into dollars. The initial exchange rate is 2.00 ringgits per dollar, and this will go up by 2 percent per year.[3] For the first year, 4.90 ringgits will be translated into 2.45 dollars. Since values are stated in millions, this will represent $2.45 million. Aftertax dividends in U.S. dollars grow from $2.45 million in year 1 to $7.92 million in year 6. The last two rows of Table 21–3 show the present value of these dividends at a 20 percent discount rate. The *total* present value of aftertax dividends received by Tex Systems adds up to $15.45 million. Repatriated dividends will be just one part of the cash flow. The second part consists of depreciation-generated cash flow accumulated and rein-

---

[2] If foreign earnings had not been repatriated, this tax obligation would not be due.

[3] The 2 percent appreciation means the dollar is equal to an increasing amount of ringgits each year. The dollar is appreciating relative to ringgits, and ringgits are depreciating relative to the dollar. Since Tex Systems earnings are in ringgits, they are being converted at a less desirable rate each year. Big Tex may eventually decide to hedge its foreign exchange risk exposure.

vested in Salaysian government bonds at 15 percent per year. The compound value of reinvested depreciation cash flows (10 million ringgits per year) is:

10 million ringgits $\times$ 8.754* = 87.54 million ringgits after six years

*Compound sum at 15 percent for six years (Appendix C at end of book).

These 87.54 million ringgits must now be translated into dollars and then discounted back to the present. Since the exchange rate is 2.21 ringgits per dollar in the 6th year (fourth line from the bottom in Table 21–3), the dollar equivalent of 87.54 million ringgits is:

87.54 million ringgits $\div$ 2.21 = $39.61 million

The $39.61 million can now be discounted back to the present, by using the present value factor for six years at 20 percent (Appendix B).

$$
\begin{array}{r}
\$39.61 \text{ million} \\
\underline{0.335 \ IF_{pv}} \\
\$13.27 \text{ million}
\end{array}
$$

The final benefit to be received is the 30 million ringgits when the plant is sold six years from now.[4] We first convert this to dollars and then take the present value.

30 million ringgits $\div$ 2.21 = $13.57 million

The present value of $13.57 million after six years at 20 percent is:

$$
\begin{array}{r}
\$13.57 \text{ million} \\
\underline{0.335 \ IF_{pv}} \\
\$ \ 4.55 \text{ million}
\end{array}
$$

The present value of all cash inflows in dollars is equal to:

Present value of dividends	$15.45 million
Present value of repatriated accumulated depreciation . . .	13.27
Present value of sales price for plant	4.55
Total present value of inflows	$33.27 million

The cost of the project was initially specified as 90 million ringgits, or $45 million. Thus we see the total present value of inflows in dollars is less than the cost, and the project has a negative net present value.

Total present value of inflows	$ 33.27 million
Cost	45.00
Net present value	$ −11.73 million

[4]Capital gains taxes are not a necessary consideration in foreign transactions of this nature.

The project is not acceptable on the basis of net present value criteria. However, before such a recommendation is made to the board of directors, the financial analyst must reconsider the project and assess its strategic importance for the firm. One must debate whether or not the specific foreign project is consistent with the firm's overall long-term goals. If the firm wants to use this foreign project as a base for its future marketing of small computers in this part of the world, then the negative net present value should not be the decisive factor in making the decision. As a next step, you need to consider any special circumstances of a nonroutine nature which may have led the firm to consider this foreign investment. For example, if Tex Systems' domestic market share is eroding, a new market penetration like the one under consideration may be crucial for the firm's future.[5]

The Tax Reform Act of 1986 and Foreign Investment Decisions

Generally, a U.S. multinational firm is allowed to take a tax credit equal to taxes paid in a foreign country (so there is not a double taxation of overall corporate income). Although the application of this principle can be somewhat complicated, the tax credit is only applicable up to comparable tax rates in the United States. For example, if a MNC pays taxes at a rate of 34 percent in Country X and the maximum tax rate in the United States is also 34 percent, then a full credit for foreign tax payments may be available.

If the foreign country's tax rate is less than the 34 percent in the United States, that also would not create a problem. If the foreign tax rate were 20 percent, the firm could get a full credit for taxes paid. But what if the foreign tax rate were 40 or 50 percent? Under this circumstance, part of foreign taxes paid (over 34 percent) may not be used as a tax credit.[6]

Prior to tax reform in 1986, the United States had one of the highest corporate marginal tax rates in the world—at 46 percent. For this reason, the foreign tax credit limitation described above was not much of a problem for U.S. multinational firms. However, now that the maximum tax

---

[5]The impact of the 20 percent rate should also not be overlooked. At discount rates commonly applied to conventional domestic investments (such as 10 percent), the project would be accepted based on net present value analysis.

[6]To a certain extent the firm may be able to average the rates in high and low tax rate countries to maintain its tax credits. Of course, many firms invest predominantly in one country or sector of the world.

Table 21–4
Selected foreign tax
rates

Belgium	a sliding scale from 31% to 43%.
Brazil	35% plus 10% surcharge.
Denmark	50%.
France	45%.
Greece	49% with several exceptions.
Ireland	a sliding scale from 40% to 50%.
Italy	36%.
Japan	31% to 43.3% on retained earnings, 25% to 33.3% on distributed earnings.
Mexico	42%.
Netherlands	42%.
Portugal	a sliding scale, 30% to 40%.
South Korea	20% for small companies and 33% for large companies, if listed on a stock exchange; 20% and 30%, if unlisted.
Spain	35%.
Taiwan	15.25%.
United Kingdom	29% for small companies and 35% for large companies.
West Germany	56% on retained profits, 36% on distributed profits.

rate on corporate income is only 34 percent in the United States, some MNCs must be concerned about full utilization of their credits for foreign tax payments. Note in Table 21–4 that West Germany has one of the highest tax rates in the world. Companies paying taxes in that country may not be able to fully offset those obligations against U.S. taxes.

The U.S. Tax Reform Act of 1986 has put pressure on other countries to lower their marginal tax rates to insure continuation of U.S. investments in those countries and to remain competitive (taxwise) on a worldwide basis. U.S. tax reform has not only influenced this country but the whole world.

Financing International Business Operations

When the parties to an international transaction are well known to each other and the countries involved are politically stable, sales are generally made on credit, as is customary in domestic business operations. If the foreign importer is relatively new or the political environment is volatile, or both, the possibility of nonpayment by the importer is worrisome for the exporter. In order to reduce the risk of nonpayment, an exporter may request that the importer furnish a letter of credit. The importer's bank normally issues the letter of credit, in which the bank promises to subsequently pay out the money for the merchandise. For example, assume that Archer Daniels Midland (ADM) is negotiating with a South Korean trading company to export soybean meal. The two parties reach agreement on price, method of shipment, timing of shipment, destination point, and the like. Once the basic terms of sale have been agreed to, the South Korean trading company (importer) applies for a letter of credit from its commercial bank in Seoul. The Korean bank, if it so desires, issues such a letter of credit, which specifies in detail all the steps that must be completed by the American exporter before payment is made. If ADM complies with all specifications in the letter of credit and submits to the Korean bank the proper documentation to prove that it has done so, the Korean bank guarantees the payment on the due date. On that date, the American firm is paid by the Korean bank, not by the buyer of the goods. Therefore, all the credit risk to the exporter is absorbed by the importer's bank, which is in a good position to evaluate the creditworthiness of the importing firm.

The exporter who requires cash payment or a letter of credit from foreign buyers of marginal credit standing is likely to lose orders to competitors. Instead of risking the loss of business, American firms can find an alternative way to reduce the risk of nonpayment by foreign customers. This alternative method consists of obtaining export credit insurance. The insurance policy provides assurance to the exporter that should the foreign customer default on payment, the insurance company will pay for the shipment. The Foreign Credit Insurance Association (FCIA), a private association of 60 U.S. insurance firms, provides this kind of insurance to exporting firms.

Funding of Transactions

Assistance in the funding of foreign transactions may take many forms.

Export-Import Bank (Eximbank) This agency of the U.S. government facilitates the financing of U.S. exports through its miscellaneous programs. In its direct loan program, the Eximbank lends money to foreign purchasers of U.S. goods, such as aircraft, electrical equipment, heavy machinery, computers, and the like. The Eximbank also purchases eligible medium-term obligations of foreign buyers of U.S. goods at a discount from face value. In this discount program, private banks and other lenders are able to rediscount (sell at a lower price) promissory notes and drafts acquired from foreign customers of U.S. firms.

Loans from the parent company or a sister affiliate An apparent source of funds for a foreign affiliate is its parent company or its sister affiliates. In addition to contributing equity capital, the parent company often provides loans of varying maturities to its foreign affiliate. Although the simplest arrangement is a direct loan from the parent to the foreign subsidiary, such a loan is rarely extended, because of foreign exchange risk, political risk, and tax treatment. Instead, the loans are often channeled through an intermediary to a foreign affiliate. *Parallel loans* and *fronting loans* are two examples of such indirect loan arrangements between a parent company and its foreign affiliate. A typical parallel loan arrangement is depicted in Figure 21–2.

**Figure 21–2
A parallel loan
arrangement**

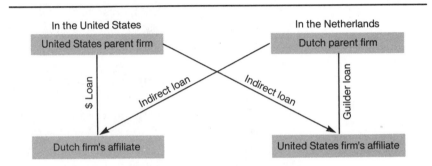

In this illustration, an American firm wanting to lend funds to its Dutch affiliate locates a Dutch parent firm, which wants to transfer funds to its U.S. affiliate. Avoiding the exchange markets entirely, the U.S. parent lends dollars to the Dutch affiliate in the United States, while the Dutch parent lends guilders to the American affiliate in the Netherlands. At maturity, the two loans would each be repaid to the original lender. Notice that neither loan carries any foreign exchange risk in this arrangement. In essence, both parent firms are providing indirect loans to their affiliates.

A fronting loan is simply a parent's loan to its foreign subsidiary channeled through a financial intermediary, usually a large international bank. A schematic of a fronting loan is shown in Figure 21–3.

**Figure 21–3
A fronting loan
arrangement**

In the example, the U.S. parent company deposits funds in an Amsterdam bank and that bank, in turn, lends the same amount to the U.S. firm's affiliate in the Netherlands. In this manner, the bank fronts for the parent by extending a risk-free (fully collateralized) loan to the foreign affiliate. In the event of political turmoil, the foreign government is more likely to allow the American subsidiary to repay the loan to a large international bank than to allow the same affiliate to repay the loan to its parent company. Thus, the parent company reduces its political risk substantially by using a fronting loan instead of transferring funds directly to its foreign affiliate.

Even though the parent company would prefer that its foreign subsidiary maintain its own financial arrangements, many banks are apprehensive about lending to a foreign affiliate without a parent guarantee. In fact, a large portion of bank lending to foreign affiliates is based on some sort of a guarantee by the parent firm. Usually, because of its multinational reputation, the parent company has a better credit rating than its foreign affiliates. The lender advances funds on the basis of the parent's creditworthiness even though the affiliate is expected to pay back the loan. The terms of a parent guarantee may vary greatly, depending upon the closeness of the parent-affiliate ties, parent-lender relations, and the home country's legal jurisdiction.

Eurodollar loans The Eurodollar market is an important source of short-term loans for many multinational firms and their foreign affiliates.

Eurodollars are simply U.S. dollars deposited in European banks. A substantial portion of these deposits is held by European branches of U.S. commercial banks. About 85–90 percent of these deposits are in the form of term deposits with the banks for a specific maturity and at a fixed-interest rate. The remaining 10–15 percent of these deposits represent negotiable certificates of deposit with maturities varying from one week to five years or longer. However, maturities of three months, six months, and one year are most common in this market.

Since the early 1960s, the Eurodollar market has established itself as a significant part of world credit markets. The participants in these markets are diverse in character and are geographically widespread. Hundreds of corporations and banks, mostly from the United States, Canada, Western Europe, and Japan, are regular borrowers and depositors in this market.

U.S. firms have more than doubled their borrowings in the Eurodollar market during the 1980s. The lower costs and greater credit availability of the Eurodollar market continue to attract borrowers. The lower borrowing costs in the Eurodollar market are often attributed to the smaller overhead costs for lending banks and the absence of a compensating balance requirement. The lending rate for borrowers in the Eurodollar market is based on the London Interbank Offered Rate (LIBOR), which is the interest rate for large deposits. Interest rates on loans are calculated by adding premiums to this basic rate. The size of this premium varies from 0.25 percent to 0.50 percent, depending on the customer, length of the loan period, size of the loan, and so on. For example, Northern Indiana Public Service Company obtained a $75 million, three-year loan from Merrill Lynch International Bank. The utility company offered to pay 0.375 points above LIBOR for the first two years and 0.50 points above for the final year of the loan. Over the years, borrowing in the Eurodollar market has been one eighth to seven eighths of a percentage point cheaper than borrowing at the U.S. prime interest rate. During a recent peak interest rate period in the United States, many cost-conscious domestic borrowers fled to the Eurodollar market. Having seen this trend, some U.S. banks began offering their customers the option of taking a LIBOR-based rate in lieu of the prime rate in order to stay competitive.

Lending in the Eurodollar market is almost exclusively done by commercial banks. Large Eurocurrency loans are often syndicated by a group of participating banks. The loan agreement is put together by a lead bank known as the manager, which is usually one of the largest U.S. or European banks. The manager charges the borrower a once-and-for-all fee or commission of 0.25 percent to 1 percent of the loan value. A portion of this fee is kept by the lead bank and the remainder is shared by all the participating banks. The aim of forming a syndicate, of course, is to diversify the risk, which would be too large for any single bank to handle by itself. Multicurrency loans and revolving credit arrangements can also be negotiated in the Eurocurrency market to suit borrowers' needs.

Eurobond market When long-term funds are needed, borrowing in the Eurobond market is a viable alternative for leading multinational corporations. The Eurobond issues are sold simultaneously in several different national capital markets, but denominated in a currency different from that of the nation in which the bonds are issued. The most widely used currency in the Eurobond market is the U.S. dollar with almost 67 percent of all the issues denominated in that currency. The next currency in importance is the deutsche mark. Eurobond issues are underwritten by an international syndicate of banks and securities firms. Eurobonds of longer than seven years in maturity generally have a sinking-fund provision.

Disclosure requirements in the Eurobond market are much less stringent than those required by the Securities and Exchange Commission (SEC) in the United States. Furthermore, the registration costs in the Eurobond market are lower than those charged in the United States. In addition, the Eurobond market offers tax flexibility for borrowers and investors alike. Since most Eurobonds are issued by a fully owned offshore finance subsidiary that is located in a tax-haven country, such as Luxembourg, there are no withholding taxes on interest paid. Wealthy investors often buy Eurobonds through Swiss bank accounts so their interest income can be kept anonymous. All these advantages of Eurobonds enable the borrowers to raise funds at a lower cost. Nevertheless, a caveat may be in order with respect to the effective cost of borrowing in the Eurobond market. When a multinational firm borrows by floating a foreign currency denominated debt issue on a long-term basis, it creates transaction exposure, a kind of foreign exchange risk. If the foreign currency appreciates in value during the bond's life, the cost of servicing the debt could be prohibitively high. Many U.S. multinational firms borrowed at an approximately 7 percent coupon interest by selling Eurobonds denominated in deutsche marks and Swiss francs in the late 1960s and early 1970s. Nevertheless, these U.S. firms experienced an average debt service cost of approximately 13 percent, which is almost twice as much as the coupon rate. This increased cost occurred because the U.S. dollar fell with respect to these currencies. Therefore, currency selection for denominating Eurobond issues must be made with extreme care and foresight. To lessen the impact of foreign exchange risk, some recently issued Eurobond issues were denominated in multicurrency units.

International equity markets   The entire amount of equity capital comes from the parent company for a *wholly owned* foreign subsidiary, but a majority of foreign affiliates are not owned completely by their parent corporations. In fact, in countries like India and Malaysia, majority ownership of a foreign affiliate must be held by the local citizens. In some other countries, the parent corporations are allowed to own their affiliates completely in the initial stages, but they are required to relinquish partial ownership to local citizens after five or seven years. In order to avoid nationalistic reactions to wholly owned foreign subsidiaries, such multinational firms as Unilever Ltd., Schlumberger, General Motors, Ford Motor Company, and IBM sell shares to worldwide stockholders. It is also believed that widespread foreign ownership of the firm's common stock encourages the loyalty of foreign stockholders and employees toward the firm. Thus, selling common stock to residents of foreign countries is not only an important financing strategy, but it is also a risk-minimizing strategy for many multinational corporations.

As you have learned in Chapter 14, a well-functioning secondary market is essential to entice investors into owning shares. To attract investors from all over the world, reputable multinational firms list their shares on major stock exchanges around the world. For instance, about 40 foreign companies are listed on the New York Stock Exchange, and the American Stock Exchange lists more than 70 foreign firms. Several hundred foreign issues are traded in the over-the-counter market. Even more foreign firms would sell stock issues in the United States and list on NYSE and AMEX were it not for the tough and costly disclosure rules in effect in this country and enforced by the Securities and Exchange Commission. Many foreign corporations, such as Hoechst, Honda, Hitachi, Sony, Magnet Metals Ltd., DeBeers, and the like, accommodate American investors by issuing American Depository Receipts (ADRs). All the American-owned shares of a foreign company are placed in trust in a New York bank. The bank, in turn, will issue its depository receipts to the American stock-holders and will maintain a stockholder ledger on these receipts, thus enabling the holders of ADRs to sell or otherwise transfer them as easily as they transfer any American company shares. Most ADRs trade in the over-the-counter market, although a few are listed on the New York Stock Exchange. ADR prices tend to move parallel with the prices of the under-lying securities in their home markets.

Looking elsewhere around the world, approximately 70 U.S. firms have listed their shares on the Toronto Stock Exchange and some 50 on the Montreal Exchange. Similarly, more than 100 U.S. firms have listed their shares on the London Stock Exchange. Approximately 160 foreign issues are listed on the Bourse de Paris, including 37 U.S. stocks. In addition, a number of foreign securities are traded on the French hors cote (OTC) market. Fully half the stocks listed on the Amsterdam stock exchange are foreign. To obtain exposure in an international financial community, listing securities on world stock exchanges is a step in the right direction for a multinational firm. This international exposure also brings an ad-ditional responsibility for the MNC to understand the preferences and needs of heterogeneous groups of investors of various nationalities. The MNC may have to print and circulate its annual financial statements in many languages. Some foreign investors are more risk averse than their counterparts in the United States, and prefer dividend income over less-certain capital gains. Common stock ownership among individuals in countries like Japan and Norway is relatively insignificant, with financial institutions holding substantial amounts of common stock issues. Insti-tutional practices around the globe also vary significantly when it comes to issuing new securities. Unlike the United States, European commercial banks play a dominant role in the securities business. They underwrite stock issues, manage portfolios, vote the stock they hold in trust accounts, and hold directorships on company boards. In Germany, the banks also run an over-the-counter market in many stocks.

As previously indicated in Chapter 14, one of the major events of the last decade has been the emergence of the Japanese equity markets. By 1987, the total value of all stocks traded in Japan exceeded that of the United States. Furthermore, Japan's share of the value of total world stock markets grew from 13.5 percent in 1977 to 36.3 percent in 1987. Over a comparable time period, the U.S. share declined from 60.8 percent to 36.1 percent. Since 1969, the average Japanese share of stock has increased by over 1,200 percent, far outstripping the 200 percent gain in the United States.

Japanese stocks typically trade at price–earnings ratios of 60–70, a value four or five times greater than that in the United States. Part of this can be attributed to accounting convention differences between the two countries; but most of the discrepancy is simply a result of a very long-term bull market (which, of course, means there is always tremendous downside potential). To give you an idea of the worth of Japanese securities, Nippon Telephone & Telegraph Company is valued at more than the entire West German stock market.

The International Finance Corporation Whenever a multinational company has difficulty raising equity capital due to lack of adequate private risk capital in a foreign country, the firm may explore the possibility of selling partial ownership to the International Finance Corporation (IFC). This is a unit of the World Bank Group. The International Finance Corporation was established in 1956 and it is owned by 119 member countries of the World Bank. Its objective is to further economic development by promoting private enterprises in these countries. The profitability of a project and its potential benefit to the host country's economy are the two criteria the IFC uses to decide whether or not to assist a venture. The IFC participates in private enterprise through buying equity shares of a business, providing long-term loans, or a combination of the two for up to 25 percent of the total capital. The IFC expects the other partners to assume managerial responsibility, and it does not exercise its voting rights as a stockholder. The IFC helps finance new ventures as well as the expansion of existing ones in a variety of industries. Once the venture is well established, the IFC sells its investment position to private investors in order to free up its capital.

Some Unsettled Issues in International Finance

As firms become multinational in scope, the nature of their financial decisions also becomes more complex. A multinational firm has access to more sources of funds than a purely domestic corporation. Interest rates and market conditions vary between the alternate sources of funds, and corporate financial practices may differ significantly between countries. For example, the debt ratios in many foreign countries are higher than those used by U.S. firms. A foreign affiliate of an American firm faces a dilemma in its financing decision: Should it follow the parent firm's norm or that of the host country? Who must decide this? Will it be decided at the corporate headquarters in the United States or by the foreign affiliate? This is a matter of control over financial decisions. Dividend policy is another area of debate. Should the parent company dictate the dividends the foreign affiliate must distribute or should it be left completely to the discretion of the foreign affiliate? Foreign government regulations may also influence the decision. Questions like these do not have clear-cut answers. The complex environment in which the MNCs operate does not permit simple and clear-cut solutions. Obviously, each situation has to be evaluated individually, and specific guidelines for decision making must be established. Such coordination, it is to be hoped, will result in cohesive policies in the areas of working capital management, capital structure, and dividend decisions throughout the MNC network.

Summary

When a domestic business firm crosses its national borders to do business in other countries, it enters a riskier and more complex environment. A multinational firm is exposed to foreign exchange risk and political risk in addition to the usual business and financial risks. In general, international business operations have been more profitable than domestic operations, and this higher profitability is one factor that motivates business firms to go overseas. International operations account for a significant proportion of the earnings for many American firms. U.S. multinational firms have played a major role in promoting economic development and international trade for several decades, and now foreign firms have started to invest huge amounts of capital in the United States.

International business transactions are denominated in foreign currencies. The rate at which one currency unit is converted into another is called the exchange rate. In today's global monetary system, the exchange rates of major currencies are fluctuating rather freely. These "freely" floating exchange rates expose multinational business firms to foreign exchange risk. To deal with this foreign currency exposure effectively, the financial executive of an MNC must understand foreign exchange rates and how they are determined. Foreign exchange rates are influenced by differences in inflation rates among countries, by differences in interest rates, by governmental policies, and by the expectations of the participants in the foreign exchange markets. The international financial manager can reduce the firm's foreign currency exposure by hedging in the forward exchange market, in the money markets, and in the currency futures market.

Multinational companies have made billions of dollars worth of direct investments in foreign countries over the years. Lower production costs overseas, tax deferral provisions, less foreign competition, and benefits of international diversification are some of the motivational factors behind the flow of direct investment between nations. Foreign direct investments are usually quite large in size and many of them are exposed to enormous political risk. Although discounted cash-flow analysis is applied to screen the projects in the initial stages, strategic considerations and political risk are often the overriding factors in reaching the final decision. One of the most important differences between domestic and international investments is that the information on foreign investments is generally less complete and often less accurate. Therefore, analyzing a foreign investment proposal is more difficult than analyzing a domestic investment project.

Financing international trade and investment is another important area of international finance that one must understand in order to raise funds at the lowest cost possible. The multinational firm has access to both the domestic and foreign capital markets. The Export-Import Bank finances American exports to foreign countries. Borrowing in the Eurobond market may appear less expensive at times, but the effect of foreign exchange risk on debt-servicing cost must be weighed carefully before borrowing in these markets. Floating common stock in foreign capital markets is also a viable financing alternative for many multinational companies. The International Finance Corporation, which is a subsidiary of the World Bank, also provides debt capital and equity capital to qualified firms. These alternative sources of financing may significantly differ with respect to cost, terms, and conditions. Therefore, the financial executive must carefully locate and use the proper means to finance international business operations.

List of Terms

multinational corporation	fronting loan
balance of payments	letter of credit
expropriation	Export-Import Bank (Eximbank)
foreign exchange rate	International Finance Corporation
foreign exchange risk	(IFC)
Foreign Credit Insurance	London Interbank Offered Rate
Association (FCIA)	(LIBOR)
purchasing power parity theory	Overseas Private Investment
interest rate parity theory	Corporation (OPIC)
currency futures contract	American Depository Receipts
transaction exposure	(ADRs)
translation exposure	Eurodollars
repatriation of earnings	Eurobonds
parallel loan	

Discussion Questions

1. What risks does a foreign affiliate of a multinational firm face in today's business world?

2. What are some allegations that are sometimes made against foreign affiliates of multinational firms and against the multinational firms themselves?

3. List the factors that affect the value of a currency in foreign exchange markets.

4. Explain how exports and imports tend to influence the value of a currency.

5. Differentiate between the spot exchange rate and the forward exchange rate.

6. What is meant by translation exposure in terms of foreign exchange risk?

7. What factors influence a U.S. business firm to go overseas?

8. What procedure(s) would you recommend for a multinational company in studying exposure to political risk? What actual strategies can be used to guard against such risk?

9. What factors beyond the normal domestic analysis go into a financial feasibility study for a multinational firm?

10. What is a letter of credit?

11. Explain the functions of the following agencies:
    Overseas Private Investment Corporation (OPIC).
    Export-Import Bank (Eximbank).
    Foreign Credit Insurance Association (FCIA).
    International Finance Corporation (IFC).

12. What are the differences between a parallel loan and a fronting loan?

13. What is LIBOR? How does it compare to the U.S. prime rate?

14. What is the danger or concern in floating a Eurobond issue?

15. What are ADRs?

16. Comment on any dilemmas that multinational firms and their foreign affiliates may face in regard to debt ratio limits and dividend payouts.

Problems

1. Using the foreign exchange rates for August 1, 1987, in Table 21–2, determine the number of U.S. dollars required to buy the following amounts of foreign currencies:
   a. 5,000 guilders.
   b. 2,000 rands.
   c. 10,000 deutsche marks.
   d. 100,000 yens.
   e. 30,000 kronas.

2. Obtain a recent copy of *The Wall Street Journal* and recalculate the currency exchanges of problem 1. How do these figures compare to those obtained in the above problem? Has the dollar strengthened or weakened against these currencies?

3. *The Wall Street Journal* reported the following spot and forward rates for the Swiss franc ($/SF) as of August 1, 1987:

Spot	$0.6502
30-day forward	$0.6519
90-day forward	$0.6558
180-day forward	$0.6610

    a. Was the Swiss franc selling at a discount or premium in the forward market on August 1, 1987?

    b. What was the 30-day forward premium (or discount)?

    c. What was the 90-day forward premium (or discount)?

    d. Suppose you executed a 90-day forward contract to exchange 100,000 Swiss francs into U.S. dollars. How many dollars would you get 90 days hence?

    e. Assume a Swiss bank entered into a 180-day forward contract with Citicorp to buy $100,000. How many francs will the Swiss bank deliver in six months to get the U.S. dollars?

4. Suppose an Austrian schilling is selling for $0.0766 and an Irish punt is selling for $1.4433. What is the exchange rate (cross rate) of the Austrian schilling to the Irish punt? That is, how many Austrian schillings are equal to an Irish punt?

5. Suppose a French franc is selling for $0.1620 and a Maltan lira is selling for $2.8329. What is the exchange rate (cross rate) of the French franc to the Maltan lira? That is, how many French francs are equal to a Maltan lira?

6. From the base price level of 100 in 1962, German and U.S. price levels in 1988 stood at 190 and 350, respectively. If the 1962 $/DM exchange rate was $0.30/DM, what should the exchange rate be in 1988? Suggestion: using the purchasing power parity theory, adjust the exchange rate to compensate for inflation. That is, determine the relative rate of inflation between the United States and Germany and multiply this times $/DM of 0.30.

7. In problem 6, if the United States had somehow managed no inflation since 1962, what should the exchange rate be in 1988, using the purchasing power parity theory?

8. An investor in the United States bought a one-year New Zealand security valued at 175,000 New Zealand dollars. The U.S. dollar equivalent was $100,000. The New Zealand security earned 12 percent during the year, but the New Zealand dollar depreciated five cents against the U.S. dollar during the time period ($0.57/NZD to $0.52/NZD). After transferring the funds back to the United States, what was the investor's return on her $100,000? Determine the total ending value of the New Zealand investment in New Zealand dollars and then translate this value to U.S. dollars. Then compute the return on the $100,000.

9. A French investor buys 100 shares of General Motors for $8,000 ($80 per share). Over the course of a year, GM goes up by 12 points.

   a. If there is a 10 percent gain in the value of the dollar versus the French franc, what will be the total percentage return to the French investor? First determine the new dollar value of the investment and multiply this figure by 1.10. Divide this answer by $8,000 and get a percentage value, and then subtract 100 percent to get the percentage return.

   b. Now assume that the stock increases by 15 points, but that the dollar decreases by 10 percent versus the French franc. What will be the total percentage return to the French investor? Use 0.90 in place of 1.10 in this case.

10. You are the vice president of finance for International Resources, Inc., headquartered in Denver, Colorado. In January 1988, your firm's Canadian subsidiary obtained a six-month loan of 100,000 Canadian dollars from a bank in Denver to finance the acquisition of a titanium mine in Quebec Province. The loan will also be repaid in Canadian dollars. At the time of the loan, the spot exchange rate was U.S. $0.7526/Canadian dollar and the Canadian currency was selling at a discount in the forward market. The June 1988 futures contract (face value = $100,000 per contract) was quoted at U.S. $0.7501.

    a. Explain how the Denver bank could lose on this transaction if it does not hedge.

    b. If the bank does hedge, what is the maximum amount it can lose?

11. Campbell Electronics Corporation has a wholly owned foreign subsidiary in Jamaica. The subsidiary earns $5 million per year before taxes in Jamaica. The foreign income tax rate is 20 percent. Campbell's subsidiary repatriates the entire aftertax profit in the form of dividends to the parent corporation. The U.S. corporate tax rate is 34 percent of foreign earnings before taxes.

    a. Complete the table below.

Before-tax earnings	$5,000,000
Foreign income tax @ 20%	− _____
Earnings after foreign income taxes	_____
Dividends repatriated	_____
Gross U.S. taxes @ 34% of foreign earnings before taxes	_____
Foreign tax credit (see line 2 above)	− _____
Net U.S. taxes payable	_____
Aftertax cash flow	_____

b. Now assume that there is a 10 percent withholding tax on dividends in Jamaica. Recompute the answer to part *a* by completing the following table.

Before-tax earnings	$5,000,000
Foreign income tax @ 20%	−_____
Earnings after foreign income taxes	_____
Gross dividends distributed	_____
Withholding tax @ 10% of dividends	−_____
Net dividends repatriated	_____
Gross U.S. taxes at 34% of foreign earnings before taxes	_____
Foreign tax credit (Foreign income tax + Withholding tax)	−_____
Net U.S. taxes payable	_____
Aftertax cash flow	_____

12. The Office Automation Corporation is considering a foreign investment. The initial cash outlay will be $10 million. The current foreign exchange rate is 2 francs = $1. Thus, the investment in foreign currency will be 20 million francs. The assets have a useful life of five years and no expected salvage value. The firm uses a straight-line method of depreciation. Sales are expected to be 20 million francs and operating cash expenses 10 million francs every year for five years. The foreign income tax rate is 25 percent. The foreign subsidiary will repatriate all aftertax profits to Office Automation in the form of dividends. Furthermore, the depreciation cash flows (equal to each year's depreciation) will be repatriated during the same year they accrue to the foreign subsidiary. The applicable cost of capital that reflects the riskiness of the cash flows is 16 percent. The U.S. tax rate is 40 percent of foreign earnings before taxes.

a. Should the Office Automation Corporation undertake the investment, if the foreign exchange rate is expected to remain constant during the five-year period?

b. Should Office Automation undertake the investment if the foreign exchange rate is expected to be as follows:

Year 0	$1 = 2.0 francs
Year 1	$1 = 2.2 francs
Year 2	$1 = 2.4 francs
Year 3	$1 = 2.7 francs
Year 4	$1 = 2.9 francs
Year 5	$1 = 3.2 francs

Selected References

Aggarwal, Raj. "International Differences in Capital Structure Norms." *Management International Review* 21, no. 1 (1981), pp. 75–88.

Alsop, Ronald. "Foreign Ventures." *The Wall Street Journal,* March 30, 1981, p. 1.

Anvari, M. "Efficient Scheduling of Cross-Border Cash Transfers." *Financial Management* 15 (Summer 1986), pp. 40–49.

Eiteman, David, and Arthur Stonehill. *Multinational Business Finance.* 3rd. ed. Reading, Mass.: Addison-Wesley, 1982.

Errunza, Vihard. "Determinants of Financial Structure in the Central American Common Markets." *Financial Management* 8 (Autumn 1979), pp. 72–77.

Flood, Eugene, Jr., and Donald R. Lessard. "On the Measurement of Operating Exposure to Exchange Rates: A Conceptual Approach." *Financial Management* 15 (Spring 1986), pp. 25–36.

Folks, William R., Jr. "Decision Analysis for Exchange Risk Management." *Financial Management* 1 (Winter 1972), pp. 101–12.

Gentry, James A; D. R. Metha; S. K. Bhattacharya; R. Cobbaut; and J. Scaringella. "An International Study of Management Perceptions of the Working Capital Process." *Journal of International Business Studies* 6 (Spring–Summer, 1979), pp. 28–38.

Hodder, James E. "Evaluation of Manufacturing Investments: A Comparison of U. S. and Japanese Practices." *Financial Management* 15 (Spring 1986), pp. 17–24.

Kester, W. Carl. "Capital and Ownership Structure: A Comparison of United States and Japanese Manufacturing Corporations." *Financial Management* 15 (Spring 1986), pp. 5–16.

Koveos, Peter, and Bruce Seifert. "Purchasing Power Parity and Black Markets." *Financial Management* 14 (Autumn 1985), pp. 40–46.

Lessard, Donald R. "World, National, and Industrial Factors in Equity Returns." *Journal of Finance* 29 (May 1974), pp. 379–91.

Misawa, Mitsura. "Financing Japanese Investments in the United States: Case Studies of a Large and Medium-sized Firm." *Financial Management* 14 (Winter 1985), pp. 5–12.

Naidu, G. N. "How to Reduce Transaction Exposure in International Lending." *Journal of Commercial Bank Lending* 63 (June 1981), pp. 39–46.

————, **and Tai Shin.** "Effectiveness of Currency Futures Market in Hedging Foreign Exchange Risk." *Management International Review* 21, no. 4 (1981), pp. 5–16.

Ricks, David A., and R. A. Ajami. "Motives of non-American Firms in Investing in the United States." *Journal of International Business* 12 (Summer–Spring 1977), pp. 24–32.

Remmers, L.; A. Stonehill; R. Wright; and T. Beekhuisen. "Industry and Size as Debt Ratio Determinants in Manufacturing Internationally." *Financial Management* 3 (Summer 1974), pp. 24–32.

Rummel, R. J., and David A. Heenan. "How Multinationals Analyze Political Risk." *Harvard Business Review* 56 (January–February 1978), pp. 67–76.

Shapiro, Alan C.   *Multinational Financial Management*. Boston: Allyn & Bacon, 1982.

Solnik, Bruno H.   "Why Not Diversify Internationally Rather than Domestically?" *Financial Analysts Journal* 30 (July–August 1974), pp. 48–54.

Stanley, Marlorie T.   "Capital Structure and Costs of Capital for the Multinational Firm." *Journal of International Business Studies* 12 (Spring–Summer 1981), pp. 103–20.

Appendixes

A Compound Sum of $1, IF_s

B Present Value of $1, IF_{pv}

C Compound Sum of an Annuity of $1, IF_{sa}

D Present Value of an Annuity of $1, IF_{pva}

E Using Calculators for Financial Analysis

Appendix A Compound sum of $1, IF_s $S = P(1+i)^n$

Percent

Period	1%	2%	3%	4%	5%	6%	7%	8%	9%	10%	11%
1	1.010	1.020	1.030	1.040	1.050	1.060	1.070	1.080	1.090	1.100	1.110
2	1.020	1.040	1.061	1.082	1.103	1.124	1.145	1.166	1.188	1.210	1.232
3	1.030	1.061	1.093	1.125	1.158	1.191	1.225	1.260	1.295	1.331	1.368
4	1.041	1.082	1.126	1.170	1.216	1.262	1.311	1.360	1.412	1.464	1.518
5	1.051	1.104	1.159	1.217	1.276	1.338	1.403	1.469	1.539	1.611	1.685
6	1.062	1.126	1.194	1.265	1.340	1.419	1.501	1.587	1.677	1.772	1.870
7	1.072	1.149	1.230	1.316	1.407	1.504	1.606	1.714	1.828	1.949	2.076
8	1.083	1.172	1.267	1.369	1.477	1.594	1.718	1.851	1.993	2.144	2.305
9	1.094	1.195	1.305	1.423	1.551	1.689	1.838	1.999	2.172	2.358	2.558
10	1.105	1.219	1.344	1.480	1.629	1.791	1.967	2.159	2.367	2.594	2.839
11	1.116	1.243	1.384	1.539	1.710	1.898	2.105	2.332	2.580	2.853	3.152
12	1.127	1.268	1.426	1.601	1.796	2.012	2.252	2.518	2.813	3.138	3.498
13	1.138	1.294	1.469	1.665	1.886	2.133	2.410	2.720	3.066	3.452	3.883
14	1.149	1.319	1.513	1.732	1.980	2.261	2.579	2.937	3.342	3.797	4.310
15	1.161	1.346	1.558	1.801	2.079	2.397	2.759	3.172	3.642	4.177	4.785
16	1.173	1.373	1.605	1.873	2.183	2.540	2.952	3.426	3.970	4.595	5.311
17	1.184	1.400	1.653	1.948	2.292	2.693	3.159	3.700	4.328	5.054	5.895
18	1.196	1.428	1.702	2.026	2.407	2.854	3.380	3.996	4.717	5.560	6.544
19	1.208	1.457	1.754	2.107	2.527	3.026	3.617	4.316	5.142	6.116	7.263
20	1.220	1.486	1.806	2.191	2.653	3.207	3.870	4.661	5.604	6.727	8.062
25	1.282	1.641	2.094	2.666	3.386	4.292	5.427	6.848	8.623	10.835	13.585
30	1.348	1.811	2.427	3.243	4.322	5.743	7.612	10.063	13.268	17.449	22.892
40	1.489	2.208	3.262	4.801	7.040	10.286	14.974	21.725	31.409	45.259	65.001
50	1.645	2.692	4.384	7.107	11.467	18.420	29.457	46.902	74.358	117.39	184.57

Appendix A (concluded)   Compound sum of $1

Percent

Period	12%	13%	14%	15%	16%	17%	18%	19%	20%	25%	30%
1	1.120	1.130	1.140	1.150	1.160	1.170	1.180	1.190	1.200	1.250	1.300
2	1.254	1.277	1.300	1.323	1.346	1.369	1.392	1.416	1.440	1.563	1.690
3	1.405	1.443	1.482	1.521	1.561	1.602	1.643	1.685	1.728	1.953	2.197
4	1.574	1.630	1.689	1.749	1.811	1.874	1.939	2.005	2.074	2.441	2.856
5	1.762	1.842	1.925	2.011	2.100	2.192	2.288	2.386	2.488	3.052	3.713
6	1.974	2.082	2.195	2.313	2.436	2.565	2.700	2.840	2.986	3.815	4.827
7	2.211	2.353	2.502	2.660	2.826	3.001	3.185	3.379	3.583	4.768	6.276
8	2.476	2.658	2.853	3.059	3.278	3.511	3.759	4.021	4.300	5.960	8.157
9	2.773	3.004	3.252	3.518	3.803	4.108	4.435	4.785	5.160	7.451	10.604
10	3.106	3.395	3.707	4.046	4.411	4.807	5.234	5.696	6.192	9.313	13.786
11	3.479	3.836	4.226	4.652	5.117	5.624	6.176	6.777	7.430	11.642	17.922
12	3.896	4.335	4.818	5.350	5.936	6.580	7.288	8.064	8.916	14.552	23.298
13	4.363	4.898	5.492	6.153	6.886	7.699	8.599	9.596	10.699	18.190	30.288
14	4.887	5.535	6.261	7.076	7.988	9.007	10.147	11.420	12.839	22.737	39.374
15	5.474	6.254	7.138	8.137	9.266	10.539	11.974	13.590	15.407	28.422	51.186
16	6.130	7.067	8.137	9.358	10.748	12.330	14.129	16.172	18.488	35.527	66.542
17	6.866	7.986	9.276	10.761	12.468	14.426	16.672	19.244	22.186	44.409	86.504
18	7.690	9.024	10.575	12.375	14.463	16.879	19.673	22.091	26.623	55.511	112.46
19	8.613	10.197	12.056	14.232	16.777	19.748	23.214	27.252	31.948	69.389	146.19
20	9.646	11.523	13.743	16.367	19.461	23.106	27.393	32.429	38.338	86.736	190.05
25	17.000	21.231	26.462	32.919	40.874	50.658	62.669	77.388	95.396	264.70	705.64
30	29.960	39.116	50.950	66.212	85.850	111.07	143.37	184.68	237.38	807.79	2,620.0
40	93.051	132.78	188.88	267.86	378.72	533.87	750.38	1,051.7	1,469.8	7,523.2	36,119.
50	289.00	450.74	700.23	1,083.7	1,670.7	2,566.2	3,927.4	5,988.9	9,100.4	70,065.	497,929.

Source: Maurice Joy, *Introduction to Financial Management* (Homewood, Ill.: Richard D. Irwin, 1977).

673

Appendix B   Present value of $1, IF_{pv} $P = S \left[\dfrac{1}{(1 + i)^n} \right]$

Percent

Period	1%	2%	3%	4%	5%	6%	7%	8%	9%	10%	11%	12%
1	0.990	0.980	0.971	0.962	0.952	0.943	0.935	0.926	0.917	0.909	0.901	0.893
2	0.980	0.961	0.943	0.925	0.907	0.890	0.873	0.857	0.842	0.826	0.812	0.797
3	0.971	0.942	0.915	0.889	0.864	0.840	0.816	0.794	0.772	0.751	0.731	0.712
4	0.961	0.924	0.885	0.855	0.823	0.792	0.763	0.735	0.708	0.683	0.659	0.636
5	0.951	0.906	0.863	0.822	0.784	0.747	0.713	0.681	0.650	0.621	0.593	0.567
6	0.942	0.888	0.837	0.790	0.746	0.705	0.666	0.630	0.596	0.564	0.535	0.507
7	0.933	0.871	0.813	0.760	0.711	0.665	0.623	0.583	0.547	0.513	0.482	0.452
8	0.923	0.853	0.789	0.731	0.677	0.627	0.582	0.540	0.502	0.467	0.434	0.404
9	0.914	0.837	0.766	0.703	0.645	0.592	0.544	0.500	0.460	0.424	0.391	0.361
10	0.905	0.820	0.744	0.676	0.614	0.558	0.508	0.463	0.422	0.386	0.352	0.322
11	0.896	0.804	0.722	0.650	0.585	0.527	0.475	0.429	0.388	0.350	0.317	0.287
12	0.887	0.788	0.701	0.625	0.557	0.497	0.444	0.397	0.356	0.319	0.286	0.257
13	0.879	0.773	0.681	0.601	0.530	0.469	0.415	0.368	0.326	0.290	0.258	0.229
14	0.870	0.758	0.661	0.577	0.505	0.442	0.388	0.340	0.299	0.263	0.232	0.205
15	0.861	0.743	0.642	0.555	0.481	0.417	0.362	0.315	0.275	0.239	0.209	0.183
16	0.853	0.728	0.623	0.534	0.458	0.394	0.339	0.292	0.252	0.218	0.188	0.163
17	0.844	0.714	0.605	0.513	0.436	0.371	0.317	0.270	0.231	0.198	0.170	0.146
18	0.836	0.700	0.587	0.494	0.416	0.350	0.296	0.250	0.212	0.180	0.153	0.130
19	0.828	0.686	0.570	0.475	0.396	0.331	0.277	0.232	0.194	0.164	0.138	0.116
20	0.820	0.673	0.554	0.456	0.377	0.312	0.258	0.215	0.178	0.149	0.124	0.104
25	0.780	0.610	0.478	0.375	0.295	0.233	0.184	0.146	0.116	0.092	0.074	0.059
30	0.742	0.552	0.412	0.308	0.231	0.174	0.131	0.099	0.075	0.057	0.044	0.033
40	0.672	0.453	0.307	0.208	0.142	0.097	0.067	0.046	0.032	0.022	0.015	0.011
50	0.608	0.372	0.228	0.141	0.087	0.054	0.034	0.021	0.013	0.009	0.005	0.003

Appendix B (concluded) Present value of $1

Percent

Period	13%	14%	15%	16%	17%	18%	19%	20%	25%	30%	35%	40%	50%
1	0.885	0.877	0.870	0.862	0.855	0.847	0.840	0.833	0.800	0.769	0.741	0.714	0.667
2	0.783	0.769	0.756	0.743	0.731	0.718	0.706	0.694	0.640	0.592	0.549	0.510	0.444
3	0.693	0.675	0.658	0.641	0.624	0.609	0.593	0.579	0.512	0.455	0.406	0.364	0.296
4	0.613	0.592	0.572	0.552	0.534	0.515	0.499	0.482	0.410	0.350	0.301	0.260	0.198
5	0.543	0.519	0.497	0.476	0.456	0.437	0.419	0.402	0.320	0.269	0.223	0.186	0.132
6	0.480	0.456	0.432	0.410	0.390	0.370	0.352	0.335	0.262	0.207	0.165	0.133	0.088
7	0.425	0.400	0.376	0.354	0.333	0.314	0.296	0.279	0.210	0.159	0.122	0.095	0.059
8	0.376	0.351	0.327	0.305	0.285	0.266	0.249	0.233	0.168	0.123	0.091	0.068	0.039
9	0.333	0.300	0.284	0.263	0.243	0.225	0.209	0.194	0.134	0.094	0.067	0.048	0.026
10	0.295	0.270	0.247	0.227	0.208	0.191	0.176	0.162	0.107	0.073	0.050	0.035	0.017
11	0.261	0.237	0.215	0.195	0.178	0.162	0.148	0.135	0.086	0.056	0.037	0.025	0.012
12	0.231	0.208	0.187	0.168	0.152	0.137	0.124	0.112	0.069	0.043	0.027	0.018	0.008
13	0.204	0.182	0.163	0.145	0.130	0.116	0.104	0.093	0.055	0.033	0.020	0.013	0.005
14	0.181	0.160	0.141	0.125	0.111	0.099	0.088	0.078	0.044	0.025	0.015	0.009	0.003
15	0.160	0.140	0.123	0.108	0.095	0.084	0.074	0.065	0.035	0.020	0.011	0.006	0.002
16	0.141	0.123	0.107	0.093	0.081	0.071	0.062	0.054	0.028	0.015	0.008	0.005	0.002
17	0.125	0.108	0.093	0.080	0.069	0.060	0.052	0.045	0.023	0.012	0.006	0.003	0.001
18	0.111	0.095	0.081	0.069	0.059	0.051	0.044	0.038	0.018	0.009	0.005	0.002	0.001
19	0.098	0.083	0.070	0.060	0.051	0.043	0.037	0.031	0.014	0.007	0.003	0.002	0
20	0.087	0.073	0.061	0.051	0.043	0.037	0.031	0.026	0.012	0.005	0.002	0.001	0
25	0.047	0.038	0.030	0.024	0.020	0.016	0.013	0.010	0.004	0.001	0.001	0	0
30	0.026	0.020	0.015	0.012	0.009	0.007	0.005	0.004	0.001	0	0	0	0
40	0.008	0.005	0.004	0.003	0.002	0.001	0.001	0.001	0	0	0	0	0
50	0.002	0.001	0.001	0.001	0	0	0	0	0	0	0	0	0

Source: Maurice Joy, Introduction to Financial Management (Homewood, Ill.: Richard D. Irwin, 1977).

675

Appendix C Compound sum of an annuity of $1, IF_{sa}

$$S = R\left[\frac{(1+i)^n - 1}{i}\right]$$

Period	1%	2%	3%	4%	5%	6%	7%	8%	9%	10%	11%
1	1.000	1.000	1.000	1.000	1.000	1.000	1.000	1.000	1.000	1.000	1.000
2	2.010	2.020	2.030	2.040	2.050	2.060	2.070	2.080	2.090	2.100	2.110
3	3.030	3.060	3.091	3.122	3.153	3.184	3.215	3.246	3.278	3.310	3.342
4	4.060	4.122	4.184	4.246	4.310	4.375	4.440	4.506	4.573	4.641	4.710
5	5.101	5.204	5.309	5.416	5.526	5.637	5.751	5.867	5.985	6.105	6.228
6	6.152	6.308	6.468	6.633	6.802	6.975	7.153	7.336	7.523	7.716	7.913
7	7.214	7.434	7.662	7.898	8.142	8.394	8.654	8.923	9.200	9.487	9.783
8	8.286	8.583	8.892	9.214	9.549	9.897	10.260	10.637	11.028	11.436	11.859
9	9.369	9.755	10.159	10.583	11.027	11.491	11.978	12.488	13.021	13.579	14.164
10	10.462	10.950	11.464	12.006	12.578	13.181	13.816	14.487	15.193	15.937	16.722
11	11.567	12.169	12.808	13.486	14.207	14.972	15.784	16.645	17.560	18.531	19.561
12	12.683	13.412	14.192	15.026	15.917	16.870	17.888	18.977	20.141	21.384	22.713
13	13.809	14.680	15.618	16.627	17.713	18.882	20.141	21.495	22.953	24.523	26.212
14	14.947	15.974	17.086	18.292	19.599	21.015	22.550	24.215	26.019	27.975	30.095
15	16.097	17.293	18.599	20.024	21.579	23.276	25.129	27.152	29.361	31.772	34.405
16	17.258	18.639	20.157	21.825	23.657	25.673	27.888	30.324	33.003	35.950	39.190
17	18.430	20.012	21.762	23.698	25.840	28.213	30.840	33.750	36.974	40.545	44.501
18	19.615	21.412	23.414	25.645	28.132	30.906	33.999	37.450	41.301	45.599	50.396
19	20.811	22.841	25.117	27.671	30.539	33.760	37.379	41.446	46.018	51.159	56.939
20	22.019	24.297	26.870	29.778	33.066	36.786	40.995	45.762	51.160	57.275	64.203
25	28.243	32.030	36.459	41.646	47.727	54.865	63.249	73.106	84.701	98.347	114.41
30	34.785	40.588	47.575	56.085	66.439	79.058	94.461	113.28	136.31	164.49	199.02
40	48.886	60.402	75.401	95.026	120.80	154.76	199.64	259.06	337.89	442.59	581.83
50	64.463	84.579	112.80	152.67	209.35	290.34	406.53	573.77	815.08	1,163.9	1,668.8

Percent

Appendix C (concluded) Compound sum of an annuity of $1

Percent

Period	12%	13%	14%	15%	16%	17%	18%	19%	20%	25%	30%
1	1.000	1.000	1.000	1.000	1.000	1.000	1.000	1.000	1.000	1.000	1.000
2	2.120	2.130	2.140	2.150	2.160	2.170	2.180	2.190	2.200	2.250	2.300
3	3.374	3.407	3.440	3.473	3.506	3.539	3.572	3.606	3.640	3.813	3.990
4	4.779	4.850	4.921	4.993	5.066	5.141	5.215	5.291	5.368	5.766	6.187
5	6.353	6.480	6.610	6.742	6.877	7.014	7.154	7.297	7.442	8.207	9.043
6	8.115	8.323	8.536	8.754	8.977	9.207	9.442	9.683	9.930	11.259	12.756
7	10.089	10.405	10.730	11.067	11.414	11.772	12.142	12.523	12.916	15.073	17.583
8	12.300	12.757	13.233	13.727	14.240	14.773	15.327	15.902	16.499	19.842	23.858
9	14.776	15.416	16.085	16.786	17.519	18.285	19.086	19.923	20.799	25.802	32.015
10	17.549	18.420	19.337	20.304	21.321	22.393	23.521	24.701	25.959	33.253	42.619
11	20.655	21.814	23.045	24.349	25.733	27.200	28.755	30.404	32.150	42.566	56.405
12	24.133	25.650	27.271	29.002	30.850	32.824	34.931	37.180	39.581	54.208	74.327
13	28.029	29.985	32.089	34.352	36.786	39.404	42.219	45.244	48.497	68.760	97.625
14	32.393	34.883	37.581	40.505	43.672	47.103	50.818	54.841	59.196	86.949	127.91
15	37.280	40.417	43.842	47.580	51.660	56.110	60.965	66.261	72.035	109.69	167.29
16	42.753	46.672	50.980	55.717	60.925	66.649	72.939	79.850	87.442	138.11	218.47
17	48.884	53.739	59.118	65.075	71.673	78.979	87.068	96.022	105.93	173.64	285.01
18	55.750	61.725	68.394	75.836	84.141	93.406	103.74	115.27	128.12	218.05	371.52
19	63.440	70.749	78.969	88.212	98.603	110.29	123.41	138.17	154.74	273.56	483.97
20	72.052	80.947	91.025	102.44	115.38	130.03	146.63	165.42	186.69	342.95	630.17
25	133.33	155.62	181.87	212.79	249.21	292.11	342.60	402.04	471.98	1,054.8	2,348.80
30	241.33	293.20	356.79	434.75	530.31	647.44	790.95	966.7	1,181.9	3,227.2	8,730.0
40	767.09	1,013.7	1,342.0	1,779.1	2,360.8	3,134.5	4,163.21	5,529.8	7,343.9	30,089.	120,393.
50	2,400.0	3,459.5	4,994.5	7,217.7	10,436.	15,090.	21,813.	31,515.	45,497.	280,256.	165,976.

Source: Maurice Joy, Introduction to Financial Management (Homewood, Ill.: Richard D. Irwin, 1977).

Appendix D Present value of an annuity of $1, IF_{pva} $A = R \left[\dfrac{1 - \dfrac{1}{(1+i)^n}}{i} \right]$

Percent

Period	1%	2%	3%	4%	5%	6%	7%	8%	9%	10%	11%	12%
1	0.990	0.980	0.971	0.962	0.952	0.943	0.935	0.926	0.917	0.909	0.901	0.893
2	1.970	1.942	1.913	1.886	1.859	1.833	1.808	1.783	1.759	1.736	1.713	1.690
3	2.941	2.884	2.829	2.775	2.723	2.673	2.624	2.577	2.531	2.487	2.444	2.402
4	3.902	3.808	3.717	3.630	3.546	3.465	3.387	3.312	3.240	3.170	3.102	3.037
5	4.853	4.713	4.580	4.452	4.329	4.212	4.100	3.993	3.890	3.791	3.696	3.605
6	5.795	5.601	5.417	5.242	5.076	4.917	4.767	4.623	4.486	4.355	4.231	4.111
7	6.728	6.472	6.230	6.002	5.786	5.582	5.389	5.206	5.033	4.868	4.712	4.564
8	7.652	7.325	7.020	6.733	6.463	6.210	5.971	5.747	5.535	5.335	5.146	4.968
9	8.566	8.162	7.786	7.435	7.108	6.802	6.515	6.247	5.995	5.759	5.537	5.328
10	9.471	8.983	8.530	8.111	7.722	7.360	7.024	6.710	6.418	6.145	5.889	5.650
11	10.368	9.787	9.253	8.760	8.306	7.887	7.499	7.139	6.805	6.495	6.207	5.938
12	11.255	10.575	9.954	9.385	8.863	8.384	7.943	7.536	7.161	6.814	6.492	6.194
13	12.134	11.348	10.635	9.986	9.394	8.853	8.358	7.904	7.487	7.103	6.750	6.424
14	13.004	12.106	11.296	10.563	9.899	9.295	8.745	8.244	7.786	7.367	6.982	6.628
15	13.865	12.849	11.939	11.118	10.380	9.712	9.108	8.559	8.061	7.606	7.191	6.811
16	14.718	13.578	12.561	11.652	10.838	10.106	9.447	8.851	8.313	7.824	7.379	6.974
17	15.562	14.292	13.166	12.166	11.274	10.477	9.763	9.122	8.544	8.022	7.549	7.102
18	16.398	14.992	13.754	12.659	11.690	10.828	10.059	9.372	8.756	8.201	7.702	7.250
19	17.226	15.678	14.324	13.134	12.085	11.158	10.336	9.604	8.950	8.365	7.839	7.366
20	18.046	16.351	14.877	13.590	12.462	11.470	10.594	9.818	9.129	8.514	7.963	7.469
25	22.023	19.523	17.413	15.622	14.094	12.783	11.654	10.675	9.823	9.077	8.422	7.843
30	25.808	22.396	19.600	17.292	15.372	13.765	12.409	11.258	10.274	9.427	8.694	8.055
40	32.835	27.355	23.115	19.793	17.159	15.046	13.332	11.925	10.757	9.779	8.951	8.244
50	39.196	31.424	25.730	21.482	18.256	15.762	13.801	12.233	10.962	9.915	9.042	8.304

Appendix D (concluded)   Present value of an annuity of $1

Percent

Period	13%	14%	15%	16%	17%	18%	19%	20%	25%	30%	35%	40%	50%
1	0.885	0.877	0.870	0.862	0.855	0.847	0.840	0.833	0.800	0.769	0.741	0.714	0.667
2	1.668	1.647	1.626	1.605	1.585	1.566	1.547	1.528	1.440	1.361	1.289	1.224	1.111
3	2.361	2.322	2.283	2.246	2.210	2.174	2.140	2.106	1.952	1.816	1.696	1.589	1.407
4	2.974	2.914	2.855	2.798	2.743	2.690	2.639	2.589	2.362	2.166	1.997	1.849	1.605
5	3.517	3.433	3.352	3.274	3.199	3.127	3.058	2.991	2.689	2.436	2.220	2.035	1.737
6	3.998	3.889	3.784	3.685	3.589	3.498	3.410	3.326	2.951	2.643	2.385	2.168	1.824
7	4.423	4.288	4.160	4.039	3.922	3.812	3.706	3.605	3.161	2.802	2.508	2.263	1.883
8	4.799	4.639	4.487	4.344	4.207	4.078	3.954	3.837	3.329	2.925	2.598	2.331	1.922
9	5.132	4.946	4.772	4.607	4.451	4.303	4.163	4.031	3.463	3.019	2.665	2.379	1.948
10	5.426	5.216	5.019	4.833	4.659	4.494	4.339	4.192	3.571	3.092	2.715	2.414	1.965
11	5.687	5.453	5.234	5.029	4.836	4.656	4.486	4.327	3.656	3.147	2.752	2.438	1.977
12	5.918	5.660	5.421	5.197	4.988	4.793	4.611	4.439	3.725	3.190	2.779	2.456	1.985
13	6.122	5.842	5.583	5.342	5.118	4.910	4.715	4.533	3.780	3.223	2.799	2.469	1.990
14	6.302	6.002	5.724	5.468	5.229	5.008	4.802	4.611	3.824	3.249	2.814	2.478	1.993
15	6.462	6.142	5.847	5.575	5.324	5.092	4.876	4.675	3.859	3.268	2.825	2.484	1.995
16	6.604	6.265	5.954	5.668	5.405	5.162	4.938	4.730	3.887	3.283	2.834	2.489	1.997
17	6.729	6.373	6.047	5.749	5.475	5.222	4.988	4.775	3.910	3.295	2.840	2.492	1.998
18	6.840	6.467	6.128	5.818	5.534	5.273	5.033	4.812	3.928	3.304	2.844	2.494	1.999
19	6.938	6.550	6.198	5.877	5.584	5.316	5.070	4.843	3.942	3.311	2.848	2.496	1.999
20	7.025	6.623	6.259	5.929	5.628	5.353	5.101	4.870	3.954	3.316	2.850	2.497	1.999
25	7.330	6.873	6.464	6.097	5.766	5.467	5.195	4.948	3.985	3.329	2.856	2.499	1.997
30	7.496	7.003	6.566	6.177	5.829	5.517	5.235	4.979	3.995	3.332	2.857	2.500	2.000
40	7.634	7.105	6.642	6.233	5.871	5.548	5.258	4.997	3.999	3.333	2.857	2.500	2.000
50	7.675	7.133	6.661	6.246	5.880	5.554	5.262	4.999	4.000	3.333	2.857	2.500	2.000

Source: Maurice Joy, *Introduction to Financial Management* (Homewood, Ill.: Richard D. Irwin, 1977)

Appendix E   Using Calculators for Financial Analysis

This appendix is designed to help you use either an algebraic calculator (Texas Instruments BA-35 Student Business Analyst) or the Hewlett-Packard 12C Financial Calculator. We realize that most calculators come with comprehensive instructions, and this appendix is only meant to provide basic instructions for commonly used financial calculations.

There are always two things to do before starting your calculations as indicated in the first table: clear the calculator and set the decimal point. If you do not want to lose data stored in memory, do not perform steps 2 and 3 in the first box below.

Each step is listed vertically as a number followed by a decimal point. After each step you will find either a number or a calculator function denoted by a box⬜. Entering the number on your calculator is one step and entering the function is another. Notice that the HP 12C is color coded. When two boxes are found one after another, you may have an ⬜ f ⬜ or a ⬜ g ⬜ in the first box. An ⬜ f ⬜ is orange coded and refers to the orange functions above the keys. After typing the ⬜ f ⬜ function, you will automatically look for an orange coded key to punch. For example, after ⬜ f ⬜ in the first Hewlett-Packard box (right-hand panel), you will punch

	Texas Instruments BA-35	**Hewlett-Packard 12C**
First clear the calculator	1. ⬜ON/C⬜ ⬜ON/C⬜ 2. 0 3. ⬜STO⬜ Clears Memory	1. ⬜CLX⬜ Clears screen 2. ⬜ f ⬜ 3. ⬜REG⬜ Clears Memory
Set the decimal point The TI BA-35 has two choices: 2 decimal points or variable decimal points. The screen will indicate Dec 2 or the decimal will be variable. The HP 12C allows you to choose the number of decimal points. If you are uncertain, just provide the indicated input exactly as shown on the right.	1. ⬜2nd⬜ 2. ⬜STO⬜	1. ⬜ f ⬜ 2. 4 (# of decimals)

in the orange color coded $\boxed{\text{REG}}$. If the $\boxed{\text{f}}$ function is not followed by another box, you merely type in $\boxed{\text{f}}$ and the value indicated.

The $\boxed{\text{g}}$ is coded blue and refers to the functions on the bottom of the function keys. After the $\boxed{\text{g}}$ function key, you will automatically look for blue coded keys. This first occurs on page 685 of the appendix.

Familiarize yourself with the keyboard before you start. In the more complicated calculations, keystrokes will be combined into one step.

In the first four calculations on pages 681 and 682 we simply instruct you on how to get the interest factors for Appendixes A, B, C, and D. We have chosen to use examples as our method of instruction.

		Texas Instruments BA-35	**Hewlett-Packard 12C**
A.	Appendix A Compound Sum of $1 i = 9% or .09; n = 5 years $IF_s = (1 + i)^n$ Sum = Present Value x IF_s $S = P \times IF_s$ Check the answer against the number in Appendix A. Numbers in the appendix are rounded. Try different rates and years.	To Find Interest Factor 1. 1 2. + 3. .09 (interest rate) 4. $\boxed{=}$ 5. $\boxed{y^x}$ 6. 5 (# of periods) 7. = answer 1.538624	To Find Interest Factor 1. 1 2. $\boxed{\text{enter}}$ 3. .09 (interest rate) 4. + 5. 5 (# of periods) 6. $\boxed{y^x}$ answer 1.5386

		Texas Instruments BA-35	**Hewlett-Packard 12C**
B.	Appendix B Present Value of $1 i = 9% or .09; n = 5 years $IF_{pv} = 1/(1 + i)^n$ Present Value = Sum $\times$ IF_{pv} $p = S \times IF_{pv}$ Check the answer against the number in Appendix B. Numbers in the appendix are rounded.	To Find Interest Factor Repeat steps 1 through 7 above. Continue with step 8. 8. $\boxed{1/x}$ answer .6499314	To Find Interest Factor Repeat steps 1 through 6 above. Continue with step 7. 7. $\boxed{1/x}$ answer .6499

		Texas Instruments BA-35	**Hewlett-Packard 12C**
C.	Appendix C Compound Sum of an Annuity of $1 i = 9% or .09; n = 5 years $IF_{sa} = \dfrac{(1 + i)^n - 1}{i}$ Sum = Receipt × IF_{sa} S = R × IF_{sa} Check your answer with Appendix C. Repeat example using different numbers and check your results with the number in Appendix C. Numbers in appendix are rounded.	To Find Interest Factor Repeat steps 1 through 7 in part A of this section. Continue with step 8. 8. $\boxed{-}$ 9. 1 10. $\boxed{=}$ 11. $\boxed{\div}$ 12. .09 13. $\boxed{=}$ answer 5.9847106	To Find Interest Factor Repeat steps 1 through 6 in part A of this section. Continue with step 7. 7. 1 8. $\boxed{-}$ 9. .09 10. $\boxed{\div}$ answer 5.9847

		Texas Instruments BA-35	**Hewlett-Packard 12C**
D.	Appendix D Present Value of an Annuity of $1 i = 9% or .09; n = 5 years $IF_{pva} = \dfrac{1 - [1/(1 + i)^n]}{i}$ Annuity = Receipt × IF_s A = R × IF_s Check your answer with Appendix D. Repeat example using different numbers and check your results with the number in Appendix D. Numbers in appendix are rounded.	To Find Interest Factor Repeat steps 1 through 8 in parts A & B. Continue with step 9. 9. $\boxed{-}$ 10. 1 11. $\boxed{=}$ 12. $\boxed{+/-}$ 13. $\boxed{\div}$ 14. .09 15. $\boxed{=}$ answer 3.8896513	To Find Interest Factor Repeat steps 1 through 7 in parts A & B. Continue with step 8. 8. 1 9. $\boxed{-}$ 10. $\boxed{CHS}$ 11. .09 12. $\boxed{\div}$ answer 3.8897

On the following pages, you can determine bond valuation, yield to maturity, net present value of an annuity, net present value of an uneven cash flow, internal rate of return for an annuity, and internal rate of return for an uneven cash flow.

Bond Valuation using both the TI BA-35 and the HP 12C.

Solve for P_b = Price of the Bond

Given:

I_t = $80 annual coupon payments or 8% coupon ($40 semiannually)
P_n = $1,000 principal (par value)
n = 10 years to maturity (20 periods semiannually)
Y = 9.0% yield to maturity or required rate of return (4.5% semi-annually)

You may choose to refer to Chapter 10 in the textbook for a complete discussion of bond valuation.

	Texas Instruments BA-35	Hewlett-Packard 12C
BOND VALUATION All steps begin with number 1. Numbers following each step are keystrokes followed by a box ☐ . Each box represents a keystroke and indicates which calculator function is performed. The Texas Instrument calculator requires that data be adjusted for semiannual compounding, otherwise it assumes annual compounding. The Hewlett-Packard 12C internally assumes that semiannual compounding is used and requires annual data to be entered. The HP 12C is more detailed in that it requires the actual day month and year. If you want an answer for a problem that requires a given number of years (e.g., 10 years), simply start on a date of your choice and end on the same date 10 years later, as in the example.	Set Finance Mode 2nd FIN Set decimal to 2 places Decimal 2nd STO 1. 40 (semiannual coupon) 2. PMT 3. 4.5 (yield to maturity) semi-annual basis 4. % i 5. 1000 (principal) 6. FV 7. 20 (semiannual periods to maturity) 8. N 9. CPT 10. PV answer 934.96 Answer is given in dollars, rather than % of par value.	Clear memory f REG Set decimal to 3 places f 3 1. 9.0 (yield to maturity) 2. i 3. 8.0 (coupon in percent) 4. PMT 5. 1.091989 (today's date month–day–year)* 6. enter 7. 1.091999 (maturity date month–day–year)* 8. f 9. Price Answer 93.496 Answer is given as % of par value and equals $934.96. If Error message occurs, clear memory and start over. _____ *See instructions in the third paragraph of the first column.

Yield to Maturity on both the TI BA-35 and HP 12C

Solve for Y = yield to maturity

Given:

P_b = 895.50 price of bond
I_t = $80 annual coupon payments or 8% coupon ($40 semiannually)
P_n = $1,000 principal (par value)
n = 10 years to maturity (20 periods semiannually)

You may choose to refer to Chapter 10 and 11 in the textbook for a complete discussion of yield to maturity.

	Texas Instruments BA-35	Hewlett-Packard 12C
YIELD TO MATURITY All steps are numbered. All numbers following each step are keystrokes followed by a box ⬚ . Each box represents a keystroke and indicates which calculator function is performed. The Texas Instruments BA-35 does not internally compute a semiannual rate, so the data must be adjusted to reflect semiannual payments and periods. The answer received in step 10 is a semiannual rate, which must be multiplied by 2 to reflect an annual yield. The Hewlett-Packard 12C internally assumes that semiannual payments are made and, therefore, the answer in step 9 is the annual yield to maturity based on semiannual coupons. If you want an answer on the HP for a given number of years (e.g., 10 years), simply start on a date of your choice and end on the same date 10 years later, as in the example.	Set Finance Mode 2nd FIN Set decimal to 2 places Decimal 2nd STO 1. 20 (semiannual periods) 2. N 3. 1000 (par value) 4. FV 5. 40 (semiannual coupon) 6. PMT 7. 895.50 (bond price) 8. PV 9. CPT 10. % i answer 4.83% 11. × 12. 2 13. = answer 9.65% (annual rate)	Clear memory f REG Set decimal f 2 1. 89.55 (bond price as a percent of par) 2. PV 3. 8.0 (annual coupon in %) 4. PMT 5. 1.091989 (today's date)* 6. enter 7. 1.091999 (maturity date)* 8. f 9. YTM answer 9.65% In case you receive an Error message, you have probably made a keystroke error. Clear the memory f REG and start over. ——————— *See instructions in the third paragraph of the first column.

Net Present Value of an Annuity on both the TI BA-35 and the HP 12C

Solve for PV = present value of annuity

n = 10 years (number of years cash flow will continue)
PMT = $5,000 per year (amount of the annuity)
i = 12% (cost of capital K_a)
Cost = $20,000

You may choose to refer to Chapter 12 in the textbook for a complete discussion of net present value.

	Texas Instruments BA-35	Hewlett-Packard 12C
NET PRESENT VALUE OF AN ANNUITY All steps are numbered and some steps include several keystrokes. All numbers following each step are keystrokes followed by a box⬚ . Each box represents a keystroke and indicates which calculator function is performed on that number. The calculation for the present value of an annuity on the TI BA-35 requires that the project cost be subtracted from the present value of the cash inflows. The HP 12C could solve the problem exactly with the same keystrokes as the TI. However, since the HP uses a similar method to solve uneven cash flows, we elected to use the method that requires more keystrokes but which includes a negative cash outflow for the cost of the capital budgeting project. To conserve space, several keystrokes have been put into one step.	Set Finance Mode 2nd FIN Set decimal to 2 places Decimal 2nd ST0 1. 10 (years of cash flow) 2. N 3. 5000 (annual payments) 4. PMT 5. 12 (cost of capital) 6. % i 7. CPT 8. PV 9. − 10. 20,000 11. = answer $8,251.12	Set decimal to 2 places f 2 f REG clears memory 1. 20000 (cash outflow) 2. CHS changes sign 3. g 4. CFo 5. 5000 (annual payments) 6. g CFj 7. 10 g Nj (years) 8. 12 i (cost of capital) 9. f NPV answer $8,251,12 If an Error message appears, start over by clearing the memory with f REG .

Net Present Value of an Uneven Cash Flow on both the TI BA-35 and the HP 12C

Solve for NPV = net present value

n = 5 years (number of years cash flow will continue)

PMT = $5,000 (yr.1); 6,000 (yr.2); 7,000 (yr.3); 8,000 (yr.4); 9,000 (yr.5)

i = 12% (cost of capital K_a)

Cost = $25,000

You may choose to refer to Chapter 12 for a complete discussion of net present value concepts.

	Texas Instruments BA-35	Hewlett-Packard 12C
NET PRESENT VALUE OF AN UNEVEN CASH FLOW All steps are numbered and some steps include several keystrokes. All numbers following each step are keystrokes followed by a box ☐. Each box represents a keystroke and indicates which calculator function is performed on that number. Because we are dealing with uneven cash flows, each number must be entered. The TI BA-35 requires that you make sure of the memory. In step 2, you enter the future cash inflow in year 1 and, in step 3, you determine its present value, which is stored in memory. After the first 1-year calculation, following year present values are calculated in the same way and added to the stored value using the SUM key. Finally, the recall key RCL is used to recall the present value of the total cash inflows. The HP 12C requires each cash flow to be entered in order. The CFo key represents the cash flow in time period 0. The CFj key automatically counts the year of the cash flow in the order entered and so no years need be entered. Finally, the cost of capital of 12% is entered and the ☐ f key and NPV key are used to complete the problem.	Clear memory ON/C 0 STO Set decimal 2 places Decimal 2nd STO Set finance mode 2nd FIN 1. 12 % i 2. 5000 FV 3. 1 N CPT PV SUM 4. 6000 FV 5. 2 N CPT PV SUM 6. 7000 FV 7. 3 N CPT PV SUM 8. 8000 FV 9. 4 N CPT PV SUM 10. 9000 FV 11. 5 N CPT PV SUM 12. RCL (answer 24420.90) 13. − 14. 25000 (cash outflow) 15. = answer −$579.10 Negative Net Present Value	Set decimal to 2 places ☐ f 2 ☐ f REG clears memory 1. 25000 (cash outflow) 2. CHS changes sign 3. g CFo 4. 5000 g CFj 5. 6000 g CFj 6. 7000 g CFj 7. 8000 g CFj 8. 9000 g CFj 9. 12 i 10. f NPV answer −$579.10 Negative Net Present Value If you receive an Error message, you have probably made a keystroke error. Clear memory with ☐ f REG and start over with Step 1.

Internal Rate of Return for an Annuity on both the TI BA-35 and the HP 12C

Solve for IRR = internal rate of return

n = 10 years (number of years cash flow will continue)
PMT = $10,000 per year (amount of the annuity)
Cost = $50,000 (this is the present value of the annuity

You may choose to refer to Chapter 12 in the textbook for a complete discussion of internal rate of return.

	Texas Instruments BA-35	Hewlett-Packard 12C
INTERNAL RATE OF RETURN ON AN ANNUITY All steps are numbered and some steps include several keystrokes. All numbers following each step are keystrokes followed by a box ☐. Each box represents a keystroke and indicates which calculator function is performed on that number. The calculation for the internal rate of return of an annuity on the TI BA-35 requires relatively few keystrokes. The HP 12C requires more keystrokes than the TI BA-35, because it needs to use the function keys ☐f and ☐g to enter data into the internal programs. The HP method requires that the cash outflow be expressed as a negative, while the TI BA-35 uses a positive number for the cash outflow. To conserve space, several keystrokes have been put into one step.	Clear memory ON/C 0 STO Set Finance Mode 2nd FIN Set decimal to 2 places Decimal 2nd STO 1. 10 (years of cash flow) 2. N 3. 10000 (annual payments) 4. PMT 5. 50000 (present value) 6. PV 7. CPT 8. %i answer is 15.10%. At an internal rate of return of 15.10%, the present value of the $50,000 outflow is equal to the present value of $10,000 cash inflows over the next 10 years.	Set decimal to 2 places f 2 f REG clears memory 1. 50000 (cash outflow) 2. CHS changes sign 3. g 4. CFo 5. 10000 (annual payments) 6. g CFj 7. 10 g Nj (years) 8. f IRR answer is 15.10% If an Error message appears, start over by clearing the memory with f REG .

Internal Rate of Return with an Uneven Cash Flow on both the TI BA-35 and the HP 12C

Solve for IRR = internal rate of return (return which causes present value of outflows to equal present value of the inflows).

n = 5 years (number of years cash flow will continue)

PMT = $5,000 (yr.1); 6,000 (yr.2); 7,000 (yr.3); 8,000 (yr.4); 9,000 (yr.5)

Cost = $25,000

You may choose to refer to Chapter 12 for a complete discussion of internal rate of return

	Texas Instruments BA-35	Hewlett-Packard 12C
INTERNAL RATE OF RETURN ON UNEVEN CASH FLOW All steps are numbered and some steps include several keystrokes. All numbers following each step are keystrokes followed by a box ☐. Each box represents a keystroke and indicates which calculator function is performed on that number. Because we are dealing with uneven cash flows, the mathematics of solving this problem with the TI BA-35 is not possible. A more advanced algebraic calculator would be required. However, for the student willing to use trial and error, the student can use the NPV method and try different discount rates until the NPV equals zero. Check Chapter 12 on methods for approximating the IRR. This will provide a start. The HP 12C requires each cash flow to be entered in order. The ☐CFo key represents the cash flow in time period 0. The ☐CFj key automatically counts the year of the cash flow in the order entered and so no years need be entered. To find the internal rate of return, use the ☐f ☐IRR keys and complete the problem.	Clear memory ☐ON/C 0 ☐STO Set decimal 2 places Decimal ☐2nd ☐STO Set finance mode ☐2nd ☐FIN 1. 12 ☐%i (your IRR est.) 2. 5000 ☐FV 3. 1 ☐N ☐CPT ☐PV ☐STO 4. 6000 ☐FV 5. 2 ☐N ☐CPT ☐PV ☐SUM 6. 7000 ☐FV 7. 3 ☐N ☐CPT ☐PV ☐SUM 8. 8000 ☐FV 9. 4 ☐N ☐CPT ☐PV ☐SUM 10. 9000 ☐FV 11. 5 ☐N ☐CPT ☐PV ☐SUM 12. ☐RCL (answer 24,420.90) 13. ☐− 14. 25000 (cash outflow) 15. ☐= Answer −$579.10. Negative NPV. Start over with a lower discount rate (try 11.15). Answer is 24999.75. With a cash outflow of $25,000, the IRR would be 11.15%	Set decimal to 2 places ☐f 2 ☐f ☐REG clears memory 1. 25000 (cash outflow) 2. ☐CHS changes sign 3. ☐g ☐CFo 4. 5000 ☐g ☐CFj 5. 6000 ☐g ☐CFj 6. 7000 ☐g ☐CFj 7. 8000 ☐g ☐CFj 8. 9000 ☐g ☐CFj 9. ☐f ☐IRR answer 11.15% If you receive an Error message, you have probably made a keystroke error. Clear memory with ☐f ☐REG and start over with step 1.

Glossary

A   **Accelerated Cost Recovery System (ACRS)**   A system that specifies the allowable depreciation recovery period for different types of assets. The normal recovery period is generally shorter than the physical life of the asset.

agency theory   This theory examines the relationship between the owners of the firm and the managers of the firm. While management has the responsibility for acting as the agent for the stockholders in pursuing their best interests, the key question considered is: How well does management perform this role?

aging of accounts receivable   Analyzing accounts by the amount of time they have been on the books.

American Depository Receipts (ADR)   These receipts represent the ownership interest in a foreign company's common stock. The shares of the foreign company are put in trust in a New York bank. The bank, in turn, issues its depository receipts to the American stockholders of the foreign firm. Many ADRs are listed on the NYSE and many more are traded in the over-the-counter market.

American Stock Exchange (AMEX)   The second largest organized security exchange in the United States.

annual percentage rate (APR)   A measure of the *effective* rate on a loan. One uses the actuarial method of compound interest when calculating the APR.

annuity   A series of consecutive payments or receipts of equal amount.

asset-based public offerings   Public offerings backed by receivables as collateral. Essentially, a firm factors (sells) its receivables in the securities markets.

asset depreciation range (ADR)   The ADR represents the expected physical life of an asset. Generally, the midpoint of the ADR is utilized to determine what class an asset falls into for depreciation purposes.

asset utilization ratios   A group of ratios that measures the speed at which the firm is turning over or utilizing its assets. We measure inventory turnover, fixed-asset turnover, total asset turnover, and the average time it takes to collect accounts receivable.

assignment   The liquidation of assets without going through formal court procedures. In order to affect an assignment, creditors must agree on liquidation values and the relative priority of claims.

automated clearinghouse (ACH)   An ACH transfers information between one financial institution and another and from account to account via computer tape. There are approximately 30 regional clearinghouses throughout the United States that claim the membership of over 10,000 financial institutions.

average collection period   The average amount of time accounts receivable have been on the books. It may be computed by dividing accounts receivable by average daily credit sales.

B   **balance of payments**   The term refers to a system of government accounts that catalogs the flow of economic transactions between countries.

balance sheet   A financial statement that indicates what assets the firm owns, and how those assets are financed in the form of liabilities or ownership interest.

banker's acceptance   Short-term securities that frequently arise from foreign trade. The acceptance is a draft that is drawn on a bank for approval for future payment and is subsequently presented to the payer.

bankruptcy   The market value of a firm's assets are less than its liabilities, and the firm has a negative net worth. The term is also used to describe in-court procedures associated with the reorganization or liquidation of a firm.

bear market   A falling or lethargic stock market. The opposite of a bull market.

beta   A measure of the volatility of returns on an individual stock relative to the market. Stocks with a beta of 1.0 are said to have risk equal to that of the market (equal volatility). Stocks with betas greater than 1.0 have more risk than the market, while those with betas of less than 1.0 have less risk than the market.

blanket inventory liens   A secured borrowing arrangement in which the lender has a general claim against the inventory of the borrower.

bond ratings   Bonds are rated according to risk by Standard & Poor's and Moody's Investor Service. A bond that is rated Aaa by Moody's has the lowest risk, while a bond with a C rating has the highest risk. Coupon rates are greatly influenced by a corporation's bond rating.

book value   (See net worth.)

break-even analysis   A numerical and graphical technique that is used to determine at what point the firm will break even (revenue = cost). To compute the break-even point, we divide fixed costs by price minus variable cost per unit.

brokers   Members of organized stock exchanges who have the ability to buy and sell securities on the floor of their respective exchanges. Brokers act as agents between buyers and sellers.

bull market   A rising stock market. There are many complicated interpretations of this term, usually centering on the length of time that the market should be rising in order to meet the criteria for classification as a bull market. For our purposes, a bull market exists when stock prices are strong and rising and investors are optimistic about future market performance.

C

call feature   Used for bonds and some preferred stock. A call allows the corporation to retire securities before maturity by forcing the bondholders to sell bonds back to it at a set price. The call provisions are included in the bond indenture.

call premium   The premium paid by a corporation to call in a bond issue before the maturity date.

capital   Sources of long-term financing that are available to the business firm.

capital asset pricing model   A model that relates the risk–return trade-offs of individual assets to market returns. A security is presumed to receive a risk-free rate of return plus a premium for risk.

capital gains taxes   Taxes on gains from holding assets. Based on the Tax Reform Act of 1986, the rate is the same as the tax on other income.

capital lease   A long-term, noncancelable lease that has many of the characteristics of debt. Under FASB Statement 13, the lease obligation must be shown directly on the balance sheet.

capital markets   Competitive markets for equity securities or debt securities with maturities of more than one year. The best examples of capital market securities are common stock, bonds, and preferred stock.

capital rationing   Occurs when a corporation has more dollars of capital budgeting projects with positive net present values than it has money to invest in them. Therefore, some projects that should be accepted are excluded because financial capital is rationed.

carrying costs   The cost to hold an asset, usually inventory. For inventory, carrying costs include such items as interest, warehousing costs, insurance, and material-handling expenses.

cash budget   A series of monthly or quarterly budgets that indicate cash receipts, cash payments, and the borrowing requirements for meeting financial requirements. It is constructed from the pro forma income statement and other supportive schedules.

cash flow   A value equal to income after taxes plus noncash expenses. In capital budgeting decisions, the usual noncash expense is depreciation.

cash flows from financing activities   Cash flow that is generated (or reduced) from the sale or repurchase of securities or the payment of cash dividends. It is the third section presented in the statement of cash flows.

cash flows from investing activities   Cash flow that is generated (or reduced) from the sale or purchase of long-term securities or plant and equipment. It is the second section presented in the statement of cash flows.

cash flows from operating activities   Cash flow information that is determined by adjusting net income for such factors as depreciation expense, changes in current assets and liabilities, and other items. It is the first section presented in the statement of cash flows.

certificates of deposit   A certificate offered by banks, savings and loans, and other financial institutions for the deposit of funds at a given interest rate over a specified time period.

clientele effect   The effect of investor preferences for dividends or capital gains. Investors tend to purchase securities that meet their needs.

coefficient of correlation   The degree of associated movement between two or more variables. Variables that move in the same direction are said to be positively correlated, while negatively correlated variables move in opposite directions.

coefficient of variation   A measure of risk determination that is computed by dividing the standard deviation for a series of numbers by the expected value. Generally, the larger the coefficient of variation, the greater the risk.

combined leverage   The total or combined impact of operating and financial leverage.

commercial paper   An unsecured promissory note that large corporations issue to investors. The minimum amount is usually $25,000.

common equity   The common stock or ownership capital of the firm. Common equity may be supplied through retained earnings or the sale of new common stock.

common stock equivalent   Warrants, options, and any convertible securities that pay less than two thirds of the average Aa bond yield at the time of issue.

common stockholder   Holders of common stock are the owners of the company. They have a residual claim to the earnings.

compensating balances   A bank requirement that business customers maintain a minimum average balance. The required amount is usually computed as a percentage of customer loans outstanding or as a percentage of the future loans to which the bank has committed itself.

composition   An out-of-court settlement in which creditors agree to accept a fractional settlement on their original claim.

compound sum   The future value of a single amount or an annuity when compounded at a given interest rate for a specified time period.

conglomerate   A corporation that is made up of many diverse, often unrelated divisions. This form of organization is thought to reduce risk, but may create problems of coordination.

consolidation   The combination of two or more firms, generally of equal size and market power, to form an entirely new entity.

constant dollar accounting   One of two methods of inflation-adjusted accounting that have been approved by the Financial Accounting Standards Board. Financial statements are adjusted to present prices, using the consumer price index. This optional information may be shown in the firm's annual report.

consumer price index   An economic indicator published monthly by the U.S. Commerce Department. It measures the rate of inflation for consumer goods.

contribution margin   The contribution to fixed costs from each unit of sales. The margin may be computed as price minus variable cost per unit.

conversion premium   The market price of a convertible bond or preferred stock minus the security's conversion value.

conversion price   The conversion ratio divided into the par value. The price of the common stock at which the security is convertible. An investor would usually not convert the security into common stock unless the market price were greater than the conversion price.

conversion ratio   The number of shares of common stock an investor will receive if he or she exchanges a convertible bond or convertible preferred stock for common stock.

conversion value   The conversion ratio multiplied by the market price per share of common stock.

convertible security   A security that may be traded into the company for a different form or type of security. Convertible securities are usually bonds or preferred stock that may be exchanged for common stock.

corporate stock repurchase   A corporation may repurchase its shares in the market as an alternative to paying a cash dividend. Earnings per share will go up, and, if the price–earnings ratio remains the same, the stockholder will receive the same dollar benefit as through a cash dividend. A corporation may also justify the repurchase of its stock because it is at a very low price or to maintain constant demand for the shares. Reacquired shares may be used for employee options or as part of a tender offer in a merger or acquisition. Firms may also reacquire part of their shares as a protective device against being taken over as a merger candidate.

corporation   A form of ownership in which a separate legal entity is created. A corporation may sue or be sued, engage in contracts and acquire property. It has a continual life and is not dependent on any one stockholder for maintaining its legal existence. A corporation is owned by stockholders who enjoy the privilege of limited liability. There is, however, the potential for double taxation in the corporate form of organization: the first time at the corporate level in the form of profits, and again at the stockholder level in the form of dividends.

cost-benefit analysis   A study of the incremental costs and benefits that can be derived from a given course of action.

cost of capital   The cost of alternative sources of financing to the firm. (See also weighted average cost of capital.)

cost of goods sold   The cost specifically associated with units sold during the time period under study.

coupon rate   The actual interest rate on the bond, usually payable in semi-annual installments. The coupon rate normally stays constant during the life of the bond and indicates what the bondholder's annual dollar income will be.

crash of 1987   The market decline on October 19, 1987, in which the Dow Jones Industrial Average declined by 22.6 percent. In the great Crash of 1929, the decline was only 12.9 percent.

credit terms   The repayment provisions that are part of a credit arrangement. An example would be a 2/10, net 30 arrangement in which the customer may deduct 2 percent from the invoice price if payment takes place in the first 10 days. Otherwise, the full amount is due.

cumulative preferred stock   If dividends from one period are not paid to the preferred stockholders, they are said to be in arrears and are then added to the next period's dividends. When dividends on preferred stock are in arrears, no dividends can legally be paid to the common stockholders. The cumulative dividend feature is very beneficial to preferred stockholders since it assures them that they will receive all dividends due before common stockholders can get any dividends.

cumulative voting   Allows shareholders more than one vote per share. They are allowed to multiply their total shares by the number of directors being elected to determine their total number of votes. This system enables minority shareholders to elect directors even though they do not have 51 percent of the vote.

currency futures contract   A futures contract that may be used for hedging or speculation in foreign exchange.

current cost accounting   One of two methods of inflation-adjusted accounting approved by the Financial Accounting Standards Board in 1979. Financial statements are adjusted to the present, using current cost data, rather than an index. This optional information may be shown in the firm's annual report.

current yield   The yearly dollar interest payment divided by the current market price.

D   **dealers**   Participants in the market who transact security trades over-the-counter from their own inventory of stocks and bonds. They are often referred to as market makers, since they stand ready to buy and sell their securities at quoted prices.

debenture   A long-term unsecured corporate bond. Debentures are usually issued by large, prestigious firms having excellent credit ratings in the financial community.

debt utilization ratios   A group of ratios that indicates to what extent debt is being used and the prudence with which it is being managed. Calculations include debt to total assets, times interest earned, and fixed charge coverage.

decision tree   A tabular or graphical analysis that lays out the sequence of decisions that are to be made and highlights the differences between choices. The presentation resembles branches on a tree.

declaration date   The day on which the board of directors officially states that a dividend will be paid.

deferred annuity   An annuity that will not begin until some time period in the future.

degree of combined leverage   A measure of the total combined effect of operating and financial leverage on earnings per share. The percentage change in earnings per share is divided by the percentage change in sales at a given level of operation. Other algebraic statements are also used, such as Formula 5–7 and footnote 3 in Chapter 5.

degree of financial leverage   A measure of the impact of debt on the earnings capability of the firm. The percentage change in earnings per share is divided by the percentage change in earnings before interest and taxes at a given level of operation. Other algebraic statements are also used, such as Formula 5–5.

degree of operating leverage   A measure of the impact of fixed costs on the operating earnings of the firm. The percentage change in operating income is divided by the percentage change in volume at a given level of operation. Other algebraic statements are also used, such as Formula 5–3 and footnote 2 in Chapter 5.

depreciation base   The initial cost of an asset that is multiplied by the appropriate annual depreciation percentage in Table 12–9 to determine the dollar depreciation.

dilution of earnings   This occurs when additional shares of stock are sold without creating an immediate increase in income. The result is a decline in earnings per share until earnings can be generated from the funds raised.

discount rate   The interest rate at which future sums or annuities are discounted back to the present.

discounted loan   A loan in which the calculated interest payment is subtracted or discounted in advance. Because this lowers the amount of available funds, the effective interest rate is increased.

disinflation   A leveling off or slow-down of price increases.

dividend information content This theory of dividends assumes that dividends provide information about the financial health and economic expectations of the company. If this is true, corporations must actively manage their dividends to provide the market with information.

dividend payment date The day on which a stockholder of record will receive his or her dividend.

dividend payout The percentage of dividends to earnings after taxes. It can be computed by dividing dividends per share by earnings per share.

dividend record date Stockholders owning the stock on the holder-of-record date are entitled to receive a dividend. In order to be listed as an owner on the corporate books, the investor must have bought the stock before it went ex-dividend.

dividend reinvestment plans Plans that provide the investor with an opportunity to buy additional shares of stock with the cash dividends paid by the company.

dividend valuation model A model for determining the value of a share of stock by taking the present value of an expected stream of future dividends.

dividend yield Dividends per share divided by market price per share. Dividend yield indicates the percentage return that a stockholder will receive on dividends alone.

dual trading Exists when one security, such as General Motors common stock, is traded on more than one stock exchange. This practice is quite common between NYSE-listed companies and regional exchanges.

Dun & Bradstreet A credit-rating agency that publishes information on over 3 million business establishments through its *Reference Book*.

Du Pont System of Ratio Analysis An analysis of profitability that breaks down return on assets between the profit margin and asset turnover. The second, or modified, version shows how return on assets is translated into return on equity through the amount of debt that the firm has. Actually return on assets is divided by $(1 - debt/assets)$ to arrive at return on equity.

E **earnings per share** The earnings available to common stockholders divided by the number of common stock shares outstanding.

economic ordering quantity (EOQ) The most efficient ordering quantity for the firm. The EOQ will allow the firm to minimize the total ordering and carrying costs associated with inventory.

efficient frontier A line drawn through the optimum point selections in a risk–return trade-off diagram. Each point represents the best possible trade-off between risk and return (the highest return at a given risk level or the lowest risk at a given return level).

efficient market hypothesis   Hypothesis which suggests that markets adjust very quickly to new information and that it is very difficult for investors to select portfolios of securities that outperform the market. The efficient market hypothesis may be stated in many different forms, as indicated in Chapter 14.

electronic funds transfer   A system in which funds are moved between computer terminals without the use of written checks.

Eurobonds   Bonds payable or denominated in the borrower's currency, but sold outside the country of the borrower, usually by an international syndicate.

Eurodollar loan   A loan from a foreign bank denominated in dollars.

Eurodollars   U.S. dollars held on deposit by foreign banks and loaned out by those banks to anyone seeking dollars.

ex-dividend date   Four business days before the holder-of-record date. On the ex-dividend date the purchase of the stock no longer carries with it the right to receive the dividend previously declared.

expectations hypothesis   The hypothesis maintains that the yields on long-term securities are a function of short-term rates. The result of the hypothesis is that, when long-term rates are much higher than short-term rates, the market is saying that it expects short-term rates to rise. Conversely, when long-term rates are lower than short-term rates, the market is expecting short-term rates to fall.

expected value   A representative value from a probability distribution arrived at by multiplying each outcome by the associated probability and summing up the values.

Export-Import Bank (Eximbank)   An agency of the United States government that facilitates the financing of United States exports through its miscellaneous programs. In its direct loan program, the Eximbank lends money to foreign purchasers of U.S. products—such as aircraft, electrical equipment, heavy machinery, computers, and the like. The Eximbank also purchases eligible medium-term obligations of foreign buyers of U.S. goods at a discount from face value. In this discount program, private banks and other lenders are able to rediscount (sell at a lower price) promissory notes and drafts acquired from foreign customers of U.S. firms.

expropriation   The action of a country in taking away or modifying the property rights of a corporation or individual.

ex-rights The situation in which the purchase of common stock during a rights offering no longer includes rights to purchase additional shares of common stock.

extension An out-of-court settlement in which creditors agree to allow the firm more time to meet its financial obligations. A new repayment schedule will be developed, subject to the acceptance of creditors.

external corporate funds Corporate financing raised through sources outside of the firm. Bonds, common stock, and preferred stock fall in this category.

external reorganization A reorganization under the formal bankruptcy laws, in which a merger partner is found for the distressed firm. Ideally, the distressed firm should be merged with a strong firm in its own industry, although this is not always possible.

F

factoring receivables Selling accounts receivable to a finance company or a bank.

federal budget deficit Government expenditures are greater than government tax revenues, and the government must borrow to balance revenues and expenditures. These deficits act as an economic stimulus.

federal budget surplus Government tax receipts are greater than government expenditures. A rarity during the last 20 years. These surpluses have a dampening effect on the economy.

federally sponsored agency securities Securities issued by federal agencies, such as the Federal Home Loan Banks and the Federal Land Bank.

Federal National Mortgage Association (Fannie Mae) A former government agency that provides a secondary market in mortgages. It is now private.

Federal Reserve discount rate The rate of interest that the Fed charges on loans to the banking system. A monetary tool for management of the money supply.

field warehousing An inventory financing arrangement in which collateralized inventory is stored on the premises of the borrower but is controlled by an independent warehousing company.

FIFO A system of writing off inventory into cost of goods sold, in which the items purchased first are written off first. Referred to as first-in, first-out.

Financial Accounting Standards Board A privately supported rule-making body for the accounting profession.

financial capital Common stock, preferred stock, bonds, and retained earnings. Financial capital appears on the corporate balance sheet under long-term liabilities and equity.

financial disclosure Presentation of financial information to the investment community.

financial futures market A market that allows for the trading of financial instruments related to a future point in time. A purchase or sale takes place in the present, with a reversal necessitated in the future to close out the position. If a purchase (sale) takes place initially, then a sale (purchase) will be necessary in the future. The market provides for futures contracts in Treasury bonds, Treasury bills, certificates of deposits, GNMA certificates, and many other instruments. Financial futures contracts may be executed on the Chicago Board of Trade, the Chicago Mercantile Exchange, the New York Futures Exchange, and other exchanges.

financial intermediary A financial institution, such as a bank or a life insurance company, that directs other people's money into such investments as government and corporate securities.

financial lease A long-term, noncancelable lease. The financial lease has all the characteristics of long-term debt.

financial leverage A measure of the amount of debt used in the capital structure of the firm.

financial sweetener Usually refers to equity options, such as warrants or conversion privileges, attached to a debt security. The sweetener lowers the interest cost to the corporation.

fiscal policy The tax policies of the federal government and the spending associated with its tax revenues.

fixed costs Costs that remain relatively constant regardless of the volume of operations. Examples are rent, depreciation, property taxes, and executive salaries.

float The difference between the corporation's recorded cash balance on its books and the amount credited to the corporation by the bank.

floating rate bond The interest payment on the bond that changes with market conditions, rather than the price of the bond.

floating rate preferred stock The quarterly dividend on the preferred stock changes with market rates. The market price is considerably less volatile than it is with regular preferred stock.

floor price   Usually equal to the pure bond value. A convertible bond will not sell at less than its pure bond value even when its conversion value is below the pure bond value.

flotation cost   The distribution cost of selling securities to the public. The cost includes the underwriter's spread and any associated fees.

forced conversion   Occurs when a company calls a convertible security that has a conversion value greater than the call price. Investors will take the higher of the two values and convert the security to common stock, rather than take a lower cash call price.

Foreign Credit Insurance Association (FCIA)   An agency established by a group of 60 U.S. insurance companies. It sells credit export insurance to interested exporters. The FCIA promises to pay for the exported merchandise if the foreign importer defaults on payment.

foreign exchange rate   The relationship between the value of two or more currencies. For example, the exchange rate between U.S. dollars and French francs is stated as dollars per francs or francs per dollar.

foreign exchange risk   A form of risk that refers to the possibility of experiencing a drop in revenue or an increase in cost in an international transaction due to a change in foreign exchange rates. Importers, exporters, investors, and multinational firms alike are exposed to this risk.

founders' stock   Stock owned by the original founders of a company. It often carries special voting rights that allow the founders to maintain voting privileges in excess of their proportionate ownership.

fronting loan   A parent company's loan to a foreign subsidiary is channeled through a financial intermediary, usually a large international bank. The bank fronts for the parent in extending the loan to the foreign affiliate.

fully diluted earnings per share   Equals adjusted earnings after taxes divided by shares outstanding, plus common stock equivalents, plus all convertible securities.

futures contract   A contract to buy or sell a commodity at some specified price in the future.

G

going private   The process by which all publicly owned shares of common stock are repurchased or retired, thereby eliminating listing fees, annual reports, and other expenses involved with publicly owned companies.

golden parachute   Highly attractive termination payments made to current management in the event of a takeover of the company.

goodwill An intangible asset that reflects value above that generally recognized in the tangible assets of the firm.

H **hedging** To engage in a transaction that partially or fully reduces a prior risk exposure by taking a position that is the opposite of your initial position. As an example, you buy some copper now but also engage in a contract to sell copper in the future at a set price.

historical cost accounting The traditional method of accounting, in which financial statements are developed based on original cost minus depreciation.

holding company A company that has voting control of one or more other companies. It often has less than a 50 percent interest in each of these other companies.

homemade leverage The use of leverage directly by investors in place of corporate leverage. It allows investors to bring into balance the value of unlevered and levered firms by providing the "missing leverage" themselves. Homemade leverage is part of the initial Modigliani and Miller approach.

hurdle rate The minimum acceptable rate of return in a capital budgeting decision.

I **income statement** A financial statement that measures the profitability of the firm over a time period. All expenses are subtracted from sales to arrive at net income.

indenture A legal contract between the borrower and the lender that covers every detail regarding a bond issue.

indexing An adjustment for inflation incorporated into the operation of an economy. Indexing may be used to revalue assets on the balance sheet and to automatically adjust wages, tax deductions, interest payments, and a wide variety of other categories to account for inflation.

inflation The phenomenon of price increase with the passage of time.

inflation premium A premium to compensate the investor for the eroding effect of inflation on the value of the dollar. In the 1980s, the inflation premium has been 3 to 4 percent. In the late 1970s, it was in excess of 10 percent.

insider trading This occurs when someone has information that is not available to the public and then uses this information to profit from trading in a company's common stock.

installment loan A borrowing arrangement in which a series of equal payments are used to pay off the loan.

interest factor (*IF*)   The tabular value to insert into the various formulas. It is based on the number of periods (*n*) and the interest rate (*i*).

interest rate parity theory   A theory based on the interplay between interest rate differentials and exchange rates. If one country has a higher interest rate than another country after adjustments for inflation, interest rates and foreign exchange rates will adjust until the foreign exchange rates and money market rates reach equilibrium (are properly balanced between the two countries).

internal corporate funds   Funds generated through the operations of the firm. The principal sources are retained earnings and cash flow added back from depreciation and other noncash deductions.

internal rate of return (IRR)   A discounted cash flow method for evaluating capital budgeting projects. The IRR is a discount rate which makes the present value of the cash inflows equal to the present value of the cash outflows.

internal reorganization   A reorganization under the formal bankruptcy laws. New management may be brought in and a redesign of the capital structure may be implemented.

international diversification   Achieving diversification through many different foreign investments that are influenced by a variety of factors.

International Finance Corporation (IFC)   An affiliate of the World Bank established with the sole purpose of providing partial seed capital for private ventures around the world. Whenever a multinational company has difficulty raising equity capital due to lack of adequate private risk capital, the firm may explore the possibility of selling equity or debt (totaling up to 25 percent) to the International Finance Corporation.

inventory profits   Profits generated as a result of an inflationary economy, in which old inventory is sold at large profits because of increasing prices. This is particularly prevalent under FIFO accounting.

inverted yield curve   A downward-sloping yield curve. Short-term rates are higher than long-term rates.

investment banker   A financial organization that specializes in selling primary offerings of securities. Investment bankers can also perform other financial functions, such as advising clients, negotiating mergers and takeovers, and selling secondary offerings.

L   **leading indicators**   The most commonly followed series of economic indicators (a series of 12 leading indicators). These are used to help forecast economic activity.

lease   A contractual arrangement between the owner of equipment (lessor) and the user of equipment (lessee), which calls for the lessee to pay the lessor an established lease payment. There are two kinds of leases: financial leases and operating leases.

letter of credit   A credit letter normally issued by the importer's bank, in which the bank promises to pay out the money for the merchandise when delivered.

level production   Equal monthly production used to smooth out production schedules and employ manpower and equipment more efficiently and at a lower cost.

leverage   The use of fixed-charge items with the intent of magnifying the potential returns to the firm.

leveraged buy-out   Existing management or an outsider makes an offer to "go private" by retiring all the shares of the company. The buying group borrows the necessary money, using the assets of the acquired firm as collateral. The buying group then repurchases all the shares and expects to retire the debt over time with the cash flow from operations or the sale of corporate assets.

LIBOR   (See London Interbank Offered Rate.)

life cycle curve   A curve illustrating the growth phases of a firm. The dividend policy most likely to be employed during each phase is often illustrated.

LIFO   A system of writing off inventory into cost of goods sold in which the items purchased last are written off first. Referred to as last-in, first-out.

limited partnership   A special form of partnership to limit liability for most of the partners. Under this arrangement, one or more partners are designated as general partners and have unlimited liability for the debts of the firm, while the other partners are designated as limited partners and are only liable for their initial contribution.

liquidation   A procedure that may be carried out under the formal bankruptcy laws when an internal or external reorganization does not appear to be feasible, and it appears that the assets are worth more in liquidation than through a reorganization. Priority of claims becomes extremely important in a liquidation because it is unlikely that all parties will be fully satisfied in their demands.

liquidity   The relative convertibility of short-term assets to cash. Thus, marketable securities are highly liquid assets, while inventory may not be.

liquidity premium theory   This theory indicates that long-term rates should be higher than short-term rates. The premium of long-term rates over short-term rates exists because short-term securities have greater liquidity, and, therefore, higher rates have to be offered to potential long-term bond buyers to entice them to hold these less liquid and more price sensitive securities.

liquidity ratios A group of ratios that allows one to measure the firm's ability to pay off short-term obligations as they come due. Primary attention is directed to the current ratio and the quick ratio.

listing requirements Financial standards that corporations must meet before their common stock can be traded on a stock exchange. Listing requirements are not standard, but are set by each exchange. The requirements for the NYSE are the most stringent.

lockbox system A procedure used to expedite cash inflows to a business. Customers are requested to forward their checks to a post-office box in their geographic region, and a local bank picks up the checks and processes them for rapid collection. Funds are then wired to the corporate home office for immediate use.

London Interbank Offered Rate (LIBOR) An interbank rate applicable for large deposits in the London market. It is a bench-mark rate, just like the prime interest rate in the United States. Interest rates on Eurodollar loans are determined by adding premiums to this basic rate. Most often, LIBOR is lower than the U.S. prime rate.

M   **majority voting** All directors must be elected by a vote of more than 50 percent. Minority shareholders are unable to achieve any representation on the board of directors.

managing underwriter An investment banker who is responsible for the pricing, prospectus development, and legal work involved in the sale of a new issue of securities.

margin requirement A rule that specifies the amount of cash or equity that must be deposited with a brokerage firm or bank, with the balance of funds eligible for borrowing. Margin is set by the Board of Governors of the Federal Reserve Board.

marginal corporate tax rate The rate that applies to each new dollar of taxable income. For a corporation, the rate is at a maximum level of 34 percent (there is also a 5 percent surtax over a limited range).

marginal cost of capital The cost of the last dollar of funds raised. It is assumed that each dollar is financed in proportion to the firm's optimum capital structure.

marginal principle of retained earnings   The corporation must be able to earn a higher return on its retained earnings than a stockholder would receive after paying taxes on the distributed dividends.

market efficiency   Markets are considered to be efficient when (1) prices adjust rapidly to new information; (2) there is a continuous market, in which each successive trade is made at a price close to the previous price (the faster the price responds to new information and the smaller the differences in price changes, the more efficient the market); and (3) the market can absorb large dollar amounts of securities without destabilizing the prices.

market maker   (See dealers.)

market risk premium   A premium over and above the risk-free rate. It is represented by the difference between the market return (K_m) and the risk-free rate (R_f), and it may be multiplied by the beta coefficient to determine the additional risk-adjusted return on a security.

market stabilization   Intervention in the secondary markets by an investment banker to stabilize the price of a new security offering during the offering period. The purpose of market stabilization is to provide an orderly market for the distribution of the new issue.

market value maximization   The concept of maximizing the wealth of shareholders. This calls for a recognition not only of earnings per share but also how they will be valued in the marketplace.

maturity date   The date on which the bond is retired and the principal (par value) is repaid to the lender.

merger   The combination of two or more companies, in which the resulting firms maintain the identity of the acquiring company.

merger arbitrageur   A specialist in merger investments who attempts to capitalize on the difference between the value offered and the current market value of the acquisition candidate.

merger premium   The part of a buy-out or exchange offer which represents a value over and above the market value of the acquired firm.

minimum warrant value   The market value of the common stock minus the option price of the warrant multiplied by the number of shares of the common stock that each warrant entitles the holder to purchase.

monetary policy   Management by the Federal Reserve Board of the money supply and the resultant interest rates.

money market accounts   Accounts at banks, savings and loans, and credit unions, in which the depositor receives competitive money market rates on a typical minimum deposit of $1,000. These accounts may generally have three deposits and three withdrawals per month, and are not meant to be transaction accounts, but a place to keep minimum and excess cash balances. These accounts are insured by various appropriate governmental agencies up to $100,000.

money market funds A fund in which investors may purchase shares for as little as $500 or $1,000. The fund then reinvests the proceeds in high-yielding $100,000 bank CDs, $25,000–$100,000 commercial paper, and other large-denomination, high-yielding securities. Investors receive their pro rata portion of the interest proceeds daily as a credit to their shares.

money markets Competitive markets for securities with maturities of one year or less. The best examples of money market instruments would be Treasury bills, commercial paper, and negotiable certificates of deposit.

mortgage agreement A loan which requires real property (plant and equipment) as collateral.

multinational corporation A firm doing business across its national borders is considered a multinational enterprise. Some definitions require a minimum percentage (often 30 percent or more) of a firm's business activities to be carried on outside its national borders.

municipal securities Securities issued by state and local government units. The income from these securities is exempt from federal income taxes.

mutually exclusive The selection of one choice precludes the selection of any competitive choice. For example, several machines can do an identical job in capital budgeting. If one machine is selected, the other machines will not be used.

N **National Association of Security Dealers (NASD)** An industry association that supervises the over-the-counter market.

National Market List The list of the best-known and most widely traded securities in the over-the-counter market.

net income (NI) approach Under the net income approach, it is assumed that the firm can raise all the funds it desires at a constant cost of debt and equity. Since debt tends to have a lower cost than equity, the more debt utilized the lower the overall cost of capital and the higher the valuation of the firm.

net operating income (NOI) approach Under this approach, the cost of capital and valuation do not change with the increased utilization of debt. Under this proposition, the low cost of debt is assumed to remain constant with greater debt utilization, but the cost of equity increases to such an extent that the cost of capital remains unchanged.

net present value (NPV) The NPV equals the present value of the cash inflows minus the present value of the cash outflows with the cost of capital used as a discount rate. This method is used to evaluate capital budgeting projects. If the NPV is positive, a project should be accepted.

net present value profile A graphic presentation of the potential net present values of a project at different discount rates. It is very helpful in comparing the characteristics of two or more investments.

net trade credit A measure of the relationship between the firm's accounts receivable and accounts payable. If accounts receivable exceed accounts payable, the firm is a net provider of trade credit; otherwise, it is a net user.

net worth, or book value Stockholders' equity minus preferred stock ownership. Basically, net worth is the common stockholders' interest as represented by common stock par value, capital paid in excess of par, and retained earnings. If you take all the assets of the firm and subtract its liabilities and preferred stock, you arrive at net worth.

New York Stock Exchange (NYSE) The largest organized security exchange in the United States. It also has the most stringent listing requirements.

nominal GNP GNP (gross national product) in current dollars without any adjustments for inflation.

nominal yield A return equal to the coupon rate.

nonfinancial corporation A firm not in the banking or financial services industry. The term would primarily apply to manufacturing, wholesaling, and retail firms.

nonlinear break-even analysis Break-even analysis based on the assumption that cost and revenue relationships to quantity may vary at different levels of operation. Most of our analysis is based on *linear* break-even analysis.

normal yield curve An upward-sloping yield curve. Long-term interest rates are higher than short-term rates.

O **open-market operations** The purchase and sale of government securities in the open market by the Federal Reserve Board for its own account. The most common method for managing the money supply.

operating lease A short-term, nonbinding obligation that is easily cancelable.

operating leverage A reflection of the extent to which fixed assets and fixed costs are utilized in the business firm.

optimum capital structure A capital structure that has the best possible mix of debt, preferred stock, and common equity. The optimum mix should provide the lowest possible cost of capital to the firm.

Overseas Private Investment Corporation (OPIC) A government agency that sells insurance policies to qualified firms. This agency insures against losses due to inconvertibility into dollars of amounts invested in a foreign country. Policies are also available from OPIC to insure against expropriation and against losses due to war or revolution.

over-the-counter markets Markets for securities (both bonds and stock) in which market makers, or dealers, transact purchases and sales of securities by trading from their own inventory of securities.

P

par value Sometimes referred to as the face value or the principal value of the bond. Most bond issues have a par value of $1,000 per bond. Common and preferred stock may also have an assigned par value.

parallel loan A U.S. firm that wishes to lend funds to a foreign affiliate (such as a Dutch affiliate) locates a foreign parent firm (such as a Dutch parent firm) that wishes to loan money to a U.S. affiliate. Avoiding the foreign exchange markets entirely, the U.S. parent lends dollars to the Dutch affiliate in the United States, while the Dutch parent lends guilders to the American affiliate in the Netherlands. At maturity, the two loans would each be repaid to the original lender. Notice that neither loan carries any foreign exchange risk in this arrangement.

participating preferred stock A small number of preferred stock issues are participating with regard to corporate earnings. For such issues, once the common stock dividend equals the preferred stock dividend, the two classes of securities may share equally (or in some ratio) in additional dividend payments.

partnership A form of ownership in which two or more partners are involved. Like the sole proprietorship, a partnership arrangement carries unlimited liability for the owners. However, there is only single taxation for the partners, an advantage over the corporate form of ownership.

payback A value that indicates the time period required to recoup an initial investment. The payback does not include the time-value-of-money concept.

percent-of-sales method A method of determining future financial needs that is an alternative to the development of pro forma financial statements. We first determine the percentage relationship of various asset and liability accounts to sales, and then we show how that relationship changes as our volume of sales changes.

permanent current assets Current assets that will not be reduced or converted to cash within the normal operating cycle of the firm. Though from a strict accounting standpoint the assets should be removed from the current assets category, they generally are not.

perpetuity   An investment without a maturity date.

planning horizon   The length of time it takes to conceive, develop, and complete a project and to recover the cost of the project on a discounted cash-flow basis.

pledging receivables   Using accounts receivable as collateral for a loan. The firm usually may borrow 60 to 80 percent of the value of acceptable collateral.

point-of-sales terminals   Computer terminals in retail stores that either allow digital input or use optical scanners. The terminals may be used for inventory control or other purposes.

poison pill   A strategy that makes a firm unattractive as a potential takeover candidate. For example, when a potential unwanted buyer accumulates a given percentage of a firm's common stock, such as 25 percent, the other shareholders receive rights to purchase additional shares at very low prices. This makes the firm more difficult to acquire. Poison pills may take many different forms.

pooling of interests   A method of financial recording for mergers, in which the financial statements of the firms are combined, subject to minor adjustments, and goodwill is *not* created.

portfolio effect   The impact of a given investment on the overall risk–return composition of the firm. A firm must consider not only the individual investment characteristics of a project but also how the project relates to the entire portfolio of undertakings.

preemptive right   The right of current common stockholders to maintain their ownership percentage on new issues of common stock.

preferred stock   A hybrid security combining some of the characteristics of common stock and debt. The dividends paid are not tax-deductible expenses of the corporation, as is true of the interest paid on debt.

present value   The current or discounted value of a future sum or annuity. The value is discounted back at a given interest rate for a specified time period.

price–earnings ratio   The multiplier applied to earnings per share to determine current value. The P/E ratio is influenced by the earnings and sales growth of the firm, the risk or volatility of its performance, the debt–equity structure, and other factors.

primary earnings per share   Adjusted earnings after taxes divided by shares outstanding plus common stock equivalents.

prime rate   The rate that a bank charges its most creditworthy customers.

private placement   The sale of securities directly to a financial institution by a corporation. This eliminates the middleman and reduces the cost of issue to the corporation.

profitability ratios   A group of ratios that indicates the return on sales, total assets, and invested capital. Specifically, we compute the profit margin (net income to sales), return on assets, and return on equity.

pro forma balance sheet   A projection of future asset, liability, and stockholders' equity levels. Notes payable or cash is used as a plug or balancing figure for the statement.

pro forma financial statements   A series of projected financial statements. Of major importance are the pro forma income statement, the pro forma balance sheet, and the cash budget.

pro forma income statement   A projection of anticipated sales, expenses, and income.

program trading   Computer based trigger points in the market are established for unusually big orders to buy or sell securities by institutional investors.

prospectus   A document that includes the important information that has been filed with the Securities and Exchange Commission through the registration statement. It contains the list of officers and directors, financial reports, potential users of funds, and the like. It is for distribution to investors.

public placement   The sale of securities to the public through the investment banker–underwriter process. Public placements must be registered with the Securities and Exchange Commission.

public warehousing   An inventory financing arrangement in which inventory, used as collateral, is stored with and controlled by an independent warehousing company.

purchase of assets   A method of financial recording for mergers, in which the difference between the purchase price and the adjusted book value is recognized as goodwill and amortized over a maximum time period of 40 years.

purchasing power parity theory   A theory based on the interplay between inflation and exchange rates. A parity between the purchasing powers of two countries establishes the rate of exchange between the two currencies. Currency exchange rates, therefore, tend to vary inversely with their respective purchasing powers in order to provide the same or similar purchasing power.

pure bond value   The value of the convertible bond if its present value is computed at a discount rate equal to interest rates on straight bonds of equal risk, without conversion privileges.

R   **real capital**   Long-term productive assets (plant and equipment).

real GNP   GNP (gross national product) in current dollars adjusted for inflation.

real rate of return   The rate of return that an investor demands for giving up the current use of his or her funds on a noninflation-adjusted basis. It is payment for forgoing current consumption. Historically, the real rate of return demanded by investors has been of the magnitude of 2 to 3 percent. However, throughout the 1980s the real rate of return has been higher; that is, 5 to 7 percent.

refunding   The process of retiring an old bond issue before maturity and replacing it with a new issue. Refunding will occur when interest rates have fallen and new bonds may be sold at lower interest rates.

regional stock exchanges   Organized exchanges outside of New York that list securities. Regional exchanges exist in San Francisco, Philadelphia, and a number of other U.S. cities.

reinvestment assumption   An assumption must be made concerning the rate of return that can be earned on the cash flows generated by capital budgeting projects. The NPV method assumes the rate of reinvestment to be the cost of capital, while the IRR method assumes the rate to be the actual internal rate of return.

repatriation of earnings   Returning earnings to the multinational parent company in the form of dividends.

replacement cost   The cost of replacing the existing asset base at current prices as opposed to original cost.

replacement cost accounting   Financial statements based on the present cost of replacing assets.

required rate of return   That rate of return that investors demand from an investment (securities) to compensate them for the amount of risk involved.

reserve requirements   The amount of funds that commercial banks must hold in reserve for each dollar of deposits. Reserve requirements are set by the Federal Reserve Board and are different for savings and checking accounts. Low reserve requirements are stimulating; high reserve requirements are restrictive.

residual dividends   This theory of dividend payout states that a corporation will retain as much earnings as it may profitably invest. If any income is left after investments, the firm will pay dividends. This theory assumes that dividends are a passive decision variable.

restructuring Redeploying the asset and liability structure of the firm. This can be accomplished through repurchasing shares with cash or borrowed funds, acquiring other firms, or selling off unprofitable or unwanted divisions.

rights offering A sale of new common stock through a preemptive rights offering. Usually, one right will be issued for every share held. A certain number of rights may be used to buy shares of common stock from the company at a set price that is lower than the market price.

rights-on The situation in which the purchase of a share of common stock includes a right attached to the stock.

risk A measure of uncertainty about the outcome from a given event. The greater the variability of possible outcomes, on both the high side and the low side, the greater the risk.

risk-adjusted discount rate A discount rate used in the capital budgeting process that has been adjusted upward or downward from the basic cost of capital to reflect the risk dimension of a given project.

risk averse An aversion or dislike for risk. In order to induce most people to take larger risks, there must be increased potential for return.

risk-free rate of interest Rate of return on an asset that carries no risk. U.S. Treasury bills are often used to represent this measure, although longer-term government securities have also proved appropriate in some studies.

risk premium A premium associated with the special risks of an investment. Of primary interest are two types of risk, business risk and financial risk. Business risk relates to the inability of the firm to maintain its competitive position and sustain stability and growth in earnings. Financial risk relates to the inability of the firm to meet its debt obligations as they come due. The risk premium will also differ (be greater or less) for different types of investments (bonds, stocks, and the like).

S **secondary offering** The sale of a large block of stock in a publicly traded company, usually by estates, foundations, or large individual stockholders. Secondary offerings must be registered with the SEC and will usually be distributed by investment bankers.

secondary trading The buying and selling of publicly owned securities in secondary markets, such as the New York Stock Exchange and the over-the-counter markets.

secured debt A general category of debt, which indicates that the loan was obtained by pledging assets as collateral. Secured debt has many forms and usually offers some protective features to a given class of bondholders.

Securities Act of 1933   An act that is sometimes referred to as the truth in securities act, because it requires detailed financial disclosures before securities may be sold to the public.

Securities Acts Amendments of 1975   The major feature of this act was to mandate a national securities market.

Securities and Exchange Commission (SEC)   The primary regulatory body for security offerings in the United States.

Securities Exchange Act of 1934   Legislation that established the Securities and Exchange Commission (SEC) to supervise and regulate the securities markets.

security market line   A line or equation that depicts the risk-related return of a security based on a risk-free rate plus a market premium related to the beta coefficient of the security.

segmentation theory   A theory that Treasury securities are divided into market segments by various financial institutions investing in the market. The changing needs, desires, and strategies of these investors tend to strongly influence the nature and relationship of short-term and long-term interest rates.

self-liquidating assets   Assets that are converted to cash within the normal operating cycle of the firm. An example is the purchase and sell-off of seasonal inventory.

semiannual compounding   A compounding period of every six months. For example, a five-year investment in which interest is compounded semiannually would indicate an *n* value equal to 10 and an *i* value at one half the annual rate.

semivariable costs   Costs that are partially fixed but still change somewhat as volume changes. Examples are utilities and "repairs and maintenance."

serial bond   A bond issued by one company or municipality with a series of different maturity dates and interest rates that correspond to rates on competitive bonds with the same maturity and risk.

shelf registration   A process which permits large companies to file one comprehensive registration statement (under SEC Rule 415), which outlines the firm's financing plans for up to the next two years. Then, when market conditions appear to be appropriate, the firm can issue the securities without further SEC approval.

simulation   A method of dealing with uncertainty, in which future outcomes are anticipated. The model may use random variables for inputs. By programming the computer to randomly select inputs from probability distributions, the outcomes generated by a simulation are distributed about a mean, and, instead of generating one return or net present value, a range of outcomes with standard deviations is provided.

sinking fund   A method for retiring bonds in an orderly process over the life of a bond. Each year or semiannually, a corporation sets aside a sum of money equal to a certain percentage of the total issue. These funds are then used by a trustee to purchase the bonds in the open market and retire them. This method will prevent the corporation from being forced to raise a large amount of capital at maturity to retire the total bond issue.

sole proprietorship   A form of organization that represents single-person ownership and offers the advantages of simplicity of decision making and low organizational and operating costs.

speculative warrant premium   The market price of the warrant minus the warrant's intrinsic value.

spontaneous sources of funds   Funds arising through the normal course of business, such as accounts payable generated from the purchase of goods for resale.

standard deviation   A measure of the spread or dispersion of a series of numbers around the expected value. The standard deviation tells us how well the expected value represents a series of values.

statement of cash flows   Formally established by the Financial Accounting Standards Board in 1987, the purpose of the statement of cash flows is to emphasize the critical nature of cash flow to the operations of the firm. The statement translates accrual-based net income into actual cash dollars.

step-up in conversion   A feature that is sometimes written into the contract, which allows the conversion ratio to decline in steps over time. This feature encourages early conversion when the conversion value is greater than the call price.

stock dividend   A dividend paid in stock, rather than cash. A book transfer equal to the market value of the stock dividend is made from retained earnings to the capital stock and paid-in-capital accounts. The stock dividend may be symbolic of corporate growth, but it does not increase the total value of the stockholders' wealth.

stock split   A division of shares by a ratio set by the board of directors—2 for 1, 3 for 1, 3 for 2, and so on. Stock splits usually indicate that the company's stock has risen in price to a level that the directors feel limits the trading appeal of the stock. The par value is divided by the ratio set, and the new shares are issued to the current stockholders of record to increase their shares to the stated level. For example, a two-for-one split would increase your holdings from one share to two shares.

stockholders' equity   The total ownership position of preferred and common stockholders.

stockholder wealth maximization   Maximizing the wealth of the firm's shareholders through achieving the highest possible value for the firm in the marketplace. It is the overriding objective of the firm and should influence all decisions.

straight-line depreciation   A method of depreciation, which takes the depreciable cost of an asset and divides it by the asset's useful life to determine the annual depreciation expense. Straight-line depreciation creates uniform depreciation expenses for each of the years in which an asset is depreciated.

Subchapter S corporation   A special corporate form of ownership, in which profit is taxed as direct income to the stockholders and thus is only taxed once, as would be true of a partnership. The stockholders still receive all the organizational benefits of a corporation, including limited liability. The Subchapter S designation can only apply to corporations with up to 35 stockholders.

subordinated debenture   An unsecured bond, in which payment to the holder will take place only after designated senior debenture holders are satisfied.

synergy   The recognition that the whole may be equal to more than the sum of the parts. The "2 + 2 = 5" effect.

T

tax loss carry-forward   A loss that can be carried forward for a number of years to offset future taxable income and perhaps be utilized by another firm in a merger or an acquisition.

Tax Reform Act of 1986   Tax legislation that eliminated many of the abuses in the tax code and, at the same time, lowered the overall tax rates.

technical insolvency   When a firm is unable to pay its bills as they come due.

temporary current assets   Current assets that will be reduced or converted to cash within the normal operating cycle of the firm.

tender offer takeover   An unfriendly acquisition that is not initially negotiated with the management of the target firm. A tender offer is usually made directly to the stockholders of the target firm.

term loan   An intermediate-length loan, in which credit is generally extended from one to seven years. The loan is usually repaid in monthly or quarterly installments over its life, rather than with one single payment.

term structure of interest rates   The term structure shows the relative level of short-term and long-term interest rates at a point in time.

terms of exchange   The buy-out ratio or terms of trade in a merger or an acquisition.

tight money   A term to indicate time periods in which financing may be difficult to find and interest rates may be quite high by normal standards.

trade credit   Credit provided by sellers or suppliers in the normal course of business.

traditional approach to cost of capital   Under the traditional approach, the cost of capital initially declines with the increased use of low-cost debt, but it eventually goes up due to the greater risk associated with increasing debt.

transaction exposure   Foreign exchange gains and losses resulting from *actual* international transactions. These may be hedged through the foreign exchange market, the money market, or the currency futures market.

translation exposure   The foreign-located assets and liabilities of a multinational corporation, which are denominated in foreign currency units, and are exposed to losses and gains due to changing exchange rates. This is called accounting or translation exposure.

Treasury bills   Short-term obligations of the federal government with maturities of up to one year.

Treasury notes   Intermediate-term obligations of the federal government with maturities from three to five years.

treasury stock   Corporate stock that has been reacquired by the corporation.

trend analysis   An analysis of performance that is made over a number of years in order to ascertain significant patterns.

trust receipt   An instrument acknowledging that the borrower holds the inventory and proceeds for sale in trust for the lender.

two-step buy-out   An acquisition plan in which the acquiring company attempts to gain control by offering a very high cash price for 51 percent of the shares of the target company. At the same time the acquiring company announces a second lower price that will be paid, either in cash, stocks, or bonds, at a subsequent point in time.

U   **underwriting**   The process of selling securities and, at the same time, assuring the seller a specified price. Underwriting is done by investment bankers and represents a form of risk taking.

underwriting spread   The difference between the price that a selling corporation receives for an issue of securities and the price at which the issue is sold to the public. The spread is the fee that investment bankers and others receive for selling securities.

underwriting syndicate   A group of investment bankers that is formed to share the risk of a security offering and also to facilitate the distribution of the securities.

unsecured debt   A loan that requires no assets as collateral, but allows the bondholder a general claim against the corporation, rather than a lien against specific assets.

V   **variable costs**   Costs that move directly with a change in volume. Examples are raw materials, factory labor, and sales commissions.

W   **warrant**   An option to buy securities at a set price for a given time period. Warrants commonly have a life of one to five years or longer and a few are perpetual.

warrant intrinsic value   (See minimum warrant value.)

weighted average cost of capital   The computed cost of capital determined by multiplying the cost of each item in the optimal capital structure by its weighted representation in the overall capital structure and summing up the results.

white knight   A firm that management calls upon to help it avoid an unwanted takeover offer. It is an invited suitor.

working capital management   The financing and management of the current assets of the firm. The financial manager determines the mix between temporary and permanent "current assets" and the nature of the financing arrangement.

Y   **yield**   The interest rate that equates a future value or an annuity to a given present value.

yield curve   A curve that shows interest rates at a specific point in time for all securities having equal risk but different maturity dates. Usually, government securities are used to construct such curves. The yield curve is also referred to as the term structure of interest rates.

yield to maturity   The required rate of return on a bond issue. It is the discount rate used in present-valuing future interest payments and the principal payment at maturity. The term is used interchangeably with market rate of interest.

Z   **zero-coupon rate bond**   A bond that is sold at a deep discount from face value. The return to the investor is the difference between the investor's cost and the face value received at the end of the life of the bond.

Index

A

ABC, 597
Accelerated Cost Recovery System (ACRS),
   369–72
Accounting flows versus cash flows, 354–56
Accounting income, 25–26, 29
Accounting Principles Board *Opinion No.
   15*, 577, 583
Accounts payable, 30, 206–7
   cost of, 206–7
   credit terms, 190, 206–7
   extending disbursements, 181
Accounts receivable, 31, 188–91, 207, 219–
   22
   aging accounts, 191
   asset backed public offerings, 221–22
   changes between the 1950s and 1980s, 188
   collection policy, 191
   credit policy, 189–92
   factoring, 220–21
   as an investment, 188–9
   pledging of, 220
   speeding up collections, 180
Accounts receivable financing, 219–22
Accounts receivable management, 188–92

Accounts receivable turnover, 57, 59–63,
   192
Accrued expense, 30
Accumulated depreciation, 31
After-acquired property clause, 474
Agency theory, 6
Allied-Signal, 558
Alpha, 355–56
American Brands, 315
American Express, 515, 558, 614
American Home Products, 33, 315
American Institute of Certified Public
   Accountants, 577
American Standard, 315
American Stock Exchange, 432–35, 579
American Telephone and Telegraph, 16, 475,
   559, 583
Amoco, 14, 515
Anacomp Inc., 571
Annual percentage rate, 214
Annuity
   defined, 242–43
   equaling a compound sum, 246
   equaling a present value, 246–48
Apple Computer, 66–67
Approximate yield to maturity, 273–74

Archer Daniels Midland, 654
Armco Steel, 263
Articles of incorporation, 12
Articles of partnership, 11
Asset backed public offerings, 221–22
Asset depreciation range, 369–70
Asset growth, nature of, 146–47
Asset structure, shifts in, 167–68
AT&T; *see* American Telephone and
    Telegraph
Atlantic Richfield, 515, 558
Automated clearing houses (ACHs), 183
Automatic data, 33
Automobile industry, 193
Average collection period, 57, 62–63, 191
Avon Products, 632

B

Babcock and Wilcox, 615
Bache Halsey Stuart Shields, 452
Balance sheet, 29–33, 98–100
    explanation of pro forma items, 98–100
    items, 30–32
    limitions, 32
    pro formas on percent-of-sales methods,
        98–100
Bank credit, 207–11
    compensating balances, 209–11
    cost of, 211–14
    interstate banking, 208
    maturity provisions, 211
    prime rates, 208–9
Banker's acceptance, 185–87
Bankers Trust, 16
Bank of America, 221
    zero coupon bonds, 448
Bankruptcy, 502–3
    Modigliani and Miller, 348–49
Bankruptcy Act, 502–3
    in court settlement, 505–8
    liquidation, 505–8
    out of court settlement, 503–4
    reorganization, 504–5
Beatrice, 461, 463, 596
Best Products, 33
Beta, 308–9, 335–39, 394–95
Bethlehem Steel, 315
Blanket inventory liens, 224
Blue Bell, 463
Board of Directors, 12
Boeing, 16, 558
Bond(s); *see* Corporate bond(s)
Bond contract, 473–75

Bond valuation and yield to maturity,
    263–76
    impact on value of changing yields to
        maturity
        decrease in inflation premium, 268–69
        increase in inflation premium, 267–68
        time to maturity, 270–71
Book value, 32, 374
    comparison of book to market value per
        share, 33
    per share, 32
Break-even analysis, 113–18
    break-even point equation, 115
    chart, 114, 117, 121
    nonliner, 121
Break-up value, 461
Bristol Myers, 515, 580, 558
Broker, 432
Brokers, mergers, 453
Burlington Industries, 558
Burroughs, 66–67
Business risk, 266

C

Call feature, 477, 529, 574–76
Call premium, 477, 484–85, 529, 475–76
Capital asset pricing model, 308–9, 335–42
    alpha, 335–37
    beta, 308–9, 335–39, 394–95
    cost of capital considerations, 308–9, 339–
        40, 342
    regression equation, 335–37
    risk-free rate of interest, 308–9, 340, 342
    security market line, 337–42
Capital budgeting, 352–78
    accounting versus cash flow, 354–56
    administrative considerations, 353–54
    bond refunding, 483–88
    capital rationing, 364
    cost of capital, 316–22
    foreign, 645–96
    incremental analysis, 376–78
    internal rate of return analysis, 357–61
    mutually exclusive, 363
    net present value analysis, 360–61, 373,
        377–78
    net present value profile, 364–68
    payback analysis, 356–57, 359–61
    portfolio considerations, 402–7
    profitability index, 361
    ranking investment proposals, 356–61
    reinvestment assumptions, 363–64
    replacement decision, 374–78

Capital budgeting—*Cont.*
  risk over time, 352–53
  sale of old asset, 374–77
  selection strategy, 361–63
  tax consequences, 374–76
  under uncertainty, 389–407; *see also* Risk
    and Risk-return tradeoffs
Capital budgeting decision
  a case example, 372–73
  relationship to time value of money, 240
Capital Cities Communications Corp., 284
Capital gains taxes, 550–51, 557
Capital lease, 493–94, 510
Capital market; *see also* Security markets
  competition for funds, 424–30
  composition of funds raised, 424–30
  corporate securities, 426–28
  equity financing, 428–30
  foreign stock exchanges, 435–36
  globalization of, 423
  government securities, 425–26
  a supply of funds, 430–32
Capital paid in excess of par, 31
Capital rationing, 364
Capital shortages, 146, 159, 214–15
Capital structure
  over the business cycle, 315–16
  debt versus equity, 315–16
  effect of warrants versus convertible debt,
    582–83
  impact on earnings, 122–26
  Modigliani and Miller, 343–51
    bankruptcy considerations, 348–49
    initial approach, 345–47
    introduction of corporate taxes, 347–48
  optimum, 312–14
  risk analysis of short- versus long-term
    debt, 156–59, 165–70
  theory of
    Durand, David, 343–47
    Miller model, 349–51
    Modigliani and Miller, 343–51
    net income approach, 343–44
    net operating income approach, 344–45
  use of debt, 126–29
Cash balance, 179–80
  excess, 179, 184
  minimum level, 94–95, 97
  negative balance, 179
Cash breakeven analysis, 118
Cash budget, 86, 91–95, 152–55
  cash payments, 92–93, 152–53
  cash receipts, 92, 152–53

Cash budget—*Cont.*
  component costs of manufactured goods, 93
Cash discounts, 191, 206–7
Cash flow, 33–45
  versus accounting flows, 354–56
  in capital budgeting, 262–63, 354–56,
    377–78
  from financing activities, 35, 39–40
  from investing activities, 35, 39–40
  from operating activities, 35–40
Cash management, 178–83
  automated clearing houses (ACHs), 183
  cost-benefit analysis, 181
  cost of not taking a discount, 207–7
  extending disbursement, 181
  float, 179–80
  improving collections, 180
  international, 183
Cash management network 182
CBS, 14, 28
Certificates of deposit, 185–86, 225–26
Cetus Corp., 579–80
Chase Manhattan, 632, 673
Chevron, 14, 515, 596, 615
Chicago Board of Trade, 226
Chicago Mercantile Exchange, 226, 436
Chrylser, 14, 193, 558
Chrysler Financial Corp., 217
CIT Financial Corp., 215, 615
Citibank of New York
  floating prime rate, 207
  leasing, 494–95
Citicorp, 494, 632
CityFed Financial, 33
Clientele effect, 550–51
Coca-Cola, 515, 558, 632
Coefficient of correlation, 403–5
Coefficient of variation, 394
Colgate Palmolive, 595
Collateral loans, short-term, 219–24
Collections, 180, 191–92
Combined leverage, 126–29
  degree of, 128–29
Commercial paper, 185–86, 215–18, 423
  dealer (industrial), 215–17
  direct (finance), 215–17
  financing advantages and limitations, 217
  rates versus bank prime, 218
Common stock, 31, 517–36
  compared to bonds and preferred, 530–32
  cost of new, 311–12
  determining required rate of return from
    price, 282–83

Common stock—*Cont.*
  different classes of, 516–18
  funds raised, 427
  valuation of, 278–86, 288
Common stock equivalents, 474–77
Common stockholder
  claim to rights, 516
  right to purchase new shares, 520–26
  voting right, 517–20
Common stock valuation
  constant dividend growth, 279–82
  no dividend growth, 279
  supernormal dividend growth, 285–86,
    297–99
  using P/E ratio concepts, 283–85
  variable dividend growth, 285–86, 297–99
Compaq, 61–62, 66
Compensating balances, 209–11
  effective cost of, 212–13
Compound sum annuity, 242–44
  example of table, 244
COMPUSTAT, 56
Conoco, 615
Consolidation, 597
Continental Illinois Bank, 578
Contribution margin, 115
Conversion premium, 569–70
Conversion price, 569
Conversion ratio, 568
Conversion value, 569–72
Convertible bonds, 476–77, 568–79
  advantages of investors, 572–73
  characteristics of, 573–74
  disadvantages to investors, 572–73
  floor value, 569–72
  forcing conversion, 574–76
  interest rate of, 572
  price pattern, 604–5
  pure bond value, 569–70
  value of, 569–72
Convertible preferred stock, 529
Convertible securities, 568–69
  accounting treatment, 574, 576–79
  advantages to corporation, 573–74
  call, 574–76
  disadvantages to corporation, 573–74
  forcing conversion, 574–76
  step-up conversion, 576
Corporate bond(s)
  advantages of debt, 490
  amount of debt, 13–14
  compared to common and preferred stock,
    526–28

Corporate bonds—*Cont.*
  coupon rate, 474, 481
  disadvantages of debt, 491
  floating rate, 489–90
  innovative forms of, 488–90
  maturity date, 474
  methods of repayment, 475–77
  new funds raised, 426–27
  par value, 473
  prices, 477–83
  priority of claims, 476
  private versus public placement, 459–62
  pure bond value (convertible bonds), 569–70
  ratings, 482–83
  refunding decision, 483–88
  security provisions, 474–75
  trustee, 474, 476
  valuation of, 263–78
  yields, 477–83
  zero coupon, 488–99
Corporate bond ratings, 482–83
Corporate bond yields, 477–83
  compared to preferred stock, 277, 526–28
  coupon rate (nomial yield), 474, 481
  current yield, 481
  yield to maturity, 303–4, 481
Corporate liquidity; *see* Liquidity
Corporate tax rates, 42–44
  average tax rate, 43
  versus individual tax rates, 44
  marginal tax rate, 43
Corporation, 12–13
  Subchapter S, 12–13
Correlation analysis, 402–5
Cost-benefit analysis, collection of
    receivables, 181
Cost of capital, 301–25
  over the business cycle, 315–6
  in capital budgeting decisions, 316–22,
    360–61
  in CAPM, 308–9, 335–42
  conceptual framework, 302–3
  marginal, 317–22
  method of weights, 312–33
  in refunding, 583–84
  review of formulas, 323–24
Cost of common stock, using CAPM, 308–9
Cost of debt, 303–5
Cost of goods sold, 24, 71–72, 89–90
Cost of new preferred stock, 306, 526–27
Cost of retained earnings, 309–11
Cost of tax deductible expenses, 44–45

Coupon rate, 474, 481
Crane Co., 575
Crash of 1987, 15, 441, 597
  international markets, 15–16
Cray Research, 66
Credit shortage; *see* Capital shortages
Credit policy administration, 189–92
  a decision example, 192
Credit standards, 190
Cumulative dividends, 528–29
Cumulative voting, 518–20
Current assets
  a financing decision, 147–56, 159–67
  financing patterns, 156–59, 165–67
  financing under varying economic
      conditions, 163–64, 166–67
  liquidity, 167–70
  management of, 178–79
  matching sales and production, 147–56
  nature of growth, 146–47, 156
  permanant, 146, 156–57
  risk, liquidity and financing, 166–68
  shifts in structure, 167–68
  temporary, 147–59
Current cost accounting, 69
Current liabilities, 31
Current ratio, 57, 63, 168–69
Current yield, 481
Cyclical sales, 147–56

D

Data General, 66
Dealer, 436
Dean Witter Reynolds, 452
Debenture, 475, 483
Debt; *see also* Corporate bonds(s)
  cost of, 303–5
  expanding use of, 472–73
  indenture, 474
  security provisions, 474–75
  short- versus long-term, 156–59
  unsecured, 475
Debt repayment methods, 475–77
  call features, 477–79
  conversion, 476
  serial payments, 475–76
  sinking fund provision, 476
Debt to asset ratios in 1960s and 1980s, 13,
    315
Debt to total assets, 57, 60–61, 64–65, 69
  industry averages, 305–6
  selected companies, 315
Decision trees, 401–2

Deferred annuity, 252–53
Deficits
  federal deficit, 15–16
  financing by foreign governments, 425,
      647
  foreign trade deficits, 15–16
Denny's, Inc., 461
Depreciation
  accelerated cost recovery system (ACRS),
      368–72
  cash flow, 34, 354–56
  categories, 369
  expense, 313
  incremental, 376–77
  percentages, 372
Depreciation expense, 31
  flow of funds, 41–42
  noncash expense, 354–56
  tax shield, 45
Deutsche Bank Capital, 459
DiGiorgio, 315
Digital Equipment, 16, 28, 66, 71, 515
Dilution of earnings per share, 450–51, 578
Discounted loans, 211–12
Discount rate
  bond refunding decisions, 483–84
  capital budgeting, 360–61
  risk-adjusting in capital budgeting, 395–
      406
  stock valuation models, 278–86
Disinflation, 55, 67
Distressed firms, 502–8
  assignment, 504
  composition, 503
  creditor committee, 503
  extension, 503
  financial alternatives, 502–8
  referee, 504
Dividend(s)
  cumulative, 528–29
  discount rate, 545
  ex-dividend date, 551–52
  holder of record date, 551–52
  informational content, 545
  life cycle growth, 543–44
  passive decision variable, 544
  payment date, 551–52
  payment procedures, 551–52
  relevence of, 545–46
  residual theory of, 544–55
  stability of, 546–48
  stock, 552–55
  stockholder preferences, 545–46

Dividend payout ratio, 100, 546
Dividend policy
  access to capital markets, 549–50
  cash position of firm, 549
  control considerations, 550
  earnings growth, 543–44
  legal rules, 548–49
  returns to company versus stockholders,
    309–11, 524–43
  selected U.S. corporations, 547
  tax position of shareholders, 500–51
  variables influencing, 548–51
Dividend reinvestment plans, 559
Dividend valuation models, 278–82, 339
  under constant dividend growth, 279–82
  under no dividend growth, 279
  under supernormal dividend growth, 285–
    86, 297–99
  under variable dividend growth, 285–86,
    297–99
Dow Chemical, 315, 475, 515, 632
Draft, 186–87
Drexel Burham Lambert, 453
Dreyfus Liquid Assets, Inc., 188
Dr Pepper, 463
Dual listing, 433
Duke Power, 483
Dun and Bradstreet, 53, 190, 206
  credit rating system, 190
DuPont Corp., 515, 595
Dupont system, 59–61

E

Earnings per share, 26–29, 122–25
Eastman Kodak, 515
Eaton Corp. 558
Economical ordering quantity, 194–97
Economic developments in the 1970s–1980s,
  13–17
Economic income, 29
Economic Recovery Tax Act of 1981, 368–
  72
Efficient frontier, 406
Efficient market hypothesis
  semi-strong form, 438
  strong form, 438
  weak form, 439
Efficient markets, 438
  criteria of, 437
Election of directors, 518–20
Electronic Data Systems, 15, 456–57, 516
Electronic funds transfer, 182–83, 216

Equity financing, 428–30
  internal versus external, 429–30
Eurobonds, 491
  convertible bonds, 576
Eurobonds market, 658–59
Euro-convertible bonds, 576
Eurodollar deposit, 183
Eurodollar loan, 218, 657–58
Eurodollars, 183, 187
Europartners, 459
Eximbank; *see* Export-Import Bank, 655
Expected value, 392–95, 401
  financing current assets, 166–67
Export-Import Bank, 697–98
External disbursement float, 181
External financing; *see* Financing decision
External growth, 19, 595–621
Extraordinary loss, accounting treatment, 72
Exxon, 14, 28, 446, 483, 515, 632

F

Factoring accounts receivable, 220–21
Farm credit bank, 426
Federal agency securities, 185–86, 425–26
Federal Home Loan Bank, 186, 426
Federal Land Bank, 186
Federal National Mortgage Association, 186,
  426
Federal Reserve
  check clearing function, 181
  margin requirements, 440
  reaction to inflation, 163, 214–15
Federal Trade Commission, 24
Fidelity Daily Income Trust, 188
Finance career opportunities, 4
Financial Accounting Standards Board
    (FASB), 33
  FASB 13 (leasing), 491–92, 510
  FASB 52 (foreign exchange), 642
  FASB 55 (convertibles), 578
  FASB 95 (cash flows), 33
Financial analysis and planning, 55, 72
  disinflation impact, 69–70
  inflation impact, 67–69
Financial capital, 27, 315
Financial forecasting, 85–100
Financial futures, 224–26
Financial intermediaries, 430–32
Financial leverage, 112, 121–26
  degree of, 125
  earnings indifference graph, 124
  earnings impact, 122–25

Financial leverage—*Cont.*
  leverage impact graph, 124
  limitations, 126
Financial management
  evolution of, 4–6
  functions of, 10
  goals of, 6–10
  relationship to accounting, 3–4, 25–26
  relationship to economics, 3–4
Financial ratios, 58–67
  asset utilization ratios, 57, 62–63
  average collection period, 57, 62–63, 191
  bad debts to credit sales, 191
  cash and equivalents to current liabilities,
    167–68
  current ratio, 57, 62, 168–69
  debt to total assets, 57, 58–61, 63–64, 69,
    315
  debt utilization ratios, 57, 64–65
  fixed asset turnover, 57, 62
  fixed charge coverage, 57, 64
  interest coverage; *see* times interest earned
    below
  inventory turnover, 57, 62
  liquidity ratios, 57, 63
  profitability ratios, 57–62
  profit margin, 58–62, 66, 100
  quick ratio, 57, 63
  receivable turnover, 57, 58–63, 192
  replacement cost ratios, 69
  return on assets, 57, 59–62
  return on equity, 57, 59–62
  return on investment, 57, 59–62
  return on net worth; *see* return on equity
    above
  times interest earned, 57, 64, 69, 473
  total asset turnover, 57–63, 65–66
  trend analysis, 65–67
Financial risk, 266–67
Financing decision, 156–67
  alternative sources, 159–60
  capital structure, 122–25, 312–16
  debt versus equity, 315–16
  effect of warrants versus convertible debt,
    582–83
  influence of term structure of interest
    rates, 159–65
  internal versus external, 429–30
  long-term financing, 157–58
  public versus private, 454–59
  short-term financing, 158–59, 165–70
  use of debt, 126–29
  use of rights, 520–26

Financing international business operations,
    654–61
  Eurobonds, 658–59
  Eurodollar loans, 657–58
  Export-Import Bank (EXIMBANK), 655
  Foreign Credit Insurance Association, 655
  fronting loans, 655–57
  international equity markets, 659–61
  International Finance Corporation, 661
  letter of credit, 654–55
  parallel loans, 656
  parent company loans, 655–57
Financing objectives, 159–60, 315–16
First Boston Corp., 452–53, 459
Fixed costs, 112–17
Float, 179–80
Floating rate bonds, 489–90
Floating rate preferred stock, 529
Flotation costs, 306, 311, 448–50, 485–86
Flow of funds, 430–32
  percentage of sales method, 98–100
Ford, 193, 515, 532, 558
  common stock class A & B, 517–18
Ford Motor Credit Corporation, 186
Foreign borrowing, 218–19, 654–61
Foreign exchange rates, 632–41
  balance of payments, 638
  cross rates, 641
  factors influencing, 636–37
  fixed rates, 636–37
  floating rates, 636–37
  forward rates, 639–41
  government policies, 638–39
  inflation, 637
  interest rates, 637–38
  other factors of consequence, 639
  relationship to U.S. dollars, 635–36
  spot rates, 639–41
Foreign exchange risk, 641–45
  accounting or translation exposure, 642
  currency futures market hedge, 644–45
  forward exchange market hedge, 642–43
  money market hedge, 643
Foreign investment decisions, 645–54
  cash flow analysis, 649–53
  example of capital budget, 649–53
  foreign investments in United States, 646–47
  joint ventures, 648
  Overseas Private Investment Corporation,
    648–49
  political risk, 647–49
  portfolio risk reduction, 646
  tax deferral, 645

Foreign stock exchanges, 435–36, 659–61
Forms of organization
   corporation, 12–13
   partnership, 11–12
   sole proprietorship, 11
Fred Meyer, 463
Fully diluted earnings per share, 578
Full service banking, 207
Futures contract, 194, 224–26, 644–45

G

Gannett, 315
Gencorp, 558
General Cinema, 28
General Electric, 16, 446, 515, 595–96
General Electric Credit, 208, 215
General Foods, 14, 596
General Motors, 12, 193, 284, 315, 515, 558
   class of stock E & H, 516–17
General Motors Acceptance Corporation,
   215–17, 221–22
Georgia-Pacific Corp, 16
Getty Oil, 596
Gillette, 632
Goals of the firm, 7–10
   profit maximization, 7
   social responsibility, 9–10
   wealth maximization, 8–9, 126; *see also*
      Valuation
Going private, 459–62
Goldman Sachs, 453, 457
Goodwill, 612–13
Government regulation, 438–41
   current legislative issues, 441
   Securities Act of 1933, 438–39
   Securities Acts amendments of 1975, 440–
      41
   Securities Exchange Act of 1934, 439–40
Government securities, 185–86, 425–26
Gross profit in production schedule, 88–89
Gulf & Western Industries, 315
Gulf Oil, 596, 615

H

Harcourt Brace Jovanovich, 148–49
Hedging, 194, 224–26, 642–45
Heinz (H. J.), 632
Henley Group, 558
Hercules, 558, 632
Hewlett-Packard, 66, 515, 558, 632
Historical cost accounting, 32–33, 67–68
Holding companies, 619–21
   drawbacks, 620–21

Holiday Corp., 28
Hospital Corp. of America, 558
Houghton Mifflin, 148–49
Houston Industries, 16
Hughes Aircraft, 516, 596

I

IBM, 16, 28, 66–67, 71, 219, 263, 451, 482,
   514–15, 558, 632
IC Industries, 558
ITT, 558
Income statement, 25–26
   elements of distortion, 70–72
   impact of leverage, 122–29
   limitations, 29
   proforma, 86–91
Income tax; *see* Taxes
Indenture, 474
Indirect investment, 430–31
Inflation, 13, 67–70
   impact on
      balance sheet, 33
      corporate liquidity, 167–70
      currency exchange rates, 637
      debt usage, 490
      financial analysis, 55, 67–70
      interest rates, 214–15
      inventory, 67–68, 194
      investment, 429–30
      prime rate, 209
      profits, 13, 67–69, 73
   interest rates, 163–64, 339–42
   inventory management under, 194
   premium, 266, 340
   rise of external funding, 429–30
Information content of dividends, 544–
   45
Inland Steel, 33
Insider trading, 9–10, 441
   Boesky, Ivan, 9, 441
   Levine, Dennis, 9, 441
Installment loans, 213
Institutional ownership of common stocks,
   515
Interest earned, 473
Interest rate parity theory, 637–38
Interest rate risk, 185
Interest rates
   economic cycles, 62–64
   effective cost of bank loans, 211–13
   effect on bond prices, 477–80
   impact of foreign exchange rates, 637–
      38

Interest rates—*Cont.*
   long-term versus short-term, 164
   long-term yields, 480
   prime commercial paper, 164, 185, 217
   prime rate, 209, 218
   short-term, 159–65, 185
   term structure of, 159–65
      expectations hypothesis, 161–62
      liquidity premium theory, 160–62
      segmentation theory, 161–62
Internal rate of return, 357–60
   reinvestment assumptions, 363
International finance; *see also* Foreign
      exchange rates; Foreign exchange risk;
      and Multinational corporations
   banker's acceptance, 185–87
   cash management, 183
   Eurobonds, 491, 701–2
   Eurodollar deposit, 183–85
   Eurodollar loans, 218, 657–58
   Eurodollars, 187
   historical background, 631–63
   sales of selected U.S. multinational firms,
      632
   Saudi Arabia, 632
   unsettled issues, 632
International Paper Co., 475, 525
Inventory, 31
   beginning and ending in production
      schedule, 88–90, 152
   carrying costs, 195–97
   fluctuating, 152
   minimum cost, 195–97
   optimum cost, 194–97
   ordering cost, 194–97
   self-liquidating, 146–47
Inventory financing, 222–24
Inventory liens, 224
Inventory management, 188–97
   under inflation and disinflation, 194
Inventory methods
   FIFO (first-in, first-out), 68, 72, 89, 194
   LIFO (last-in, last-out), 71
Inventory models; *see* Economical ordering
   quantity
Inventory profits, 67–68
Inventory trust receipts, 224
Inventory warehousing, 224
   field, 224
   public, 224
Investment banking, 445–56
   advisor, 447
   after-market, 451–52

Investment banking—*Cont.*
   agency functions, 447
   best efforts, 446
   changes in, 452
   dilution, 450–51
   distribution process, 447–50
   functions of, 446–47
   leading underwriters 1987, 453
   pricing, 450–52
   public versus private, 454–59
   role of, 445–46
   spread, 448–50
   syndicates, 447–48, 452–53
   underwriter, 446
Investments, 31
   accounts receivables, 188–89
   ranking proposals, 356–63
Investment tax credit, 371, 495

J–K

Johnson & Johnson, 16, 515
Junk bonds, 614
Kidder Peabody, 208, 453
Kimberly-Clark, 558
K Mart, 148, 558
Kraft, 558

L

Lazard Freres, 459
Lease versus purchase analysis, 510–13
Leasing
   advantages of, 494–95
   aftertax cost, 512
   capital versus operating, 493–94
   FASB statement, 491–92
   as a form of debt, 491–95
   income statement effect, 494
   sale and leaseback, 495
Leasing revenues: treatment of, 71
Leslie Fay, 463
Level production, 93, 193–94
   an example, 151–56
Leverage; *see also* Financial leverage *and*
      Operating leverage
   the risk factor, 116–17
Leveraged buyouts, 459–62, 615
Levi Strauss & Co., 461
Liabilities, 31
LIBOR; *see* London Interbank Offered
      Rate, 185, 187, 658
Life cycle curve, 543–44

LIFFE; *see* London International Financial
        Futures Exchange, 644
Lilly (Eli) & Co., 33, 315, 515
Lily Tulip, 463
Lines of credit, 217
Liquidation
    an example, 506–8
    priority of claims, 505–6
Liquidity, 30, 166–70
    ratios, 63
    risk versus financing plan, 167–70
    securities markets, 431–32
Litton Industries, 16, 598
Loan repayment, using present value of
        annuity, 247–48
Lock box, 180
London Interbank Offered Rate (LIBOR),
        185, 187, 658
London International Financial Futures
        Exchange (LIFFE), 644
Long Island Lighting, 33
Long-term financing; *see also* Financing
        decision
    of current assets, 157–58
Long-term yields, 480
Lotus, 33
LTV Corp., 263, 579, 598
Lyon Furniture Mercantile Agency, 190

M

McDermott, J. Ray, 615
McDonald's Corp., 28
McDonnell-Douglas Corp., 16
McGraw-Hill, 614
Mack Truck, 221–23
MacMillan, 28, 148–49, 597
Managing underwriter, 447–48, 451
Marathon Oil, 615
Marginal cost of capital, 317–22
Marginal principle of retained earnings,
        542–46
Margin requirements, 440
Marketable securities, 31, 184–88
    factors influencing selection, 184
    risk of holding long-term, 184
Market efficiency, 437–38
Market maker, 447
Market risk premium, 337–39
Market stabilization, 451
Matching sales and production, 147–56
Merger arbitrageur, 617–18
Merger premiums, 604, 616–18

Mergers, 595–619
    accounting considerations, 612–14
    cash purchase, 601–2
    definition of, 597
    effect on EPS, 603–10
    expected growth in EPS, 605–11
    financial motives, 598–600
    with high P/E company, 607–10
    long-term considerations, 605–7
    maximization of market value, 605
    motives for, 598–600
    motives of selling stockholders, 600–601
    negotiated versus tender offers, 614–16
    nonfinancial motives, 600
    portfolio diversification, 598, 611–12
    present value analysis of, 601–2
    stock for stock exchange, 603–7
    tax effects, 612–13
    tax loss carry forward, 599
    terms of exchange, 601–5
Merck & Co., 515, 558, 632
Metro-Media, 463
Merrill Lynch, 452–53, 489
Merrill Lynch Capital Markets, 459
MGM, 597
Midwest Stock Exchange, 433
Miller Beer, 14
Minimum cost of capital, 312–14
Minnesota Min. & Mfg., 515
Mobil Oil Corp., 515, 615, 632
Money market, 423
Money market accounts, 188
Money market investment funds, 187–88
Monsanto, 558
Monte Carlo simulation, 399–401
Moody's Bond Record, 482
Moody's Investor Service, 56, 482
Morgan (J. P.), 632
Morgan Stanley, 453
Mortgage agreement, 474
Multinational corporations, 633–34
    definition of, 633
    exporters, 644
    foreign affiliate, 634
    fully owned foreign subsidiary, 634–35
    joint venture, 634
    licensing agreement, 634
    nature and environment, 633–35
Mutually exclusive projects, 361–63, 374

N

National Association of Securities Dealers,
        436–38

National Bankruptcy Act, 503
National Credit Office, 190
National Hardware Association, 56
National Retail Furniture Association, 56
National securities market, 440–41
Navistar International, 580–81
NCR, 66, 558
Negotiated offers, 614
Net credit position, 207
Net present value, 360–61, 373, 498–99
   bond refunding, 483–88
   compared to internal rate of return, 361
   in leasing, 510–13
   reinvestment assumptions, 377–78
Net present value profile, 364–68
Net worth; *see also* Book value, 32
New York Stock Exchange, 432–35, 579
   demand and supply of equity capital, 430–31
   listing requirements, 434–35
   size and liquidity, 432, 434
   warrant trading, 582–83
Northwest Industries, Inc. 461
Notes payable, 31
Nynex, 558

O

Ohio Edison Co., 16, 304–5
Operating lease, 493–94
Operating leverage, 113–21
   degree of, 118–19
   limitations of analysis, 21
   risk in, 116–17
Opportunity cost, 543
Optimal capital structure, 312–14
Outboard Marine, 33
Over-the-counter markets, 433, 436–37
Owens-Illinois, 558

P

Pacific Coast Stock Exchange, 433
PaineWebber, 453
Pan American Corp., 580
Parsons Corp., 461
Participating preferred stock, 529
Partnership, 11–12
Par value, 473, 530
   splits, 555–56
Passbook savings account; *see* Savings
   account
Payback method, 356–57, 360–61
Penn Central Railroad, 217

Penney (J. C.), 148–50
Pepsi Co., 575
Percent-of-sales method, 98–100
Permanent current assets, 147, 157–59
Perot, H. Ross, 456–57
Pfizer Inc., 571, 632
Phillip Morris, 14, 515, 558
Phillips Petroleum, 14, 315
Pickens, T. Boone, 14, 596, 615
Plant and equipment, 31
Playboy, 33
Pledging accounts receivable, 220
Point of sale terminals, 151
Poison pills, 596, 525–26
Polaroid, 315
Pooling of interests, 612–14
Portfolio effect, 598, 611–12
Portfolio evaluation, 404–6
   efficient frontier, 405–6
Portfolio risk, 402–5
   correlation analysis, 402–5
   correlation coefficient, 402–7
Preemptive right, 520–6
Preferred stock, 31, 427, 526–30, 575
   call feature, 529
   compared to common stock and bonds, 530–38
   conversion feature, 529
   cost of, 306, 526
   cumulative dividends, 528–29
   investors in, 527–28
   justification for, 526–27
   new funds raised, 427
   participating, 529
   par value, 530
   required return, 277–78
   right to dividends, 526
   tax considerations, 528
   valuation of, 276–78
   voting rights, 518, 531
   yield compared to Aa bond, 528
Premium offers, 616–18
Prentice Hall, 597
Prepaid expense, 31
Present value analysis; *see* Net present value
   and Time value of money
Present value of annuity, 244–45
   example of table, 245
Present value of bond, 265
Present value of single amount, 241–42
   example of table, 243
   relationship to compound sum, 242
Presprich, P. W., 456

Price-earnings ratio, 28–29, 465–67
  selected U.S. corporations, 28
  valuation, 283–84
Primary earnings per share, 576–79
Primary offering, 451–56
  EDS example, 208–9, 456–59
Prime Computers, 66
Prime rate, 163, 208–9, 216–18
Private placement, 456–59
Probability, 392–94, 396–98, 399–401
  current asset financing under varying
    conditions, 166–67
Probability distribution, 391, 393–94, 397,
    400, 403
  portfolio effect, 402–3
Procter & Gamble, 515, 558
Production costs, 88–90
Production schedule, 88–89, 152
  level production, 92–93
  seasonal production, 193–94
Profitability ratios, 58–52
Profit maximizing, 7
Pro forma financial statements, 86–98
Prospectus, 439
Proxy, 517
Prudential-Bache, 452–53
Public financing
  advantages, 454–55
  disadvantages, 455–56
  example EDS, 456–59
Public Service New Hampshire, 580
Purchase of assets, 612–14
Purchasing power parity theory, 637

Q–R

Quaker State, 315
Ralston Purina Co., 575
Rapid Data Systems, 353
Ranking investment proposals, 356–61
Ratio analysis; *see also* Financial ratios
  classification system, 57–58
  comparative analysis, 56
  the DuPont System, 59–61
  the Saxton Company, 58–67
  trend analysis, 65–67
RCA, 596, 616
Real rate of return, 266
Refunding corporate bonds, 483–88
  capital budgeting analysis, 484–88
Regional stock exchanges, 432–33
Regulation of security markets, 438–41
Reinvestment assumptions; *see* Capital
  budgeting

Reorganization
  external, 504
  internal, 504
Replacement cost accounting, 32–33, 69
Replacement decisions, an example, 374–78
  in capital budgeting, 374–78
  tax consequences, 374–78
Required rate of return on bond, 263–74,
    481
  approximation method, 273–74, 303–5,
    481–82
  determination from bond price, 271–72
  influences on
    business risk, 266
    financial risk, 266
    inflation premium, 266
    required real rate of return, 266
    risk-free rate of return, 266
    risk premium, 266
    time to maturity, 270–71
Restructuring, 14–15, 459–62
  leverage buyouts, 459–62
  mergers, 14
  stock repurchase, 14
Retained earnings, 27, 30, 542–46
  active decision variable, 544
  and capital structure, 319–20
  cost of, 309–10
  marginal principle of, 542–46
  required returns, 309–10
  statement of, 27
Return to capital, 27
Revlon, 14
Rights offering, 520–26
  desirable features, 524–25
  effect on stockholder's position, 523–24
  ex-rights, 522
  rights-on, 522
  value of a right, 521–23
Risk
  in capital budgeting, 389–407
  portfolio effect, 402–6
  premium, 266
  risk-adjusted discount rate, 395–99
Risk averse, 390–91
Risk-free rate of interest, 266–67, 308–9,
    337–42
Risk measurement, 392–95
  beta, 308–9, 335–39, 394
  coefficient of variation, 392–94
  expected value, 392–95
  probability, 392–94
  qualitative factors, 397–98
  standard deviation, 392–95

Risk-return tradeoffs, 6, 10, 390–91
    in asset management, 166–70
    in capital asset pricing model, 325–42
    in capital budgeting, 389–90
    in capital markets, 424
    in foreign exchange, 641–54
    in portfolio combinations, 402–5
    in securities, 530–32
    use of hedging, 56
    with use of leverage, 115–17
  Robert Morris Associates, 56
  Rockefeller Centers Properties, 457–59
  Royal Dutch ADR, 515

S

SFN, 463
Safeway Stores, 596
Sale and leaseback, 495
Sale of old asset, 374–77
Sales
  projection, 86–88, 98–100, 146–47
  recognition of, 71
Salomon Brothers, 451, 453, 459, 558
Sante Fe Southern Pacific, 558
Saturday night special, 615
Savings account ,185, 187
Schlumberger, 558
SCOA Industries, 461
Scovill, Inc, 461
Sears Roebuck, 452, 515
Secondary offering, 455
Secondary trading, 432
Secured debt; *see* Bankrupcy *and* Debt
Securities Act of 1933, 5, 438–39
Securities Acts amendments of 1975, 440–41
Securities Exchange Act of 1934, 438, 439–40
Securities and Exchange Commission, 24, 69, 433
  financial reporting standards, 33, 69
  regulation of securities markets, 438–41
Security market line, 337–39
Security markets, 432–38
  efficiency of, 437–38
  liquidity, 432
  organization of, 432–37
  organized exchanges, 432–35
  over-the-counter markets, 436–37
  role of, 431–32
Self-liquidating assets, 146–47
Self-liquidating loan, 207
Semivariable costs, 113
Serial payments, 475–76

Share price effect, 406–7
Shearson Lehman Hutton, 452–53, 457
Shelf registration, 454
Shell Oil Co., 596
Sherwin-Williams, 575
Short-term financing
  of current assets, 158–59
  foreign borrowing, 218–19
  marketable securities, 184–88
  use of collateral, 219–24
Simulation models, 399–401
Sinking fund provisions, 476
Small business financing, 158
Social responsibility, 9–10
Sole proprietorship, 11
Sources of funds
  bank loans, 207–15
  depreciation as a source of funds, 41–42, 45
  external forecast, 98–100
  float, 179–80
  foreign borrowing, 218–19, 654–61
  spontaneous, 99, 205
Stages of production, 223–24
Standard & Poor's, 28
Standard and Poor's Corporation, 28–29, 56, 482–83
Standard deviation, 392–95, 402–5
Standard Oil of California, 14
State and local securities, 426
Statement of cash flow
  depreciation, 34
  developing a statement, 34–35
  from financing activities, 35, 39–40
  from investing activities, 35–39–40
  from operating activities, 35–40
Stifel, Nicolaus & Co., 459
Stock dividends, 552–55
  accounting considerations, 552–53
  informational content, 555
  possible increase in cash dividends, 554–55
  utilization of, 555
  value to investor, 553–54
Stock exchange membership, financial institutions, 440
Stock repurchase, 14, 556, 559
  effect on earnings per share, 557
Stockholder's equity, 32
Stockholders in the United States, 514
Stock split, 555–56
  accounting treatment, 555–56
  purpose of, 556
Storer Communications, Inc., 461

Straight-line depreciation, 376
Subchapter S Corporation, 12–13
Subordinated debentures, 475
Superior Oil Co., 596
Supernormal growth dividend model, 285–86, 297–99
Swiss Bank Corporation International Securities, Inc., 459

T

Tandy, 66
Tax(es)
  benefits on stock repurchase, 557
  capital gain, 550–51
  capital structure, 347–48
  corporate, 42–43
  cost of tax deductible expense, 44–45
  deductibility of interest on debt, 427, 490, 526–28
  dividend policy, 550–51
  in leasing, 494–5
  loss carry forward, 599
  on sale of assets, 374–77
  preferred stock, 526–28
  sole proprietorship, 11
Tax loss carryforward, 599
Tax position of shareholders, 550–51
Tax reform act of 1986
  asset depreciation range, 369–70
  capital gains, 557
  depreciation percentages, 372
  leasing, 495
  new depreciation rules, 369–70
Tax shield, 45
Technical insolvency, 502
Tektronix, 558
Temporary current assets, 147–59
  under level production, 151–56
Tender offer takeover, 516–19
  leveraged takeover, 615
  negotiated versus tendered, 614–16
  "poison pill," 596
  "saturday night special," 615
  two step buyout, 618–19
  "white knight," 596, 615
Tenneco, 16
Term loan, 211
Terms of exchange, 601–5
Terms of trade, 190–91
Term structure of interest rates, 159–65
  a comparison over time, 163
Texaco, 596
Texas Instruments, 284, 353

Texas Utilities, 28
Tight money, 145, 166–67, 214–15, 451
Times interest earned, 57, 64, 69, 473
Time value of money, 239–53
  interpolation, 295–97
  patterns of payment, 251–53
  review of formulas, 253–56
  semiannual, quarterly or montly compounding, 250–51
Timing financial policy, 15, 156–65, 315–16
Trade credit, 158, 190–91, 205–7
  cash discounts, 206–7
  payment period, 190–91, 206
Treasury bills, 185–86, 225, 423
  sold at a discount, 185–86
Treasury notes, 185–86
Trend analysis, 65–67
Tri-Continental Corporation, 579
Tri Star Pictures, 580
Trust Indenture Act of 1939, 474
Truth in Lending Act of 1968, 214
Turner Broadcasting, 580
Two-step buyout, 618–19

U

U.S. government securities, 184–87, 225–26
U.S. Leasing International, 494
U.S. Steel, 33, 615
U.S. Treasury, 185–86, 425
Underpricing, 450, 572–73
Underwriting, 446
Underwriting costs, 434, 450
Underwriting syndicate, 447–48, 452–53
Uniform Commercial Code, 219
Uniroyal, Inc., 461, 463
Unisys, 66–67, 221, 632
United Airlines, 579
United Technologies, 615
Unocal, 596
Unsecured debt, 475
Upjohn, 28

V

Valuation
  common stock, 278–86
  corporate bonds, 263–78
  goals of the firm, 7–8
  market value to book value, 33
  preferred stock, 276–78
  price earnings ratios, 28–29
  risk in capital budgeting, 389
  supernormal growth firm, 297–99
  use of constant growth dividend model, 279–80

Valuation of common stock, 278–86
Value Line Investment Survey, 56
Variable cost, 113
Volcker, Paul, 451
Volume-cost-profit analysis, 115–17

W

Wang Laboratories, 66, 516–17
Warner Lambert, 632
Warrants, 579–84
  accounting considerations, 583–84
  detachable feature, 579
  intrinsic value, 580–82
  minimum value of, 580
  speculative premium, 581–82
  step-up in option price, 583
  usage of, 583
  valuation of, 580–82
Wealth maximization, 8–10, 389
Weighted average cost of capital, 302–3,
  312–13
Westinghouse, 16
West Shore Railroad, 475
Weyerhaeuser, 315
White Knight, 596, 615
Wickes Companies, 580
Winn Dixie, 28
Wire Transfer, 182–83
Wood Gundy Corp., 459

Working capital and the financing decision,
  145–70
Working capital management, 18, 145–46,
  165–70

Y–Z

Yamaichi International, 459
Yield
  of common stock dividends, 307–8
  using present value of an annuity, 250
  using present value of a single amount,
    248–50
Yield curve; *see* Term structure of interest
  rates
Yield on investment using time value of
  money, 248–50, 357–60
Yield to maturity, 263–74, 481
  approximation method, 273–74, 303–5,
    481–82
  determination from bond price, 271–72
  influences on
    business risk, 266–67
    financial risk, 266–67
    inflation premium, 266
    required real rate of return, 266
    risk-free rate of return, 266
    risk premium, 266–67
    time to maturity, 270–71
  using interpolation, 295–97
Zero coupon rate bonds, 488–89